THE DEEP SPRINGS COOKBOOK

THE DEEP SPRINGS COOKBOOK

The Deep

A Guide for

Springs Cookbook:
Ambitious Beginners, with 600 Recipes

by Tom Hudgens
Artwork by Justin Kim

PUBLISHED FOR THE DEEP SPRINGS CENTENNIAL CELEBRATION, 2017

Copyright © 2017 by Tom Hudgens.

All rights reserved. No part of this book may be reproduced in any form without written permission from the author.

Library of Congress Cataloging-in-Publishing Data available.

ISBN 978-0-9989557-0-4

Formerly published, in slightly different form, as *The Commonsense Kitchen: 500 Recipes Plus Lessons for a Hand-Crafted Life,* by Chronicle Books, San Francisco, 2010.

Cover image: "The Big Deep Springs," Justin Kim, mixed media on paper, 2016.

Designed by Jena Scholten

Illustrations and cover art by Justin Kim

page 154: "Modern Man" by Ann Applegarth, originally published in *West Wind Review*, Spring 1992. Used by permission of poet.

page 18: Excerpt from "All at One Point," a story in the collection *Cosmicomics* by Italo Calvino, translated by William Weaver, copyright 1978, published by Harvest Books, an imprint of Houghton Mifflin Harcourt.

page 374: Excerpt from *Invisible Cities* by Italo Calvino, translated by William Weaver, copyright 1978, published by Harvest Books, an imprint of Houghton Mifflin Harcourt

10 9 8 7 6 5 4 3 2 1

CONTENTS

Introduction 19

About Deep Springs 20

The College and Ranch 21

The Rhythms of a Day 22

The Boardinghouse 24

The Author 24

CHAPTER 1
Kitchen Basics 26

Culinary Terms 30

Essential Equipment 32

Essential Ingredients 37

Measuring 45

Metric Equivalents of U.S. Measurements 47

CHAPTER 2
Breakfast: Oats, Grits, Bacon, & Eggs 50

Oatmeal 51

Steel-Cut Oats 51
    Other Cooked Breakfast Cereals 51

Dried Fruit Compote 52

Grits 52
    Elaine's Baked Grits 52

Granola 52

Griddle Toast 53
    Milk Toast 53
    Bready Egg 53
    Gashouse Egg, Knothole Egg, or One-Eyed Egyptian 53

French Toast 53

Simple Breakfast Potatoes 54

Baked Bacon 54

Fresh Breakfast Sausage 55

Chicken-Fried Steak 55

Grapefruit for Breakfast 56

Eggs 56

Scrambled Eggs 57

Fried Eggs 57
    Fried Egg Sandwich 58

Omelet 58

Sorrel Omelet 59

Poached Eggs 60

Soft-Boiled Eggs 60

Shirred Eggs 60

CHAPTER 3
Pancakes, Biscuits, & Cornbread 62

Jack's Buttermilk Pancakes 63
    Cowboy Pancakes 63
    Whole-Wheat Pancakes 63
    Buckwheat Pancakes 63
    Blueberry or Huckleberry Pancakes 63

Eloise's Cornmeal-Buttermilk Pancakes 63

Ricotta Pancakes 64

Biscuits 65
    Whole-Wheat Cheddar Biscuits 65
    Cream Biscuits 65
    Sour Cream Biscuits 65
    Cornmeal Biscuits 65
    Griddle Biscuits 66
    Drop Biscuits 66

Biscuits and Gravy   66

Skillet Cornbread   67

Dutch Babies   68
   Apple Dutch Babies   68

Oatmeal Scones   68

Cream Scones   69

Cornmeal Cherry Scones   69

Joan's Irish Soda Bread   70

Pumpkin Bread   70

Grandma Z.'s Coffeecake   71
   Blueberry Coffeecake   71

Banana Bread   72

Doughnuts   72

Funnel Cakes   73

CHAPTER 4
BREAD, BUTTER, CRACKERS, & CHEESE   74

Dinner Bread   76
   Rich Dinner Bread   77
   Wheaty Dinner Bread   77
   Sesame Bread   77
   Potato Bread   77
   Bread for Lunch   77
   Bread for the Next Day   77
   Hamburger Buns   77

Focaccia   77
   Potato Focaccia   78
   Longer-Rise Focaccia   78
   Other Variations   78

Farm Butter and Buttermilk   79

Cheese Crackers   79
   Black Pepper Cheese Crackers   79

Whole-Wheat Crackers   80

Puffy Salties   80

Thyme Crackers   80

Serving Cheese   81

Queso Blanco   82
   Whey Lemonade   82

CHAPTER 5
GREAT LUNCHES   84

Reatha's Macaroni and Cheese   85
   Spicy Macaroni and Cheese   85

Baked Potatoes   85

Pizza   86
   Egg Pizza   88

Fresh Clam Chowder   88
   Corn Chowder   89

Grilled Cheese Sandwich   89

Good Sandwiches   89

Tuna Salad   90
   Mediterranean Tuna Salad   90

Curry Tofu Salad   91

Hard-Boiled Eggs   91

Deviled Eggs   92
   Kimchi Deviled Eggs   92

Egg Salad   92

Asparagus and Mushroom Frittata   93
   Chard and Mushroom Frittata   93
   Leek and Gruyère Frittata   93
   Bacon and Onion Frittata   93

Tortilla Española   94

Gâteau de Crêpes (Stacked Crêpe Cake with Spinach, Gruyère, and Béchamel)   94

My Mother's Enchiladas   96

Green Chile Enchiladas   97

Red Chile Enchiladas   98

New Mexico Posole with Pork and Green Chile   98
   Red Chile Posole   99

Gumbo   99

Gunhild's Chicken Curry   100

Curry Powder   102

Papadums or Papads   102

Raitas   102

Falafel   102

Hummus   104

Avocado Toast and Avocado Tortilla   104

Minted Iced Tea   104

Hibiscus Iced Tea   105

Lemonade   105
Limeade   105

CHAPTER 6
BEANS   106

Pinto or Black Beans   108
Variations   108

Refried Beans   108

Mama Nell's Chili con Carne   108
Frito Pie   109

Black Bean Chili   110

Pork and White Bean Chili   111

Red Beans and Rice   111

Lima Bean and Ham Soup with Kale   112

White Bean Soup with Fried Sage   114
Rosemary Oil   114

White Bean and Escarole Soup   114

White Bean Gratin with Fennel   115

Split Pea Soup   116

Chickpeas with Tomatoes, Lemon, and Mint   116

CHAPTER 7
HOT VEGETABLES & VEGETABLE SOUPS   118

Artichokes   119
Stuffed Artichokes   119

Fresh Artichoke Hearts   120

Pan-Roasted Asparagus   120
Broiled or Grilled Asparagus   121
Asparagus Pasta   121

Sautéed Green Beans   121
Sautéed Romano Beans   122

Green Beans Cooked in Bacon Fat   122

Southern-Style Braised Green Beans   122

Fresh Shell Beans   122

Broccoli   123

Brussels Sprouts with Brown Butter   123

Cabbage with Juniper   124

Honey-Glazed Rainbow Carrots   125
Italian Tzimmes   125

Carrot Soup with Ginger   125

Cauliflower   126

Mashed Cauliflower   126

Chayote   127

Corn on the Cob   127
Jalapeño-Lime Butter   127

Sautéed Corn   128

Catherine's Corn Soup   128

Roasted Eggplant   129

Fennel, Celery Root, and Potato Gratin   130

Slovenian Fennel and Potatoes   131

Roasted Garlic   131

Garlic Soup   131

Greens   132

Sautéed Kale and Corn   133

Leek Gratin   133

Leek and Vegetable Purée Soup   133

Irish Leek and Oat Soup   134

Sautéed Mushrooms   135

Nettle Broth   135

Cornmeal-Fried Okra   136

Grilled Okra   136

Sweet Onions Cooked in Cream   136

Red Onion Galette   136

Parsnip Soup with Toasted Almond Olive Oil   138

Boiled Peanuts   138

Peanut Soup   139

Minty Peas   139

Snap Peas   139
    Spring Pasta with Snap Peas and Asparagus   139

Roasted Red Peppers   140

Scalloped Potatoes   140
    Variations   141

Simple Roasted Potatoes   141
    Roasted Potatoes, Apples, and Onions   141
    Roasted Potatoes and Fennel   141
    Potatoes, Tomatoes, and Pesto   141

Scallion-Buttermilk Potatoes   142

Mashed Potatoes   142

Roasted Radicchio   142

Jota (Sauerkraut, Sausage, and Bean Soup)   143

Sautéed Spinach   143

Butternut Squash Soup with Diced Pear   144

Butternut Squash Chips   145

Cornmeal-Fried Summer Squash   145

Grilled Summer Squash   145

Priscilla's Fried Green Tomatoes   146

Tomato Soup   146

Tomato Cobbler   147

Tomato Concassé   148
    Summer Tomato Pudding   148

Watercress Soup   148

Roasted Yams or Sweet Potatoes   149

Roasted Yams with Pears and Bourbon   149

Ratatouille   150

Soupe au Pistou   151

Vegetable Stock or Broth   151

Poem: "Modern Man"   154

CHAPTER 8
SALADS & DRESSINGS 156

LEAFY GREEN SALADS   157
    How to Wash Salad Greens   158
    Dressing a Green Salad   158
    Salad Toppings   158

Bowl-Dressed Salad   159

Greek Salad   159

Fig and Feta Salad   160

Chef's Salad   160

Arugula Salads   161

Spinach Salads   161

Tracy's Caesar Salad   161
    Creamy Caesar Dressing   162

Watercress Salad   162

Vegetable and Fruit Salads 163

Apple and Pear Salad   163

Fuji Apple Coleslaw   163

Asparagus Salad   164

Green Bean Salad with Cherry Tomatoes and Basil   164

Marinated Beets   164

Carrot-Raisin Salad   165

Celery Root Salad   166

Corn Salad   166

Summer Cucumber Salad   166

Shaved Fennel   167
   Shaved Fennel with Pears and Parmesan   167

Fennel, Blood Orange, and Toasted Almond Salad   167
   Fennel, Orange, and Black Olive Salad   168

Gazpacho   168

Jícama   168

Black Kale, Golden Beets, and Leeks with Orange Oil   169

Kohlrabi-Apple Slaw   169

Orange and Date Salad   170

Potato Salad   170

Vinaigrette Potato Salads   171

Radishes   171

Summer Squash Carpaccio   171

Tomatoes with Salt   172

Summer Tomato Sandwich   173

Thyme Salt   173

Watermelon, Feta, and Basil Salad   173

Shallot Vinaigrette   173
   Other Vinaigrettes   174

Lemon Vinaigrette   174

Ranch Dressing   174

Blue Cheese Dressing   175

Toasted Cumin–Mint–Yogurt Dressing   175
   Improvised Creamy Dressings   175

Croutons   175

Toasted Nuts   176

Mixed Salted Nuts   176

Blanched Almonds   176

Pan-Toasted Seeds   176

CHAPTER 9
Beef, Lamb, & Pork   178

Marinated Steak   180

Steak Fried in Beef Tallow   180

Flank Steak with Blue Cheese   181

Grilled Skirt Steak with Salsa Verde   181

Porcini-Dusted Steak   182

Carne Asada   182
   Tacos de Carne Asada   182

Roast Beef   183
   Roast Beef Salad   184
   Roast Lamb   184

Beef Stew, with Nine Variations   184
   Elizabeth's Winter Beef Stew   186
   Russian Borscht   186
   Goulash   186
   Carbonnade Flamande   186
   Italian Beef Stew   186
   Boeuf Bourguignonne   186
   Mexican Braised Beef (or Goat)   187
   Lamb Stew   187
   Shepherd's Pie   187

Allspice-Scented Pot Roast   188

Green Chile Beef Stew   188

Glazed Meatloaf   189

Italian Meatballs   190

Mediterranean Meatballs   191

Skillet Hamburgers   192
   Burger Steak Salad   192

Rico's Tacos   192

Steak Tartare   193

Beef Carpaccio   194

Beef Liver with Bacon, Onions, and Mushrooms   196

Apple-Marinated Pork Chops   197

Tender Cured Pork Chops   197
   Quick Brine for Pork Chops   198

Pork Chops Slow-Cooked in Olive Oil   198

Pork Tenderloin   199

Cynthia's Garlic-Studded Milk-Braised Pork Loin   199

Slow-Roasted Pork   200
   Crispy Pork   201

Glazed Ham   201

My Mother's Polish Sausage Stew   202

CHAPTER 10
CHICKEN & TURKEY   204

Roast Chicken   205
   Holiday Roast Chicken   205
   Quick Brine for Chicken   206

Marmalade Chicken   206

Sautéed Chicken Breast   206

Double-Herbed Grilled Chicken   207

Cayenne-Rubbed Chicken with Potatoes and Garlic   208

Crispy Pan-Fried Chicken   209

Tarragon-Roasted Chicken with Tomatoes   210

Chicken Cooked Under a Brick   210
   Bacon-Wrapped Chicken Cooked Under a Brick   211

Herbed Braised Chicken, with Five Variations   212
   Braised Chicken with Fennel   213
   Chicken Paprikash   213
   Braised Chicken in Red Wine with Mushrooms   213
   Chicken, Chorizo, and Chickpeas   213
   Chicken Curry   213

Shoyu Chicken   214

Chicken and Dumplings   214
   Chicken Pot Pie   216

Matzoh Ball Soup   216

Gin Chicken Liver Pâté   217

Chicken Stock   217
   Stock from Leftover Roast Chicken   218
   Turkey Stock   218

Apple- and Rosemary-Scented Roast Turkey   218

CHAPTER 11
FISH & SHELLFISH   220

Clay's Broiled Trout   221

Whole Roasted Trout with Herb Salad   221

Baked Salmon   222
   Three More Simple Cooking Methods for Salmon   222

Gravlax   223

Pan-Fried Sole   223

Sole Stuffed with Leeks   224

Pan-Fried Cod or Snapper   225

Fried Catfish   225

Seared Tuna   225

Mussels   225
    Moules Marinière de Bretagne   226
    Mussels with Leeks and Orange Zest   226
    Mussels with Spicy Tomato Sauce   226

Oysters on the Half-Shell   226
    Mignonette Sauce   226

Seared Scallops with Gremolata   227

Boiled Shrimp   227
    Cocktail Sauce   228

Grilled Shrimp with Shrimp Essence   228

Sautéed Spicy Squid   229

CHAPTER 12
PASTA, DUMPLINGS, RICE, & STUFFING   230

Handmade Egg Noodles with Cream   231

Ricotta Ravioli with Sage Brown Butter   232

Whole-Wheat Pappardelle with Corn and Chiles   233

Manicotti   234

Pasta Cookery   235

Toasted Pasta with Garlic   236

Wide Noodles with Broccolini, Feta, Lemon, & Pine Nuts   236

Garlic Bread   237

Pecan Couscous   237

Spaetzle   237

Cornmeal-Egg Soup Dumplings   238

Rice   238

Golden Basmati Rice Pilaf   239

Brown, White, and Wild Rice Pilaf with Mirepoix   240

Green Rice with Peas and Pea Greens   240

Risotto   241
    Saffron Risotto   241
    Wild Mushroom Risotto   241
    Butternut Squash Risotto   241
    Black Truffle Risotto   242

Polenta   242

Southern Spoon Bread   243
    Variations   243

Quinoa   243

Farro Salad with Cherry Tomatoes and Pecorino   244

Clio's Stuffing   244
    Stuffed Winter Squash   245

CHAPTER 13
SAUCES, RELISHES, PICKLES, & JAM   246

Dad's Steak Sauce   247

Tomato Sauce   247
    Thick Tomato Sauce   248

Tomato Sauce with Meat   248

Fresh Summer Tomato Sauce   249

Fresh Salsa   249
    Guacamole   249
    Mediterranean Avocado Dip   249
    Horseradish-Tomato Relish   249

Fresh Horseradish Cream   250
    Slovenian Horseradish Sauce   250

New Mexico Red Chile Sauce   250

New Mexico Green Chile Sauce   251

Green Chile Relish   251

Lime-Pickled Red Onions   252

Yogurt-Shallot Sauce   252

Lemon Butter Sauce   252

Mayonnaise   252
   Garlic Mayonnaise   253
   Mustard Mayonnaise   253

Aioli   253

Toasted Nut Olive Oil   254

Pesto   254

Meyer Lemon–Olive Relish   254

Green Chimichurri Sauce   255

Dill Pickles   255

Pickled Summer Vegetables   256
   Pickled Winter Vegetables   256

Blond Barbecue Sauce   257

Oven Applesauce   257

Cranberry Sauce   257
   Cranberry Relish   258

Pickled Plums   258
   Other Pickled Fruit   258

Pickled Black Grapes   258

Kevin's Apricot Jam   259

Marmalade   260

Quince Jam   260

CHAPTER 14
PIES & FRUIT DESSERTS   262

Butter Piecrust   263
   Lard Piecrust   264
   Vegetable Oil Piecrust   264
   Vegetable Oil–Butter Piecrust   265

DOUBLE-CRUST PIES   265

Apple Pie   265
   Apple and Candied Orange Pie   266
   Apple and Candied Lemon Pie   266
   Apple and Quince Pie   266
   Bacon-Apple Pie   266

OTHER DOUBLE-CRUST FRUIT PIES   267

Pear Pie   267

Blackberry Pie   267

Blueberry Pie   267

Peach, Nectarine, Apricot, or Plum Pie   268

Diana's Cherry Pie   268

Rhubarb Pie   268

SINGLE-CRUST PIES   269

Lemon Meringue Pie   269

Chocolate Cream Pie   270

Custard Cream Pie   271
   Banana Cream Pie   271
   Banana Pudding   271

Pumpkin Pie   271

Sweet Potato Pie   272

Pecan Pie   272

Rhubarb Custard Pie   273

Jam Pie   273

Maple Syrup Pie   274

Aunt Lela's Buttermilk Pie   274

Cheesecake   274
   Gingersnap Crust   275

OTHER FRUIT DESSERTS   276

David's Baked Apples   276

Orange Bread Pudding   276

Ginger Peach Crisp   276

Pear, Ginger, and Lemon Crisp   277
   Other Fruit Crisps   278

Poached Pears with Chocolate Sauce   278

My Mother's Strawberry Shortcake   279

Canned-Fruit Cobbler   280

SIMPLEST FRUIT DESSERTS   280

Apples and Oranges   280

Cherries with Almond Paste   280

Citrus Compote   280

Dulce De Leche with Fresh Fruit   281

Dried Fruit in Sweet Wine   281

Figs, Honey, and Feta   281

Melon with Rosewater   281

Nuts from the Shell   281

Peaches and Cream   282

Warm Pears with Chocolate Ice Cream   282

Persimmons   282

Pineapple   282

Pomelo   282

Rhubarb   283

Watermelon   283

Story: "The Strawberry"   284

CHAPTER 15
CAKES   286

Goose Egg Pound Cake   288
    Goose Egg Pound Cake Cinnamon Toast   288

Carrot Cake   289

Parsnip Cake   290

Whipped Cream Cake   290

Chocolate Mayonnaise Cake   291

Pinky's Jewish Apple Cake   292

Elge's Three-Ginger Gingerbread   292

Fresh Ginger Cake   293

Currant Cake   294

Cherry-Pork Cake   294

Prune Cake   295

Milk and Honey Cake   296

Poppyseed Cake   296

Big Pink Cake   297

CHAPTER 16
GOOEY DESSERTS   300

Chocolate Pudding   301

Butterscotch Pudding   301

Pearl Tapioca Pudding   302

Peach Leaf Custard Sauce   303

Vanilla Bean Crème Brûlée   303

Baked Custard   304
    Colostrum Custard   304

Gooseberry Fool   304
    Other Fruit Fools   304

Vanilla Ice Cream   305
    Coffee Ice Cream   305
    Strawberry Ice Cream   305
    Peach Ice Cream   305
    Buttermilk Ice Cream   305
    Cinnamon Ice Cream   306
    Whiskey Ice Cream   306
    Butter Pecan Ice Cream   306

Lemon Ice Cream   306

Blackberry Ice Cream   307

Pear Sherbet   307
    Pear and Black Pepper Sherbet   307

Snow Ice Cream   308
    Maple Snow Ice Cream   308

Gelatin Desserts 308

Tangy Lemon Sour Cream Gelatin   309

Lime Yum   309

Creamy Orange Gelatin   309

Carol's Fresh Fruit Gelée   310

Blood Orange Gelée   310

Almond Cream   311
  Rose-Scented Cream with Raspberries   311
  Fresh Bay Leaf Cream with Citrus   311

Goat Milk Panna Cotta with Cherries   312

CHAPTER 17
Cookies & Candy 314

Chocolate–Chocolate Chip Cookies   315
  Chocolate–White Chocolate Chip Cookies   315
  Chocolate-Peanut Cookies   315
  Dark Chocolate Wafers   315

Ella's Chocolate Chip Cookies   315

Pistachio Chocolate Chip Cookies   316
  Fruit and Nut Cookies   317

Chocolate Chip–Hazelnut Shortbread Bars   317

Sheet Pan Brownies   317

Mexican Chocolate Cookies with Almonds   318

Peanut Butter Cookies   319
  Almond-Butter Cookies   319

Oatmeal-Coconut Bars   319

Wedding Cookies   320

Sesame Cookies   320

Cashew Cookies   321

Walnut Biscotti   321

Lemon-Anise Biscotti   322

Lime Bars   322

Lemon Slice Cookies   323

Italian Orange Cookies   324

Gingersnaps   324
  Gingersnaps, Vanilla Ice Cream, and Boysenberries   325

Ginger Cookies   325

Butter Cookies   325
  Cardamom Butter Cookies   325

Biscochitos   326

Vanilla Wafers   327

Old-Fashioned Vinegar Taffy   327

English Toffee with Sea Salt   328

Sesame Candy   328

Mama Nell's Kentucky Bourbon Balls   329

CHAPTER 18
Menus 330

CHAPTER 19
Aftermath: Leftovers, Dishes, Soap, & Stains 338

Non-Edible Recipes 342

Toothbrushing Powder   342

Cut Flower Solution   342

Hummingbird "Nectar"   343

Deep Springs Soap   343

CHAPTER 20
Bibliography 346

Index 352

"It was enough for her to say, at a certain moment: 'Oh, if I only had some room, how I'd like to make some noodles for you boys!' And in that moment we all thought of the space that her round arms would occupy, moving backward and forward with the rolling pin over the dough, her bosom leaning over the great mound of flour and eggs which cluttered the wide board while her arms kneaded and kneaded, white and shiny with oil up to the elbows; we thought of the space that the flour would occupy, and the wheat for the flour, and the fields to raise the wheat, and the mountains from which the water would flow to irrigate the fields, and the grazing lands for the herds of calves that would give their meat for the sauce; of the space it would take for the Sun to arrive with its rays, to ripen the wheat; of the space for the Sun to condense from the clouds of stellar gases and burn; of the quantities of stars and galaxies and galactic masses in flight through space which would be needed to hold suspended every galaxy, every nebula, every sun, every planet, and at the same time we thought of it, this space was inevitably being formed..."

—Italo Calvino, Cosmicomics

INTRODUCTION

Welcome to *The Deep Springs Cookbook*. Not simply a record of the meals I served to the Deep Springs College community of fifty people during my years as chef, this book was originally conceived to inspire the students' ongoing discovery of the vital craft of cooking as they embarked upon their adult lives. If you are just beginning to cook for yourself and your family, I hope this book will spark your culinary imagination while introducing you, recipe by recipe, to many essential kitchen practices. If you are a seasoned cook, I hope it will inspire you to see a familiar ingredient, technique, or dish in a new light. *The Deep Springs Cookbook* is an eclectic, working repertoire of dishes and democratic culinary philosophies. You'll find recipes for many familiar American "comfort food" favorites: big Boardinghouse breakfasts with eggs, bacon, pancakes, and grits; Southern and Southwestern dishes, including authentic New Mexico red and green chile sauces; a whole chapter on pies, including a thorough run-down on piecrust and the recipe for my Great-Aunt Lela's famous buttermilk pie. There are recipes for pinto beans, skillet cornbread, steak fried in beef tallow, pork chops marinated with fresh apple, and ten different versions of beef stew. I have included many of my mother's and grandmother's recipes: baked custard, cornmeal-fried summer squash, chicken enchiladas, Kentucky bourbon balls. Alongside such old-fashioned dishes, there are many modern, lighter recipes: oatmeal, granola, and other healthful morning grains; lean meats and fish; and vegetables, soups, and salads galore. In fact, two of the largest chapters in the book are devoted entirely to vegetables: Hot Vegetables and Vegetable Soups, and Salads and Dressings. Both are arranged alphabetically by type of vegetable.

In keeping with the Deep Springs spirit of self-sufficiency, you'll learn how to churn fresh butter, bake homemade crackers, prepare a simple cheese from whole milk and vinegar... there's even a recipe for homemade soap. Most of these recipes were developed in the busy Deep Springs kitchen, where there is little time for fussy preparations, little money for expensive or exotic ingredients, and little regard for food trends or snobbery, but where a great appreciation for any good, soul-satisfying food abides. Long before the terms "farm-to-table" or "locavore" came into use, meals of beef, vegetables, and milk produced on the ranch were being served in the Boardinghouse. Deep Springs is the only place I know where a tobacco-chewing mechanic from rural Oklahoma might be served black truffle risotto on the same day that a distinguished governmental scholar from France is served cherry Jell-O with canned fruit cocktail.

About Deep Springs

What is Deep Springs? Stated very simply, Deep Springs is a college on a ranch: a very small, fully accredited, two-year college program for academically advanced young men (only twelve are admitted each year), situated on a real, working cattle ranch in an isolated, high-desert California valley.

In addition to rigorous academic coursework and the responsibility of self-governance, the students put in about twenty hours of physical labor each week at a variety of jobs on the ranch. Though it's not a vocational school, the young men who attend Deep Springs get a good taste of many professions: rancher, laborer, farmer, mechanic, cowboy, butcher, cook.

Over the years, Deep Springs has been profiled in *The New Yorker, The Chronicle of Higher Education, The Los Angeles Times, The Wall Street Journal,* and many other respected publications. *The New York Times* once called Deep Springs "one of the most selective and innovative colleges in the world." But to describe Deep Springs effectively, it's necessary to first set the scene, to describe the timeless physical place that existed, nameless, eons before human eyes ever traced its contours.

For hundreds of miles along California's eastern side runs the enormous Sierra Nevada mountain range, like a dragon's spine. Yosemite, Kings Canyon, Mount Whitney, Lake Tahoe: all these renowned places are part of the Sierra Nevada. The western approach to the Sierra peaks is slow and gradual—the Foothills, California's Gold Country. But to approach the peaks from the east is to be astonished: they are sudden, towering, startling. On the eastern side, in the Sierra's "rain shadow," the terrain is desert, with alkali lakes, salt flats, and sagebrush. The beauty is vast, austere, at times brutal, nothing obscuring the near-impossible distances. Death Valley is nearby. You love rocks? You'll love the eastern Sierra. Deep Springs Valley is small by the standards of the region, roughly twelve miles long and half as wide, running northeast-southwest, ringed by mountains. The weather is extreme—scorching summers, biting-cold winters, violent winds, torrential downpours, snowstorms.

From the college you can see several jagged peaks of the Sierra in the distance. At the southern end of the Valley is an alkali lake. Its water is not only bitter but unapproachable, skirted by moonlike acres of salt-crusted alkali mud. While the land—the lake, the mountains, the canyons, the intermittent streams—is fascinating (botanists, zoologists, and, especially, geologists flock there), it's the sky, the light, that gives the place such a haunting voice. A desert landscape might seem harsh and forbidding to the uninitiated, but with time, experience, and attention, you come to experience the land as a frame for a never-ending, ever-changing show of light. The light of a clear summer midday in the Valley is overwhelming, so bright your vision dims, colors wash out. You squint, even wearing your darkest sunglasses and widest-brimmed hat. The harsh rays reflect up off the light-colored ground and burn your face. It's almost too much to bear.

Or consider the opposite: occasionally a thick cloud cover blankets the Valley. On a moonless night in such conditions, if no artificial light is near, you literally can't see your hand in front of you. It is darker than any closet, as impeccably dark as a deep cave. Between these extremes, the stark land and light interplay in a perpetual spectacle that is anyone's for the noticing. If you are up early enough, when there are thin, high morning clouds over the Valley, you might see them turn from gray to orange to fierce pink, then settle back to white, all within a ten-minute span.

Some rare winter mornings, a low blanket of fog covers the Valley floor, softly but completely obscuring the low hills, the college buildings, the corrals. You go for a walk and the fog encloses you, allowing only the higher peaks and the sharply clear sky to be seen in a circle above you. The climbing sunlight bounces off the blinding white fog, illuminating the peaks to a dazzling gold that lasts but a moment, saturating the sky's blue to an intensity you never could have imagined. Notice well—the conditions that create this white, blue, and gold may not be repeated for years, or in your lifetime, or ever again.

In the fall, if forest fires are burning in the Sierra, early-afternoon winds often blow a strange, thick haze into Deep Springs Valley. Faraway mountains look like paper cutouts. Sunlight filters coldly through the haze, bathing everything in a wan, white, sad light. If you are happy in that moment, this peculiar light gives you pause, as though sadness lurked nearby, but if you are sad in that moment, this bleached, shadowless light affirms and reinforces your mood, as if happiness abided in some far-off place.

Later in the afternoon, after the haze—and the mood—has dissipated, the angled light brings the mountains near the lake into sharp relief, every canyon and furrow revealing itself. If there has been a rain and the air is freshly charged and super-clear, you can discern individual sagebrush bushes dotting the slopes, ten miles away.

Sunsets delight everyone; never confined to one part of the sky, they stretch all around in a cyclorama of color. Pink columns of mile-high cumulus clouds dwarf the mountains; jet vapor trails crisscross the sky; wispy cirrus clouds break into a geometric pattern, unfolding like a Chinese fan. When afternoon rains dissipate at dusk, the resulting sunsets are extraordinary—charcoal blacks next to indigo, fuchsia impossibly fading into cobalt blue, a melon-colored cloud with a pale-green sky behind it. On rare occasions, there is thunder and lightning; on even rarer occasions, the lightning is pink.

Finally, the full moon over Deep Springs Valley is unlike a full moon anywhere else. The pale-colored Valley floor reflects and intensifies the light. You can see every detail as you walk down the road—pebbles and beetles, the color red. You could read a book without straining your eyes in such moonlight. On moonless nights, the starlit sky is spectacular. Many newcomers to the Valley really see the Milky Way for the first time—its shape, its edges, its gap and spur.

How, you may ask, does all this relate to food and cooking? Well, Deep Springs' landscape and *The Deep Springs Cookbook* both repeatedly invite you to pay close attention. Whether you are walking a trail in the Valley at sunset or frying eggs, there is a lot going on and a great deal to be learned, simply by noticing and paying attention to all the details. Drift off into a reverie, and your eggs might turn brown and rubbery in an instant, or you might miss that fleeting shaft of light on Mount Nunn.

The College and Ranch

In this austere, spectacular setting, Deep Springs College was founded on an existing cattle ranch in 1917 by American educator and entrepreneur Lucien L. Nunn. Twenty-six young men attend Deep Springs; twelve to thirteen arrive each summer for two years of rigorous college coursework and physical labor on the ranch. The students govern themselves and make important decisions in the life of the college, assuming much of the responsibility for hiring faculty, admitting new students, and deciding which courses should be taught.

Students perform a variety of jobs during their two years: irrigating alfalfa fields, feeding livestock, milking cows, answering phones in the office, running the bookstore, maintaining the computer networks, toiling in the gardens and orchard, preparing rooms for guests, butchering meat for the kitchen, washing up after meals, and cooking meals for the entire community. Meals in the Boardinghouse are an important part of community life, bringing students, faculty, staff, and families together, marking the rhythm of the day. Everyone works hard and comes to meals hungry. A hired chef prepares many of the meals, while the students, rather adventurously, cook the others. Students approach the daunting job of cooking at Deep Springs the same way they approach most of their endeavors—what they lack in practical experience they make up for with enthusiasm, ambition, interest, and intelligence.

Deep Springs can be a wonderful place to cook. Because it is a cattle ranch, free-range, grass-fed beef is in abundant supply, and a dairy herd of about four cows is milked by student hands twice daily. There are pigs, lambs, and goats. Small flocks of chickens, rabbits, and turkeys are raised "for the table." There is a fruit orchard—apples, pears, peaches, plums, and a lone almond tree (though it's a rare year when all these trees manage to bear, due to the harsh winter weather and winds). In summer, the student gardeners harvest onions, garlic, carrots, lettuce, leeks, beets, tomatoes, basil, eggplant, corn, potatoes, cucumbers, and squash. A raspberry hedge thrives. The henhouse flanks the garden; students gather about six dozen eggs a day from the chickens and geese.

Among the many unique—and perhaps anachronistic—aspects of Deep Springs is the fact that the college never has admitted women as students (there are female faculty, administrators, and staff). Although most people in the greater Deep Springs "family" hope that the college will soon become coeducational, many also appreciate the deep camaraderie and nurturing that develops among "the guys." A sense of ease and humility characterizes Deep Springs' all-male student environment. They knit during meetings. They perhaps don't shower or change clothes as frequently as they would elsewhere. They cook for each other; when one student is sick, the others take care of him, bringing him soup or cookies.

In Deep Springs' accredited academic program, there are standard courses in English composition, public speaking, subjects all over the math/science spectrum, history, literature, political science, and philosophy. But there are elective-type courses, too, not only photography, painting, sculpture, pottery, and music, but also, on occasion, saddlery, auto mechanics, breadmaking, and culinary arts.

After Deep Springs, most students finish their college degrees at four-year universities such as Harvard, Cornell, Berkeley, Oxford, and Yale. Deep Springers go on to become college professors, teachers, writers, doctors, lawyers, engineers, farmers… and chefs.

The Rhythms of a Day

A typical day at Deep Springs starts at 4:30 a.m. A student's alarm goes off; it's time to milk the cows. He rolls out of bed, bleary from too little sleep, and wakes the other "dairy boy." (Deep Springs students in general don't like being called boys, but the "dairy boy" moniker has long endured.) The two silently leave the dorm and walk to the Boardinghouse to collect empty six-gallon stainless-steel milk containers, or "shotguns," from the walk-in refrigerator. They trudge toward the dairy barn, about a quarter-mile from the Boardinghouse, pulling the shotguns on a cart. For much of the year, it's below freezing at this coldest time of day. Frost coats the grass, and a lawn sprinkler's slow leak has formed an elaborate ice sculpture overnight. Sometimes one of the dogs—there are always several at Deep Springs—will get into the habit of accompanying the dairy boys on their twice-daily labor.

The dairy cows are well-accustomed to their routine, but the students always have to prompt them. The enormous animals rise from the cold ground and huff and puff a bit, taking their time getting to the barn. Each cow has her own stanchion in the low rock-and-concrete barn (thought to be the oldest building on the ranch). Her head goes through a gap in a whitewashed wooden stand, and the students slide a slat into place to prevent her from backing out. As the dairy boys settle down to work, they invariably put on music—Brahms or Chopin, or maybe some Metallica.

Sitting on low stools, one student on each side of the cow, they first clean the cow's teats and udder with a disinfecting solution, then position a sterilized bucket underneath and begin milking. To milk a cow, you pinch a teat at its top with your thumb and forefinger, then squeeze all the way down the length of the teat with a slight tug: warm milk streams out in a short squirt. After only a short time on the job, the young men develop a fast, skilled, musical rhythm. Sometimes the cows will disrupt things, kicking over the bucket or copiously urinating or defecating, spoiling the milk.

The first milk to emerge is mostly nonfat, but later in the milking, it comes out creamier. Once the pinching-squeezing yields no more milk, they clean the cow's udder and teats again and rub them with Bag Balm, a classic ranch salve the dairy boys don't hesitate to rub on their own chapped hands.

The milk is carefully weighed, the weight recorded in a log. The dairy boys pour the warm milk through a simple device using cooling coils—like an air conditioner—to rapidly cool the milk, then separate the cream using a centrifugal separator. They thoroughly hose down the concrete floor of the milking area, wash and sterilize all the equipment, then finally wheel the milk, sloshing in the shotguns, back to the Boardinghouse in time for breakfast. They greet the Student Cook, who, to the low sounds of classic Chicago blues, is laying bacon out on a sheet pan or cracking brown eggs into a bowl. The dairy boys go to the big refrigerator and empty yesterday's milk into a bucket (this old milk will be fed to the pigs), then fill clean pitchers with fresh milk and set them out on the tables in the dining room.

A quarter-hour before breakfast is served, the cook rings the giant iron bell mounted outside the Boardinghouse; this first bell serves as an alarm clock for most of the community. But many people, not just the cook and the dairy boys, are already up. During the summer alfalfa-growing season, the student irrigation team is moving sprinkler lines on the fields, the student "feed man" is throwing hay to the horses, the student gardeners are harvesting vegetables for that day's meals, the Writer in Residence is preparing for a reading she will give that evening, a designated student is recording the night's high and low temperatures for the National Weather Service, and the art professor is out in the desert, capturing the sunrise on canvas.

The final breakfast bell rings, and students, staff, administrators, faculty, and families gather for pancakes, scrambled eggs, bacon, oatmeal, fruit, coffee, and fresh milk. On Mondays the college president, the academic dean, the ranch manager, and the Student Body president will meet at a back table over breakfast, coordinating all the goings-on in the Valley.

Shortly after breakfast, the morning's classes begin. Some students might spend the whole morning in the biology lab, while others, following an hour of intermediate Spanish or first-year composition class, will be expected to probe deeply into Melville's *Moby-Dick* or deTocqueville's *Democracy in America*. By the time the final lunch bell rings, everyone's stomach is growling as the professors wrap up spirited class discussions.

Afternoons at Deep Springs are usually devoted to working: the general labor crew builds fences, mows lawns, and hauls garbage; the butcher blasts Prince's *Purple Rain* as he cuts roasts, steaks, and chops; the cooks hurry to get the meatloaf in the oven so there will be enough time to bake the cookies and rolls. The student "office cowboy" processes requests for applications to Deep Springs. Students who don't have afternoon work duties spend their hours studying—or sleeping. The dairy boys typically take a nap before going out for the evening's milking. Sometimes, when there is a surfeit of milk, they will forgo the nap and spend the time in the kitchen, making yogurt or cheese (see page 82 for a basic, easy cheese made from fresh milk, vinegar, and salt).

The last bell of the day—the dinner bell at 6 p.m.—signals for many Deep Springs community members the time to relax and unwind. Everyone loves to linger over dinner, but often the Applications or Curriculum committees must meet, or the morning's class schedule is so tight that some classes must be held in the evenings. On Tuesday evenings, the student dishwashers rush to finish scrubbing the pots so they can attend Public Speaking, a long-standing Deep Springs institution where several students give short speeches to the assembled community, to be critiqued and graded afterward. On Fridays, the entire Student Body gathers for their weekly meeting. These meetings often go late into the night as they democratically tackle the many problems that arise or decisions that must be made in community life.

Many guys find the late-night hours the only time available for studying; to be sleep deprived is a Deep Springs tradition. They spend weekends studying or organizing special work projects (building a grape arbor, painting a mural on the basketball court), but sometimes there is time for relaxing, recharging activities, such as reading for pleasure, riding horses, hiking the many trails in the Valley and surrounding mountains, or just catching up on sleep.

The Boardinghouse

The human-built environment at Deep Springs consists of roads, fences, reservoirs, pipelines, power lines, treelines, irrigated fields, gardens, an orchard, corrals, pens, coops, and some twenty buildings. College activities center around the Main Circle: the student dorm, faculty cottages, Boardinghouse, and buildings containing the library, classrooms, science labs, and administrative offices all surround a big green lawn. Across a field from the Main Circle is the Lower Ranch, with barns, corrals, garden, and ranch staff housing. The dairy barn is nestled at the base of a rocky hill between the two. All these places are important parts of Deep Springs life, but the Boardinghouse, affectionately abbreviated as "B.H.," with its big kitchen and community dining room, could be considered the true "heart" of daily activity at Deep Springs. Like the kitchen in a big family home, it's subjected to constant, intensive use. Even apart from mealtimes, the dining room is a favorite hangout and study space for both students and faculty, where the proverbial "conversations deep into the night" often take place. Between Friday evening poker games, "postmortem" critiques following Public Speaking, midnight meals cooked from care packages sent from home, long political roundtable discussions, loud "cut-loose" dance parties, or simply coffee available 24 hours a day, the B.H. is rarely empty.

The original Boardinghouse was likely little more than the kitchen and dining room. Right from the college's beginning in 1917, the demands placed upon the building subjected it to such constant tinkering and adding-to that today it's difficult, if not impossible, to determine when components were added: a laundry room, a small apartment and office for the cook, a butchering room, and a dugout root cellar in the back all seem to have been added early on. Later came additional dry-storage areas, walk-in refrigerators and freezers, and expanded dining areas, including a stone fireplace hand-built from beautifully rough, angular specimens of almost-black Deep Springs Valley basalt. In my own three decades of deep acquaintance with the B.H., I've seen two major kitchen renovations, including turnover of every piece of kitchen equipment; I've seen porches built, deteriorate, and rebuilt; I've seen at least three new floors put in, and countless new paint jobs. Today, this worn-and-torn, patched-together building has reached the end of its functional life, and plans are underway for an all-new Boardinghouse in the same spot. This edition of The *Deep Springs Cookbook* has been prepared, in part, to commemorate that project.

The Author

I've been fortunate to be associated with Deep Springs in many capacities. I attended as a student: Deep Springers are identified by the year they arrive in the Valley; I arrived in 1988, so I'm a member of the class of 1988, abbreviated as "DS'88." I returned to the Valley a decade later to work as the Boardinghouse Chef/Manager, and a few years later taught a one-term culinary arts class.

Early in my two years as a student, I signed up for the job of Student Cook, considered the hardest job on the ranch, and loved it. Deep Springs alumnus David Tanis (DS'71), then chef at the renowned Berkeley, California, restaurant Chez Panisse, now a *New York Times* columnist, celebrated cookbook author, and culinary mentor, once visited the Valley during that time and cooked several meals for the community. I hovered at his side as he generously wielded his culinary wizardry, roasting peppers, chopping garlic with anchovies, pitting olives, shaving fennel and Parmesan, butchering lambs, roasting whole chickens, simmering black beans with herbs, peeling apples with a paring knife—all new to me. On the final evening of his visit, David braised thirty pounds of lamb shoulder with Moroccan spices, steamed a mountain of couscous, threw together a salad of grated carrots with fresh ginger and green olives, and baked a round loaf of fennel-seed bread for each table. As the community gathered for dinner, we blasted Umm Kulthum on the Boardinghouse stereo and offered platters of spicy lamb tartare on little toasts. From that point on, I was deliciously hooked on the craft of cooking.

After Deep Springs, while finishing my liberal arts degree at Cornell University, instead of the usual student work-study jobs, I cooked in restaurants and did a good deal of private catering, once even planning, cooking, and serving a sumptuous wedding banquet for a hundred guests. My friend Elge and I met in a class called "The Social History of Food and Eating" and became fast friends. We cooked for each other: we'd make tangerine-juice–injected leg of lamb, steak tartare, fresh egg noodles, gazpacho, Greek salad, and almond-crusted cherry pie when perhaps we should have been studying for exams. No matter—in a broader sense, we were still pursuing our education. After graduating in 1992, I moved to Berkeley, where, thanks to my experience at Deep Springs with David Tanis, I got a job washing lettuce and rolling out pasta dough at the extraordinary Chez Panisse, the famous, influential restaurant that emphasizes beautiful, fresh ingredients and simple, classic techniques. Later, with new skills and experience, I lived and cooked in Hawaii. I was excited and inspired by the rich patchwork of island cultures and culinary traditions.

In 1998 I returned to the Valley for a three-year stint as Deep Springs' chef, feeding the community and working closely with students every day. Once, early on, someone asked me for a couple of my recipes, so I wrote them down, plus a few others. At the end of that year, I compiled the first 40-page edition of *The Deep Springs Cookbook* and gave a copy to each graduating student; the book also became indispensable to us in the kitchen. Each year, with each graduation, the cookbook expanded—the final 2001 edition was almost 200 pages long. A few years later, I returned to Deep Springs once more to teach a course in culinary arts, using the old cookbook as a reference.

I continued compiling the book and testing recipes for some years, then in 2009 I learned of San Francisco publisher Chronicle Books' interest in a Deep Springs cookbook, and sent them my manuscript. It was beautifully published as *The Commonsense Kitchen: 500 Recipes Plus Lessons for a Hand-Crafted Life* the following year, and found a place in many peoples' kitchens beyond the Deep Springs community. This revised edition restores the book's original title, and brings it "back home" for Deep Springs' 2017 Centennial Celebration.

For more information on Deep Springs College:

Website:
www.deepsprings.edu

Mailing Address:
HC 72 Box 45001
Dyer, NV 89010
Telephone:
(760) 872-2000

CHAPTER 1

KITCHEN BASICS

Learning to cook is a lifelong process. Every time I mix a batter, slice an onion, or peel an apple, I'm learning to cook, provided I'm paying attention. You want to learn to cook? Go into the kitchen and start cooking. Keep cooking. Let your hunger and appetite guide you; cook what you want to eat.

Pay close attention to every step in the process, and to your results. Food is our primary, fundamental connection to nature. Even urban dwellers who rarely see the sun or set foot on soil must still eat food grown in the sun, in soil. What is the most highly-processed food you can think of? Whatever it is, it is still ultimately based on plants, grown in a field somewhere under the sun.

Cooks perform a kind of alchemy, transforming natural products—plants, animals, water, salt—into food that builds and nourishes the body and soul. I believe the dawn of human civilization occurred not at the moment we learned to build a fire, nor at the moment of killing and butchering an animal, but rather at the moment we learned to carefully cook bits of that animal's flesh over the fire without burning it, to brown, smoky, juicy perfection.

Learning to cook, like learning any craft or skill, is a matter of learning to pay attention, to ask questions. *The best first step is developing close attention to what you eat.* What tastes good to you? Why? What we eat affects not only our bodies, but ultimately the whole, interconnected world. To open a can of green beans creates a different result, both in your body and in the world, than if you bought and cooked a handful of fresh green beans. Each choice, no matter how small, makes a difference. Appreciate your food before eating it. Take a moment to be aware of the colors and aromas. Be aware of all the people who worked to produce the food. Use whatever has been made available to enhance your experience of eating. Sprinkle a little salt, if it makes the food taste better. Pepper. Condiments. Squeeze the lemon or lime. Help yourself to any sauce the cook has provided. Spread a little butter on your bread. Be aware of how the different foods offered complement one another. Relish every bite. Lick your fingers. Stop when you're full. Compliment the cook.

Pay attention to your food likes and dislikes. With time, they may change. Foods I once hated I now love. When I was a kid, each summer my mother would implore me to taste *just one* cherry tomato she had grown in our New Mexico backyard: "Just try it," she'd say, "they're sweet as candy!" I'd dutifully pop one in my mouth, bite into it…and gag. Now, as an adult, I love tomatoes of every size, stripe, and hue. A friend once insisted on his dislike for cherry tomatoes—until he tasted them simply cut in half with a knife, and then he loved them. He hadn't liked the way the little tomatoes squirted their juice when bitten whole. Halved, their good flavor was more accessible. "I never knew anything so simple could make such a difference," he said. Welcome to the craft of cooking.

The second step in learning to cook is developing close attention to ingredients. Notice their qualities, their properties, their inherent beauty. I can't decide which is more beautiful, the finished pot of Gumbo (page 99) or the gleaming bell peppers, fat yellow onions, celery like temple columns, fuzzy okra pods, bits of thyme and dried hot red pepper, raw pink chicken with yellow skin, smoked sausages, and vibrant bunch of parsley, all laid out on the counter. Develop the habit of asking yourself, "Where do these ingredients come from?" For those of us living in modern, industrialized society, answering that question can be extraordinarily complex. Parts of virtually any modern American meal could come from all over the globe. Nonetheless, as we take a greater interest in preparing our own food, the question naturally arises.

Each summer at Deep Springs a new group of students arrives. It doesn't take long before some of them recognize, innately, the possibility of a meal composed entirely of Deep Springs–grown ingredients. This always excites them greatly, as it excited me. Once, when I was first learning to cook as a Deep Springs student, I made a shepherd's pie from a James Beard recipe, containing lamb, onions, garlic, rosemary, potatoes, milk, and butter—all grown or produced in the Valley. It was a revelatory moment: the rich, homely, old-fashioned dish came out well, but it also possessed a kind of deep authority. It belonged right there, where we were. It tasted appropriate and immediate.

Ingredients are infinitely variable. Food is nature, it is life, it is plants and animals, and therefore it is ever-changing, dynamic. Food is always a product of its place and time and circumstance; food is always in the present moment. Cooking, by its concrete nature, resists over-intellectualization. Rather than thinking about it conceptually, ask yourself what is happening right there in the moment: sometimes the lettuce is sweet, sometimes it's bitter, so the sharpness of the dressing has to be adjusted accordingly. The tomatoes were watery last year, needing vinegar to perk up their flavor; this year they are deeply colored, plummy and concentrated, needing nothing but salt. Last week's burgers were deliciously beefy, but these today are a little flat, needing more black pepper and hot sauce.

The third step in learning to cook is, simply, to do it: cook, cook, cook, and keep cooking. Work to satisfy your hunger. Follow recipes. Each recipe in this or any other cookbook offers a lesson and will contribute to your growing culinary knowledge. When following a new recipe, it's important to sit down and read the recipe through — every word, from beginning to end

— before you begin. Sometimes, while cooking, things happen very quickly and there is no time to leave the stove and check the recipe. When the dish is finished, and the actual, physical experience of having cooked it is under your belt, go back and read the recipe through again. Take notes in the margins. Remember that a recipe is not a guarantee that the result will be exactly what you imagine. A recipe is to the finished dish as a written invitation is to the party itself. Anything could happen. Even the simplest recipe is subject to a host of variables, including your own expectations.

Consider a dish as simple as a grilled cheese sandwich. Many questions arise, should you care to ask them. First, what are your expectations? Did you eat and love grilled cheese sandwiches as a child? Were it possible to exactly replicate those grilled cheese sandwiches today (it isn't), would you still love them? Is the bread white, wheaty, soft, chewy; the cheese sharp, mild, grainy, creamy? Will it be Cheddar, bouncy American, or something more "sophisticated," whatever that means? Will the cheese melt creamily, or will it separate and release some of its oil? What fat, if any, will you use to toast the sandwich? Butter? Olive oil? Mayonnaise? Do you spread the outside of the bread thinly with butter and very slowly toast it over low heat in a pan until the bread is golden and the cheese is just melted? Or will you cook it more quickly, over higher heat, and then finish melting the cheese for a few moments in the microwave? Is there another element to the sandwich, a slice of onion, a slice of tomato (do you salt the tomato?), the slightest smear of mustard? Is the bread toasted to a deep brown or just a pale gold? Are you going to sit down and eat your sandwich by yourself as soon as it comes out of the pan, or are you making several for a crowd? Is the sandwich cut in half or in quarters, diagonally or crosswise? What, if anything, will accompany your grilled cheese sandwich? Tomato soup? From a can or homemade? Applesauce? A fresh, crisp apple? A shaved fennel and radish salad? Will you serve the sandwich on a room-temperature plate, a warmed plate, or just a napkin or paper towel? Each option will affect your grilled cheese sandwich experience. Since each question could have any number of answers, an infinite variety of grilled cheese sandwiches is possible. My recipe for a grilled cheese sandwich (page 89) reflects my own biases and answers a few of these questions, but it still leaves plenty of them up to you. Successfully following a recipe not only requires your attention, it requires your good judgment and common sense.

You will find lots of rules in this or any other cookbook, but I hasten to point out that for every cooking rule, there exist several delightful, delicious exceptions. "Be lamps unto yourselves," the dying Buddha told his students. Paying close attention to your own experience as you cook is far more important than following rules just because they are printed on a page. Ruining food is a tiny tragedy and is almost always the result of a lapse of attention somewhere along the way. Simply resolve to pay closer attention the next time, and keep cooking. Learn from your mistakes, and learn how to correct your mistakes whenever possible. If you are given to improvisation, know that the more adept you are with the basics, the more successful your improvisations will be. Cooking is not so much a systematically acquired body of knowledge as a series of intricate, interwoven understandings of ingredients and procedures, each taken on its own terms, each its own idiosyncratic universe.

Finally, learning to cook well is learning how to coax the best out of a few ordinary ingredients, developing the knack for making "something out of nothing." Constraints and limitations often stimulate creativity and new ideas. All good cooks remember a time when, faced with a poorly equipped kitchen and a virtually bare cupboard, they nonetheless produced something delicious. Once I had a job where I cooked vegan dinners in a squalid little café kitchen equipped with only a glass-topped electric stove, an electric oven, and a few poor-quality pots and pans. The stove was no good for anything but boiling water, so I did most of my cooking in the oven—slowly roasting onions instead of sautéing them—and managed to turn out some really good food.

Keep cooking. Honest, nourishing, delicious food is a universal right, not a luxury reserved for the privileged, the greedy, or the righteous. Food, though perhaps not all-important, is still important. Remember: if you're irritable, you're probably hungry. Food can strengthen, embolden, invigorate, empower, restore, refresh, recharge, comfort, balance, collect, soothe, gratify, entertain, cheer, amaze, surprise, and delight us. May you find this book instructive and inspiring. May it help you discover your own, unique culinary principles and philosophies, helping you to write, as it were, your own cookbook.

Culinary Terms

Someone once said that the essence of education is learning new words. A bit reductive, perhaps, but every art, craft, or discipline comes with its own vocabulary; a single word may efficiently connote a complex process or product. Whether you aspire to highly-skilled chefdom or simply to putting an honest meal on your family's table, knowing these words will help you on your path.

BOIL (NOUN OR VERB):
Put tap water into a pot, put the pot on a stove burner, and turn the burner to its highest setting. The water will come to a boil, with many large bubbles briskly breaking the surface of the water. (Contrast with *simmer*.) How long will it take for water to come to a boil? That depends on many things: the thickness and material of the pot, the size and shape of the pot, whether the pot is covered, the form and intensity of the burner's heat, the pot's proximity to the flame, the initial temperature of the water, the amount of water, and the altitude. At higher altitudes (such as Deep Springs' altitude of 5,200 feet), water boils at a lower temperature and remains at that lower temperature while it boils. Therefore, certain foods, such as beans, take longer to cook at higher altitudes. Added pressure raises the boiling point, so foods will cook faster. This is the principle behind pressure cookers.

A *low boil* is characterized by a few large bubbles rapidly breaking the surface of the water here and there. A *rolling boil*, by contrast, is characterized by many large bubbles very rapidly breaking everywhere on the surface of the water.

BRAISE (NOUN OR VERB):
A cooking method whereby food is cooked slowly in a small amount of flavorful liquid. See the recipes for Herbed Braised Chicken, page 212, and Beef Stew, page 184.

BRINE (NOUN OR VERB):
A saltwater solution, often also containing sugar and aromatic ingredients, that penetrates, flavors, and tenderizes meat. See the recipe for Tender Cured Pork Chops, page 197. Brining produces a more radical transformation than marinating. See also *cure*.

CHIFFONADE (NOUN OR VERB):
To cut an herb or a leaf into fine ribbons with a sharp knife.

CHILE (NOUN; PRONOUNCED "CHEE-LAY"):
The proper Spanish term for what are commonly called "hot peppers." Chile is all-important in Southwestern cooking, particularly in the traditional cooking of New Mexico, used either green (typically roasted, peeled, and seeded) or red (typically dried and ground).

CHILI (NOUN; RHYMES WITH "SILLY"):
A stew containing beans (or meat, or both), onions, and a hefty quantity of chile. "Chili powder" is usually a spice blend containing cumin, oregano, and other spices in addition to ground chile.

CHUNK (NOUN OR VERB):
To cut into large, cube-shaped pieces, from ½ inch to 1 inch. See also *dice*.

CREAM (VERB):
To whip or beat butter or other fat, either alone or in combination with sugar, until much air is incorporated into the butter. Creamed butter is light in color and texture, very pliable, and fluffy. When sugar and butter are creamed together, the water in the butter partially dissolves the sugar.

CRUSH (VERB):
In this book, *crush* means to finely mash until the food (usually garlic) is reduced to a purée or, in the case of dry foods such as crackers, to crumbs.

CURE (VERB):
To transform a food's original texture or structure using salt—either dry salt (see the recipe for Gravlax, page 223) or a saltwater solution; see also *brine*. In both methods, the salt penetrates the meat over time.

DEGLAZE (VERB):
To dissolve, using a small amount of liquid (water, wine, or stock), the flavorful, caramelized brown residue (see *fond*) that forms in a pan when sautéing meat, mushrooms, onions, or other savory foods.

DICE (NOUN OR VERB):
To cut into small, cube-shaped pieces. *Fine dice* means to cut into about ¼-inch cubes, and *medium dice* means to cut into about ½-inch cubes.

EMULSIFY (VERB; EMULSION IS THE NOUN):
To smoothly combine two substances that wouldn't normally mix, usually a water-based mixture (for instance, vinegar in salad dressing) with an oil-based one. This is done by means of an *emulsifier*—such as mustard, garlic, egg yolks, or potatoes. Mayonnaise (page 252) is a familiar example of an emulsion.

FILLET (NOUN):
A boneless piece of meat or fish.

FOLD (VERB):
To gently combine a mixture that contains a lot of air (usually whipped egg whites or whipped cream) with another, heavier mixture, so that relatively little of the air is lost from the first mixture.

To fold, place the lighter mixture on top of the heavier one. Using a whisk or a rubber spatula, gently sweep large folds of the heavier mixture up from the bottom of the bowl. Continue until the mixture is uniform. The whisk or spatula is held almost parallel to the vessel's bottom. Mere stirring, by contrast, involves holding the utensil perpendicular to the vessel's bottom.

FOND (NOUN):
The flavorful, caramelized brown residue that forms in the pan when sautéing meat or other foods. The fond is an important source of the finished dish's flavor. See Beef Stew, page 184, or Sautéed Chicken Breast, page 206. See also *deglaze*.

JULIENNE (NOUN OR VERB):
To cut into small, uniform matchstick-shaped pieces (see Kohlrabi-Apple Slaw, page 169).

KNEAD (VERB):
To stretch and fold a mixture, usually bread dough, repeatedly for the purpose of developing the elastic wheat protein known as gluten. The basic motion involves stretching the dough out, then folding it over, rapidly, again and again. Kneading may be done in a sturdy electric mixer or by hand.

MACERATE (VERB):
To soak shallots or onions in vinegar with salt, flavoring the vinegar. Also to sprinkle sugar over cut fruit in order to draw out the fruit's juices.

MARINATE (VERB; MARINADE IS THE NOUN):
To flavor food by letting it sit submerged in, rubbed with, or tossed with flavorful ingredients.

MINCE (VERB):
To chop very finely.

MIREPOIX (NOUN; PRONOUNCED "MEER-EH-PWA"):
Classically, the trio of aromatic vegetables—onion, carrot, and celery—that gives a fundamental "structure" to the final flavor of many a dish (see the recipe for Brown, White, and Wild Rice Pilaf with Mirepoix, page 240).

NONREACTIVE (ADJECTIVE):
In this book, *nonreactive* refers to a vessel made of (or lined with) a material that will not react with acidic foods: glass, ceramic, or enamel, and in some cases, plastic or stainless steel.

POACH (VERB):
To cook food in very hot, but not boiling, water (or wine, or other flavorful liquid). Typically, the water is brought to a boil, the food is put into the water, and then the pot is taken off the heat; the residual heat of the water cooks the food. See the recipes for Poached Eggs, page 60, and Boiled (technically poached) Shrimp, page 227.

ROAST (NOUN OR VERB):
To cook food in the oven, uncovered, for a sufficient length of time and at a sufficiently high temperature to produce an appetizing brown exterior. "*Bake*," by contrast, simply means to cook food in the oven.

ROUX (NOUN; PRONOUNCED "ROO"):
A blend of flour and fat (vegetable oil, lard, butter, or other fat) that is cooked together for the purpose of thickening and enriching liquid. See the recipes for Biscuits and Gravy, page 66, and Gumbo, page 99.

SAUTÉ (NOUN OR VERB):
Means "jump" in French, evoking the intensity of the heat and the way skilled chefs toss ingredients around in a pan with a deft flick of the wrist. *Sauté* means to quickly cook food in an uncovered pan over high heat in a little oil or butter. The pan must be wide enough so the food browns appetizingly. If the cook attempts to sauté too great a volume of food at a time relative to the surface area of the pan, the food will not brown; in this case, the action is closer to *stewing*.

SEASON (VERB; SEASONING IS THE NOUN):
1. To salt food.

2. To apply salt and/or other flavorings to food.

3. To prepare a cast-iron pan for use by applying a thin coat of oil or fat and heating it in the oven (see page 34). The oil polymerizes and fuses to the pan, creating a nonstick coating.

SHAVE (VERB):
To slice food paper-thin.

SIMMER (NOUN OR VERB):
A specific heat level for a deep pot of liquid, at which small bubbles appear here and there intermittently on the liquid's surface. (Contrast with *boil*.)

SPONGE (NOUN):
In breadmaking, a *sponge* is made by combining the recipe's liquid (water or milk), yeast, and only a portion of the flour, mixing it to a batterlike consistency, and allowing it to sit so the yeast naturally proliferates. After the sponge has developed sufficiently, the recipe's salt, fat, and remaining flour are mixed in, resulting in a dough.

STEW (VERB):
To slowly cook food in a covered pan without allowing the food to brown. Steam plays a significant role in the cooking. (Contrast with *sauté*.)

WHIP (VERB):
To beat a substance rapidly in such a way that air is incorporated into it. Examples: whipped cream (page 290), whipped egg whites, and whipped butter.

ZEST (NOUN OR VERB):
The flavorful, oil-rich, pigmented outer skin of citrus fruits, used to give bright flavor to many dishes. Usually removed by means of a fine grater, zester, or rasp (page 34); zest may also be taken in long strips with a vegetable peeler. Care is usually taken to avoid the bitter white pith between the zest and the fruit's juicy flesh.

Essential Equipment

Extraordinary food does not depend on extraordinary kitchen equipment, and extraordinary kitchen equipment does not guarantee extraordinary food. People often assume that my kitchen drawers and cupboards are filled with the finest, most expensive culinary gadgets. Actually, I have quite ordinary stuff, most of it battered from years of use: a few good knives (and some not-so-good ones); heavy, heat-conducting pots and pans; various utensils; and a few basic time-saving electric appliances.

On one hand, I don't place too much emphasis on tools and equipment. Once you develop good knife skills and attention to temperatures and timing, many manufactured kitchen thingamajigs become superfluous. On the other hand, it's important to remember that "no job is difficult if you have the right tool." To that I might add "and the right skill." A few good tools are important if you want to learn to cook well. Your hands are always your primary kitchen tool. The physicality of all your kitchen skills resides in your hands—your strength, your gentle touch, your delicate control. A steady hand, a light hand, a practiced hand—these can all be cultivated. Tactile sensations always tell you a great deal about the food you are working with. Tools are just extensions of your hands.

So, assuming you have a good pair of hands, and that your kitchen has a stove, an oven, a sink, and a refrigerator, what tools do you need to begin cooking, to follow the recipes in this book? Well, you need a couple of knives, a cutting board, and a steel to keep the knives sharp. You need a few sturdy pots and pans that conduct heat evenly, and a few utensils: spoons, spatulas, sieves....

Quality kitchen equipment might be expensive, but in some cases the expense is well justified. I once saw a sign in a shop window in Reno, Nevada, that read, "*The burden of poor quality far outlasts the thrill of the bargain.*" Considering something as simple as cooking your morning oatmeal, the recipe in this book calls for lightly toasting the oats in the pan in a little butter before adding the water and milk. In an inexpensive, thin-bottomed pot, if you keep the flame very low and stand over the stove, constantly and patiently stirring the oats, you just might be able to toast them successfully without scorching them, but it won't be easy. On the other hand, a thick-bottomed pot diffuses the stove's heat well; toasting oats in such a pot will demand much less of your attention—the oats will gently toast and acquire flavor without burning, thanks to the quality of the pot. I know folks who routinely burn food in their inexpensive pans, necessitating the pans' frequent replacement. If you take all that ruined food into account, as well as the expense of new pans, paying $100 for a pan of excellent quality that will last a lifetime doesn't seem so outrageous.

On the other hand, sometimes the cheaper item is every bit as good. I have a few different vegetable peelers, but I bought my favorite one at a grocery store twenty years ago for $1.75—it peels thinly; its blade has stayed razor-sharp.

KNIVES AND CUTTING IMPLEMENTS

It would be difficult to argue that any kitchen tool is more essential than a good, sharp knife. If I were forced to use only one knife, it would be a *chef's knife* (also sometimes called a *cook's knife*) with an 8- to 10-inch blade. A chef's knife of excellent quality will last for a very long time. To learn about knives before you invest in one, go to a knife store, look at your various options, hold them in your hand, and ask questions. Stainless-steel knives are the easiest to use, though in Europe, carbon-steel knives are more common—they sharpen readily, but they pit and discolor easily and may react with acid foods. I've always used stainless-steel knives. When I was a brand-new Student Cook at Deep Springs, I asked ranch manager Geoff Pope if we could order a new knife—all the existing knives were hopelessly dull. He agreed, and when the new knife arrived, it was a revelation: suddenly, kitchen tasks were easy, even pleasurable. I sailed through piles of onions, easily trimmed beef for stew, chopped herbs with abandon. As I developed skill, I remember the joy of making a giant batch of salsa—every tomato, onion, and jalapeño finely diced by hand. Around that time, my mother gave me my own German chef's knife for my birthday, a knife I used steadily for ten years.

Knives are made by one of two processes: forged or stamped. Fully forged knives are crafted one at a time and are better balanced in the hand. They are also more expensive. Stamped knives are made by cutting a knife shape from a sheet of stainless steel, then sharpening it. Stamped knives are cheaper, typically about half the price of forged knives, though some brands are still well-balanced and sturdy enough to withstand heavy use. Pay attention to all parts of any knife you are considering purchasing. Look closely at the blade, how it curves. Pay attention to how the handle feels in your hand, how easy it is to grip. Notice its overall weight and balance—a good knife will balance when held at the point where blade and handle meet, or will tip slightly toward the handle. Look closely, too, at the back edge of the knife blade. On sturdy, well-made knives, this right-angled back edge is sharp, good for crushing small amounts of garlic to a smooth, juicy purée.

After your chef's knife, the next-most-used knives are smaller *paring knives*, with 4- to 5-inch blades, both straight and serrated. These need not be forged. Once I bought an expensive forged paring knife and promptly lost it—I swept it into the garbage along with a pile of lettuce trimmings while washing salad at Chez Panisse. I realized my mistake only when retrieving it would have meant sifting through the entire day's garbage. I find most stamped paring knives to be perfectly adequate.

I rely on *serrated knives* a good deal: a smaller one (with a 4- to 5-inch blade) for cutting tomatoes or sectioning citrus fruit, and a larger one for bread. On the large serrated bread knife, an offset handle is preferable, enabling you to cut all the way through a loaf without smashing your knuckles.

A *sharpening steel* is necessary for keeping your knife sharp. A steel won't put a new edge on a dull knife, but it will maintain an existing good edge for a long time. You can acquire the skill necessary for using the steel. Ask the person at the knife store—or a chef—to show you how. Some cooks prefer a wide angle for steeling their knives, creating a sturdier edge that will last longer, while others prefer a narrower angle, creating a very sharp, but shorter-lived, edge. Find your own balance between these two, and stick with it; changing angles will wear your knife blade away more quickly. If you love sharp knives and intend to use yours a lot, you may also want to get—and learn to use— a *sharpening stone*. I prefer water-lubricated stones (also called *whetstones*); they are cleaner and easier to maintain than those lubricated with oil. When to use a sharpening steel and when to use a stone? The steel maintains the edge on your knife, while a stone restores it. Your steel is for everyday use—it's a good idea to steel your knife every time you use it. But for household cooks, stone sharpening is necessary only occasionally. If you need to create an entirely new edge on your knife, it's time to take it to a professional knife sharpener who uses an electric stone wheel. Knife stores or kitchen-supply stores often offer sharpening services.

An important, constant companion to your knife is a *wooden cutting board*. Maple, thanks to its hardness, is the best wood for cutting boards. Like a knife, a good-quality cutting board might be expensive, but also like a knife, with care it may last a lifetime or longer. Cutting boards should never be submerged in water. They should be nice and big; I have an 18-by-24-inch one that always sits on the counter (caveat: clean underneath it frequently, and ensure that it never gets wet underneath). Smaller cutting boards that fit in a drawer are good to have for tasks like slicing a tomato for a sandwich. Flexible plastic cutting mats are handy (I often use them when trimming meat), especially when cut down with scissors to more manageable sizes, but these should not take the place of a larger cutting board.

Kitchen shears are essential for many tasks, and shears whose blades come apart are the easiest to clean. *Vegetable peelers* are also essential and come in many designs. I prefer a peeler that peels quite thinly. A now-common kitchen tool, the *"fine-plane" rasp* is like a grater, except with a grating surface of tiny, precisely sharpened cutting holes. It was originally manufactured and used as a woodworking tool, but chefs discovered its keen ability to finely grate citrus zest, Parmesan cheese, and chocolate. Such a grater is also very good for reducing a clove of garlic to a smooth mush, or horseradish to a sinus-clearing cloud, though lots of the latter will quickly dull the tiny blades.

POTS AND PANS

Many recipes in this book specify a *heavy* skillet, saucepan, or pot. Why? Heavier cookware conducts heat more evenly; you want the heat from the stove burner to evenly distribute over the cooking surface of the pan. You don't want pans that have hot spots; thin, cheap pans make the cook's job much harder. Any cookware that has an aluminum core clad in stainless steel will likely perform well; there are many brands—and prices. Though sturdy, these are still lighter weight (and a bit easier on the wrists) than most alternatives.

French-style *enameled cast iron* is beautiful and performs well, but it's especially heavy and the enamel is prone to chipping. If the inner enamel surface becomes stained, you might be tempted to bleach it, but too much bleach will make the enamel porous. I especially enjoy using low-tech American *cast iron*. Antique cast-iron skillets are readily found, and you have to wonder, while you are cooking your dinner in them, what stories they could tell, what histories they have mutely witnessed. New (or long-neglected) cast-iron cookware must first be "seasoned" before it is used: wash with soap and water, dry thoroughly, then rub the entire surface—inside and out—with a very light film of cooking oil. Put the skillet upside down in a 400°F oven for about an hour, then turn off the oven and let the skillet cool overnight. The oil coating should now be "fixed" and dry on the surface of the pan. If it seems tacky or sticky, heat it again. Acidic foods may disintegrate the seasoning and react with the pan, so I usually cook tomato sauces and other acidic foods in stainless-steel or coated cookware. I occasionally give a cast-iron skillet a brief scrub with a soapy dishcloth, but most often the skillet needs only to be wiped out with a paper towel. Deep-frying is excellent for maintaining the seasoning on cast iron. When food is burned onto a cast-iron pan, scrub the residue with salt. If you end up scrubbing the seasoning off, you can easily re-season it.

A couple of *nonstick-coated skillets* are nice to have, especially for cooking eggs, but I have found that the coating disintegrates after several years of use, regardless of how well made the pan itself is.

Your pots and pans should have *well-fitting lids*, and ideally, most of them—and their lids—should be able to withstand oven heat. It is a great convenience to be able to start cooking a dish on top of the stove and finish it in the oven, in the same pan.

UTENSILS AND MISCELLANY

Wooden spoons are indispensable—they will not mar the surfaces of your cookware. The *heatproof silicone spatula* is my mother's favorite kitchen tool (her mother called them "child cheaters" because they get all the cake batter out of the bowl, with none left to lick!). An *instant-read thermometer* is a very useful tool, especially for beginning cooks. It's essential for roasting whole chickens, turkeys, roast beef, pork loin, or other large cuts of meat, and if you bake bread, it helps you tell when the bread is done. The old-fashioned meat thermometers, the kind you stick in the roast and leave there during baking, are not as useful.

If you love pesto, *a heavy stone mortar and pestle* (see illustration on page 247; look for these in well-stocked Asian food stores) will coax the truest flavors out of the garlic and basil, but it's practical only for working with small quantities. A food processor makes a large batch of pesto in a jiffy, or if you don't mind adding a great deal of oil, so will a blender, but the violent mechanical action of these devices may subtly diminish some flavors—the flavor of good olive oil, for instance.

As for larger appliances, a *toaster* makes better toast than a *toaster oven*, but the toaster oven is more versatile—you decide. If you bake a lot, a *stand mixer* is convenient, especially a sturdy one that will knead bread dough. A *slow cooker* is like a low-temperature mini-oven. It's good for keeping stews and sauces warm at parties, or for cooking a large quantity of steel-cut oatmeal, but I prefer using an actual oven to slow-cook meats. A *blender* purées liquids, while a *food processor* purées more-solid substances. A blender is necessary for silky puréed soups, but a food processor is necessary for certain other things—pulverizing soaked chickpeas for falafel, for instance. An *immersion blender* is especially versatile, much easier to use and store than a standard jar-type blender.

I've become quite attached to cooking on an *outdoor gas or charcoal grill*—it provides high heat and flame-kissed flavors that can't be duplicated indoors. Among the many new recipes in this edition of the book, several specify use of a grill.

Supplies needed for the kitchen, and called for in this book, are most conveniently thought of as items that come in rolls: *paper towels, plastic wrap, aluminum foil, baking parchment paper, wax paper, cheesecloth,* and *butcher's twine*. Of these, parchment paper is the newcomer to home kitchens. It's very good for baking cakes and other items that tend to stick to their pans. A sheet can be lightly crumpled, then re-flattened and placed over stewing vegetables, permitting just the right amount of steam to escape. Certain acidic foods will eat holes in aluminum foil, but a sheet of parchment between food and foil will prevent this.

CHAPTER 1: KITCHEN BASICS — 35

EQUIPMENT LIST

The following list of equipment encompasses everything you will need to cook all the recipes in this book. Items with * are nice to have but not essential. Items in [ ] are necessary only for making the dish in question (ice cream maker, meat grinder, doughnut cutter...).

Blades, steels, and boards

chef's knife
paring knife
small serrated knife
offset bread knife
boning knife *
[oyster knife]
kitchen shears
pizza cutter (not just for pizza—also for cutting fresh pasta noodles or homemade crackers)
zester or modern "fine-plane" grater *
vegetable peeler
sharpening steel
sharpening stone *
hardwood cutting board
small cutting board(s) or flexible plastic mats *

Pots and pans

large (about 4-quart capacity) saucepan with tight-fitting lid
2 small (about 1½-quart capacity) saucepans with tight-fitting lids
smaller saucepan *
stockpot (deep, 8-quart capacity)
steamer insert *
braising pot or soup pot (heavy, oven safe, at least 4 quarts; a Dutch oven is an ideal example), with tight-fitting, oven-safe lid
small nonstick * sauté pan (omelet pan), 6 to 8 inches in diameter
medium (9- to 10-inch) nonstick * skillet
large (10- to 12-inch) nonstick * skillet with tight-fitting lid
griddle * (flat, like a skillet, but no sides, for cooking pancakes and such)
teakettle (metal or glass; for boiling water)
[teapot] (ceramic or glass; for brewing tea)
pressure cooker * (great for cooking beans at high altitudes)
roasting pans (with sides about 2 inches high, one of sufficient capacity to hold a whole chicken, another larger one to hold a whole turkey *)
baking dishes (9 by 13 inches, 8 by 8 inches)
2 round cake pans (9 inches in diameter)
1 springform pan * (10 to 12 inches in diameter)
[1 large tube-style cake pan]
2 or 4 * loaf pans
2 sheet pans (12 by 17 inches, with rim)
2 baking sheets * (also called cookie sheets, without rim)
[pie plates] (10 inches in diameter, one regular for single-crust pies, one deep for double-crust pies)

Utensils

4 or 5 wooden spoons, assorted sizes
heatproof rubber spatulas
skimmer (wide, perforated spoon)
slotted or perforated spoon
wire whisk
ladle
metal spatula (pancake turner)
tongs
wooden rolling pin
instant-read thermometer (powered by a small battery; range should be from freezing to 400°F)
candy/deep-fry thermometer *
perforated colander
screen sieves, one fine-mesh *
sifter * (screen sieves work well)
pastry brush *
[nutcracker and picks]
corkscrew/bottle opener
potato masher *
melon baller *

Other equipment

pepper grinder
cruet for olive oil *
4 or 5 stainless-steel mixing bowls (assorted sizes)
box grater (with two or three sizes of blade-type holes)
large stone mortar and pestle * (good for many things, but especially if you love garlic)
wire cooling racks
measuring spoon set (two *)
measuring cup set (two *)
salad spinner (not just for salad—good for spin-drying leafy herbs or shaved potatoes for potato chips)
[ice cream maker]
food mill * (can take the place of a food processor and blender in many cases)
potato ricer * (a food mill is more versatile)
[pasta roller-cutter] (hand crank)

[meat grinder with interchangeable blades]
spatter screen * (to reduce the mess in high-heat stovetop cooking)
[ramekins] (individual porcelain custard cups, necessary for crème brûlée)
propane blowtorch * (for crème brûlée)
jars with lids, various sizes
terrycloth kitchen towels
flour sack–type kitchen towels
[doughnut cutter]
[coffee cone] (for holding filters)
kitchen scale, accurate to the quarter-ounce, up to 5 pounds *
sealable storage containers (plastic, or glass with sealable plastic lids; assorted sizes)

Appliances
toaster and/or toaster oven *
blender (more essential than a food processor)
food processor (necessary for some recipes)
stand mixer *
slow cooker *
electric hand-held mixer *
coffee grinder *
another coffee grinder for grinding whole spices *
outdoor gas or charcoal grill (specified in a few recipes)

Essential Ingredients

Author Mark Kurlansky, in his book *Salt*, tells of a thousand-year-old Chinese children's song listing the seven necessary kitchen staples needed every day: firewood, rice, oil, salt, soy sauce, vinegar, and tea. What a great list! Can we modern Westerners come up with a similar one? What are the minimal pantry staples needed to cook in North America? Narrowing down the possibilities (for instance, flour and sugar are certainly staples in the Deep Springs kitchen, where baked goods are prepared every day, but not when I cook just for myself or my family), here is an easy-to-remember list of seven items I always have on hand, and that are called for in this book constantly: salt, pepper, olive oil, butter, lemons, garlic, and onions. With these items, you can prepare virtually any fresh food (vegetables, fruit, nuts, grains, meat, eggs, dairy) simply but deliciously, whether you are making appetizers, soup, salad, a main course, dessert…or all of the above.

Many meats need no seasoning besides salt and pepper; fish and shellfish usually need only salt and perhaps a little lemon; garlic and onions enhance virtually any savory food; butter and lemon are the foundation for many sauces and desserts. These fundamentals, plus several other common ingredients frequently called for in this book, deserve further mention and explanation.

BAKING POWDER AND BAKING SODA

Most of the recipes in Chapter 2 (Pancakes, Biscuits, and Cornbread), as well as the Cakes and Cookies chapters, contain *baking powder* or *baking soda*. What is the difference? When baking soda, called *bicarbonate of soda* in old cookbooks, is combined with an acid ingredient such as buttermilk, little bubbles of gas form, thereby leavening the dough or batter. Baking powder is simply baking soda combined with a powdered acid. As soon as baking powder comes into contact with moisture, the chemical reaction begins. Over time, especially in moist climates, baking powder's leavening capability may deteriorate, so it's wise to buy small containers and use them within a year of purchase. *Always use a perfectly dry measuring spoon to measure baking powder*—the moisture from a wet spoon could ruin the whole container. If you are in doubt as to the potency of your baking powder, just drop a spoonful into a glass of hot water—if this results in an immediate, lively fizz, it's still good.

If you detect a metallic taste in biscuits, cornbread, and other plainly-flavored preparations that use baking powder, try substituting *home-mixed baking powder*, using the following ratio: 1⅓ teaspoons cream of tartar (a powdered acid), 1 teaspoon baking soda, and ¼ teaspoon salt. This is best mixed as needed—its leavening power deteriorates over time. Use the same measurements you would use for regular baking powder.

BUTTER

When people ask me what my favorite food is, I love to say, "Butter." For a lavish Christmas party, my friend Elge and I once offered a "butter bar"—a black marble slab with several different kinds of "artisan" butter for guests to taste on plain French bread. If you love butter, try some of these more expensive butters—they're delicious. Or, best of all, churn your own, as we do at Deep Springs—the recipe is on page 79. A few of the recipes in this book specify salted or unsalted butter, but most simply say "butter," and you may use whatever you have on hand.

Are there any differences between salted and unsalted butter, other than the obvious? Yes: unsalted butter, also known as "sweet butter," has a shorter shelf life, so if you purchase it within the "sell by" date printed on the package, you will usually have fresher butter. Salted butter, with its slightly longer shelf life, usually has a more intense butter flavor.

Sometimes you might find "European-style" butter, with a lower moisture content (and a correspondingly higher fat content) than American butter. The cream used to make it is first cultured, like sour cream, resulting in a richer, deeper flavor. Butter is not pure fat, but *clarified butter* is, and so is Indian *ghee*. Melt a stick of unsalted butter over a low flame, undisturbed. As soon as the butter is completely melted and a thick white foam has formed on top, carefully skim off all the foam with a wide spoon (save this in a bowl; it's very good on toast). What remains in the pan is a thick layer of pure butterfat over a thin layer of milk solids and water. Were you to pour off the pure fat and heat it again in a clean pan, again skimming the foam to remove residual water, you would have clarified butter, which is excellent for pan-frying (see page 253). To make ghee, continue heating the butter after you have skimmed off the foam. As the layer of water evaporates out of the fat, you will hear a merry sizzling sound. Once all the water cooks off, the sizzling quiets. The milk solids remaining on the bottom of the pan will then toast to a nutty brown and flavor the butter. At this point, when the butter releases a nutty, toasted aroma, pour the ghee out of the pan and into a metal bowl to cool. If you simply melt a pat of butter in a wide pan until it turns toast brown, you have made *brown butter*, great on Brussels sprouts (see page 123).

BUTTERMILK

Many recipes in this book call for buttermilk; its gentle tanginess and full dairy flavor make for tender, tasty baked goods. In the Deep Springs kitchen we use 3 gallons of it each week, for breakfast baking, for cornbread and biscuits for lunch, for dinner dessert cakes, and for creamy salad dressings. People who don't like to drink buttermilk by itself may be reluctant to commit to a whole quart of it (pints are rare outside the South). Keep in mind, however, that a quart is 4 cups—two or three recipes' worth—and that it has a much longer refrigerator shelf life than milk. If you like plain yogurt, you may easily acquire a taste for buttermilk—it's lightly salted, tangy and refreshing, but fortifying. Like yogurt, it's very good for you, more easily digested than milk. For the ultimate buttermilk experience, follow the Farm Butter and Buttermilk recipe on page 79—to me, the "true" buttermilk produced is as prized as the butter. Can you substitute plain yogurt for buttermilk in these recipes? Not always—yogurt contains less liquid than buttermilk, so it could yield a drier product.

CANNED FOOD

Canned food was hailed as a miracle when the technology was first developed in the late 1800s and early 1900s. Nowadays it receives a great deal of disdain, but we needn't turn up our noses at canned food completely; some of the recipes in this book call for various canned tomato products, a couple of lunch dishes call for canned condensed soup, canned tuna is, of course, a convenient American staple, and I love my grandmother's canned pear cobbler (page 280). But for the most part, the high-heat canning process causes the flavor and nutritive quality of foods to deteriorate to such an extent that manufacturers must add enormous quantities of sugar, salt, and other substances to make them taste good. Fresh or frozen food is almost always better.

CITRUS

Lemons, oranges, limes, and other citrus are essential for lively-flavored food, as important for the intense oils in their zest, or outer colored skin, as for their sweet or tart juice. Though major varieties of citrus fruit are available in supermarkets year-round, the season for the best citrus is December through March, peaking in January. Some citrus varieties, such as blood oranges, have even shorter seasons. The juiciest specimens are heavy for their size and have smaller pores. I use lemons and limes year-round, but I make a practice of avoiding oranges and other citrus during summer and early fall, when many other fruits are in season to be enjoyed. Then, in the darkest, coldest time of the year, the sweet, vibrant taste of the first oranges seems like a gift.

CHOCOLATE

Theobroma, food of the gods! Visiting an arboretum, I once saw a cacao (chocolate) bush and a coffee bush growing side by side; they are clearly botanical cousins. The dessert chapters in this book contain recipes for chocolate pudding, chocolate cakes, chocolate sauce, chocolate cream pie, brownies, and several different kinds of chocolate chip cookies, all relying on the most readily available and least expensive forms of chocolate: unsweetened cocoa powder and chocolate chips. But chocolate has developed a wine-like connoisseurship recently; many varieties are available, some quite expensive. If you wish to use bars of high-quality chocolate in place of chocolate chips in any of these recipes, you will not be disappointed. Try chocolate chip cookies made with bittersweet Belgian or Swiss chocolate, hand-chopped with a knife into rough, uneven "chips." A little of the chocolate may melt and ooze out, showing a different character. In Mexico and the rest of Latin America, chocolate has always been thought of primarily as a beverage, what we call "hot chocolate," rather than as a solid candy. Solid sweet Mexican chocolate, usually flavored with cinnamon and almonds, is rough and grainy with sugar crystals, designed to be dissolved in rapidly boiling water. Once dissolved, the brew is whipped with a traditional wooden whip called a *molinillo* until an appealing froth forms on the top (chocolate naturally contains a bit of starch, enabling this froth to form). In some parts of South America, a hot drink of chocolate is customarily served unsweetened, with sugar packets on the side for those who like it sweet, and milk for those who like it creamy. In this form, and in the caffeine jolt you will quickly receive, chocolate's kinship with coffee once again becomes apparent.

Chocolate is composed of two substances, chocolate liquor and cocoa butter. Unsweetened cocoa powder is mostly chocolate liquor (the name has nothing to do with alcohol), containing most of the pigments and characteristic flavor compounds we know as "chocolate." Cocoa butter, on the other hand, contains all the fatty richness we associate with solid chocolate but few of the flavor compounds. White chocolate, devoid of chocolate liquor, is made of cocoa butter, sugar, and vanilla. Many of the chocolate dessert recipes in this book call for unsweetened cocoa powder, and all will be perfectly good if made with a leading brand. However, sometimes you may find other cocoa powders that are richer and darker than the leading supermarket brands, labeled "Dutch-processed," "high-fat," or "extra-dark." These yield excellent results.

In a practice reaching far back into pre-Columbian times, chocolate is also occasionally treated as a spice, deepening the roasty-toasty flavor of chiles—a little is called for in some of this book's Mexican and Southwestern recipes. Conversely, a pinch of cayenne pepper (or other hot chile) curiously piques and enhances the flavor of many a chocolate dessert.

COFFEE

A couple of the cake recipes in the book call for brewed coffee, and the breakfast chapters mention it frequently. If you love coffee, it would be a worthwhile experiment to purchase green coffee beans to roast and grind yourself, as was the common practice of yesteryear. Roasting, during which myriad flavor compounds are formed, is simple enough to do but exceedingly complex chemically. Since many of these compounds are quite unstable, the most flavorful coffee is made of very freshly-roasted beans. The darkest roast is not necessarily the most flavorful; medium-roast coffee often has a wonderful complexity of aromas and flavors.

To make a great cup of coffee, consider the following ideal scenario: toast your green coffee beans slowly in a pan in a 300°F oven, tossing and redistributing them frequently, until they are deep brown. Finely grind your beans in a coffee grinder and put a kettle of cold water on to boil. Position a paper filter in a filter cone over your favorite mug. Put 2 heaping tablespoons of ground coffee in the filter (more if your mug is abnormally large). The moment the water reaches a boil, pour the water over the coffee, thoroughly moistening the grounds. You will see tiny rainbow-y bubbles coming off the grounds as the water seeps through; this is called "bloom." Once the first pour of water has filtered through, pour another, enough to fill your cup. Stir the grounds gently with a spoon, being careful not to rip the filter. Once your second pour has filtered through, your coffee is ready to enjoy.

CORNMEAL

Perhaps it's my Southern ancestry—I love cornmeal. Odes to cornmeal can be found throughout the book. Although natural, whole-grain cornmeal has a superior flavor, it's a perishable product—it can readily go rancid or moldy. In the South, where delicious cornmeal is especially valued, it's often kept in the refrigerator or freezer. Most supermarket cornmeal has been treated for long shelf life and tastes flat and bland compared to fresh, stone-ground cornmeal. Once I mail-ordered some extraordinarily delicious stone-ground yellow cornmeal from Louisiana. It came in an assortment of five grinds: *grits* (the coarsest), *polenta, cornmeal, fish fry,* and *flour* (the finest). These days, I get a reliably good organic stone-ground cornmeal at the supermarket, and following the Louisiana mill's example, I sieve it into different grinds, and use it for everything. Most often, using a fine screen sieve, I sift it into just two grinds, coarse and fine. The coarse I use for polenta (page 242). It takes a little longer to cook than packaged polenta, but has a deep, delicious corn flavor. I sometimes put the finer grade through an extra-fine sieve, separating it into fluffy corn flour that's great swapped out for some of the all-purpose flour in biscuits and cakes, and a medium–grind meal that's ideal for cornbread.

GARLIC, ONIONS AND SHALLOTS

Cook your way through the savory chapters of this book, and you will be reaching for members of the Allium family—garlic, onions, leeks, scallions, and shallots—constantly. Garlic and onions have been very successfully grown at Deep Springs for years—and used with abandon by the Student Cooks. Chopping and sautéing onions are fundamental kitchen tasks—it's the first thing I teach Student Cooks. When I taught a culinary arts class, the first thing I demonstrated was dicing an onion; afterward, the students liked to say, "Tom made us cry on the first day of class." Actually, if your knife is quite sharp, fewer fumes will be released, whereas a dull knife crushes more of the onion's cells, releasing more fumes. To lessen the effect of the fumes, light a candle nearby. Watch out for onions with any soft or rotten parts—cut these away entirely.

Garlic is an almost addictive ingredient—it not only tastes good in its own right, but it enhances the flavors of everything else. To peel fresh garlic, separate the head into cloves, and then with a small knife, cut the stem end off a clove. Often the skin will peel right off—lightly crushing the clove helps release the skin. If the clove of garlic seems dry, shrunken, or yellowed, or has a granulated surface, it has not stayed fresh—throw it out. Cut out any brown spots. Unless the garlic is freshly harvested, I always cut each clove in half and pry out the tough little sprout in the center. This part tastes especially harsh and bitter. Garlic can be minced with a knife, but crushing it allows more of its flavor to be released and dispersed throughout the dish.

Many good cooks swear by a garlic press. A heavy stone mortar and pestle does a beautiful job of crushing a small handful of garlic to a smooth, flavorful purée. When a recipe calls for just a clove or two or three, you can deploy a trick I learned from chef David Tanis: crush the split cloves to a juicy purée with the back edge of your chef's knife, and there's no extra equipment to wash.

Shallots have a finer, smoother, more intense savor than onions—some cuisines of the world use them exclusively. Use shallots in recipes that call for them—then try the same recipe with onion and note the difference. A small shallot, grated into a cup of yogurt, with a little salt and pepper stirred in, makes a superlative sauce for any simple food (see page 252).

Avoid using pre-peeled, pre-chopped onions, garlic, or shallots. Since the flavor compounds in these vegetables are so volatile, such products must be heavily treated with preservatives. For the same reason, don't be tempted to chop your onions and garlic far ahead of time. There simply is no substitute or shortcut for peeling and chopping fresh onions and garlic yourself, as you need them—all that is required is your knives, a little practice, and patience. The flavors in your cooking will have a deep, complex sweetness and savor.

FLOUR

Wheat flour is the staple grain of half the world, playing a fundamental role in many cuisines. As grains go, wheat is high in protein and sustained many of our forebears. There are numerous types of wheat flour on the market: all-purpose, unbleached, whole wheat, white whole wheat, bleached, bread flour, cake flour, semolina flour, self-rising flour. Choosing flour can be confusing to a beginner. What we commonly know as "white flour" is more properly known—and labeled—as *all-purpose flour*. To keep things simple, all the recipes in the book have been tested using this basic flour. If you like, you can use *bread flour* in the bread recipes (bread flour has a higher protein content than all-purpose; wheat's elastic protein gives bread its characteristic springy texture). You can also use *cake flour* in the cake and quick bread recipes (cake flour has a lower protein content than all-purpose, and so makes for lighter, softer-textured baked goods).

I highly recommend choosing *unbleached* all-purpose flour (not to be confused with whole-wheat flour) over flour labeled "bleached." In my experience, name-brand flour will perform more consistently than bargain brands or store brands. In the American South, *self-rising flour* is popular for biscuits and such. It is made of softer wheat than all-purpose flour, and has baking powder and salt already mixed in.

Semolina flour is made from pale yellow, high-protein durum wheat (the same wheat used in macaroni, spaghetti, and other dried pasta) and has a sandlike texture. This granular texture makes it good for dusting fresh pasta noodles, and it can be added to bread doughs (see Pizza, page 86).

Learning to make *fresh pasta* (see page 231) is a particularly good, direct way to learn about the properties of flour. Knowledge thus gained will carry over into breadmaking and the baking of quick breads, piecrust, and cakes.

OILS AND FATS

While olive oil is much touted for its health benefits, it's important to remember that other vegetable oils contain many of the same beneficial compounds. Olive oil has become the primary cooking oil of many American kitchens for good reason—it tastes so delicious. *Extra-virgin olive oil* is pressed from olives using only mechanical extraction—no heat or solvents are used. Extra-virgin olive oil has the deepest olive flavor. *Pure olive oil* is extracted from olives using heat or solvent extraction methods—it doesn't have as strong an olive flavor, but it's fine for frying. Sometimes in food-service settings, you will see something labeled "olive pomace oil." This flavorless oil is extracted from olive pits and the residue left over from olive oil pressing; under international law it is not allowed to be labeled as olive oil. *Extra-light olive oil* costs the same as regular olive oil but has no flavor or aroma. If you want a lighter-tasting olive oil, just blend a little extra-virgin into a larger quantity of vegetable oil. Even among extra-virgin oils, you'll find many varieties and prices. I tend to buy less-expensive extra-virgin olive oil and use it for both cooking and salads. When I have a bottle of great extra-virgin olive oil, I use it where its flavor will be most appreciated: in delicate green salads, on hot pasta with garlic, in mashed potatoes in place of the butter, or simply drizzled on bread.

When sold in their typically refined state, *sunflower, safflower*, and *peanut oils* are excellent for deep-frying. Sometimes you can find them unrefined, and their flavors can be excellent, with as much character as olive oil. *Coconut oil's* reputation has improved of late, along with other saturated fats, and it is a superb cooking oil—it gives dishes' flavors a particular roundness and richness. In many recipes, the whiff of coconut it may impart is not unwelcome.

Speaking of saturated fat, *lard, beef tallow*, and *chicken fat* make appearances throughout this book, and have always been a part of my cooking, even when they were unfashionable. It's hard to explain exactly how, but pure, preservative-free, freshly-rendered lard from well-raised hogs is a particular joy to cook with. It gives many dishes—beans, soups, stews, Mexican food, even piecrust—a deep, authoritative presence.

PEPPER

Black pepper is by far the most commonly used spice in European-derived cooking. History books say that demand for it ultimately led to the Europeans' "discovery" of the Americas. It not only provides a little spicy kick, but actually acts as a flavor enhancer, too. Even foods rich with other hot spices, such as chili or curry, often reach their balance with a touch of black pepper. Black pepper is made by soaking and drying unripe pepper berries after harvest. A naturally occurring enzyme causes the outer skin to shrivel and blacken (you have probably noticed that the inside of a peppercorn is white). This process creates many complex flavor compounds. These, in turn, enhance other flavors. *White pepper* is made by soaking off the peppercorn's outer skin in water, leaving only the inner seed. The peppercorns undergo a slight fermentation in this process, so their flavor is different, a bit cheeselike. White pepper is much used in Chinese cooking. *Green peppercorns* are freeze-dried and have a mild, fresh, almost floral scent. They are the least-processed form of pepper, being neither fermented nor soaked. As pepper is an essential kitchen seasoning, so a pepper grinder is an essential kitchen tool. Many of those aforementioned complex flavor compounds evaporate when ground pepper sits around for too long; only freshly ground pepper fulfills pepper's full promise. In addition to grinding pepper, I sometimes even sieve it: using two strainers, one fine-mesh and the other regular-mesh, I sift the pepper into three grades: fine, coarse, and cracked. I always try to use the coarse grind in egg salad (page 92) and other preparations where the powdery fine grind would turn the dish gray.

What is "red pepper"? It's a common name for *cayenne*—small, very hot, bright red chile pods that are dried and then used whole, or crushed coarsely, or finely ground. Many recipes in this book call for a pinch. Its intense heat is bright, clean, and forward, without lingering in the mouth the way many other hot chiles do. When small, hot, red chile pods are crushed coarsely, they are referred to as *hot red pepper flakes* and are important in Italian cooking.

SALT

In the first terrifying, frustrating, but ultimately rewarding weeks of cooking for the entire Deep Springs community when I was a student, I remember learning two extremely important things: (1) to *turn the stove burner down*, and (2) to *add salt until the food tasted good*.

Why do we, like many animals, crave salt? Why does it taste so good to us? I have a theory: it has to do with trace minerals. Pure salt, or sodium chloride, is relatively rare in nature. A host of other minerals, many of which are essential to our body chemistry, exist in trace quantities alongside the sodium chloride in seawater and salt deposits (which are ancient dried seawater). This same mineral balance exists in our blood; we are, literally, the salt of the earth or, more directly, the salt of the oceans. Until quite recently in our evolutionary history, we humans consumed unrefined salt from these natural sources. Nowadays, industries extract and use the minerals, one reason why pure salt—the leftover—is so cheap. Virtually all salt on the market today is refined, even if it's labeled "sea salt." And so, even if we consume a lot of refined salt, we continue craving salt *because our bodies require the trace minerals that always accompany salt in its natural state*.

The salt craving reaches a zenith with professional cooks (especially men), who, tasting food all day, typically become inured to the taste of salt, and so tend to oversalt their food. Many years ago, I started using truly unrefined sea salt in all my cooking at home. Of course, such salt is more expensive than refined salt, though not prohibitively so. Most varieties are pale gray and somewhat moist. I've found that when I use this salt consistently, I don't use too much—I enjoy undersalted or even unsalted food much more than I used to.

Judicious use of salt is fundamental to good cooking. Salt is the great balancer—it offsets acidity (for example, tomatoes need a lot of salt) and balances sweetness (most of the dessert recipes in this book call for a pinch). If you oversalt a dish, you can sometimes correct your error by adding an acidic component—lemon juice or tomatoes.

When sautéing many vegetables together, add them to the pan one at a time, beginning with the one that needs the longest cooking. With each addition, add a pinch of salt to the pan—this is called "salting from the bottom up" and allows the individual flavors to remain distinct. Many recipes in this book direct you to do this. It is important to salt all or most of the elements in composed dishes—all the components of lasagna, for instance, are individually seasoned, and potatoes to be added to soup taste best when boiled separately in well-salted water.

A few recipes (for pickles and brines) in this book specify *kosher salt*. This is especially pure, refined salt with a unique crystalline structure that makes it lighter than other kinds of salt; a tablespoon of kosher salt weighs much less than a tablespoon of regular table salt. Use kosher salt in recipes that specify it—the minerals in other salts could adversely affect the recipe.

SPICES (AND HERBS)

By "spice," we mean dried, intensely aromatic plant material, usually used in small quantities, such as seeds (mustard, fennel, coriander), berries (pepper), fruits (cayenne, paprika), buds (cloves), flowers (saffron), and bark (cinnamon). Aromatic leaves, fresh or dried, are, of course, called *herbs*.

With herbs, fresh is most often better, though dried forms of some (such as thyme, bay, oregano, and sage) are traditional in many a dish. Some cooks use spices and herbs cautiously, aiming to enhance, not dominate, a food's inherent flavors, while other cooks—and other cultures—use them much more liberally. Whichever approach you prefer, balance is always key: even spice-heavy preparations such as Indian curry must be carefully balanced to be good.

Dried spices are best stored in a dark cabinet; they lose their flavor and aroma over time, especially if exposed to heat and light. I think standard spice jars are too big. Whenever possible, buy spices in quantities you are likely to use up within a year. Most of my spice jars are quite small, and I keep larger quantities of spices—and lesser-used ones—well wrapped and sealed in the freezer, to better preserve their volatile aromas. I usually buy whole spices, grinding them as needed in a coffee grinder designated for the purpose. Here is a list of all the spices (and dried herbs) called for in this book:

Whole spices and herbs:
black peppercorns (used very frequently if you have a pepper grinder)
caraway seed (occasional)
cardamom (occasional)
celery seed
cinnamon sticks (occasional)
cloves
coriander
cumin
fennel seed
juniper berries (occasional)
marjoram (occasional)
mustard seed (yellow or black)
nutmeg
oregano
red pepper flakes
saffron (occasional)
star anise (occasional)
thyme
white pepper

Ground or powdered spices and herbs:
black pepper (used very frequently if you do not have a pepper grinder)
cayenne pepper (used frequently)
cinnamon
cloves
cumin
curry powder (see page 102 for a recipe)
ginger
mace (occasional)
dry mustard
paprika
sage
turmeric (for blending curry powder)
white pepper

SUGAR

My friend Elge calls granulated sugar "the white menace." Indeed, the wide distribution of highly-refined sugar throughout the world's food systems, and the ill health caused by its overconsumption, is one of the iconic (and ironic) stories of our industrialized world today. That said, sweets are delicious, gratifying, and an essential part of our culinary heritage. In developing the sweet recipes for this book, I've always aimed to use sugar with as restrained a hand as possible. We generally favor less-sweet desserts nowadays than did our forebears; cookie, cake, and jam recipes from old cookbooks are often too sweet for modern tastes.

Sugar is a fascinating ingredient. In many Asian cuisines, it is carefully used in many savory foods to balance salty, sour, or spicy flavors (see the recipe for Shoyu Chicken, page 214—the large amount of soy sauce requires a hefty dose of sugar to balance it). In baked goods, sugar not only provides sweetness, it retains moisture. Compare the recipes for Biscuits (page 65) and Oatmeal Scones (page 68)—the biscuits contain no sugar, while the scones contain a generous amount. Biscuits, the recipe urges, must be consumed warm, while the scones are delicious hours after being baked, owing to their sugar content. Sugar also helps keep ice cream creamy, deterring the formation of grainy crystals, because it "binds" with the water in the cream. However, a large ratio of sugar to cream is required to accomplish this effect. Instead, in the Vanilla Ice Cream recipe (page 305), I use a little cornstarch—it also suppresses crystal formation by binding with the water, without adding unnecessary sweetness. In that recipe, I also include a tablespoon of honey, to impart a subtle, extra character to the sweetness. Honey, by volume, is sweeter than sugar.

Sugar also preserves flavor and aroma—it is essential to fruit jam. If you dial back the sugar in jam too much, you'll end up with cooked-tasting, sour fruit paste that would rather mold than not. Sugar allows good fruit to be cooked rapidly while retaining the fruit's vibrant, fresh flavor and color. The precisely-timed addition of sugar "fixes" the elusive flavor of freshly-brewed coffee in the Coffee Ice Cream recipe (page 305), and of Earl Grey tea in the Marmalade recipe (page 260).

Best of all, sugar caramelizes. The recipes for Butterscotch Pudding (page 301), Toffee (page 327), Dulce de Leche (page 281), and Crème Brulée (page 303), all owe their goodness to caramelization, a transformative and complex chemical process. As sugar caramelizes, it develops into myriad compounds with new aromas that together form the flavor we know and love as caramel.

To make simple *caramelized sugar*, combine a cup of granulated (white) sugar with about ¼ cup of water in a clean, heavy saucepan. Have a lightly-oiled metal sheet pan ready, for pouring the finished caramel. Heat the sugar and water over a medium-high flame, stirring only until the sugar dissolves. Stir gently to avoid getting any of the mixture on the sides of the pan—it can trigger recrystallization. Let the sugar cook without stirring, watching it carefully: once the water has evaporated, the sugar can then reach the temperatures required for caramelization. If the sugar "seizes up" and recrystallizes before it begins to darken, start over. The color of the molten sugar progresses from clear to pale yellow, to light amber, then to reddish amber, then dark brown, then finally to smoky, burned black. The trick is to remove the sugar from the heat the moment it reaches the desired level of darkness. Too dark, and the caramel is bitter and burned; too light, and the caramel flavor is too faint. Look for the beginnings of a red color, after the yellow and light amber stages, then quickly pour the caramel onto the prepared sheet. Don't be tempted to touch the sugar until it has cooled—it's *extremely* hot. When partially cooled, caramel can be stretched into fine threads, or molded or shaped. When completely cool, it can be broken into shards, or pulverized into coarse powder, excellent for topping ice cream or flavoring whipped cream.

A different and little-known way of caramelizing sugar is to toast it at a low temperature in the oven: simply spread a ¼-inch layer of granulated (white) sugar on a baking sheet, and place it in a 325°F oven. Let the sugar bake for several hours, removing the sheet and stirring the sugar around a few times. Depending on the ability of your oven to maintain a steady 325°F, the sugar should begin to change color, from snow-white to pale beige, after about 3 or 4 hours. This *toasted sugar* may be used in any recipe calling for regular granulated sugar, but having undergone some caramelization, it results in a much more interesting, complex sweetness in the final product. (You can toast the sugar even longer to achieve a darker color—at this stage, the sugar is very complex, but markedly less sweet, and therefore not as versatile. If you let the sugar continue toasting, it will finally liquefy.) The simplest baked goods, such as plain cake or cookies, take on a subtle but unmistakable complexity when made with toasted sugar; the sweetness practically dances on your tongue.

Brown sugar is simply white, granulated sugar with a little molasses added back (molasses is the by-product of sugar refining). For *home-mixed brown sugar*, blend dark molasses into granulated sugar (or toasted sugar), using anywhere from a teaspoon to a tablespoon of molasses for each cup of sugar, depending on how dark you want it. Blend with your clean fingers until the mixture is uniform.

You may find other specialty sugars, in varying degrees of refinement: *demerara sugar, turbinado sugar*, Mexican *morena sugar*, and many brands of *organic sugar* are less refined, retaining a little more residual molasses than standard granulated sugar, while *Muscovado sugar* and Mexican *piloncillo* are even darker. All are delicious, and useable in a wide range of recipes, but they may not perform well for standard candy-making, or for recipes requiring the caramelization of sugar—the impurities in these sugars affect the rate of caramelization unpredictably. For making the toasted sugar above, or any of the candy recipes in this book, standard, name-brand granulated (white) sugar is the only sugar sufficiently refined to deliver predictable results.

VINEGAR AND OTHER FLAVORFUL THINGS IN BOTTLES

The word vinegar comes from the French *vinaigre*, literally meaning "sour wine." Alcohol in wine (or cider, or other fermented juice) may, when exposed to air over a long period, convert into acetic acid. Whatever characteristics the wine or cider had will contribute to the character of its corresponding vinegar.

Vinegar, even vinegar of good quality, is relatively cheap, and a little goes a long way, so I like to have several varieties on hand. This book frequently calls for the following three vinegars: *red wine vinegar, balsamic vinegar* (made by a more complex process than other vinegars), and *apple cider vinegar*. Other types of vinegar, such as the wonderfully complex *sherry vinegar*, bright *champagne vinegar*, or yeasty *malt vinegar*, are also worth experiencing. Vinegars flavored with herbs or fruit may be appealing, but I find that they are not as versatile as those above. I keep *white distilled vinegar* under the kitchen sink, with the cleaning products—I prefer vinegar with more character for use in food.

Alongside the vinegars in my kitchen pantry, I keep a few other flavorful bottled items: *Worcestershire sauce*, a timeless, curious blend of molasses, tamarind, anchovies, and shallots; *soy sauce*, occasionally used in non-Asian recipes; Tabasco or other fiery *hot sauce*; and various pure extracts—*vanilla, almond*, and *lemon extract* are all called for in this book's dessert recipes. Finally, I'm particularly fond of flower waters, frequently used in Middle Eastern cookery, particularly *rosewater* and *orange flower water*. These intensely perfumy waters are best used sparingly—sprinkled lightly over food just before serving. They are delicious on sweet summer melon (see page 281). Rosewater is called for in some very old American baking recipes; there is a little in this book's pound cake (see page 288). And I find that a few drops of rosewater or orange flower water often improve the taste of a glass of cheap wine.

Measuring

MEASURING FLOUR

When a recipe in this book specifies "sifted flour," it means that the flour must be sifted prior to measuring. Since we in the United States prefer our volume measurements (cups and teaspoons and tablespoons) to the more accurate weighing common in Europe, sifting flour before measuring will ensure that you get the same amount each time. But I cheat a little—I simply "fluff up" any flour I'm about to measure by sifting it through my hand or with a spoon. Then I gently spoon the flour into the measuring cup and level the cup off with a straight-edged object such as the back of a knife. Don't tap the cup or pack the flour down into the cup. This is especially important when multiplying a recipe—I always advise Deep Springs student cooks to measure the flour for cakes cup by cup, or to weigh it.

MEASURING OTHER INGREDIENTS

Liquids are best measured in glass or plastic liquid measuring cups, with clearly marked gradations. Dry ingredients are best measured in metal or plastic measuring cups that can be leveled off. Substances like brown sugar must be firmly packed into the cup. Sticks of butter as usually packaged are easy to measure with the aid of the markings on the wrapper and your good eye. If you have butter that is not conventionally packaged, use the displacement method: to measure ½ cup of butter, take a 1-cup liquid measuring cup and put ½ cup of cold water in it. Add butter, pressing the butter just below the surface of the water. When the water reaches the 1-cup mark, pour off the water and you have ½ cup of butter.

When a recipe calls for ⅛ teaspoon of a dry ingredient (usually salt), measure out ¼ teaspoon of the ingredient onto a plate, then divide the pile in half evenly with a knife.

Useful equivalents:
1 cup = 16 tablespoons
1 cup (liquid) = 8 ounces
2 cups = 1 pint
1 pint = 1 pound; "A pint's a pound the world around."
4 cups = 2 pints = 1 quart
4 quarts = 1 gallon
1 tablespoon = 3 teaspoons
4 tablespoons = ¼ cup
1 ounce butter = 2 tablespoons
1 stick butter = ½ cup
1 cup grated cheese = about 4 ounces, or ¼ pound
2 cups sugar = 1 pound
2 cups butter = 1 pound
4 cups sifted flour = 1 pound
4 jumbo eggs = about 1 cup
5 large eggs = about 1 cup
1 cup whole almonds = 4½ ounces
1 cup walnut halves and pieces = 3¼ ounces
1 cup chopped walnuts = 3¾ ounces
2 cups dry beans = about 1 pound
1 cup chocolate chips = 6 ounces
6-ounce portion of meat = about the size of two decks of cards
1 ounce of cheese = about the size of your thumb

Metric Equivalents of U.S. Measurements

VOLUME

U.S. Measure	Metric Equivalent	Round To
¼ teaspoon	1.233 ml	1 ml
½ teaspoon	2.465 ml	2.5 ml
1 teaspoon	4.929 ml	5 ml
1 tablespoon	14.787 ml	15 ml
2 tablespoons	29.574 ml	30 ml
3 tablespoons	44.361 ml	45 ml
¼ cup	59.148 ml	60 ml
⅓ cup	78.815 ml	80 ml
½ cup	118.30 ml	120 ml
⅔ cup	157.63 ml	160 ml
¾ cup	177.44 ml	175 ml
1 cup	236.59 ml	240 ml
1 pint (2 cups)	473.18 ml	475 ml
1 quart	946.08 ml	950 ml
2 quarts	1.89 L	1.9 L
3 quarts	2.838 L	2.85 L
1 gallon	3.784 L	3.8 L

WEIGHT

U.S. Measure	Metric Equivalent	Round To
¼ ounce	7.087 g	7 g
½ ounce	14.175 g	14 g
1 ounce	28.35 g	28 g
4 ounces	113.4 g	113 g
6 ounces	170.1 g	170 g
8 ounces	226.8 g	227 g
12 ounces	340.19 g	340 g
1 pound	453.59 g	454 g
2 pounds	907.19 g	907 g
3 pounds	1.361 kg	1.4 kg
4 pounds	1.814 kg	1.8 kg
5 pounds	2.268 kg	2.25 kg
10 pounds	4.536 kg	4.5 kg

LENGTH

U.S. Measure	Metric Equivalent	Round To
¼ inch	6.35 mm	6.5 mm
½ inch	1.27 cm	1.25 cm
¾ inch	1.905 cm	1.9 cm
1 inch	2.54 cm	2.5 cm
6 inches	15.24 cm	15.25 cm
8 inches	20.32 cm	20 cm
9 inches	22.86 cm	23 cm
10 inches	25.4 cm	25 cm
1 foot	30.48 cm	30.5 cm

TEMPERATURE

U.S. Measure	Metric Equivalent	Round To
0° F	-17.78° C	-18° C
40° F	4.444° C	4° C
100° F	37.778° C	38° C
125° F	51.667° C	52° C
135° F	57.222° C	57° C
140° F	60° C	60° C
160° F	71.111° C	71° C
170° F	76.667° C	77° C
180° F	82.222° C	82° C
190° F	87.778° C	88° C
200° F	93.333° C	93° C
212° F	100° C	100° C
225° F	107.22° C	107° C
250° F	121.11° C	121° C
275° F	135° C	135° C (Gas Mark 1)
300° F	148.89° C	149° C (Gas Mark 2)
325° F	162.78° C	163° C (Gas Mark 3)
350° F	176.67° C	177° C (Gas Mark 4)
375° F	190.56° C	190° C (Gas Mark 5)
400° F	204.44° C	204° C (Gas Mark 6)
425° F	218.33° C	218° C (Gas Mark 7)
450° F	232.22° C	232° C (Gas Mark 8)
475° F	246.11° C	246° C
500° F	260° C	260° C

CHAPTER 2

BREAKFAST: OATS, GRITS, BACON, & EGGS

Deep Springs students have legendarily hearty appetites, even for young men, thanks to all the hard physical work and long periods of mental concentration. Therefore, the big carbohydrate- and cholesterol-laden American ranch breakfast is alive and well every day at Deep Springs; eggs, bacon, quick breads, and pancakes are all mainstays. However, at the behest of older, more sedentary, health-conscious community members, the cooks often make a pot of oatmeal and set out yogurt and a tray of cut fresh fruit. While much of the oatmeal may go uneaten, ending up as slop for the pigs, no matter how much bacon the cooks make, there is rarely any left over.

In this chapter, you'll find recipes for wholesome, lighter, everyday breakfasts for adult metabolisms alongside old-fashioned ranch breakfast recipes for young hard workers and hard thinkers.

Oatmeal

serves 2

A bowl of piping-hot oatmeal, cooked with a little milk, topped with butter, and augmented with dried fruit, seeds, and other flavorful accompaniments, is a breakfast of particular savor.

1 tablespoon butter

1 cup rolled oats *(regular or old-fashioned, not quick or instant)*

2 cups water

¼ teaspoon salt

1 cup milk

FOR SERVING (ANY COMBINATION)

butter

milk, half-and-half, cream, buttermilk or yogurt

Dried Fruit Compote *(page 52)*

almonds, walnuts, pecans, or other nuts

sunflower, sesame, or flax seeds

brown sugar, honey, maple syrup, jam, or fruit preserves

bananas, blueberries, peaches, pears, Fuyu persimmons, or other fresh sweet fruit *(acidic fruit doesn't marry well)*

dates, raisins, dried cherries, dried cranberries, or other dried fruit, cut small

Melt the butter in a medium-sized, heavy saucepan over medium-high heat. Add the dry oats and lightly toast the oats, stirring and tossing constantly, keeping everything moving, until a nutty smell emerges from the pan. Some of the grains may turn pale gold, but otherwise the grains should not visibly darken. Immediately add the water, salt, and milk, and cook until the mixture comes to a boil. Reduce the heat to medium-low and cook, stirring frequently, until thick and creamy, about 10 minutes.

Add more milk or water if you like a soupier consistency. For richer oatmeal, use half water, half milk. If you like raisins cooked with your oatmeal, add them when you add the liquid. Serve with any combination of the suggested toppings.

Steel-Cut Oats

serves 3 to 4

If you love oatmeal but have never tried steel-cut oats, you are in for a treat. Steel-cut oats are used for the classic "porridge" of Ireland and Scotland. Rolled oats (the type most familiar in the United States) are made by steaming oat berries before they are flattened by rollers, whereas steel-cut oats, as the name suggests, are simply unprocessed oat berries cut into small pieces with powerful steel cutters. Steel-cut oats, being less processed, are more nutritious and delicious. What's more, this type of oatmeal can be reheated with almost no loss of integrity.

1 tablespoon butter

1 cup steel-cut oats

4 cups water *(part milk may be used)*

½ teaspoon salt

Follow the directions for toasting and cooking regular oatmeal (preceding recipe), and simmer the oatmeal for about 20 minutes. Taste to determine if the grains are tender to your liking or if they need more time. Stir frequently, going over the bottom of the pan with your wooden spoon to make sure nothing is sticking.

Steel-cut oats can also be made successfully in a slow cooker for larger groups: toast 2 cups steel-cut oats in 1 tablespoon butter as specified in the preceding recipe, then put the toasted oats in the bowl of the slow cooker. Add 8 cups of cold water (or 6 cups water and 2 cups milk), ½ teaspoon salt, stir well, and turn the cooker on high. The oatmeal is finished after about 4 hours. Stir in a final tablespoon of butter, and serve.

OTHER COOKED BREAKFAST CEREALS

Oats are naturally sweet, readily releasing their unctuous starch in the cooking—hence oatmeal's perennial popularity. You might also find rolled rye flakes or barley flakes or spelt flakes, or the steel-cut or cracked form of these grains. These can be cooked like oats and have their own unique nutty flavors and degrees of starchiness. Just like rye bread, cooked rye cereal is excellent with a touch of orange zest. Polenta (page 242) also makes a satisfying breakfast porridge that is particularly tasty with dried cherries.

Dried Fruit Compote

This compote is excellent atop oatmeal or other cooked breakfast cereals, but for a simple dessert, serve it chilled in a bowl, with some of the juices, topped with a dollop of sour cream. You can use a blend of dried fruit, or a single type. I like plenty of dried apricots: I prefer sweet dark brown Turkish apricots to the sulfured orange variety. Put any combination of pitted prunes, dried apricots, dried cherries (both sweet and sour types, if possible), dried pears, and raisins in a saucepan. Add sufficient cold water to cover the fruit by about 2 inches. If you like, add a cinnamon stick, a couple of slices of peeled fresh ginger, and a strip of orange zest to the pan. Heat over a medium flame, stirring occasionally. As soon as the liquid is hot and steaming and bubbles are barely beginning to form, remove from the heat. Let sit, covered, for about ½ hour, then it's ready to be spooned over hot oatmeal, including a couple of spoonfuls of the sweet liquid. Transfer any remaining fruit and liquid to jars, and refrigerate. Leave the cinnamon, ginger, and orange zest in to flavor the compote, but pick them out prior to serving.

Grits

serves 4 to 6

Dear to the heart of many a Southerner. Serve with sausage and fried eggs. Stone-ground grits have a wonderful corn flavor that is brought out by long cooking. If quick grits are what you have, they cook in a very short time—about 5 minutes.

2 cups water

2 cups milk

1 cup stone-ground grits *(see page 25: Cornmeal)*

½ teaspoon salt

2 tablespoons butter

freshly ground black pepper *(optional)*

Bring the water and milk to a boil in a medium-sized, heavy saucepan, being careful not to let it boil over. Reduce the heat a bit and slowly whisk in the grits. Stirring constantly, let cook until slightly thickened. Reduce the heat to low and let cook, stirring frequently (being careful the grits are not burning on the bottom), until the grains are tender, about 45 minutes. (Rather than using the stovetop, you may finish the grits in a 325°F oven, requiring less attention.) Cover the pan, remove from the heat, and let sit for about 5 more minutes. Add the salt and butter. Pass the pepper grinder at the table.

ELAINE'S BAKED GRITS

Make a recipe of Grits as directed above, and let cool until you can hold your hand on the bottom of the pan. Using a whisk, blend in salt, pepper, cayenne, and paprika to taste, and add a dash of Worcestershire sauce. Whisk in 2 eggs, a good handful of roasted, peeled, chopped green chile (page 251), and about 4 ounces of grated sharp Cheddar cheese, blending until the cheese melts. Pour into a buttered baking dish. Top with 4 additional ounces of grated sharp Cheddar, and bake at 375°F for about 45 minutes. Let rest about 10 minutes before serving.

Granola

makes about 12 cups

My longtime friends (excellent home cooks who once worked as librarians at Deep Springs) make a version of this delicious, basic, not-too-sweet granola once a month. If you want to add raisins, stir them in after the granola has cooled. Sometimes, in summer, I make a huge batch of granola for breakfast at Deep Springs, serving it alongside fresh homemade yogurt.

½ cup vegetable oil

¾ cup honey

10 cups rolled oats

½ cup unsweetened flaked coconut

½ cup raw sunflower seeds

¼ cup sesame seeds

¼ cup coarsely ground flax seeds

1 heaping cup coarsely chopped raw almonds

¼ cup wheat germ

½ teaspoon salt

FOR SERVING

fresh fruit

yogurt, milk, or buttermilk

Heat the oven to 275°F. Warm the oil and honey together to a simmer in a small pan, and toss thoroughly with the oats in a large mixing bowl. Add the coconut; sunflower, sesame and flax seeds; almonds; wheat germ; and salt, and toss thoroughly. Spread the mixture onto 2 large rimmed baking sheets and toast slowly in the oven, tossing and redistributing every 15 minutes, until the oats and coconut are an appealing golden color, about 1 hour. Watch the granola carefully, especially toward the end. Let cool completely on the sheets (tossing a few times as it cools), then carefully transfer to zipper-lock bags or a storage container.

Serve with fresh fruit and yogurt, milk, or buttermilk.

Griddle Toast

Just set a skillet over a medium flame (or use the pancake griddle as we do at Deep Springs), generously butter a thick slice of bread on both sides (the basic dinner bread recipe in this book, page 76, is excellent for toast), and toast the bread in the skillet, checking it carefully and turning it a few times, until it is golden brown.

MILK TOAST
Cut a slice of Griddle Toast into quarters, and put the pieces in a bowl. Heat a cup of milk until hot and steaming, and pour it over the toast. Salt lightly and serve with a spoon. Sometimes this is all you want.

BREADY EGG
The childhood stay-home-sick-from-school favorite. Tear a piece of Griddle Toast into bite-sized pieces, dropping them into a warmed bowl. Scoop a fresh, warm soft-boiled egg (page 60) out of its shell and over the toast. Mix to coat the bread with egg. Salt lightly and serve.

GASHOUSE EGG, KNOTHOLE EGG, OR ONE-EYED EGYPTIAN
Cut a 2-inch round hole in the center of a slice of bread with a cookie cutter, or cut a diamond-shaped hole with a knife. Toast on one side as for Griddle Toast, then flip the bread. Put a small pat of butter into the bread's hole, then immediately crack an egg into the hole. Cook carefully to set the underside of the egg, and flip again to cook the white of the egg through, letting the yolk remain runny. Salt and pepper to taste. Serve with ham or sausage. This egg-and-toast dish goes by many other names, including moon egg, egg in a nest, chicken in a basket, and one-eyed jack.

French Toast

serves 2 to 3

The plain Dinner Bread recipe (page 76) works beautifully for French toast; the richer variation—with eggs and extra butter in the dough—is even better.

2 eggs, lightly beaten

1 cup milk

¼ teaspoon sugar

¼ teaspoon vanilla extract

pinch of salt

6 or 7 thick slices bread

butter for cooking

FOR SERVING (CHOOSE ONE)

butter and maple syrup

jam and powdered sugar

yogurt and fresh fruit

In a wide, flat-bottomed dish (I use an 8-by-8-inch glass baking dish), whisk together the eggs, milk, sugar, vanilla, and salt. Submerge the slices of bread in the milk mixture and let them soak for 10 to 15 minutes. Melt a pat of butter in a wide skillet over medium-high heat, swirling to coat the bottom. When the butter's sizzling subsides, lay in 2 to 3 slices of the saturated bread. Cook until brown on one side, then flip and cook the other side, turning the flame down to medium to allow the French toast to cook all the way through without burning on the outside. Wipe out the skillet with a paper towel, raise the heat again, add another pat of butter, and cook the remaining pieces in the same manner.

Serve with butter and maple syrup, or jam and powdered sugar, or yogurt and fresh fruit.

Simple Breakfast Potatoes

serves 3 to 4

Whether hash browns or home fries, I judge breakfast restaurants on the quality of their potatoes. This is an easy method for delicious, crispy potatoes to accompany your bacon and eggs.

1½ pounds medium red potatoes

1 tablespoon salt, plus more for seasoning

2 to 3 tablespoons vegetable oil

1 small yellow onion, finely diced

1 tablespoon butter

black pepper

Scrub the potatoes and put them in a large pot. Cover with water 1 inch over the tops of the potatoes, add 1 tablespoon salt, and bring to a boil. Cook until the potatoes are soft throughout but not falling apart. Drain the potatoes well and put them on a large sheet pan. Using 2 forks, quickly break up the hot potatoes into rough ½-inch chunks, taking care not to mash them. Let the potatoes cool and release steam for about 20 minutes.

Heat a griddle, a large nonstick skillet, or a seasoned cast-iron skillet over a medium-high flame. Oil the griddle with some of the vegetable oil. Throw the onion onto the griddle, with a good sprinkling of salt. Toss the onions around and let cook until just beginning to brown. Add a bit more oil to the griddle and scatter the potatoes over the onion. Toss everything around with the spatula. Melt the butter into the potatoes. Continue cooking, tossing occasionally, until the potatoes are browned and crisped to your liking. Add thin streams of oil as necessary (more oil will help the potatoes brown and crisp). Salt and pepper well to taste, and serve immediately.

Baked Bacon

What could be better than a cast-iron skillet of slowly cooking bacon, mingled with the sweet, heady scents of pancakes and biscuits and the "drip-drip" of strong coffee? I love bacon cooked a bit unevenly, with crisp spots and chewy spots all on the same strip. The skillet does a lovely job, provided you pay close attention as the bacon slowly browns, poking and turning the strips as necessary. But what if the skillet, or your attention, is already well-occupied? What if you are cooking lots of bacon, or you want to avoid the sputtery stovetop mess? Here's what to do:

Heat the oven to 350°F. Cover a large sheet pan (with a 1-inch rim) with aluminum foil (shiny side up), and lay out strips of bacon, leaving a 2-inch zone free on one end of the sheet pan. Put the pan in the oven and place 2 small metal measuring cups or other small heatproof objects under the other end of the pan, so the pan is tilted and the grease flows into the empty space as the bacon cooks. Bake slowly in this manner for about 30 minutes, or

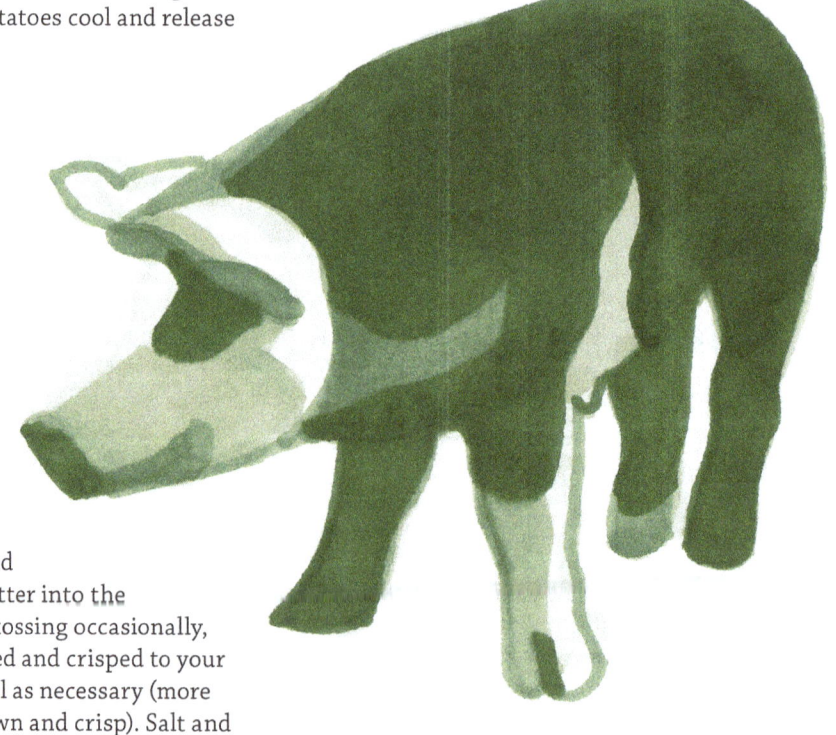

until the bacon is as crisp and golden as you like; the cooking time will depend on the thickness of the bacon. For thicker bacon, turn the strips over with tongs and cook for a few minutes more. If you like your bacon very crisp, it's best to buy thinner bacon, or to let thick bacon cook longer and slower, in a 300°F oven. When the bacon is cooked to your liking, carefully pour off the grease into a metal cup (reserving it for cooking vegetables, if you like), and serve the bacon hot, on a platter well lined with paper towels.

Fresh Breakfast Sausage

makes 1 pound; serves 5 to 6

This is one of the simplest sausages to make, and it's an ideal opportunity to make Biscuits and Gravy (page 66). As with any meat grinding, *make sure both the meat and the grinder are very cold*. Cold meat grinds more cleanly and retains more juice when cooked.

If you do not have a meat grinder but do have a large, sharp knife, you can still make this sausage, with even better, juicier results. Chill your cutting board as well as the meat, shore up your patience, and chop the meat very finely, to roughly ⅛-inch dice, in small batches.

EQUIPMENT/SUPPLIES

meat grinder

ice

rock salt

FOR THE SAUSAGE

1 pound boneless pork butt, 30% to 40% fat

1 teaspoon salt

¼ teaspoon sugar

1 teaspoon black pepper

1 teaspoon dried sage

1 teaspoon ground ginger

Cut the pork butt into chunks small enough to fit through the feed tube of your meat grinder, and toss with all the seasonings in a medium bowl. Put in the freezer for up to 30 minutes while you ready the grinder. Chill the grinding apparatus, disassembled, including the grinding plate with the largest holes (coarsest), in a bath of 1 gallon of cold tap water, up to 1 gallon of ice, and a cup of rock salt. Mix these well, then completely submerge all parts of the grinder. Let the grinder chill for about 20 minutes, then assemble it and grind the sausage.

Heat a big skillet over medium heat, gently form the sausage into small patties, about ½ inch thick, and fry slowly on both sides until the patties are cooked through and appealingly browned.

Chicken-Fried Steak

serves 3 to 4

Early German settlers brought their beloved schnitzel with them to Texas, where it gradually became chicken-fried steak, a dish emblematic of Texas and readily found on breakfast, lunch, and dinner menus in informal restaurants all over the American West. Once, at Deep Springs, the Student Cooks wanted to make chicken-fried steak for dinner. They told me they'd set some steaks aside, and I gave them this basic recipe. I had to miss that dinner—I was spending the evening in town. The next morning, I came in to make lunch and found a pan of leftover chicken-fried *rib-eye* steaks! I hadn't thought to ask what cut of steak they intended to use—rib-eyes are luxurious, tender, fatty steaks that are best suited to the simplest cooking methods, not for breading and frying. No doubt it was the best chicken-fried steak ever served!

Although this recipe specifies round steak, you may use any lean, flavorful, tough cut of steak.

about 1 pound round steak

½ teaspoon salt, plus more for seasoning

black pepper

1 cup flour

pinch of cayenne pepper

1 cup buttermilk

about 2 cups safflower oil, peanut oil, or other oil appropriate for frying

FOR SERVING

gravy from Biscuits and Gravy recipe *(page 66)*

Fried Eggs *(facing page)*

Cut the steak into 3 or 4 portions. Using a meat pounder, pound the steaks well, until very thin and translucent (hold them up to the light to check). Using paper towels, pat the steaks dry, then salt and pepper them generously. In a shallow bowl, season the flour with ½ teaspoon salt, black pepper to taste, and the cayenne. Pour the buttermilk into another shallow bowl. Dip the steaks in the buttermilk, shaking off the excess, then dredge them well in the flour. Put the steaks on a rack set over a tray and refrigerate for about 30 minutes. This allows the coating to set.

Fill a large cast-iron skillet halfway with oil, and set it over a medium-high flame. When the oil is very hot and just beginning to smoke, put the steaks in the skillet. Don't crowd the steaks in the pan, lest you cool down the oil too much—fry one at a time if necessary. Fry to a golden brown, 1 to 2 minutes, then turn carefully and cook the other side. Drain the steaks on a couple of brown paper grocery bags, or on paper towels. Serve hot with fried eggs and sausage gravy. Make the gravy first, keeping it hot, then cook the steaks, and finally quickly fry the eggs, and serve everything immediately.

Grapefruit for Breakfast

Choose a large grapefruit that's heavy for its size. Cut it in half *crossways*, and place a half on a small plate. Using a special grapefruit knife or a small serrated knife, patiently loosen each individual grapefruit section from the membrane. Serve with a small spoon. After eating all the cut sections from their pockets, pick up the grapefruit shell and squeeze its juice into your spoon, slurping up one spoonful at a time, until you have consumed all the juice. Sometimes, I like a sprinkle of sea salt on the grapefruit—it brings out the sweetness.

Eggs

Egg cookery is exacting. To make good eggs requires attention and precision, whatever the cooking method. Among cooking professionals, short-order breakfast cooks are in a class of their own—their position is inescapably unglamorous, yet their skills and timing are put to the test every day.

Here are essential methods and preparations for breakfast eggs in all their glory: scrambled eggs, fried eggs, omelets, poached eggs, soft-boiled eggs, and shirred eggs. I say "breakfast eggs," keeping in mind that eggs may be served at any meal: an omelet is very good for lunch or dinner, and scrambled eggs with lots of butter and salt are the classic midnight snack, perfect for settling the body after a marathon Student Body meeting, or when you've arrived home late from a party and you're still too giddy to sleep. For more egg recipes, including a run-down on hard-boiled eggs, egg salad, deviled eggs, and Italian *frittate*, see the Great Lunches chapter (beginning on page 84).

For scrambled eggs, fried eggs, or omelets, I observe three rules:

The eggs must be at room temperature. Cold eggs will cool down your pan, making them stick. To warm refrigerated eggs, put them in a bowl of hot tap water for a few minutes.

The pan must be hot enough. If it's not, the eggs will likely stick, even with plenty of butter. But it should not be so hot that the eggs brown immediately. Let the butter be your guide: when butter melts, first it sizzles and foams, then the sizzling quiets and the foam begins to subside, and soon the butter will brown. For most egg methods, put the eggs in the pan as soon as the foam subsides. For omelets, you want the pan a bit hotter: add the eggs the moment the butter begins to brown. If you put butter in the pan and it immediately sizzles, foams, and browns before it's even finished melting, the pan is too hot. Egg pans (also called omelet pans) are small sauté pans with sloped sides, about 8 inches in diameter, usually nonstick, preferably of a sturdy, heat-conducting material. A nice, new nonstick pan makes all these egg preparations easier.

Don't let eggs brown. Browned egg is indigestible and a sure indicator of overcooking. Omelets are frequently browned, in an attempt to cook the center through, but they are much more delectable when they are finished on gentler heat.

Scrambled Eggs

serves 1

Eggs need a good sprinkle of salt, but due to the nature of the protein in egg white, adding the salt at the end of cooking will help keep the egg tender.

2 large, fresh eggs

2 teaspoons buttermilk *(yogurt or sour cream may also be used)*

1 tablespoon butter

salt

FOR SERVING

black pepper

hot sauce, such as green Tabasco sauce

Warm the eggs to room temperature before cracking them: put them in a bowl of hot tap water for a few minutes, or leave them at room temperature for an hour. Crack the eggs into a small bowl, add the buttermilk, and beat briefly with a fork, just enough to break up the yolks—the mixture need not be uniform. Heat a small, heavy omelet pan or skillet over medium-high heat. It is important that the pan is hot enough. Melt the butter—it should melt quickly and bubble without burning—and swirl it to coat the bottom of the pan. As soon as the butter's foam subsides, pour in the eggs. Move the eggs about with your spatula constantly as they cook. Do not let them brown. Cook just until the eggs have set—the mass should be moist but not liquidy. Scrambling 2 eggs takes about 30 seconds once the eggs go into the pan. Season judiciously with salt (eggs need a good amount of salt), and turn out onto a plate or warmed serving dish immediately. Do not let the eggs sit in the pan, or they will overcook. Some people prefer their eggs cooked drier, until the curds have lost their sheen of moisture. Let diners season to taste with additional salt, black pepper, or hot sauce (a Deep Springs favorite is green Tabasco).

Fried Eggs

serves 1

2 large, fresh eggs

1 tablespoon butter

Warm the eggs before cracking them: put them in a bowl of hot tap water for a few minutes, or leave them at room temperature for an hour. Heat a small, heavy omelet pan or skillet over a medium-high flame. It is important that the pan is hot enough. Melt the butter in the pan, swirling it around, until the sizzling quiets and the foam subsides. At that point, break open the eggs very close to the surface of the pan (this will help keep the yolks from breaking). Jostle and swirl the pan gently to keep the eggs moving smoothly on the film of butter as they cook. Cook the eggs in this way for about 30 seconds, then remove the pan from the heat.

For *sunny-side-up eggs*, put a lid on the pan, and let the eggs continue cooking in the residual heat of the pan until the whites have just set, about 1 minute more. Return to a low flame if necessary. Gently slip the eggs out of the pan, or lift them out carefully with a spatula. The yolks will be very runny, the whites tender.

For *over-easy* (or *over-medium*) eggs, flip the eggs, and continue cooking in the pan's residual heat to the desired yolk texture, about 30 seconds more for over-easy or about 1 minute for over-medium. Check and return the pan to a low flame if necessary.

Flipping an egg without a utensil, only a flick of the wrist, requires the right pan shape—an omelet-style pan with gently sloping sides—and practiced skill. If you are lacking either of these, use a spatula, be gentle, and accept a broken yolk.

Though I usually consider it the cook's responsibility to season food, breakfast fried eggs are an exception; people customarily salt and pepper fried eggs at the table.

FRIED EGG SANDWICH

An over-medium egg is best for a sandwich; the yolk should be gooey, not runny. When you flip your egg, salt and pepper it generously, then place a thin slice of cheese on top to soften while the egg finishes cooking. I like wheat bread, sharp cheese, a generous amount of mayonnaise, just a little mustard, and lettuce, tomato, and thinly sliced onion. Fried egg sandwiches are excellent fare for a Sunday afternoon hike.

Omelet

serves 1

Omelets take practice to make well—several steps happen in quick succession, so don't be discouraged if your first attempts don't meet your expectations. An omelet could be considered a sophisticated variation on scrambled eggs. You can make an omelet without a filling and it would still be an omelet, but omelets are usually filled. A nonstick pan is highly recommended for omelets.

There are three rules for omelet fillings:

Don't overfill your omelet. For a 3-egg omelet, about ⅓ cup of filling is about right; for a 2-egg omelet, use ¼ cup.

Fillings should be precooked and well-seasoned, and should go into the omelet warm (except for cheese; see next rule). Throwing a heap of cold filling into your partly cooked omelet will cool everything down. Even if you manage to turn out a solid-looking omelet, a tepid, unappetizing mix of raw egg and filling will run out when you cut into it. Vegetables—onions, peppers, mushrooms—should be sautéed until completely cooked and seasoned well with salt before being used in an omelet.

Cheese for omelets should be grated and at room temperature. This ensures that the cheese will not cool down the eggs. About 1¼ ounces of cheese per omelet is ample.

3 large, fresh eggs, at room temperature

½ teaspoon milk

pinch of salt, plus more as needed

1 heaping tablespoon butter *(most for the pan, a small pat for the finish)*

⅓ cup filling of your choice *(see the following list)*

Warm the eggs before cracking them: put them in a bowl of hot tap water for a few minutes, or leave them at room temperature for an hour. Crack the eggs into a small bowl, add the milk and a big pinch of salt, and beat briefly with a fork, just enough to break up the yolks. The total cooking time for an omelet, once the eggs go into the pan, is about 2 minutes. Therefore, have everything in position before you begin: butter, a spatula, your prepared (warm) filling, and the warmed serving plate nearby.

Heat a small, heavy omelet pan over medium-high heat. Melt most of the butter—it should melt quickly and bubble without burning—and swirl it to coat the bottom of the pan. As soon as the foam has subsided and the butter is just beginning to brown, pour in the eggs. Let the eggs cook undisturbed for a few seconds, then start pushing folds of cooked egg to the center of the pan, allowing uncooked egg to run under. After about 20 seconds, when half the volume of egg is cooked, add about ⅓ cup of warm filling, scattering and spreading it in the center of the omelet. Enclose the filling by folding the omelet in half or thirds, using a flick of your wrist and a spatula, if necessary, and remove it from the heat. Let the omelet cook in the pan's residual heat for a moment to set its folded shape, then flip to cook the other side. Peer into the center of the omelet—when finished, the egg should be solid but still very creamy inside. Return it to a low flame if necessary. Try not to let it brown. Give the omelet another light sprinkle of salt. Turn the omelet onto a warmed plate, then run the remaining butter over the surface; this gives a wonderful aroma, flavor, and shine. Serve immediately.

TRADITIONAL OMELET FILLING INGREDIENTS; USE YOUR FAVORITE COMBINATION:

sautéed diced onion

sautéed diced sweet peppers *(bell peppers, pimentos, and other sweet varieties)*

Sautéed Mushrooms *(page 135)*

sautéed tomatoes *(take care to cook most of the moisture away)*

crumbled cooked bacon or sausage

chopped ham

grated cheese *(such as fontina, Cheddar, Jack, Swiss, feta, Gruyère, or smoked Gouda)*

SPECIAL OMELET FILLINGS AND PRESENTATIONS:

- chopped fresh herbs—parsley, chives, sage, thyme, dill—beaten into the eggs, and the omelet filled with delicate cheese
- cream cheese with sautéed bacon and minced jalapeños
- chopped green chile (canned or freshly roasted, page 251) and grated Jack cheese (Scatter cubes of avocado over the finished omelet.)
- feta cheese (Include a little chopped fresh dill in the eggs; in summer serve with slices of ripe tomato on the side.)
- Ratatouille (page 150), heated (Finish with a drizzle of good olive oil.)
- smoked salmon and chives or dill (For a special occasion, garnish with sour cream and a bit of salmon caviar.)
- whole yolk omelet (A feat of culinary skill for runny-yolk lovers, cook a plain omelet, but let one of the egg yolks remain whole and unbroken, keeping it in the omelet's center while the omelet cooks; the runny yolk enhances the rest of the omelet like a sauce.)

Sorrel Omelet

serves 2

A special springtime dish, this omelet is an excellent way to appreciate the gentle, tart flavor of this unusual herb. Because sorrel cooks and readily softens at a low temperature, it can be mixed into the eggs raw. For a great lunch, toss a mixed green salad, rub hot toast with a cut clove of fresh garlic, and cook up a sorrel omelet.

5 large, fresh eggs

2 heaping cups coarsely chopped sorrel leaves *(from 1 small bunch)*

½ teaspoon salt

1 tablespoon butter, plus more for finishing

freshly grated Parmesan cheese

Warm the eggs in a bowl of hot tap water. Crack them into a bowl, beat them lightly, and mix in the sorrel and salt. Heat a small, heavy omelet pan over a medium flame. Melt 1 tablespoon butter—it should bubble without burning—and swirl it to coat the bottom of the pan. As soon as the foam has subsided, pour in the eggs. Let the eggs cook undisturbed for a few seconds, then start pushing folds of cooked egg to the center of the pan, allowing uncooked egg to run under. There is no need to fold this omelet; it can simply be flipped flat when the first side is cooked. As sorrel cooks, it turns a dull green—using a small knife, peek inside the omelet and look for telltale patches of bright green sorrel and undercooked egg. Continue cooking gently, flipping as necessary, until the omelet is just cooked through, but still creamy and moist inside. The total cooking time will be about 5 minutes. Turn the finished omelet onto a plate, run a pat of butter over the surface, then sprinkle lightly with Parmesan. Cut in half and serve.

Poached Eggs

Poached eggs are "shreddy" by nature. I don't bother to trim or otherwise neaten their appearance. Bring 4 cups of water to a boil in a saucepan. When the water is at a full rolling boil, break in 2 large eggs, holding them right above the surface of the water. Slap on the cover and remove the pan from the heat. Let the eggs cook in the hot water for exactly 3 minutes, gently jostling the pan once or twice, then remove the eggs with a slotted spoon. The yolks will be runny; for firmer eggs, leave them in the water for another minute. Drain the eggs for a moment, then place on hot buttered toast, crispy-browned corned beef hash, your *salade de frisée aux lardons*, or whatever they are to be served with, and serve immediately.

Soft-Boiled Eggs

On occasional Sunday mornings at Deep Springs, I'll forgo the usual student-cooked brunch, instead opting to walk across the road to the henhouse and reach under an obliging bird for a couple of freshly laid eggs for my breakfast: two salt-and-peppered soft-boiled eggs, nothing else. Put on some old blues records, and I'm ready to clean the whole house.

A soft-boiled egg is the most direct egg experience—you eat it right out of its shell. If you come by the pastel blue-green eggs produced by black-and-white Araucana chickens, this is the best way to serve them, so the beauty of their shells can be appreciated. To serve soft-boiled eggs in the traditional manner, you need egg cups and small spoons.

Put large eggs in a saucepan and cover with cold water. (For smaller or larger eggs, adjust the cooking time in 20-second increments.) Bring to a boil over high heat. When the water comes to a boil, immediately remove from the heat, slap on the cover, and let the eggs sit in the hot water for 3 minutes and 15 seconds for a cooked but tender white and a warm but runny yolk. (This is the correct time for sea-level kitchens; at Deep Springs' altitude, to compensate for the lower boiling point of water, I leave the eggs in the water for about 25 seconds longer, for a total of 3 minutes and 40 seconds.) Dump the hot water out of the pan and cover the eggs with cold tap water to stop the cooking. Remove after several seconds, lest they cool down too much, and serve immediately.

To eat, put the warm eggs, pointy side up, into egg cups, and have pats of butter, salt, and pepper nearby. With a small spoon, gently tap the side of the pointed end near the top, all around to break the shell. Lift off the top part of the egg and scoop out the bit of white. Eat the egg in small bites, buttering, salting, and peppering each bite. Eating a soft-boiled egg neatly is a delicate, meditative, developed skill.

Shirred Eggs

This is one of the easier ways to prepare breakfast eggs, provided you watch them carefully to prevent overcooking. The same procedure can be used whether you are preparing just a few eggs for an intimate breakfast or several dozen for Sunday brunch. Heat the oven to 325°F. Grease the cups of a muffin tin well with melted butter. Into each cup, pour about 2 teaspoons of heavy cream or half-and-half (I've also successfully used a mixture of equal parts sour cream and buttermilk). Break an egg into each cup. Place the tin in the oven and bake until the whites of the eggs are set but the yolks are still runny, anywhere from 10 minutes for small eggs to 15 minutes for jumbo eggs: *check frequently*. Don't overcook—once the yolks cook solid, they have lost much of their saucy savor. Run a small knife around the edge of each egg, then use a wide soup spoon to lift out the eggs.

CHAPTER 3
PANCAKES, BISCUITS, & CORNBREAD

Most of the recipes in this chapter, based on flour and dairy, and leavened with baking powder or baking soda, are categorized as "quick breads." Yeast breads, on the other hand, take considerable time to rise and have an entirely different character. There are three rules to keep in mind with any quick bread:

Mix the dough or batter just until blended, and treat it gently. Overmixing results in dry, tough bread. With biscuits and scones, this requirement is even more extreme: mix just until the flour is barely moistened, no more.

Bake or cook quick breads just until "set" and cooked through. These breads lack the moisture-retaining properties of yeast breads, and so are prone to drying out.

Serve savory quick breads, such as biscuits and cornbread, while still warm. Sugar retains moisture in baked goods; therefore low-sugar quick breads are especially prone to dryness.

For *home-mixed baking powder,* blend 1½ teaspoons cream of tartar, 1 teaspoon baking soda, and ¼ teaspoon salt together in a small bowl. This is best mixed as needed—its leavening power deteriorates over time. Use the same measurements you would use for regular baking powder.

For *home-mixed brown sugar* that possesses more character than the storebought variety, blend dark molasses into granulated (white) sugar. For light brown sugar, use 1 teaspoon molasses for each cup of sugar. For darker brown sugar, use 1 tablespoon molasses. Blend with your clean fingers until the mixture is uniform.

Beginning bakers may wish to consult the sections on Baking Powder and Baking Soda, Buttermilk, Cornmeal, Flour, and Sugar in the Essential Ingredients section at the beginning of the book, pages 37 to 45.

Jack's Buttermilk Pancakes

serves 6 to 7

Here is the all-time favorite, everyday classic, from Jack Aldworth, my predecessor in the Boardinghouse kitchen. These pancakes have been a part of Deep Springs breakfasts for many years.

3 cups sifted all-purpose flour

½ cup sugar

1 tablespoon baking powder

1½ teaspoons baking soda

1½ teaspoons salt

3 eggs, at room temperature, beaten

4 cups buttermilk, at room temperature

4 tablespoons butter, melted

vegetable oil for cooking the pancakes

FOR SERVING

softened butter

warmed maple syrup

Thoroughly whisk together the flour, sugar, baking powder, baking soda, and salt in a medium bowl. Whisk together the eggs, buttermilk, and melted butter in a large, deep bowl. Over a medium-high flame, heat a griddle (or a wide skillet) for several minutes. Add the dry ingredients to the wet ingredients and combine just until mixed.

Oil the griddle lightly with vegetable oil, and begin cooking: gently drop spoonfuls of batter onto the griddle. For the easiest dispensing of the batter, transfer it to a pitcher or other vessel with a spout. I like to make pancakes that are on the small side, using about ¼ cup of batter, the better to make a tall stack. Let the pancakes cook until the impressions of bubbles remain in the uncooked top surface, then flip and cook on the other side for a few moments more. Press lightly on the top of a pancake—if your finger leaves an impression, it needs a bit more time. If it springs back, it's done. The side cooked first is considered the more attractive "top" side. Serve immediately with soft butter and warm maple syrup.

COWBOY PANCAKES
Instead of serving them with syrup, roll up the buttered pancakes with brown sugar and a hot slice of bacon. Eat like a taco.

WHOLE-WHEAT PANCAKES
For the tastiest 100 percent whole-grain pancake, spelt, an ancient form of wheat, delivers a sweeter taste and none of the bitterness of whole wheat. Simply substitute whole-grain spelt flour for the all-purpose flour in the master recipe, adding 3 to 4 tablespoons of wheat germ. Alternatively, use half whole-wheat flour, half all-purpose, plus 3 to 4 tablespoons wheat germ and a tablespoon or two of honey.

BUCKWHEAT PANCAKES
These are especially good in cool weather, with marmalade or another citrusy topping. Substitute 1½ cups buckwheat flour for 1½ cups of the all-purpose flour in the master recipe.

BLUEBERRY OR HUCKLEBERRY PANCAKES
Proceed with the master recipe, adding 1 to 2 cups fresh or frozen blueberries or huckleberries (if using frozen, do not thaw) when combining the wet and dry ingredients. Or sprinkle the berries directly on the wet batter of each pancake before flipping it. Huckleberries are a wild delicacy: tiny berries, intensely pigmented, with a distinctively intense sweet-zingy flavor.

Eloise's Cornmeal-Buttermilk Pancakes

serves 4 to 5

My friend Eloise once ran a breakfast café in San Francisco; these Southern-style pancakes—the centerpiece of her menu—go superbly with sausage, syrup, and good, strong coffee.

One morning at Deep Springs, I had a whole batch of cornmeal-buttermilk pancakes cooking on the griddle, when Linda Newell, the college's general projects manager, ran into the Boardinghouse, pale and shaken. "Did you listen to the news this morning?" she asked, her voice trembling.

"No," I said.

"Something major has happened. Do you want to sit down?" she asked.

"No," I said, "I have to keep cooking the pancakes. Just tell me."

While I carefully flipped the pancakes, she told me what had happened on the East Coast that morning of September 11, 2001.

1 cup sifted all-purpose flour

1 cup medium-grind cornmeal

1 teaspoon baking soda

1 teaspoon salt

¼ cup firmly packed brown sugar

3 large eggs, at room temperature, beaten

2 cups buttermilk, at room temperature

½ cup plain whole-milk yogurt

4 tablespoons butter, melted

vegetable oil for cooking the pancakes

FOR SERVING

softened butter

warmed maple syrup

Whisk together the flour, cornmeal, baking soda, and salt in a medium bowl. In a large, deep bowl, mix together the brown sugar, eggs, buttermilk, yogurt, and melted butter. If the wet ingredients are cold, place the bowl in a basin of hot water to bring the contents to room temperature.

Over a medium-high flame, heat a griddle (or wide skillet) for several minutes. Oil the griddle with a bit of vegetable oil.

Whisk the dry ingredients into the wet mixture just until there are no lumps of flour left, and begin cooking: carefully drop spoonfuls of batter onto the griddle. Or transfer the batter to a pitcher or other vessel with a spout, and pour measures of batter onto the griddle. These cook a bit faster than regular pancakes and are rather delicate; I think it's easiest to make them on the small side, using about ¼ cup batter. When the impressions of bubbles remain in the uncooked top surface of the pancakes, they are ready to flip. After flipping, to determine whether they are cooked through, press lightly on top of a pancake—if your finger leaves an impression, it needs a bit more time. If it springs back, it's done. The side cooked first is considered the more attractive "top" side. Serve immediately with soft butter and warm maple syrup.

Ricotta Pancakes

serves 2

These rich little pancakes have a lovely brown exterior and a delicate, custardy interior. Ripe pears are a natural choice, but sliced, sugared strawberries or other juicy fruit are good, too. If you are serving these pancakes as a dessert, add a few drops of vanilla extract to the wet ingredients for the batter.

3 tablespoons all-purpose flour

2 tablespoons sugar

¼ teaspoon baking powder

¼ teaspoon salt

¾ cup ricotta cheese

1 egg

¼ cup milk

TOPPING

½ cup ricotta cheese

2 teaspoons sugar

2 to 3 tablespoons butter for cooking the pancakes

slices of ripe pear, or sliced, sugared strawberries, for serving

In a small bowl, whisk together the flour, sugar, baking powder, and salt. In a pitcher or other spouted vessel, whisk the ricotta, egg, and milk together until uniform. Add the dry ingredients, whisk the two mixtures together thoroughly, and let rest for 20 minutes to allow the flour to absorb liquid.

For the topping, mix together the ricotta and sugar in a small bowl and keep at room temperature.

Heat a griddle or wide skillet over a medium-high flame. Melt a small pat of butter on the griddle and begin cooking, using about 2 tablespoons of batter for each pancake. Let the pancakes cook until deep golden brown on one side, then flip and cook on the other side for a few moments more. Serve immediately, topped with the sweetened ricotta and fruit.

Biscuits

serves 4 to 6

This recipe yields buttery biscuits with a layered texture. For especially fluffy, delicate biscuits, use a blend of cake flour and all-purpose flour. For a good, nutty flavor, use a blend of whole-wheat and all-purpose flour.

2 cups sifted all-purpose flour

2½ teaspoons baking powder

½ teaspoon baking soda

½ teaspoon salt

6 tablespoons cold unsalted butter

¾ cup cold buttermilk

Heat the oven to 450°F. Sift together the flour, baking powder, baking soda, and salt into a medium bowl. Cut the butter into slices and rapidly work the butter into the dry mixture with your hands. Work until the flour is somewhat moistened and there are no large, but many small, pieces of butter in the mixture. Pour in the buttermilk and gently combine with a wooden spoon just until mixed.

Turn the dough out on a floured board and knead (in other words, flatten, fold over, flatten, fold over) only four or five times, sprinkling flour on the board as necessary to prevent sticking. In flattening and folding, work the dough into a rectangle, about 8 by 6 inches. Gently roll the dough, using flour as necessary to keep it from sticking, to a ¾-inch thickness and cut with a sharp, round cutter dipped in flour or into squares with a long, sharp knife dipped in flour. (To the irritation of traditionalists, I almost always make square biscuits, as it uses 100 percent of the dough with no scraps to bother with.)

Place 1 inch apart on an ungreased baking sheet, and let rest for a few moments. Once the biscuits are cut and placed on the sheet, they may be refrigerated until you are ready to bake them. Bake in the center of the oven until golden brown on the bottom and top, 8 to 10 minutes. Biscuits must be consumed warm from the oven. "Take two and butter 'em while they're hot!" my mother likes to say as she passes the napkin-lined basket of biscuits.

WHOLE-WHEAT CHEDDAR BISCUITS

These are good with brothy soups. Replace the flour in the master recipe with a blend of 1 cup whole-wheat flour, ¾ cup all-purpose flour, and ¼ cup wheat germ. Work 1 cup (4 ounces) grated sharp Cheddar cheese into the dry ingredients along with the butter, using only 4 tablespoons butter.

CREAM BISCUITS

These are more cakey and less flaky than regular biscuits, with a creamy, tender flavor.

2 cups sifted all-purpose flour

2½ teaspoons baking powder

½ teaspoon salt

1 cup heavy *(whipping)* **cream**

Proceed as for regular biscuits, except, of course, there is no butter to work in. As this dough is a bit stickier, bake the biscuits on a greased baking sheet.

SOUR CREAM BISCUITS

Slather these with butter and honey.

2 cups sifted all-purpose flour

1½ teaspoons baking powder

¾ teaspoon baking soda

½ teaspoon salt

1¼ cups natural sour cream *(no binders or thickeners)*

Proceed as for Cream Biscuits (above).

CORNMEAL BISCUITS

For when you can't decide whether to make biscuits or cornbread.

1½ cups sifted all-purpose flour

½ cup medium-grind cornmeal

2 teaspoons baking powder

½ teaspoon baking soda

¾ teaspoon salt

6 tablespoons cold butter

¾ cup buttermilk

Follow the instructions in the master Biscuits recipe.

GRIDDLE BISCUITS

Any of these biscuits may be "baked" on a hot griddle set at pancake temperature or a little cooler. The outer texture will be crispier and the insides more dense than oven biscuits. Roll them ½ inch thick rather than ¾ inch, and gently turn them after they are nicely browned on the first side. In my experience they are cooked when both sides are brown; this will depend, of course, on the thickness of the biscuits and the temperature of the griddle. Cornmeal Biscuits are my favorite for griddle cooking; serve with gravy or maple syrup.

DROP BISCUITS

If you are really in a hurry, make drop biscuits; they eliminate the rolling and cutting step. Use any of the recipes here, adding about ¼ cup more liquid than is called for—the dough will be wet and sticky. Using an ice cream scoop (a small one—1 ounce—if possible), drop neat, uniform scoops of dough 1 ½ inches apart on *well-greased* baking sheets. I like to serve drop biscuits with their attractive browned undersides facing up.

Biscuits and Gravy

serves 4 to 6

Some brisk mornings, this is exactly what you want for breakfast. If you have a meat grinder, you could even make your own breakfast sausage (see page 55).

SAUSAGE GRAVY

- 3 tablespoons fat in skillet from cooking breakfast sausage or bacon
- 3 tablespoons all-purpose flour
- 3 cups milk
- ½ teaspoon salt
- ¼ teaspoon freshly ground black pepper
- 1 or 2 pinches of cayenne pepper
- about ½ cup crumbled cooked breakfast sausage *(optional)*
- 1 recipe Biscuits *(preceding page)*, split and buttered

Cook breakfast sausage (or bacon, though I prefer the taste and heft of sausage here) in a cast-iron skillet, retaining

all the browned bits and 3 tablespoons fat in the skillet. Stir the flour into the fat with a wooden spoon, scraping up any stuck browned bits. Cook this roux over medium-low heat for a few minutes, stirring constantly, until it bubbles well and has begun to turn a shade darker. Remove from the heat, continuing to stir for a moment more as the roux cools. Let stand for 10 minutes, then return to medium-high heat and add the milk slowly, whisking constantly. Cook until thickened, then reduce the heat to low and simmer, whisking frequently, for 2 to 3 minutes. Season carefully with salt, black pepper, and cayenne. If you like, stir in a handful of crumbled cooked breakfast sausage. Ladle the gravy generously over piping-hot, split, buttered biscuits. Serve with breakfast sausage and fried eggs.

Skillet Cornbread

serves 6 to 8

Southern cornbread tends to be savory, not sweet, and has a greater proportion of cornmeal, while Northern, or "Yankee" cornbread, very good in its own right, is cakier and sweeter. Though some recipe writers insist that "true" Southern cornbread contains only cornmeal, no flour, most recipes do call for a small amount of all-purpose flour. This recipe uses both polenta, or coarse-grind cornmeal, and medium-grind cornmeal. The polenta adds a little extra toothsome texture. If you don't have polenta, just eliminate the first step of soaking it in buttermilk, and use 1½ cups cornmeal.

Fresh stone-ground cornmeal is very perishable and difficult to find outside the South, but it makes heavenly cornbread— see page 40 for more information on cornmeal. Sugar is controversial: some Southern cooks shun it entirely, while others pour it in with abandon. I think a small amount is necessary for its moisture-retaining properties. As for the cheese, this recipe is good without it, but it enhances the flavor of the corn. Butter gives the cornbread a round, full flavor, but bacon drippings can be used for part of the fat, too, resulting in a slightly drier but delicious cornbread.

Perhaps the most important part of this recipe is the *hot cast-iron skillet*. I never bake cornbread in anything else. The crusty exterior is a great part of the charm, much like the skin on a roast chicken. A deep golden, steaming-hot round of skillet-baked cornbread is a beautiful sight to behold.

- **½ cup polenta** (*coarse cornmeal; preferably stone-ground*)
- **1 cup buttermilk**
- **1 cup medium-grind cornmeal** (*white has a subtly finer taste, but yellow is prettier; preferably stone-ground*)
- **½ cup sifted all-purpose flour**
- **2 teaspoons baking powder**
- **1 teaspoon baking soda**
- **1 teaspoon salt**
- **½ cup** (*2 ounces*) **finely grated sharp white Cheddar cheese** (*optional*)
- **2 eggs, lightly beaten**
- **2 tablespoons brown sugar**
- **½ to ¾ cup sweet corn kernels** (*optional*)
- **5 to 6 tablespoons butter** (*3 or 4 tablespoons for the batter, 2 tablespoons for the skillet*)

Heat the oven to 400°F. For best results, have all ingredients at room temperature. In a medium bowl, stir the polenta into the buttermilk and set aside. Sift the cornmeal, flour, baking powder, baking soda, and salt together into a large bowl. If you are using the cheese, toss it with the dry ingredients. Into the polenta-buttermilk mixture, stir the eggs and the sugar (and the corn, if you are using it). Meanwhile, in the oven, melt the butter in a well-seasoned, 10-inch cast-iron skillet. Stir all but 2 tablespoons of this melted butter into the wet ingredients, returning the hot skillet, with the remaining 2 tablespoons of butter, to the oven. Carefully add the wet ingredients to the dry, stirring just until the dry ingredients are moistened—do not overmix.

When the butter in the skillet is just beginning to brown, spoon the thick batter into the skillet—it should sizzle happily. Bake for 15 minutes, or just until a toothpick inserted in the center comes out clean. Let the cornbread rest in the skillet for a moment, then invert it onto a plate. Since the skillet will retain a great deal of heat, it's best not to leave the cornbread in it, lest it overcook and dry out. Serve immediately.

Dutch Babies

serves 2 to 4

My mother made Dutch babies, or German pancakes, for the occasional weekend breakfast when I was a kid. Inevitably, I asked, "Why are they called Dutch babies?" We imaginatively figured it was because the pancake, puffed as it emerges from the oven, looks somewhat like a roasted baby, all golden and crispy in the skillet.

This recipe can't really be multiplied—success depends on the specified amount of batter, made from room-temperature eggs and milk, baked in a preheated, household-sized skillet. If you'd like to make several batches of Dutch Babies for a crowd, you'll need several skillets, several vessels to mix each batch of batter individually, and ample oven space.

This same batter is used to make *Yorkshire pudding*, a traditional savory English dish to accompany Roast Beef (page 183): to the butter in the skillet, add the strained fat and "drippings" from the roast beef, pour in the batter and bake as directed here, and serve at once with the beef, horseradish, and watercress.

3 large eggs *(or 4 smaller ones)*

¾ cup milk

¾ cup all-purpose flour, sifted

½ teaspoon salt

3 tablespoons butter

FOR SERVING (CHOOSE ONE)

maple syrup

powdered sugar

fresh fruit with jam or jelly

Heat the oven to 450°F. Bring all the ingredients to room temperature. Beat the eggs, milk, flour, and salt in a medium bowl until very smooth. Melt the butter in a heavy 10-inch or 12-inch oven-safe skillet. As soon as the butter is hot and bubbling, pour in the batter and put the skillet into the oven. After 15 minutes, lower the oven temperature to 350°F and continue baking for another 8 to 9 minutes. The pancake will be a deep golden brown, with crisp edges. If the pancake puffs up in large bubbles in the first 10 to 15 minutes, pierce the bubbles with a fork. Cut the pancake into wedges and serve immediately with maple syrup, or sifted powdered sugar, or a quick compote of fresh fruit tossed with melted jam or jelly.

APPLE DUTCH BABIES
This traditional variation is superb with "frizzled" ham (thick slices of ham steak quickly sizzled in a little butter in a hot skillet) and plenty of strong drip coffee. Pears are good, too, with nutmeg or ginger.

4 tablespoons butter

3 tart apples, cored, peeled if you like, and thinly sliced

½ teaspoon ground cinnamon

⅛ teaspoon salt

1 tablespoon sugar

batter for Dutch Babies

Heat the oven to 450°F. In a cast-iron skillet over a medium-high flame, melt the butter. When it is hot and bubbling, throw in the apples, cinnamon, salt, and sugar. Cook the apples, stirring frequently, until soft but still holding their shape, about 10 minutes. Whisk the batter ingredients together, pour over the apples in the skillet, and bake as directed in the master recipe. This is delicious cooled to room temperature; the apple flavor becomes stronger as it sits.

Oatmeal Scones

makes 8 large scones

You need not serve butter and jam with these great scones—they are perfect just as they are, with a cup of tea or strong coffee. They're sweet and buttery enough to remain delectable even hours out of the oven.

2 cups sifted all-purpose flour

⅓ cup firmly packed brown sugar

1½ teaspoons baking powder

¾ teaspoon baking soda

¾ cup rolled oats, plus ¼ cup more for shaping and cutting the scones

¾ cup cold salted butter *(1½ sticks)***, cut into thick slices**

½ cup Zante currants or raisins

½ cup buttermilk, or more as needed

Heat the oven to 425°F. Combine the flour, brown sugar, baking powder, baking soda, and ¾ cup of the oats in a large bowl. Rapidly work the butter into the dry mixture with your hands, lightly smearing the slices between your palms. Break the butter into smaller pieces, dispersing it throughout. The flour will become somewhat moistened, and the visible pieces of butter will resemble small peas. Stir in the currants. Pour in the buttermilk and mix the dough until just combined. If the dough still seems very dry, sprinkle in a tablespoon or so more buttermilk.

Scatter the remaining ¼ cup oats on a cutting board. Gather the dough into 2 equal-sized balls. On the oat-strewn board, gently pat each ball into a 1-inch thick disk. With a sharp knife, cut each disk into 4 wedges. Place the scones about 1 inch apart on an ungreased baking sheet and bake in the center of the oven until they are a rich golden brown on the outside and are cooked in the center, 12 to 15 minutes. Let the scones rest on the sheet for a few minutes before removing them to a cooling rack—they are very crumbly when they emerge from the oven.

Cream Scones

makes 8 medium scones

Made with the extra-thick, double-rich cream from the Deep Springs cows, these scones won a blue ribbon at the regional Tri-County Fair.

2 cups sifted all-purpose flour

⅓ cup sugar

1 tablespoon baking powder

½ teaspoon salt

¾ cup Zante currants

1 teaspoon grated orange zest

1¼ cups heavy *(whipping)* **cream**

Heat the oven to 425°F. Lightly grease a baking sheet. Whisk the flour, sugar, baking powder, and salt together in a medium bowl. Stir in the currants and zest. Mix in the cream just until the dry ingredients are moistened. Gather the dough into a ball, transfer it to a lightly floured surface, and pat into an 8-inch round, about ¾ inch thick. Cut into 8 wedges and place at least ½ inch apart on the baking sheet. Bake until the tops are golden brown, 12 to 15 minutes. Transfer the scones to a rack and let cool slightly before serving.

Cornmeal Cherry Scones

makes about 14 small scones

Lightly sweetened, dried tart cherries are hard to find in the Eastern Sierra; on vacations from Deep Springs, I always stock up on them so that I can make these scones frequently. They're inspired by a famous scone baked at the Cheese Board Collective in Berkeley. For information on cornmeal, see page 40.

6 tablespoons fine cornmeal, preferably stone-ground, plus more for dusting the baking sheet

1 cup all-purpose flour

3 tablespoons sugar

¾ teaspoon baking powder

¼ teaspoon baking soda

⅛ teaspoon salt

6 tablespoons cold butter, cut in small pieces

⅓ cup dried cherries

¼ cup sour cream

¼ teaspoon almond extract

Heat the oven to 425°F. Sift 6 tablespoons fine cornmeal, flour, sugar, baking powder, baking soda, and salt into a bowl. Using your hands, thoroughly work the butter into the dry mixture, until the butter is evenly dispersed and the mixture is moist. Toss in the cherries, breaking up any that are stuck together. Make a well in the center and add the sour cream and almond extract, blending them together in the well. Gently fold the sour cream into the dough, blending just until uniform.

Dust a baking sheet lightly with a little fine cornmeal. Using two spoons (or a small ice cream scoop), shape 1-ounce balls of dough, and place 1½ inches apart on the sheet. Bake in the center of the oven for 8 to 9 minutes, or until brown on the bottom and barely golden on top. Let the scones sit a moment—they are very crumbly when hot—then transfer to a rack.

Joan's Irish Soda Bread

makes 2 medium loaves

If you've never tasted caraway seeds in anything but rye bread, you'll be surprised at their entirely different character when combined with raisins in this lightly sweetened soda bread. For the most tender texture, don't overmix the batter—combine the dry and wet ingredients just until there is no dry flour left. (My friend Joan, who makes many loaves of this soda bread every St. Patrick's Day, mixes for only as long as it takes to say an "Our Father," a "Hail Mary," and a "Glory Be.")

3 cups all-purpose flour

⅔ cup sugar

1 teaspoon baking soda

2 teaspoons baking powder

1 teaspoon salt

2 cups buttermilk

2 eggs

2 tablespoons caraway seeds

2 tablespoons sunflower oil or other vegetable oil

1½ cups raisins

Heat the oven to 350°F. Grease and flour 2 medium (4-cup) loaf pans. Whisk the flour, sugar, baking soda, baking powder, and salt together in a large bowl. Whisk the buttermilk, eggs, caraway seeds, and oil together in a medium bowl. Pour the wet ingredients into the bowl with the dry ingredients, and sprinkle the raisins over. Sweeping your whisk thoroughly over the bottom of the bowl, mix the batter only until uniform; do not overmix. Scrape into the prepared pans and bake for 30 to 35 minutes, until a toothpick inserted in the center comes out clean. Let the soda bread rest in the pans for 10 minutes, then turn out onto a rack to cool. A toasted, buttered slice is delicious the next day.

Pumpkin Bread

one 9-by-13-inch cake; serves 4 to 6

Come December, the holiday baking bug bites. The measuring cups practically spring out of the drawer, wanting to be used. The air in the house demands to be warmed by the oven's heat, and to be laced with cinnamon and vanilla. Here, from my friend Elge's kitchen, is just the recipe you need to prime your holiday baking pump—a quick, easy, not-too-rich, not-too-sweet pumpkin bread that is reliably delicious and stays moist for days. It's exactly the thing to make on a Saturday morning, enjoy warm, then return to throughout the weekend—a little square with a glass of milk, a nice big piece with your tea or your bourbon.

For the pumpkin in this recipe, I favor the kabocha pumpkin, a Japanese variety with dark green rind and deep orange flesh. Its flavor is sweet and pumpkin-true, its texture dense and smooth. If a kabocha pumpkin is what you're using, cut it in half, scrape out the seeds with a spoon (I save them for vegetable stock), and bake cut side–down on a baking sheet in a 350°F oven until soft. If you're mixing the cake right away, go ahead and measure out your 2 cups of pumpkin (no need to purée it), then whisk in your spices—the warm pumpkin will "bloom" the spices.

This cake may be varied in many ways: you can use a little more molasses (or honey) and a little less brown sugar. You can substitute pureed roasted sweet potato, or applesauce, for the pumpkin. The spices may be varied however you wish—allspice or mace could be used instead of cinnamon, cloves, and nutmeg. You can add a cup of coarsely-chopped walnuts or pecans, or raisins or other dried fruit. You can halve the recipe and use an 8-by-8-inch pan. Do whatever you wish to make this recipe yours—it's a keeper.

2½ cups all-purpose flour

1 teaspoon baking soda

1 teaspoon baking powder

½ teaspoon salt

2 cups cooked pumpkin *(or a 15-ounce can of pumpkin)*

2 teaspoons cinnamon

- **½ teaspoon ground cloves**
- **½ teaspoon ground ginger**
- **¼ teaspoon grated nutmeg**
- **½ teaspoon finely grated orange zest** (optional)
- **4 eggs**
- **1½ cups brown sugar**
- **2 tablespoons molasses**
- **1 cup sunflower oil or other vegetable oil**

Heat the oven to 350°F. Butter and dust with flour a 9-by-13-inch glass baking dish. Into a medium bowl, sift together both kinds of flour, baking soda, baking powder, and salt. In a large bowl, vigorously whisk together the pumpkin, cinnamon, cloves, nutmeg, ginger, orange zest, eggs, brown sugar, molasses, and oil. Add the dry ingredients and whisk gently until the batter is uniform. Scrape the batter into the prepared dish, smooth the top, and bake for 30 to 35 minutes, or until a toothpick inserted in the center comes out clean. Let the cake cool, then keep covered with plastic wrap. The spice flavors are at their best the next day.

Grandma Z.'s Coffeecake

serves 8

This crumb cake is somehow much more than the sum of its parts. It is based on a recipe from the grandmother of one of my oldest friends, whose name is also Tom.

- **1 cup granulated** (*white*) **sugar**
- **1 cup firmly packed brown sugar**
- **3 cups sifted all-purpose flour**
- **1 cup cold butter** (*2 sticks*)
- **¼ teaspoon salt**
- **½ teaspoon baking powder**
- **½ teaspoon baking soda**
- **2 eggs, beaten**
- **1 cup buttermilk**
- **½ teaspoon vanilla extract**

Heat the oven to 375°F. Grease and flour a 9-by-13-inch baking dish. In a large bowl, mix the granulated sugar, brown sugar, and flour. Cut the butter into thin slices and toss the slices in the flour-sugar mixture. With your hands, rapidly work the butter into the mixture, smearing the butter slices between your palms, to the point that the mixture is somewhat moistened and only small pieces of butter are visible.

Reserve 1 firmly packed cup of this mixture for the topping. Mix the salt, baking powder, and baking soda into the remainder. Combine the eggs, buttermilk, and vanilla in a medium bowl. Add to the flour mixture and, with a rubber spatula, fold together both mixtures just until smooth. Scrape into the prepared baking dish. Sprinkle the reserved topping evenly over the top. Bake just until a toothpick inserted in the center comes out clean, 20 to 25 minutes. Let cool for at least 15 minutes before cutting into squares.

BLUEBERRY COFFEECAKE

Omit the brown sugar and use 2 cups granulated sugar. Include ¼ teaspoon ground nutmeg and/or 1 tablespoon finely grated lemon zest in the batter. After spreading the batter in the pan, but before you sprinkle on the topping, scatter 2 cups fresh or frozen (if frozen, do not thaw) blueberries over the top. Sprinkle the topping over the berries and bake. Frozen blueberries will cool everything down, so if you're using them, allow an extra 5 to 10 minutes of baking time.

Banana Bread

makes 2 loaves or 1 large cake

This is bread in name only; with a cup each of butter and sugar, it's really cake. Your bananas should be fully ripe—thoroughly yellow with many brown speckles.

2½ cups mashed ripe bananas *(4 or 5)*

2 teaspoons fresh lemon juice

1 cup butter *(2 sticks)***, at room temperature**

½ cup granulated *(white)* **sugar**

½ cup firmly packed brown sugar

3 large eggs

1 teaspoon vanilla extract

1 cup pecans or walnuts *(about 3¼ ounces)***, lightly toasted** *(page 176)* **and coarsely chopped**

2½ cups sifted all-purpose flour

1 teaspoon salt

2 teaspoons baking soda

Heat the oven to 350°F. Grease and flour 2 loaf pans or 1 large tube pan. Stir the lemon juice into the mashed bananas. In a large bowl, using an electric mixer, cream the butter until light. Add both kinds of sugar and cream again. Add the eggs, one at a time, beating after each one. Mix in the banana–lemon juice mixture, the vanilla, and the nuts. Sift together the flour, salt, and baking soda, and fold into the wet ingredients. Mix just until the batter is uniform. Pour the batter into the prepared pans. Bake for about 45 minutes, until a toothpick inserted in the center comes out clean. Let cool for 10 minutes in the pan, then remove and cool on a rack.

Doughnuts

makes about 30 medium doughnuts

As far back as I can remember, I was fascinated by the transformation of ingredients. When I was a toddler, we had an old refrigerator with the freezer compartment on the bottom. I often froze the milk left in my breakfast cereal bowl—I loved to come back later and find the bowl of frozen milk, with a few stray Froot Loops or Cocoa Puffs embedded in it. A bowl of milk, looking almost the same, but cold and rock-hard: extraordinary. When I was six or seven, I made my mother breakfast in bed for Mother's Day. The first thing I did was make the coffee, but I didn't serve it until the French toast and blueberries were finished: she drank it stone-cold, dutifully, and waited decades to tell me. On my eleventh birthday, I made a batch of these cake doughnuts from a recipe in *The Betty Crocker Picture Cookbook*. I ate most of them and had a stomachache by evening. It was worth it, though; they were the best doughnuts I'd ever had. Making them twenty years later at Deep Springs, I discovered they still are.

Deep-frying requires a large amount of oil, so that the oil's temperature will remain stable when the doughnuts are dropped in. If the oil cools down too much, the doughnuts will absorb more of it. A candy or frying thermometer, the glass kind that clips over the rim of the pot and stays there throughout the cooking, is useful for maintaining the oil's temperature.

EQUIPMENT/SUPPLIES

doughnut cutter

deep-fry thermometer *(or instant-read thermometer)*

FOR THE DOUGHNUTS

1 cup sugar

2 tablespoons butter, melted

4 egg yolks

½ cup buttermilk

¼ cup plain yogurt

1 teaspoon vanilla extract

3½ cups sifted all-purpose flour

2 teaspoons baking powder

1 teaspoon baking soda

½ teaspoon salt

¼ teaspoon ground mace

5 to 6 cups safflower oil, peanut oil, or other appropriate oil for frying

FOR DUSTING (OPTIONAL)

¾ cup sugar

1 tablespoon ground cinnamon

Beat the sugar and melted butter into the egg yolks in a large bowl. Beat in the buttermilk, yogurt, and vanilla until the mixture is uniform. Sift together the flour, baking powder, baking soda, salt, and mace, and add to the wet ingredients, stirring just until thoroughly combined. Cover the dough and refrigerate for at least 1½ hours, preferably overnight.

On a generously floured surface, gently roll out the dough to a ⅓-inch thickness, handling it as little as possible. It is a very delicate dough and easy to overwork. Dip the doughnut cutter in flour before cutting each doughnut. Using a thin metal spatula, transfer the cut doughnuts to a floured plate, the holes to another. Reroll the scraps gently, and cut a few more doughnuts. If you will be coating the doughnuts in cinnamon sugar, combine the sugar and cinnamon in a wide, shallow dish.

In a large, heavy saucepan over a medium-high flame, heat 5 to 6 cups of fresh oil (oil that has not been previously heated) to about 360°F—it's best to keep the oil between 350° and 375°F. Fry the doughnuts in small batches, turning once, until they are a medium-deep golden brown on both sides. The timing will depend on the size of the doughnuts. Break open a doughnut to be sure they are cooked all the way through. Allow the oil to return to the correct temperature before frying the next batch. Fry the holes and any remaining scraps of dough separately. Drain briefly on plenty of paper towels, then dredge them in cinnamon sugar, if desired, while still warm. I like to make half the doughnuts cinnamon-sugared and leave half plain.

Funnel Cakes

serves 6

Funnel cakes, another utterly gratifying deep-fried treat, are much simpler than doughnuts: the batter can be mixed and ready by the time the oil is hot. As with doughnuts, you need to keep a large amount of oil at a stable temperature, to ensure that the funnel cakes don't absorb too much of it. At home, it is easiest to fry the funnel cakes one at a time in a heavy, 6- to 8-inch-deep saucepot, filled at least 3 inches deep with oil. At Deep Springs we fit four large food service–sized #10 cans, both ends removed, into our commercial deep-fryer to achieve the round shape. As for the funnel, one that holds ½ cup is ideal—that's about how much batter you'll need for each cake.

EQUIPMENT/SUPPLIES

deep-fry thermometer (*or instant-read thermometer*)
funnel

FOR THE FUNNEL CAKES

4 to 5 cups safflower oil, peanut oil, or other appropriate oil for frying
2 cups sifted all-purpose flour
¼ cup granulated (*white*) **sugar**
1 teaspoon baking powder
½ teaspoon salt
¼ teaspoon ground mace
2 eggs
1½ cups whole milk
1½ teaspoons vanilla extract
powdered sugar for dusting (*optional*)

In a deep, heavy saucepan over a medium-high flame, heat the oil to 375°F. Meanwhile, sift together the flour, sugar, baking powder, salt, and mace. Whisk the eggs, milk, and vanilla together in a large bowl. Whisk the dry mixture into the wet mixture just until uniform. Ladle ½ cup of batter into a funnel, your finger stopping the hole. Release the batter into the hot oil, "scribbling" the stream of batter evenly over the surface of the oil. The frying batter will rise to the top in a tangled mass. After about a minute, when the cake is golden brown on the underside, gently flip it and cook the other side until golden brown, about a minute more. Drain on plenty of paper towels for a few moments. Allow the oil to return to 375°F before frying the next funnel cake.

I like funnel cakes unsugared, but most people prefer them dusted lightly with powdered sugar: put a spoonful of powdered sugar in a sieve and tap the sieve over the warm cakes. Consume immediately.

CHAPTER 4

BREAD, BUTTER, CRACKERS, & CHEESE

Deep Springs students have always loved making and eating bread. Once, master baker Cecilia Lopez taught a very popular course, "Breads of Europe and the Middle East," in which each student baked many, many loaves of bread, including some made with sourdough cultures they had "caught" themselves.

Breadmaking can become wonderfully complex, but don't forget that it's also quite simple. I'll always remember one of my classmates at Deep Springs, making bread for that evening's dinner in the Boardinghouse kitchen, being struck with an epiphany: "You just take powder and germs, mix in some water, and you get bread!"

A warm loaf of home-baked bread makes the simplest meal quite special. In the world of food and cooking, bread occupies its own sovereign kingdom. Making good bread requires a different sort of attention: precisely timed moments between long periods of simply leaving it alone. The few recipes here provide a good, basic introduction to breadmaking. If memories of past bread failures still haunt you, begin afresh with the easy recipes in this chapter. Like other arenas of cookery, breadmaking requires close attention to timing and temperature. Making bread takes time. When bread dough rises slowly, a more delicious yeasty, wheaty flavor develops. These recipes presuppose an ambient kitchen temperature of about 70°F; your dough will rise more quickly in a warmer kitchen. I have found that it's easy, when making bread on warm days, to inadvertently let the dough rise for too long, to the point that the yeast is exhausted and the loaf emerges denser and not as well-textured. At Deep Springs we always make our tastiest loaf bread in the colder months. Focaccia, an olive oil–rich flatbread with a quicker rise, is a good choice for warmer weather.

Bread's characteristic structure comes from the protein in wheat, called gluten. You knead bread dough for a long period of time to fully develop this gluten into long, elastic strands. In contrast, the quick bread recipes in the previous chapter, leavened with baking powder or baking soda, require very brief mixing, so little elastic gluten is formed. See Butter Piecrust (page 263) or Handmade Egg Noodles (page 231) for further perspective on gluten. All these breads are superb warm from the oven and stay good and moist for the rest of the day. Left at room temperature, they are good as toast the next day. *Never refrigerate bread*;

it goes stale in the refrigerator faster than at room temperature. Once cooled completely, wrap extra whole loaves of bread well with plastic wrap. Immediately freeze any loaves you will not be using that day. Thaw the bread, wrapped, for several hours at room temperature, then unwrap, brush with water, and heat in a 400°F oven for about 5 minutes, until the crispiness of the crust is restored. It will taste almost fresh-baked.

Don't let bread get moldy. At Deep Springs we put stale bread scraps in a deep pan that sits on the back of our big convection oven. The bread dries quickly and is easily pulverized to make fine breadcrumbs, good for frying. Sometimes, using a food processor, I pulse chunks of moister, day-old bread to coarse crumbs and toast them until golden in a 325°F oven with olive oil and salt, as a topping for pasta. See Italian Meatballs, page 190, for more about breadcrumbs. Make crumbs, croutons (page 175), or French Toast (page 53) out of bread that is more than two days old. If bread develops mold, toss it in the compost.

Dinner Bread

makes 4 loaves, 1¼ pounds each

Warm bread at dinner. The talented Cecilia Lopez developed this easy, basic recipe for the Deep Springs kitchen. It fits perfectly into our cooking schedule: we make the "sponge" right after breakfast and mix the dough first thing when we come in to prepare dinner. Each step takes only minutes. The use of a sturdy, large-capacity electric mixer is specified in this recipe, but if your strength and stamina are good, you can knead your bread dough by hand. The recipe may be halved.

SPONGE

- 2 cups warm low-fat milk *(bath temperature—110° to 115°F)*
- 2 cups warm water
- 4 cups all-purpose flour, preferably unbleached, or 2 cups whole-wheat flour and 2 cups all-purpose flour
- 2 tablespoons brown sugar
- 1½ tablespoons active dry yeast *(2 packets, or ½ ounce)*

DOUGH

- 2 tablespoons salt
- 6 tablespoons butter, at room temperature
- 7 to 8 cups all-purpose flour
- melted butter for brushing the tops *(optional)*

7:30 A.M.: SPONGE

Thoroughly combine the warm milk, warm water, 4 cups flour, brown sugar, and yeast in a large bowl, or in the bowl of a large-capacity electric mixer. Cover the bowl and let the sponge develop at room temperature (about 70°F—not in a particularly warm place) for 5 to 7 hours.

2:00 P.M.: MIX

Add the salt, butter, and 7 cups flour to the sponge. Mix with the paddle attachment until the dough is uniform—it should leave the sides of the bowl. If the dough is still very soft and sticky, add another cup of flour. (Some of the variations will produce a stickier dough; these are more difficult to knead by hand.) Switch to the dough hook and knead the dough at low speed for about 10 minutes, stopping the mixer and turning the dough over once or twice to ensure even kneading.

Lightly oil a large bowl and put the dough in it, turning it over once. Cover with plastic wrap (or enclose in a large, clean garbage bag) and let the dough rise at room temperature until doubled in bulk, a little over an hour.

3:30 P.M.: SHAPE

Grease 4 loaf pans, or dust 2 flat baking sheets well with cornmeal. Punch down the dough and divide evenly into 4 pieces. Take a piece of dough and gently flatten it into a rectangle. Choose its smoothest side and fold the dough in on itself in thirds, smooth side out, pinching the seam closed on the bottom. Place smooth side up in one of the bread pans, or on the cornmeal-dusted sheet. Shape the other 3 loaves. Cover the loaves with plastic wrap (or enclose in the inflated garbage bag) and leave them at room temperature for the second rise. Ensure that the oven will be at 400°F by baking time.

5:00 P.M.: BAKE

Have the oven at 400°F. (Optional: using a razor-sharp blade, slash the tops of the loaves lengthwise—this will help the bread expand in the oven and make for a lighter texture. A regular knife is not sharp enough and will just deflate the bread.) For a crispy crust, spray the loaves well with a water mister before putting them in the oven, and spray once or twice during the first 10 minutes of baking. Bake the bread in the hot oven for 25 to 30 minutes, until deep golden brown all over and lightly browned on the bottom. When done, the loaf will sound hollow when thumped on the bottom. If you have an instant-read thermometer, the internal temperature of the bread should be about 190°F. Remove from the pans and put on a rack to cool. (Optional: for a softer crust, brush the tops of the hot loaves with melted butter.) Let cool for at least 20 minutes before slicing.

RICH DINNER BREAD

Follow the master recipe, reducing the water in the sponge by ½ cup. Add 2 tablespoons more butter and 2 whole eggs when you mix the dough.

WHEATY DINNER BREAD

In a covered saucepan, combine 1 cup bulgur wheat and 2 cups water. Bring to a boil and let boil for 2 minutes. Drain well, saving the water, and let cool. Use the water as part of the liquid in the sponge in the master recipe, and stir the bulgur into the sponge. In the sponge, use all whole-wheat flour. When you mix the dough, add ½ teaspoon more salt and 2 tablespoons honey.

SESAME BREAD

With its haunting sesame flavor, this is a good bread to accompany beef. Use half whole-wheat flour and half white flour in the sponge in the master recipe. When mixing the dough after the sponge has developed, replace half the butter with 3 tablespoons of strong, dark Asian sesame oil. After the first rising, shape the loaves into rounds, then press the tops of the loaves into a wide bowl of sesame seeds, coating the tops thoroughly with the seeds. The seeds toast as the bread bakes.

POTATO BREAD

Scrub a small russet potato and cut into cubes. Put in a small saucepan with 2 cups water, and bring to a boil. Reduce the heat, cover, and boil gently until the potato is completely soft and falling apart. Drain, saving the liquid. Rub the potato chunks through a screen sieve back into the liquid, and use this warm liquid for the 2 cups of water in the sponge in the master recipe. The potato's starch will produce a stickier dough, but it gives the bread a wonderfully moist texture.

BREAD FOR LUNCH

Using the master Dinner Bread recipe or any of the variations, make the sponge the night before, using only 1½ teaspoons of yeast. Let it develop, covered, at room temperature overnight. Mix and knead the dough right after breakfast at 8:00, shape the loaves at 10:00, then bake at 11:30—the loaves will be finished and ready to slice at 12:30, when lunch is served.

BREAD FOR THE NEXT DAY

Often, this 2-day process is much more convenient—and the bread that results has a deeper yeasty flavor but is perhaps a little denser. Using the master Dinner Bread recipe or any of the variations, cover and refrigerate the dough immediately after mixing/kneading. The following day (12 to 24 hours later), take out the dough and shape it into loaves. Cover (or put in an inflated garbage bag) and let come to room temperature and rise for about 2 hours. Bake as usual.

HAMBURGER BUNS

For good, soft, homemade hamburger buns, follow the master recipe or (if you like) any of the above variations, keeping the dough on the wet and sticky side. After the first rise, using well-floured hands (and a rolling pin, if necessary), form the dough into disks about 6 inches in diameter and about ½ inch thick. Thoroughly dredge the buns in flour before placing them on a baking sheet about 2 inches apart. Let rise, and bake the buns at 400°F for about 15 minutes, until golden on the outside and light and springy throughout. Brush off the excess flour and let the buns cool on a rack.

Carefully split the buns with a sharp bread knife. Use them the same day you make them, or if they are a day old, butter and toast them first.

Focaccia

makes 2 flatbreads; serves 6 to 8

For years, easy, forgiving focaccia was the only bread I made. The soft, olive oil–rich dough is rolled or stretched into a sheet and baked on a sheet pan, somewhat like a pizza with much simpler toppings. This master recipe can be started and baked in a single afternoon. It's a good yeast bread to make in hot weather—the Dinner Bread is a little more heat sensitive. Once you gain experience, the potato and longer-rise variations are as instructive as they are delicious. Substituting white wine for some of the water adds a subtle dimension to the yeastiness. You can use whole-wheat flour for part of the all-purpose flour if you prefer.

SPONGE

2 tablespoons yeast *(2½ packets)*

¼ teaspoon brown sugar

2 cups warm water *(bath temperature—110° to 115°F)*

2 cups all-purpose flour, preferably unbleached

DOUGH

2 teaspoons salt

6 tablespoons extra-virgin olive oil

1 tablespoon finely chopped fresh rosemary

about 3 cups all-purpose flour

TOPPING

4 tablespoons extra-virgin olive oil

1 tablespoon coarse sea salt

To make the sponge, in a large mixing bowl, stir the yeast and brown sugar into the water. Mix in 2 cups flour, and cover the bowl tightly with plastic wrap. Let the sponge develop at room temperature for 30 to 40 minutes.

To make the dough, mix the salt, olive oil, and rosemary into the sponge, then add enough flour to make a dough that just leaves the sides of the bowl, about 3 cups. Knead the dough for about 7 minutes, or until it is soft, shiny from the oil, and elastic. Put the dough in a large bowl coated with olive oil, turn once, cover with plastic wrap, and set aside to rise at room temperature for about 30 minutes.

Heat the oven to 450°F. Punch the dough down and cut it in half. Oil 2 baking sheets (about 12 by 17 inches) not too skimpily with olive oil. Gently stretch the halves of dough into rough rectangles of similar size, placing each onto a baking sheet. Cover loosely with plastic wrap (or place in an inflated garbage bag) and let rise for 30 minutes. Uncover and dimple the dough heavily, all over, by pressing your oiled fingers all the way down into the dough, almost piercing it. Drizzle each focaccia with about 2 tablespoons of olive oil, and sprinkle evenly with the coarse sea salt. Cover and let rise again for about 30 minutes. Bake in the hot oven until the bread is golden brown all over and light brown underneath, about 20 minutes. Rotate the pans once or twice during baking to ensure even browning. When done, remove the focaccia from the pans and place on a rack to cool.

POTATO FOCACCIA

Scrub a russet potato and cut into chunks. Cover with water in a small saucepan and gently boil, covered, until the potato is completely soft. Pass the potato and its water through a food mill or a sieve. Add enough water to this thin potato purée to measure 2 cups. Let cool to warm bath temperature, if necessary, and proceed with the master recipe, substituting the purée for the water in the sponge. You will still need a total of about 5 cups flour, but this potato dough should be a little stickier than a regular dough—it will probably stick to the sides of the mixer bowl. Top this focaccia with paper-thin slices of unpeeled potato—use various sizes and colors—blanched in lightly salted water just until tender. After you dimple the dough, place the potato slices between the dimples, pressing them lightly into the dough, and brush each with olive oil. Make sure each slice gets some sea salt. This is one of the ways we celebrate our abundant Deep Springs potato crop.

LONGER-RISE FOCACCIA

A longer rise promotes the development of more-complex wheat flavor and a springier texture. Following the master recipe or the potato variation, use only 1 tablespoon of yeast. Let the sponge develop for 3 hours. Let the finished dough rise for 1 hour.

OTHER VARIATIONS

Substitute sage for the rosemary. Or strew sautéed onions, thyme, and pitted oil-cured black olives over the dough. Or lightly press thin slices of red, ripe tomato into the dough after you dimple it. Beautiful.

Farm Butter and Buttermilk

Much equipment has come and gone from the Deep Springs Boardinghouse kitchen over the years, but the same old wooden 1-pound butter mold, its corners rounded from many decades of use, is still used to shape small quantities of Deep Springs' own butter. Occasionally we bake with it, but most often it is reserved simply for lavishing on freshly baked bread.

Cream to be churned into the most delicious butter must first be ripened, or cultured. Mix ¼ cup of fresh, cultured yogurt or buttermilk into each quart of fresh cream. A quart of cream will yield a scant pound of butter and about a pint of buttermilk. Put the cream in a jar with a well-fitting lid, and put the jar in a larger basin of hot water, sloshing the cream around in the jar occasionally. Heat the cream gently in this way until it reaches 80°F, barely lukewarm to the touch. Wrap the jar in towels to insulate it, and let stand overnight. When the cream is cultured, it should have a light, yogurty tanginess.

Once cultured, cool the cream to about 60°F. Put the cultured cream in the bowl of an electric mixer and whip on medium-low speed. At first, the cream will thicken as for whipped cream. Continuing to whip, you will begin to see flaky granules of butter. When the granules stick together in clumps the size of corn kernels, stop the churning. Immediately drain off the liquid. This liquid is the original, "true" buttermilk, different from the cultured-milk product we buy at the store. Salt the buttermilk very lightly, and save it for drinking or baking.

Wash the butter in a large bowl, in water that is about 50°F. Use only as much water as necessary to wash out the excess buttermilk. Take handfuls of the butter and squeeze gently to remove as much water as possible.

Finally, lightly salt the butter with about ½ teaspoon fine sea salt per pound. Knead the butter 20 or 30 times to work in the salt and to give it a good texture. Pack the butter into a mold lined with plastic wrap, and chill. Remove from the mold and wrap well. To serve, bring to room temperature.

Cheese Crackers

makes about 30 crackers; serves 6

This recipe and those that follow make enough crackers to generously serve 6 people as a soup or cheese accompaniment. These crackers are also good with Quince Jam (page 260).

1 cup all-purpose flour

½ teaspoon salt, plus more for sprinkling

½ teaspoon dry mustard

¼ teaspoon cayenne pepper

1 tablespoon butter

1½ cups *(6 ounces)* **grated extra-sharp Cheddar cheese, at room temperature**

1 egg

1 egg yolk

In a medium mixing bowl, whisk together the flour, salt, mustard, and cayenne. Work in the butter and cheese with your hands very well, until the mixture is crumbly and uniform. Mix in the egg and yolk, and knead the dough a few times, until it is uniform. Wrap tightly and let rest, refrigerated, for at least 1 hour, to allow the flour to absorb the liquid.

Heat the oven to 375°F. Lightly grease a baking sheet. Divide the dough into fourths. Working with one piece of dough at a time, on a lightly floured board with a lightly floured rolling pin (or using the rollers of a hand-crank pasta machine), roll the dough thin. Prick all over with a fork, cut into squares or diamonds (a pizza cutter works well), and carefully place on the baking sheet. Sprinkle the crackers lightly with salt. Bake until they are pale golden brown, 8 to 10 minutes. The crackers will crisp as they cool on a rack.

BLACK PEPPER CHEESE CRACKERS

Add coarsely ground black pepper, about 1 teaspoon, to the dry ingredients, and reduce the cayenne to a pinch. These are excellent with fresh corn soup.

Whole-Wheat Crackers

makes about 30 crackers; serves 6

These crackers and the following Puffy Salties are based on recipes from Diana Kennedy's cookbook *Nothing Fancy*—one of my favorites. Try them with a generous schmear of soft homemade cheese (page 82).

¼ cup fine bulgur wheat

1 cup whole-wheat flour *(whole-grain spelt flour may also be used)*

1 cup minus 2 tablespoons sifted all-purpose flour

3 tablespoons wheat germ

1 teaspoon salt

¼ teaspoon baking powder

6 tablespoons cold butter

½ cup buttermilk

Toast the bulgur wheat in a small dry skillet over a medium-high flame, tossing constantly, until light brown with an appealing nutty scent. Transfer to a small plate to cool. Mix the bulgur with the whole-wheat and all-purpose flours, wheat germ, salt, and baking powder in a medium bowl, then thoroughly work in the butter until evenly dispersed throughout the mixture. Add the buttermilk and blend just until the dough is uniform. Wrap tightly and let rest, refrigerated, for 30 minutes.

Heat the oven to 375°F. Lightly grease a baking sheet. Divide the dough into fourths. Working with one piece of dough at a time, on a lightly floured board with a lightly floured rolling pin (or using the rollers of a hand-crank pasta machine), roll the dough thin—as thin as the bulgur will allow. Prick all over with a fork, and cut into squares (a pizza cutter works well). Carefully place on the baking sheet. Bake just until light brown, about 10 minutes; watch carefully. The crackers will crisp as they cool on a rack.

Puffy Salties

makes about 75 small crackers; serves 6

These simple crackers are good with soups of all types. You will need a clean spray bottle filled with water.

2 cups sifted all-purpose flour

½ teaspoon salt

3 tablespoons butter, at room temperature

½ cup cold water

coarse sea salt or kosher salt for sprinkling

In a medium bowl, thoroughly mix the flour, salt, and butter. Mix in the cold water and knead the dough well, until it is very elasticized. Wrap and let rest for 10 minutes.

Heat the oven to 400°F. Divide the dough into fourths. On a lightly floured board with a lightly floured rolling pin (or using the rollers of a hand-crank pasta machine), roll the dough very thin—a little thinner than a tortilla. Spray lightly with water, then evenly sprinkle sea salt or kosher salt over the dough—not too much! Using a pizza cutter, cut the dough into 1-inch squares. Transfer to a lightly greased baking sheet. Bake until puffed and light brown, 5 to 6 minutes; watch carefully.

Thyme Crackers

makes about 20 large crackers; serves 6

These large crackers, with their beautiful scattering of whole thyme leaves baked into the dough, go well with clam chowder (or any kind of chowder), but they are also superb with soft goat cheese and honey for dessert. You will need a clean spray bottle filled with water for spraying the surface of the crackers.

7 or 8 sprigs fresh thyme

2 cups sifted all-purpose flour

2 tablespoons wheat germ *(optional)*

1 tablespoon sugar

1 teaspoon salt

2 tablespoons butter, at room temperature

⅔ cup milk

coarse sea salt or kosher salt for sprinkling

To prepare the thyme, carefully strip the tiny individual leaves and clusters of leaves off the stems. Pick apart any large clusters of leaves. You should have about 1 tablespoon. In a large bowl, blend the thyme, flour, wheat germ (if using), sugar, and salt. Thoroughly work in the butter with your hands—it should be evenly dispersed throughout the mixture. In this process you will bruise many of the thyme leaves, releasing their scent into the dough. Mix in the milk, enough to make a pliable dough, and mix the dough just until it is uniform. Wrap the dough well with plastic wrap and let rest in the refrigerator for at least 1 hour.

Heat the oven to 400°F. On a lightly floured board with a lightly floured rolling pin (or using the rollers of a hand-crank pasta machine), roll one-third of the dough at a time into an oblong or rectangle, a little thinner than a tortilla. With a sharp knife or pizza cutter, cut into long strips 1 to 2 inches wide. Place the strips on a lightly greased baking sheet, spray lightly with water, and sprinkle lightly with coarse or kosher salt. Bake the crackers in the center of the hot oven for 5 to 6 minutes. Watch them carefully—they should have many golden brown spots but not be browned throughout. They burn easily because of the sugar in the dough and the high heat of the oven. Remove the crackers from the sheet to cool on a rack.

Serving Cheese

Cheese is a universe unto itself. Western Europe is a cheese lover's paradise, with many hundreds of traditional varieties still made there today, each a unique expression of its place. Happily, many of these European cheese traditions are gradually taking root in North America.

Serve cheese on a wooden board, with a small knife of appropriate strength and sharpness for the type of cheese being served. Cut slices of cheese to go on good bread or crackers, or just cut or break cheeses into chunks to eat by themselves. The French love a bite or two of cheese after a meal, before or instead of dessert. Here are some guidelines for serving cheese:

Serve cheese at room temperature. The fat in cheese carries much of its flavor, but cold fat doesn't accomplish this as well.

Serve cheese simply. The simple cracker recipes in this chapter (the ones that don't already contain cheese) beautifully accompany cheese, as would a loaf of home-baked bread. Apples, pears, grapes, and dates complement the flavor of many cheeses, while citrus and most other acid fruit may detract from it. Nuts—especially sweet nuts right out of the shell—are also a good accompaniment (see page 281).

Many fine cheeses may be expensive, but a little goes a long way. An ounce of cheese is about the size of your thumb. Though it's very easy to eat more, *an ounce per person is usually enough*, especially of cheeses high in fat. If you wish to serve an inexpensive cheese in an elegant way, feta cheese is a great possibility: let a block of feta come to room temperature for an hour or two, then drizzle it with fragrant olive oil and grind black pepper over it. This is marvelous in summer with fresh ripe figs, or at other times of year with sweet dates (Medjool, Khadrawi, and Black Sphinx are all good date varieties).

Queso Blanco

makes about 2 cups

This is one of the simplest cheeses you can make. When all the Deep Springs dairy cows are in full production, there is more milk than the community can drink, so naturally cheesemaking enters everyone's mind. There is always a lot of talk of Roquefort and Gouda and Brie, but this milk cheese, known in Latin American cooking as *queso blanco* (and in Indian cookery as *paneer*) is what usually gets made. Keep in mind that cheesemaking is a form of food preservation. As such, for best results, make sure your raw ingredient (in this case, milk) is absolutely fresh, and that your surfaces and utensils are absolutely clean. This simple cheese will keep, refrigerated, for a few days if made with whole milk, longer if made with skim. If you make it with whole milk, a soft, creamy, spreadable cheese results. With nonfat milk, you will have a much firmer, slightly rubbery product (also delicious, but different). It does not readily melt in either case, but if made with lower-fat milk, it can be crumbled and browned in a nonstick skillet in a little oil. The whey, the by-product, may be made into a tasty and unusual lemonade (recipe follows).

EQUIPMENT/SUPPLIES

instant-read thermometer

cheesecloth *(or clean cotton "flour sack" towel)*

FOR THE CHEESE

8 cups *(½ gallon)* **very fresh whole, low-fat, or skim milk**

¼ cup vinegar *(cider vinegar or red wine vinegar; the label should specify 5% acidity)*

1 teaspoon salt

Heat the milk in a heavy pot over a medium-high flame, stirring and scraping the bottom frequently with a wooden spoon, until the milk reaches 180°F. Stir in the vinegar—the milk will curdle; in other words, the soft curds will separate from the liquid whey. Set a colander over a large stockpot. Wet the cheesecloth with cold tap water, and wring it out. Line the colander with cheesecloth. Pour the hot curds and whey through the cheesecloth, using a rubber spatula to scrape any bits of stuck curd off the bottom of the pot. If you like, pour the hot whey into a pitcher and make whey lemonade.

Drain the curds for a moment, then turn them back into the pot. Stir in the salt thoroughly, then pour the cheese back into the cheesecloth-lined colander. If necessary, arrange the cheese into a nice round shape. Cover the top with plastic wrap, put the colander, set over a bowl, in the refrigerator, and let the cheese continue to drain for 1 to 2 days, turning once. When the cheese has drained sufficiently, remove it from the cloth and wrap it tightly. Keep refrigerated.

This cheese has many uses. Its fresh, uncomplicated flavor is best enhanced by other flavorful elements: on little toasts with ripe tomatoes and herbs, or crumbled into spicy dishes. It is particularly good crumbled and sizzled in a little hot olive oil in a nonstick skillet until it browns.

Serve immediately by itself, or alongside a salad, or topped with a relish...possibilities abound.

WHEY LEMONADE

The Queso Blanco recipe will yield about 8 cups of milky whey. While it is still warm, stir in 1 cup of sugar. Add the juice and grated zest of 3 lemons and a big sprig of fresh mint. Let cool, then let steep and chill in the refrigerator for several hours. Strain into ice-filled glasses, garnish with slices of fresh lemon, and enjoy.

CHAPTER 5

GREAT LUNCHES

Enthusiastic class discussions often spill over into the lunch hour, and afternoon ranch work begins immediately after lunch, so Deep Springs lunches must deliver a powerful, quickly-consumed nutritional punch, satisfying the hunger that comes after a morning of intense classes and fueling the body for an afternoon of sweaty outdoor work.

What constitutes a great lunch is limited only by your taste, appetite, and imagination. Of course, dishes for many other great lunches may be found in several neighboring chapters; this one gives a sampling of dishes—usually meals in themselves, inexpensive to prepare and appealing in hot or cold weather—that I rely on most heavily at Deep Springs: pizza, pasta, macaroni and cheese, enchiladas, sandwiches….

Lunch, served at the hottest time of the day, is when Deep Springers like to consume vast quantities of cool, refreshing beverages such as iced tea and lemonade; you will find recipes for those at the end of the chapter.

Reatha's Macaroni and Cheese

serves 6 to 8

My friend Reatha, originally from South Carolina, is a great Southern cook. This is my written-down version of her renowned "mac & cheese." I've adapted and changed a couple of things over the years, but it still evokes her generous spirit.

This macaroni and cheese is rich. Serve it with something tart and refreshing, like a green salad, sliced summer tomatoes, or Apple and Pear Salad (page 163), and follow with a nice nap. The crumb topping is optional but excellent—we all love something creamy underneath something crunchy.

1 pound dry large elbow macaroni

4 tablespoons butter

12 ounces extra-sharp Cheddar cheese, grated *(about 3 cups)*

4 ounces mozzarella cheese, grated *(about 1 cup)*

4 ounces Gruyère cheese, grated *(about 1 cup)*

two 12-ounce cans evaporated milk

3 eggs, beaten

1 teaspoon salt

1 teaspoon dry mustard

⅛ teaspoon cayenne pepper

¾ teaspoon white pepper

CRUMB TOPPING (OPTIONAL)

1½ cups plain breadcrumbs

3 tablespoons butter, melted

1 or 2 pinches salt

black pepper

paprika for sprinkling on top

Heat the oven to 350°F. Cook the macaroni in a large pot in plenty of boiling salted water (the water should taste lightly salty) until soft but not falling apart. Drain well, shaking the colander, but do not rinse. Dump the hot macaroni into a large bowl or, if there is ample room to mix, back into the pot, and toss it gently with the butter. Combine the cheeses in a medium bowl, and toss three-quarters of the cheese with the hot buttered macaroni.

In a medium bowl, whisk together the milk, eggs, salt, and spices to make a savory custard. Dump the macaroni mixture into an ungreased 9-by-13-inch baking dish and pour the custard over it. Top with the remaining cheese. Make the topping, if you opt for it, while the macaroni bakes: combine the crumbs, melted butter, salt, and pepper to taste in a medium bowl and toast carefully in the oven on a baking sheet, or toss in a medium-hot skillet, until the crumbs are golden brown, about 5 minutes.

Bake the macaroni and cheese for 7 to 8 minutes, then bring the dish out of the oven and quickly stir the whole thing around to evenly distribute the heat. Immediately return the dish to the oven and bake for another 7 to 8 minutes, then take it out and stir it again. When the cheese is melted and the sauce is smooth and creamy, remove it from the oven. *Do not overbake:* if the cheese gets too hot it will separate and the creaminess will turn to greasiness. You can check the temperature of the sauce with an instant-read thermometer; at 140°F, the cheese will be melted and the eggs cooked. Sprinkle lightly with the optional topping and paprika, and serve.

SPICY MACARONI AND CHEESE

Among the many options for spicing up macaroni and cheese, here are a few: when mixing the macaroni and cheese together, add several hot New Mexico green chiles that have been roasted, peeled, and chopped (page 251). Or substitute 1½ cups of New Mexico Red Chile Sauce (page 250) for one can of the evaporated milk. Or briefly sauté minced fresh hot chiles in some of the recipe's butter. Or substitute pepper jack cheese for the Cheddar.

Baked Potatoes

serves 6

More than toddlers love candy, Deep Springs rancher and office manager Iris Pope loves baked potatoes. "My mouth is watering!" she always yells into the kitchen after seeing "Baked Potatoes" on the lunch menu board. These baked potatoes emerge with a light, fluffy texture and tender, flavorful skin.

Alongside baked potatoes and the array of toppings, I like to serve an abundant green salad and something rich in protein: hard-boiled eggs or chicken salad.

6 large russet potatoes

1 tablespoon vegetable oil

1½ teaspoons salt

½ teaspoon black pepper

FOR SERVING

butter

sour cream

thinly sliced green onions or chives

crumbled cooked bacon

grated Cheddar cheese

Sautéed Mushrooms (page 135)

chopped cooked broccoli

Heat the oven to 450°F. Scrub the potatoes under running water with a clean cloth and let them briefly air-dry. Combine the oil, salt, and pepper and rub this mixture all over the potatoes with your hands: the abrasion of the salt tenderizes the skin. Prick each potato in two places with a small knife. Arrange the potatoes on a baking sheet and bake for 40 minutes to an hour, or until thoroughly soft inside. Slit the top of each potato. Let people add the toppings of their choice.

Pizza

serves 3 to 4

You could easily find more sophisticated recipes for pizza, but this, baked in a rectangular sheet pan and cut into squares, evokes the perennial lunchtime favorite of generations of Deep Springs students. Green salad with abundant creamy dressing is a good accompaniment.

To accommodate the rising time for the dough, start 3 hours before you intend to serve the pizza. A little semolina flour, made from high-protein durum wheat, makes a good crust with a nice straw color, but you can successfully use more all-purpose flour in its place. Many suggestions for toppings are given below, both with and without tomato sauce. A list giving a quick overview of the assembly instructions is also provided.

SPONGE FOR DOUGH

1 cup warm water (bath temperature—115°F)

pinch of brown sugar

1 cup semolina flour

½ cup whole-wheat flour

2¼ teaspoons active dry yeast (1 packet)

FINISHING THE DOUGH

1¾ cups all-purpose flour, or more as needed

1 tablespoon extra-virgin olive oil

1½ teaspoons salt

GARLIC OIL

2 cloves garlic, crushed to a purée

pinch of salt

2 tablespoons olive oil

ASSEMBLY

about 1 cup Thick Tomato Sauce (page 248)

2 to 2½ cups (8 to 10 ounces) **grated mozzarella cheese**

about 2 cups toppings of choice (see the list on page 88)

FOR SERVING

freshly grated Parmesan cheese

hot red pepper flakes

To make the sponge, pour the warm water into a large bowl and stir in the brown sugar, semolina flour, whole-wheat flour, and yeast. Cover the bowl and let the sponge develop for 1 hour.

To finish the dough, mix the all-purpose flour, olive oil, and salt into the sponge. If it seems overly sticky, add a bit more all-purpose flour, enough to produce a soft, silky dough. Knead for 8 to 10 minutes. Put the dough in a large, oiled bowl, turn to coat with oil, cover, and let rise for 45 minutes. This is a good time to grate the cheese and make the sauce.

Heat the oven to 450°F. Position a rack near the center of the oven. Line a sheet pan with parchment paper well-rubbed with olive oil and dusted with semolina flour or cornmeal; if you have no parchment, just oil the pan well and dust generously. On a floured surface, gently stretch and shape the dough to an evenly thick rectangle (it's okay to use a rolling pin), and lay it in the pan. Lightly press the dough to fill out the sides and corners of the pan, making a rim. Cover (an inflated garbage bag works well) and let rise for 20 minutes while you ready the toppings.

To make the garlic oil, in a small bowl, mix the garlic with a pinch of salt and the olive oil. Brush over the surface of the crust. To assemble the pizza, top it first with the sauce, then with about a third of the grated mozzarella cheese, then the topping of your choice, and finish with the remaining mozzarella.

Bake the pizza for about 20 minutes, or until the crust is cooked through and browned on the bottom and the cheese is bubbly and brown on top. Let the pizza rest and "set up" for about 5 minutes before cutting. Serve with Parmesan and hot red pepper flakes.

ASSEMBLY, BOTTOM TO TOP

- oiled pan, or pan lined with oil-rubbed parchment paper
- dusting of semolina or cornmeal
- dough
- garlic oil
- sauce
- one-third of the grated mozzarella
- topping
- remaining grated mozzarella

FAVORITE TRADITIONAL THIN-SLICED TOPPINGS WITH TOMATO SAUCE

- pepperoni
- mushrooms and parsley
- zucchini (lightly salted/peppered) and red onion
- fresh tomato (lightly salted/peppered) and oil-cured olives *(With tomatoes, use less sauce.)*
- sausage and sautéed Greens (page 132) *(Precook loose Italian sausage and pour off the excess fat.)*
- fresh tomato (lightly salted/peppered) and fresh basil *(With tomatoes, use less sauce.)*

FAVORITE UNUSUAL TOPPINGS WITHOUT TOMATO SAUCE

- lightly sautéed fennel, oil-cured olives, lemon zest, a little mozzarella, and Parmesan at the end (cool weather)
- cream-simmered leeks, a scraping of nutmeg, and Gruyère cheese (good with cornmeal in the crust instead of semolina—excellent in cooler weather, when leeks are in season)
- fresh, raw spinach tossed with olive oil, salt, pepper, and grated mozzarella, topped with dollops of ricotta cheese (the spinach wilts and cooks in the oven)
- small cubed boiled potatoes, pesto, mozzarella and Parmesan cheeses (warm weather)
- ripe pear with blue cheese and dollops of ricotta seasoned with nutmeg (cool weather)
- chopped cooked bacon, chopped fresh escarole tossed with olive oil, and mozzarella, topped after baking with grated hard-boiled egg

EGG PIZZA

To make the meal more substantial, crack up to 4 eggs onto this pizza—evenly spaced; each in its own quadrant—during the last 5 to 6 minutes of baking, and let cook until the whites are just set, the yolks still gooey.

Fresh Clam Chowder

serves about 6

Fresh clams are a rare luxury in the eastern Sierra, so at Deep Springs I typically make this thick chowder using canned clams, and it never fails to please—especially the more senior members of the community. I always make corn chowder (see the variation following) at the same time and serve both chowders with homemade crackers (such as Thyme Crackers, page 80).

If you'd like to use canned clams, use three 6.5-ounce cans chopped clams with juice, and two 8-ounce bottles clam juice. When adding the milk and cream to the pot with the roux, add the clam juice and the juice from the cans of clams, but add the clams themselves at the end.

FOR STEAMING THE CLAMS

3 pounds fresh clams

2 cups water

1 bay leaf

½ cup chopped onion

2 cloves garlic, lightly crushed

2 to 3 sprigs of fresh thyme

3 to 4 sprigs of fresh parsley

FOR THE CHOWDER

4 tablespoons butter

3 strips bacon or 3 ounces salt pork, finely diced

½ cup all-purpose flour

1 large yellow onion, cut into small dice

2 teaspoons coarsely chopped fresh thyme, or ½ teaspoon dried thyme

3 cups whole milk

½ cup heavy (whipping) **cream**

1 tablespoon salt

1 pound boiling potatoes (gold, white, or red)**, scrubbed, cut into small dice**

¼ cup chopped parsley

freshly ground black pepper

Scrub the clams thoroughly with a brush, and rinse well in cold water. Put them in a large, heavy pot with 2 cups water, bay leaf, ½ cup chopped onion, crushed garlic, thyme sprigs, and parsley sprigs. Place over a high flame, let the water come to a boil, and steam until the clams have opened, about 3 minutes. Using a slotted spoon, transfer the clams to a large, wide bowl to cool. Strain and reserve the cooking liquid. When the clams are cool, remove the meat from the shells, and set the meat aside.

In a heavy soup pot, melt the butter over medium-high heat, stir in the diced bacon, then stir in the flour to make a roux. Stirring with a wooden spoon, let the mixture come to a full, bubbly boil. As soon as the color begins to change from a pasty white to a pale beige, add the onion and thyme with a good pinch of salt. Let cook, stirring constantly, until the onion softens. Gradually add the milk and cream, then add the salt, potatoes, and the cooking liquid from the clams. Bring to a simmer, stirring frequently, and continue to cook gently for 10 to 15 minutes, or until the potatoes are cooked. Stir in the clam meat, parsley, and pepper to taste. Taste for salt, and adjust as necessary. Some say this is even better reheated the next day, and in fact, many traditional chowder recipes call for aging the chowder on the back of the stove for a period of time before reheating and serving.

CORN CHOWDER

Replace the clams (and the aromatics for steaming them) in the master recipe with about 4 ears' worth of fresh sweet corn kernels. Shuck the corn, remove the silks, and cut off the kernels into a large bowl, then thoroughly scrape the cobs with the back of your knife to extract all the germ and milk. Make the bacon roux as directed in the master recipe. When adding the milk, cream, salt, and potatoes to the pot with the roux, add the corn kernels and 2 cups of water, simmering, stirring frequently, until the potatoes are cooked. Since the flavors go so well together, I often can't resist adding a small can of chopped roasted green chiles to corn chowder, or a good dollop of Green Chile Relish (page 251). Serve with Black Pepper Cheese Crackers (page 79). Compare this old-fashioned corn chowder with the sleeker, more modern Catherine's Corn Soup on page 128.

Grilled Cheese Sandwich

This dish fulfills, perhaps more than any other, that primal gastronomic desire for something crisp on the outside and creamy within. It is delicious with a crisp, spicy-tart apple, or a beer, or a bowl of Tomato Soup (page 147). For each sandwich, lightly butter 2 slices of good brown bread on one side. Place sharp white Cheddar cheese between them, buttered sides out, and carefully toast on both sides in a skillet over low heat. It takes about 10 minutes to cook properly, so the cheese is perfectly melted and the bread perfectly toasted. Cut in half diagonally and serve immediately.

Good Sandwiches

Whole books have been written about sandwiches, and many more could be. At Deep Springs we rarely use purchased bread or pre-sliced deli meat, so sandwiches for lunch are a labor of love: I'll be roasting extra beef the night before (which takes hours; see page 183); hand-slicing the beef paper-thin (the old electric meat slicer has sat in the repair shop for years); starting the bread dough; mixing, rising, shaping, baking, and cooling the bread; and then slicing it by hand, along with tomatoes, onions, lettuce, and cheese. Furthermore, the lunch line in the Boardinghouse moves with excruciating slowness on sandwich day, as each person must assemble his or her own sandwich.

Nonetheless, the results are a dream; how often do you get such a fresh sandwich? The lesson to be learned here is that even something as simple as a sandwich benefits from the same care and close attention as any other food. Even a "boring"-sounding sandwich—wheat bread, sliced turkey, Cheddar, mayonnaise, mustard, lettuce, tomato, and onion—will be startlingly good if all elements are fresh and treated with care. Here are a few pointers for very good sandwiches:

Fresh bread: choose bread that is soft, flavorful, and baked that day. Chewy, artisan-style breads, baguettes, large rolls—all these are wonderful to eat on their own, but they are rarely my first choice for a sandwich. Sliced packaged bread is often pointedly sweet. Focaccia is an ever-popular sandwich bread in upscale cafés, but I find it overly rich and oily. The basic Dinner Bread recipe in this book (page 76), and all its variations, makes good sandwiches. If your bread is not fresh, toast it, and put on a little more spread.

Flavorful spread: mayonnaise carries flavors beautifully and also helps keep moisture from your filling (tomatoes are often the culprit) from soaking into the bread and making it soggy. Mustard enhances the flavor of virtually any cold meat. A little apricot jam mixed into mayonnaise is great with ham, pork, or turkey. Also consider chutney, or any type of relish, or soft cheese. Whatever your choice, take care to spread it all the way to the edges of the bread.

Green: a little fresh, tender greenness is essential to a sandwich. Like any salad, it needs to be washed and dried (see page 158). If you want a lot of lettuce on your sandwich, and you intend to eat it immediately, consider tossing it with vinaigrette or other dressing first. Choices are legion— leaf lettuce, watercress, arugula, even herbs (I like a few mint leaves on a sliced lamb sandwich).

Tomato: in summer, I slice ripe tomatoes into every sandwich, but outside of tomato season, I opt for extra greens and onions, or pickles, in their place. For the best flavor, salt the tomato, but if you're wrapping the sandwich for later, wait to salt it until just before you eat it, or else the tomato will throw off much of its juice, sogging the bread. On a ham sandwich, try a few slices of leftover fried green tomato (see page 146).

Onion: thinly sliced red onion is beautiful, a health tonic, and a flavor enhancer.

Meat/cheese: meat and cheese for sandwiches should be thinly sliced. Try a vegetable peeler, rather than a knife, to dispense cheese onto a sandwich, if a block of cheese is all you have. Home-roasted meats make sandwiches with singular character, especially roast beef, but good-quality ham, turkey, and other deli meats—prepared specifically for use in sandwiches—rarely disappoint.

Finally, enjoy your sandwich at *room temperature*, not refrigerator-cold—it will taste much better.

Tuna Salad

serves 3 to 4

When Deep Springs students wander into the Boardinghouse kitchen and notice I'm mixing up a giant bowl of tuna salad, they know that tuna melts will be on the menu for lunch: generous scoops of tuna atop thick slices of homemade bread, with mild, creamy Muenster cheese melted over the top. This tuna salad calls for celery and onion, but chopped pickles may be added, too: a finely-diced handful of either the simple Dill Pickles (page 255), or the sweeter Pickled Summer Vegetables (page 256), along with a few drops of the pickling brine.

two 5-ounce cans solid white tuna packed in water

¼ cup finely diced red onion

juice of ½ lemon, plus more as needed

½ teaspoon red wine vinegar

½ teaspoon Dijon mustard

⅛ teaspoon salt, plus more as needed

⅛ teaspoon freshly ground black pepper

⅓ cup finely diced celery (optional)

pinch of cayenne pepper

3 to 4 tablespoons mayonnaise

Remove the tuna from the can and drain well in a screen sieve. Put the tuna in a medium bowl and flake it not too finely with a fork, then toss with the onion, lemon juice, vinegar, mustard, salt, black pepper, celery (if using), and cayenne, and let marinate for 10 minutes. Mix in the mayonnaise. Taste for salt and acidity, adding more salt and another squeeze of lemon, if necessary.

MEDITERRANEAN TUNA SALAD

In place of the mayonnaise in the master recipe, use 2 to 3 tablespoons olive oil. Add a handful of coarsely chopped green olives, a few chopped capers, some coarsely chopped parsley, and an extra squeeze of lemon. This mixture is delightful and healthful atop a green salad.

Curry Tofu Salad

serves 4 to 6

This makes an excellent sandwich filling, but I also like it piled on cucumber slices or stuffed in celery sticks. Nothing else but tofu works for this recipe—its light, mellow character is the perfect foundation for building an intense and lively curry flavor. I first devised it to have something to serve the non–tuna eaters when I make tuna melts for lunch at Deep Springs, but it became popular with everyone, even people who thought they didn't like tofu.

- 1 pound firm tofu
- ¾ teaspoon salt, plus more as needed
- 1-inch piece fresh ginger, peeled and thinly sliced
- 2 cloves garlic
- 2 tablespoons sunflower oil or other vegetable oil
- 6 large white mushrooms, wiped clean, trimmed, halved, and sliced
- 1½ teaspoons mild or hot Curry Powder *(page 102)*
- 1 small carrot, peeled and finely shredded
- 2 green onions, thinly sliced
- 1 medium stalk celery, finely diced
- ¼ cup mayonnaise, plus more as needed
- 1 tablespoon yellow mustard
- 1 teaspoon soy sauce
- 1 tablespoon fresh lemon juice, plus more as needed
- freshly ground black pepper
- 3 to 4 tablespoons chopped fresh dill, parsley, or cilantro *(optional)*

Crumble the tofu finely in a medium bowl, sprinkle with ¾ teaspoon salt, and mix well. Finely mince together the ginger and garlic. In a wide skillet over a medium-high flame, heat the oil. Throw in the garlic and ginger with a pinch of salt and sauté, stirring, for 20 to 30 seconds. Add the mushrooms with a pinch of salt, then add the curry powder and cook, stirring, for another minute. Add the tofu, continuing to stir as the tofu heats through and excess water evaporates, 4 to 5 minutes. When there is no more excess water, remove from the heat and let the tofu cool completely in the pan, about 30 minutes.

Add the remaining ingredients: carrot, green onion, celery, mayonnaise, mustard, soy sauce, lemon, black pepper to taste, and optional herbs. Taste for seasoning, adding more salt, pepper, lemon juice, or mayonnaise to balance. Serve immediately or refrigerate.

Hard-Boiled Eggs

This method produces an egg that is cooked through, but no more; the yolk is bright colored and creamy, with no gray ring, and the white is firm but tender. Very fresh eggs, when hard-boiled, can be difficult to peel. If your eggs are very fresh, age them at room temperature for a day.

Place eggs gently in a saucepan and cover with cold water. Quickly bring to a boil over high heat. The moment they come to a boil, slap on the lid and remove them from the heat. Let sit, undisturbed, for exactly 7 minutes (for large eggs), 7½ minutes (for extra-large eggs), or 8 minutes (for jumbo eggs). At high altitudes, add 30 seconds to the sitting time.

(If you are cooking a large quantity of eggs in a large pot over a small burner, it will take a long time for the water to reach a boil. In this case, the eggs may need to cook for only a minute or two after the water boils: break open an egg to check, and judge how much more time is needed to cook the yolk through.)

Pour off the hot water and run cold water over the eggs for a minute, then dump enough ice into the pan to cover the eggs. Chill thoroughly in the ice bath for about 10 minutes. To peel, gently crack the shell all over, then start removing the shell at the blunt end. The shell and the filmy membrane should easily peel away.

Hard-boiled eggs are excellent in your lunch for any kind of outdoor excursion, but don't forget to pack some salt and pepper—simply fold a little into a small sheet of aluminum foil. The best hard-boiled eggs I ever ate were enjoyed in the company of good friends on the 14,246-foot summit of White Mountain Peak near Deep Springs.

Deviled Eggs

makes 1 dozen; serves 4 to 6

Deviled eggs are among the most popular hors d'oeuvres. The procedure for cooking the eggs in this recipe produces a firm white, without overcooking the yolk. "Deviled" should refer to the spicy seasonings, not the sulfury smell of overcooked eggs!

6 large eggs

¼ cup mayonnaise

1 teaspoon Dijon mustard

pinch of salt

⅛ teaspoon cayenne pepper

⅛ teaspoon paprika

TOPPINGS

paprika

freshly ground black pepper

minced fresh chives (optional)

Cover the eggs with water in a saucepan and set on a high flame. Bring to a boil, reduce the heat to low, and cook, covered, for 30 seconds. Remove the pan from the heat and let stand, still covered, for 10 minutes. Drain and run cold water over the eggs for a few minutes. Plunge the eggs into an ice-water bath, leaving them for several minutes, to chill thoroughly. Carefully peel the eggs, first tapping the egg all over on a hard surface to evenly break the shell, then peeling from the blunt end. Rinse each one to remove tiny specks of shell.

Cut the eggs in half lengthwise, carefully removing the yolks to a medium bowl and placing the whites on a tray. Mash the yolks with the mayonnaise, mustard, salt, cayenne, and paprika. Put the mixture in a sturdy plastic bag, cut a small hole in a corner of the bag, and pipe the yolk mixture into the whites, almost touching the egg with the tip of the bag as you squeeze. Dust with more paprika and some black pepper, and sprinkle with chives, if you like.

KIMCHI DEVILED EGGS

Kimchi encompasses a vast array of fermented Korean pickles, but the most popular is made of Napa cabbage and specially-grown red chile flakes. I love kimchi with scrambled eggs and rice for breakfast; here it adds surprising depth to deviled eggs. Squeeze the liquid out of a fistful of spicy, well-aged kimchi, letting the liquid fall back into the kimchi jar. Chop the kimchi finely, and add three-quarters of it to the yolk mixture in the master recipe, plus a spoonful of the kimchi liquid. Top each deviled egg with the remaining chopped kimchi and thinly sliced green onions.

Egg Salad

serves 6 to 8

A Deep Springs classmate of mine, now a rabbi and teacher, married with children, makes this egg salad for his wife when she is in need of gustatory comfort. She is always very appreciative. If you'd like to further embellish your egg salad, chopped fresh dill is wonderful and traditional, as are coarsely chopped green olives.

1 dozen perfectly cooked Hard-Boiled Eggs (preceding page), **cooled and peeled**

2 tablespoons finely diced red onion

½ cup finely diced celery (optional)

3 tablespoons fresh lemon juice, plus more if needed

¾ to 1 cup mayonnaise

½ teaspoon salt, plus more if needed

¼ teaspoon coarsely ground black pepper

Chop the eggs in large dice or put them through a large wire grid (I use a cooling rack). Place in a medium bowl and gently blend in the onion, celery (if using), lemon juice, mayonnaise, salt, and pepper. Taste, and add more salt and lemon juice if necessary. This is best served immediately.

Asparagus and Mushroom Frittata

serves 4 to 6

There are many kinds of frittata, or Italian baked omelet, but asparagus, mushrooms, and eggs make an especially good partnership. Have all the vegetables cut and ready to go before you start cooking. This is good at room temperature and so makes ideal picnic food. Serve a big green salad alongside.

1 bunch fresh asparagus

3 tablespoons olive oil

1 medium yellow onion, finely chopped

2 large cloves garlic, finely crushed

about ½ teaspoon salt

8 ounces white or brown mushrooms, wiped clean, trimmed, halved, and thinly sliced

8 large eggs, at room temperature

freshly ground black pepper

pinch of hot red pepper flakes

2 tablespoons chopped parsley

3 tablespoons freshly grated Parmesan cheese

Heat the oven to 300°F. To prepare the asparagus, rinse it, then peel the bottom 3 to 4 inches of each stalk with a vegetable peeler. Snap the tough bottom off each stalk (peeling it first yields a greater quantity of tender asparagus), and diagonally slice the asparagus, tips and all, as thinly as possible.

In a 10-inch oven-safe skillet (if you wish to unmold the frittata onto a platter, a nonstick skillet is recommended), heat 2 tablespoons of the olive oil over a medium-high flame. Add the onion and garlic with a couple of pinches of salt and sauté, stirring frequently, until the onion is translucent—it shouldn't brown. Add the mushrooms with a generous pinch of salt and sauté for a few moments more. Once the juice from the mushrooms begins to subside, add the asparagus with a generous pinch of salt, and sauté until the asparagus is tender (adding salt with each addition keeps the various flavors distinct).

Crack the eggs into a large bowl and beat lightly, just enough to break up the yolks. Stir the warm mushroom-asparagus mixture into the eggs. (Keep the skillet nearby—it will be used to cook the frittata.) To the egg mixture, add freshly ground pepper to taste, ¼ teaspoon salt, a pinch of red pepper flakes, and the parsley and Parmesan. Beat lightly just until everything is combined.

Clean the skillet, and add oil it with the remaining tablespoon of olive oil. Gently pour in the egg mixture and put the skillet in the oven. Bake until the frittata is set in the center, about 20 minutes. Remove from the oven and let the frittata "set up" for about 5 minutes before turning it out onto a plate or a board. Serve warm or at room temperature, cut into wedges.

CHARD AND MUSHROOM FRITTATA
Substitute a bunch of chard for the bunch of asparagus in the master recipe. Remove the leafy green part from the chard and slice the stems finely. Sauté the stems with the onion, then chop the leaves and add them at the end. Cook until the vegetables are just tender, then mix as directed in the recipe. This variation is good with crumbled feta cheese substituted for the Parmesan.

LEEK AND GRUYÈRE FRITTATA
Omit the chard, mushrooms, and Parmesan from the master recipe, and add 1 to 2 leeks that have been trimmed, cleaned, diced, and gently stewed in butter until tender, and a cup of grated Gruyère cheese.

BACON AND ONION FRITTATA
Omit asparagus, mushrooms, and parsley from the master recipe, and add ½ pound of finely diced cooked bacon. Use two onions, and cook them in the bacon fat.

Tortilla Española

serves 4 to 6

In Spain, *tortilla* is a slowly cooked omelet of onions and potatoes fried in olive oil, usually served as a *tapa*, or hors d'oeuvre. Since we use the same word for the delectable staple of Mexican cooking, the name of this Spanish dish confuses the uninitiated, and the clunky name "potato omelet" never sounds good. Despite these nomenclatural difficulties, *tortilla española* is one of the touchstones of a good cook, transforming cheap, humble ingredients into something that even ardent carnivores will happily devour as the main dish of a meal. I make tortilla española for lunch at Deep Springs several times a year, served always with a plentiful green salad and, in summer, with Gazpacho (page 168). The Spanish recipes I've seen call for no pepper, garlic, or thyme, and they always call for the tortilla to be cooked entirely on top of the stove and flipped once or many times in the cooking. Unless strict authenticity is my goal, I find it much easier to use the oven, and as for the extra seasonings, they taste delicious. I have even included such things as mushrooms and anchovies in tortilla española.

- 2 cups olive oil for frying
- 2 large white or yellow onions, diced
- 1½ to 2 teaspoons salt
- 3 medium russet potatoes, peeled, halved lengthwise, and sliced in 1/8-inch-thick slices
- 1 large clove garlic, crushed
- 7 large eggs, at room temperature
- 2 teaspoons chopped fresh thyme *(3 to 4 sprigs' worth)* or ¼ teaspoon dried thyme
- ½ teaspoon white pepper

Heat the oven to 325°F. Heat the olive oil in a 10-inch heavy, oven-safe skillet (if you wish to unmold the tortilla onto a platter, a nonstick skillet is recommended) over a medium-high flame until a bit of onion bubbles excitedly when dropped in. Gently drop in the onions with ¼ teaspoon salt, and fry gently until the onions are almost translucent, 3 to 4 minutes. Stir in the potatoes with about ½ teaspoon salt and fry-sauté the mixture, stirring from time to time. When the potatoes are nearly tender, stir in the garlic with another pinch of salt. Continue to cook until the potatoes are cooked through, 6 to 7 minutes. Using a screen sieve set over a metal bowl or pot, drain the potatoes and onions of all excess oil for several minutes, reserving the oil: it will impart its delicate potato and onion scent to almost anything else you cook (store it in the refrigerator).

Wipe out the skillet and add back about 1 tablespoon of the olive oil. Using a whisk, beat the eggs briefly in a large bowl, just to break up the yolks, then stir in the thyme, pepper, and about ¾ teaspoon salt. Fold in the hot drained potatoes and onions. Dump the mixture into the warm skillet, smoothing the top if necessary, and bake until the eggs are set, 10 to 12 minutes. Let the tortilla rest in the skillet for about 5 minutes, then invert it onto a plate. Let cool for a bit longer before cutting it into wedges. Serve slightly warm or at room temperature.

Gâteau de Crêpes (Stacked Crêpe Cake with Spinach, Gruyère, and Béchamel)

serves 6 as a main course or 8 as a smaller course

One Sunday afternoon at Deep Springs, a student mixed up a vat of crêpe batter and made stacks and stacks of crêpes. Then he sautéed mushrooms, onions and spinach, chopped ham, grated Swiss cheese, and whipped up some béchamel sauce. He stacked the crêpes into 4 or 5 "cakes" with the various fillings and cheese, covered the stacks with béchamel and more cheese, and stuck them in the oven for half an hour, until the cheese and the béchamel browned a bit. *Et voila*, there, along with a green salad, was a simple, but nourishing and wonderfully satisfying dinner, equally *magnifique* for its frugality and economy as for its richness and flavor.

The crêpes may be made the day before for greater convenience, and in fact, leftover *gâteau de crêpes* is delicious. For the crêpe batter, you may omit the wine and simply use ½ cup water, and lacking buckwheat flour, just use a full cup of all-purpose flour.

CRÊPES

2 eggs

1 cup whole milk

¼ cup dry white wine

¼ cup water

½ teaspoon salt

½ cup all-purpose flour

½ cup buckwheat flour

3 tablespoons vegetable oil

about ¼ cup melted butter for cooking crêpes

BÉCHAMEL

2 cups milk

3 to 4 tablespoons finely diced shallot or onion

1 bay leaf

2 pinches dried thyme, or 3 to 4 sprigs fresh thyme

4 tablespoons butter

4 tablespoons all-purpose flour

¼ teaspoon salt

¼ teaspoon grated nutmeg

freshly ground pepper to taste

FILLING

12 ounces cleaned spinach

1 tablespoon butter

1 large yellow onion, thinly sliced

pinch of salt

8 ounces Gruyère cheese, grated

First, make the crêpe batter: combine eggs, milk, wine, water, salt, all-purpose flour, buckwheat flour, and vegetable oil in a blender. Buzz for a full 30 seconds to thoroughly blend the batter. Cover and let rest, refrigerated, for at least 1 hour (overnight is ideal).

Next, make the béchamel: In a small heavy saucepan, heat the milk with the shallot, bay leaf, and thyme, until the milk is hot and steaming. Cover the pan and set aside. In a larger saucepan over a medium flame, melt the butter and add the flour. Cook, stirring frequently with a wooden spoon, for 3 minutes—the color of the roux should not visibly darken. Remove from the flame and let the roux rest for 5 minutes. Strain the hot milk and gradually whisk it into the roux, a little at a time. Return the pan to a medium flame. Continuing to stir, let the sauce come to a boil. Reduce the heat to very low, and let the sauce gently cook for ½ hour, whisking frequently (I sometimes use the oven for this step—I just put the whole saucepan in a 350°F oven, and take it out to stir a few times). Add the salt, nutmeg, and pepper to taste. The béchamel should only be moderately salted for this dish—the sweetness of the milk should be evident, too.

While the béchamel is cooking, make the filling: wash the spinach and drain in a colander. Heat a wide skillet over a high flame and add the spinach all at once (or in batches, if the pan isn't big enough), stirring it around constantly until it wilts. Transfer the spinach to a big shallow bowl, spreading it out to cool. As soon as the spinach is cool enough to handle, take up fistfuls of spinach and squeeze out all the excess water (I drink this—the minerals are just what a busy cook needs). Chop the spinach coarsely. In a skillet, melt the butter over medium-high heat. When it sizzles, throw in the onion with a pinch of salt and sauté until the onion browns lightly. Add the spinach, stirring it thoroughly into the onions. Let cook for a moment, then transfer to a bowl.

Now make the crêpes: heat a 7- to 10-inch pan with gently sloping sides over a medium-high flame, then brush lightly with melted butter. Use about 3 tablespoons of batter per crêpe: drizzle the batter in a swath across the bottom of the pan, then swirl and tilt the pan so the batter completely coats the bottom. Cook for about 30 seconds on the first side, or until lightly browned. Slide a knife or spatula under the crêpe's edge to loosen it, then flip and cook the other side about 10 seconds. Stack the crêpes on a plate as they're done.

Finally, assemble the gâteau. First, heat the oven to 375°F. In the center of an ovenproof plate (with at least ½-inch lip), put a small dab of béchamel. Center a crêpe on the plate, then spread about ¼ cup of béchamel over it. Put a second crêpe atop the first—this is the base of the gâteau. Top the second crêpe with about 3 tablespoons of the spinach-onion mixture, and about 2 tablespoons of cheese. Repeat with crêpes, spinach, and cheese until all are used up, finishing with a crêpe. Pour the remaining béchamel over the top, spreading it on the sides. Top the gâteau with the remaining cheese, and bake in the oven for about 30 minutes, or until the gâteau is heated through and the béchamel and cheese are bubbling. Let the gâteau set a few minutes, then cut in wedges and serve with a simple green salad.

My Mother's Enchiladas

serves 4 to 6

Between this recipe and the two that follow, the imaginative cook will see a world of possibility in the enchilada. The word *enchilada* means "imbued with chile"—the thing imbued with chile being, of course, corn tortillas. Enchiladas may be rolled, stacked, baked like a casserole, or "built" directly on the plate; the tortillas may be fried in oil or just heated on a burner; enchiladas may have a savory, meaty filling or no filling but cheese; the cheese may be a traditional variety, such as Jack, or may be borrowed from another ethnic tradition, such as feta or fontina; the chile sauce may be red or green, creamy or lean, mild or hot.

For many years, mostly in Texas and New Mexico in the 1970s, this was one of my mother's most prized company dishes. It is elegant, rich, distinctive, and universally loved. Accompany with a big tossed green salad and a bowl of radishes chilled in ice water. This recipe calls for frying the tortillas, an authentic New Mexico touch. A brief dip in boiling oil helps the tortillas retain their texture, and the end result is succulently rich. However, for a leaner dish, I often merely heat the tortillas in a hot, dry skillet until they take on appealing brown spots. Sometimes I brush them with a little oil first (see the next recipe, Green Chile Enchiladas). If you use tortillas cold, they will disintegrate, and the enchiladas will emerge too puddingy.

SAUCE

2 teaspoons vegetable oil or lard

1 medium yellow onion, diced

pinch of salt

2 cloves garlic, crushed

¾ teaspoon ground cumin

¾ teaspoon dried oregano

one 14-ounce can cream of chicken soup

one 8-ounce can diced fire-roasted green chiles *(or use 1 cup chopped, freshly roasted chiles, page 251)*

¼ teaspoon freshly ground black pepper

1 to 2 cups diced cooked well-seasoned chicken *(optional; to cook chicken, see Green Chile Enchiladas, facing page)*

1 cup safflower oil or other light vegetable oil for frying

12 corn tortillas

2 cups *(8 ounces)* **grated Jack cheese**

Heat the oven to 375°F. To make the sauce, warm the oil or lard in a medium-sized, heavy saucepan over a medium-high flame. Add the onion and sauté with a pinch of salt for 3 to 4

minutes, stirring frequently, until mostly translucent. Add the garlic, cumin, and oregano and cook slowly without browning, stirring frequently, for 2 to 3 minutes. Add the can of soup, ½ can of water, and the green chiles. Heat, stirring frequently, until the mixture reaches a simmer. Reduce the heat and let simmer for 5 minutes, stirring occasionally. Stir in the black pepper (and the chicken, if you opt for it) and remove from the heat, but keep warm.

To fry the tortillas, heat the oil in a deep, heavy pot over a medium-high flame until a bit of tortilla dropped in sizzles and bubbles fiercely. Drop in a tortilla, using a slotted spoon or tongs to immerse it completely, and fry for about 10 seconds, or only until softened—the tortillas should not get crispy. Lift the tortilla out of the oil and allow to drain over the pot for a few seconds. Lay it on a thick bed of paper towels to drain further. Continue with the remaining tortillas. Blot the tortillas with more paper towels.

Spread a ladleful of the sauce on the bottom of a 9-by-13-inch baking dish. Arrange a single layer of tortillas over the sauce, top with a little more sauce, then sprinkle lightly with cheese. Repeat layers of sauce, tortillas, more sauce, and cheese until everything is used up. Finish with a generous amount of sauce and cheese, with no tortilla exposed. Bake until the cheese is melted and the top is bubbly, 20 to 25 minutes. Let rest for about 10 minutes, then cut into squares or wedges and serve.

Green Chile Enchiladas

serves 4 to 6

This superb dish from New Mexico is more laborious than the previous recipe, but it tastes more authoritatively of green chile. Since the flavor is so haunting, a simple green salad is all you need alongside. To save time on the day you want to serve, you may make the sauce and cook the chicken a day ahead. For a meatless variation, try filling the enchiladas with sautéed fresh summer corn, cut off the cob (page 128).

In this recipe, the tortillas are lightly rubbed with oil and heated in a skillet. If you want a rich, authentically New Mexican flavor, fry the tortillas briefly in oil as described in the previous recipe.

12 ounces boneless, skinless chicken breast *(2 medium-sized breast halves)*

pinch of dried oregano

¼ teaspoon salt

black pepper

vegetable oil or lard for heating tortillas

12 corn tortillas

1 recipe New Mexico Green Chile Sauce *(page 251)*

1½ cups *(6 ounces)* **grated Jack cheese**

1 cup *(4 ounces)* **grated sharp white Cheddar cheese**

1 medium onion, finely chopped

Season the chicken with oregano, salt, and pepper. Rub with a little vegetable oil and cook in a medium skillet over medium heat until browned on both sides and cooked through, about 4 minutes on each side. Let cool to room temperature on a plate, then chop into small dice.

To assemble and bake the enchiladas, heat the oven to 350°F. Heat the green chile sauce. Heat the tortillas by rubbing them lightly on one side with vegetable oil (or melted lard, or a mixture) and heating them in a hot, dry skillet until they get appealing brown spots here and there. Place a tortilla in the skillet, flip, place another on top, flip both, place another on top of that, flip all three, and so forth, building up the stack and giving each tortilla its moment of direct contact with the heat. The accumulated heat will steam and soften the tortillas. When all are heated, cut the stack in half with a sharp knife to make half-moons.

Spread a little warm green chile sauce on the bottom of a 9-by-13-inch baking dish. Put down a layer of tortillas, top with more sauce, a little cheese, a bit of chicken, and a little chopped onion. Repeat until the tortillas and chicken are used up, and finish with a generous amount of sauce and cheese. Bake for about 30 minutes, until the cheese is browned and bubbly. Let rest for about 10 minutes, then cut into squares or wedges and serve.

Red Chile Enchiladas
serves 3 to 4

Here is another approach to enchiladas: rather than assembling the elements into a casserole and baking it, the tortillas, sauce, cheese, and filling are assembled "to order" on individual plates. In New Mexico, these enchiladas are often topped with a fried egg. Yellow Cheddar cheese on enchiladas may seem unsophisticated or inauthentic, but it's what our mothers often used, and it tastes delicious with red chile.

1 recipe New Mexico Red Chile Sauce *(page 250)*

1½ cups filling of choice: cooked seasoned ground beef, or cooked turkey or chicken, or Slow-Roasted Pork *(page 200)*, **or Sautéed Corn** *(page 128)*

8 or 9 corn tortillas

vegetable oil or lard for heating tortillas

1 small onion, finely diced

1½ cups grated cheese of choice: sharp yellow Cheddar, jack, fontina

3 or 4 Fried Eggs *(page 57; optional)*

Warm the sauce and the filling, if necessary. Heat the corn tortillas in either of the ways described in the previous two recipes: fry them briefly in oil or rub them lightly with oil and heat in a hot, dry skillet. Or you can merely heat them directly on the gas flame of your stove until they develop brown spots here and there. On each plate, put a dab of chile sauce. Lay a hot tortilla over the sauce. Put a spoonful of filling on the tortilla. Drizzle more sauce over. Sprinkle with some chopped onion and a little cheese. Repeat with another tortilla, more filling, sauce, onion, and cheese. For each person, a 2- or 3-tortilla stack is usually ample. Top each serving with a fried egg, if you like, and more chopped onion. Serve immediately.

New Mexico Posole with Pork and Green Chile
serves 6 to 8

Posole is a rich brothy soup of Mexican hominy and pork, flavored with chiles. While many versions are enjoyed in Mexico (and spelled "*pozole*"), I prefer the more austere types that prevail in New Mexican kitchens. It is very simple to cook, requiring a short list of ingredients.

Once, when the rabbi came for lunch, I couldn't serve pork, so I made *beef posole* instead: I seasoned short ribs and brisket with salt and crushed cumin seed ahead of time, and cooked them exactly like the pork shoulder—it was delicious.

Finding the posole itself, the particular kind of hominy, can be tricky. By definition, hominy is whole, dried corn kernels that have been soaked and treated with a mild alkali solution, then washed, and either used fresh or re-dried. This ancient process tenderizes the corn's tough skin, and increases its nutrient availability. For posole, calcium oxide (or "lime"), is used for the alkali solution. Corn thus treated is called *nixtamal*. If you grind nixtamal finely, you have the *masa*, or dough, that corn tortillas are made of. Mexican markets that make their own tortillas may have fresh nixtamal available—it's excellent for posole, and it cooks fairly quickly. If the more widely available dried posole is what you have, it must be soaked in water first, then cooked like beans. Dried posole kernels are white and slightly translucent—they don't look like regular corn. Caveat: Mexican markets sometimes carry untreated dried corn meant for grinding and label it "posole," but these will never soften in cooking and the flavor is completely different.

1 pound dried posole

2 pounds boneless pork shoulder, cut in 5 or 6 equal-sized chunks, or approximately 5 pounds meaty pork neck bones

1 tablespoon lard or vegetable oil

1 large white onion, coarsely chopped

5 to 6 cloves garlic, crushed

½ teaspoon dried oregano, crumbled

1 teaspoon salt

about 10 to 15 New Mexico green chiles, roasted, peeled, seeded, and coarsely chopped (page 251)

The posole is cooked like beans: soak the kernels in water overnight, then put both the posole and its soaking water in a large, heavy pot. If necessary, add sufficient fresh water to cover the posole by about 2 inches. Lightly salt the water, bring to a boil, and simmer for about 2 hours, by which point the kernels should be almost tender.

Meanwhile, in an extra-large, heavy pot, cover the pork with cold, lightly-salted water, bring to a boil, skim off the scum (but not too much of the fat) that forms on top, then reduce to a simmer. Let the pork simmer for about 2 hours. Add the posole and all its liquid to the pot with the pork, and continue simmering.

In the emptied pot, heat the lard or vegetable oil on a medium flame, and gently stew the onion, garlic, oregano, and teaspoon of salt, until the onion is soft. Once the onion has softened, add as much roasted, peeled, seeded, and coarsely chopped New Mexico green chile as you care to, and cook a minute or two more. Add the onion-chile mixture to the posole, and continue simmering very slowly for up to an hour more. If you like, remove the pork, let cool slightly, then cut or break up into more manageable pieces, then return it to the pot. If you have used pork neck bones, remove, let cool, pick off the meat, and return the meat to the pot. Add salt and pepper to taste. Posole is excellent reheated the next day.

RED CHILE POSOLE

In place of the green chile, you may simmer 10 to 15 dried whole New Mexico red chile pods with the pork. When the pork is cooked, fish out the chiles and let cool. Carefully scrape out the scant flesh from each chile, chop it if it's stringy, and add it back to the posole. Or, for a more elegant presentation, omit the chiles from the posole altogether, leaving it "white," and serve a pot of New Mexico Red Chile Sauce (page 250), alongside, letting each person top their posole with the sauce.

Gumbo

serves 6 to 8

Gumbo is a way of life, a unique cultural expression—a bit of France and a bit of Africa, cultivated in the soil of the American South. It's best defined as a stew of peppers, tomatoes, onions, celery, and usually okra, thickened with roux or filé powder, flavored with thyme, parsley, and cayenne, and enriched with poultry, sausage, or shrimp. I believe the heart and soul of good gumbo resides in the roux, vegetables, and herbs; meatless gumbo is still delicious. Smoked turkey necks, wings, drumsticks, and even fatty tails are available in supermarkets wherever there is a large African American population. Andouille sausage, seasoned with hot dried red peppers and thyme, is the real thing, but try any medium-spicy smoked sausage.

Six cups of chicken stock or water will make a thick, soupy gumbo, to be served in a bowl, over a little rice—this is how I like it best. Four cups of chicken stock or water will make a thicker, more stewlike gumbo. Either way, gumbo is a meal in itself; no accompaniment is needed. Green bell peppers are required for gumbo—red or yellow bell peppers will make the dish too summery-sweet.

Gumbo can be varied in many ways: add a pound of shrimp, shelled or not (the shells will impart more flavor, but your guests will get their fingers messy peeling them), in the last 10 minutes of simmering. Or add a pound of picked crabmeat at the very end (for the liquid, use half water, half chicken stock). Or, follow the recipe up to the point of adding the sausage, and use this "base" as a medium for braising chicken (see page 212). Add the okra after the chicken is tender. Or, if you opt for a meatless gumbo, eggplant, surprisingly, tastes right at home—omit all meat from the recipe and throw a coarsely chopped eggplant into the pot along with the peppers.

½ cup sunflower oil or other vegetable oil

½ cup all-purpose flour

2 medium onions, finely chopped

3 to 4 stalks celery, finely chopped

salt as needed

- 2 green bell peppers, finely chopped
- ¾ teaspoon dried thyme, or 2 to 3 teaspoons chopped fresh thyme
- ½ teaspoon hot red pepper flakes
- 6 cups chicken stock or water (use 4 cups for a thicker gumbo)
- 1 smoked turkey neck or ham shank
- one 14-ounce can whole plum tomatoes, chopped, or 2 cups Tomato Concassé (page 148)
- about 1 pound andouille sausage
- 12 ounces fresh young, tender okra, sliced ¼ inch thick (see page 136 for how to detect tough okra pods)
- ½ cup chopped parsley
- ½ teaspoon black pepper
- Tabasco or other hot sauce

FOR SERVING

- ⅛ teaspoon filé powder for each serving (optional)
- steamed long-grain white rice (see page 238)

First make the roux. In a large, heavy saucepan over medium-high heat, blend the oil and flour with a wooden spoon. Stir constantly as the mixture heats and begins to bubble. When it is vigorously bubbling, turn down the heat to medium-low, and keep stirring. The roux will turn from pasty white to pale ivory, then will darken by degrees to the color of peanut butter. At this point, and not a moment later, throw in the onions and celery with a large pinch of salt. Raise the heat to medium and cook, stirring constantly, for about 5 minutes, then throw in the bell pepper with a pinch of salt. Cook for another 7 to 10 minutes, stirring constantly, until the vegetables are tender. Taste a bit of the onion—there should be no crunch left. Add the thyme, pepper flakes, chicken stock, turkey neck, tomatoes, and whole sausage to the pot. If you used water instead of chicken stock, add a teaspoon of salt. Bring to a simmer and cook for about 30 minutes, stirring frequently. Add the okra and simmer for another 10 minutes, stirring frequently, until the okra is tender.

Remove the turkey neck, pick the meat off the bones, chop the meat coarsely, and return it to the pot. Remove the sausage, slice it thickly, and return to the pot. Stir in the parsley and black pepper. Taste for salt and add Tabasco to taste; gumbo should be warmly spicy, never hot.

Both the roux and the okra thicken the gumbo, but filé powder will also provide a little thickness, and its own unique flavor. If you like, stir ⅛ teaspoon of filé into each bowl just before serving. Serve the gumbo in wide bowls over a small amount of hot steamed long-grain white rice.

Gunhild's Chicken Curry

serves 4 to 6

Indian food is a wholly different and exciting culinary idiom. Fresh ginger, basmati rice, and whole spices are no longer hard to find, as they were early in my cooking days. Once you learn a few of the basic dishes and procedures, Indian food lends itself to flights of improvisation, especially when you have access to a variety of vegetables. Vegetables are closer to the heart and soul of Indian food than meat; in fact, it may be perfectly expressed without any meat at all. For an added touch of authenticity, use *ghee*, a kind of clarified butter (see page 38), instead of vegetable oil.

I learned to make this curry early in my days as Student Cook at Deep Springs. One of my classmates had a Danish mother and a father from northern India; soon after they married, she went to India to take cooking lessons from his family. When they visited Deep Springs during my tenure as Student Cook, my classmate's mother enthusiastically showed me how to make their basic family curry, with all the accompaniments. She didn't use a written recipe. All her spices were from India, and very freshly ground. She used two blends: a simple mix of ground cumin and coriander, and a complex *masala* (meaning "spice blend") that was red from hot chiles. What we know as "curry powder" is only one example of many different masalas used in the various regions of India. A recipe for home-ground curry powder follows this curry recipe.

The lemon and red onion, served separately on a plate, are meant to be eaten like a relish with everything else; an occasional strong crunch of onion or zingy burst of lemon only makes the curry taste better. The curry may be made well ahead of time, up to the point of adding the spinach. For the spinach to retain its vivid green freshness, stir it into the hot curry just before serving.

RICE

- **2 cups uncooked basmati rice**
- **1 teaspoon vegetable oil or ghee**
- **1 teaspoon salt**
- **3 cups plus 2 tablespoons water**

CURRY

- **1 tablespoon ghee or vegetable oil**
- **1 large yellow onion, thinly sliced lengthwise**
- **¼ teaspoon plus several pinches salt, or more as needed**
- **4 cloves garlic, finely chopped**
- **1 ounce** *(a 2- to 3-inch piece)* **fresh ginger, peeled and finely chopped**
- **½ teaspoon ground cumin**
- **½ teaspoon ground coriander**
- **4 teaspoons curry powder** *(to grind your own, see recipe below)*
- **¼ teaspoon black pepper**
- **8 boneless, skinless chicken thighs** *(about 2 pounds)*
- **one 14-ounce can condensed cream of chicken soup**
- **1 large bunch fresh spinach, washed well and coarsely chopped**

FOR SERVING

- **1 lemon, thinly sliced**
- **1 small red onion, thinly sliced**
- **Indian naan or other flatbread, warmed and brushed lightly with ghee or oil** *(sometimes I use whole-wheat tortillas)*
- **papads** *(see recipe below)*
- **raita** *(see recipe below)*

To make the rice, first rinse it well in a colander until the water runs clear, then soak the rice for about 30 minutes in a large bowl, and drain well. Put the rice, oil, salt, and water in a medium-sized, heavy saucepan with a well-fitting lid. Set the pan on high heat, bring to a boil, reduce to a simmer, slap on the lid, and let the rice cook, undisturbed, for about 20 minutes, or until all the water is absorbed. To tell if the rice is done without lifting the lid, tilt the pan slightly and listen carefully: if you hear the hissing, sizzling sound of water hitting the sides of the pan, it needs more time. If you don't hear anything, the water is all absorbed and the rice is done.

To make the curry, heat the tablespoon of ghee or vegetable oil in a large, heavy soup pot over a medium flame. When the oil shimmers, throw in the onion with ¼ teaspoon salt and sauté, stirring frequently, until the onion is translucent, 5 to 6 minutes. Add the garlic and ginger with a pinch of salt and cook, stirring frequently, for another minute. Stir in the spices, then the chicken, with a final big pinch of salt. Cook for about 5 minutes, stirring frequently, while your kitchen fills with a wonderful aroma. Add the can of soup and about ½ can of water. Bring the mixture to a simmer. Reduce the heat and cover the pan. Simmer slowly, stirring occasionally, until the chicken is tender, about 20 minutes. Stir in the spinach, and let cook for 3 to 4 minutes more. Taste for salt—the curry should be well-seasoned.

Serve with the hot basmati rice, and the thinly sliced onion and lemon on a platter. Serve warmed flatbread, papadums, and a raita on the side.

Curry Powder

makes about 3 tablespoons

You can make your own *masala*, or curry powder, if you have a coffee grinder designated for spices. This medium-spicy blend is flavorful and well balanced.

2 teaspoons coriander seed

2 teaspoons cumin seed

1 teaspoon fennel seed

1 teaspoon brown mustard seed

½ teaspoon white peppercorns

7 cloves

2 teaspoons hot red pepper flakes *(add more for a spicier curry powder)*

½ teaspoon ground cinnamon

1 teaspoon ground turmeric

Grind the whole spices and red pepper flakes to the finest powder in your grinder, then stir in the cinnamon and turmeric.

Papadums or Papads

These thin, lentil-flour wafers are a delectably crispy, savory accompaniment to an Indian meal. Many brands of papad are made in India by collectives entirely run and staffed by women. They are sold in packages, ready to be quickly fried. Over a medium flame, heat about 2 inches of vegetable oil in a large saucepan. The oil is ready when a papad, dipped in the oil, begins to blister immediately. Immerse papads in the oil one at a time, let them puff and blister for only a few seconds, then immediately remove with tongs, shake off the excess oil, and put the papads on a bed of paper towels to drain. If the papads visibly brown, the oil is too hot.

Raitas

These cool yogurt salads aid in the digestion of a spicy Indian meal. All three recipes serve 4 to 6, and are best served at cool room temperature, not refrigerator-cold.

For a *mustard seed raita*, heat a tablespoon of ghee (page 38) or vegetable oil in a small skillet. Add a tablespoon of brown mustard seed, swirling the seeds in the ghee. As the seeds heat, they slightly lighten in color and pop. When all the seeds have "popped," stir ghee and seeds into 2 cups of plain whole-milk yogurt. Season with a pinch or two of salt and a squeeze of fresh lime or lemon juice. Let sit for about ½ hour before serving.

To make *cucumber raita*, grate an English cucumber into a medium bowl, using the coarse holes of a box grater. Squeeze out the excess liquid (I love to drink this). Mix in 1½ cups plain whole-milk yogurt, a pinch or two of salt, and a handful of chopped mint. Chill and stir again before serving.

If you like your curry especially spicy, the sweetness of a *cantaloupe and black pepper raita* will temper the heat most agreeably. Peel, seed, and dice half of a sweet cantaloupe, and mix into 1½ cups plain whole-milk yogurt. Season with ½ teaspoon salt, ½ teaspoon coarsely ground black pepper, and a small handful of chopped fresh mint. Serve soon after mixing.

Falafel

serves 4 to 6

Everyone—even meat eaters—loves a meal of falafel, hummus, and pita bread. Despite the frying, it is a simple meal to put together; the result is somehow more beautiful and festive than one would imagine, given the ordinary ingredients.

FALAFEL

- 1½ cups dry chickpeas, soaked overnight in 4 cups water, drained
- ¾ cup chopped onion
- ⅓ cup coarsely chopped parsley
- 2 medium cloves garlic, sliced
- ¾ teaspoon ground cumin
- ¾ teaspoon ground coriander
- 1½ teaspoons salt
- scant ½ teaspoon baking powder
- large pinch of cayenne pepper
- 2 medium eggs
- 1 tablespoon toasted sesame seeds *(optional)*

TAHIN SAUCE

- ¾ cup roasted sesame tahini
- ¾ cup cold water
- 3 tablespoons fresh lemon juice
- ¼ teaspoon salt

ACCOMPANIMENTS

- ¼ bunch flat-leaf parsley
- ¼ bunch fresh mint
- ¼ small onion
- about 1 cup sliced cucumber
- about ½ cup chopped fresh ripe tomato
- about ½ cup chopped green onion
- 1 to 2 cups shredded lettuce
- sliced fresh oranges *(optional; good in winter)*
- Hummus *(optional; recipe below)*
- about 8 yeasted flatbreads *(pita or other type; sometimes in a pinch I just use whole-wheat flour tortillas)*
- safflower oil, peanut oil, or other light oil for frying

To make the mix for the falafel, in a food processor, pulse the soaked chickpeas, onions, parsley, garlic, cumin, coriander, salt, baking powder, cayenne, and egg to a coarse, grainy mush. Do not process until completely smooth—coarse particles of chickpea are part of the charm of good falafel. Stir in the sesame seeds, if desired.

To make the *tahin* sauce, whisk the tahini, cold water, lemon juice, and salt together in a small bowl until smooth. Whisk together again, if necessary, just before serving.

Before frying the falafel, have all the accompaniments chopped and ready: very finely chop the parsley, mint, and onion together. Put the herb-onion mixture, cucumber, tomato, green onion, and lettuce in small dishes on the table—these all are better at room temperature than chilled. In winter, a platter of sliced oranges enhances everything. If you are also serving hummus, make sure it's at room temperature, and heat the flatbreads while frying the falafel.

Heat 1 inch of oil in a wide, heavy skillet over medium-high heat until a dab of falafel mix sizzles merrily when dropped in. Slip neat spoonfuls of the falafel mix into the oil (I use a small ice cream scoop). I like falafel made on the small side, with 2 to 3 tablespoons of batter—the more crispy surface area, I think, the better. Smaller falafel are also easier to cook through. Fry, turning once, until the falafel are a deep brown, 2 to 3 minutes per side. Break one open to make sure they are cooked through—they will look doughy and be lighter colored in the centers if they are not (sometimes I finish them in a 350°F oven if I have made the falafel large or gotten the oil too hot). Drain on paper towels. Serve immediately or keep warm.

To eat, stuff pockets or pieces of flatbread with falafel and vegetables (and hummus, if you opt for it), moistening well with spoonfuls of tahin sauce. Falafel is the most forgiving of fried foods and can be held, eaten at room temperature, or even reheated.

Hummus

serves 4 to 6

I admit that sometimes I just buy prepared hummus, enlivening it with a few pinches of powdered New Mexico red chile. This popular dip may be made with canned chickpeas, but it's especially good if you cook them yourself: start with 1 heaping cup of dry chickpeas, add a bay leaf, a strip of orange zest, and half of a small onion to the cooking water, and follow the guidelines for cooking beans on page 106. For especially delectable hummus, blend and serve it while the chickpeas are still slightly warm.

2 cups cooked chickpeas

¼ to ⅓ cup of the chickpea cooking water

¼ cup roasted sesame tahini

1 clove garlic, crushed

1 teaspoon salt, plus more as needed

pinch of cayenne pepper (or ground New Mexico red chile)

juice of 1 large lemon

⅓ cup extra-virgin olive oil, plus 2 to 3 tablespoons more as needed

TOPPING

1 tablespoon extra-virgin olive oil

paprika

Purée the chickpeas, 2 tablespoons of the cooking water, tahini, garlic, salt, and cayenne in a food processor, scraping down the sides of the bowl as necessary, until you have an ultra-smooth paste. Stir in the lemon juice and ⅓ cup olive oil. Adjust the consistency and richness with more olive oil or more of the chickpea-cooking water, if needed. Taste for seasoning, adjusting if necessary—this will depend on the saltiness of the chickpeas. Transfer to a serving dish and swirl the surface so there are deep furrows and ridges. Drizzle with 1 tablespoon more olive oil, and sprinkle a bit of paprika over.

Avocado Toast and Avocado Tortilla

Good avocados require a little timing and attention, but once you have a perfectly ripe one, a simple, great lunch is practically already made. A ripe avocado yields to gentle pressure around the stem, has no soft or hard spots, and slices cleanly. But it won't stay in that state for very long—ripe avocados readily ferment, producing an unpleasant flavor. I love avocados in practically any salad or sandwich, or made into guacamole, but these two simple preparations allow a more direct experience of avocado's subtle flavor and silken texture.

For *avocado toast,* brown a slice of bread in a skillet with a little olive oil, or brush it with olive oil and grill it on your outdoor grill. Rub the toast with a cut clove of garlic. Place slices of ripe avocado atop the bread, and drizzle lightly with extra-virgin olive oil and a few drops of lemon juice. Salt and pepper the avocado, and sprinkle lightly with hot red pepper flakes and toasted sesame seeds. Eat immediately.

For an *avocado tortilla,* heat a corn tortilla directly over a gas flame, until brown speckles appear here and there. Place slices of avocado in the warm tortilla, sprinkle with sea salt, lemon juice, and red pepper flakes, and eat immediately.

Minted Iced Tea

makes 1 gallon

Here we have fresh mint both used in the brewing of the tea and added with lemons to flavor the tea as it cools. This tea is barely sweetened with honey—add sugar to taste to make "sweet tea."

2 lemons, washed and thinly sliced

1 large bunch mint, washed thoroughly

6 cups water

5 English Breakfast or Earl Grey teabags

⅓ cup honey

lots of ice

Take a large square of cheesecloth, and tie the lemons and half of the mint together into a bundle.

Bring the water to a boil in a large saucepan. Throw in the teabags, immediately remove the pot from the heat, and add the loose mint. Let steep for 5 minutes, then gently remove the mint and the teabags and discard—without squeezing them. Immediately stir the honey into the brew to fix the fresh tea flavor. Pour the tea into a gallon pitcher. Add the bundle of lemons and mint to the pitcher to further infuse the tea. Once cool, squeeze a little of the lemon juice from the bundle into the tea, then discard the bundle. Add sufficient ice and cold water to fill the pitcher. Stir and serve.

Hibiscus Iced Tea

makes 1 gallon

A favorite in Mexico, this deep ruby-red brew has a unique, pleasant, tart flavor. The Spanish word for hibiscus is *jamaica*. One of my successors in the Deep Springs kitchen, Donna Blagdan, makes a similar version of this tea with a couple of dried *chiles de arbol* added.

3 cups packed dried hibiscus flowers (*4 ounces*)

8 cups cold water

zest of ½ orange, taken in strips with a vegetable peeler

1 cup sugar, plus more as needed

lots of ice

Put the hibiscus flowers into a large saucepan. Add 4 cups of the water and the orange zest and bring to a boil. Remove from the flame and let steep for 10 minutes. Strain the tea into another container, leaving the hibiscus flowers in the pan. Add 4 more cups cold water to the pan with the flowers, and bring to a boil. Let steep for 10 minutes, then strain the second batch of tea into the container with the first. Add the sugar, stirring to dissolve. Taste—if the brew is still very tart, add more sugar to taste, just enough to balance the tartness and sweetness. Let cool to room temperature. Pour the tea into a gallon pitcher filled with ice, adding more ice or cold water as necessary to fill the pitcher, and serve. If you are making the tea ahead of time, add the ice just before serving.

Lemonade

makes 1 gallon

You want a big glass of this good, tart, refreshing lemonade in the late afternoon, when you've been working out in the sun. For an unusual *whey lemonade*, see page 82.

7 medium lemons

1 cup plus 2 tablespoons sugar

6 cups water

lots of ice

Wash and dry the lemons. In a medium saucepan, stir together the sugar with 3 cups of the water, bring to a boil, and remove from the heat. Finely grate the zest of 6 of the lemons into the hot syrup.

Let cool to room temperature. If you wish, strain the zest out of the syrup (I like the little bits of zest). Squeeze about 1¼ cups of lemon juice from the 6 zested lemons, and mix into the syrup. Fill a gallon pitcher with ice. Pour the lemonade base over the ice. Add the 3 additional cups cold water, plus more if necessary to fill the pitcher. Stir well and taste the lemonade, adjusting with more lemon juice if necessary. It will taste strong at this point—it mellows as the ice melts. Slice the remaining lemon and immerse the slices in the lemonade. Serve.

LIMEADE
For some delightfully zippy limeade, follow the above instructions, using the juice and the zest of 8 to 9 limes instead of the lemons. Where's the tequila?

CHAPTER 6

BEANS

Beans, a staple of Deep Springs cooking, are nutritious, inexpensive, and among the tastiest of foods. It is easy to cook beans badly, which is not necessarily to say that it is difficult to cook beans well. Having a good dish of beans is simply a matter of following a series of steps. Selecting beans in the market is the first step; try, whenever possible, to buy and cook beans, lentils, or split peas from the current crop—no more than a year old. For about a year after harvest, beans retain a trace amount of moisture. When they are old and bone-dry, they not only take forever to cook but have also lost some of their flavor. Supermarkets that have a large Latin American clientele will have fresh, good-quality beans. Don't buy beans containing a lot of splits.

The following guidelines work for virtually any type of dry bean: pinto, black, pink, chickpeas, white navy, dry lima, or, for a proper New Year's Day in the American South, black-eyed peas.

Guidelines for Cooking Beans

1. Before measuring, pour the beans out onto a clean counter or platter and run through them with your fingers, meticulously picking out stones, dirt clods, moldy or discolored beans, and splits. Moldy beans will muddy the flavor of the whole pot, and split beans are especially dry and flavorless. Measure the beans, rinse them well in a colander, then put them in a deep bowl or other large vessel. To allow room for expansion, they should fill the bowl by no more than a third.

2. Fill the bowl with cold water (2 to 3 inches above the level of the beans) and soak the beans, refrigerated, for at least 6 hours, or overnight. Put the beans and their soaking water into a large, heavy, oven-safe pot.

3. Top off the pot with enough fresh water to cover the beans by about 2 inches, and bring to a boil over high heat, skimming off any light-colored foam that rises to the surface. Let the beans boil fairly rapidly for a few minutes, then reduce the heat to a low boil (not a simmer). Add bay leaf, if the recipe calls for it, or other flavorings except salt. After several minutes of cooking, the skins of the beans will start to wrinkle. Add oil or fat. Cover the pot and continue cooking over medium-low heat at a gentle simmer. I often put the whole thing in a 300°F oven at this point, especially when preparing a large quantity. The oven provides indirect, even heat—no frequent stirring required. Cook for 1 to 3 hours, according to your altitude

and the type of bean you have, stirring occasionally. Because the boiling temperature of water lowers with higher altitude, beans take considerably longer to cook (up to 3 hours) at Deep Springs' altitude of 5,200 feet (a pressure cooker may be a great time and energy saver if you frequently cook beans at high altitudes). Check the water level occasionally—the beans should always stay well covered. If you need to add water, bring it to a boil first. When the beans are done, they should be completely soft and yielding. Most recipes say "until soft but not mushy" and I concur, but I am always happy to err on the side of mushy if error is unavoidable.

4. Once the beans are soft, add salt. Stir in the salt and taste the broth—it should taste savory enough to be eaten on its own—perhaps a tiny bit on the salty side, as the beans will absorb some salt. Return the beans to the oven for ½ hour more. Taste the beans again for salt. They are now ready to be served plain, with hot sauce and vinegar, or made into chili or soup. If you are using the beans in a room-temperature bean salad, cool them in their broth, then drain them well and make the salad. If you let hot beans cool out of their broth, they will dry out.

5. Beans' combination of protein and starch makes them very perishable—they "hold onto their heat," providing a ready medium for potentially harmful microorganisms to grow. *Cool the beans quickly* if you will not be using them right away: at home, I put the pot of beans into a shallow sink of cool tap water, just deep enough to come two-thirds up the side of the pot, sometimes with ice added. Stir the beans from time to time; they are usually cool enough to refrigerate in under an hour. With larger quantities of beans, pour them into large, shallow pans (at Deep Springs we use food-service "hotel" pans) and let cool on a rack to room temperature, stirring occasionally, then promptly refrigerate. Reheat leftover beans thoroughly.

The chapter begins with basic pinto and black bean recipes, followed by several hearty chilis, and other substantial bean dishes. The latter part of the chapter contains lighter bean dishes that fit in a menu with other foods.

Many of the recipes use white navy beans; taken together, they are not necessarily meant to sing the praises of that particular bean, but rather to show how versatile beans can be in general. Between several rich and spicy chilis, hearty soups, a bean casserole, and a minty chickpea salad, inspired cooks will see a world of possibility in the humble bean. Consider all these recipes as templates for imaginative use of the many bean varieties available.

Lentil cookery is similar to bean cookery, but these smaller legumes require no soaking and cook in less time. Cook lentils in water until they are soft, and then, off the heat, add salt to taste and a glug of olive oil. Stir the pot frequently as it cools. The lentils will absorb salt and oil richness from the broth. They may be used for soup, or well drained and added to a salad.

Pinto or Black Beans

serves 4 to 6

Not only are *frijoles* an indispensable part of any Mexican or Southwestern meal, they may be the meal itself, along with a couple of warm corn tortillas. A bowl of plain, freshly cooked pinto beans in their broth is surprisingly good. If you have a pot of leftover beans, you're halfway to a good soup. Generally speaking, black beans are served in the southern states of Mexico, while pinto beans are served in the northwestern states of Mexico and throughout the southwestern United States. Black beans were completely unfamiliar in my Texas–New Mexico growing-up years but were a great discovery in early adulthood. Black beans appeal in summer, whereas pinto beans are often exactly what you crave when the weather is cold. Pink beans are quite similar to pintos and may be used in these recipes.

3 cups dry pinto or black beans (about 1½ pounds)

1 cup finely chopped white onion

2 tablespoons vegetable oil or lard

1 tablespoon salt

Follow the guidelines for cooking beans in the preceding section, stirring in the onion at the same time as the oil, when the skins of the beans start to wrinkle.

VARIATIONS

Sometimes I include meat, a small, bony cut of fresh beef or pork, to add richness and flavor. Or, using pinto beans, you may throw in a couple of strips of raw bacon once the beans settle to a simmer, and West Texans will feel right at home (these are known as *cowboy beans* or *Texas beans*). In both cases, the fat on the meat will suffice to enrich the beans, and the oil may be omitted. Or you may dump in a cup of beer in the last 30 minutes of cooking; then you will have *frijoles borrachos* (drunken beans).

Refried Beans

serves 4 to 6

"Refried beans" does not mean that the beans were fried once and are now being fried again. The term is a direct, if misleading, translation of the Spanish *frijoles refritos*, meaning cooked pinto beans that have not been merely reheated but cooked down with a generous amount of fat, richly concentrating their flavor. You may also make *refritos* from black beans.

1 recipe Pinto or Black Beans (preceding recipe)

3 to 4 tablespoons vegetable oil or lard

salt

black pepper

Cool the beans in their broth and refrigerate overnight. Drain off and reserve any bean broth above the level of the beans. Heat the oil in a wide cast-iron skillet over a medium-high flame. When hot but not smoking, spoon in the beans. Cook the beans, mashing them (a potato masher with a flat bottom is ideal) and stirring them constantly until some of the liquid is evaporated away and the beans are richer tasting. Reduce the heat to low. To develop the flavor, allow the beans to gently brown on the bottom, then scrape the crust up into the rest of the mass, using a wooden spoon. Repeat this a few times, but do not let the beans burn or become too dry—add reserved bean broth as necessary to keep them almost pourable. Season the beans with salt, if necessary, and pepper. For a good Mexican touch, if you feel the flavor needs piquing, stir in the juice of half a lime.

You may also refry your beans in the oven. Heat the oil in an oven-safe skillet on the stovetop, add the beans, and stir until the beans are thoroughly hot and bubbly. Put the skillet in a 350°F oven. Stir every 15 minutes or so, scraping up the crust that forms on the bottom, for a total of 30 to 45 minutes. This method requires much less of your time and attention.

Mama Nell's Chili con Carne

serves 4 to 5

This is my version of my grandmother's chili; the square of chocolate is her beautiful and fascinating touch. *Chili* (spelled with an "i" at the end) is a thoroughly Anglo-American stew flavored with *chile* (spelled with an "e" at the end) and other ingredients, sometimes meat, sometimes beans, sometimes both. This recipe is best made with pure ground chile, not chili powder. Chili powder is a spice blend containing other spices and sometimes salt in addition to mild ground red chile. If you like, you can start with 8 to 10 whole dried chile pods, cooking and straining them as detailed in the Red Chile Sauce recipe (page 250). Whole chiles deliver a wonderfully pure, clean flavor, and the result is easier on the stomach, as ground chile and chili powder contain tiny glasslike shards of chile skin. When I follow this recipe I often omit the tomatoes, and use a little more chile in their place.

My grandmother served this one of two ways: (1) In bowls, with grated cheese, chopped green onion, and chopped dill pickle on top. Or (2) she used corn tortillas, grated cheese, and fresh chopped white onion and made stacked enchiladas, using the chili as the sauce. She topped my grandfather's serving with a fried egg.

1¾ cups dry pinto beans

1 tablespoon vegetable oil or lard

3 teaspoons salt, plus more as needed

about 1 pound ground beef, about 80% lean

1 large onion, cut in medium dice

3 to 4 cloves garlic, crushed

1 teaspoon ground cumin

½ teaspoon dried crumbled oregano

⅓ cup pure ground red chile *(New Mexico chile is, of course, preferred: mild, medium, or hot)*

a 14-ounce can of diced tomatoes in juice, or 2 cups of Tomato Concassé *(page 148)*

1 square *(1 ounce)* **unsweetened chocolate**

2 teaspoons cornmeal

¼ teaspoon freshly ground black pepper

FOR SERVING (2 OR 3 ARE AMPLE)

grated cheese

chopped onion

sliced green onion

chopped fresh tomatoes

sour cream

saltine crackers

Cook the beans according to the guidelines on page 106-107, adding oil or lard at the beginning of cooking, and adding 2 teaspoons of the salt in the last 20 minutes of cooking.

Meanwhile, heat a large, heavy pot over a medium-high flame. Add the ground beef, stirring to break up the meat. As soon as the meat releases some liquid, add the diced onion with 1 more teaspoon of the salt. Cook, stirring, until the beef is no longer pink and the onion is beginning to look translucent. Add the garlic with a pinch of salt, and cook a moment more. Add the cumin, oregano, and ground chile, and let cook, stirring frequently, about 5 minutes. Add the tomatoes and all their juice, and bring to a simmer while the beans finish cooking.

When the beans are done, add them to the beef mixture, then stir in the cornmeal and the chocolate. Let the chili simmer for another 20 minutes, stirring frequently. Stir in the black pepper, and taste for salt, correcting if necessary. Serve with the toppings of your choice: grated cheese, chopped white onion, sliced green onion, chopped tomatoes, sour cream, or saltine crackers. This chili is even better the next day, after the chile flavor has permeated the beans.

FRITO PIE

This pure Southwestern comfort food meal is worthy of being served in a real china bowl, not, as some insist, in the cut-open Fritos bag. Arrange a bed of Fritos corn chips in a wide bowl. Ladle a serving of Mama Nell's Chili (recipe above, or use the meatless Black Bean Chili recipe that follows) over the Fritos. Top with more Fritos, grated cheese, sour cream, and onion. As my grandmother often exclaimed, regarding delicious food, "This'll make you slap your daddy!"

Black Bean Chili

serves 6 to 8

This modern classic is based on a recipe in a book I've always loved, Deborah Madison's *The Greens Cookbook*. A Deep Springs visitor gave the Boardinghouse kitchen a copy when I was a student, and it became one of my primary culinary guides. A favorite standard Deep Springs lunch consists of a big pot of this chili, a big pot of Pork and White Bean Chili (facing page), condiments, green salad, and huge Skillet Cornbreads (page 67).

2 cups dry black beans (about 1 pound)

1 bay leaf

2½ teaspoons salt, plus more as needed

2 teaspoons ground cumin

2 teaspoons dried oregano

1 tablespoon paprika

2 tablespoons sunflower oil or other vegetable oil

2 medium yellow onions, cut into small dice

4 cloves garlic, crushed

2 to 3 tablespoons ground dry chile: ancho (medium-hot), **pasilla** (medium-hot), **New Mexico** (hotter), **or California** (milder), **or 2 to 3 tablespoons chili powder**

2 to 3 teaspoons chopped canned chipotle chile

pinch of ground cinnamon

pinch of ground cloves

1 ounce (1 square) **unsweetened baking chocolate or 2 triangles Mexican chocolate**

one 28-ounce can diced tomatoes (or 4 cups of Tomato Concassé, page 148)

1 to 2 teaspoons red wine vinegar

black pepper

¼ cup chopped cilantro

FOR SERVING (2 OR 3 ARE AMPLE)

onion chopped with cilantro

grated pepper Jack cheese

sliced green onions

diced ripe tomatoes

minced jalapeños

sour cream thinned with milk

lime wedges

Soak the beans overnight and cook with the bay leaf, following the guidelines on page 106. Once the beans are soft, add 2 teaspoons of the salt and simmer for about 20 minutes more. Remove the bay leaf. Leave the beans in their broth. Toast the cumin in a small, dry skillet over high heat, stirring constantly, until fragrant. Add the oregano and toast for a few seconds more. Add the paprika, and immediately remove from the heat. Stir the mixture for a few more seconds as the skillet cools. Transfer the spices to a bowl.

Heat the oil in a large, heavy pot over a medium-high flame and throw in the onions with ½ teaspoon salt. Cook, stirring frequently, until the onions have begun to wilt. Reduce the heat to medium, cover the pot, and cook until the onions are soft, about 10 minutes, lifting the lid to stir from time to time. Add the garlic with a pinch of salt, the toasted spices, the ground chile, chipotle chile, cinnamon, cloves, and chocolate. Cook for a minute, stirring constantly, then stir in the tomatoes. Bring to a simmer, and let cook for 5 minutes.

Pour 2 to 3 cups of the bean broth out into a separate pot and set aside. Add the tomato mixture to the beans, and adjust the consistency with the reserved broth. Simmer the chili for 10 minutes, then remove from the heat and add enough wine vinegar to enliven the flavors. Add black pepper to taste, together with the cilantro. Taste for salt and serve with the accompaniments of your choice.

Pork and White Bean Chili

serves 6 to 8

A Deep Springs student brought this recipe from his mom. I adapted it and adopted it immediately. What's the secret? It's the cheese.

2 heaping cups dry white navy beans (*a little over a pound*)

1 bay leaf

2½ teaspoons salt, plus more as needed

2 teaspoons ground cumin

2 teaspoons ground coriander

1½ teaspoons dried oregano

2 pounds ground pork (*on the lean side, if possible*)

¼ teaspoon black pepper, or more as needed

2 medium yellow onions, cut into small dice

4 cloves garlic, minced

pinch of ground cloves

pinch of hot red pepper flakes

three 4-ounce cans chopped fire-roasted green chiles (*or about 2 cups roasted, peeled, and seeded New Mexico green chile, page 251*)

1½ cups (*6 ounces*) **grated jack cheese**

½ cup coarsely chopped cilantro

FOR SERVING (2 OR 3 ARE AMPLE)

chopped green onions

diced ripe tomatoes

minced jalapeño

sour cream thinned with milk

lime wedges

white onion chopped with cilantro

Soak and cook the beans with the bay leaf, following the guidelines on page 106. When the beans are tender, add 2 teaspoons of the salt and simmer for ½ hour more. Remove the bay leaf. Leave the beans in their broth.

Over medium heat, toast the cumin and coriander in a small skillet until their fragrance is released. Add the oregano and toast for a few seconds more. Transfer the spices to a small bowl. In a large skillet over medium-high heat, cook the pork with ½ teaspoon salt, ¼ teaspoon pepper, and the reserved toasted spices until it is no longer pink, 6 to 7 minutes. If your pork is fatty, drain off as much of the fat as you like. Add the onions with another pinch of salt and cook for 10 minutes, or until the onions are soft. Add the garlic, cloves, red pepper flakes, and green chiles with their juice, and cook for a few minutes more.

Drain and reserve 3 cups of broth from the beans. Stir the pork mixture into the beans, adding back enough broth to achieve a thick, soupy consistency. Simmer for 10 minutes to allow the flavors to combine, then remove from the heat and add the cheese and cilantro, stirring to melt and incorporate the cheese. Add salt and pepper to taste and serve immediately with the accompaniments of your choice. You can make the chili, up to the point of adding the cheese and cilantro, well ahead of time.

Red Beans and Rice

serves about 6

This dish, perhaps more than any other, is emblematic of New Orleans. Louis Armstrong closed his letters with the phrase "Red beans and ricely yours." It's still served at places up- and downscale all around the city, any time of day, but continues to be especially prevalent on Mondays—the traditional laundry day. The idea is that the beans can slowly simmer all day with a minimum of fuss and attention, allowing the housewife or servants to concentrate on the laundry. And therein is a hint to successfully making red beans and rice—*the beans must not be hurried*. It takes time for the flavors to marry, for the delicious, deep porkiness of the sausage and the seasonings in the broth to permeate the beans. Red beans have sturdier skins than other bean types, lending themselves to longer cooking.

Note: In southern Louisiana, by all means use the region's celebrated andouille sausage, stronger smoked sausage, and the marvelous smoked pork known as *tasso*; in other places, if these products are not available, any garlicky, lightly smoked, medium-spicy sausage may be used. In place of tasso, you may substitute cubes of slab bacon, or a ham hock or two, or a meaty ham shank.

1 pound red kidney beans, picked over, rinsed, and soaked overnight

2 bay leaves

1 or 2 whole cayenne pepper pods (or ¼ teaspoon ground cayenne)

½ pound andouille sausage, whole (see Note above)

1 smoked sausage (about ¼ pound; see Note above)

½ pound tasso, chopped (see Note above)

1 tablespoon lard or vegetable oil

2 medium yellow onions, cut in small dice

5 cloves garlic, crushed

¾ teaspoon dried thyme

⅛ teaspoon celery seed, ground in spice grinder

about 1 teaspoon salt, plus more to taste if necessary

½ teaspoon ground black pepper

1 tablespoon red wine vinegar

2 teaspoons molasses

RICE

1 cup uncooked long-grain white rice, rinsed well and drained

1½ cups water

scant ½ teaspoon salt

2 teaspoons butter

FOR SERVING

3 or 4 scallions, trimmed, washed well, and sliced thinly

¼ bunch parsley, finely chopped

Tabasco or other hot sauce (passed at the table)

Put the beans in a large, heavy pot with their soaking water, and add sufficient fresh water to cover the beans by about 2 inches. Bring to a boil over a high flame, then reduce the heat to a lively simmer. Skim off any foam that forms on the top. When the beans have settled to a simmer, add the bay leaves and pepper pod. Continue cooking for about 1 hour, until the beans are beginning to soften. Add the sausage and tasso. Reduce the flame to very low, cover the pot, and let the beans cook slowly, stirring occasionally, for another hour. Remove the sausages and tasso and let cool. Slice the sausages, dice the tasso, and return them to the pot.

Meanwhile, in a large saucepan, heat the lard or oil over a medium flame. Add the onions with a pinch of salt and sauté, stirring frequently, until the onions are just beginning to soften, about 5 minutes. Add the garlic, thyme, and celery seed with a pinch of salt, and cook about 5 minutes more. Add the onion mixture to the beans. The beans should always be submerged in the liquid; if more water is necessary, bring it to a boil first. When the beans are thoroughly soft, add the vinegar and molasses. Taste the bean broth for salt, adding about a teaspoon or more, or less, depending on the saltiness of the sausage. Fish out and discard the pepper pod and bay leaf. Before serving, mash a few of the beans slightly with a potato masher, thickening the liquid.

Meanwhile, cook the rice: in a heavy saucepan, put the rice, water, salt, and butter. Bring to a boil, then reduce the flame to low and cover the pot. Let the rice cook about 20 minutes, or until all the liquid is absorbed.

To serve, arrange a ring of hot rice in a shallow soup bowl. Spoon the hot beans into the center, allowing plenty of liquid. Sprinkle over the scallions and parsley, and serve immediately, passing hot sauce for those who want more kick.

Lima Bean and Ham Soup with Kale

serves 6 to 8

Big buttery beans, ham, bacon, and vitamin-loaded greens—this is February food. Serve with brown bread and a big green salad. You can make this soup in stages, cooking the beans and ham hock the day before. Though the kale will lose its vibrant color, this soup is very good reheated. The ham shank is cooked separately from the beans because the salt it releases while cooking will slow the softening of the beans.

- **1 smoked ham shank**
- **2 cups dry large lima beans** (about 1 pound), **soaked overnight** (see guidelines for cooking beans, page 106)
- **1 bay leaf**
- **salt**
- **2 to 3 strips thick-sliced bacon, cut into medium dice** (or 2 to 3 tablespoons olive oil)
- **1 medium yellow onion, cut into medium dice**
- **1 small carrot, peeled and cut into medium dice**
- **2 stalks celery, cut into medium dice**
- **1 large bunch kale, thickest stems removed, washed and chopped into bite-sized pieces**
- **2 cloves garlic, crushed**
- **one 14-ounce can diced tomatoes in juice** (or 2 cups Tomato Concassé, page 148)
- **black pepper**
- **1 to 2 teaspoons cider vinegar or fresh lemon juice**

Cover the ham shank with water in a large saucepan. Bring to a boil, skim off any scum that rises to the surface, and reduce the heat to a simmer. Let simmer for 1 hour, or until the meat is tender and can be easily removed from the bone. Meanwhile, put the soaked beans in a large, heavy soup pot with the bay leaf and fresh water to cover the beans by about 2 inches. Bring to a boil, skim off the scum that rises to the surface, and reduce the heat to a simmer. Cook the beans until they are completely buttery-soft and yielding, 30 to 40 minutes (longer at high altitudes). Carefully add salt until the broth tastes good, like a thin soup. Cook over low heat for about 20 minutes longer so the salt penetrates the beans. Remove the bay leaf.

When the ham shank is tender, remove it to a plate to cool, saving the broth. Discard the bones, fat, and gristle. Break up the meat into chunks, and add the meat and ham broth to the beans. In a large saucepan, cook the bacon over medium-low heat to render out the fat. When the bacon is beginning to brown and there is ample fat (2 to 3 tablespoons; you may replace some of this fat—or the bacon altogether—with olive oil), throw in the onion, carrot, and celery with a good pinch of salt and cook, stirring occasionally, until the onion is no longer translucent, about 10 minutes. Add the kale in batches—it will cook down—and the garlic. When everything is simmering, add the tomatoes and their juice. Bring the mixture back to a simmer and cook, stirring every so often, until the kale is tender, about 20 minutes. Stir the vegetable mixture into the beans, and simmer for about 10 minutes more. Taste for salt. Add pepper to taste. To brighten the flavors, add 1 to 2 teaspoons of cider vinegar or lemon juice. This soup is also excellent *sans* meat, using olive oil to stew the vegetables.

White Bean Soup with Fried Sage

serves 4 to 6

While I think of chili and the heartier bean soups above as meals in themselves, this and the following recipe are examples of more refined, lighter, bean soups, easier to fit into a menu with other foods.

2½ cups dry white navy beans (about 1¼ pounds)

1 bay leaf

4 tablespoons extra-virgin olive oil

2 teaspoons salt, plus more as needed

1 medium yellow onion, cut into small dice

2 stalks celery, cut into small dice

3 cloves garlic, crushed or minced

chicken stock, vegetable stock, or water for thinning the soup, if needed

1 to 2 teaspoons fresh lemon juice

freshly ground black pepper

TOPPING

¼ cup olive oil for frying

12 to 16 large sage leaves

Soak and cook the beans with the bay leaf and a tablespoon of the olive oil, following the guidelines on page 106. Since the beans are for soup, use ample water when cooking them. When the beans are soft, add 1½ teaspoons salt and simmer for about 20 minutes more. Leave the beans in the broth.

In a small, heavy saucepan over a medium flame, heat 2 tablespoons of the olive oil. Gently sauté the onion, celery, and garlic with a few pinches of salt until the vegetables are soft and sweetened, about 5 minutes—do not let them brown. Add the vegetables to the beans and simmer for about 10 minutes more. Purée the soup in batches in a blender. Be careful when blending hot liquids; fill the blender jar only half full, hold the lid in place with a kitchen towel, and start the blender on lower speeds. For the smoothest texture, pass the soup through a screen sieve, using the back of a ladle. Add some chicken stock, vegetable stock, or water if the soup needs thinning. Stir in a teaspoon or two of lemon juice to brighten the flavor. Add more salt to taste, and pepper. Enrich with a final tablespoon of olive oil.

To fry the sage, heat ¼ cup olive oil in a small skillet over medium-high heat until the tip of a sage leaf sizzles when dipped in. Fry the sage leaves until crisp, 5 to 10 seconds—they will turn a darker shade of green and release a puff of fragrance. Remove immediately with a slotted spoon and drain on paper towels. Float a couple of fried sage leaves in each bowl of soup, plus a drizzle of the sage-scented oil.

ROSEMARY OIL

Instead of fried sage, you can garnish this soup with rosemary oil. Strip the needles off a small branch of rosemary until you have about 2 tablespoons of needles. Put the needles in a blender jar with ½ cup olive oil and blend on high speed until the herb is completely pulverized. Pour the mixture into a small cup and allow it to sit for an hour. Strain through a sieve, and drizzle ½ teaspoon of the scented oil over each bowl of soup just prior to serving. (Use the remaining rosemary slurry to marinate chicken or scent focaccia bread or, with garlic, nuts, and Parmesan added, to garnish pasta, pizza, or rice.)

White Bean and Escarole Soup

serves 6 to 8

This simple, elegant soup contains escarole, a lettucelike green that tastes pleasantly bitter and satisfyingly crunchy raw, but nutty and fortifying cooked. Like all members of the chicory family, escarole is especially tasty with savory beans. Once you have chicken stock and cooked beans on hand, the soup is practically already made. We served it at Deep Springs one Christmas to begin a sumptuous Italian dinner featuring glazed Deep Springs–raised ham.

1 large head escarole

2 teaspoons olive oil

1 medium yellow onion, cut into small dice

1 medium carrot, peeled and cut into small dice

1 small stalk celery, cut into small dice

- **2 pinches of salt, plus more as needed**
- **6 cups good chicken stock**
- **3 cups cooked, well-seasoned white navy beans in their liquid** *(start with 1½ cups of dry beans, and follow the guidelines on page 106)*

Remove any wilted or blemished outer leaves of the escarole; remove the remainder of the leaves from the core and cut into bite-size squares. Briefly immerse the escarole in a basin of cold water and drain. Heat a teaspoon of the olive oil in a large, heavy soup pot over medium heat. Add the onion, carrot, celery, and a good pinch of salt and cook slowly, covered, stirring occasionally, until the vegetables are completely tender, about 5 minutes—they shouldn't brown. Add the chicken stock, and bring to a simmer. Let this soup base simmer gently for about 5 minutes while you wilt the escarole. Heat another teaspoon of olive oil in a large saucepan. When it just begins to smoke, add half the escarole with a pinch of salt and immediately stir. It will quickly wilt and turn a vivid green. Let the escarole cook, stirring two or three times, for about 1 minute, or until nutty and tender. Add it to the soup, and repeat with the remaining escarole.

Drain the beans, saving their flavorful liquid for another purpose, and add them to the soup. Bring to a simmer. If the chicken stock was well seasoned, the soup should not need salt—taste. Serve immediately, stirring the pot from the bottom when ladling up each serving.

White Bean Gratin with Fennel

serves 6 to 8

This casserole is superb served with lamb, or pork or chicken, or by itself with fresh brown bread and a big, vegetable-y salad.

- **2 cups dry white navy beans** *(about 1 pound)*
- **1 bay leaf**
- **4 tablespoons extra-virgin olive oil**
- **2 teaspoons salt, plus more as needed**
- **1 fennel bulb, cut into medium dice, reserving the feathery fronds for topping**
- **1 large yellow onion, cut into medium dice**
- **2 tablespoons coarsely chopped fresh sage**
- **1½ teaspoons red wine vinegar, plus more if needed**
- **¼ teaspoon hot red pepper flakes**
- **black pepper**

TOPPING

- **¾ cup dry breadcrumbs**
- **2 tablespoons extra-virgin olive oil**
- **feathery fennel fronds, coarsely chopped**
- **salt and black pepper**

Soak and cook the beans with the bay leaf, following the guidelines for cooking beans on page 106. When the beans are tender, remove from the heat and stir in 2 tablespoons of the olive oil and the salt. Taste the broth: it should be pleasantly seasoned, like soup. Let the beans sit in the broth while you prepare the vegetables and the topping.

Heat the oven to 350°F. In a medium saucepan, in the remaining 2 tablespoons olive oil, cook the fennel and onions with a pinch of salt over a medium flame until tender. Add the sage and cook for 1 minute more. Drain off sufficient liquid so that the beans are still very moist, but not soupy. Add the onion-fennel mixture, vinegar, red pepper flakes, and salt and pepper to taste. Taste; the flavors may need brightening with a judicious touch more vinegar. Combine the ingredients for the topping—breadcrumbs, olive oil, chopped fennel fronds, and salt and pepper to taste—in a small bowl. Spread the beans in a 9-by-13-inch baking dish, and sprinkle the topping evenly over the surface. Bake until the topping is golden brown, 20 to 25 minutes.

Split Pea Soup

serves 4 to 6

This hearty split pea soup contains marjoram, a flowery herb similar to oregano. Lacking marjoram, you may approximate its flavor with a couple of pinches of oregano and a pinch of dried mint. Why the rice? It somehow lightens the peas' starchiness, invisibly. You can make this soup with yellow or green split peas—I often use a combination. Serve with a warm loaf of wheat bread.

- **2½ cups dry green or yellow split peas** *(about 1¼ pounds)*
- **½ cup uncooked brown rice**
- **9 cups water**
- **1 bay leaf**
- **2 to 3 pinches of hot red pepper flakes**
- **1 tablespoon butter**
- **1 medium carrot, peeled and cut into medium dice**
- **1 medium yellow onion, cut into medium dice**
- **1½ teaspoons salt, plus more as needed**
- **1 teaspoon dried marjoram, or 1 tablespoon chopped fresh marjoram**
- **2 tablespoons soy sauce**
- **freshly ground black pepper**
- **2 teaspoons red wine vinegar**

In a large, heavy soup pot, soak the split peas and rice in 9 cups water for about 1 hour. Bring to a boil over high heat, skim off the foam that collects on the surface, and add the bay leaf and pepper flakes. Reduce the heat to a lively simmer. Cook, stirring frequently, until the peas and rice have dissolved into a purée, about 50 minutes. Watch carefully at the end—as it thickens, it will tend to stick to the bottom and burn. Remove the bay leaf.

In a medium saucepan, melt the butter over medium-high heat. Add the carrot and onion with the salt and cook, stirring frequently, until the onion is soft, 8 to 10 minutes. Add these vegetables to the peas and simmer slowly for 20 minutes more. Add the marjoram, soy sauce, and pepper to taste. Stir in the vinegar to brighten the corners. Taste for salt and serve. This soup is very good reheated.

If you want ham in your split pea soup, either cut up a packaged ham steak and throw it into the soup near the end or separately braise a ham shank to tenderness, adding the chunks of meat and broth to the soup in the last 20 minutes of cooking.

Chickpeas with Tomatoes, Lemon, and Mint

serves 4 to 6

This summer Mediterranean salad is excellent with Cumin Roast Chicken (page 205). Serve Melon with Rosewater (page 281) for dessert. To cook the chickpeas, see the guidelines for cooking beans on page 106.

- **1 tablespoon olive oil**
- **½ red onion, diced**
- **1 clove garlic, crushed**
- **salt**
- **2 cups cooked chickpeas, well drained**
- **about 1 cup diced ripe red tomatoes, drained**
- **juice and grated zest of ½ lemon**
- **pinch of hot red pepper flakes**
- **½ cup loosely packed mint leaves, coarsely chopped**
- **¼ cup coarsely chopped parsley**
- **black pepper**
- **extra-virgin olive oil**
- **lemon slices for garnish**

In a large skillet, heat the olive oil over a medium-high flame until it shimmers. Add the onion and garlic with a little salt and sauté for 1 to 2 minutes. When the onion is mostly cooked, add the chickpeas and cook until the chickpeas are dry. They are now ready to absorb moisture and flavor from the other ingredients. Turn the chickpeas out onto a shallow serving dish to cool to room temperature. Just before serving, gently toss in the tomatoes, lemon, pepper flakes, mint, parsley, and plenty of salt and pepper to taste. Drizzle well with extra-virgin olive oil, and arrange lemon slices over the top.

CHAPTER 7
HOT VEGETABLES & VEGETABLE SOUPS

Every vegetable has its own natural history. Over millennia, people encouraged certain traits such as sweetness and tenderness, very gradually transforming wild plants into modern cultivars. The bunch of green chard sitting on your kitchen counter mutely contains within its cells epochs of human history. Because some of chard's modern cultivars were developed in fertile cattle-grazing valleys in northern Italy and Switzerland, chard tastes especially good cooked with a little cream and Parmesan or Gruyère cheese. That zucchini squash tastes "truest" when cooked quickly in a little olive oil is a clue that it developed in warmer southern European climates, where olives thrive. Chilly weather brings out the natural sugars in cabbage, and cooks know that cabbage tastes best when braised slowly in a little butter or pork fat, with maybe a chopped apple thrown in. So we might hazard a guess that what we know today as cabbage developed in colder northern climates. Each vegetable, each embodying its own individual story, must be considered on its own terms; there aren't many universal vegetable-cookery rules….

I know many people who, like me, are not vegetarians but who nurture a great love for vegetables. It's the produce section, not the meat counter, that most inspires me when I'm shopping to cook a meal. Any vegetable can be delicious, especially if grown with care, bought fresh, and cooked thoughtfully. It's gratifying to serve people vegetables they thought they hated—beets or Brussels sprouts or cabbage—and see them discover for the first time how good they can be.

Technically, there are three vegetable chapters in this book. Beans are certainly a vegetable, and their chapter precedes this one. This chapter contains recipes and ideas for hot vegetable dishes, including many soups (the preceding Beans chapter also contains several soup recipes). The next chapter deals with salads and cold vegetable preparations, including a terrific approach to gazpacho, a chilled soup.

Artichokes

serves 6

Artichokes are traditional in the spring, but they grow well in California's cool coastal climate in all but the hottest months. When I serve whole artichokes at Deep Springs, I often give a demonstration of how to eat them, since there are always one or two students who have never encountered them before. An interesting fact: one of the flavor compounds in artichokes causes some people to perceive sweetness in plain water, or even in inhaled air. While lemon butter is traditional with warm artichokes, they may also be served at room temperature, with Mayonnaise (page 252), Aioli (page 253), or Lemon Vinaigrette (page 174). And although the carrot, celery, and other aromatic flavorings are delicious, adding an extra layer of savoriness, I don't always include them. Often, I just use water, salt, olive oil, and lemon juice to counteract the artichokes' characteristic bitterness.

6 large globe artichokes, with stems

1 strip lemon zest, taken with a vegetable peeler

juice of ½ lemon

½ small onion, cut into large dice

1 carrot, peeled and coarsely chopped

1 stalk celery, thickly sliced

1 bay leaf

1 sprig fresh tarragon or mint

10 peppercorns

3 tablespoons olive oil

salt

LEMON BUTTER

½ cup butter *(1 stick)*

juice of ½ lemon

Rinse the artichokes well. With a large bread knife or other serrated knife, cut off the top inch of the artichokes, revealing the lighter-colored inner leaves. Pull off the outer layer of leaves from around the base, and then, using kitchen scissors, snip the sharp thorn off the remaining outer leaves. Cut the stems off at the base so the artichoke sits straight. Trim the brown tips from the stems. As you finish, plunge the artichokes and stems into water with a little vinegar added—this will keep them from browning.

Arrange the artichoke stems on the bottom of a large, heavy pot. Add the lemon zest, lemon juice, onion, carrot, celery, bay leaf, tarragon or mint, peppercorns, and olive oil. Arrange the artichokes on top, adding just enough water to submerge the bottom thirds of the artichokes. Add enough salt to the water to make it taste slightly salty. Cover the pot and bring to a boil. Lower the heat slightly and cook the artichokes at a low boil for 20 to 30 minutes, or just until a knife can be inserted into the base with no resistance. Drain the artichokes.

To make the lemon butter, melt the butter in a small saucepan, add the lemon juice, and serve in small cups with the artichokes. Provide a large bowl for the discarded leaves. To eat an artichoke, begin with the outer leaves. Pull a leaf off with your fingers, dip the lower, pale-colored tip into the butter, then scrape off the edible flesh from the bottom of each leaf with your teeth. The leaves become more tender the closer you get to the heart. When all the leaves are consumed, scoop out the bristly "choke" with a spoon. Take up your knife and fork and enjoy the succulent heart, dipping slices into the remaining lemon butter. Artichoke stems, when peeled, are as tender and flavorful as the heart.

STUFFED ARTICHOKES

This special-occasion dish is lots of work for the cook, but heaven for the eater. Using large artichokes, follow the procedure for cleaning and trimming them in the master recipe above, but remove the inedible part from the inside, also: pull out the small inner lavender leaves, and using a small spoon, carefully scrape out the fibrous choke from each artichoke. Cook just until tender as described in the master recipe—the hollowed-out artichokes will take less time. Reserve the cooking water, unless it tastes very bitter.

Take the cooked artichoke stems, peel off the outer fibrous layer, and chop the tender cores into a medium bowl. In a large skillet, sauté a cup of finely-diced onion in ample butter with salt; when the onion is tender, add about 2 cups of coarse breadcrumbs to the skillet, and continue sautéing until the breadcrumbs and onions begin to brown slightly. Add the breadcrumb mixture to the artichoke stems, and add freshly chopped parsley, freshly ground pepper, and salt if necessary. Moisten this mixture with a few spoonfuls of reserved artichoke cooking water, or with chicken stock. Taste—the stuffing should be rich and savory. Fill each artichoke cavity with the stuffing. Bake for about 20 minutes in a 350°F oven to heat through. If necessary, you can hold the artichokes for up to half an hour in the turned-off oven. Serve with Lemon Butter. Eat the artichoke leaves with your fingers, dipping the pale-colored tip into the butter, then scraping the edible flesh from each tough leaf with your teeth. When all the leaves are consumed, pour the rest of the butter over the stuffing, take up your knife and fork, and eat the prized artichoke heart with the stuffing.

Fresh Artichoke Hearts

serves 6

Homemade artichoke hearts, prepared from fresh artichokes, require a measure of patience and dexterity with a knife, but their flavor and texture far exceeds anything purchased in a jar or can. I serve these artichokes with simple Baked Halibut (page 222), and drizzle both artichokes and fish with Lemon-Olive Relish (page 254), but they may be served alongside other fish varieties, or with other meats—chicken, slow-braised beef, or lamb. They can go into a salad or onto an assorted antipasto platter. Or try them tossed with pasta, along with sautéed mushrooms, olive oil, and herbs. The broth from cooking the artichokes is savory and delicious, not bitter—it may become the basis of a soup, pasta, or risotto.

3 large artichokes, with 2- to 3-inch stems

juice of 1 lemon

2 to 3 strips lemon zest, taken with a vegetable peeler

½ teaspoon fennel seed

1 sprig fresh tarragon or mint *(optional)*

12 whole peppercorns

1 carrot, peeled and cut diagonally in 6 pieces

1 teaspoon salt

3 tablespoons extra-virgin olive oil

Don't cut off the artichoke stems; the stems contains the same flavorful "heart" as the body of the artichoke. Using a large serrated knife, cut off the pointy top third from the body of the artichoke. Switch to a sharp, small paring knife, and working systematically around the artichoke and down the base, trim off all green parts from the leaves, base, and stem: only the yellow and white parts should remain.

Cut the trimmed artichokes in half lengthwise, then scoop out the fuzzy, fibrous choke in the center, and any lavender-tinged leaves near the choke. Cut each half in thirds lengthwise, making question-mark–shaped wedges. Rinse the prepared artichokes, and plunge them into a saucepan of water, just enough to cover them, acidulated with the juice of a fresh lemon. Add the lemon zest, fennel seed, tarragon or mint (if using), peppercorns, carrot, salt, and olive oil. Over a high flame, bring the artichokes to a simmer, then reduce the heat to maintain a simmer. Taste the liquid for salt (it should taste nicely seasoned, like broth), and cook the artichokes gently just until tender, about 10 minutes—test with a knife. Remove the artichokes from the liquid with a slotted spoon, cool both liquid and artichokes separately, then return the artichokes to the liquid, and refrigerate.

Pan-Roasted Asparagus

serves 2 to 4

Asparagus, with its little shoots popping up out of the ground, is the quintessential spring vegetable. I cook, eat, and serve lots of asparagus in spring and otherwise do without. Air-shipping and prolonged cold storage rob asparagus of much of its flavor and character. I read somewhere that legendary architect Frank Lloyd Wright (who visited Deep Springs in the early days) would sometimes have nothing for dinner but a heap of spring asparagus with butter and lemon.

Pencil-thin asparagus is not necessarily the best. If you take the time to peel the stalks before snapping off the bottoms, even the thickest asparagus turns out tender and succulent. I used to boil asparagus in salted water, but I have come to prefer slowly pan-roasting the whole spears on top of the stove, or simply broiling or grilling them.

1 pound asparagus

1 tablespoon butter or olive oil

salt

black pepper

Rinse the asparagus. Using a vegetable peeler, peel each stalk, starting about 3 inches away from the tip and going down. Then, grasping only the bottom inch of the stalk, snap off the bottom part of the stalk—the asparagus will break where its tenderness and toughness meet. Heat a wide skillet over a medium-high flame. Melt a tablespoon of butter or olive oil and lay the asparagus in the skillet in a uniform line. Sprinkle lightly with salt. Let the asparagus cook—it will gently sizzle—for 2 to 3 minutes. Using tongs, turn the spears and cook on the other side for about 1 minute, until tender but still crisp. Sprinkle with pepper to taste.

BROILED OR GRILLED ASPARAGUS

Peel spears of asparagus as described above, then toss in olive oil and salt, arrange on a baking sheet, and put the sheet under a hot broiler for about 5 minutes, or until there are appealing brown spots here and there. If the spears are thick, they will need to be turned and broiled on the other side. Or lay the spears directly on a hot grill, opposite the direction of the grill's grates so they don't fall through, and let cook for about 5 minutes, turning with tongs if necessary.

ASPARAGUS PASTA

Peel spears of asparagus as described above, then thinly slice on the diagonal. Sliver the tips. Sauté with a little crushed garlic and salt in plenty of olive oil just until tender, then toss with freshly cooked medium shell pasta or another similar pasta shape. When draining the pasta, save a little of the pasta cooking water, in case moisture is needed in the finish. Add salt and pepper, grated lemon zest, and Parmesan. Taste and adjust. Lemon Butter Sauce (page 252) is also superb on asparagus pasta, perhaps with a few Sautéed Mushrooms (page 135). See the recipe for Snap Peas (page 139) for a similar pasta.

Sautéed Green Beans

serves 2 to 4

Although green beans are a year-round supermarket staple, they are at their sweetest and best in summer. Yellow wax beans may also be used, alone or in combination with a green variety. This method results in beans that are crisp-tender, slightly wrinkly in appearance, and bright green. They are almost as good cold as freshly cooked. For a beautiful summer lunch, serve these green beans alongside Grilled Skirt Steak (page 181) and a spoonful of Roasted Peppers (page 140).

There are two distinct camps in the United States regarding green beans—those who like them thin and young, cooked just until tender but still retaining a little crunch (this recipe is an example), and those who like them grown a bit larger, and cooked to a softer texture with bacon or salt pork (see the following recipes).

1 pound slender fresh summer green beans

2 tablespoons olive oil

1 small red onion, thinly sliced lengthwise *(optional)*

2 cloves garlic, crushed fine *(optional)*

½ small red bell pepper, sliced into long, thin strips *(optional)*

salt

black pepper

Rinse the beans well in a colander and snip the tops and tails off. I arrange handfuls of green beans, aligning the ends to be cut off against the counter surface and cutting the lot with my chef's knife, but it takes only a little more time to sit at the kitchen table and top and tail them one by one, getting a fast rhythm going.

In a wide skillet with a well-fitting lid, heat the olive oil over a medium-high flame. When it shimmers, add the optional onion, garlic, or red bell pepper with a pinch of salt and sauté quickly for a few seconds. Throw in the green beans with another pinch of salt. There should be just a little water left on the beans from rinsing, which will help them to cook. Stir everything around to distribute a light coating of oil on the beans, then slap on the lid. If the pan seems very hot, reduce the flame a little. If the pan seems dry, add a tablespoon or so of water. Keep cooking the beans, stirring every so often, until they are tender but still crisp (taste one). On average, pencil-sized beans are tender after 8 to 10 minutes of sautéing. Don't stir them constantly; they are especially good if they brown lightly here and there. Grind a little black pepper over the beans and serve.

SAUTÉED ROMANO BEANS

I especially love these larger, flatter, sturdier relatives of green beans, with their hint of lima bean flavor. Snip the tops and tails off a pound of romano beans, and snap them in half. Follow the master recipe above, but blanch the beans first in a large pot of rapidly boiling, salted water, for about 1 minute. Drain the beans well, scatter on a tray, and let cool slightly. Proceed with sautéing the blanched beans as described in the master recipe.

Green Beans Cooked in Bacon Fat

For this Southern summer garden delicacy, you need beans that are bred to be grown a little larger, the better to withstand long cooking. Large romano beans (see preceding recipe) work very well, but Kentucky Wonder, an heirloom pole bean variety, is ideal for this (and the following) method. Top and tail 1 pound of large green beans. Boil in well-salted water until tender, but not mushy, and let drain. Heat a tablespoon of good fresh bacon fat in a saucepan until it sizzles. Throw in the drained beans and sauté them in the bacon fat for a few minutes. Pepper and serve.

Southern-Style Braised Green Beans

This is an old recipe of my mother's, in her words, with my amendments in parentheses: "*Snap 1 pound Kentucky Wonder beans* (or use romano beans, pinch off their tops and tails, and cut in half or thirds). *Boil ¼ lb. salt pork in a big pot* (in about 2½ cups of water) *for about 20 minutes. Add beans, pepper, and a pinch of sugar. Cover and cook* (stirring frequently at the beginning, but not stirring at all once the beans become tender) *until liquid is almost gone, about 2 hours, over low heat* (Check after 1½ hours)." Be sure and serve a round of Skillet Cornbread (page 67) alongside.

Fresh Shell Beans

Shell beans are the "bridge" between fresh green beans and dry beans. If you have very overgrown, bulging bean pods in your summer green bean patch, the pods are no longer edible, but the beans inside can be shelled out, cooked, and enjoyed. And any variety of bean cultivated for use as a dry bean may also be used fresh, as a shell bean. When beans have just matured but the pods are still fresh, pop the beans out of the pods and simmer them in water, as you would dry beans. A strictly summer crop, shell beans are sometimes available at farmers markets and well-stocked produce markets. Japanese *edamame* are fresh shell soybeans—simply boil the whole pods in well-salted water until the beans within are tender.

Cranberry shell beans are beloved by Italians, and American Southerners dote on fresh shell *black-eyed peas* and *runner beans*, but *lima beans* are perhaps the best-known shell bean. I am sure millions of children still grow up eating mixed vegetables from frozen packages: always those same cubed carrots, inch-long green beans, peas, corn, and a lima bean here and there. And I'm sure many of those millions still hate the lima beans and pick them out, or swallow them whole with milk, as I once did. But I also remember discovering that the smaller, greener lima beans were actually quite good.

You may occasionally see *fresh garbanzo*, or chickpea, shell beans. I bought a large bunch once, with only one or two beautiful green garbanzo beans to each pod. After more than an hour of work, I had produced a preciously small amount of light and fresh-tasting green hummus.

If you find shell beans, sit at your kitchen table and remove the beans from the pods. Put the beans in a heavy saucepot, and cover with cold water by about 1 inch. Bring to a boil and skim off any scum that collects on the surface. Reduce the flame, maintaining a lively simmer. Add half an onion to the pot, plus a bay leaf and a small peeled carrot. Depending on the variety, shell beans will be tender after 30 to 40 minutes of cooking—taste one to determine doneness. When the beans are soft, remove the pot from the flame and immediately stir in enough salt to season the liquid well. Also add a good shot of olive oil. Stir frequently as the beans cool—they will absorb salt and oil from the broth. Cooked shell beans are quite perishable: refrigerate them promptly after they are cool.

Cooked shell beans and their flavorful broth may form the backbone of a delicious, hearty vegetable soup (see Soupe au Pistou, page 151). Or add sautéed corn, freshly cut from the cob, and stewed onion to drained shell beans, with perhaps a little chopped fresh savory or other herb, and you have a wonderful *succotash*. Or toss shell beans and some of their broth with fresh tomatoes, herbs, and an appropriately shaped pasta, and scatter with Parmesan and golden-toasted breadcrumbs.

Broccoli

Bursting with vitamins and calcium, broccoli, a cool-weather crop, is one of the most popular vegetables in the United States. Many people steam broccoli; I usually find steamed vegetables bland, but I admit, sometimes I just artlessly throw a crown of broccoli whole into my smallest saucepan with a splash of water and turn the heat up high. Often, I am amazed at how sweet it tastes with no salt or seasoning.

Most of the time I "steam-sauté" broccoli. Cut the florets off the central stem, but don't throw away the stem: peel it, and it's as tender as the rest. Cut the smaller florets in half, the larger ones in quarters. Cut the stem into uniform pieces; all the cut broccoli should cook at about the same rate.

For each pound of broccoli, melt a tablespoon of butter or olive oil and 2 tablespoons of water in a large saucepan with a well-fitting lid over a medium-high flame. When the water begins to boil, throw in all the broccoli with ¼ teaspoon salt, and stir to coat. Cook, stirring frequently but otherwise keeping the lid on, until the broccoli is as tender as you like. Some like it soft; others prefer a little crunch remaining.

If you want to use cooked broccoli in a salad, use olive oil in the cooking, spread the hot broccoli on a tray to cool, and dress it at the last minute—the acidic vinegar will turn broccoli a dull army green. For an excellent picnic salad, toss cooked, cooled broccoli with Aioli (page 253) and halved cherry tomatoes. Broccoli to be served warm is enhanced by dark Asian sesame oil and a sprinkle of lightly toasted sesame seeds, or by sizzling crushed garlic in the oil before adding the water and broccoli. You can top cooked broccoli with Roasted Red Peppers (page 140) and a handful of Toasted Walnuts (page 176). Or toss sautéed small-cut florets with pasta, hot red pepper flakes, olive oil, toasted breadcrumbs, and grated Parmesan.

Brussels Sprouts with Brown Butter

serves 4 to 6

Brussels sprouts and brown butter were made for each other, as I learned from my friend Adra long ago. Making a frequent appearance on my Thanksgiving table, they win everyone over, even the alleged Brussels sprout haters. The toastiness of the butter enhances the naturally meaty, cabbagey flavor of the Brussels sprouts. Sometimes, in fall and winter, you may find them on their stalk, resembling 2-foot-tall Muppet-trees. Pre-cut Brussels sprouts, ideally, should have no yellow. I have eaten Brussels sprouts that had yellowed on the outside, but I peeled them down to the green before cooking. Lots of brown butter on those, please, and I hope your kitchen has good ventilation.

Once you get the hang of it, brown butter is one of the easiest sauces there is. The French call it *beurre noisette*—"hazelnut butter." You simply take the butter to within a few seconds of burning, then toss it with hot food.

1 pound Brussels sprouts, stems trimmed, tough or discolored outer leaves removed

1 cup water

¼ teaspoon salt, plus more as needed

2 to 3 tablespoons butter

freshly ground black pepper

Cut each sprout in half lengthwise. Put the water and ¼ teaspoon salt in a medium saucepan and bring to a boil over a high flame. Throw in the sprouts, stirring well to distribute. Let the water come back to a boil, slap on the lid, and let the Brussels sprouts cook for about 4 minutes, stirring once or twice. To test for doneness, rinse a sprout in cold water and bite into it. When they are just tender to the bite, they are done. Avoid undercooked, crunchy sprouts or overcooked, mushy sprouts. Drain the liquid from the pan and transfer the sprouts to a serving dish. Give the pan a quick rinse and set it back on the burner.

To make the brown butter, turn the flame to medium-high and let the pan dry for a few seconds, then throw in the butter. When the butter melts and bubbles and the foam subsides, swirl the pan and watch carefully until the butterfat (the liquid on the bottom) and the remaining foam turn a toast brown. It will first smell raw and dairylike, then it will take on a toasty and savory aroma as it browns. When the butter is well browned and smells tantalizing, dump in the Brussels sprouts, tossing gently to distribute. Let the sprouts sizzle in the butter for a few moments. Add a pinch or two of salt, if necessary, and a few twists of pepper, then slide them back into their serving dish. Serve immediately.

Cabbage with Juniper

serves 2 to 3

This splendid, unusual combination makes an elegant accompaniment to a winter dinner. In the fall, I harvest blue juniper berries from the tree in front of the Deep Springs faculty duplex; they are the size of peppercorns and very fragrant. Taste the cabbage when you're cutting it; if it's not sweet, use the half-teaspoon of sugar.

½ small green cabbage

¼ teaspoon juniper berries

pinch of salt, plus more as needed

1 tablespoon water

2 tablespoons butter

½ teaspoon sugar, if cabbage isn't sweet

1 tablespoon dry white wine

freshly ground black pepper

Cut the core from the cabbage, and cut the leaves into bite-size strips. In a small bowl, crush the juniper berries well with a pinch of salt. Add the tablespoon of water. In a medium saucepan over medium heat, melt 1 tablespoon of the butter with the juniper-water mixture. When the water boils, add the cabbage, the sugar, if using, and the wine. Cook the cabbage, stirring frequently, until tender, 6 to 8 minutes. Stir in the remaining tablespoon of butter, and add salt and pepper to taste.

Honey-Glazed Rainbow Carrots

serves 4 to 6

Purple carrots could scarcely have been imagined in American supermarkets decades ago. When I was a student at Deep Springs, husband-and-wife team Rex and Susan Mongold farmed organic potatoes in the neighboring Fish Lake Valley. Once, a group of us went over to help them harvest potatoes, including the astonishingly pigmented Peruvian purple potatoes, a variety new to all of us. Discussing purple vegetables, Susan said that purple carrots were grown in Turkey, but she knew no one who could procure the seed. After that, I started seeing purple potatoes in markets, then many years later, purple carrots began to emerge. Now carrots are readily available in multicolored "rainbow" bunches—purple, orange, yellow, and white. Someone must have finally gotten seed from Turkey.

1 pound multicolored "rainbow" carrots

salt

1½ tablespoons honey

coarse black pepper

Peel the carrots, trim the ends, and cut them into small bite-size pieces on the diagonal, rotating the carrot a bit each time you cut, producing uniform, attractive, jewel-like chunks. Melt the butter over medium heat in a wide skillet. When it is bubbling, throw in the carrots with a good sprinkling of salt and cook them, tossing frequently, until they are cooked on the outside but still raw on the inside, about 2 minutes. Raise the heat to medium-high and add the honey, tossing the carrots to coat. Cook quickly, tossing frequently, until the liquid in the pan reduces to a syrup and a few of the carrots have lightly caramelized, about 10 minutes. Sprinkle the carrots lightly with coarsely ground pepper. If necessary, these may be held briefly in a warm oven.

ITALIAN TZIMMES

One of the traditional dishes served at a Jewish Passover dinner, or seder, *tzimmes* usually consists of a sweet vegetable, such as carrots or sweet potatoes, with dried fruit and spices. In Yiddish, tzimmes means "mess." I found this particular combination in an Italian-Jewish cookbook. Plump ¼ cup golden raisins in hot chicken stock or water, and lightly toast ¼ cup pine nuts (see page 176). Following the preceding Honey-Glazed Carrots recipe, add ¼ teaspoon ground cinnamon to the pan when adding the honey, and sprinkle the raisins and pine nuts over the finished dish just before serving. This was good with lemon-and-rosemary roast lamb at a seder I hosted at my house one year at Deep Springs. We used pine nuts we had harvested the previous fall up in the White Mountains.

Carrot Soup with Ginger

serves 4

Found on the menus of socially progressive cafés, this simple soup is a modern classic. This version ends up thick, with a clean, subtle ginger flavor. For a richer, more elegant soup, dress it up with ½ cup of heavy cream at the end. Or for an entirely different effect, use half a can of coconut milk. If your carrots are ordinary, you may slip a small red bell pepper (seeded and chopped) in with the carrots—it will perk up their flavor without announcing its own presence. Similarly, a teaspoon or two of curry powder (see page 102) harmonizes well, added at the same time as the carrots. But if you have super-fresh, sweet carrots, these amendments are unnecessary.

2½ pounds sweet, crisp, tender carrots

about 2 tablespoons butter

1 large yellow onion, cut into medium dice

4 cloves garlic, minced

2-inch piece of fresh ginger, peeled and finely chopped

about 1 teaspoon salt

black pepper

Peel the carrots and cut on the diagonal into even ½-inch slices. In a large, heavy pot with a well-fitting lid, melt a tablespoon of the butter over a medium-high flame. Throw in the onion, garlic, and ginger with ¼ teaspoon of the salt, and stew, stirring frequently but keeping the pot covered between stirrings, until the onion is almost tender, about 5 minutes. The vegetables shouldn't brown—reduce the flame if necessary. Add the carrots with another ¼ teaspoon of salt and stew, stirring frequently, for about 5 more minutes. Add enough cold water to cover the carrots by 1 inch, and add another ½ teaspoon salt. Bring to a boil, and simmer gently until the carrots are completely soft, about 15 minutes.

Purée the soup in batches in a blender, adding a small pat of cold butter to each batch while blending. Be careful when blending hot liquids: fill the blender jar only half full, hold the lid in place with a kitchen towel, and start the blender on lower speeds. Pass the soup through a screen sieve using the bottom of a ladle to press on the solids. Discard any stringy material left in the sieve. Thin the soup with water, if necessary. Taste for salt—it will probably need a pinch more. Reheat gently, and garnish each bowl with a light twist of black pepper.

Cauliflower

A cool-weather vegetable, cauliflower has its own particular savor, more delicate yet somehow meatier than broccoli or other cruciferous vegetables. Cauliflower may be "steam-sautéed" like broccoli (see page 123); however, it tastes especially good when allowed to brown slightly. Rinse a large head of cauliflower thoroughly and drain, then halve lengthwise. Cut off all dark or blemished leaves, and trim any brown spots. Include any unblemished pale green leaves, and the tender core as well. Cut the cauliflower into uniform, bite-sized pieces.

For buttery *sautéed cauliflower*, melt a tablespoon of butter in a large skillet over a medium-high flame. When it sizzles, add about 2 cups of cut cauliflower with a big pinch of salt. Toss to coat, and sauté for about 5 minutes, tossing occasionally, allowing the cauliflower to brown a little. Check the doneness by tasting a piece. Very freshly picked cauliflower will cook more quickly. I like it cooked until it has just lost its crunch but is not mushy. Add freshly ground pepper, for which cauliflower has a particular affinity. Transfer to a serving dish, wipe out the skillet, and repeat with more butter and the remaining cauliflower.

For *broiled cauliflower*, toss cut cauliflower with a little olive oil, salt, and pepper. Arrange on a baking sheet so the pieces are not too crowded, and stick under a hot broiler for 8 to 10 minutes, or until the cauliflower is tender, and its edges are beginning to deliciously blacken here and there.

Whole roasted cauliflower makes an especially dramatic presentation. Heat a cast-iron skillet in a 350°F oven. Leaving the cauliflower whole, rub it with olive oil and sprinkle lightly with salt. Place it in the hot skillet and put the skillet in the oven. Raise the heat to 375°F, and roast the cauliflower, basting once or twice with the juices that collect on the bottom of the skillet, until it is golden brown and tender, about 1 to 1½ hours. Grind pepper over the hot cauliflower. Serve whole, carving the cauliflower at the table.

Mashed Cauliflower

serves 4 to 6

This is like mashed potatoes, only made with cauliflower.

1 medium cauliflower (about 1¾ pounds)

¼ cup heavy (whipping) **cream** (or half-and-half, or sour cream)**, warmed**

1 tablespoon butter

salt and freshly ground black pepper

Cut the cauliflower in half, and boil both halves in a large saucepan in lightly salted water until quite soft, 12 to 15 minutes (poked with a knife, it should offer no resistance). Drain well. Gently mash the cauliflower to a purée with a potato masher, adding the cream and butter. If the mixture isn't as smooth as you'd like, purée a portion of it in a blender or food processor, then fold this purée back into the remainder of the cauliflower. Add salt and, of course, freshly ground black pepper to taste.

Chayote

serves 4 to 6

Chayote, known as *mirliton* in southern Louisiana, and by many other names around the world, is a hardy member of the Curcurbitaceae family that includes gourds, cucumbers and squash. Often sold in Latin American markets, it grows like a weed in warm climates. Here is a simple recipe for chayote cooked Italian-style, with olive oil, garlic, and hot red pepper flakes.

2 chayotes *(about 5 ounces each)*

1½ tablespoons olive oil

2 or 3 cloves garlic, crushed fine

½ teaspoon salt, plus a pinch

2 or 3 pinches of hot red pepper flakes

Peel the chayotes carefully—they exude a unique, slippery liquid that makes them hard to hold onto. Use a towel if necessary. Cut into medium dice. If the seed within offers little resistance to your knife, it is tender and need not be removed—just cut right through it. If it feels tough, cut it out. Heat the olive oil in a medium saucepan over medium-high heat, add the garlic and ½ teaspoon salt, and cook, stirring rapidly, just until the garlic turns opaque—do not let it brown. Add the chayote with the pepper flakes and the pinch of salt, reduce the heat to medium, and cook, covered, stirring frequently, until the chayote is tender, 6 to 8 minutes.

Corn on the Cob

Fresh corn on the cob is a summer ritual dear to the heart of many an American. Is there a point to all that fuss about freshness? Yes, when the corn in question is any of the old heirloom varieties, such as Golden Bantam or Silver Queen. The sugars support a rich, milky corn flavor, but you must cook the corn very soon after it is picked, before the sugars turn to starch.

My grandmother always said you should bring your big pot of water to a boil and then, and only then, send "your fastest boy" out to the cornfield and have him pick the corn and "shuck it as he runs back to the kitchen." I'm not sure who my grandmother's "fastest boy" was, as she had three daughters.

In recent decades, "supersweet" varieties of corn have emerged, and now almost nobody grows anything else. Though these varieties are indeed sweet and stay sweet through prolonged storage, their flavor is not as rich and nuanced as the old varieties. If your corn isn't as sweet as you'd like, add a bit of sugar to the boiling water.

Like asparagus and tomatoes, corn is quite particular to its season. Eat lots of corn in the summer, but don't be tempted by corn your supermarket offers in the colder months, when you know it grew halfway around the world. Just wait until next summer—the corn will taste all the sweeter for your patience.

Get as many ears of corn as will fit in your largest pot—it's fine if they are crowded. Peel back the husks and remove the silks. Rub off any excess silk with a damp kitchen towel. Fold the husks back over the kernels. The husks not only intensify the corn flavor and keep the corn hot before serving, they provide a handle by which to hold the ear.

Fill your largest pot about half full with water. Don't add salt; it will toughen the corn. Bring to a boil, and plunge in the corn. Let the water return to a boil, then boil for 3 to 4 minutes. Drain and serve. As much as I like butter and salt, I love corn unadorned. However, fresh lime juice, salt, and powdered chile is delicious on corn, as you will discover on any trip to Mexico. Sometimes, remembering those flavors, I make the following butter.

JALAPEÑO-LIME BUTTER

Mix in a bowl the finely grated zest and juice of a lime, a stick of room-temperature butter, a minced jalapeño (seeds and light-colored pith removed if you want it mild), and ¼ teaspoon each salt and pepper. Keep stirring—the butter and lime juice will eventually emulsify. Serve with hot corn on the cob.

Sautéed Corn

serves 4 to 6

Corn sweetens any plate; this sauté goes well with meat, seafood, or cheese dishes and is easy company with many other vegetables. It may even induce people to eat kale and other greens (see page 133).

To vary this simple recipe, throw in some Jalapeño-Lime Butter (recipe above) or a little cooked, crumbled bacon. Or pep things up with a handful of chopped Roasted Red Peppers (page 140) and a pinch of cayenne to further the red pepper flavor. For elegant *creamed corn*, add ½ cup heavy cream to the pan along with the corn. Cook until the cream is reduced somewhat and is coating the corn.

6 ears fresh sweet corn

3 tablespoons butter

1 small onion, finely diced

¼ teaspoon salt, plus more to taste

freshly ground black pepper

Shuck the corn and rub the silks off with a damp kitchen towel. Using a chef's knife, cut the kernels off the corn. Cut away from you onto a large cutting board. Once the kernels are cut off, scrape the bare cobs with the back of the knife to extract all the germ and milk.

Melt the butter in a wide skillet over medium-high heat. When it sizzles and foams, throw in the onion and ¼ teaspoon salt. Sauté the onion for about a minute, stirring and tossing frequently, until it is mostly transparent. Do not let the onion brown—remove the pan from the heat for a moment if necessary. Throw in the corn kernels with all their liquid and sauté, keeping everything moving. After a minute or two, reduce the heat to medium and continue to cook for about 5 minutes, or until the onion is tender and the corn kernels are cooked but still a little crisp. Season with pepper to taste and additional salt, if necessary. Serve immediately.

Catherine's Corn Soup

serves about 6

The pure essence of corn is realized in this smooth, exquisite soup. It always reminds me of Catherine Brandel, one of the best chefs I've ever known—she cooked at Chez Panisse for many years. She always pointed out what a laborious soup it is to make, like many worthwhile things. To better preserve the sweetness of the corn, the soup is only salted at the very end. It is also good chilled.

12 large ears fresh, sweet summer corn

about 6 tablespoons butter

1 large onion, diced

salt

freshly ground black pepper

GARNISH (CHOOSE ONE)

1 tablespoon chopped basil or cilantro sprinkled over each bowl

some Jalapeño-Lime Butter *(page 127)*

chopped Roasted Red Peppers *(page 140)*

a spoonful of Green Chile Relish *(page 251)*

a swirl of either the New Mexico Red or Green Chile Sauces *(page 250 or 251)*

Shuck the corn, and rub the silks off with a kitchen towel. Using a chef's knife, carefully cut the kernels off the cobs into a wide bowl. With the back of your knife, scrape all the juice and germ out of the cobs into the bowl with the corn. Put the cobs in a large pot, cover with cool water, and bring to a boil. Reduce the heat to a simmer. Meanwhile, heat 4 tablespoons of the butter in a heavy soup pot over medium-high heat, and throw in the onion with a good pinch of salt. Cook the onion for a few minutes, stirring frequently, until it begins to soften. Stir in the corn with all its accumulated juice and stew for several minutes, stirring frequently, until the corn is thoroughly heated. Pour in enough of the hot corncob water to barely cover the corn kernels. Bring the soup to a boil, reduce the heat, and boil gently for about 5 minutes.

Adding a small pat of cold butter to each batch, purée the soup in batches in a blender. Be careful when blending hot liquids: fill the blender jar only half full, hold the lid in place with a kitchen towel, and start the blender on lower speeds. If you would like a little texture to remain in the soup, purée only about two-thirds of it. Let the blender run for a full minute for each batch. Press the soup through a screen sieve, using the bottom of a ladle and extracting as much liquid as possible. Discard the dry, fibrous material remaining in the sieve. Salt the soup lightly, tasting it carefully, and add freshly ground black pepper to taste. Reheat gently, ladle into warmed bowls, garnish, and serve.

Roasted Eggplant

Always an abundant summer staple, eggplant needs a blast of dry, high heat to taste silky and succulent; I always roast or broil or grill it. In the past, I followed recipes that instructed the cook to salt and drain the eggplant prior to cooking to remove the bitter juices, but I'm not convinced this is necessary, especially with fresh summer eggplant. Rather than entirely peeling eggplant, I "half-peel" it, in alternating, zebra-like strips, so that some peel remains.

Heat the oven to 450°F. Cut a large, half-peeled globe eggplant into 1-inch chunks, and toss with a little olive oil in a large bowl. Exercise judgment when adding oil: eggplant will readily absorb and retain any oil you throw its way, and too much will make the eggplant heavy. Sprinkle with salt and toss again, then arrange the chunks in a single layer on a baking sheet and put in the oven, roasting the eggplant until deep brown and soft throughout, 15 to 20 minutes. Eggplant thus cooked is delicious mashed up with a little fresh garlic, coarsely chopped cilantro, and more olive oil and served as a dip or relish; or tossed with penne or other similar sturdy pasta, spicy tomato sauce, lots of fresh basil, and Parmesan or feta cheese.

One Deep Springs summer, despite the heroic efforts of the student gardeners in battling ferocious winds, dust devils, late frosts, and gophers, a huge crop of eggplant was the only successful harvest. In the Boardinghouse kitchen, as Student Cook, I developed the habit of throwing a couple of whole eggplants and whole unpeeled heads of garlic into whatever simmering meat stock I had on the back stove burner, and letting them cook until soft. The eggplant and garlic gave something to the stock, and

vice versa. I'd drain and quickly peel and mash the eggplant and garlic together with salt, and serve it as a sauce with whatever was for dinner that night. Did I put in olive oil, herbs, and pepper? I hope so, but I don't remember—and though boiled eggplant doesn't sound like something I'd approve of today, I remember it as a light, delicate, flavorful condiment.

Fennel, Celery Root, and Potato Gratin

serves 4 to 6

Fresh fennel bulb, sometimes sold in stores as anise, is best in the cooler months of the year. It is much loved in southern France and Italy, where it is called *fenouil* and *finocchio*, respectively. (Incidentally, *finocchio* is Italian slang for a gay man, and was the name of a famous old San Francisco nightclub where the entertainers were all female impersonators.) Looking vaguely like celery, fennel has fat, pale green bulbs; thin, darker, fibrous stalks; and feathery dill-like fronds. Very fresh fennel has a marvelous faint sweetness and a delicate anise scent. I love fennel raw, shaved paper-thin on a mandoline slicer and tossed with enough lemon juice to keep it from turning brown (see page 167). But cooked fennel has its own particular savor, more subtle and far-reaching than celery. I have never put it in a soup or stew and wished I hadn't. Thick slices of fennel can be brushed with olive oil and grilled like a steak, or browned in butter in a skillet.

Fennel and celery root are, in fact, botanical cousins; the Umbelliferae family gives many cuisines around the world a plethora of highly flavored roots, stalks, leaves, flowers, and seeds: ajwain, angelica, anise seed, caraway seed, carrots, celery, celery root, chervil, cilantro, coriander, cumin, dill, fennel, fennel seed, lovage, parsley, parsley root, parsnip, and many more. This gratin is wonderful with roast lamb. Serve Apple and Candied Orange Pie (page 266) for dessert.

2 pounds yellow or russet potatoes, peeled and cut into bite-sized chunks

1 large celery root, peeled and cut into bite-sized chunks

2¼ teaspoons salt, plus more as needed

1 scant tablespoon olive oil

1 large sweet onion, cut into medium dice

1 large fennel bulb, trimmed, stalks and fronds removed, cut into medium dice

1½ cups heavy (whipping) **cream**

¼ teaspoon freshly ground black pepper, plus a little more

Heat the oven to 400°F. Put the potatoes and celery root in a large pot, and cover with water by ½ inch. Add 2 teaspoons of the salt and bring to a boil. Lower the heat to medium and cook until the vegetables are soft, about 10 minutes; the cut edges of the potato should start to look a little rounded, and it should be quite easy to crush a potato cube with the back of a spoon. Drain well in a colander.

Meanwhile, stew the onion and fennel: heat the olive oil in a small, heavy saucepan over a medium-high flame. Add the onion with a pinch of salt and cook, stirring frequently, for 2 to 3 minutes. The onion should not brown—lower the heat if necessary. Add the fennel with a pinch of salt and cook, covered, stirring occasionally, until the onion and fennel are tender, about 10 minutes. Heat the cream in a small pot on the stove with ¼ teaspoon each salt and black pepper. Butter a large (9-by-13-inch) glass or ceramic baking dish and dump in the drained potatoes and celery root, and the stewed onions and fennel. Toss gently to combine the two mixtures. Pour the heated cream over all, gently pressing the vegetables down into the cream. Bake, uncovered, until brown and bubbly, 30 to 35 minutes. Use a small knife to peer into the center of the gratin: what liquid cream remains (there should be some but not a lot) should be thick. Twist a bit more black pepper on top and let the gratin rest for about 10 minutes in a warm place before serving.

Slovenian Fennel and Potatoes

Cut peeled gold potatoes into uniform large dice, and cover with cold water in a saucepot. Salt the water and bring to a boil. As soon as the water boils, add an equal amount of fennel bulb, trimmed and cut into large dice. Let the potatoes and fennel cook together until the cut edges of the potatoes are beginning to look rounded. The potatoes should be soft, but not falling apart, and the fennel should be tender. Drain the potatoes and fennel briefly in a colander, then transfer to a large bowl. Gently toss with good olive oil, and additional salt, if necessary. The edges of the cooked potatoes will break down a little, and their starch will emulsify the olive oil into a sauce. Serve immediately. In Slovenia, this light and simple dish is served alongside fried fish.

Roasted Garlic

Garlic is one of Deep Springs' most dependable crops. As long as we plant it at the correct time, it seems to thrive in the hot sun, winds, and temperature extremes, and the rapacious gophers and birds leave it alone. Most garlic is harvested in midsummer, staying especially tender and succulent for 2 to 3 months afterward. That's when I am most inclined to roast whole heads of garlic.

Although garlic heads may be roasted whole and naked with no prior treatment, here is a way that maximizes their softness and sweetness. Choose firm, sound heads of garlic. Heat the oven to 350°F. Remove the outer layers of papery skin on the garlic, but leave the cloves intact. Using a paring knife, gently shave the skin from the top ends of the cloves, so just a bit of each clove is exposed. Rub the whole head well with olive oil. Arrange the heads snugly in a baking dish. Take a piece of baking parchment that will fit over the dish, crumple it tightly into a wad, then flatten it out and press it down on top of the garlic. Put a sheet of aluminum foil (shiny side down) over the dish and seal well, crimping the foil around the edges of the dish. The parchment holds in an extra measure of steam and flavor, but if you have no parchment, just use foil. Bake for 30 to 40 minutes, or until the garlic is soft throughout.

After your guests have admired the garlic's beauty and symmetry, advise them to squeeze out the purée from the bottom, as they would a tube of toothpaste. Cut thick slices of warm bread (or toasted or grilled bread), drizzle with olive oil, then squeeze and spread the roasted garlic purée over the bread. Sprinkle with salt. This is an excellent hors d'oeuvre with fresh soft goat cheese, or is a beautiful accompaniment to Roast Chicken (page 205).

Garlic Soup

serves 2

This very old European peasant dish is a good use for any day-old bread that's not too sweet; well-textured, chewy, artisan-style bread, such as a baguette, is ideal. Any of the savory bread recipes in this book (see the chapter beginning on page 74) work well, too.

3 cups water

½ teaspoon salt

pinch of dried sage, thyme, or rosemary

2 thick slices good bread

1 large clove garlic, halved

extra-virgin olive oil

grated Parmesan cheese

freshly ground black pepper

Bring the water to a boil in a medium saucepan with the salt and a pinch of the dried herb of your choice. Toast the bread until the surface is golden brown. Rub the raw garlic into the rough toasted surfaces of the bread. Put the toast in each of 2 wide soup bowls, and drizzle with extra-virgin olive oil. Pour the boiling-hot herb broth over the bread. Grate Parmesan over the top, and twist that peppermill. A poached egg (page 60) is very good atop the toasted bread. You can use chicken stock or vegetable stock instead of water, and you can also fortify the soup with a handful of cooked Greens (following recipe).

Greens

serves 2 to 4

By "greens" I mean cooked leafy greens: kale, chard, spinach, collards…. Many Americans, other than Southerners, are still unfamiliar with the idea of eating cooked greens (besides spinach) as a vegetable, but greens are powerfully nutritious and equally delicious if grown and cooked with care. Although they may be grown year-round, greens are best when they have undergone a frost; cold temperatures stimulate the plant to produce sugars you can taste. In Deep Springs' garden, the greens remain for some time, still producing, long after the tomatoes and other summer crops have been turned under. Once you acquire a taste for greens, you will find that your body craves them when you need an extra boost of vitamins and minerals in cold weather.

Greens are easy to incorporate into all kinds of foods, such as pasta, rice, soups, stir-fries, omelets, and scrambled eggs. Cooking times for greens depend on three factors: the variety, the maturity of the plant, and how the leaves are cut. Mature, large-leaved kale and collard greens will withstand lengthy cooking if cut into large pieces. But those same leaves will become tender much more quickly if cut into fine ribbons first. Tender greens such as spinach are almost always best just wilted or quickly sautéed.

Most cooking greens, such as kale, collards, arugula, mustard greens, and many Asian greens, including choi sum, bok choy, and tatsoi, belong to the huge Brassicaceae family, which also includes cabbage, broccoli, and cauliflower. A second significant greens family includes spinach, chard, and beet tops. Finally, certain lettuces and chicories (radicchio, endive, and escarole), though most familiar raw in salads, are also very good cooked. My favorite accompaniment to greens is hot, creamy Polenta (page 242) and a pork chop.

Here is a method that, in my experience, works for all greens. It's especially suited to the greens varieties listed here, but other types work, too:

¾ to 1 pound *(1 large bunch)* **leafy cooking greens, such as chard, collards, kale, mustard, turnip, or beet greens**

2 tablespoons olive oil or bacon fat

½ small onion, finely diced *(extra-fine if the greens will not need much cooking time)*

about ½ teaspoon salt

1 or more cloves garlic, crushed *(optional; or use instead of onion)*

black pepper

a few drops fresh lemon juice or red wine vinegar

Separate the leaves of the greens. Immerse the leaves in a clean basin of cool water and swirl gently to thoroughly rinse off dirt. Lift the greens out of the water and heap them into a colander to drain. If your basin is small and the greens were crowded in it, you may have to repeat this process a couple of times until the water is clear. (My grandmother always washed her spinach three times.) Let the greens drain in the colander. If you are using collards, chard, or kale, gently strip the leafy parts off the stems. To easily do this, form an "O" shape with your thumb and forefinger and pull the stem of the leaf through the O, tearing the leaves from the stems. Cut or tear the leaves into bite-size pieces. Using a knife, slice a handful of the most tender stems paper-thin and combine with the leaves—this way, the stems will cook at the same rate as the leaves.

Heat the olive oil in a wide, heavy skillet over medium heat until it shimmers. Throw in the onion with a pinch of salt and sauté quickly until the onion begins to soften, 3 to 4 minutes. Stir in the garlic, if you opt for it, with another pinch of salt. Add the greens—the water still clinging to them will create steam and aid in the cooking. Add ¼ teaspoon salt and stir until the greens are coated with oil and beginning to wilt. A splash of water may be necessary if the pan seems hot and the greens seem dry—greens should not brown. Continue to cook, stirring frequently, until the greens are tender—this could take anywhere from a few seconds for tender young spinach to 15 minutes for cabbage or kale—to check the doneness, taste a piece. Do not cover the pan if you are cooking spinach, chard, or beet greens, as certain compounds in these vegetables, once volatilized, may precipitate back into the pan and dull the color of the greens to an uninspiring olive drab. Add more salt, if necessary, and black pepper to taste. Most varieties of greens benefit from a touch of acidity—vinegar or lemon juice.

Sautéed Kale and Corn

serves 4 to 6

This sauté is a great way to get people to eat their kale. Any variety may be used: black kale (also known as lacinato, Italian, or dino kale), green curly kale, or Red Russian kale.

1 tablespoon olive oil

½ small yellow onion, cut into medium dice

1 fat clove garlic, crushed

about ¼ teaspoon salt

1 large bunch kale, washed, stemmed, and cut into bite-sized pieces

kernels cut from 2 ears fresh sweet corn

¼ teaspoon hot red pepper flakes

black pepper

Heat the olive oil over a medium flame in a large, heavy pot. Add the onions and garlic with a little salt, and sauté until the onion is tender, about 5 minutes. Don't let the onion brown. Raise the heat to medium-high and add the kale in two or three batches, each with a pinch of salt, letting each batch wilt before adding another. Add a splash of water if the pan seems too dry—the kale shouldn't brown. When the kale is tender, add the corn, red pepper flakes, additional salt, and black pepper to taste. Heat to bubbling and serve.

Leek Gratin

serves 4 to 6

Leeks, highly prized by the French for their haunting flavor and tonic health benefits, take center stage in this rich, simple dish. When I cooked at Liberty Café in San Francisco following my stint at Deep Springs, this is one of the dishes I first learned from chef Cynthia Shea. I still make it a couple of times each winter.

2 or 3 large leeks, enough to make 5 cups diced leeks

¾ cup heavy (whipping) **cream**

1 tablespoon Dijon mustard

¼ teaspoon salt

Heat the oven to 350°F. Tear off the outer dark green leaves of the leeks. Using a small, sharp knife, "whittle" away the dark green parts from the leeks, leaving only the white and pale green parts. Cut the leeks in half lengthwise, and rinse each half very well under cool running water, rinsing between all the layers to remove all dirt. Drain well, and cut the leeks into large dice. In a large bowl, toss the leeks, cream, mustard, and salt together thoroughly. Scrape leeks and all liquid into a buttered 9-by-13-inch baking dish, or ceramic baking dish of similar capacity, spreading the leek mixture evenly in the dish. Cover tightly with foil, and bake in the center of the oven for about 40 minutes. Remove the foil, and bake on the top rack of the oven about 20 minutes more, until the top surface of the leeks is golden brown. Let the gratin rest a moment, then serve portions with a wide metal server—make sure each serving has plenty of the delicious browned top.

Leek and Vegetable Purée Soup

serves 4 to 6

Leeks really come into their own in soups. This recipe could be considered a template for using all manner of cool-weather vegetables. A bowl of thick, silky puréed soup, using leeks as the backbone, goes a long way to restore one's vitality in the long winter months. Cauliflower, winter squash, fennel bulb, potato, or celery root may all be used in place of, or in addition to, the turnips.

2 large leeks

about 3 tablespoons butter

½ medium onion, cut into medium dice

about 1 teaspoon salt

4 to 5 medium turnips or 1 large rutabaga (about 1½ pounds)**, peeled and cut into medium dice**

2 carrots, peeled and cut into medium dice

black pepper

pinch of cayenne pepper

½ teaspoon balsamic vinegar or fresh lemon juice, if necessary

CHAPTER 7: HOT VEGETABLES & VEGETABLE SOUPS

First, clean the leeks: cut off any brown or withered parts, and remove the outermost layer. With a knife, carefully "whittle" off the dark green tops of the leek using an upward motion, leaving the white and pale green parts intact. The trimmed leek will be pointed like a pencil. Reserve the dark green tops. Cut the dirty root end off the leek, then cut the leek in half lengthwise. Under cold running water, thoroughly rinse each layer of the leek—dirt and mud might lurk between the layers. Also rinse the reserved dark green tops. Cut the white and pale green leek bottoms into medium dice. Chop the dark green leek tops coarsely, put in a small saucepan, and cover with water. Bring to a boil to make a simple stock.

Meanwhile, in a large, heavy soup pot over a medium-high flame, melt 1½ tablespoons of the butter. When it is bubbling, throw in the diced leeks and onion with a pinch of salt. Cook, stirring frequently, for about 2 minutes, then add the turnips and carrots with another pinch of salt. Cook all the vegetables, stirring frequently, until they are slightly softened. Pour the leek stock through a strainer over the vegetables, then add enough extra water to just barely cover the vegetables. Bring the soup to a boil, then reduce to a simmer. Let simmer until all the vegetables are tender, about 10 minutes. Using a blender, purée the soup in batches, adding a small pat of butter to each batch. Be careful when blending hot liquids: fill the blender jar only half full, hold the lid in place with a kitchen towel, and start the blender on lower speeds. Purée until completely smooth and silky. Return the soup to the pot and add salt to taste. Start with ½ teaspoon; it might need more. Carefully add a few twists of black pepper and a pinch of cayenne. If the soup tastes quite sweet and needs a little oomph, add a tiny amount—about ½ teaspoon—balsamic vinegar or lemon juice to balance. Reheat gently, and serve.

When a *brothy vegetable soup*—not a purée, but a soup with chunks of vegetables—is called for, simply follow the recipe above, taking care to cut the vegetables into evenly sized medium dice, and skip the puréeing step. Such a soup may be enriched with chopped cooked Greens (page 132), with Handmade Egg Noodles (page 231), or with Cornmeal-Egg Soup Dumplings (page 238). While this leek-based recipe is most appropriate in the cooler months of the year, Soupe au Pistou (page 151) is a delicious brothy soup made of warm-weather vegetables.

Irish Leek and Oat Soup

serves 4 to 6

This soup is pure comfort food—it's like something your grandmother might have made, even if she didn't. The oats thicken the soup slightly, and add their own sweetness. It's closely based on a recipe in Colman Andrews' marvelous cookbook *The Country Cooking of Ireland*. You could substitute nutmeg for the mace, but really, it's worth picking up a small jar of mace—its heady perfume is excellent here, and besides, you need it to make this book's Doughnuts and Funnel Cakes recipes (pages 72 and 73).

4 medium leeks, to yield about 6 cups sliced

3 tablespoons butter

¼ teaspoon salt, plus more to taste

4 cups chicken stock

1 pint *(2 cups)* **whole milk**

½ cup steel-cut Irish oatmeal, uncooked

½ teaspoon ground mace

freshly ground black pepper to taste

Tear off the outer dark green leaves of the leeks. Using a small, sharp knife, "whittle" away the dark green parts from all the leeks, leaving only the white and pale green parts. Cut the leeks in half lengthwise, and rinse each half very well under cool running water, rinsing between all the layers to remove all dirt. Drain the leeks and slice them thinly, crossways, with a sharp knife.

In a heavy soup pot, melt the butter over medium-high heat. When it bubbles, throw in the leeks with ¼ teaspoon salt. Cook the leeks, stirring often, until they are wilted. Reduce the flame and continue cooking, stirring often, until the leeks are soft, about 10 minutes. Add the stock, raise the flame, and bring to a boil. Slowly add the oatmeal, stirring all the while, then stir in the mace. Turn down the heat to low, and let the soup simmer for about 20 minutes, stirring frequently. Slowly stir a cupful of the hot soup into the milk, to temper it, then stir the tempered milk into the soup. Bring the soup back to a simmer, and let simmer 10 minutes more. Add the pepper. Taste, adding salt or more pepper if necessary.

Sautéed Mushrooms

serves 2 to 3

Mushrooms, it must always be remembered, are a life form as different from plants as you and I are. Thanks to the glutamic acid within their cells, mushrooms enhance the flavors of the foods they accompany. The following basic technique works for virtually all fresh mushrooms. *If you are consuming fresh wild mushrooms, be certain of the expertise of whoever picked them.*

Sautéed mushrooms are a source of deep, satisfying flavor in many dishes. When fresh, cultivated white or brown mushrooms look clean, with closed gills. *Portobello* mushrooms are simply brown mushrooms grown large—they may be diced and used in this recipe. If you are using fresh *shiitake* mushrooms, completely pull off the tough stem of each mushroom before slicing (reserve the stems to enrich chicken or vegetable stock). Unless they are very dirty, don't rinse mushrooms in water: they will absorb a lot of the water, making them quite difficult to brown in the pan, and will end up soggy. To slice white or brown mushrooms evenly, first cut them in half lengthwise, then arrange the two halves so you can slice them lengthwise at the same time.

4 ounces white, brown, or shiitake mushrooms

2 teaspoons butter

1 or 2 generous pinches salt

freshly ground black pepper

Trim off and discard all but ⅛ inch of the mushroom stems (for shiitakes, discard the stems entirely), then wipe clean, halve, and slice the mushroom caps thickly. You should have about 2 cups. Melt the butter in a wide skillet over a high flame. When it just begins to brown, throw in the mushrooms with 1 or 2 generous pinches of salt (mushrooms need a good amount of salt). Toss to coat with butter, then let the mushrooms cook, undisturbed, for several seconds. Continue sautéing the mushrooms, stirring and tossing every 20 seconds or so, letting them brown appetizingly. Taste—they are usually cooked after 1 to 2 minutes. Twist a little black pepper over them.

The Italians add chopped garlic and parsley at the end and cook for a moment more. Thyme is also a very good mushroom herb. For a great *mushroom steak sauce*, add a splash of red wine to the skillet once the mushrooms are cooked, let it reduce for a moment or two until syrupy, swirl in another pat of butter, then pour both mushrooms and sauce over your cooked steak. Or use white wine in the sauce, and serve with fish or chicken.

Nettle Broth

A green forest of stinging nettles grows each summer under the leaky hilltop water tower behind the mechanic's shop at Deep Springs. Climb the steep rocky slope up to the water tower. Using thick leather gloves or tongs and your pocket knife, grab and lop off a large bunch of nettle tops and take them down to the kitchen. Keeping the gloves on, rinse the nettles, chop them coarsely, and put them in a pot. Now take off the gloves. Cover the nettles with water and add a peeled, chopped carrot and a peeled, chopped onion. Bring to a boil, reduce the heat, and simmer for about 20 minutes. Cooking deactivates nettles' sting. Add salt to taste and a good drizzle of olive oil. Strain. This makes a deep, powerfully nutritious, surprisingly meaty-tasting, bright green broth. To make it into a more substantial soup, add some gently-cooked leeks and some diced boiled potatoes. Younger, more tender spring nettles may be prepared and eaten like any tender green: quickly cooked in olive oil or butter and served as a vegetable, or added to brothy soups, pasta, risotto, or omelets. The eleventh-century Tibetan ascetic Milarepa lived in a mountain cave for twelve years, eating nothing but nettle broth; his skin and beard were said to be tinted green from this austere but sustaining diet.

Cornmeal-Fried Okra

serves 2

This easy and delicious method will persuade you of okra's worth. After this, okra initiates should try the Gumbo on page 99, then finally the Grilled Okra recipe below. Summer squash is also excellent when cornmeal-fried (see page 145).

about 12 ounces fresh okra *(about 4 cups sliced)*

about 2 tablespoons cornmeal

2 tablespoons vegetable oil and/or bacon fat

salt and freshly ground black pepper

Rinse the okra, cut the caps and tips off, and slice crosswise, about ¼ inch thick. Pay attention as you cut—if a particular okra pod seems tougher under the knife than the rest, throw it out. (You can't detect the tough ones visually.) Toss the okra in a bowl with the cornmeal. Heat the oil or fat in a wide, heavy skillet over medium-high heat and sauté the okra, stirring and tossing gently, until browned and tender, 5 to 7 minutes. Salt and pepper to taste, and serve.

Grilled Okra

Select firm, fresh, unblemished okra pods, preferably all the same size. Wash the okra, and carefully thread the pods on two parallel metal skewers, creating a sturdy "raft" of okra that is easy to place and flip on the grill. Get your grill nice and hot, and clean and oil the grates. Brush the okra with olive oil, and sprinkle lightly with salt. Grill the okra about 3 or 4 minutes, or until it is lightly browned on one side, then flip and grill the other side until lightly browned. Put the okra on a plate, pull out the skewers, season lightly with additional salt and freshly-ground pepper, and serve hot.

Sweet Onions Cooked in Cream

serves 3 to 4

The onions undergo two distinct cooking processes in this very simple recipe: first, in the liquid cream, the onions simmer and soften. But as the cream's water evaporates, only its fat remains, and the onions begin to fry.

¼ cup heavy *(whipping)* **cream**

3 sweet yellow onions, halved, cored, and thickly sliced lengthwise

salt and freshly ground black pepper

Heat the cream to boiling in a wide skillet over a high flame. Throw in the onions with a couple of pinches of salt and cook, stirring constantly, until the onions wilt and the cream reduces to a thick sauce. Reduce the heat and continue cooking, stirring frequently, letting the onions brown lightly as the liquid evaporates. Add salt and freshly ground pepper to taste.

Red Onion Galette

serves 4 to 6

What is a galette? It's a pie baked freeform on a flat sheet, not in a pie pan. At Deep Springs, we first made these to simultaneously accompany roast beef and serve as a satisfying, meatless main dish for the herbivores. We like them so much that we often serve them as the backbone of a meatless dinner with, for instance, risotto, vegetable sauté, green salad, tomatoes, hard-boiled eggs, warm bread, and ice cream for dessert.

Leftover galette is delicious, even cold. This recipe is a little more elaborate than many; to streamline the process, you may make the various elements—the dough for the crust, the onions, and the cheese filling—on the first day, then assemble and bake the galette the next day. The amount of cheese may seem small, but it plays a supporting role, bolstering and deepening the rich flavor of the caramelized onion. You can also try other kinds of soft fresh cheese, including goat cheese.

Sometimes I make two smaller pies rather than one large one. These take a little less time to bake and may be cut into hors d'oeuvre–sized wedges, whereas a piece of the large pie is most appropriately served on a plate with a fork.

CRUST

1 cup all-purpose flour

¼ cup whole-wheat flour

3 tablespoons wheat germ

scant ½ teaspoon salt

6 tablespoons cold butter

about ¼ cup cold apple juice, orange juice, or milk

ONION FILLING

1½ tablespoons olive oil

3 large red onions, thinly sliced (about 1¾ pounds; about 8 cups sliced)

¾ teaspoon salt, plus more as needed

¼ teaspoon brown sugar

½ teaspoon red wine vinegar

1 teaspoon balsamic vinegar

freshly ground black pepper

CHEESE FILLING

4 ounces cream cheese

pinch of salt

pinch of ground nutmeg

freshly ground black pepper

1 egg, beaten

If you are unfamiliar with making piecrust, see page 263. Mix both kinds of flour, wheat germ, and salt in a medium mixing bowl. Cut the butter into small pieces, and toss with the flour. Using your hands (or a pastry blender), rapidly work the butter into the flour, breaking up the pieces of butter, until the flour is somewhat moistened and there are pea-sized pieces of butter in the mixture. Stir in the cold juice; the mixture should cohere. Squeeze the dough into a ball, and wrap well with plastic wrap. Flatten the wrapped dough into a disc, and refrigerate for 1 to 2 hours, or overnight.

To cook the onions, first heat the olive oil in a wide, heavy skillet over medium-high heat. Pile in the onions with ¾ teaspoon salt and cook, turning and stirring as the onions cook down. When a browned, caramelized residue, called fond, forms in the pan, take the pan off the heat for a moment and allow the fond to dissolve, stirring it into the onions; this careful caramelization is the key to full, sweet flavor. Return to the heat, let another fond form, then stir it into the onions. Repeat a few times. Do not let the mixture burn—watch carefully, stirring often. Cook until the onions are completely tender, darkened in color, and sweet, 30 to 40 minutes. Season the onions with the brown sugar, red wine vinegar, balsamic vinegar, a pinch or two of additional salt, and freshly ground pepper to taste. Let cool in the pan.

To make the cheese filling, in a medium bowl, gently work the cream cheese with the salt, nutmeg, and pepper until smooth. Gradually add half the egg to the cheese, blending until smooth. Reserve the rest of the egg.

When you are ready to assemble and bake the galette, heat the oven to 375°F. On a floured surface with a flour-dusted rolling pin, roll the dough out into a circle. Continue rolling out the dough until it is about 14 inches in diameter, leaving the center somewhat thick, the edges thinner. For a neat final appearance, trim any rough outer edges of the circle. Place the rolled-out crust on a baking sheet lightly dusted with flour, and lightly brush the inner surface of the dough with some of the reserved egg. Spread the cream cheese mixture into a 6- to 7-inch circle in the center of the crust, leaving about 3 inches of dough around the edge. Spread the onions evenly atop the cream cheese. Fold the crust partway over the filling in 6 even folds, tucking the final fold under the first, making a roughly symmetrical, hexagon-shaped galette. A small window of onion filling will show in the center.

Brush the crust on the top of the galette with the remaining egg. Bake, rotating the sheet once or twice, for 40 minutes to an hour. The crust should be a nice golden brown. Before slicing, let the galette cool on the sheet to room temperature or until just warm—it's fragile when hot.

Parsnip Soup with Toasted Almond Olive Oil

serves 4 to 6

Parsnips, a winter crop, have a pronounced banana-like flavor that can be cloying. When chunked and roasted with other root vegetables, they tend to dominate. This elegant, velvety soup, however, showcases all their best qualities. Your guests will be surprised that it contains no cream.

TOPPING

¼ cup whole almonds, lightly toasted *(see page 176)* and coarsely chopped

3 tablespoons extra-virgin olive oil

pinch each of salt and black pepper

SOUP

about 3 tablespoons butter

5 large parsnips, peeled and cut into 1-inch chunks *(about 2 pounds)*

1 medium yellow onion, cut into medium dice

3 cloves garlic, crushed

¾ teaspoon salt, plus more as needed

5 to 6 cups vegetable stock

black pepper

To make the topping, in a small bowl stir the toasted, chopped nuts into the 3 tablespoons olive oil with a pinch of salt and pepper.

To make the soup, in a heavy soup pot, melt 1½ tablespoons of the butter over medium-high heat. When it sizzles, throw in the parsnips, onion, and garlic with ¾ teaspoon salt. Stew the vegetables, stirring frequently, until they are beginning to soften, 7 to 8 minutes. Add the stock and bring to a simmer. Simmer until the parsnips are completely soft, about 15 minutes. Purée the soup in batches in a blender, adding a pat of cold butter to each batch as it blends. Be careful when blending hot liquids: fill the blender jar only half full, hold the lid in place with a kitchen towel, and start the blender on lower speeds. Blend until completely smooth. Carefully season the soup to taste with salt and pepper. Top each bowl of soup with a spoonful of toasted almond olive oil.

Boiled Peanuts

serves 3 to 4

An Asian farmer at my local market sells fresh raw peanuts in the shell in summer and early fall—they are still moist inside, not dry. I love to bring a bag home and boil them in brine for an excellent snack popular in the deep South and Hawaii, too. Although "boiled" is a thoroughly unfashionable food descriptor, these peanuts are a revelation to anyone tasting them for the first time—a fresher, more vegetable-y side of the peanut's character comes forth. And the boiling, it is said, drives minerals and other nutrients from the peanut's shell into the nutmeat.

1 pound raw fresh peanuts in the shell

5 cups water

3 tablespoons salt *(heaping if kosher)*

Rinse the peanuts well in cold water. Put peanuts, water, and salt into a heavy saucepan, cover, and bring to a rolling boil. If the peanuts insist on floating on the water's surface, use the lid of a smaller-sized saucepan as a weight to keep them submerged. Reduce the flame slightly, and boil, stirring frequently. Adding fresh boiling water to the pot, if necessary, to maintain the water level, cook the peanuts until the nuts inside the pods are tender. Fresh peanuts, that have not been dried, take very little time, only about 20 minutes. Thoroughly dried peanuts can take much longer, up to several hours, according to some recipes. If prolonged cooking is necessary, put the covered saucepan into a 300°F oven, and check the water level every half hour or so, topping off with additional boiling water as necessary. When the peanuts are tender, remove from the heat, but let the pot sit, stirring occasionally but otherwise keeping the pot covered, until they are just warm. To allow the salt to penetrate all the way to the nutmeat, let the peanuts cool completely in the water. If you like, you can reheat them in the water to serve warm. Drain thoroughly, dump into a bowl, and serve, providing an empty bowl for the shells.

Peanut Soup

serves 3 to 4

This unusual, delicate soup is a specialty of the American South, with hints of Africa and France. If you have a fresh jar of natural peanut butter, before stirring it up, use a little of the oil on top to sauté the vegetables.

- **1 tablespoon peanut oil from the jar of peanut butter, or any vegetable oil**
- **1 medium leek, white and light green parts only** *(see page 133)***, cleaned and cut into medium dice**
- **1 medium carrot, peeled and cut into medium dice**
- **pinch of salt, plus more as needed**
- **4 cups chicken stock**
- **⅔ cup natural peanut butter, well stirred**
- **½ teaspoon honey, or more as needed**
- **½ teaspoon apple cider vinegar, or more as needed**
- **¼ teaspoon Tabasco or other hot sauce, or more as needed**
- **black pepper**

Heat the oil in a large saucepan over a medium flame and sauté the leeks and carrots with a pinch of salt until they are softened, 5 to 6 minutes—don't let the vegetables brown. Add the chicken stock and bring to a boil, letting the soup cook until the leeks are completely soft, about 10 minutes. Whisk in the peanut butter, honey, vinegar, and Tabasco. Blend the soup smooth in a blender. Be careful when blending hot liquids: fill the blender jar only half full, hold the lid in place with a kitchen towel, and start the blender on lower speeds. Return the soup to the pan, reheat gently, and add salt and pepper to taste. The salt added will depend on whether the peanut butter is salted or not, and on the saltiness of the chicken stock. If necessary, judiciously add more honey, vinegar, or Tabasco to balance the flavors.

Minty Peas

These peas make a good accompaniment to springtime grilled meats (especially lamb) or roast beef (page 183). Shell fresh English peas, if it's springtime (or just take a bag of frozen peas out of the freezer), and cook them in a covered pot with a splash of water, a bit of butter, and a mint teabag sitting right on top of the peas. Take out the teabag when you stir the peas, then put it back on top. Cook until the peas are tender. Season with salt and pepper and more butter, if you like. Remove the teabag once it has scented the peas to your liking. For a stronger mint flavor, tear open the teabag and stir the dried mint into the peas.

Snap Peas

These springtime treats have a sweet, edible pod. Just rinse a handful in cool water and then pinch the tough ends off, pulling away any tough strings along the edges of the pod. Cut each pea in half on the diagonal, so the pieces look like little boats. For each big handful of snap peas, put a scant teaspoon of butter, a tablespoon of water, and a pinch of salt in a small covered skillet or omelet pan. Set the pan over high heat. When the butter is melted and the water is bubbling, throw in the peas, tossing to coat. Cook quickly, tossing a few times but otherwise keeping the pan covered, for about 45 seconds, or just until the peas are steaming hot and have lost their raw flavor. Larger, late-season snap peas may require 2 to 3 minutes. They should be pleasantly crisp-tender—taste to check. Serve immediately.

SPRING PASTA WITH SNAP PEAS AND ASPARAGUS

For a lovely springtime pasta, trim and cut snap peas as described in the master recipe. Cut a handful of asparagus into 2-inch lengths. Cut up a few small spring onions. Cook the onions, peas, and asparagus together as described above, then toss them with a serving of cooked Handmade Egg Noodles (page 231) or penne, medium shells, or other similar-sized pasta, a spoonful of the pasta cooking water, a gob of butter, freshly grated Parmesan, and a few good twists of black pepper. Slide onto a warmed plate and grate more Parmesan over.

Roasted Red Peppers

serves 8 to 12

These peppers enhance many things: you can strew them over pork chops, chicken, or skirt steak, or toss a handful into sautéed sweet corn. Peppers are available in supermarkets all year round, but are most succulent in summer and early fall.

6 large, sound, fleshy red bell peppers, or a combination of colors

1 teaspoon olive oil

¼ teaspoon balsamic vinegar

¼ teaspoon salt

¼ teaspoon black pepper

1 sprig fresh basil

Arming yourself with tongs, roast the peppers directly over the gas flame of your stove, or put them on a baking sheet and roast them close to your oven broiler, or char them over a charcoal fire while the fire is still too hot to cook the meat. Whichever heat source you use, allow the peppers to blacken and char evenly on all sides. Watch carefully—do not let them burn so much that the outer skin turns ashy gray. When the peppers are evenly charred, transfer them to a sealable glass or plastic container. Seal the container and let the peppers sweat for 20 to 30 minutes.

When removing the peppers from the container, be careful not to lose any of the juice that has accumulated. Break open the peppers and allow any juice inside to run into the container. Using your hands, remove the skin from the peppers, as well as the stems and seeds. Do not rinse the peppers in running water—a few bits of charred skin are part of the charm. Sometimes it helps to wipe your hands with paper towels a couple of times during the process. Cut the pepper flesh into strips and put in a bowl. Pour the reserved liquid through a strainer to catch the seeds—pour it over the peppers, if you like your peppers juicy (I do), or reserve for another use. Season the peppers with very small amounts of olive oil and balsamic vinegar, and the salt and pepper. Pick the leaves off a sprig of basil, cut them into fine ribbons (called *chiffonade*) with a sharp knife, and toss with the peppers.

Scalloped Potatoes

serves 6 to 8

Serve this classic right from its baking dish; a glazed ceramic oval casserole, about 1½ quarts in capacity, is ideal. A 9-by-13-inch glass baking dish works well, too.

If you're making scalloped potatoes for a crowd, use multiple baking dishes to achieve the same ratio of volume to surface area as specified in this household-sized recipe. For example, if you multiply the recipe by 6 to serve the Deep Springs community, and you intend to bake it in large "hotel" pans, you'll need to use 3 shallow hotel pans, each pan holding 2 recipes' worth of potatoes. While it might be tempting to bake it all in one deep pan, it would require hours of baking to cook the potatoes through, and even then, the potatoes would have a mushy, steamed quality. Furthermore, there would be a lesser proportion of the golden-brown top, which is much of this recipe's appeal.

2 pounds russet potatoes

1 tablespoon butter

1 cup heavy (whipping) **cream**

¼ cup milk

1¼ teaspoons salt

freshly ground black pepper

Heat the oven to 400°F. Under cool running water, rinse the potatoes well, scrubbing the skins with a clean cloth. Leave on any smooth, light-colored skin. Peel away any rough or blemished spots. (For an especially classic appearance, peel the potatoes completely.) Slice the potatoes in even, $\frac{1}{16}$-inch slices—this is quick work with a mandoline slicer. If slicing by hand, I find it easiest to cut the potatoes in half lengthwise first. Take your time to produce even slices—any thick pieces might still be raw when the rest of the potatoes are done.

Rub the tablespoon of butter all over the inside of your baking dish. In a large bowl, thoroughly toss together the potato slices, cream, milk, salt, and pepper to taste. Separate any stuck-together clumps of potatoes—you want all the potato surfaces to get a coating of cream. Dump the potatoes and all liquid into the baking dish and pat the potatoes down to make an even layer, with no pieces sticking up. Cover the potatoes with aluminum foil (shiny side down), taking care not to let the foil touch the potatoes but making sure the foil is well-crimped around the rim, sealing the dish. Bake for about 40 minutes, or until the potatoes are bubbling around the edges and cooked through. Test by inserting a small knife into the center of the dish—the potatoes should feel completely soft.

Remove the foil and bake for another 10 to 15 minutes, or until the top is golden. Let your scalloped potatoes set for about 10 minutes in a warm place before serving.

VARIATIONS

A well-executed, golden, bubbly dish of scalloped potatoes seasoned with nothing but cream, salt, and pepper could never be considered dull. Sometimes plainly-flavored food is a revelation; your guests will be amazed that anything with so few ingredients could be so delicious. Your skill and technique shine through. Nonetheless, there are infinite possibilities for embellishing scalloped potatoes. Try one or two of the following additions:

- 1 to 2 teaspoons chopped fresh thyme
- 1 teaspoon chopped fresh rosemary
- about 1 cup sliced sautéed onions
- about 1 cup sliced sautéed fennel
- about 1 cup sliced sautéed turnips
- about ¾ cup Sautéed Mushrooms (page 135)
- about ¾ cup grated Gruyère cheese

You may also substitute, for an equal amount of the potatoes, up to 8 ounces of other cool-weather vegetables, thinly sliced: sweet potatoes, butternut or other winter squash, rutabagas, or celery root.

Simple Roasted Potatoes

serves 4 to 6

Potatoes come in myriad shapes, sizes, colors, and degrees of starchiness. For the creamiest mashed potatoes or crispiest fries, russets or other "starchy" varieties are always recommended. For this recipe, red or white "waxy" types give the best results. Yellow potatoes, such as Yukon gold, have a medium level of starch and may be successfully used for any recipe.

1½ pounds red, white, or yellow potatoes
1 teaspoon salt
black pepper
1 tablespoon olive oil
1 teaspoon chopped fresh rosemary *(optional)*

Heat the oven to 450°F. Scrub the potatoes and trim away any blemishes. Cut into 1-inch chunks. In a large bowl, toss the potatoes vigorously with the salt, pepper to taste, and olive oil. Vigorous, thorough tossing is specified so that the oil and salt combine with the cut potatoes' starch to form a thin paste that will coat the potatoes. Scatter on a parchment-lined baking sheet and bake, tossing and redistributing occasionally, for about 30 minutes, until the potatoes are browned and soft. If you like, sprinkle the rosemary over the potatoes, toss, and return to the oven for 2 to 3 minutes more.

ROASTED POTATOES, APPLES, AND ONIONS

This variation is excellent with pork chops. Replace some of the potato in the master recipe above with chunks of tart, firm, flavorful cooking apple. Add a diced onion, too. Omit the rosemary, or not, or use thyme or sage.

ROASTED POTATOES AND FENNEL

These are particularly good with fish, pork, or poultry, and invite a dollop of Aioli (page 253). Omit the rosemary and include 2 large fennel bulbs, trimmed of any brown spots, stalks removed (reserve the fronds), and cut into ½-inch chunks, adding a good extra pinch of salt. Once the potatoes and fennel are tender, toss them with the coarsely chopped feathery inner green fronds of the fennel. Serve immediately.

POTATOES, TOMATOES, AND PESTO

This simple summer dish makes good use of three of the most abundant Deep Springs garden crops: potatoes, tomatoes, and basil. Roast potatoes with olive oil and plenty of salt as described in the master recipe. Cut ripe summer tomatoes into chunks, place in a colander, sprinkle lightly with salt, and let drain, being sure to save the salty tomato liquid for a soup or other recipe. Scatter the drained tomatoes over the hot potatoes. Drizzle pesto (see page 254) lightly over everything, serving extra pesto in a dish on the side. Serve immediately.

Scallion-Buttermilk Potatoes

serves 4 to 6

These are like mashed potatoes, except with chunky potatoes and bits of green onion. ("Scallion" is simply another word for green onion.) The bulk of the liquid must be heated; cold liquid will seize up the potatoes' starch and make for a less creamy texture. Though white pepper is traditional in mashed potatoes so they keep their pristine whiteness, I like black pepper too much not to include it. For a special treat, make Farm Butter (page 79), saving the buttermilk, and use both the butter and the "true" buttermilk in this recipe.

- **2 pounds yellow or russet potatoes, trimmed but left unpeeled, cut into chunks**
- **1 tablespoon butter, plus 1 to 2 more tablespoons for finishing**
- **1 bunch green onions, trimmed, white and green parts thinly sliced on the diagonal**
- **2 big pinches salt, plus more as needed**
- **½ cup half-and-half**
- **½ cup buttermilk, at room temperature**
- **freshly ground black pepper**

Put the potatoes in a large pot with just enough water to cover. Bring to a boil over a high flame. Melt 1 tablespoon butter in a small pan over medium-high heat. Add the green onions with a big pinch of salt, and cook until softened, 1 to 2 minutes. Add the half-and-half and heat until steaming; set aside. The potatoes are done when a chunk yields easily to gentle pressure with the back of a spoon. When they are done, pour off the water completely (this unsalted potato water is excellent for making bread, by the way); add the green onion/half-and-half mixture, buttermilk, 1 to 2 tablespoons additional butter, and salt and pepper to taste. Stir gently; the potatoes will break up somewhat and emulsify the liquid. If the potatoes seem too liquidy, keep mashing until the mixture thickens. Taste for salt and pepper. Transfer to a warmed serving dish, and serve immediately.

Mashed Potatoes

For classic mashed potatoes, use the proportions and methods in the previous recipe, omitting the green onions, and peeling the potatoes. For a perfectly smooth texture, put the potatoes through a ricer or a food mill. If you like a few lumps, mash with a potato masher. Don't whip mashed potatoes for long or the starch could break and the potatoes will be sweaty and gummy. You may boil the potatoes whole—they will take quite a bit longer to cook but will retain, some say, a bit more potato flavor. Waxy potato types, such as red potatoes, do not mash well. You can omit the buttermilk and use all half-and-half, though I love the bit of tang that buttermilk gives. If you are feeling luxurious, use cream in place of the half-and-half or sour cream in place of the buttermilk. Use white pepper if you want a classic appearance. My sister Diana always adds a very small amount of freshly grated nutmeg to mashed potatoes. For a delicious, unusual change of pace, use a hefty shot of fragrant extra-virgin olive oil in place of the butter and some of the liquid.

Roasted Radicchio

This cool-weather dish, perfect with any simple meat, doesn't sound—or look—remotely as good as it tastes. Raw radicchio's ("ra-DEEK-ee-yo") brilliant burgundy color fades to an unfortunate dull brown, but the vegetable's characteristic bitterness softens into melting, savory sweetness under the broiler. A large head of radicchio will serve about three people.

Heat your oven's broiler. Remove any withered leaves from a fat, tight head of radicchio. Trim the discolored surface from the base. Cut the head lengthwise through the base into about 16 wedges. Carefully toss the wedges with a good drizzle of extra-virgin olive oil and a good pinch of salt. Arrange the radicchio wedges in a single layer, flat, on a baking sheet. Put the sheet a couple of inches under the broiler flame and broil for 4 to 5 minutes, or until the radicchio is tender and blackened here and there. Serve immediately.

Jota (Sauerkraut, Sausage, and Bean Soup)

serves 4 to 6

This wintertime soup (pronounced "YO-tah") is traditional in Slovenia, and in the neighboring regions of Istria in Croatia and Friuli in Italy. It is hearty, substantial, and wonderfully healthy from the sauerkraut. Many different versions are made and enjoyed. You may add onions or potatoes if you wish, or chopped parsley at the end, but I prefer this straightforward version. The recipe calls for readily-available pink beans, but cranberry beans, an heirloom Italian variety, are excellent here, if you can find them; pinto beans could be successfully used, too, although they would make the soup browner than is characteristic.

For the sauerkraut, choose a refrigerated type made of nothing but cabbage and salt, that has not been heat-treated. The sauerkraut juice is as important as the cabbage itself. At farmers markets, sometimes you can find artisan-made sauerkraut—this will be excellent. (These vendors often also sell the juice by the shot, as a health tonic.) As for the sausage, it needs to be smoked, like kielbasa, with tender skin. Sausage and sauerkraut of excellent quality, plus beans cooked with care, will yield an extraordinary soup indeed.

1½ cups pink beans *(dry cranberry beans are excellent, if available)*, **picked over and soaked overnight**

1 bay leaf

3 cups fresh sauerkraut in its liquid

2 strips bacon, cut in small strips

4 cloves garlic, well-crushed

about 9 ounces smoked, lightly-spiced sausage *(kielbasa-type)*

Put the beans and their soaking water in a heavy soup pot. If necessary, add sufficient water to cover the beans by 2 inches, and bring to a boil. Skim off any foam that forms on the surface. Add the bay leaf, reduce the flame, and simmer the beans gently until they are soft. (Do not add salt to the beans—the sauerkraut and sausages likely provide all the salt the soup needs.)

Meanwhile, gently squeeze some of the juice out of the sauerkraut, reserving the juice. Chop the sauerkraut coarsely. In a small saucepan over a medium flame, sizzle the bacon until some of its fat has been released. Stir in the garlic and cook for a moment. Add the chopped sauerkraut, plus ½ cup of the reserved kraut juice, and cook until the sauerkraut is heated through. Add 1½ cups of water, and bring to a simmer. When the beans are soft, add the contents of the sauerkraut pan to the beans. Put the sausages in the pot, whole, and bring the soup to a simmer. Simmer for about 20 minutes, or until the sauerkraut is tender. Remove the sausages, cool them slightly, slice them, and return them to the pot. Taste the soup carefully for salt, adding judicious amounts of the reserved sauerkraut juice until the broth tastes balanced, savory, and well-seasoned. Reheat and serve. Delicious the next day, naturally.

Sautéed Spinach

serves 2 to 3

Spinach is easy—it's almost always available in markets, it's easy to cook, it's loved even by finicky eaters, and it's good company to many other foods. This simple sauté can be served as is or tossed into pasta, folded into rice, thrown into soup, strewn over pizza, or stirred into curry. I don't recommend using bags of prewashed baby spinach, especially for this recipe—baby spinach cooks down to a surprisingly minuscule volume, and its flavor is not as well-developed as the more mature bunched spinach specified.

2 bunches fresh spinach

butter or olive oil

small amount of chopped onion or garlic (optional)

salt

freshly ground black pepper

Cut most of the stems from the spinach, and wash the leaves well in a large basin of water, as you would lettuce—spinach tends to be muddy and gritty. Drain the spinach briefly in a colander. Heat a skillet over medium-high heat, and throw in the spinach to wilt it—the water clinging to the leaves will create sufficient steam. Stir the spinach around for about 30 seconds, until it is all wilted. Turn the clump of spinach out onto a plate and let cool for a few minutes. When cool enough to handle, with clean hands, gently squeeze some of the excess water out of the spinach. (Sometimes I save this mineral-rich liquid and drink it as a tonic.) Chop the spinach coarsely. Heat a little butter or olive oil in the skillet over a medium-high flame (you may cook a little chopped onion or garlic in the butter first, if you like). When hot, add the spinach and sauté briefly to concentrate the flavor, just a minute or two. Add salt and pepper to taste and serve immediately.

Butternut Squash Soup with Diced Pear

serves 4 to 6

This cool-weather soup requires going at a big, hard squash with your kitchen knife, but the deeply flavored, velvety result is worth the effort.

TOPPING

1 small, ripe, fragrant pear

3 tablespoons extra-virgin olive oil

pinch each of salt and black pepper

SOUP

1 medium butternut squash *(about 2½ pounds)*

4 cups water

1 large onion, cut into medium dice

¼ teaspoon salt, plus more as needed

about 2 tablespoons butter

1 small carrot, peeled and cut into medium dice

freshly ground black pepper

To make the pear topping, halve the pear and cut out the core and stem. Don't peel it. Patiently cut the pear into small dice. Put it into a small bowl and add the extra-virgin olive oil. Stir in a pinch each of salt and pepper. Set aside while making the soup.

Wash the squash and pop off the stem. Arming yourself with a large chef's knife, cut the bulbous portion off the bottom of the squash. Cut the meaty top section in half, into two big cylindrical pieces. With your knife, carefully peel all 3 sections of the squash, reserving all the peel. Cut the bulbous bottom section in half and scoop out the seeds, reserving them with the peels. Cut the flesh of the squash into 1-inch chunks.

Put the peel and seeds in a small saucepan. Add the water and bring to a boil over high heat. Add about one-fourth of the onion (including any scraps from chopping it) and ¼ teaspoon salt. Reduce the heat somewhat and let this simple stock boil not too violently for 10 to 15 minutes. Meanwhile, in a large, heavy soup pot, melt a tablespoon of butter over a medium-high flame. Add the remaining onion with a pinch of salt and cook, stirring frequently, until the pieces of onion are clear around the edges, about 2 minutes. Add the carrots with another pinch of salt and cook for a minute or so more. Reduce the heat to medium and stir in the squash cubes with a big pinch of salt. Continue to cook, stirring frequently, for about 5 minutes as the stock finishes cooking. Strain the stock into the soup pot—it should just cover the vegetables. If not, bring the required amount of water to a boil and add it. Bring the soup to a lively simmer and cook, stirring occasionally, for 5 more minutes, or until the squash is completely soft. Purée the soup to a uniform smoothness in batches in a blender, dropping a small pat of cold butter into each batch as it blends. Be careful when blending hot liquids: fill the blender jar only half full, hold the lid in place with a kitchen towel, and start the blender on lower speeds.

Unlike other vegetable purée soups, this one does not need straining—it will be silky smooth. Carefully add salt and pepper to taste. Gently place spoonfuls of pear and oil into the center of each bowl of hot soup, and serve immediately.

Butternut Squash Chips

At Deep Springs everyone cheers when butternut squash chips are on the menu. Peel and seed a butternut squash as described in the previous recipe. Cut the thickest pieces down to long, inch-thick blocks. Using a swivel-bladed vegetable peeler or a mandoline slicer, shave paper-thin strips from the squash (save the thick scraps for another use). In a large, heavy pot, heat 4 to 5 cups of safflower, peanut, or other fry-friendly vegetable oil to 325°F. Fry the strips in batches, stirring gently to submerge the squash as it fries, until crisp but not deeply browned, 2 to 3 minutes. Remove with a skimmer and drain on paper towels or brown paper. While the chips are still hot, sprinkle with fine salt, and a little pepper if you like. They will crisp as they cool.

The above technique is also how you make *potato chips*, if you have a mandolin slicer. Scrubbed, unpeeled russet potatoes work well; red potatoes do not. Feel free to experiment with other types of potato. Most varieties will fry more satisfactorily if you rinse out their heavier starch in cool running water after slicing them. Drain and dry these washed chips very well, using a salad spinner, before frying them.

Cornmeal-Fried Summer Squash

serves 2 to 3

Like many mothers, mine encountered great success in growing zucchini and other summer squash in her garden. This was our supper many a summer night in New Mexico when I was quite young.

If you have squash blossoms in your garden that you want to use but don't want to make a big fuss with, chop a couple of them up coarsely and throw them into your fried squash, as you would an herb, in the last minute or so of cooking.

1 pound assorted summer squash: zucchini, yellow crookneck, pattypan, or other varieties

¼ teaspoon salt, plus more as needed

2½ tablespoons yellow cornmeal

2 tablespoons olive oil, bacon fat, or a combination

black pepper

There are two ways to make this: you can cook large slices of squash over a medium flame, turning them once like steaks, or you can toss smaller bits around in the pan. Some of the cornmeal will fall off the squash while cooking, but it fries up into crispy crumbs in the oil and still tastes delicious. Okra is also excellent prepared in this manner (see page 136).

Wipe the summer squash clean with a kitchen towel, or rinse briefly and towel-dry. (Squash has a tendency to absorb water if rinsed, making the final result mushy.) Cut into ¼-inch slices or ½-inch chunks. In a large bowl, toss the squash with ¼ teaspoon salt and the cornmeal. Heat the oil in a big skillet (a nonstick skillet is ideal) over a medium-high flame, and throw in the squash, as well as the cornmeal in the bottom of the bowl. Cook, tossing occasionally, until the squash is tender and the cornmeal golden. Let the squash cook undisturbed for moments at a time to allow an appealing golden-brown crust to develop. Season with 1 to 2 big pinches of salt, and black pepper to taste.

Grilled Summer Squash

serves 4 to 6

Summer squash contains a great deal of water. In the preceding recipe, the cornmeal wicks and absorbs excess water as the squash cooks. Grilled squash always sounds appealing—the smoky flavor, the nice brown grill marks—but without prior treatment, it ends up soggy, mushy, and bland. Here, a generous amount of salt and sugar draws the water out of the squash, without making the final product taste overly salty or sweet. Then the squash is blotted with paper towels, seasoned with nutty cumin and hot red pepper flakes, and grilled. It comes out tender but firm, with lively seasoning that enhances the squash's good delicate flavor without overpowering it.

- **1½ pounds summer squash: zucchini, yellow crookneck, pattypan, or other varieties**
- **1 tablespoon kosher salt**
- **2 teaspoons sugar**
- **1 teaspoon whole cumin seeds, coarsely crushed in a mortar**
- **½ teaspoon hot red pepper flakes**
- **2 teaspoons olive oil**

Rinse the squash briefly and dry it with a towel. With a long knife, cut the squash into even planks, a little thinner than ¼ inch. In a wide, shallow bowl, toss the squash with the salt and sugar, and let sit, tossing occasionally, for about 30 minutes. Drain the squash well, and arrange it on a double layer of paper towels. Cover with more paper towels, pressing to blot excess liquid from the squash. Wipe out the shallow bowl, return the squash to it, and toss the squash with the cumin, hot pepper flakes, and olive oil. Get your grill nice and hot, and clean and oil the grates. Grill the squash on one side until it develops brown grill marks, 1 to 2 minutes, then turn the pieces and grill the other side 1 to 2 minutes more. Remove the squash to a warmed plate and serve immediately.

Priscilla's Fried Green Tomatoes

serves 4 to 6

When frost threatens Deep Springs Valley in the early fall, we harvest all the tomatoes and put flats of green tomatoes on every conceivable surface in the pantry area of the Deep Springs Boardinghouse. Many continue to ripen for use in salads, but we are also compelled to make fried green tomatoes. They are never better than when made by Priscilla Freeman, one of my successors in the Deep Springs kitchen.

- **1½ pounds green** *(unripe)* **tomatoes**
- **1 egg**
- **2 tablespoons milk**
- **pinch of brown sugar**
- **½ cup all-purpose flour**
- **½ cup cornmeal**
- **1¼ teaspoons salt**
- **black pepper**
- **pinch of cayenne pepper**
- **2 to 3 tablespoons vegetable oil**
- **2 to 3 tablespoons bacon fat**

Slice the tomatoes a little thinner than ¼ inch. Beat the egg, milk, and sugar in a shallow bowl, and combine the flour, cornmeal, salt, black pepper to taste, and cayenne in another shallow bowl. Dip the tomatoes in the egg, then dredge them in the flour mixture. Place the tomatoes on a sheet pan in a single layer, not touching. Don't let the prepared tomatoes sit for more than about 20 minutes, or the coating will become soggy. Heat a wide, heavy skillet over a medium-high flame. Add a tablespoon each of oil and bacon fat. Heat until the surface of the oil shimmers. Carefully lay in about a third of the tomato slices without crowding. Cook until the underside is an appetizing golden brown, 1 to 2 minutes, then flip and cook the other side. Drain on paper towels. Taste a slice, and sprinkle extra salt and pepper over the hot tomatoes if necessary. Drain the used oil from the pan, wipe clean, and add fresh oil and bacon fat to fry the remaining tomatoes. Serve hot.

Use the leftovers in the next day's ham sandwiches.

Tomato Soup

serves 4 to 6

This simple soup evokes, but updates, the tomato soup of our youth. It's perfect with a Grilled Cheese Sandwich (page 89). The recipe uses both fresh and canned tomatoes, and may be multiplied to serve a crowd. The better and sweeter the fresh tomatoes, the better the soup; you can even use a portion of cherry tomatoes, if you like. If your supply of ripe summer tomatoes is abundant, you can use 4 pounds of them for this soup, omitting the canned tomatoes; conversely, if you are craving tomato soup in the cooler months, use 2 cans of good-quality whole plum tomatoes. For a classic flavor, a sprig of tarragon may be used instead of basil.

- **2 pounds ripe, red summer tomatoes**
- **3 tablespoons olive oil**
- **1 small red onion, chopped finely**
- **3 cloves garlic, smashed**

1¼ teaspoons salt, in all, or more as needed
1 28-ounce can whole plum tomatoes
1 cup chicken stock or vegetable stock
2 to 3 large sprigs fresh basil
3 tablespoons cold butter
freshly ground black pepper to taste
½ teaspoon sherry vinegar
(sugar if necessary)

Trim the stem-end of the fresh tomatoes, and cut them into large chunks, reserving all juice. If you're using some cherry tomatoes, cut them in half. In a heavy soup pot, heat the olive oil over a medium-high flame, and sauté the onion with 1 teaspoon of salt for a moment, then add the garlic with a pinch of additional salt, and continue sautéing, stirring constantly, until the onion is tender—the onion should not brown, only soften. Add the fresh tomatoes. Gently break up the canned tomatoes with your hands, then add them, and all liquid from the can, to the pot, along with the stock. Bring the soup to a simmer, then plunge the fresh basil sprigs into the pot. Lower the heat and simmer gently for about 15 minutes, stirring occasionally. Fish out and reserve the basil. Purée the soup in three batches in a blender, dropping a tablespoon of cold butter into each batch as it blends. Be careful when blending hot liquids: fill the blender jar only half full, hold the lid in place with a kitchen towel, and start the blender on lower speeds. Let each batch blend on high speed until thoroughly smooth, at least a full minute. Pass the soup through a screen sieve, using the back of a ladle. Press on the solids in the sieve to extract as much liquid and flavor as possible. Return the soup to the pot, and season with black pepper, ¼ teaspoon additional salt, and the sherry vinegar. Taste carefully for balanced flavors—if the soup is very acidic, add a small pinch of sugar. Or, if it tastes very sweet, a little more salt and sherry vinegar can balance it. Reheat gently and serve. If there is any soup left over, return the reserved sprigs of basil to it before refrigerating—they will continue to perfume the soup as it sits.

Tomato Cobbler

serves 4 to 6

Use an assortment of full-flavored, peak-of-season summer tomatoes in this savory dinner cobbler, including a couple of Roma (plum) tomatoes for their firm texture and good, sweet flavor. Serve alone, with a green salad, or alongside burger steaks or any other simple meat. You can substitute a cup of fresh basil for the parsley and rosemary.

1 tablespoon butter
1 medium yellow onion, cut in medium dice
6 cloves garlic, peeled and crushed or finely slivered
4 cups ripe summer tomatoes, cut in large chunks
1 teaspoon salt, plus 2 pinches more
1 cup coarsely chopped fresh parsley
1 teaspoon finely chopped fresh rosemary
2 dashes Tabasco or other hot sauce
1½ teaspoons balsamic vinegar
freshly ground black pepper to taste
2 tablespoons fine cornmeal or all-purpose flour

BISCUIT TOPPING

1 cup medium-grind cornmeal *(for more information on cornmeal, see page 40)*
1 cup extra-fine cornmeal or all-purpose flour
1 teaspoon brown sugar
1 teaspoon baking powder
½ teaspoon salt
6 tablespoons chilled butter, cut in small cubes
1½ cups grated Gruyère cheese *(or whatever cheese you have)*
1 cup cold buttermilk

In a small skillet over a medium flame, melt the tablespoon of butter. When it bubbles, throw in the onions with a pinch of salt and sauté, tossing frequently, for 2 to 3 minutes. Add the slivered garlic with another pinch of salt and sauté 2 to 3 minutes more, until the onion is tender. The onion and garlic shouldn't really brown. Remove from the flame and let cool in the pan.

Heat the oven to 375°F. Put the cut tomatoes (and all the accumulated tomato juice) in a 9-by-13-inch baking dish. Add the warm onion-garlic mixture, a teaspoon of salt, the basil, Tabasco, balsamic vinegar, black pepper, and 2 tablespoons of fine cornmeal. Stir well to combine.

In a large bowl, whisk together the cornmeal, fine cornmeal or flour, brown sugar, baking powder, and salt. Cut in the butter rapidly with your hands until the dry mixture is somewhat moistened and there are small flecks of butter in the mixture. Stir in the cheese. Stir in the buttermilk to make a thick batter; spoon the batter in about 12 big scoops over the tomato mixture. Put in the hot oven and bake for 35 to 40 minutes, until the biscuits are golden brown and cooked through (test with a small knife) and the tomatoes are bubbling. Let rest 10 minutes to settle the tomato juices, then serve with a wide spoon.

Tomato Concassé

Not really a dish in itself, tomato concassé, or fresh ripe tomatoes that have been peeled and diced, is an important building block for many a summer recipe. Wherever canned diced tomatoes are called for, tomato concassé may be used, making the dish even more special. It's part of this book's recipe for Soupe au Pistou, (page 151), and is the starting point for Gazpacho (page 168). Fresh tomatoes made into concassé can be used for Tomato Sauce (247) in place of the canned diced tomatoes called for, but may result in a thinner (but very flavorful) sauce. Tomato concassé can be added to chili, beef stew, gumbo, curry, or braised chicken; it can be stirred into beans or tossed with pasta along with garlic, olive oil, and herbs.

Use only vine-ripe summer tomatoes for concassé. Plunge a few tomatoes at a time, whole, into a pot of boiling water. Gently roll the tomatoes around for 20 to 30 seconds, making sure all sides come in contact with the boiling water, especially the stem end. Remove the tomatoes with a slotted spoon. (Many cooks plunge the tomatoes into a basin of ice water at this point to stop the cooking; I rarely do.) With a small knife, make an incision in the blossom end of each tomato, and peel the skin away—it should slip off easily. (I save the peels for vegetable stock—they contain a lot of flavor.) Working over a large bowl to catch all the juice, carefully cut out the stem end of each tomato to remove any white, tough core. Once all the tomatoes are peeled and cored, halve them crosswise with a knife, and gently squeeze each half over the bowl to release the juice and seeds. Dice the tomato halves to the desired size. I usually let the seeds remain, but if you want to strain them out, pass the juice through a screen sieve, pressing hard to extract all the flavorful gel from around the seeds. Mix the diced tomato solids with the juice, and your tomato concassé is ready to use.

SUMMER TOMATO PUDDING

A supremely comforting dish to accompany grilled meat and green salad. Season a bowl of tomato concassé carefully with salt, sherry vinegar, and black pepper. Make an equal volume of Croutons (page 175), using the oven, or by tossing the bread and oil in a hot pan on the stove. When the croutons are golden and crisp, mix them into the tomatoes along with a little coarsely-chopped basil or other herb of choice. Taste for seasoning. Let the pudding sit, so that the bread absorbs the tomato juices, and serve at room temperature.

Watercress Soup

serves 6 to 8

A small bowl of this very simple, intense green soup alongside a freshly made egg salad sandwich on wheat bread makes a savory, invigorating winter lunch. The soup may also be made with spinach.

¼ **cup olive oil**

1 small onion, diced

1 carrot, peeled and diced

1 small stalk celery, diced

2 teaspoons salt, plus more as needed

4 cups water

8 to 10 ounces watercress *(2 small bunches)*, **washed, largest stems removed, and coarsely chopped**

freshly ground black pepper

In a large, heavy soup pot over a medium-high flame, heat the olive oil until fragrant. Throw in the onion, carrot, and celery with a pinch of salt and cook, stirring frequently, until the vegetables are sweetened and beginning to soften. Add the water and bring to a boil. Stir in the watercress, bring back to a boil, and boil for about a minute. Add 2 teaspoons salt and pepper to taste. Transfer the soup to a blender and blend at high speed (in batches, if necessary), until the soup is completely smooth. Be careful when blending hot liquids: fill the blender jar only half full, hold the lid in place with a kitchen towel, and start the blender on lower speeds. If it seems very fibrous, pass the soup through a wire-mesh sieve, using the back of a ladle to press through as much liquid and purée as possible. Serve immediately.

Roasted Yams or Sweet Potatoes

In common usage, *yams* are orange-fleshed and *sweet potatoes* are yellow-, white-, or purple-fleshed, but the two are essentially interchangeable. These delicious, healthy tubers are in season in the fall and winter. Scrub yams well under running water, and bake on a foil-covered baking sheet in a 400°F oven until they are completely soft, about 1 hour. The foil is necessary because yams expel syrup as they cook, which burns onto whatever surface they are baked on. Allow the yams to cool until you can handle them. Peel off the skins, but retain as much of the syrup as possible. Gently fold in butter, salt, and pepper to taste. A little brown sugar or cane syrup can be added, if you want to be especially Southern. Or, instead of butter, virgin coconut oil is especially good on yams.

Roasted Yams with Pears and Bourbon

serves 6 to 8

This marvelous holiday dish comes from the repertoire of Eve Felder, a chef at Chez Panisse when I worked there, and later, a chef-instructor at the Culinary Institute of America. I've only added the bourbon. Strict measurements aren't necessary in recipes such as this—follow your own taste and good sense of judgement.

about 3 pounds orange-fleshed yams *(Jewel or Garnet varieties)*

salt

freshly ground pepper

about 2 tablespoons butter, plus a little more for reheating

about 2 ripe Bosc pears, peeled and cut into medium dice

about 3 tablespoons bourbon

Heat the oven to 400°F or whatever temperature is convenient. Scrub the yams well, place on a foil-lined baking sheet, and put them in the oven. Bake until the yams are thoroughly soft and beginning to expel juice—this will take about an hour, or longer at lower oven temperatures. Allow to cool until you can handle them. Remove the skin and any blemishes, or any hard, fibrous, or discolored parts. To the extent it's possible to slice the soft yams, slice them into a bowl (this takes care of the occasional long fibers found in yams). Lightly season with salt and freshly ground pepper to taste, folding the yams gently into a coarse puree.

In a skillet over a high flame, melt the butter. When it sizzles, throw in the diced pears with a pinch of salt. Sauté the pears for a moment, then splash in the bourbon, allowing the mixture to cook until the bourbon's sharp alcohol aroma subsides, leaving only a tantalizing, bourbon-buttery-caramel smell. Fold the warm pears, and all liquid from the pan, into the yams. Leave at room temperature, then dot lightly with additional butter and reheat in a hot oven at serving time.

Ratatouille

serves 4 to 6

This traditional dish of stewed summer vegetables from southern France, like many Mediterranean summer dishes, is very good reheated the next day, or simply served at room temperature, like a salad, with a fresh drizzle of olive oil. It is happy company with many simple foods: pork chops, steaks, roasts, chicken, wide noodles, and eggs.

There are many methods for making ratatouille. On one end of the spectrum, you could just stew everything together in a big pot with lots of olive oil until the vegetables are all cooked into a mush. On the other end, I have seen fussy recipes in which each vegetable is cooked separately and then blended only at the end. This recipe is a compromise: the vegetables are initially cooked in a couple of simple, separate processes, then the whole thing is baked together like a casserole. Each vegetable retains something of its own identity, but there is also a lovely blending of the various flavors. Ratatouille is a bit more work than many other vegetable dishes, but well worth the effort.

1 globe eggplant *(about 1¼ pounds)*, **cut into 1-inch chunks**

about ⅓ cup extra-virgin olive oil

1 teaspoon salt, plus more as needed

1 medium yellow onion, cut into 1-inch dice

2 red bell peppers *(about 8 ounces)*, **cut into 1-inch dice**

1 tablespoon red wine vinegar

3 cloves garlic, crushed

1 to 2 pinches hot red pepper flakes

2 or 3 assorted summer squash *(about 1 pound)*, **cut into 1-inch chunks**

2 or 3 red ripe tomatoes *(about 1½ pounds)*

8 to 10 fresh basil leaves, coarsely chopped

1 tablespoon coarsely chopped parsley

3 or 4 oil-cured black olives, pitted and coarsely chopped

freshly ground black pepper

Heat the oven to 450°F. Toss the eggplant in a medium bowl with a good drizzle of the olive oil and ¼ teaspoon of the salt. Scatter the eggplant on an oiled baking sheet and bake until it is well browned on the edges and silky soft, 15 to 20 minutes. Remove from the oven.

While the eggplant is baking, heat 1½ tablespoons olive oil in a large, heavy skillet over a medium-high flame. Add the onions with a pinch of salt and cook for 1 to 2 minutes, stirring constantly, until they begin to soften. Add the bell peppers with ¼ teaspoon of the salt and cook, stirring frequently, for about 5 minutes, until the peppers are soft. The onions and peppers should brown slightly. Transfer the onions and peppers to a 9-by-13-inch baking dish. Let the skillet cool for a moment, then add the red wine vinegar. The vinegar will deglaze all the flavorful brown residue that formed while the onions and peppers were cooking. Taste— if the vinegary liquid tastes burned and bitter, throw it out. If it tastes good and savory, add it to the peppers and onions.

Wipe the skillet clean and add another 1½ tablespoons of olive oil. When the oil is hot, add the crushed garlic with a pinch of salt. Let the garlic cook for just a few seconds, then add the hot red pepper flakes and the squash with another ¼ teaspoon salt and cook, stirring frequently, just until the squash is browned here and there, and softened, but not falling apart. Transfer the garlicky squash to the dish with the onions and peppers. (Don't wash the skillet yet; you might need it to reduce the juices when the ratatouille is finished.)

Reduce the oven's heat to 375°F. Bring a small pot of water to a boil and plunge the tomatoes in for 15 to 20 seconds, then remove them. The skins should now slip off easily with the aid of a small knife. Cut the peeled tomatoes into 1-inch chunks, and add them, with their juice, to the vegetables in the baking dish. Add a final ¼ teaspoon salt. Add the eggplant (and any accumulated juices) to the dish, gently tossing all the vegetables together. Bake for about 30 minutes. Remove from the oven and let cool for about 15 minutes. If the ratatouille is swimming in juice, drain off the juice and reduce it in your skillet, over a medium flame, to a thin, syrupy consistency. Drizzle it back over the vegetables. Gently toss the vegetables with the basil, parsley, olives, and salt and pepper to taste. Serve warm or at room temperature, with a fresh drizzle of olive oil.

Soupe au Pistou

serves 6 to 8

Another southern French summer classic, this soup is full of good things from the summer garden: tomatoes, beans, green beans, squash, sweet corn (quite un-French, but delicious), and basil. *Pistou* is the southern French term for the pesto, made without nuts, that tops the soup. I like the deep, satisfying flavor that chicken stock gives this soup, but vegetable stock (following recipe) is fine to use, too.

12 ounces ripe summer tomatoes, different colors if possible

¼ cup olive oil

½ medium onion, finely diced

1 small inner rib celery, finely diced

1 small carrot, peeled and finely diced

3 pinches of salt, or more as needed

handful of fresh green beans, tops and tails cut off, cut into ⅛-inch pieces

8 ounces summer squash, different colors if possible, finely diced

½ cup fresh corn kernels (*or cooked small pasta such as small shells*)

1 cup cooked beans, preferably fresh shell beans (*page 122*)

5 cups chicken or vegetable stock

black pepper

one recipe of Pesto (*page 254*)**, omitting the nuts, at room temperature**

First, peel and seed the tomatoes, following the method for Tomato Concassé on page 148. Cut the peeled tomatoes into medium dice. (If you like, infuse the stock with the tomato peels.)

In a large, heavy soup pot, heat the olive oil over medium-high heat. When it is fragrant, add the onion, celery, and carrot with a pinch of salt. Stew these vegetables, stirring frequently, until they are beginning to soften, 3 to 4 minutes. Add the cut green beans with another pinch of salt and cook, stirring, for 1 to 2 minutes more. Add the squash with a pinch of salt and continue to stew the vegetables, stirring, until the squash is just tender, 2 to 3 minutes more. Add the corn (if using), beans, tomato concassé, and strained stock, and bring to a boil, then reduce the heat to a simmer. Simmer until the squash is soft but not falling apart, about 10 minutes. (If you're using pasta instead of corn, add the cooked pasta in the last few minutes of simmering.) Taste for salt, and add a little pepper. Ladle the hot soup into bowls, and spoon a generous tablespoon of *pistou* into each bowl. Serve.

Vegetable Stock or Broth

makes 12 cups

What is the difference between broth and stock? *Broth* implies a liquid suitable for consuming on its own, whereas *stock* implies "something out of which other things are made." This is an all-purpose vegetable stock, flavorful enough to be served on its own as a broth. When fresh, it tastes almost as substantial and satisfying as good homemade chicken stock. I often use it for risotto, meatless borscht, and many other vegetable soups. Do not be tempted to use onion skins or any other vegetable trimmings that should go in the compost. If it's not something you'd eat yourself, don't put it in your stock. Always peel carrots, even for this recipe; because carrot skin is often slightly bitter, the end result will taste cleaner. Feed carrot peels to the horses or goats.

Stock is infinitely variable, depending on what it will be used for. You can vary the herbs, use wine in place of some of the water, or add small amounts of dried mushrooms (dried porcini are especially good). If you save the rinds from chunks of Parmesan cheese, these give excellent flavor and body to vegetable stock. You may sauté the onions—or the mushrooms—separately until they are deep brown. Or add garlic, stewing it with the vegetables. Clean potato peelings will give the stock a little body and good flavor. You may add other vegetables, such as leeks (including the greens) or the clean peelings and seeds of winter squash in cool weather, or tomatoes or corncobs (after you've cut off the kernels) in warm weather.

- 2 tablespoons butter or olive oil
- 1 large yellow onion, halved, peeled, and thickly sliced lengthwise
- 1 large carrot, peeled and cut into chunks
- 3 stalks celery plus 1 inner rib of celery with the leaves, thickly sliced
- ½ teaspoon salt, plus more as needed
- 5 or 6 large white or brown mushrooms, wiped clean, trimmed, halved, and thickly sliced
- 1 bay leaf
- 2 sprigs fresh thyme, or ½ teaspoon dried
- 1 sprig parsley
- 1 teaspoon whole black peppercorns
- 10 cups cold water
- soy sauce

In a large soup pot, melt the butter over medium-high heat, and add the onion, carrot, celery, and ½ teaspoon salt. Lower the heat slightly and cook for about 5 minutes, uncovered, stirring the vegetables frequently and allowing them to stew and sweeten. Add the mushrooms with a pinch of salt, and stew for 5 minutes more. Add the bay leaf, thyme, parsley, peppercorns, and water to the pot. Cover, raise the heat to high, and bring the stock to a boil. Reduce the heat and gently boil for 30 minutes. Season with salt and soy sauce until it tastes good—the soy sauce provides depth. Strain the stock through a sieve. Use it or freeze it on the day you make it—its freshness fades if it's kept.

Modern Man

*Old farmer
down the road
a ways,
wife died
last March,
says he got hisself
a microwave
in May,
says
at sundown
he just totes
a beet
or a potato
big 'uns, no pesticides,
from the west field,
stops to wash
hands,
food,
the day's accumulation
of memories,
pops that beet in,
or potato,
hacks off chunks of
rat cheese,
bread,
cold butter,
and
there,
by gum,
is a dandy
supper.*

—Ann Applegarth

CHAPTER 8

SALADS & DRESSINGS

Refrigeration technology is a recent development in our evolution. Food writers often herald ice cream as refrigeration's greatest gift to mankind, but I'd nominate the ubiquity of fresh, cool, crunchy, healthful salads. But refrigeration is a double-edged sword: food may seem fresh under refrigeration when actually it could be quite old and unfit for consumption. Ironically, widespread refrigeration, coupled with the demands of commerce, means we frequently eat food that is far less fresh than what our forebears consumed, when surely the opposite was intended as refrigeration developed. In any case, we are fortunate to have fresh, green salads readily available year-round. Salads are a superb medium for inspired cooks to practice their ingenuity.

So vast is the field of salad possibilities, it is challenging to exactly define the word "salad." A salad may be composed of leafy greens, or only of chopped or shaved vegetables. Salads usually contain a fresh, raw element, but not always. A salad may be cold or warm, a side dish or a main course, rich or lean. Someone once told me his favorite salad was a live oyster with a drop of fresh lemon juice. An acidic element (citrus or vinegar) is the rule for most salads, but a handful of pristine baby lettuces, just picked from the garden, may be so delicate that no dressing is needed beyond a drizzle of olive oil and a whisper of salt. And some relishlike salads contain no oil at all.

The recipes in this chapter provide examples of all these salad types. It begins with recipes and methods for leafy green salads, followed by many fruit- or vegetable-based salads, including old-fashioned potato salad and coleslaw. At chapter's end are recipes and methods for vinaigrettes and creamy salad dressings, and for toasted nuts and croutons.

LEAFY GREEN SALADS

Green salad occupies the same place that bread and butter did in generations past—it's an everyday thing. Serving it as part of every lunch and dinner at Deep Springs, I always vary the greens, toppings, and dressings. A general overview of green salad follows, with many recipes for specific green salads, such as Caesar Salad (page 161) and Chef's Salad (page 160).

Salad greens are among the easiest vegetables to grow. Throughout the spring and summer we enjoy beautiful, though sometimes weather-damaged, lettuces from the greenhouse and garden. There is a vast spectrum of salad greens, from fragile yellow-green butter lettuce to deep purple-red radicchio, from the easy sweetness and crunch of head lettuce to peppery mustard or succulently bitter endive.

Though bagged, washed, ready-to-use salad greens are a great convenience, whole heads of lettuce or bunches of greens that you have cut and washed yourself will always taste fresher and more vibrant. For an intriguing salad blend that will surpass, with clear, individual flavors, any bagged store-bought variety, include something from each category below, balancing the various flavor characteristics.

Iceberg lettuce, though lacking in the vitamins and minerals so rich in other greens, has an unparalleled crunchiness. Although not particularly good in mixed salads, it's delicious served by itself, cut in a dramatic wedge, generously topped with a creamy dressing and flavorful toppings, and served with a knife and fork—see the Blue Cheese Dressing recipe on page 175. Although most Mexican restaurants in the United States serve shredded iceberg lettuce alongside their enchiladas, super-nutritious *shredded cabbage* is more commonly served in Mexico, and tastes much better.

Radicchio, endive, escarole, dandelion, frisée, and other members of the chicory family are cool-weather salad greens cultivated for their distinct bitter-sweet flavor. I have come to prefer them in salads over sweet lettuces. A taste for them is readily acquired: the bitterness adds great depth and balance to the tart, sweet, savory, and salty flavors ubiquitous in salads. In many Asian cuisines, bitter vegetables are especially valued for their healthful, "cleansing" qualities, and in fact, after a rich meal, a well-balanced, lightly dressed salad of bitter greens can taste wonderfully refreshing. If stronger-flavored greens are controversial with some of your diners, serve them at first in small quantities and proportions, and cut them small.

Lettuce *(sweet)*
- butter lettuce
- red- or green-leaf lettuce
- oak leaf lettuce
- romaine lettuce (best in Caesar salad)

Chicory family *(bitter, but compellingly good once the taste is acquired)*
- radicchio
- escarole
- Belgian endive
- frisée
- young dandelion

Brassica family *(spicy and strong)*
- arugula (page 161)
- green and red cabbage
- savoy cabbage
- tatsoi
- mizuna
- baby kale
- baby mustard greens

Spinach family *(minerally taste)*
- spinach (page 161)
- very young chard
- very young beet greens

Cresses *(peppery)*
- watercress (see page 162)
- garden cress
- curly cress

Herbs *(aromatic)*
- flat-leaf parsley leaves and sprigs
- mint leaves
- cilantro leaves and sprigs
- basil leaves, coarsely chopped
- dill fronds
- chervil fronds
- tarragon (coarsely chopped)
- chives (chopped into 1-inch batons)

A salad mix heavy on the sweet lettuces stands up well to a creamy dressing, and benefits from the addition of other vegetables, such as shredded carrots, sliced mushrooms, radishes, cucumber, celery, and fennel. A more varied mix, containing bitter, peppery, or aromatic greens, is better suited to a simple vinaigrette.

HOW TO WASH SALAD GREENS

1. Use a large, clean basin and fill with cool water.

2. Cut large leaves into bite-size pieces with a sharp knife, or tear them. Especially strong-tasting lettuces are best cut into smaller pieces.

3. Immerse the lettuce in the water, swirling it around gently with your hands.

4. Drain the lettuce in a colander. (Bunch spinach tends to be very dirty; you might need to wash it twice.)

5. Spin the greens dry in a salad spinner (or roll in a large, dry kitchen towel).

6. Chill the greens in a covered bowl, if you won't be serving the salad soon.

DRESSING A GREEN SALAD

Recipes for vinaigrettes and creamy dressings are on pages 173 to 175; also see the method for Bowl-Dressed Salad on the following page. A green salad tossed with dressing just before serving is tastier—and lighter—than one that gets drizzled with dressing on a plate (the usual practice in the Boardinghouse line at Deep Springs).

Allow about 2 tablespoons of vinaigrette for a large plate of green salad. Put the greens and toppings in a large bowl, add the well-stirred dressing, and with your clean hands, gently toss until all the dressing is evenly distributed over the greens. If you are serving individual salads, pile the dressed greens high in the center of each plate. If you are serving family style, serve from the bowl, or gently transfer the salad to a large, shallow bowl, piling the salad in the center. *Serve tossed salad immediately.*

SALAD TOPPINGS

A simple salad of only mixed greens is wonderfully satisfying, especially in the context of a multicourse menu containing complexly flavored dishes. But there are endless possibilities for topping your salads: croutons, vegetables, fruit, cheese, bacon, nuts, beans, meats…. As with any composed dish, however, it's best to keep it simple. One, two, or three harmonious garnishes are usually ample.

Croutons *(page 175)*

Thinly sliced vegetables
- onion
- radish
- fennel
- cucumber
- mushroom
- summer squash
- carrot
- celery
- young turnip

Other vegetables
- avocado
- halved cherry tomatoes
- chunked large tomatoes
- cut corn
- lightly cooked broccoli or cauliflower
- julienned kohlrabi
- blanched green beans
- Marinated Beets (page 164)
- Fresh Artichoke Hearts (page 120)

Nuts
- lightly toasted (page 176), then tossed with a few drops of olive oil and a little salt

Sunflower seeds, sesame seeds, or pumpkinseeds
- lightly pan-toasted (page 176)

Cheese
- hard cheeses (such as Parmesan), shaved with a vegetable peeler or grated
- medium-hard cheeses (such as Cheddar), cut into small cubes
- soft cheeses (such as goat cheese), spread generously on little toasts or crackers
- crumbled blue cheese
- crumbled feta cheese
- (Avoid combining cheese with fish.)

Fruit
- apples, peeled and sliced
- pears, all types, peeled and sliced
- stone fruit, all types, sliced
- Fuyu persimmons, peeled and sliced
- oranges or other sweet citrus, peeled and sliced or sectioned with a knife
- figs, halved or quartered
- grapes, seeded and halved
- Zante currants or sultana raisins plumped in wine
- (Sweet fruit is generally good with nuts and cheese, but be careful when combining it with vegetables or meat; certain combinations are better than others. Summer berries are good in green salads with a little soft, fresh cheese such as goat cheese or ricotta, but they don't combine well with other toppings. Avoid combining fruit with most vegetables, beans, egg, or fish.)

Bacon *(page 54)*
- strip bacon cooked until crisp, well-drained, and chopped or crumbled
- slab bacon cut into medium dice, cooked, and drained (called *lardons* in French)

Other meat/poultry
- cooked and chilled, trimmed of skin or fat, cut into bite-size chunks or slices

Fish
- cooked and chilled, gently flaked over the finished salad (Avoid combining fish with cheese or non-citrus fruit.)

Beans *(pages 106 to 108)*
- any type of bean, cooked and cooled in its broth, then well drained (avoid combining beans with fruit.)

Hard-Boiled Eggs *(page 91)*
- halved or quartered; for the best presentation, arrange over the finished salad, giving each egg a pinch of salt and pepper (avoid combining egg with fruit)

Bowl-Dressed Salad

This is how I usually make salads at home. Once you have made vinaigrettes and other dressings using recipes and have a sense of the right proportions, you may successfully make dressings "to order," right in the salad bowl. Put your washed greens, vegetables cut just so, croutons, and other toppings into your big, wide salad bowl. Carefully but generously drizzle in olive oil (a cruet allows a thin, even, easily controllable stream of oil), and toss gently. With utmost care, sprinkle in just enough vinegar to sparkle the flavor of the greens and oil: toss and taste. Sprinkle salt cautiously, but twist the peppermill more freely. Toss and taste again. Toss thoroughly and serve at once.

Greek Salad

On sweltering summer days, sometimes all you want for dinner is a big Greek salad. Make a simple vinaigrette with fresh lemon juice, red wine vinegar, extra-virgin olive oil, salt, and pepper. Toss a blend of green and red leaf lettuce, romaine, spinach, mint, dill, and parsley with a small amount of the vinaigrette. Mound the lettuce onto plates, and liberally top each salad with sliced sweet ripe summer tomatoes, sliced cucumber, thinly sliced red onion, coarsely crumbled feta cheese, and whole kalamata olives (or other black Mediterranean olive of your choice—warn your guests that the olives have pits). Drizzle a little more dressing over the toppings. Serve with an extra lemon wedge, and hunks of bread to mop up the extra vinaigrette.

Fig and Feta Salad

Toss a blend of arugula and sweet lettuces with a little Lemon Vinaigrette (page 174) and a little chopped fresh thyme. Top with ripe summer figs, cut lengthwise into wedges, and crumbled feta cheese. Drizzle a little more vinaigrette over the figs.

Chef's Salad

serves 6 abundantly

Traveling through Wyoming one rainy spring, I ate in a classic American, pretense-free restaurant and ordered a chef's salad and chicken soup with rice. Though the salad was made with ordinary ingredients—iceberg lettuce and perhaps not the freshest crinkle-cut carrot sticks—it hit the spot, and I quickly introduced my version into the Deep Springs lunch repertoire. The community loved it so much that for a time it became our special-occasion lunch—huge, fresh, colorful trays of chef's salad welcomed Deep Springs trustees, alumni gatherings, visiting scholars, and families for graduation. The particular specified components, including deli meats and cheeses, are classic and familiar to everyone, but you may vary the suggested lettuces, vegetables, toppings, and dressings to suit any circumstance.

In warm weather, serve chef's salad alone with freshly baked bread or biscuits; in cold weather, include a hot vegetable soup as well.

GREENS

1 small head red-leaf lettuce

1 small head butter lettuce

1 small bunch spinach

1½ cups shredded red cabbage

TOPPINGS

½ small red onion, shaved thin

4 slices turkey breast, cut into bite-size ribbons

4 slices ham, cut into bite-size ribbons

4 slices sharp Cheddar cheese, cut into bite-size ribbons

4 slices provolone cheese, cut into bite-size ribbons

½ English cucumber, sliced into rounds

4 large red radishes, thinly sliced

2 small, tender stalks celery, thinly sliced on the diagonal

½ cup white or brown mushrooms, wiped clean, trimmed, halved, and sliced

1 small carrot, peeled and shaved into strips with a vegetable peeler

1½ cups Croutons (page 175)

24 cherry tomatoes, halved with a serrated knife

4 Hard-Boiled Eggs (page 91), **cut into quarters**

FOR SERVING

Ranch Dressing (page 174)

Blue Cheese Dressing (page 175)

Lemon Vinaigrette (page 174)

Wash and spin the greens dry, and Cut into bite-sized pieces. Chill while preparing the other ingredients. Lay out 6 large plates. In your large salad bowl, toss the greens with a little of the lemon vinaigrette, and mound in the center of the plates. Evenly scatter all the other toppings, in the order listed, on and around the greens, letting things fall as they will, with no fussy arranging. Serve the salads immediately, passing bowls of creamy dressings and lemon vinaigrette, letting your guests drizzle their dressing of choice over their salad.

Arugula Salads

Although I didn't grow up eating arugula, once the taste was acquired, it became—and remains—one of my favorite fresh greens. Arugula salads need only a few additions and enhancements, so delicious is the nutrient-rich arugula itself. Quite often I will dress a handful of arugula with only a squeeze of lemon, a drizzle of olive oil, a pinch of salt, and a half-twist of pepper. Arugula suffers in very hot weather but is otherwise available year-round.

Here are some ideas:

- sliced fresh oranges, toasted pistachios, Citrus Vinaigrette (page 174)
- summer tomatoes, Croutons (page 175), shaved Parmesan, mustard vinaigrette (page 174)
- shaved pecorino romano cheese, fresh mint leaves, lemon-oil dressing
- crisp sweet apples, toasted walnuts, Shallot Vinaigrette (page 173)
- peeled and sliced Fuyu persimmon, toasted pecans, apple cider vinaigrette (page 174; perfect for Thanksgiving!)
- sliced ripe pears, shaved Parmesan, Lemon Vinaigrette (page 174)
- sliced fresh plums, dried cherries, toasted almonds, Shallot Vinaigrette (page 173)

Spinach Salads

Bagged ready-to-use baby spinach, though fresh, is still a processed product; for the most flavorful spinach salad, buy bunches of spinach (preferably with a little dirt still on them). Spinach is available in all but the hottest months. Very fresh, well-grown spinach sometimes tastes faintly chocolaty. Cut off the leafy top half of a bunch, discarding the stems. In plenty of water, carefully wash the leaves and spin dry. (Spinach in my grandmother's day was very dirty—she always washed it three times.) If the leaves are large, cut them into bite-size pieces.

Warm spinach salads are as fortifying as they are delectable. The spinach should be at room temperature. Warm the dressing slightly, place it in a large metal bowl, add hot components (such as bacon) and then the spinach, and toss over a very low flame until the spinach just barely begins to soften and wilt. Quickly mound on a plate and serve immediately. Add cheese to warm salads at the end.

Here are three good spinach salads, the first warm, the rest cold:

- hot bacon, warm soft-boiled egg, Croutons (page 175), slightly warmed mustard vinaigrette (page 174) or Lemon Vinaigrette (page 174), and chunks of Gruyère cheese
- lemon juice and zest, freshly grated Parmesan, extra-virgin olive oil, crushed garlic, salt and pepper, and Croutons (page 175)
- crisp apples, dried Zante currants plumped in red wine, crumbled blue cheese, and sherry vinaigrette (page 174)

Tracy's Caesar Salad

serves 4 to 6

This is a good, fresh, lemony-garlicky, old-fashioned Caesar salad from my sister Tracy's recipe file.

2 large heads romaine lettuce *(about 1½ pounds)*

about ½ cup extra-virgin olive oil, in all

2½ cups day-old bread cubes

3 or 4 cloves garlic, finely crushed

¼ teaspoon salt for dressing, plus more as needed

freshly ground black pepper

3 or 4 anchovy fillets, drained and well crushed

¼ cup fresh lemon juice, plus more as needed

1 teaspoon red wine vinegar

1 egg

⅓ cup freshly grated Parmesan cheese, plus at least another ¼ cup for sprinkling

Discard any large, blemished outer leaves of romaine. Wash (see page 158), gently tear by hand into bite-size pieces, and spin dry.

In a wide skillet, heat 1 tablespoon of the oil over a medium-low flame, and add the bread cubes. Sauté, stirring and tossing constantly, until the cubes are golden brown, 7 to 8 minutes. Blend another tablespoon of olive oil with a third of the garlic, and toss this with the croutons. Cook for a minute more. Salt and pepper the croutons, transfer them to a plate, and set aside.

In a small bowl, combine the remaining garlic, anchovy, lemon juice, vinegar, and ¼ teaspoon salt. Put the egg in a small pot of cold water and bring to a boil. Remove from the heat and let the egg sit in the hot water for 3 minutes. Transfer the egg to a bowl of cold water to stop the cooking.

Put the romaine in a very large salad bowl. Drizzle with 3 tablespoons of the oil and toss well. Using a spoon, scoop the warm egg from its shell into the lemon juice mixture, mash well, and add to the salad. Add 2 to 3 tablespoons more oil, croutons, freshly ground pepper to taste, and Parmesan, and toss very well. Taste a piece of romaine to see if the flavors are balanced; if necessary, add more salt, pepper, Parmesan, or lemon juice. Pile the salad onto large plates, grate extra Parmesan over each one, and serve immediately.

CREAMY CAESAR DRESSING

This is a more modern method for making a creamy, emulsified Caesar dressing. Put 2 or 3 cloves garlic, 3 anchovy fillets, ¼ cup fresh lemon juice, 1 teaspoon red wine vinegar, ¼ teaspoon salt, and a soft-boiled egg (page 60) into the jar of a blender. While blending at low speed, slowly drizzle in 6 to 7 tablespoons extra-virgin olive oil, as if you were making mayonnaise (see page 252). Stir in ⅓ cup freshly grated Parmesan and freshly ground black pepper to taste. Taste for salt—the amount required will depend on the saltiness of the anchovies and Parmesan. When abundant quantities of kale were being grown in the Deep Springs garden, one of my successors in the Boardinghouse kitchen, Jon "Dewey" DeWeese (DS'07), often served *kale Caesar*, with thinly-sliced red onions and homemade focaccia croutons. He would toss the kale with the dressing ahead of time, so that the kale softened a little, then he'd toss it again with the onions and croutons just before serving.

Watercress Salad

serves 2 to 3

The bracing, peppery savor of watercress perfectly balances roast beef, steak, and many other rich meat dishes. After something rich and gratifying, such as cheese soufflé, a simple fluff of watercress tossed with olive oil, lemon juice, salt, and a tiny bit of pepper may be all that is wanted.

Watercress is strictly a cool-weather crop; summer temperatures cause it to be overly hot. Separate a bunch of watercress into large, bite-size sprigs, discarding only the fattest stems. Wash and dry (see page 158). Toss with a drizzle of olive oil, a squeeze of lemon juice, a pinch of salt, and just a little black pepper (watercress is already peppery). Serve immediately, in fluffy mounds on individual plates, or mounded high in the middle of a platter.

Vegetable and Fruit Salads

Apple and Pear Salad

serves 4

There are many apple and pear trees in the Deep Springs orchard; I serve this salad frequently when there is a bumper crop. This autumn recipe uses about a pound of fruit but may be multiplied successfully. It's good with Reatha's Macaroni and Cheese (page 85). Excellent additions to this salad are thinly sliced fennel bulb, lightly toasted nuts (page 176), shredded red cabbage, chopped radicchio, or crumbled blue cheese.

1 shallot or ¼ small red onion, sliced lengthwise, paper-thin

juice of ½ lemon

¼ teaspoon salt

1 crisp, flavorful apple

1 ripe, sweet pear

1 small rib celery, split lengthwise and thinly sliced on the diagonal

1 tablespoon extra-virgin olive oil

freshly ground black pepper

In a medium bowl, combine the shallot, lemon juice, and salt, and let sit. Leave the apple and pear unpeeled. Cut 4 big sections of flesh away from each piece of fruit, leaving box-shaped cores. Using a sharp knife and a patient, steady hand, slice the fruit lengthwise into thin slices. Toss with the lemon juice mixture. Add the celery, olive oil, and pepper to taste, tossing gently to combine. Serve immediately.

Fuji Apple Coleslaw

serves 6 to 8

In this coleslaw, the crisp, sweet Fuji apple provides enough sugar to bring out the natural sweetness of the cabbage. Both cabbage and apples are especially good in the cooler months of the year. This recipe calls for cutting the apple into julienne, or fine matchsticks—excellent knife practice.

Although I love coleslaw with mayonnaise, cabbage also tastes great with a vinaigrette dressing, such as the Shallot or Lemon Vinaigrettes (page 173). I prefer using plain vegetable oil in such dressings, as strong olive oil tastes out of place on cabbage. My friend Elge makes a brilliant red-cabbage coleslaw sweetened with shredded carrot and flavored with crushed fennel seeds.

½ small red onion, thinly sliced

juice of ½ lemon, plus more as needed

1 teaspoon apple cider vinegar

¼ teaspoon salt, plus more as needed

1 large Fuji apple, peeled, quartered, and cored

1 small green cabbage, finely shredded

freshly ground black pepper

1 teaspoon celery seed

½ cup mayonnaise *(page 252)***, or to taste**

In a large bowl, combine the onion with the lemon juice, vinegar, and salt. Using a sharp knife, cut the apple into fine julienne, and toss it with the onion and lemon juice. Add the cabbage, pepper to taste, celery seed, and mayonnaise. Toss well and taste, adding more salt and lemon juice if necessary. Serve right away, or chill for an hour or two, tossing again before serving.

If you'd like to make the coleslaw in advance, lightly salt the shredded cabbage first, let it sit in a bowl for 20 to 30 minutes, and then, taking up the cabbage in handfuls, gently squeeze some of the excess liquid out of the cabbage before tossing it with the other ingredients.

Asparagus Salad

For asparagus to be served cool with a vinaigrette, first peel the bottom third of each asparagus stalk with a peeler, and snap off the end. Blanch the asparagus in a large pot of boiling, lightly-salted water, only to heat it through and brighten the color, 30 seconds to 1 minute. Plunge the asparagus into cold water for a moment to stop the cooking, then drain, pat dry, chill, dress, and serve. Any vinaigrette may be used; a citrusy one is traditional and delicious. Homemade Mayonnaise (page 252) or Aioli (page 253) are also superb on asparagus. Pristinely fresh asparagus may be cut into fine matchsticks and served raw, tossed with a little Lemon Vinaigrette (page 174).

Green Bean Salad with Cherry Tomatoes and Basil

serves 6 to 8

To make this summer garden picnic salad extra-special, procure a colorful assortment of green beans and cherry tomatoes. It can be made more substantial with the addition of a cupful of cooked, well-drained beans (page 106) or fresh shell beans (page 122).

- about 1½ pounds assorted summer green beans: blue lake, yellow wax, romano, etc.
- salt for blanching beans, plus ½ teaspoon for dressing
- about ½ pound assorted cherry tomatoes: red, yellow, pear, etc.
- 2 sprigs green basil
- 2 sprigs purple basil
- ½ shallot, minced
- 1 small clove garlic, crushed
- 2 tablespoons red wine vinegar
- 1 tablespoon balsamic vinegar
- 3 to 4 tablespoons extra-virgin olive oil
- freshly ground black pepper to taste

Pinch the tops and tails off the beans. Arrange them in 3 to 4 batches according to size and variety. Bring a large pot of water to boil, and have a large bowl of ice water close at hand. Salt the boiling water until it tastes slightly salty, and dissolve a similar amount of salt in the ice water, too. Plunge the first batch of beans into the boiling water, stir them around, and let cook just until tender. Taste a bean to tell—the beans should be neither crunchy nor mushy. Using a skimmer, transfer the beans to the ice water—this stops the cooking and "locks in" their fresh flavor. Add an extra pinch of salt to the water (the first batch of beans will have absorbed some salt), and cook the next batch of beans, repeating until all the beans are cooked. Remove the beans from the ice water when cool, let drain thoroughly, then arrange the beans on a couple of thicknesses of paper towels to blot away all excess water.

Cut the cherry tomatoes in half lengthwise, or "pole to pole"—this helps them retain more of their juice. Pick the leaves from the sprigs of basil, and chop coarsely. In a cup, combine the shallot, garlic, both kinds of vinegar, and ½ teaspoon salt.

To serve, make sure all the components are at room temperature. Toss the beans, tomatoes, basil, vinegar mixture, olive oil, and pepper together. Mound the salad on a platter, and serve immediately.

Marinated Beets

serves 4 to 6

Beets are maybe not universally loved, but we beet lovers love beet salads with especial zeal, to which this recipe attests. I almost never prepare beets any other way, and over the years, I've won over many a beet hater—those who insist beets taste like dirt or recall bad childhood experiences with canned or overcooked beets. Well-cooked beets are appealingly sweet and yet, well, earthy tasting. (Of course, they taste particularly good if they are grown in good earth.) To keep the earthiness in check, I always include at least a little orange, and often a fennel-y thing as well: shaved fennel (page 167), or a bit of tarragon or chervil.

Somehow, beets taste more broad and substantial than many other vegetables. Grown year-round, they are especially welcome in the fall, winter, and spring. Serve a pile of these beets atop a green salad, or on a bed of shaved fennel tossed with lemon juice.

Or topped with a few slices of peeled fresh orange and strewn with crushed toasted walnuts. Or sprinkled with fresh chervil sprigs (or chopped tarragon) and draped with prosciutto. Or dolloped with Fresh Horseradish Cream or Slovenian Horseradish Sauce (page 250). Sliced beets can be layered with rounds of goat cheese, or simmered in beef stew to make Russian Borscht (page 186). Possibilities abound.

If not only red beets but Chioggia (pink striped) beets or golden beets are available, cook, peel, slice, and dress all three varieties separately and keep them in separate bowls until serving time—a salad or composed dish with all three colors (the Chioggia sliced horizontally to show off the bull's-eye pattern) is one of the most spectacularly colorful sights of cool-weather cookery. Although the yellow and Chioggia varieties taste very good, plain old red beets, awash in pigment, are still my favorite.

1½ pounds beets *(if possible, choose beets of even size)*

2 teaspoons olive oil

¼ teaspoon salt, plus more as needed

¼ cup water

¼ teaspoon finely grated orange zest

2 tablespoons fresh orange juice

2 tablespoons red wine vinegar

freshly ground black pepper

1 tablespoon chopped tarragon, chervil, or wild fennel flowers *(optional)*

Heat the oven to 400°F. Cut off all but ½ inch of the beet greens and, if fresh and leafy, save for another use (see page 132). Scrub the beets well under running water. Toss them with the olive oil and ¼ teaspoon salt, and arrange them in a baking dish in which they will fit comfortably in one layer. Pour ¼ cup water into the dish and cover with aluminum foil (shiny side down), tightly—otherwise the water will evaporate and the beets will burn. Bake for 40 minutes (for golf ball–sized beets), or until the biggest beet offers no resistance when pierced to the center with a small knife. In my experience, large beets might take as long as 1½ hours. Remove the foil very carefully—the steam can burn your hand. Let the beets cool in the dish for about 20 minutes, then cut off the tops and tails and slip off the skins. Wipe any remaining bits of skin off with your hand—do not rinse the beets in running water.

Sometimes the skin is stubborn and must be peeled off with a paring knife.

Slice the beets lengthwise into wedges and place in a medium bowl. Add the orange zest and juice, red wine vinegar, additional salt, and pepper to taste. Toss well, and taste for balanced sweet, acidic, and salt flavors. Toss the beets again in their dressing just before serving.

Carrot-Raisin Salad

serves 6 to 8

The old church-potluck classic, new and improved with citrus and black pepper! One November, the Deep Springs gardeners pulled a bumper crop of carrots when an early hard freeze threatened. The Boardinghouse walk-in refrigerator was filled with crates and crates of carrots, dirt still clinging to the fat orange roots—the smell was powerfully fresh, sweet, and earthy.

Feel free to try variations of this salad using beets or parsnips in place of the carrots—these tougher vegetables require a fine, sturdy grater, but their flavors are excellent.

⅓ cup golden raisins or Zante currants

4 cups grated rainbow carrots *(or regular orange carrots)*

grated zest and juice of ½ orange

grated zest and juice of ½ lemon

1 teaspoon red wine vinegar

⅔ cup mayonnaise, or to taste, or a blend of yogurt and mayonnaise

¼ teaspoon salt

freshly ground black pepper

Pour boiling water over the raisins in a small bowl. Let plump for about 15 minutes, then drain and cool. Take handfuls of the grated carrots and gently squeeze out some excess juice (I always drink this). In a medium bowl, combine the drained raisins and carrots with the orange zest and juice, lemon zest and juice, vinegar, mayonnaise, salt, and pepper to taste. Taste: there should be just enough salt and lemon juice to temper the inherent sweetness of the other ingredients. Serve, or chill if serving later.

Celery Root Salad

serves 2 to 3

If you want a light, lunchtime accompaniment for steak in the cold months, try this simple herbed celery root salad from my friend Mona Talbott, a wonderful chef who cooked at Chez Panisse and the American Academy in Rome. Celery root, also known as *celeriac*, is more versatile in its uses and more subtle and complex in flavor than stalk celery. A common vegetable in northern Europe, it can be cooked like a potato; many potato dishes are enhanced by substituting celery root for some of the potato. It makes marvelous soups. Instead of the herbs in this recipe, the julienned celery root can be combined with crisp apples, walnuts, and a little mayonnaise to make a sophisticated *Waldorf salad*.

1 medium celery root, scrubbed and peeled

juice of ½ lemon

½ teaspoon sunflower oil or other vegetable oil

salt and freshly ground black pepper

2 to 3 tablespoons chopped fresh dill

2 to 3 tablespoons chopped fresh parsley

With your chef's knife, cut the celery root into fine julienne. Toss in a medium bowl with the lemon juice, oil, a pinch of salt, pepper to taste, and the dill and parsley. Serve alongside your favorite steak.

Corn Salad

serves 2 to 4

Cooking corn "locks in" the sweetness, so I prefer to cook it first for salad, rather than just using it raw. I love to eat this alongside a simple piece of Baked Salmon (page 222).

3 ears cooked corn on the cob (page 127)**, chilled**

about 2 tablespoons Lemon Vinaigrette (*page 174, substituting lime for the lemon, if you like*)

1 small green jalapeño, seeded and minced

1 small red jalapeño, outer dark red part only, minced

¼ teaspoon salt

few twists freshly ground black pepper

Cut the corn kernels from the cobs with a knife. Scrape the bare cobs with the back of the knife to extract all the germ and milk. In a medium bowl, toss the corn with the vinaigrette, green and red jalapeño, salt, and pepper. Taste for salt, piquancy, and acidity.

Summer Cucumber Salad

serves 2 to 3

This refreshing, simple salad contains no oil. It's a great opportunity to use the variety of cucumbers that grows each year in the Deep Springs garden (or that you find at your summer farmers market): lemon cucumbers, Persian cucumbers, English cucumbers, Armenian cucumbers…. Peel only if the skin is tough or bitter; scoop out the seeds only if they are big. White balsamic vinegar has a singular sweetness that is especially well-suited to cucumbers. If you don't have any, just mix a few drops of honey into red wine vinegar. These cucumbers are good company to a spoonful of Marinated Beets, page 164. Sweet summer red onion, thinly sliced into rings, may be included, in addition to or instead of the garlic.

1 small clove garlic, finely crushed to a purée

2 teaspoons white balsamic vinegar (*or 1¾ teaspoons red wine vinegar mixed with ¼ teaspoon honey*)

- **heaping ¼ teaspoon salt**
- **2 cups bite-size cucumber chunks** *(from an assortment of cucumbers)*
- **6 basil leaves, coarsely chopped**

Mix the garlic, vinegar, and salt together in a medium bowl. Toss in the cucumbers and basil. Serve immediately.

Shaved Fennel

Raw shaved fennel, seasoned only with a little lemon juice, is an excellent base for many salads, or served by itself with pork, chicken, or fish. Fennel is best in cool weather; hot weather dulls its flavor and appeal. Try it with a sandwich, instead of chips; it may be successfully eaten with your fingers. Fennel is best freshly cut but will hold in an airtight container or bag, refrigerated, for a few hours. It pairs well with artichokes, beets, pears, nuts, citrus, and shellfish. For more information on fennel, see page 130.

Fennel bulbs that are flatter tend to have a more pronounced fennel flavor than ones that are more bulbous. Trim the outer layer and dark green stalks from a large bulb of fennel. Reserve a small bunch of fronds from the top, preferably the feathery inner fronds. Using a mandoline slicer, shave the fennel bulb across the grain in paper-thin slices. If you don't have a mandoline, use a knife to first cut the fennel bulb in half lengthwise, then slice crosswise on the diagonal as thinly as possible, being patient but decisive. Chop the reserved fronds coarsely. Toss the fennel and fronds with a squeeze (about a teaspoon per fennel bulb) of lemon juice.

SHAVED FENNEL WITH PEARS AND PARMESAN

Gently toss a big handful of shaved fennel with 2 sliced sweet, ripe pears (peeled or not), a squeeze of lemon juice, ample shavings of Parmesan, a pinch of salt, a twist of pepper, and a good drizzle of extra-virgin olive oil. Slices of prosciutto are great with this salad.

Fennel, Blood Orange, and Toasted Almond Salad

serves 3 to 4

Blood oranges are a great winter treat. They don't come into their season until January, and they are usually finished by March. They look and taste as if the cells of an ordinary small, tart orange had been injected with the juice of fresh raspberries. This salad is one of the blood orange's nicest manifestations. The unusual marriage of flavors will continue to haunt you long after you have licked the plate clean.

- **½ cup whole almonds, lightly toasted** *(see page 176; walnuts are also good)*
- **3 tablespoons extra-virgin olive oil**
- **1 fennel bulb**
- **½ lemon**
- **2 to 3 blood oranges**
- **salt and freshly ground black pepper**

When the toasted almonds are cool, chop them haphazardly (with many coarse pieces, but also plenty of fine pieces), then mix them well with the olive oil in a small bowl. Shave the fennel thinly and chop a good handful of the inner fronds coarsely (as described in the previous recipe) and toss with a squeeze of lemon juice in a medium bowl. Wash the blood oranges in cool water, towel dry, then finely grate the outer colored zest of one or two of the oranges into another bowl. Using a small, sharp, serrated knife, peel the oranges, cutting all the white pith away from the flesh. Cut the oranges lengthwise in half, then crosswise into thin half-moons, removing any seeds. Collect all the juice as you cut the oranges, combining it in the bowl with the zest.

Gently but thoroughly toss together the shaved fennel, an extra squeeze of lemon, the oranges with all their juice and zest, and the almond-oil mixture, with a couple of good pinches of salt and a twist of pepper. Mound the salad on individual serving plates (or serve family style, heaped on a big platter) and serve immediately.

FENNEL, ORANGE, AND BLACK OLIVE SALAD
For a delicious southern French variation, use good, regular navel oranges, substitute black oil-cured olives for the almonds, and include thinly sliced rings of sweet red onion.

Gazpacho

serves 4

Here is a magnificent version of the famous Andalusian summertime chilled soup. For best results, your tomatoes should be dead-ripe and bursting with flavorful juice. For variations of this soup, try a *gazpacho californiano*, adding a little fresh, cooked corn and a little cubed avocado, and using cilantro instead of parsley. If you have tomatoes in assorted colors, you can serve a spectacular *double-tomato gazpacho:* make a batch of gazpacho using yellow tomatoes, and another batch using red tomatoes. Using 2 ladles and a mustering of confidence, simultaneously fill each bowl with both colors of soup. The gazpachos will remain separate in the bowl.

SOUP BASE

2½ pounds sweet, red, ripe tomatoes

1¾ teaspoons salt, or more as needed

freshly ground black pepper

4 teaspoons red wine vinegar, or more as needed

1 teaspoon balsamic vinegar

1 small clove garlic, finely crushed

5 tablespoons extra-virgin olive oil, or more as needed

GARNISHES

1 tablespoon minced red onion

2 tablespoons chopped cucumber

1 tablespoon minced red or yellow bell pepper

2 to 3 teaspoons minced jalapeño or other hot pepper

½ cup Croutons *(page 175)*, lightly crushed

1 to 2 tablespoons chopped parsley

Following the method on page 148, make Tomato Concassé from 2½ pounds of ripe summer tomatoes, dicing the tomato solids finely, and catching every drop of tomato juice. You should have about 4 cups of tomato solids swimming in juice. Season this base with 1¾ teaspoons salt, pepper to taste, the red wine vinegar, balsamic vinegar, and garlic. Gently whisk in about 5 tablespoons of extra-virgin olive oil. Taste for balanced acidity, salt, and oil, adjusting as necessary. Stir in the garnishing ingredients: minced red onion, chopped cucumber, minced sweet bell pepper, minced hot pepper, lightly crushed croutons, and chopped parsley. Chill well, taste again for salt, and serve the same day in chilled, wide, white bowls.

Jícama

This big, round, buff-colored tuber is sold year-round in most supermarkets (usually next to the hot chiles) or Latin American markets. Easy to grow in warm climates, it has a mild sweetness and a satisfying, crunchy texture. Kids love jícama once they try it. In Mexico, jícama is often served dressed with fresh lime juice, salt, and powdered chile, but I am usually so taken with just the lime and salt that I never get to the chile. As part of a festive table of Mexican dishes, you can mimic the colors of the Mexican flag with a relish tray of red radishes, green lime wedges, and lovely snow-white jícama.

Select a large jícama with smooth skin and no blemishes. Peel it with a knife—the outer layer of skin is tough. Slice the jícama in ¼-inch-thick slices, then cut the slices to make large matchsticks. Squeeze the juice of a lime into a medium bowl, add the jícama, and toss with enough salt to balance the sweetness of the jícama and the acidity of the lime; taste small pieces until you get it right.

For a more complex dish, you can toss this seasoned jícama with peeled, sliced oranges and orange zest, sliced red radishes, and coarsely-chopped cilantro, echoing a wonderful recipe in *The Greens Cookbook*.

Black Kale, Golden Beets, and Leeks with Orange Oil

This splendid, room-temperature winter vegetable dish triangulates very well with roast lamb and a sprightly green salad with mint leaves and shaved fennel. The proportions of the three vegetables are flexible; I aim for about 40% kale, 30% beets, and 30% leeks by volume. First, prepare the golden beets using the Marinated Beets recipe (including the orange and vinegar dressing) on page 164.

Wash a Seville orange (a sour variety with uniquely flavorful zest, used in English marmalade; lacking a Seville, blood oranges, tangerines, or navel oranges may be used), and finely grate its zest into a small cup containing a few tablespoons of high-quality extra-virgin olive oil. Stir, cover, and set aside at room temperature to let the orange flavor infuse the oil.

Trim the root and all dark green parts off the leeks, leaving the leek bottoms intact. Soak the leeks in cool water to ensure they are free of dirt. Bring a large pot of water to a boil, and salt the water well, until it tastes lightly salty. Boil the leeks for several minutes (this depends on the size and freshness of the leeks), or until they can be easily pierced on the bottom with a small knife. The leeks should be completely tender, but not falling apart. Remove the leeks to a plate to cool. Keep the water hot for blanching the kale. Once cool, cut smaller leeks crosswise in half, and larger ones in quarters. Line up the leeks on a platter, cover, and set aside.

Meanwhile, wash the kale (black kale is ideal, and is also known as lacinato kale, Italian kale, or dino kale), and remove the leafy parts from the stems: form an "O" with your thumb and index finger, and pull each kale leaf through by its stem, stripping off the leafy parts, discarding the stems. Tear each leafy part in two slim pieces. In the same boiling water as the leeks, blanch the kale leaves for about a minute, or until just tender but still vibrant, with only a hint of crunch remaining. Dip the kale in a bowl of ice water to halt the cooking, then spread out on a tray covered with a towel to dry. Cover and set aside.

To serve the dish, ensure all vegetables are at room temperature. Strain the orange olive oil. Toss the kale with a little orange oil, and arrange on a serving platter. Toss the beets with their dressing, and scatter the beets over and around the kale, reserving the extra dressing. Drizzle a little orange oil over the leeks, carefully tossing them to distribute the oil, then arrange them over and around the kale and beets. Drizzle the remaining dressing from the beets over everything, and serve.

Kohlrabi-Apple Slaw

serves 3 to 4

A crunchy, elegant slaw, made from an almost-forgotten winter vegetable. Like other members of the cabbage family, kohlrabi tastes sweetest when grown in cool weather.

- ½ large Fuji apple, cut into julienne *(matchsticks)*
- 1 large kohlrabi *(about 12 ounces)*, peeled and cut into julienne *(matchsticks)*
- ¼ cup finely diced shallot or red onion
- juice of ½ lemon
- ½ teaspoon apple cider vinegar
- ¼ teaspoon salt
- ¼ teaspoon celery seed
- 1 tablespoon sunflower oil or other vegetable oil

If you are slow at cutting the apple, douse it with a bit of the lemon juice so it doesn't brown. Combine the apple, kohlrabi, shallot, lemon juice, vinegar, salt, celery seed, and oil in a medium bowl. Serve chilled. It will still be good and crisp the next day.

Orange and Date Salad

serves 4 to 6

This salad, based on a recipe I found in an antique American fruit cookbook, is timelessly delicious in the cooler months, served with pork, poultry, or lamb.

8 ounces Medjool dates

2 large navel oranges

⅓ cup Shallot Vinaigrette (page 173)**, made without the optional garlic**

lettuce leaves for serving

Halve the dates, remove the pits, and cut each half lengthwise in two. Wash and dry the oranges, and finely grate the colored outer zest of one of the oranges into the vinaigrette. Using a small, sharp, serrated knife, peel the oranges, removing all the bitter white pith. With the knife, cut each orange section from the membrane. Gently toss the dates, orange sections, and vinaigrette together in a medium bowl. Serve immediately (before the orange throws off too much of its juice), atop lettuce leaves on individual plates or piled in the center of a platter lined with lettuce leaves.

Potato Salad

serves 8 to 10

When freshly made with ample mayonnaise, this is your potato salad dream come true. I first started making it while cooking at a neighborhood deli in Hawaii (a job I loved, after years of more formal restaurant work). One morning, when I hadn't been at the job long, I found myself with little to work with besides a large bunch of dill, a red cabbage, some cucumbers, and a box of russet potatoes. Knowing that the islanders don't fool around with their potato salad—they like lots of hard-boiled eggs and mayonnaise—I decided we couldn't go wrong with a big bowl of it in the deli case, laced with bright-tasting vegetables and tinted an appealing golden yellow with a bit of American mustard. Lo and behold, it was an instant favorite. Fresh cucumber and fresh dill replace the usual pickle, and the cabbage adds crunch and more fresh flavor. Though most potato salad recipes call for waxy-type potatoes instead of russets, here is a case where the texture and starchiness of russets are better suited.

6 eggs

6 large russet potatoes, peeled and cut into ¾-inch chunks

1 tablespoon salt, plus more as needed

1 small red onion, finely diced

2 tablespoons red wine vinegar, or more as needed

¾ cup finely diced celery

1 cup diced seedless cucumber

½ cup chopped green cabbage

½ cup chopped red cabbage

½ cup coarsely chopped fresh dill

¼ cup yellow mustard or other mustard

about 1 cup mayonnaise, or more as needed

½ teaspoon freshly ground black pepper, or more as needed

Hard-boil the eggs according to the directions on page 91. Peel and chop them coarsely. (To chop eggs easily, I press them through the grid of a cooling rack or other wire grid.)

Put the potatoes in a pot and cover them with cold water. Add the 1 tablespoon salt and bring to a boil. Reduce the heat to medium-high and skim off any scum that rises to the surface. After 7 or 8 minutes, check the potatoes: when done, the corners and edges will have rounded a little, and a cube will yield easily without melting to a mush when gently crushed with a fork. Drain the potatoes well in a colander for about 5 minutes, then scatter on a tray to cool completely. This method results in potatoes that are dry and ready to absorb moisture and flavor from the dressing. In a small bowl, macerate the diced red onion in the red wine vinegar with a pinch of salt while you prepare the other vegetables.

In a large bowl, mix together the cooled potatoes, eggs, onion-vinegar mixture, celery, cucumber, green and red cabbage, dill, mustard, mayonnaise, and pepper, tasting to make sure the salt, pepper, and vinegar are balanced. Add more mayonnaise if you would like a creamier salad. This potato salad is best served immediately, when the potatoes still have their freshly cooked texture and the mixture is just slightly cooler than room temperature. If made of sound ingredients (mayonnaise from a newly opened jar, for instance), it will still be perfectly fit to eat after an hour of sitting, covered, at room temperature. Otherwise, it's best to chill it immediately. If you plan on having leftover potato salad, refrigerate the amount you want left over as soon as you make it.

Vinaigrette Potato Salads

Red, white, yellow, or even purple potatoes make good potato salads with vinegar-based dressings. This type of potato salad may be served warm or at room temperature, and is lighter than the preceding recipe. Cook the potatoes whole unless they're very large, and peel them only if you want an especially refined result. Always start the potatoes in cold water and bring to a boil, and salt the water well. When the potatoes can be easily pierced with a fork, they're done. Drain well. As soon as the potatoes are cool enough to handle, slice or dice them, and immediately toss them with a few spoonfuls of vinaigrette, allowing them to absorb the vinaigrette. (Vinaigrette recipes are found on pages 173 to 174.) Add a little extra mustard and toss again. Add whatever further augmentations you like: onion, green onion, shallot, celery, capers, cabbage, lettuces, cooked green beans, pickles, olives, hard-cooked eggs, bacon, herbs…then toss with more vinaigrette and black pepper, tasting carefully and adjusting as necessary.

For *German potato salad*, use coarse-grain mustard in the dressing, include plenty of cooked bacon, onions, and parsley, and serve warm. For a *French-style potato salad*, use shallots, cornichon pickles, Dijon mustard, and parsley. Include cooked, sliced pork sausage, and serve warm or at room temperature.

Radishes

When the weather starts to cool, watch the radishes in your market: when they appear nice and fresh, with few cracks, their greens vibrant, buy a bunch, pull off the greens, pinch off the little roots, wash well, and chill in a shallow bowl with a little water added. Drain off the water and serve in their bowl with a good loaf of bread (a French baguette is ideal), butter, and salt. To eat, dip a radish lightly in the salt and eat bites of radish between bites of generously buttered bread.

Summer Squash Carpaccio

serves 2 to 3

This quick, simple, beautiful salad is best made with very fresh, young (but not "baby") summer squash, in a variety of colors and shapes, such as dark green zucchini, yellow crookneck, and pale green pattypan. See page 194 for a classic beef carpaccio recipe.

2 or 3 very fresh young summer squash

salt and freshly ground black pepper

1 piece of Parmesan or Pecorino Romano cheese *(for shaving over the carpaccio)*

extra-virgin olive oil

¼ cup chopped, lightly toasted walnuts *(optional)*

several leaves of fresh mint or basil

Wipe the squash clean with a damp towel, and shave it paper-thin with a mandolin slicer. Arrange the slices, overlapping slightly, on large, individual plates, or on a very large platter if serving several people. Sprinkle evenly with salt and pepper. With a vegetable peeler, shave some strips of Parmesan over the squash. Drizzle everything with extra-virgin olive oil. If you like, scatter a handful of chopped, lightly toasted walnuts (see page 176; for excellent flavor, rub the excess skin off the walnuts, and toss them in a drop or two of olive oil and a sprinkling of salt). Arrange the mint leaves into a stack and cut into fine ribbons (chiffonade) with a sharp knife. Strew over the carpaccio and serve immediately.

Tomatoes with Salt

One of my Deep Springs classmates used to quote his Tennessee grandfather: "Ain't but two things in this world money can't buy—true, true love and homegrown tomatoes." In late summer, the Deep Springs community revels in the garden's inevitably abundant tomato crop. Some students, in fact, taste their first homegrown tomato at Deep Springs. During tomato season, rarely do I serve a meal that does not include a slice or two of tomato with a sprinkling of sea salt. That includes breakfast—tomatoes are very good with eggs, bacon, and toast.

Tomatoes are in season, depending on the climate of your area, from roughly mid-July through October. Ripe summer tomatoes are extraordinarily good with nothing more than salt. Balanced sweet and acid, juicy, and succulent—few other fruits or vegetables possess such dynamics within their skin. There are dozens of varieties, of all shapes, sizes, and colors. Each has its own characteristics and balance. Though an assortment is beautiful to behold, the cultivation, not the variety, determines the goodness of the tomato. The plant itself needs ample water to grow, but as it fruits, less water is needed. Once the plant sets fruit, some growers allow the roots to find water deep in the ground, letting the soil's surface remain dry. Such "dry-farmed" tomatoes are excellent, with deeply concentrated flavors and pigments.

As assorted, colorful "heirloom" tomatoes have grown in popularity (and price), commercial growers have profited from such practices as overwatering the tomatoes to increase weight, shipping them long distances, cold-storing them for long periods, and even growing them in hothouses for year-round availability—all deleterious to quality. *The most delicious tomatoes are grown in warm soil, with minimal water, in summer, close by.* Finally, keep tomatoes at room temperature whenever possible. They should be refrigerated only when you suspect they might go bad before you can use them.

Slice ripe summer tomatoes thickly and arrange them, slightly overlapping, on a plate. Sprinkle evenly with salt. Tomatoes benefit from rather a lot of salt. Pepper lightly, if you like. After salt, if you want to enrich this simplest of salads, drizzle with a little extra-virgin olive oil. If you wish, sprinkle with a thoughtfully chosen herb—while coarsely chopped basil is, like olive oil, an old, familiar friend of the tomato, other herbs, such as dill, mint, marjoram, and thyme, are equally persuasive. Serve tomatoes very soon after you salt them; they will throw off liquid—and flavor—as they stand.

Summer Tomato Sandwich

Spread mayonnaise generously on a slice of soft bread. Place thick, juicy slices of summer tomato over the mayonnaise, sprinkling well with salt, and a little pepper if you like. Eat over the sink.

Thyme Salt

You may enhance tomatoes—or many other foods such as eggs, mushrooms, steak, chicken, rice, or beans—with this lovely green, aromatic salt. Take 4 or 5 fresh sprigs of thyme and tear off the tiny leaf clusters, discarding the tough stems. Pound the thyme in a mortar and pestle with about 3 tablespoons of salt (ideally, coarse sea salt) until the herb is pulverized and the salt is green. If the mixture seems very moist, add a tablespoon more salt. If there are visible pieces of herb left in the salt, you may strain them out by rubbing the salt through a screen sieve. Keep the thyme salt in an open bowl on the counter for several days, allowing the mixture to dry completely, then keep in an airtight container.

Watermelon, Feta, and Basil Salad

The combination of salty feta and sweet summer watermelon is startlingly good in this simple, modern salad. Break or cut a large, chilled watermelon in half (page 283). Using a small knife, cut around the perimeter of the large central seedless heart of the melon, and carefully ease the heart out. Slice the heart into thin slices. Arrange the melon, overlapping, on individual salad plates, allowing several slices per plate. For each plate, slice about 1½ ounces of feta cheese in thinnish slices, and intersperse them with the slices of watermelon. Tuck a few basil leaves here and there. Squeeze fresh lime juice over the salad, then drizzle with extra-virgin olive oil. Salt the watermelon lightly, twist a little black pepper over the whole salad, and serve immediately.

Shallot Vinaigrette

makes about 1½ cups

First, pronunciation: "vinaigrette" has only three syllables, not four; it is pronounced "vin-ay-GRET," not "vin-e-gar-ette." But however you say it, it's a terrifically tasty and versatile salad dressing. I make this and the lemon vinaigrette that follows constantly at Deep Springs. Both recipes contain a small amount of Dijon mustard. If the oil is added slowly while whisking, the mustard emulsifies the dressing. Even after it has sat for awhile and separated, the dressing will re-emulsify when shaken if it was correctly made the first time. The ratio of oil to vinegar varies. Use the lesser amount of olive oil at first, then taste the vinaigrette by dipping the tip of a lettuce leaf into it. Depending on the flavor of your salad greens and your own taste, you may want a sharper vinaigrette (less oil) or a smoother one (more oil).

1 small shallot, finely minced *(or 2 to 3 tablespoons finely diced red onion)*

1 small clove garlic, crushed to a purée *(optional)*

¼ cup red wine vinegar

2 tablespoons balsamic vinegar

¾ teaspoon salt

¼ teaspoon freshly ground black pepper

1 tablespoon Dijon mustard or other type of mustard

½ teaspoon chopped fresh thyme, or ¼ teaspoon dried thyme

¼ cup sunflower oil or other vegetable oil

½ to ¾ cup extra-virgin olive oil

In a deep bowl, mix the shallot, garlic (if using), red wine and balsamic vinegars, salt, pepper, mustard, and thyme with a whisk or a fork. Let stand for about 15 minutes. Slowly whisk in the oils, beginning with the vegetable oil. The technique is similar to that for making a mayonnaise (see page 252): drizzle the sunflower oil into the bowl in a thin stream while whisking constantly; the mixture should thicken slightly. After adding the vegetable oil, whisk in the olive oil in a thin stream. Taste for balanced salt and vinegar—it should not be so vinegary that it burns the back of your throat. Add more oil if necessary. The correct amount of oil can never be specified exactly; it depends on the flavor of your salad greens, the acidity level of the vinegar, the season, the temperature...and your mood. Sometimes you will want a very tart vinaigrette, other times a more oily one. Vinaigrette is best used the day it's made but will taste good for a few days if kept refrigerated (let it come to room temperature if the oil congeals).

OTHER VINAIGRETTES

For a good tart *balsamic vinaigrette*, reverse the amounts of balsamic and red wine vinegar (¼ cup balsamic vinegar, 2 tablespoons red wine vinegar). For a *sweet balsamic vinaigrette*, use all balsamic vinegar. Use a tablespoon more of mustard, and a tablespoon less of vinegar, for a *mustard vinaigrette*. Sherry vinegar, apple cider vinegar, and champagne vinegar will yield, respectively, *sherry vinaigrette*, *apple cider vinaigrette*, and *champagne vinaigrette*.

Lemon Vinaigrette

makes about 1¼ cups

This vinaigrette is tasty and bright, with a good lemon color, not from the lemon but from the olive oil. It is excellent tossed with spinach salad with hard-boiled egg, with arugula and other "assertive" greens, or with sweet lettuces (such as romaine) and shaved Parmesan. Good on many cooked vegetables, it is ideal with asparagus or artichokes. For a more complex *citrus vinaigrette*, use zest and juice from a blend of flavorful tart and sweet citrus, such as limes, Seville oranges, blood oranges, kumquats, and tangerines.

1 small clove garlic, crushed to a purée

finely grated zest of 1 lemon

juice of 2 lemons (about ⅓ cup)

2 tablespoons champagne vinegar, red wine vinegar, or cider vinegar

¾ teaspoon salt

¼ teaspoon white pepper

1 tablespoon Dijon mustard

¼ cup sunflower oil or other vegetable oil

½ cup extra-virgin olive oil

In a deep bowl, combine the garlic, lemon zest, lemon juice, vinegar, salt, white pepper, and mustard. Slowly whisk in the oils, beginning with the sunflower oil. The technique is similar to that for making mayonnaise (see page 252): drizzle the sunflower oil into the bowl in a thin stream while whisking constantly; the mixture should thicken slightly. After adding the sunflower oil, whisk in the olive oil in a thin stream. Taste for balanced flavors—if the vinaigrette is too tart, add a little more oil.

Ranch Dressing

makes about 1 cup; serves 4 to 5

Delectable when freshly made, this dressing is also still good the next day. For greater speed and convenience, you may omit any or all of the herbs and call it simply *buttermilk dressing*. It will still taste good and ranchy. To make a ranch dip, substitute sour cream for the buttermilk.

½ clove garlic

⅛ teaspoon salt, or more as needed

¾ cup mayonnaise

2 tablespoons fresh lime juice, or more as needed

⅓ cup buttermilk

1 heaping tablespoon finely chopped cilantro

1 heaping tablespoon finely chopped parsley

1 heaping tablespoon finely chopped chives

¼ teaspoon black pepper, or more as needed

In a deep bowl, crush the garlic well with ⅛ teaspoon salt. Mix in the mayonnaise, then whisk in the lime juice, buttermilk, herbs, and pepper until smooth. Or shake the ingredients together in a jar. Taste, and adjust the salt, pepper, and lime juice as necessary.

Blue Cheese Dressing

makes about 3 cups; serves 10 to 12

For a treat, heavily drizzle this dressing over a standing-up wedge of iceberg lettuce on a plate, and serve with a knife and fork, and scatter warm, crispy bite-size chunks of bacon over the top. You could pack up to 8 ounces of blue cheese into this, but at that point you would have a *blue cheese dip*, not a dressing.

- 1½ cups mayonnaise
- 1 cup buttermilk
- 1 cup crumbled blue cheese *(about 6 ounces)*
- 1½ tablespoons apple cider vinegar, or more as needed
- ¼ teaspoon dry mustard
- ¼ teaspoon white pepper

In a medium bowl, whisk together, one by one, the mayonnaise, buttermilk, blue cheese, vinegar, dry mustard, and white pepper, or shake together in a jar. Taste for salt and acidity, adding salt and more cider vinegar if needed.

Toasted Cumin–Mint–Yogurt Dressing

makes 2 cups; serves about 8

Two strong, distinctive flavors—cumin and mint—marry beautifully in this creamy dressing, complementing and tempering one another.

- 1 tablespoon ground cumin
- 1 cup yogurt
- ¾ cup mayonnaise
- ½ cup buttermilk
- ¼ cup chopped fresh mint
- ¼ teaspoon black pepper, or more as needed
- ½ teaspoon salt

Toast the cumin in a small skillet over a medium-high flame until it releases a nutty fragrance; do not let it scorch. In a medium bowl, combine the cumin, yogurt, mayonnaise, buttermilk, mint, pepper, and salt with a whisk until smooth, or shake together in a jar. Taste and adjust the seasoning as necessary.

IMPROVISED CREAMY DRESSINGS

Using the previous three recipes as a rough guide, you may easily improvise a quick creamy dressing. Start by blending mayonnaise with either yogurt or buttermilk—you decide the proportions. Add a bit of vinegar or lemon or lime juice for added tartness, salt for balance, and freshly ground black pepper. Throw in a minced shallot for a creamy shallot dressing, or ripe avocado, crushed anchovy, and lots of finely chopped herbs for a Green Goddess–style dressing. Taste and adjust the seasoning as necessary.

Croutons

I am inordinately fond of croutons: I can eat them like potato chips. If I want to add a single element to a simple mixed green salad, I choose croutons. Different kinds of bread result in different kinds of croutons; most sliced sandwich bread is decidedly sweet and will taste odd in salads. Baguettes or other sturdy-textured, artisan-style breads make good croutons, as do any of the savory breads in this book (see the chapter beginning on page 74).

Heat the oven to 325°F. Cut the crust from a loaf of day-old bread. Tear the loaf into bite-size pieces (or cut into evenly sized cubes). Toss the pieces in plenty of olive oil—about ½ cup for a large loaf of bread—and a little salt. Bake on a rimmed baking sheet, tossing and redistributing every 7 to 8 minutes (even after many years of cooking professionally, I always set a timer for croutons). Be patient and vigilant. Bake just until pale gold and crispy throughout. The moment you take them from the oven, gently toss them in a tablespoon or two more olive oil (this time, use your best extra-virgin) and salt (if necessary) and pepper to taste. When you make tossed salads, toss the croutons with everything else, so the croutons absorb some of the dressing.

Toasted Nuts

You may toast nuts at 300°F, 325°F, or 350°F, or even a low 250°F. The lower the temperature, the longer it takes, but the less chance there is of burning them. Scatter raw, shelled nuts on a sheet pan, and put in the oven. At 350°F, check them every 5 minutes or so, tossing and redistributing the nuts on the sheet. At 250°F, check every 10 minutes. As with croutons (preceding recipe), I always set a timer when toasting nuts. I think all nuts are best toasted until they are a very pale brown; darker brown nuts take on a toasted-grain flavor, and the characteristic fragrance of their variety is lost. Once nuts begin to brown, they quickly burn. *Almonds,* loved by everyone when freshly toasted, take about 10 minutes in a 350°F oven and 45 to 50 minutes in a 250°F oven. *Hazelnuts* (also called *filberts*) take about as long as almonds. *Walnuts* take less time, depending on the size of the pieces. Walnuts and hazelnuts have papery, shiny, bitter skin that may be partly rubbed off after they are toasted—take up handfuls and rub lightly, letting the bitter skins fall out. *Pecans* must be watched carefully, as their skins are dark to begin with.

While the nuts are still warm, toss them with a few drops of olive oil—just enough to coat, then toss them with fine salt. For each pound of nuts, allow about 2 teaspoons of salt. To make fine salt, grind regular salt to a powder in a mortar, or in a cup with the handle of a wooden spoon. In addition to the salt, a pinch of cayenne is often good, as is black pepper.

Mixed Salted Nuts

For a superb, luxurious mix, use equal parts whole almonds, blanched almonds (see below), hazelnuts, and pecans. Following the instructions for Toasted Nuts in the preceding recipe, lightly toast, oil, and salt each variety of nut separately, then mix them when cool.

Blanched Almonds

For an especially refined result, almonds can be blanched before toasting or using them in recipes. Bring a small pot of water to a boil. Working with small handfuls of almonds at a time, throw them in the boiling water for about 30 seconds, remove with a slotted spoon, and slip off the skins while they're still warm. Let the blanched almonds drain on a kitchen towel, then lightly toast them as you would regular almonds.

Pan-Toasted Seeds

You can use the oven to toast *sesame seeds*, *sunflower seeds*, or iron-rich *pumpkinseeds* as directed in the Toasted Nuts recipe above, but more often, I simply toast seeds in a shallow, heavy pan on the stove, tossing them in the pan constantly over a medium flame, until they are lightly and evenly toasted.

CHAPTER 9
BEEF, LAMB, & PORK

There is no question: to an omnivorous food lover, red meat is a primary gustatory pleasure. Whether we eat meat or not, our ancestors certainly did. Although eating large quantities of meat may cause health problems, meat consumption is nonetheless an inherent component of our evolutionary history.

Living and working at Deep Springs, we are lucky to be so close to many sources of our food: we grow fruits and vegetables in the garden, orchard, and fields; we obtain eggs from the chickens and milk from the dairy cows; and we maintain small "slaughter herds" of cattle, hogs, lambs, goats, and fowl. Deep Springs students, with supervision from the ranch staff, take responsibility for the tough work of slaughtering cattle and other animals. Some Deep Springs community members even bring their young children to slaughters, so the kids will see the source of the meat they enjoy so much. We always strive to grow more of our own vegetables, but, being a cattle ranch, we have all the good range beef we want. We attempt never to forget how fortunate we are. To feed the Deep Springs community of some fifty people, we use about ten head of cattle each year. The cattle eat quantities of nutritious, organically grown hay, but they also dine on the scrubby desert plants of the Valley floor during the colder months, and are taken up into the White Mountains to feast on the lush upper-elevation flora in the summers. Though we finish the animals on grain, our beef still has a rich, full, distinctive flavor—the effect, perhaps, of the rugged desert plants.

And many a spring, we buy a few young hogs, fatten them on kitchen scraps from the Deep Springs kitchen throughout the summer, and finish them on windfall apples from the orchard and the mash left over from cider pressing in the fall. The meat is uncommonly sweet and succulent; once we tasted a Deep Springs pork chop side by side with a commercial one, and the Deep Springs chop was unmistakably sweeter and cleaner tasting. Sometimes, an enterprising student will fire up the smoker and treat the grateful community to delicious home-smoked hams, bacon, and sausage.

Pork is an excellent, versatile meat. Three great cuisines of the world—those of China, the American South, and Germany—have fully realized, in completely different ways, the glories of pork cookery. Yet pork also suffers image problems: a couple of major world religions proscribe it, it is saddled with the reputation of being heavy or fatty, and until recently most people drastically overcooked it, fearing trichinosis. It doesn't help that the intelligence of pigs is well documented, or that beloved children's movies feature personable pigs narrowly avoiding slaughter. However, hogs are now bred to be less fat than they once were, certain cuts of pork are leaner than many other more commonly consumed meats, and the trichina parasite is not only all but eradicated in commercial hogs but is killed at a low 137°F. And children grow up to face their inherited human omnivory.

Not long ago, the Deep Springs ranch staff maintained an edict that meat had to be served at all three meals each day. But now the community often enjoys a meal with no meat. Nutritional science affirms this middle ground; it is not nutritionally necessary to eat meat every day, or to avoid it entirely. As a chef, I take satisfaction in very gently discouraging extreme eating of any kind. I consider it a small triumph when a self-proclaimed vegetarian enjoys a morsel of meat, or when a die-hard meat-and-potatoes man enjoys a meatless meal.

Marinated Steak

serves 6

Really great steak cuts, such as rib-eye or T-bone, to my mind need only salt and pepper, even if I'm just pan-frying them. Tougher, cheaper steaks benefit from a tart marinade. Once, in a Turkish cookbook, I found a recipe for lamb chops marinated in freshly squeezed onion juice and thyme sprigs, a discovery that led to much experimentation (see Carne Asada, page 182). The sharpness of onion juice gives meat a wonderful tenderness and succulence. This recipe gives instructions for pan-frying, but you can grill the steaks over a fire, too.

- **2 large yellow onions**
- **6 small sirloin steaks** (about 6 ounces each)**, about 1 inch thick**
- **10 sprigs fresh thyme**
- **salt and black pepper**
- **about 2 tablespoons olive oil**
- **about 6 tablespoons dry red wine or water**

Peel the onions, trim off any brown or dry spots, and rinse clean. Grate the onions, using the medium or large holes of a box grater (burn a candle close by to lessen fumes!), or chop them coarsely and then pulverize to a smooth slush in a food processor. Take a large, clean, flour-sack-type cotton kitchen towel (or 2 or 3 layers of cheesecloth) and rinse it well in warm water. Wring the towel out well, then drape it over a large bowl. Dump the onion slush into the towel. Take up the corners of the towel and squeeze out as much liquid from the onion into the bowl as possible.

Discard the onion solids left in the towel (or toss them into simmering stock). Add the steaks and thyme sprigs to the bowl and toss everything together well. Let the steaks marinate at room temperature for about an hour, turning and tossing them a few times.

Heat a wide, heavy skillet over a medium-high flame. Remove the steaks from the onion juice and pick off any bits of thyme. Pat the steaks dry with paper towels. Salt and pepper the steaks well on both sides. Add a tablespoon of olive oil to the skillet, enough to coat the bottom. The moment the oil begins to smoke, lay in 3 of the steaks. Let them sizzle, undisturbed, for about 3 minutes, then flip and cook on the other side for another 3 minutes, or until juices collect on the top side. The steaks should be medium-rare; cook for another 30 seconds for medium. Remove the steaks to a clean, warmed platter, then pour off any excess fat in the skillet. Splash in about 3 tablespoons of wine or water and scrape up the browned bits in the bottom of the skillet. Let the liquid reduce for a few seconds, then pour this scant sauce over the cooked steaks. Wipe out the skillet with a damp paper towel and heat it up again with fresh olive oil; repeat with the remaining 3 steaks.

Steak Fried in Beef Tallow

If you love steak, render some beef tallow (see the Deep Springs Soap recipe on page 343) and try this method, a favorite of longtime Deep Springs ranch manager Geoff Pope. Fat provides a perfectly even and very hot medium in which to cook steak. Any tender cut of steak (T-bone or rib-eye) may be used, but New York steak is ideal. The steak's fat cap emerges ethereally crackly-crisp and golden. Be assured that cooking it this way doesn't mean that more fat gets into the steak than was already there. Select a 1-inch-thick steak with a nice band of fat on the edge. Pat dry with paper towels. Season well with salt and pepper, pressing the seasoning into the meat. Take care to season the fat also. Heat about ½ inch of beef tallow in a heavy skillet over a medium-high flame until it is very hot—about 375°F. The fat should sizzle and bubble fiercely when you dip the tip of the steak in it. Using tongs, lay the steak carefully into the fat. For a medium-rare steak, let it cook for about 3 minutes on the first side, then flip carefully and cook on the other side for another 3 minutes, or until juices begin to collect on the top side of the steak. Drain the steak on several layers of paper towels for about 5 seconds on each side. Transfer the steak to a warmed plate or platter and let it rest for 1 minute. Serve.

If you'd like to serve the steak with potatoes, have ready cubes of peeled russet potato that have been boiled in salted water until tender. While the steak is resting, fry these in the hot fat until they are golden brown, about 1 minute. Drain on paper towels, and give them a final sprinkle of salt, some freshly ground pepper, and a tiny bit of finely chopped parsley. Serve alongside the steak.

Flank Steak with Blue Cheese

serves 3 to 4

Flank steak is not the most tender or expensive cut, but it is excellent if cooked carefully, with a far-reaching, true beef flavor. It must be thinly sliced before serving. Any simple steak or burger can be enhanced with a crumbled blue cheese topping. In summer, accompany your steak with sliced ripe tomatoes, lightly salted, and strew the blue cheese over steak and tomatoes both.

- **1 small flank steak** (*about 1¼ pounds*)**, about ½ inch to ¾ inch thick**
- **1 teaspoon salt**
- **1 teaspoon olive oil, plus 1 tablespoon**
- **¼ teaspoon dried thyme**
- **3 pinches cayenne pepper**
- **black pepper**
- **2 tablespoons water or wine**
- **small pat of butter** (*optional*)
- **about 3 ounces blue cheese, crumbled, at room temperature**

Cut the oval-shaped flank steak into 3 or 4 evenly sized pieces. Pat dry with paper towels, and rub the meat well with the salt, 1 teaspoon olive oil, thyme, cayenne, and black pepper. Let sit at room temperature for ½ hour, or refrigerate for several hours. Bring the meat back to room temperature before cooking.

Heat a wide, heavy skillet over a medium-high flame—a 12-inch cast-iron skillet is ideal. Swirl the remaining tablespoon of olive oil in the skillet to coat the bottom. When the oil just begins to smoke, lay the steaks in the skillet; they should not crowd or touch each other. Let sizzle for 4 minutes on the first side, then flip and cook on the other side for another 3 to 4 minutes. The steaks are best cooked to medium-rare—they will still be pink in the middle. Very rare flank steak is a bit tough.

Remove the steaks to a warmed platter to rest, and keep warm. Add about 2 tablespoons water or wine to the skillet, scraping up the browned bits from the pan with a spatula and letting the liquid reduce to a syrup. As the steaks rest, juice will collect on the platter. Add this to the sauce in the skillet. If you want a richer sauce, swirl in a small pat of cold butter. Slice the rested steaks thinly across the grain, arrange on the platter, and drizzle with the sauce. Scatter the blue cheese over the steak, and serve.

Grilled Skirt Steak with Salsa Verde

serves 4 to 6

Skirt steak is the heavily-used diaphragm muscle on cattle; it's an extremely flavorful cut. If the steak has a distinct, outer layer of fat, trim some of this off with a small, sharp knife.

- **1½ pounds skirt steak**
- **1½ teaspoons salt**
- **freshly ground black pepper**
- **1 recipe Salsa Verde** (*page 254*)**, or Green Chimichurri Sauce** (*page 255*)

Cut the skirt steak into manageable pieces that are easy to turn on the grill. Pat the steak dry with paper towels, season with the salt and pepper to taste, and let rest at room temperature for about 30 minutes.

Prepare a hot fire in your gas or charcoal grill. Clean the grates well with a grill brush, then oil the grates with a paper towel moistened with olive oil. Place the pieces of steak on the grill, about 2 inches apart. Thinner pieces of skirt steak will cook for about 3 minutes on each side for medium-rare, while thicker pieces may take 5 minutes on each side. The steaks should brown well on both sides. When you have flipped the steaks, watch for beads of steak juice that collect on the top side. At that point, the steaks should be medium-rare. Remove the steaks from the grill to a warmed platter, cover loosely with foil, and let rest for about 10 minutes. With a sharp knife, slice the steaks across the grain, into bite-sized slices. Arrange on a platter, drizzle with some of the salsa verde and serve immediately. Pass the rest of the salsa verde at the table.

Porcini-Dusted Steak

Among wild mushrooms, *boletus edulis,* known in France and Britain as *cepes* and in Italy as *porcini,* are the most prized—extremely rich in glutamates, they possess a deep, meaty, *umami* flavor. Dried porcini, used with a restrained hand, can deepen the flavor of broths, braises, risotto, tomato sauce, polenta, and many other foods, whether in the form of dried mushroom slices, or ground into a potent powder. For any of the preceding steak preparations, when seasoning the steaks with salt, dust them also with a little porcini powder, about ¼ teaspoon per pound of meat. Let the steaks sit, then cook as directed. Your guests will not be able to discern a specific "mushroomy" flavor, only a remarkably far-reaching beefiness.

Carne Asada

serves 2 to 3 as an entrée, 4 to 5 as tacos

This is my own version of Mexican grilled steak, or *carne asada,* but the taste is true. There are two steps in marinating the meat: first you rub ground dried chiles and cumin into the meat and let it sit for several hours, then you drench it with freshly made onion-garlic-cilantro juice and let it sit for a couple of hours more before cooking it. This makes superlative tacos (see the following recipe). You can cook the meat in a skillet as specified here, or you can grill it on your outdoor grill.

- **1 pound** (*trimmed weight*) **beef skirt steak, trimmed of excess fat if necessary**
- **2½ teaspoons ground chile or chili powder** (*see page 108*)
- **½ teaspoon ground cumin**
- **¼ teaspoon black pepper**
- **1 large white or yellow onion, peeled and coarsely chopped**
- **2 or 3 cloves garlic, peeled**
- **several sprigs cilantro, stems and leaves torn into small pieces**
- **½ teaspoon salt**
- **1 scant tablespoon sunflower oil or other vegetable oil**

Trim the meat of excess fat, if necessary, and cut into 3 pieces. Mix together the ground chile, cumin, and black pepper, and rub all over the steak. Put the meat in a deep, nonreactive (glass, porcelain, or plastic) bowl. Cover the bowl and marinate the meat, refrigerated, for several hours or overnight.

A few hours before you want to start cooking, put the onion, garlic, and cilantro in the bowl of a food processor and process to a juicy purée. (Or grate the onions and garlic with a box grater and chop the cilantro fine.) Lay a couple of large squares of cheesecloth or a clean dish towel, dampened and wrung out, over a medium bowl, and dump in the onion purée. Gather up the ends of the cheesecloth and squeeze the onion juice into the bowl. Discard the dry solids left in the cheesecloth. Pour the onion juice over the meat, turning the meat to coat it with juice. Marinate the meat at room temperature for about 1 hour, turning occasionally. Remove the meat from the marinade, pat the meat dry with paper towels, and season it with salt on both sides, using about ½ teaspoon of salt in all.

Set a large, heavy skillet over a medium-high flame. The skillet should be wide enough to accommodate all the pieces of meat without touching. When the skillet is hot, add a scant tablespoon of oil and lay in the steaks—they should sizzle loudly. Cook until well browned on one side, about 4 minutes, then turn and cook on the other side for another 3 to 4 minutes, until juices begin to collect on top. The total cooking time will be 8 to 10 minutes. The meat should be medium-rare inside; however, if you want to be authentically Mexican, cook it through to well-done. Remove the meat to a board or platter and let it rest for about 5 minutes before slicing thinly across the grain.

TACOS DE CARNE ASADA

Often, here in what Frida Kahlo liked to call *Gringolandia,* tacos are crispy deep-fried tortilla shells with a ground beef filling. Although they are delicious, the joys of the simpler soft tacos served in Mexico are also well worth discovering. At its simplest, a taco is a flavorful bit of protein with a sauce, wrapped in one or two warm, soft corn tortillas. There are few things better than a good *carne asada* taco, found in taquerías and taco trucks in all parts of the United States, wherever there is a large

Mexican population. In San Francisco's Mission neighborhood, there are a few taquerías that serve especially tasty *tacos de carne asada*. The gruff men shout behind the counter, the mariachi music blares over the sirens and traffic outside, a drug addict collapses in a corner, but a bite of one of their tacos is like coming home to *Mamá*.

For each taco, heat 2 corn tortillas directly over your stove's flame (or on a hot, ungreased griddle) until they are floppy and steaming, with appealing brown spots here and there. Put them on a plate, stacked together. Pile about ⅓ cup of chopped warm carne asada in the center of the tortillas. Top with a spoonful of salsa (see Fresh Salsa, page 249), and strew with chopped white onions and chopped cilantro. Serve immediately, with the traditional accompaniments: a whole, crisp, red radish and a lime wedge. To eat, first squeeze lime juice over the taco. Then pick the whole thing up, holding in the meat, and start nibbling at one end. Use plenty of napkins. Tacos are messy; eating them neatly is an acquired skill. The scent of lime oil on your hands enhances the whole experience. Munch the radish.

Roast Beef

serves 10 to 12 (6-pound roast), or 3 to 4 (2-pound roast)

Roast beef has become uncommon on American home tables, yet its preparation is absurdly easy, requiring simple attention to timing and little else. I make and serve it all the time at Deep Springs—the hardest part is getting it into the oven early enough so that it roasts to tenderness, unhurried, and rests sufficiently before slicing. There is nothing more satisfyingly elemental. Whether you choose a large strip loin, top sirloin, top round, or a smaller tri-tip, the meat should have a nice layer of fat on top, called a "fat cap," for the most succulent results.

Leftover roast beef is so good in sandwiches or salads that I sometimes make it expressly for those. For a splendid, authentic English dinner, serve hot slices with Horseradish Cream (page 250), Yorkshire Pudding (page 68), and Watercress Salad (page 162). In summer, I like to serve fresh Horseradish-Tomato Relish (page 249) with roast beef.

If you are roasting beef for sandwiches, let the cooked roast cool to room temperature, then wrap well and refrigerate overnight. Slice the cold roast as thinly as possible across the grain. Cold roast beef sandwiches are superb with the same accompaniments: horseradish and watercress.

FOR A 6-POUND, BONELESS STRIP LOIN, TOP SIRLOIN, OR TOP ROUND ROAST:

2 tablespoons salt

1 tablespoon freshly ground black pepper

pinch of celery seed

1 large yellow onion, sliced

6 cloves garlic, peeled and halved

3 or 4 bay leaves *(or a few sprigs of fresh thyme or rosemary)*

FOR A 2-POUND, BONELESS TRI-TIP ROAST:

2 teaspoons salt

1 scant teaspoon freshly ground black pepper

small pinch of celery seed

½ medium yellow onion, sliced

2 cloves garlic, peeled and halved

1 or 2 bay leaves *(or a couple of sprigs of fresh thyme or rosemary)*

FOR SERVING

Yorkshire Pudding *(page 68)*

Watercress Salad *(page 162)*

Fresh Horseradish Cream *(page 250)*

Bring the meat to room temperature. For a 6-pound roast, this will take about 3 hours. (Once it has begun to come to room temperature, don't change your mind and decide to roast it another day!) Heat the oven to 325°F. Pat the roast dry with paper towels, and rub it all over with the salt, pepper, and celery seed. Make a bed in a roasting pan of the sliced onions, halved garlic cloves, and bay leaves. Place the meat on top, fat side up, and place in the oven.

Remove the roast from the oven when an instant-read thermometer inserted in the center registers 125°F for rare, 135°F for medium-rare, or 140°F for medium. It should take a little over 2½ hours for a 6-pound roast, or about 1 hour for the first pound and 20 minutes for each additional pound. A smaller tri-tip roast can take as little as 40 minutes—check carefully. A very rare roast will still feel very springy inside when pressed with a finger; a more thoroughly cooked roast will be firmer. Let the roast rest for 15 to 20 minutes before slicing. (Make Yorkshire pudding with the fat and drippings in the pan while the roast is resting.) Serve hot slices with a fluff of watercress to one side of the meat and horseradish cream on the other.

ROAST LAMB

You may successfully roast a leg of lamb by following the directions and timing for roast beef. A boneless leg will be easier to carve than a bone-in one, but the bone contributes flavor and helps the meat cook more evenly, so if possible, ask the butcher to carve the bone free but rewrap and tie the meat around it. You can then easily remove the bone after roasting. Cook to an internal temperature of 135°F for tender, medium-rare meat. Instead of celery seed, flavor the lamb with a restrained amount of chopped fresh rosemary. Include, if you like, a strip or two of orange zest in the bed of onions.

In my student days at Deep Springs, ranch mechanic Wendell Brizendine kept a flock of lambs. I will never forget the sight—or the delicious smell—of legs of lamb marinating in red wine in large roasting pans on a shelf in the Boardinghouse pantry, to be cooked by Wendell's wife Ginny that evening. Deep Springs lamb has a rich, definitive "lamb-y" flavor that I love. Only lamb imported from Australia or New Zealand has that great gamy flavor—much American-raised lamb is mild to the point of blandness. No matter how much you have finessed the seasonings, if you are serving roast lamb to older Americans, they are likely to expect a dish of bright green, sweet mint jelly served alongside.

Beef Stew, with Nine Variations

serves 6 to 8

Homemade beef stew is increasingly rare in American kitchens and, therefore, increasingly special. It takes inexpensive ingredients and a bit of work, time, patience, and watchfulness, and yields a result that is incomparably soothing and restoring.

Rarely does a week go by in the Deep Springs kitchen when we don't serve beef stew in some form or another. This one has big, tender chunks of beef, carrots, and potatoes. The vegetables are well cooked but not falling apart. If you were to pare down beef stew to its barest essentials, it would contain little

ROAST BEEF SALAD

To serve about 4 people, toss together bite-size slices of roast beef, a little red onion sliced paper-thin, a big ripe tomato cut into chunks, a cup of croutons, and 2 or 3 big handfuls of mixed salad greens with enough mustard vinaigrette (page 174) to thoroughly moisten all the components. Taste and adjust the seasonings as necessary. Serve immediately.

beyond beef, onions, and stock. Feel free, then, to decrease, vary, or omit the supporting ingredients; exact quantities are not as crucial as following the basic steps. The recipe directs you to finish cooking the stew in the oven, as we do at Deep Springs, but you may simply continue cooking it on the stovetop, if you carefully adjust the heat so the stew simmers gently. Or finish it in a slow cooker, if you have one.

2½ pounds beef chuck, not too lean, cut into 1-inch chunks

1½ teaspoons salt, plus more as needed

½ teaspoon coarsely ground black pepper, or more as needed

pinch of ground cloves

3 to 4 tablespoons sunflower oil, olive oil, or other vegetable oil

1 cup good-tasting, fruity red wine

3 cups chicken stock, vegetable stock, beef stock, or water

1 bay leaf

¼ teaspoon dried thyme, or 2 sprigs fresh thyme, leaves picked and chopped

one 14-ounce can diced tomatoes

1 large yellow onion, cut into medium dice

3 cloves garlic, crushed

3 medium carrots, peeled and cut on the diagonal into 1-inch chunks

1 long stalk celery, cut into medium dice

12 ounces yellow, red, or white potatoes, unpeeled, trimmed and cut into 1-inch chunks

few drops of red wine vinegar *(optional)*

¼ cup chopped parsley

(OPTIONAL, FOR THICKENING)

¾ cup cold water

⅓ cup all-purpose flour

Heat the oven to 300°F. To brown the meat, it must first be dry; if it's sitting in juice, transfer it to a plate and pat dry with paper towels. Put a large skillet over a medium-high flame. In a large bowl, toss the beef chunks with 1½ teaspoons salt and the pepper and cloves. Warm about a tablespoon of the oil in the skillet and scatter half or a third of the beef evenly in the pan—it should sizzle when you add it. Don't crowd the meat. Let it attain a nice mahogany brown on one side before turning it. Ideally, all sides of the beef chunks should be this rich brown. In practice, if you accomplish two sides, you're golden. Transfer the browned meat to a large, heavy stew pot (a pot that can go in the oven as well as on the stovetop). Deglaze the hot skillet with a splash of the wine, scraping up any browned bits with a wooden spoon. Add this flavorful liquid to the pot with the beef. Add more oil and brown the remaining beef in one or two more batches, deglazing the skillet after each batch. As the vegetables will eventually take their turn in the skillet, there is no need to wash it yet.

To the pot with the beef, add the chicken stock, any remaining wine, bay leaf, thyme, and tomatoes. Bring the stew just to a simmer over medium-high heat, skimming off any scum that rises to the surface. Taste the liquid for salt. Cover the pot and put it in the hot oven. After ½ hour, reduce the oven heat to 250°F and let simmer for another hour, or until the beef is still chewy but beginning to become tender. The stew should only simmer—it must never boil hard or the beef will be dry.

In your skillet over a medium flame, warm a final tablespoon of oil and gently cook the onion, garlic, carrot, and celery with a pinch of salt, stirring frequently, for 3 to 4 minutes, or until they lose their crunch—do not let the vegetables brown. Put a lid on the skillet when you're not stirring. Add the potatoes with a large pinch of salt and cook, continuing to stir frequently, for another 3 to 4 minutes. Add the vegetables to the pot with the beef, along with a flour slurry for thickening, if desired (see the next paragraph), and continue to simmer until the beef, vegetables, and potatoes are tender, about ½ hour more.

This recipe gives a flavorful broth with plenty of body as it is; however, you may want to thicken the stew, especially if you want to serve it on plates over potatoes, noodles, or rice. In a jar with a tight-fitting lid, vigorously shake together the cold water and flour until the flour is completely dissolved. Stir this mixture into the stew when adding the vegetables, and bring the stew back up to a simmer—the remaining ½ hour of simmering will cook the flour thoroughly. If you have decided to thicken your stew late in the game, just drain the liquid from the stew, thicken it in a separate pot, and return the thickened liquid to the beef and vegetables.

Taste the finished stew for salt and pepper—the salt will depend on the saltiness of the chicken stock, and you may well want a fresh shot of pepper. If you feel that the flavors need brightening, sprinkle in a few drops of red wine vinegar. Beef stew is perhaps even better reheated the next day. In either case, stir in the parsley just before serving. Serve in wide bowls.

ELIZABETH'S WINTER BEEF STEW

This variation pays homage to my friend Elizabeth—her beef stew was legendary, and she had a masterful, encyclopedic knowledge of produce and of cooking appropriately to the season. I think of beef stew as cold-weather fare anyway, but you may make it even more warming and hearty by omitting the tomatoes and adding 2 medium turnips, peeled and cut into 1-inch chunks, and 1 medium bunch of kale, stemmed (see page 132) and coarsely chopped. Cook these vegetables along with the onion, celery, and carrots. Peeled winter squash, cut into 1-inch chunks, is a good option too, but add it later, in the last 40 minutes of simmering.

RUSSIAN BORSCHT

Longtime Deep Springs residents Geoff and Iris Pope are big fans of this borscht. Once I overheard Geoff say to Iris, "No, I don't want any dessert—I'm having another bowl of borscht instead." The natural meatiness of beets melds beautifully with beef. Even people who are not fond of beets "straight" often love borscht. Proceed with the master Beef Stew recipe, omitting the thyme and tomatoes, and adding a teaspoon of crushed caraway seeds. Use an additional 1½ cups of stock. With the onion, carrot, and celery, include half a small cabbage, cut into bite-sized squares. In the last ½ hour of cooking, add ½ recipe of Marinated Beets (page 164), cut into chunks. The hint of orange is wonderful with the beef. Accompany with platters of both pickled and fresh cucumbers, good rye bread, and lots of sour cream. Slovenian Horseradish Sauce (page 250) is also excellent atop borscht.

GOULASH

Substitute 1 teaspoon caraway seeds for the thyme in the master Beef Stew recipe. Omit the wine (use water to deglaze the skillet), tomatoes, carrots, and celery. For the oil, substitute fresh lard or bacon fat, and include some chunks of bacon, if you like. With the onion and garlic, include half a small cabbage, coarsely chopped. Add ¼ cup sweet Hungarian paprika (or a combination of sweet and hot paprika) to the pot before putting it in the oven. Serve over egg noodles (to make your own, see page 231) or Spaetzle (page 237). For a Slovenian-style goulash, serve over hot soft Polenta (page 242). Goulash hails from Hungary, polenta from Italy; Slovenia is nestled between the two. This just might be my favorite version of beef stew.

CARBONNADE FLAMANDE

For a version of the famous Belgian dish, proceed with the master Beef Stew recipe, omitting the carrots, celery, tomatoes, and potatoes. Double the amount of onion. For the wine and chicken stock, substitute a smooth-tasting ale (a rich Belgian ale is ideal, preferably made by Trappist monks). Finish with a teaspoon of cider vinegar or malt vinegar. Serve boiled potatoes on the side, tossed with butter and finely chopped parsley, or serve with Herbed Spaetzle (page 237).

ITALIAN BEEF STEW

This lighter, brighter stew appeals in hotter weather. Follow the master Beef Stew recipe, substituting white wine for the red wine. Double the amount of garlic. With the bay leaf and thyme, include 1 strip of lemon zest and 1 teaspoon chopped fresh rosemary. Omit the potatoes, celery, and carrots, and use fresh Tomato Concassé (page 148) instead of canned tomatoes. Don't thicken the stew, and finish with a squeeze of fresh lemon juice instead of red wine vinegar. Shower each bowl with freshly chopped Italian parsley.

BOEUF BOURGUIGNONNE

For a simple version of this French classic, follow the master Beef Stew recipe, substituting bacon fat for the vegetable oil, and using an entire bottle of good, fruity red wine (merlot, pinot noir, and zinfandel are all good candidates) instead of a combination of red wine and chicken stock. Omit the tomatoes and potatoes and, for an authentic touch, use pearl onions. If you like, add chunks of thick bacon (2 to 3 ounces) that you have slowly browned in a skillet. In the last 15 minutes of cooking, add 8 ounces of fresh mushrooms that have been sliced and sautéed in butter with salt and pepper. Swirl a small pat of cold butter into the stew just before serving. Serve alongside boiled and buttered potatoes.

MEXICAN BRAISED BEEF (OR GOAT)

Omit the thyme, carrots, celery, potatoes, and parsley in the master Beef Stew recipe. Double the amounts of cloves, onion, and garlic. In a small, dry skillet, toast 2 teaspoons ground cumin. When it has released its fragrance, add 1 teaspoon dried oregano. Remove from the heat and add 3 to 4 tablespoons ground chile or chili powder. Stir this spice mixture, 1 corn tortilla torn into small bits, and 1 square of unsweetened chocolate into the stew before putting it in the oven to simmer. The tortilla and chocolate not only contribute wonderful flavor, but also conspire to slightly thicken the stew. If you like, stir in a little chopped cilantro. Serve with warm corn tortillas.

When we kept milk goats at Deep Springs, an inevitable fate awaited all the young male goats. Should you, too, be lucky enough to have or find fresh goat meat (known in Spanish as *cabrito* or *chivo*), this spicy stew is an ideal use for it.

LAMB STEW

When I arrived at Deep Springs as a student, I had eaten lamb only a couple of times in my life. By the time I left, I had eaten it many different ways, cooked it in almost as many, and taken the opportunity to observe lamb's transition from animal in the field to "quarters" hanging in the walk-in refrigerator to chops and roasts to that warm, satisfied feeling of a good dinner in my belly.

Occasionally we let the lambs get just a bit past lambhood, making their richly gamy flavor even more pronounced. One evening at dinner in the Deep Springs Boardinghouse, a visiting scholar who had just returned from Mongolia looked down into her bowl of stew and said, "Mutton. I feel like I'm back in Mongolia."

Substitute chunks of lamb shoulder for the beef in the master Beef Stew recipe, and omit the thyme, tomatoes, carrots, celery, and potatoes. With the bay leaf, add a bit of rosemary and a strip of orange zest. This makes a lovely, light Mediterranean-style lamb stew, good served with White Bean Gratin with Fennel (page 115), and Fresh Artichoke Hearts (page 120).

SHEPHERD'S PIE

For a rich, traditional English shepherd's pie, make a simpler lamb stew, omitting the wine, tomatoes, carrots, celery, and potatoes from the master Beef Stew recipe, doubling the onions, and adding 2 teaspoons of chopped fresh rosemary with the bay leaf. Thicken well with a flour slurry, as described in the master recipe. Without the liquid from the tomatoes or the wine, the thickening will produce an appropriate gravy-like consistency. Season the stew well with salt and pepper, put in a wide casserole dish, and cover with a blanket of hot, fresh Mashed Potatoes (page 142). Bake in a 400°F oven for about half an hour to brown the potatoes.

Allspice-Scented Pot Roast

serves 5 to 6

If spices were party guests, allspice usually arrives with a raucous crowd—cinnamon, cloves, nutmeg, and ginger—but its own, subtler voice is seldom heard. Only when you get it alone do you realize what terrific company it is for many other flavors. Here is a pot roast recipe, a delicious way to get to know allspice's personality. Rather than conveying a spicy taste, the allspice enhances the beef's "beefiness." The aroma of the braising meat is both tantalizing and comforting.

Pot roast is akin to Beef Stew, only there is less liquid, and the meat is all in one piece. The seasonings and aromatics may be varied: use the Beef Stew recipes on the preceding pages for more pot roast ideas.

one 2½-pound chuck roast, about 1½ inches thick

1 tablespoon salt, plus more as needed

1 tablespoon whole allspice berries, ground

generous amount of freshly ground black pepper

1 tablespoon vegetable oil

2½ cups water

1 bay leaf

2 medium onions, cut in large dice

2 medium carrots, peeled and cut in large dice

2 stalks celery, cut in large dice

Season the beef with salt, allspice, and a generous amount of black pepper. Cover the roast and let rest at room temperature for about 1½ hours, so the seasoning penetrates the meat. (You can season the roast a day ahead; refrigerate it, covered, overnight, and bring it to room temperature the next day.)

Heat the oven to 300°F. In a Dutch oven or other wide, ovenproof pot, heat the tablespoon of oil over a medium-high flame until it shimmers. Place the roast in the hot oil, letting it sear and brown for about 3 to 4 minutes on each side. Pour in the water with a good pinch of salt, and add the bay leaf. Bring to a simmer on the stovetop, then cover the pot and place it in the oven. Let the roast slowly braise for about 2 hours—the meat should be just tender.

Carefully transfer the meat to a plate, and pour the scant liquid from the pot into a bowl. Spoon some of the clear fat on top of the liquid back into the pot. Place the pot back on a medium-high flame, and heat the fat until it begins to sputter and sizzle. Throw in the onion, carrot, and celery with a large pinch of salt, and cook the vegetables, stirring frequently, until they are crisp-tender, about 6 minutes. Pour the reserved liquid back into the pot, then place the roast atop the vegetables. Return the pot to the 300°F oven for another 30 minutes, or until the roast and vegetables are tender. Let the pot roast rest for about 10 minutes, then serve chunks of tender meat, vegetables, and a little juice to each person. Accompany with the starch of your choice: potatoes, rice, polenta, or noodles.

Green Chile Beef Stew

serves 4 to 5

This particular combination of beef, potatoes, and green chile is especially characteristic of southern New Mexico, where I spent some of my growing-up years. Serve in wide bowls, with sour cream and hot corn tortillas heated directly over the flame.

1¾ pounds stew beef (chuck is ideal), **cut into 1-inch chunks**

½ teaspoon dried oregano, crumbled

1 teaspoon salt, plus more as needed

2 tablespoons all-purpose flour

3 to 4 tablespoons lard, or safflower oil, or other vegetable oil

1 large onion, cut into medium dice

6 cloves garlic, crushed

4 medium yellow, red, or white potatoes, unpeeled, cut into 1-inch chunks

2 cups chicken stock or beef stock

2 cups water

½ to ¾ cup coarsely chopped roasted New Mexico green chiles (see page 251)

¼ teaspoon black pepper

FOR SERVING

sour cream

corn tortillas

Pat the beef dry with paper towels. Combine the oregano, ½ teaspoon of the salt, and the flour in a large bowl, add the beef, and toss together. In a heavy soup pot over a medium-high flame, heat a scant tablespoon of oil. Brown about a third of the beef in the oil, letting the pieces brown well on each side. Remove the browned beef to a large bowl and deglaze the pot with a little water, scraping the browned bits from the bottom of the pot. Add this liquid to the beef. Repeat with the remaining beef in two more batches, adding fresh oil to the pot for each batch. Add a final scant tablespoon of oil to the pot and stew the onion with a pinch of salt. When the onion is partly cooked, add the garlic with another pinch of salt, and cook for a moment more. Add the reserved beef and deglazing liquid, potatoes, stock, water, ½ teaspoon salt, and chiles to the pot, and bring to a simmer. Gently simmer the stew until the beef and potatoes are tender, 1 to 1½ hours. Add the pepper and more salt to taste.

Glazed Meatloaf

serves 6 to 8

Let me assure you that this is the classic juicy and flavorful meatloaf of your dreams, adapted from a great recipe in the pages of *Cook's Illustrated*. Meatloaf is best baked on a rimmed baking sheet, rather than in a loaf pan, so that more of the surface browns appealingly. Wrap leftover meatloaf tightly in plastic wrap, place it between two trays or baking sheets with a heavy object on top, and refrigerate it, weighted, overnight. It will then slice neatly for sandwiches.

6 ounces fresh mushrooms

2 teaspoons olive oil

1 large onion, finely diced

2 cloves garlic, peeled and crushed

1¼ teaspoons salt

1 pound lean ground beef

1 pound ground pork

⅓ cup chopped parsley

⅔ cup crushed saltine crackers

⅓ cup plain yogurt or buttermilk

2 large eggs, beaten

½ teaspoon dried thyme, or 1 teaspoon fresh thyme or rosemary

½ teaspoon black pepper

1 tablespoon Worcestershire sauce

1 tablespoon Dijon mustard

¼ teaspoon hot sauce

GLAZE (IF YOU LOVE GLAZE, DOUBLE THE QUANTITY)

¼ cup bottled "chili" sauce or ketchup

2 tablespoons brown sugar

1 tablespoon cider vinegar

Heat the oven to 350°F. Line a shallow roasting pan or rimmed baking sheet with aluminum foil (shiny side up), and grease the foil lightly. Wipe the mushrooms clean, and grate them using the coarse holes on a box grater. Scatter the grated mushrooms on the foil, and bake for about 20 minutes in the preheating oven, to evaporate some of their moisture. The mushrooms should darken in color and reduce in volume, but they shouldn't get crispy-dry. Transfer the mushrooms to a large bowl. Heat the olive oil over a medium-high flame in a medium-sized skillet, and sauté the onion and garlic with ¼ teaspoon of the salt until the onion is transparent and no longer crunchy, about 5 minutes. Transfer the onion mixture to the large bowl with the mushrooms, and let cool.

Add the meats to the bowl, along with the parsley, crushed saltines, yogurt, eggs, thyme, remaining 1 teaspoon salt, pepper, Worcestershire sauce, mustard, and hot sauce. Without smashing, kneading, or otherwise overworking the meat, lightly but thoroughly combine all the ingredients until amalgamated. If you have used different proportions of the listed ingredients and want to taste the mixture, fry a bite-sized piece in a small skillet until cooked through, and taste. Pat the meat into a narrow, free-form loaf (about 15 inches long, 4 inches wide, and 2 inches high) in the pan.

To make the glaze, mix the ketchup, brown sugar, and vinegar in a small bowl and spoon the glaze in a stripe down the center of the meatloaf. Bake for 40 to 45 minutes. Crank up the oven's heat to 500°F and bake for about 15 minutes more to brown the top and set the glaze. Using a small knife, peek at the interior of the meatloaf—no pink should remain. The internal temperature of the meatloaf, taken with an instant-read thermometer, should register 165°F. Let rest for about 10 minutes before slicing.

Italian Meatballs

serves 4 to 6

For years I tended to bake meatballs and wonder how I could make them better. Then I learned to sauté them in olive oil—now that's-a-great-a-meatball! A student brought this method to the Deep Springs kitchen from his Italian family. The coarse breadcrumbs are essential to the recipe: cut the crust off a loaf of white Italian bread with a serrated knife, then tear the bread with your fingers into raisin-sized chunks.

Structurally, meatballs and meatloaf have much in common: ground meats bound with egg, breadcrumbs, seasonings, and liquid. Once you have successfully followed a recipe, you are well equipped to improvise. Good-quality ground turkey and turkey sausage work well in this recipe, standing in for the beef and pork sausage. If you want to use ground pork rather than pork sausage, season it up with salt, pepper, hot red pepper flakes, and crushed fennel seeds. For a good all-beef meatball, see the following recipe for Mediterranean Meatballs.

3 to 4 tablespoons olive oil

1 medium yellow onion, finely diced

2 large cloves garlic, minced or crushed

1½ teaspoons salt

¼ teaspoon dried oregano, crumbled

1 cup coarse day-old breadcrumbs

⅓ cup buttermilk or plain yogurt, or more as needed

1 pound lean ground beef

1 pound fresh Italian sausage, hot or sweet

2 large eggs

¼ teaspoon black pepper

FOR SERVING

cooked rice *(page 238)* **or pasta** *(page 235)*

about 4 cups Tomato Sauce *(page 247)*

3 to 4 tablespoons chopped Italian parsley

freshly grated Parmesan cheese

Heat a tablespoon of the olive oil in a small saucepan over a medium flame, and gently cook the onion and garlic with ¼ teaspoon of the salt for about 5 minutes, or until the onion has turned translucent—it should not brown. Stir in the oregano and set aside to cool. In a large bowl, toss the breadcrumbs with the buttermilk. Add the cooled onion mixture, the beef, the sausage (casings removed), eggs, remaining 1¼ teaspoons salt, and black pepper. Mix with your clean hands, gently breaking up the meats to amalgamate with the other ingredients. Don't whip or beat or knead the mixture. Rinse your hands well; you should be able to form 1½-inch balls (handling lightly; it's fine if the meatballs are not perfectly smooth or perfectly round) with damp hands without the mixture sticking. If the mixture is sticky, add a little more buttermilk. Heat the oven to 350°F. Heat 2 to 3 tablespoons of olive oil in a wide, heavy skillet over medium-high heat. When the oil is hot but not smoking, put in the meatballs without crowding (it may be necessary to cook them in batches). The meatballs should sizzle merrily upon contact with the oil. When they have nicely browned on the underside, gently turn them with tongs. They should not get crispy-brown—at that point they're overcooked.

Drain the meatballs on several thicknesses of paper towels, then arrange them in a shallow roasting pan. Put the pan in the oven for a few moments to finish cooking the meatballs through—no pink should remain. Serve the meatballs with rice or pasta and, always, tomato sauce. If you are serving individual plates, the rice or pasta should be on the bottom with 3 to 4 meatballs sitting on the rice, tomato sauce spooned over the meatballs, and a scattering of chopped parsley over all. If you are presenting the meatballs in a dish to be passed at the table or on a buffet, serve the rice or pasta in a separate dish. Choose a large, wide dish for the meatballs, make a pool of red sauce on the bottom, arrange the meatballs over the red sauce, spoon more red sauce over the meatballs (not coating them completely; let bits of the brown meatballs show through), and sprinkle parsley over all. In any case, serve extra sauce and freshly grated Parmesan cheese on the side.

Mediterranean Meatballs

serves 3 to 4

This tender and flavorful all-beef meatball dish is good in hot weather, with gentle Middle Eastern flavors everyone loves. Ground lamb could be used in place of the beef.

5 tablespoons olive oil

1 small yellow onion, finely diced

2 to 3 large cloves garlic, crushed

1½ teaspoons salt

1¼ pounds lean *(but not extra-lean)* **ground beef**

½ cup medium breadcrumbs

2 tablespoons plus ¾ cup plain yogurt, at room temperature

1 egg

¼ teaspoon cayenne pepper

½ teaspoon paprika

1 teaspoon cumin seed, toasted lightly and coarsely ground

2 teaspoons sesame seed, toasted lightly and coarsely ground

1 or 2 dashes Tabasco or other hot sauce

few twists of black pepper

3 to 4 heaping tablespoons chopped fresh mint

2 to 3 tablespoons chopped parsley

Heat the oven to 300°F. Heat a tablespoon of the olive oil in a small skillet and sauté the onion and garlic with ½ teaspoon of salt until tender, about 3 minutes, then let cool. Transfer the onion mixture to a large bowl and add the beef, breadcrumbs, 2 tablespoons of the yogurt, egg, cayenne, paprika, cumin, sesame, Tabasco, remaining 1 teaspoon salt, black pepper, and mint. Using your clean hands, mix everything lightly but thoroughly. Don't smash the meat or knead the mixture. Form into 1½-inch balls.

Heat 4 tablespoons of olive oil over a medium flame in a very large skillet until the oil shimmers. Arrange the meatballs in the pan without crowding (it may be necessary to cook them in batches), and let them cook, undisturbed, until they are golden brown on the underside. Turn with tongs to gently brown all sides. Put the skillet in the oven and let the meatballs gently cook about 20 minutes. Carefully spoon off most of the oil in the skillet, keeping as much of the juice and browned bits as possible. Pushing the meatballs to the side, whisk the final ¾ cup yogurt, plus a pinch of salt and pepper, into the meat juices. Toss the meatballs in the sauce, and return to the oven or a low flame for a few moments to warm the sauce through. Sprinkle with parsley and serve.

Skillet Hamburgers

For each person, obtain 6 to 7 ounces of ground chuck, about 80 percent lean. Ideally, the meat has been ground that day with a very sharp, cold grinder. Gently shape the meat into a ¾-inch-thick patty, taking care that you don't rearrange the structure of the meat too much; otherwise the burger will be tough. It's fine if the patty is not perfectly shaped. The center of the patty should be a bit thinner than the edges—this prevents the burger from puffing in the middle as it cooks. Over a medium-high flame, heat a heavy skillet for a few minutes. Place the meat in the skillet—it should sizzle on contact—and gently press down. (Don't press the meat at any other point after this; you'll just squeeze out the juices.) Let cook for 4 to 5 minutes, then flip and cook the other side. Amply salt and pepper the cooked side. (Burgers are juiciest, I think, if salted after cooking, not before.) At this point you may put a thin slice of cheese on top, or a crumble of blue cheese. Cook for another 3 to 4 minutes, then transfer the burger to the prepared bun or plate. Lightly toast the buns—in the same pan if there's room (I like it when the buns get a little sheen of meat-grease). Don't be too stingy with the mayonnaise or too generous with the ketchup or mustard. Top with red onion sliced paper-thin, leaf lettuce, and ripe tomato sprinkled with salt.

Salting the tomato is as important as seasoning the meat. I remember a good old burger place in Oakland, California, run by an Afghani family. There was nothing remarkable about their ingredients; they used frozen patties, premade buns, and supermarket lettuce and tomatoes. The burgers were good because they were prepared with care; the cooks grilled the burgers and toasted the buns side by side on a gas grill. They cut the iceberg lettuce into ribbons. They were generous with their tasty mayonnaise-based, ketchup-laced sauce. And they salted the tomato on every burger.

For a recipe for *homemade hamburger buns,* see page 77.

BURGER STEAK SALAD

For a direct and satisfying answer to the burger craving, arrange lettuce leaves, sliced tomatoes, and chopped onion on a plate, drizzle with a little vinaigrette or aioli, and place the cooked burger patty on top. Strew with crumbled blue cheese and go at it with a knife and fork, bun forgotten.

Rico's Tacos

serves 4 to 6

A beloved, recurrent, simple dinner in our household, these tacos evoke our childhood in New Mexico. The meat filling is quite plain, inviting a generous topping of spicy salsa. Authentically, the tortillas are briefly sizzled and softened in a shallow pan of hot oil, but I prefer the lighter result when the tortillas are simply heated over a flame. The ratio of meat to potato is quite variable—sometimes I use less potato than is called for here, sometimes more.

2 to 3 tablespoons sunflower oil or other vegetable oil, or lard

1 medium white or yellow onion, finely diced

1 teaspoon salt, plus more as needed

2 medium yellow potatoes, unpeeled, finely diced

2 pounds lean ground beef

pinch of celery seed

black pepper

FOR SERVING

12 corn tortillas

2 cups salsa, mild or hot (use Fresh Salsa, page 249, or your favorite prepared salsa)

avocado slices (optional)

1 cup natural sour cream, well stirred

Heat the vegetable oil in a heavy skillet over medium-high heat. Add three-quarters of the onion with a pinch of salt and cook, stirring frequently, until the onion begins to soften, about 5 minutes. Set aside the rest of the onion to top the tacos. Add the potato with another pinch of salt and cook, stirring frequently, for about 3 minutes. Add the ground beef and celery seed. Stir to combine the beef, onion, and potato. Reduce the flame to medium, and let the mixture cook, stirring frequently, for about 10 minutes, or until the meat is cooked completely and the potato is soft, releasing starch to thicken the meat juices somewhat. Add 1 teaspoon of salt and pepper to taste, and reduce the flame to medium-low. Allow the mixture to brown slightly on the bottom of the skillet, then stir it up, scraping up any browned residue that adheres to the bottom. Let it brown again, continuing to brown, stir, and scrape for another 10 to 15 minutes, building up the flavor. Taste again—it may need more salt and pepper. When finished, the mixture should taste deeply savory.

When you are ready to eat, heat corn tortillas directly on the flame of a gas burner (or in a hot, dry skillet) until they get appetizing brown spots. Place a tortilla on the flame or skillet, turn, place another on top, turn both, place another on top of that, turn all three, and so forth, building up the stack and giving each tortilla its moment of direct contact with the heat. The accumulated heat will steam and soften the whole stack. Put a hot tortilla on a warmed plate, scoop about ⅓ cup of the meat mixture on top, then top with a bit of diced onion, salsa, avocado (if desired), and a dollop of sour cream. Eat immediately: pick up the filled tortilla and take a bite from one end, holding up the other end with your finger so the filling won't fall out. This dinner is messy, requiring a little skill and plenty of napkins, but it is well worth it.

Steak Tartare

serves 6 as a light course, 8 to 10 as an hors d'oeuvre

Steak tartare's allure is tantalizingly laced with danger and taboo. Something of a Deep Springs tradition, it is a culinary rite of passage, much like one's first raw oyster: if you are able to eat *that* and love it, you are no longer the picky little kid you once were; what other previously shunned delicacies await?

There is something vitally appealing about raw meat. Chefs always particularly appreciate a good raw beef or raw fish dish. I once knew a cook who told me how her mother, on grocery-shopping trips, used to buy a quarter-pound of ground round for the two of them to share, raw, in the car on the way home as a reward for completing the shopping. The mother carried a salt shaker in her purse for the purpose.

Raw meat is more easily digested than cooked meat. A knob of steak tartare wrapped in a lettuce leaf is my definition of health food. All that said, a word to the wise: *eating raw meat is potentially hazardous to your health*. Please don't make this dish unless you are absolutely certain of the freshness and quality of your beef. Honor a good butcher with your steadfast business. I completely trust the quality of our beef at Deep Springs.

I first encountered *tartarski biftek* when I was an exchange student in Slovenia, where it was always very finely ground and always served with mayonnaise (on the side, or piped decoratively over the mound of meat) and toast points. I don't see mention of mayonnaise in any American cookbook recipes, but the older ones do specify grinding the meat to a uniform paste. The more contemporary chef-ly versions of steak tartare always call for hand-chopping the meat fine. I like a compromise: a spreadable paste with a portion of the meat hand-chopped. And finally, I briefly sear the piece of meat on all sides to guard against any kind of surface contamination.

Raw lamb is also delicious: once, when chef and Deep Springs alumnus David Tanis was visiting, I made a Middle Eastern–inflected *lamb tartare,* with a little cilantro and cayenne.

TOASTS

1 medium loaf good white bread, thinly sliced

melted butter

SAUCE

½ cup mayonnaise

2 tablespoons extra-virgin olive oil

1 tablespoon fresh lemon juice

pinch of salt

MEAT

1½ pounds beef tenderloin, perfect quality, visible fat trimmed off, well chilled

salt and black pepper

1 tablespoon olive oil

2 high-quality, freshly shelled egg yolks
(traditional, but 1 to 2 tablespoons of olive oil may be substituted)

3 anchovies, blotted of excess oil

3 tablespoons minced onion

1 tablespoon finely chopped capers

¼ teaspoon salt

several twists of black pepper

juice of ¼ lemon

1 tablespoon coarsely chopped parsley

10 to 15 small lettuce leaves, washed and spun dry, for serving

To make the toasts, heat the oven to 350°F. Cut the bread into small rectangles the size of dominos, arrange on a baking sheet, brush lightly on one side with melted butter, and toast in the oven until pale golden brown, about 10 minutes. Let the toasts cool on a rack.

To make the sauce, slowly whisk the olive oil into the mayonnaise in a small bowl, then add the lemon juice and salt. Cover and refrigerate.

To prepare the meat, season the beef well with salt and pepper, keeping it well-chilled. Over a high flame, heat the olive oil in a heavy, medium-sized skillet until it smokes, and carefully lay the cold beef in the sizzling oil. Cook for about 20 seconds per side, turning until all sides—including the ends—are seared. Put the beef on a plate and stick it in the freezer for about 10 minutes. Remove from the freezer and chop a third of the beef very finely by hand with your sharpest knife. Cut the rest into chunks and process in the food processor with the egg yolks (or olive oil) and anchovies until it is reduced to a fine paste. In a medium bowl, combine the beef-egg-anchovy mixture with the chopped beef, onion, capers, salt, pepper, lemon juice, and parsley. Mound the mixture in the center of a platter, surrounded by the little toasts and lettuce leaves, the dish of mayonnaise sauce close by. Serve immediately.

To eat, spread a generous layer of meat on a piece of toast and top with a small blob of mayonnaise sauce. Or wrap a ball of meat and a bit of sauce in a lettuce leaf.

Beef Carpaccio

serves 6 as a light course, 8 to 10 as an hors d'oeuvre

Whole slices of raw meat! Simpler and lighter than tartare, and therefore more elegant, yet also more crude (in a good way) and respectful of the integrity of the good product from which it is made: that defines good Italian food. Carpaccio was conceived in 1950 at the renowned Harry's Bar in Venice, Italy, during a major exhibition of the Renaissance painter Vittore Carpaccio. The deep red of the beef and the white of the mayonnaise sauce is said to echo the painter's famous reds and whites. At Harry's Bar, this still-popular dish is served simply: raw, well-trimmed shell steak, thinly sliced, served with a mayonnaise sauce—no other embellishments. Carpaccio now refers to any thinly sliced food tiled over a plate and sprinkled with seasonings—see Summer Squash Carpaccio, page 171. Lamb may also be used for carpaccio; instead of the mayonnaise sauce, drizzle with a vinaigrette to which you have added a few pitted, chopped oil-cured black olives.

Please use only *impeccably fresh, high-quality meat* for this recipe (see the Steak Tartare recipe, above). *Eating raw meat is potentially hazardous to your health.*

SAUCE

use the same sauce ingredients and procedure as in Steak Tartare, preceding recipe

MEAT

1½ pounds beef tenderloin, perfect quality, trimmed of fat, well-chilled

salt and black pepper

1 tablespoon olive oil

3 anchovies, blotted of excess oil and finely chopped

3 tablespoons minced green onion

1 tablespoon finely chopped capers

salt and freshly ground black pepper

juice of ¼ lemon

1 tablespoon coarsely chopped parsley

Make the mayonnaise sauce; cover and refrigerate.

To prepare the meat, season the beef well with salt and pepper, keeping it well-chilled. Heat the olive oil in a skillet until it smokes, and carefully lay the cold beef in the sizzling oil. Cook for about 20 seconds per side, turning until all sides—including the ends—are seared. Put the beef on a plate and stick it in the freezer for about 20 minutes.

Slice the beef crosswise as thinly as possible, using your sharpest knife. (I find this easier if the cylinder of meat is first halved lengthwise.) Place the slices between two layers of wax paper and gently roll to a translucent thinness, using a rolling pin. This may be done a few hours ahead of serving time.

Peel off one layer of the wax paper, put one slice of the meat facing down on an individual plate, and peel off the top layer of wax paper from the slice. Continue until the center of the plate is attractively "tiled" with meat. Repeat with the remaining plates. Put the mayonnaise sauce in a plastic bag, cut a tiny hole out of the corner, and squirt the mayonnaise in fine threads in a crosshatch pattern over the meat. Don't be too lavish with the mayonnaise. Evenly sprinkle the anchovies, green onions, capers, salt, pepper, lemon juice, and parsley over the meat. Serve immediately; eat with a knife and fork.

Beef Liver with Bacon, Onions, and Mushrooms

serves 6

I love runny egg yolks and bloody meat, mayonnaise oozing out of sandwiches, steak tartare. I love bitter things: chicory lettuces and English marmalade, candied citrus peel. I find there is more good fruitcake in the world than many people think. I love all the "icky" vegetables: Brussels sprouts and beets, turnips, rutabagas, and kale. I love all the strange things in the deli case, even the headcheese, the olive loaf, and especially the mortadella with chunks of white fat. I love anchovies and capers. I love the fat on roast beef, the skin on roast chicken. I love pickled pigs' feet and fried-tripe tacos.

Nonetheless, as a child, I was a very picky eater indeed. When I was seven or eight, I wouldn't eat much beyond Rice Krispies, peanut butter, hamburgers with ketchup only, and celery. I eventually discovered that you can acquire a taste for just about anything. Why dislike something when you could instead just enjoy it? In Hawaii, I first learned to appreciate the gray, sticky, cold, watery taro root paste known as poi only in the context of a whole, traditional island meal, alongside rice, salty pit-cooked pork, and braised cabbage. Until recently, I did not like beef liver, black-eyed peas, dill, or spaghetti squash. But now I like them all. Well, maybe not every day. The following preparation finally won me over to liver.

We always serve liver the day after a slaughter at Deep Springs, along with any other organ meats the cook is ambitious enough to prepare ("Organ Meat Festivals" we call such meals). Liver is quite rich and should be served in small portions—3 or 4 ounces. A single beef liver is huge, and far more than the community will eat. With a controversial menu item such as liver, I always include familiar, guaranteed-to-please foods: a big tossed green salad, roasted potatoes, pasta with cheese, warm bread, and a dessert such as Chocolate Mayonnaise Cake (page 291).

six 3- or 4-ounce slices of well-trimmed, very fresh beef or calves' liver, about ½ inch thick

milk for soaking

2 to 3 tablespoons butter

1 large yellow onion, thinly sliced with the grain

2 pinches of salt, plus more for seasoning

8 ounces white or brown mushrooms, wiped clean, trimmed, halved, and thickly sliced

3 to 4 thick-cut strips bacon, cut into bite-size squares

black pepper

In a wide, shallow bowl, soak the liver in enough milk to barely cover for 1 hour prior to cooking it. Meanwhile, make the accompaniments. Take a wide skillet and melt a tablespoon of butter over a medium-high flame. Throw in the onion with a big pinch of salt. Sauté, stirring and tossing constantly, allowing the onion to brown. Reduce the heat to medium-low and let the onion continue to brown and caramelize. If a brown, caramelized residue forms on the bottom of the pan, slap the lid on the pan and remove from the heat for a few moments—the steam from the onions will melt this residue back into the onions, making them more tasty and savory. The total cooking time will be about 20 minutes. When the onions are tender and taste good, transfer them to a dish, and keep warm. Sauté the mushrooms in two batches in butter with a pinch of salt until brown and flavorful (page 135). Set the mushrooms aside in a bowl. Rinse out the skillet if necessary, and cook the bacon slowly in the skillet until browned and crispy. Pour the fat into a metal cup, reserving it for cooking the liver. Drain the bacon on paper towels and set aside. You may prepare the mushrooms, bacon, and onion ahead of time, but they should be warm when you start cooking the liver.

Drain the pieces of liver and pat dry with paper towels. Season the liver on both sides with salt and pepper. Wipe out the skillet, and heat 1 tablespoon of bacon fat over medium-high heat until the liver sizzles merrily upon contact. Cook 3 pieces of the liver until brown on one side, turn, and cook until just beginning to brown on the other side. If the liver is about ½ inch thick, this should take 40 to 50 seconds on each side. Do not overcook. The liver should still be barely pink in the middle. Remove the liver to a warmed plate or platter. Repeat with the remaining 3 pieces of liver. Spoon the onions over the liver, sprinkle the mushrooms and bacon on top, and serve right away. Now, what wouldn't taste good with onions, bacon, and mushrooms strewn over it?

Apple-Marinated Pork Chops

serves 3

These pork chops are seasoned with salt and marinated with fresh apple a day ahead. The salt penetrates and tenderizes the meat much as a brine does, and the apple's sugars help the pork brown beautifully in the pan. They are perfect with Roasted Potatoes, Apples, and Onions (page 141). After the chops are cooked, the apples and onions in which the pork marinated are simmered briefly in apple cider or apple juice. The onions remain a little crunchy, but if they taste good to you, you may serve them with the chops or use them in another dish: once I tossed the apples and onions into sautéed Swiss chard—the combination was delicious.

Strictly speaking, the word *cider* refers not to fresh apple juice, but to what we in the U.S. call "hard cider"—apple juice that has been allowed to ferment into a light alcoholic beverage. In the days before refrigeration, fresh-pressed apple juice could not be kept for long without spontaneously fermenting into cider. Apples grown for eating, the sweet apples we're familiar with, make bland, watery cider. Seed-planted apples express the fruit's full genetic diversity, yielding sour, bitter, or astringent fruit in addition to sweet specimens. A careful blending of such apples yields cider that is complex, well balanced, and delicious. For this recipe, cider will make a deeper, more savory sauce, while apple juice will make a sweeter one—both are good.

3 center-cut pork chops, about 1 inch thick, a little fat left on

1 teaspoon salt

½ teaspoon freshly ground black pepper

½ flavorful apple, unpeeled, thinly sliced

¼ small yellow onion, thinly sliced

1 tablespoon olive oil

1 cup apple cider or apple juice

Rub the pork chops with the salt and pepper. Place the apple slices over the top and bottom surfaces of each chop, put the chops in a shallow bowl, and scatter the onion over them. Cover tightly with plastic wrap, pressing the wrap down on the surface of the chops, and refrigerate overnight.

Set the chops out at room temperature for about 1 hour before cooking. Remove and reserve the apples and onions. Pat the chops dry with a paper towel. Heat the olive oil in a wide, heavy skillet over a medium-high flame and brown the chops for about 4 minutes on each side, or just until they feel firm when pressed with a finger. If they don't seem cooked, lower the flame and continue cooking for a few minutes more. They are thoroughly cooked, but still juicy, when they have reached an internal temperature of 150°F. Remove the chops to a warmed plate, and loosely cover with foil to keep warm.

Reheat the skillet over a medium-high flame. If there is excessive fat left in the skillet, pour it off. Add the apples and onions and pour in the apple cider. Bring to a boil, scraping the browned, flavorful bits from the bottom of the skillet with a wooden spoon and letting them dissolve into the cider. After everything has boiled for about a minute, strain out the apples and onions. Or, if you prefer, leave them in. Boil until the liquid is reduced to a thin syrup, just a few tablespoons. Pour over the warm chops and serve.

Tender Cured Pork Chops

serves 8

The meat fibers in lean cuts of pork often "seize up" and may be very tough if not cooked with care. One way of counteracting this tendency is simply to cook the meat over very gentle heat (see the following recipe, Pork Chops Slow-Cooked in Olive Oil). Another way is to brine the meat. A brine is not simply a marinade—the salt solution actually penetrates the meat and alters the structure of the protein, curing the meat. Once cured, chops may be cooked on high heat and will remain tender. This brine will also flavor and tenderize chicken (page 205) as well as other cuts of pork, such as a whole boneless loin—allow an extra 24 hours for each extra inch of thickness, for cuts up to 4 inches thick.

In this recipe, the water, salt, sugar, and soy sauce are essential, but the aromatic flavorings may be varied to suit the occasion. Garlic, fennel, allspice, coriander, thyme, red pepper, citrus zest—any of these could be delicious.

BRINE

6 tablespoons kosher salt (see page 42)

6 tablespoons firmly packed brown sugar

8 cups water

⅓ cup soy sauce

1 small, leafy stalk celery, thinly sliced

1 small carrot, peeled and thinly sliced

½ small yellow onion, thinly sliced

4 large leaves fresh sage, bruised and torn up

several sprigs of parsley, bruised and torn up

3 bay leaves, crushed in your hand

2 teaspoons crushed juniper berries

½ teaspoon crushed black peppercorns

8 bone-in pork chops, about ¾ inch thick

about 2 tablespoons sunflower oil or other vegetable oil

To make the brine, stir the salt and sugar into the water in a large bowl until completely dissolved. Add the soy sauce, celery, carrot, onion, sage, parsley, bay leaves, juniper berries, and peppercorns, then add the pork chops. Refrigerate the chops in the brine, stirring and redistributing several times, for at least 24 and preferably 36 hours (½-inch pork chops take only 24 hours; 1-inch chops take about 48 hours). Remove the chops from the brine, and pat dry with paper towels. Heat the oven to 350°F.

Over a medium-high flame, heat about a tablespoon of oil in a wide, heavy skillet. Cook 4 of the chops until well browned on one side, about 4 minutes. Flip and cook on the other side for another 3 to 4 minutes. Repeat with the remaining 4 chops. If necessary, you may finish cooking the chops in the oven once they have been browned on the stovetop. They are best cooked to medium, until the meat is firm and a faint rosy pink color. These chops may also be grilled, to wonderful effect, over a charcoal fire.

QUICK BRINE FOR PORK CHOPS

If you have only an hour or two, a 30- to 60-minute soak in this strong brine effectively seasons pork chops for roasting or grilling: 4 cups cool tap water, 2 ounces salt, ⅓ to ½ cup sugar. Weighing the salt is more accurate, as the volume-to-weight ratio of different salt types vary considerably. Two ounces of kosher salt is equivalent to a scant ½ cup. If the pork is to accompany robustly flavored dishes, use the greater amount of sugar; for more subtly flavored accompaniments, use the lesser.

Pork Chops Slow-Cooked in Olive Oil

serves 3

These tender pork chops require no chopping or peeling of ingredients and no marinating or brining, making them perfect for a quick weeknight supper. They can be cooking in the pan just minutes after you walk into the kitchen. To keep them tender, you cook them slowly over a low flame. The lower temperature results in less spattery mess than most other pan-cooked meat. Although they don't brown, paprika, balsamic vinegar, and soy sauce provide a good stand-in for browned flavor.

3 center-cut boneless or bone-in pork chops, about 1 inch thick (*bone-in chops will need a minute or two more in the pan*)

¾ teaspoon salt

½ teaspoon black pepper

2 or 3 pinches of cayenne pepper

1 teaspoon paprika

½ cup olive oil

2 teaspoons balsamic vinegar

2 teaspoons soy sauce

2 teaspoons honey

Rub the chops all over with the salt, black pepper, cayenne, and paprika. Over a low flame, heat the olive oil in a wide, heavy skillet for a minute. Gently lay the pork chops in the warm oil. Raise the heat slightly. Listen carefully: as soon as you hear a low, gentle sizzle, turn the heat down slightly, adjusting it as necessary to maintain this slow sizzle. Let the chops cook in this manner for 6 to 7 minutes on each side—the precise timing depends on the chops' thickness and the intensity of the heat. When done, they should feel firm throughout when pressed with a finger. The interior of the chops will be a juicy, pale pink. Remove the chops to clean plates.

Pour the oil from the pan into a metal cup or other heatproof container, reserving it for cooking more pork chops or for another use—it's very good for cooking vegetables. Add the balsamic vinegar, soy sauce, and honey to the warm pan, bring to a bubbling boil, and drizzle over the chops.

Pork Tenderloin

serves 5 to 6

When you want lean, tender, succulent meat that requires little advance preparation, you want pork tenderloin. Though the seasonings suggested here are lively and classic, you can vary them to suit your taste. Serve pork tenderloin amid an array of simple vegetable dishes and salads, such as beets with orange, artichokes, watercress, and boiled new potatoes dressed with olive oil.

2 pork tenderloins, each a little over a pound

1 teaspoon salt

¼ teaspoon cayenne pepper

scant ¼ teaspoon black pepper

¼ teaspoon rubbed sage

about 1 tablespoon olive oil

1 to 2 tablespoons water or wine

Pat the tenderloins dry with a paper towel. Cut each tenderloin crosswise into 2 pieces of equal weight. With a meat pounder, rolling pin, or other heavy object, pound the bulbous-end piece until it is flattened and only slightly thinner than the tapered-end piece—this way, the two differently shaped pieces will cook at about the same rate. Rub the salt, cayenne, black pepper, and sage into the meat. Let sit at room temperature for 20 to 30 minutes.

Heat a wide, heavy skillet over a medium flame. Add half of the olive oil to the skillet, and rub the pieces of pork with the remaining olive oil. Lay the pork in the oil, and put a loose cover on the skillet. Let the meat cook, turning several times, for a total of 15 to 20 minutes, or until the thickest pieces are beginning to feel firm. (The internal temperature should register 150°F on an instant-read thermometer.) Remove the pork to a clean plate and let rest for 5 minutes before slicing on the diagonal, across the grain. The meat will be rosy pink but cooked throughout. Add a couple of tablespoons of water or wine to the skillet and return to the flame, scraping the flavorful brown bits on the bottom of the skillet with a wooden spoon and letting them dissolve into the liquid. Boil until the liquid is reduced to just a spoonful, and pour this scant sauce over the sliced pork.

Cynthia's Garlic-Studded Milk-Braised Pork Loin

serves 4 to 6

The pork emerges tender, juicy, and milky white in this lovely Italian recipe, taught to me by Cynthia Shea, a terrific chef I worked with at Liberty Café in San Francisco.

1 boneless pork loin roast, about 2 pounds, with some fat left on

2 to 3 cloves garlic, cut into matchstick-sized slivers

1 teaspoon salt

about ½ teaspoon black pepper

1 tablespoon olive oil

4 cups whole milk

2 strips lemon zest, taken with a vegetable peeler

5 or 6 fresh sage leaves

Pat the pork dry with paper towels. Using a small knife, poke holes all over the surface of the meat and insert slivers of garlic, until the garlic is used up. Salt and pepper the meat well on all sides.

Choose a heavy pan that will comfortably accommodate the meat. Heat the olive oil in the pan over medium-high heat and brown the pork loin well on all sides (sturdy tongs are a great help here). Pour in the milk, and submerge the lemon zest and sage. Lower the heat to medium. Slowly bring the milk to a low simmer, reducing the heat further, if necessary, and cook the pork, turning several times, just until the meat is cooked through, 30 to 40 minutes. For very good results, if you are patient, you may prolong the cooking further, taking up to an hour over very low heat—in effect slowly poaching the loin in the milk.

When the pork is cooked, it should feel firm when gently squeezed and should register about 145°F in the center with an instant-read thermometer. If the internal temperature is much higher than 145°, the meat might be overcooked and dry. The inside of the meat should still be a faint rose color, but it should be thoroughly opaque, not raw looking. Remove the meat from the liquid and let rest for about 10 minutes. Slice thinly across the grain. Return any unsliced pork to the liquid, and refrigerate it in the liquid when cool. The gray, milky, curdled liquid left over from cooking the pork looks hideous but tastes savory and delicious. How to serve it without letting anyone see it? One strategy is to hide it underneath the meat, spooning a little into the serving dish or plate before laying down the sliced pork. Or incorporate it into your chosen starch: fold it into cooked rice, toss with cooked pasta, or stir into polenta. Finally, be sure your accompaniments are bright and colorful: bright green vegetables, beets, citrus….

Slow-Roasted Pork

serves 8 to 10

Consider this recipe only one of many potential pathways to a delectable pork roast so tender it can be cleaved with two forks. While a bone-in roast with plenty of fat is specified, you can cook leaner, boneless pieces of shoulder in a similar fashion. Lacking a good covering of fat, adding a splash of wine and more olive oil, and loosely wrapping the roast in baking parchment, will help keep the meat moist. You can cook the pork in a slow cooker instead of the oven. You can cook it for a little less time—5 to 6 hours—at a slightly hotter temperature—300°F—and still achieve excellent results. Rather than the seasoning specified here, you can immerse the pork in a brine (page 198) for about 3 days instead. The pork shoulder, also known as pork butt, is well-marbled, tender, and ideally suited to this low-and-slow method.

1 bone-in pork shoulder *(butt)* **roast with a nice covering of fat, about 6 pounds**

about 5 teaspoons salt

1 teaspoon crushed fennel seeds

1 teaspoon hot red pepper flakes

1 teaspoon black pepper

1 medium onion, thinly sliced

1 tablespoon honey

1 tablespoon olive oil

lemon wedges, for serving

Pat the pork dry with paper towels. Rub all over with salt. Judge the amount of salt—big pieces of meat need a good amount; use more if necessary. Rub with the fennel seeds, pepper flakes, and black pepper, and let rest, refrigerated, preferably overnight, but at least for an hour or two.

Bring the pork to room temperature, and heat the oven to 275°F. Arrange the sliced onion in a pile in a rimmed roasting pan large enough to accommodate the pork comfortably. Place the pork fat-side-up atop the onion. Rub the fat side of the pork all over with the honey, then drizzle with the olive oil. Roast in the center of the oven for about 7½ hours, basting with the pan juices once or twice, until tender throughout and deep brown all over. Pour off any pan juices into a cup and carefully spoon off the fat from the top (reserve the fat for cooking vegetables, if you like). Serve the pork with the defatted pan juices and wedges of lemon. Salsa Verde (page 254) is an excellent and traditional accompaniment.

CRISPY PORK

One of the great benefits of Slow-Roasted Pork is being able to make Crispy Pork the next day. Using your hands, break up the chilled roast into rough, bite-sized pieces, plus a few smaller pieces. Heat a skillet over a medium-low flame. The leftover pork should contain sufficient fat to brown; if it's lean, add a little oil to the skillet first. Arrange the pieces of meat in the skillet without crowding. Let the pork sizzle slowly in the skillet, rather like cooking bacon, turning the pieces as necessary, until they are crispy and golden brown all over. Taste, and season with salt if necessary. Akin to the Mexican dish of *carnitas*, this crispy pork makes an excellent taco filling: for each taco, heat 2 corn tortillas over a flame until softened, fragrant, and blackened here and there. Stack them together, place a good amount of sizzling-hot crispy pork in the center, top with spicy salsa, squeeze fresh lime juice over, fold the tortillas around the filling, and eat immediately.

Glazed Ham

serves 8 to 10 with leftovers

In this Christmas recipe, a fully-cooked ham is first simmered in milk to temper the saltiness, then glazed in the oven. The palette of aromatic ingredients—onion, ginger, garlic, allspice, peppercorns, and thyme in the initial cooking of the ham, and cardamom, Worcestershire, white pepper, and cloves in the glaze—is lively, balanced, and traditional, enhancing the excellent flavor of ham, but may, of course, be varied to suit your taste. Serve hot slices of ham with assorted types of mustard, and a fruit-based accompaniment such as Pickled Fruit or Quince Jam (pages 258 to 260). Serve leftover ham cold and thinly sliced, with mustard, either alongside Reatha's Macaroni and Cheese (page 85), or tucked into sandwiches with leftover Priscilla's Fried Green Tomatoes (page 146).

½ **gallon whole milk**

1 small onion, thinly sliced

6 cloves garlic, peeled and split

1 small piece of peeled fresh ginger

1 tablespoon whole allspice berries

10 whole black peppercorns

2 to 3 sprigs fresh thyme

1 bone-in half ham, fully cooked *(not spiral-sliced; the butt end is meatier than the shank end)*, **8 to 10 pounds**

GLAZE

6 whole green cardamom pods

1 stick butter

¾ **cup honey**

2 teaspoons Worcestershire sauce

1 teaspoon apple cider vinegar

2 teaspoons Dijon mustard

½ **teaspoon white pepper**

big pinch ground cloves

FOR SERVING

assorted mustards and chutneys

Pickled Fruit *(page 258)*, **Quince Jam** *(260)*, or **Applesauce** *(257)*

Choose a large stock pot with a heavy bottom for the initial cooking of the ham—slow, even heat is necessary. Pour the milk in the pot, and add the onion, garlic, ginger, allspice, peppercorns, and thyme. Give the ham a quick rinse, and ease it down into the pot. Place the pot on a medium-low flame, checking and stirring often as the milk heats. When the milk begins to simmer, lower the heat to maintain a simmer—the milk shouldn't boil hard. Continue to monitor the ham, turning it several times throughout the process, until an instant-reading thermometer registers 160°F in the thickest, meatiest part of the ham, about 1 hour.

Meanwhile, to make the glaze, first remove the black seeds from the cardamom pods, and crush them finely in a mortar. Throw the cardamom husks into the pot with the simmering ham. Put the cardamom seeds and all the other glaze ingredients in a small saucepan, and heat over a medium flame until bubbling.

About 45 minutes before serving time, glaze the ham: heat the oven to 375°F. Drain the ham from the milk. (My friend Elge suggests straining and saving the milk to make a sumptuous gravy for ham biscuits [page 65] for Boxing Day brunch.) Pick off any bits of onion or other aromatic ingredients that may be adhering to the ham. Put the ham, fat side up, on a rimmed baking sheet. Blot the ham with paper towels to help the glaze adhere. Using a barbecue brush, apply one third of the glaze, and put the ham in the hot oven. Bake 20 minutes, allowing the first layer of glaze to darken and set, then remove the ham and apply half the remaining glaze. Bake another 10 minutes, then apply the remainder of the glaze. Return to the oven for another 10 minutes, carefully transfer the ham to a serving platter, and bring it, with fanfare, to the dining table.

My Mother's Polish Sausage Stew

serves 3 to 4

Absolutely simple and restorative, this is one of the best winter-warming suppers. The term "stew" is used loosely here; New Englanders will find this dish similar to their beloved, corned beef–based "boiled dinner." Serve with mustard, rye crackers and cucumbers.

1 pound kielbasa *(Polish smoked pork/beef sausage)*, **cut into 6 pieces**

1 small head green cabbage, cut lengthwise, through the stem, into 6 wedges

6 to 7 boiling onions, peeled, or 2 small onions, peeled and quartered

3 carrots, peeled and each cut in thirds

6 small red or yellow potatoes, about golf ball-size, unpeeled

8 cups cold water

1 tablespoon salt, plus more as needed

grainy mustard, for serving

Throw all the ingredients into a large pot and bring to a boil. Reduce the heat to low and simmer for about 10 minutes. Taste the broth for salt, adding more if necessary. Poke some of the potatoes and other vegetables with a small knife to make certain they are tender. Simmer longer if necessary. Let stand, covered, off the heat for about 5 more minutes. To each guest serve a couple of pieces of sausage and an assortment of vegetables swimming in plenty of broth in a large bowl. Serve with knife, fork, and spoon, and a small dish of grainy mustard on the side.

CHAPTER 10

CHICKEN & TURKEY

I've kept egg-laying chickens at various times and once raised one to eat—it was delicious. I've also raised turkeys, beginning with one in Hawaii. That Thanksgiving, we thanked the turkey, we thanked the universe, and we thanked each other. A few years later, at Deep Springs, I enjoyed raising a flock of two dozen Bourbon Red turkeys, letting them have free run of my yard. But alas, tragedy struck, at least from my perspective: half the flock was picked off by some very lucky coyotes in a single night. I found turkey feathers strewn across an alfalfa field.

I am grateful to know the satisfaction of producing my own food, but it's a lot of work. I am grateful to know, quite intimately, how much energy goes into producing just a little meat. I am also grateful for all those birds, raised from chicks, in all their incarnations: their youth, their life, their corporal selves. We took the lives of these animals and incorporated them into our own.

If you use *kosher chicken or turkey,* reduce the salt in these recipes to a pinch: kosher poultry is already salted.

Roast Chicken

serves 2 to 3 (3-pound chicken), or 4 to 6 (5-pound chicken)

Once, as a fascinating experiment, I raised a chicken "for the table." Wanting to cook it very simply, I used this method, based on what Paul Bertolli, in *Chez Panisse Cooking,* calls his "tribute to roast chicken." Seasoned like fresh Italian sausage, this chicken has become many people's favorite over the years. At Deep Springs I serve whole roast chickens family-style—I put the birds on oval platters, garnish with sliced lemons and parsley sprigs, place a carving knife and fork alongside, and put one on each table in the Boardinghouse. In this way, the students gradually learn how to carve a chicken.

If you would like to roast a cut-up chicken or an equivalent amount of chicken parts, increase the oven heat to 450°F—the chicken will take only about 30 to 45 minutes to cook (depending on their size), and the higher heat will help the skin to crisp in this shorter amount of time.

Sometimes I substitute cumin seeds for the fennel, and it's an entirely different bird.

FOR A 2½- TO 3-POUND CHICKEN:

1½ teaspoons salt

¾ teaspoon black pepper

1½ teaspoons fennel seed, coarsely crushed

¼ teaspoon red pepper flakes

¼ teaspoon dried thyme

FOR A 3½- TO 4-POUND CHICKEN:

2¼ teaspoons salt

1 heaping teaspoon black pepper

2¼ teaspoons fennel seed, coarsely crushed

heaping ¼ teaspoon red pepper flakes

heaping ¼ teaspoon dried thyme

FOR A 4½- TO 5-POUND CHICKEN:

1 tablespoon salt

1½ teaspoons black pepper

1 tablespoon fennel seed, coarsely crushed

½ teaspoon red pepper flakes

½ teaspoon dried thyme

Pull the excess fat out of the cavity and around the neck flap of the chicken. Tie the legs together with a length of butcher twine. Tuck the wings behind the neck. Mix the salt, pepper, fennel seed, red pepper, and thyme together in a small bowl. Rub the seasoning all over the chicken, inside and out. Rub a greater proportion of seasoning on the breast. You may season the chicken several hours ahead of time, or the day before—if so, keep it covered and refrigerated.

When you're ready to cook the chicken, set it out at room temperature for about 1 hour. (Once the chicken has begun to come to room temperature, don't change your mind and decide to cook it another day!) Heat the oven to 425°F. Roast the chicken, breast side up, on a rack (or simply on a foil-covered rimmed baking sheet, with the foil's shiny side facing up) for about 1 hour (for a 3-pound chicken) to about 1½ hours (for a 5-pound chicken), or until an instant-read thermometer inserted in the thickest part of the breast or thigh registers 165°F. Using a small knife, you may peek into the interior of one of the thighs—no pink should remain, nor should any pink-colored juices run out. Let the chicken rest for 10 minutes before carving.

HOLIDAY ROAST CHICKEN

Here, the chicken undergoes a light cure for two days in a brine before being roasted. This festive treatment tenderizes and seasons the meat deliciously down to the bone. Use the brine recipe for Tender Cured Pork Chops (page 197). The juniper berries in the brine will impart a flavor evocative of wild game—especially appropriate with pork but a bit unusual with chicken; you decide whether or not to include them. Let the chicken—either parts or a whole bird—soak in the brine, completely submerged, for 36 hours. Remove the chicken, pat dry with paper towels, and put on a rack, uncovered, in the refrigerator for several more hours or overnight (this helps the skin dry and emerge crisp after roasting). Roast the chicken (as directed in the previous recipe, but omitting the spice rub) for about 1 hour (for a 3-pound chicken) to about 1½ hours (for a 5-pound chicken), or until an instant-read thermometer inserted in the thickest part of the breast or thigh registers 165°F. For parts, roast at 450°F for about 30 to 45 minutes.

QUICK BRINE FOR CHICKEN

If you have only an hour or two, a 30- to 60-minute soak in this strong brine effectively seasons chicken for roasting or grilling: 4 cups cool tap water, 2 ounces salt, ⅓ to ½ cup sugar. Weighing the salt is more accurate, as the volume-to-weight ratio of different salt types vary considerably. Two ounces of kosher salt is equivalent to a scant ½ cup. If the chicken is to accompany robustly flavored dishes, use the greater amount of sugar; for more subtly flavored accompaniments, use the lesser.

Marmalade Chicken

serves 3 to 4

To prepare this delicious chicken, you allow salt and pepper to penetrate into the meat for several hours or overnight but apply the marmalade just before baking. Why not just marinate the chicken in the marmalade, too? Because the concentration of sugar in the marmalade will draw moisture out of the chicken, ultimately resulting in tougher, drier, less flavorful meat. What's more, the marmalade, now diluted, will fail to coat the chicken and will merely pool in the pan.

This is very good with Pecan Couscous (page 237).

1 large chicken, about 4 pounds, cut up into 8 pieces

2 teaspoons salt

few pinches of cayenne pepper

plenty of black pepper

1 large red onion, thinly sliced

½ cup citrus marmalade, any type *(to make your own, see page 260)*

Pat the chicken dry with paper towels. Rub with salt, cayenne, and black pepper, putting a slightly larger proportion of the seasoning on the breasts. Let the chicken sit, covered and refrigerated, for several hours or overnight.

Heat the oven to 350°F. Line a large, rimmed baking sheet with aluminum foil (shiny side up), and scatter with the sliced onions. In a big bowl, toss the chicken with the marmalade and place, skin side up, on the sheet, evenly spaced, tucking the onions underneath the chicken. Scrape all the remaining marmalade from the bowl onto the top surfaces of the largest pieces of chicken. Bake for an hour. Let the pan rest at a slight tilt for about 10 minutes so the juice pools. Transfer the chicken (and the onions, if you like) to a warmed platter or plates. Carefully pour off the liquid into a cup, then spoon off and discard the clear fat from the top. Use the remaining flavorful brown sweet-salty juice as a sauce.

Sautéed Chicken Breast

serves 2 to 3

Here is a thorough run-down on how to sauté a chicken breast. It's elegant, quick, easy, reliable, and universally loved and appreciated. Once you get the hang of cooking chicken breasts this way, you can infinitely vary the flavors by including in the seasoning, or in the sauce, judicious amounts of lemon zest, fresh herbs, cayenne, ground chile, cumin, fennel seed, or other aromatic ingredients. Much effort is made in this recipe to cook the skin to an appealing brown crispiness. However, if you choose to use skinless breasts, they too can emerge from the pan savory and juicy, provided you don't overcook them.

1 boneless, skin-on whole chicken breast or 2 boneless, skin-on breast halves, about 1 pound total

¾ teaspoon salt, plus a pinch

several twists of black pepper

2 teaspoons olive oil

2 tablespoons dry white wine or chicken stock

1 tablespoon cold butter

1 teaspoon fresh lemon juice

A whole, boneless chicken breast is heart-shaped; remove the tough seam down the middle and you have two teardrop-shaped chicken breast halves, each with a tapering "tenderloin"—a small, separate strip of meat loosely attached to the underside. I usually pull these tenderloins off and cook them alongside the breasts. Using a small, sharp knife, trim off any excess fat, tendon, or bit of bone. Trim out the tough little tendon in the center of the rounded end of each breast. Put the chicken breasts in a heavy plastic bag. Using the smooth side of a meat pounder or other heavy object, gently pound the rounded, fatter end of each breast half until it is the same thickness—about ¾ inch—as the pointed, thinner end. Pat the chicken dry with a paper towel, and season all over with the ¾ teaspoon salt and the pepper. Put the breasts on a plate, skin side up, and put in the refrigerator, uncovered, for several hours or overnight—this will help dry out the skin slightly, so that it crisps nicely.

Set a wide, heavy skillet over a medium flame. Let the pan heat for about 2 minutes. Raise the heat to medium-high, and add the olive oil. When the oil just begins to smoke, place the chicken breasts in the pan, skin side down—they should sizzle.

Cook the breast halves on the skin side for 4 to 5 minutes, or until the skin has crisped to a nice deep golden brown. Turn and cook the skinless side for 2 to 3 minutes, or until the breast is just cooked through (if the breast is thicker than ¾ inch, it might take more time). The texture of the breast, when pressed with a finger, will have progressed from squishy to just springy. Transfer the chicken, skin side up, to a warmed plate, and cover loosely with foil to keep warm, while you make a pan sauce. Pour off any fat in the pan. Add the wine or stock—it will boil up furiously. With a spatula or a wooden spoon, scrape the browned bits from the bottom of the pan—they will dissolve into the sauce. This brown flavor residue is called the *fond*, most conveniently translated as "flavor base." When the wine has reduced by half, swirl the tablespoon of cold butter into the sauce, off the heat. Squeeze lemon juice—1 to 2 teaspoons—into the sauce and add a pinch of salt. Using a sharp knife, slice the chicken breasts into slices about 1 inch wide. Pour the pan sauce over the chicken breasts and serve immediately.

Double-Herbed Grilled Chicken

serves about 4

A good recipe if you have a summer herb garden and an outdoor grill, this chicken is first marinated with strong thyme, bay, and oregano, then tossed with more delicate parsley, basil, and chives while it's hot off the grill. Don't feel bound by the herb profile suggested here: savory, sage, rosemary, mint, cilantro, and dill would also be delicious. Lacking a grill, you can roast the chicken in a 450°F oven.

one 4-pound chicken, cut into quarters

½ lemon

2½ teaspoons salt

¼ teaspoon cayenne

several sprigs fresh oregano

several sprigs fresh thyme

1 bay leaf, crumbled coarsely

1 tablespoon olive oil

several sprigs fresh parsley

several sprigs fresh basil

finely grated zest of ½ lemon

1 small handful fresh chives, cut in ¼-inch pieces, or 1 green onion, thinly sliced

freshly-ground black pepper

Trim away any excess fat on the chicken around the neck and body cavities—it can cause flare-ups during grilling. Rub each piece of chicken all over with the half lemon, squeezing to release the juice. Blot the chicken dry with paper towels, place in a large bowl, then season evenly with the salt and cayenne. Bruise the oregano and thyme sprigs well, chop roughly, and add to the chicken along with the bay leaf and a tablespoon of olive oil. Toss the chicken well. Take some of the tenderer leaves of thyme and oregano and stuff them under the skin of the breasts and legs. Let the chicken marinate, refrigerated, for several hours or overnight.

Bring the chicken to room temperature for cooking. Thoroughly heat the grill to medium-high, clean the grates, and brush the grates with a wad of paper toweling moistened with olive oil. Pick any large pieces of herbs off the chicken, place the chicken skin-side down on the grill, and cook until nicely marked, about 3 minutes. Turn the chicken 90 degrees, and cook another 2 minutes, or until marked. Flip the chicken, and reduce the grill's heat to medium. Let the chicken finish cooking over medium heat until cooked through, about 20 minutes. While the chicken is grilling, chop the parsley and basil coarsely, and scatter in a large serving bowl that will accommodate the chicken. Grate the lemon zest over the herbs, scatter over the chives, and grind several twists of black pepper. When the chicken is cooked, transfer each piece directly from the grill to the bowl, tossing and coating the hot chicken in the herbs. Let the chicken rest for a few minutes, and serve.

Cayenne-Rubbed Chicken with Potatoes and Garlic

serves 4 to 6

This roast chicken is a simple and much-loved dinner in our household, served with a salad or a simply prepared green vegetable. The cayenne pepper (extremely healthful, by the way) is present but not overpowering.

2¾ teaspoons salt

2 teaspoons paprika

½ teaspoon cayenne pepper

½ teaspoon black pepper

3 medium yellow, red, or white potatoes, cut into ½-inch chunks

about 15 cloves garlic or more, unpeeled

1 tablespoon olive oil

3 to 4 bone-in, skin-on chicken breast halves, or whole legs, or a 4-pound chicken cut into quarters

In a small bowl, combine the salt, paprika, cayenne, and black pepper. Divide this mixture in half. Rub half of the mixture all over the chicken, and let sit for ½ hour, or for several hours or overnight, covered and refrigerated. If you've seasoned the chicken ahead of time, bring it to room temperature before roasting.

Heat the oven to 450°F. In a large bowl, toss the potatoes and garlic with the olive oil and the remaining seasoning mixture. Arrange the potatoes in a 13-by-9-inch baking dish in an even layer. Place the chicken skin-side up, atop the potatoes. Bake for about 25 minutes for large chicken breasts; leg-thigh pieces may take longer. The chicken should feel firm all the way through when pressed with a finger, and should register about 150°F at its thickest point with an instant-reading meat thermometer. Remove the chicken to a plate.

Give the potatoes and garlic a gentle stir, and return to the oven to finish cooking, 5 to 8 minutes more. If there is a lot of fat at the bottom of the baking dish, let the dish rest for a few minutes at a slight tilt so the fat pools to one side; scoop the potatoes from the other side. (Save this flavorful fat for sautéing vegetables.) Serve chicken, potatoes, and garlic to each person, letting them squeeze the roasted garlic over everything.

Crispy Pan-Fried Chicken

serves 2 to 3

This recipe uses the classic three-step breading process, in which you dredge the seasoned chicken first in flour, then in egg, then in breadcrumbs. The coating adheres well, can be done hours ahead of time, and emerges from the pan irresistibly golden and crispy. Certain varieties of mild white fish, such as snapper or cod, are also good treated this way. Whether served with chicken or fish, Meyer Lemon–Olive Relish (page 254) is a superb accompaniment.

Homemade breadcrumbs will lend their own character to the finished product, but be assured that packaged Japanese breadcrumbs, called *panko,* are made exactly for this purpose and will produce an incomparably light and crispy coating. Finally, for a rich, luxurious flavor, use clarified butter instead of vegetable oil to fry the chicken.

2 boneless, skinless chicken breast halves

1 clove garlic, crushed

1 or 2 pinches of dried thyme

½ teaspoon salt

black pepper

BREADING (APPROXIMATE AMOUNTS)

⅓ cup all-purpose flour

1 egg

1 teaspoon Dijon mustard

1 cup dry breadcrumbs *(use Japanese panko for best results)*

sunflower oil or other vegetable oil or clarified butter *(see page 37)* **for frying**

Trim any fat or gristle from the chicken breast. Gently pull away the "tenderloin"—the tapered strip of meat—from underneath each breast. Put the chicken breasts in a plastic bag, and with a meat pounder or other heavy object, gently pound the breasts to an even ½-inch thickness. Cut each breast in half lengthwise, or in thirds if especially large. Pat the breasts and tenderloins dry with paper towels, and season with the crushed garlic, a pinch or two of dried thyme, the salt, and pepper to taste.

To bread the chicken, sprinkle the flour over a wide plate. Beat the egg with the mustard in a wide, shallow bowl. Spread the breadcrumbs over another wide plate. First, dredge the chicken in the flour, then dip it in the egg, coating all sides, then coat with the breadcrumbs. Lay the pieces of breaded chicken on a rack set atop a baking sheet and let rest for about 20 minutes (or longer, refrigerated). This "sets" the breading, allowing the crumbs and flour to thoroughly hydrate, for fewer spatters while frying.

In a wide, heavy skillet or sauté pan, heat about ½ inch of vegetable oil or clarified butter over a medium-high flame. To test whether the oil is hot enough, throw in a breadcrumb: if it sizzles excitedly right away and browns after 15 to 20 seconds, the oil is ready. Gently lay the chicken in the pan. If your pan is on the small side, cook the chicken breasts in batches. Crowding the chicken in the pan cools down the oil too much, allowing it to saturate the coating. Let the chicken fry on one side until golden brown. Check the underside after about 30 seconds—if it has browned too quickly, just turn the chicken, lower the heat, and continue to cook, turning the chicken a few more times. It should take about 2 minutes on each side to cook the chicken through, 4 to 5 minutes in all. You may cut into a piece of the chicken to make sure it is cooked through. Drain briefly on paper towels and serve immediately.

Tarragon-Roasted Chicken with Tomatoes

serves 6

This is a superb way to prepare light or dark meat. Serve with bread to soak up the flavorful tomato-chicken juices. In the cooler seasons, Roma tomatoes, ripened on a windowsill, are fine to use. Once, to celebrate the last day of a semester at Deep Springs, we accompanied this chicken with Stuffed Artichokes (page 119) and Wild Mushroom Risotto (page 241)—a great menu.

You may substitute 1 to 2 tablespoons of fresh thyme leaves, or ½ cup chopped fresh basil, for the tarragon. Both, like tarragon, are good with both chicken and tomatoes.

- 6 bone-in, skin-on chicken breast halves or 1 whole chicken, cut into parts
- 2 teaspoons salt
- 2 tablespoons olive oil
- ½ teaspoon freshly ground black pepper, plus more for seasoning tomatoes
- 3 tablespoons coarsely chopped fresh tarragon, plus an extra sprig for garnish
- 1 teaspoon finely grated lemon zest
- 1 pound red, ripe tomatoes

In a large dish, rub the chicken breasts all over with 1½ teaspoons of the salt, olive oil, pepper, 2 tablespoons of the tarragon, and lemon zest. Cover the chicken with plastic wrap, and leave it to marinate at room temperature for 30 minutes, or refrigerate overnight. If refrigerated, set the chicken out at room temperature for about 1 hour before serving.

Heat the oven to 450°F. Lightly oil a large, shallow roasting pan. Arrange the breasts in the pan, pat the skin dry with paper towels, and roast for 25 to 30 minutes, or just until firm and no longer pink in the middle. An instant-read thermometer inserted into the middle of the thickest part should register 165°F. The skin should be golden and crispy. Remove the chicken to a warmed serving platter. While the chicken is roasting, cut the tops out of the tomatoes and cut them into quarters. As soon as the chicken is out of the roasting pan, drain off most of the fat that has accumulated in the pan, and return the pan to the hot oven. After it has heated for a moment or two, throw in the tomatoes with the remaining ½ teaspoon salt, pepper to taste, and the remaining tablespoon of tarragon, and gently toss the tomatoes in the hot pan drippings, scraping up any brown bits on the bottom of the pan. The tomatoes will release juice. After a couple of minutes, when the tomatoes are barely warmed through, distribute them evenly over the chicken and pour some of the juice over all. Garnish with a sprig of tarragon. Make sure everyone gets some of the flavorful juices in serving.

Chicken Cooked Under a Brick

serves 4

Deep Springs students like this flavorful chicken, but they love the name. Once, a student baked some sourdough bread that utterly failed to rise, so the Student Cooks were inspired to make "Chicken cooked under Michael's bread."

This is an elegant treatment for the good old chicken leg, as festive as a sautéed chicken breast, but cheaper…and more laborious. It's luxuriously boneless, with browned, crispy skin and deeply flavored meat. The aluminum foil–wrapped brick is not heated, but its weight helps the meat to cook rapidly, the fat to render, and the skin to crisp. Serve with Parmesan polenta and vegetables of the season.

"Chicken leg" denotes the entire leg: the drumstick and the thigh, still attached to one another. One large chicken leg is enough for a serving. Perhaps you have the good fortune to know a butcher who will expertly bone the chicken legs but keep the skin on for you. More probably, you will have to bone the legs yourself. You may also use thighs, allowing two per serving; see the variation at the end of the recipe for skinless thighs.

EQUIPMENT

2 standard-sized, clean bricks *(they should fit into your skillet)*

4 whole chicken legs, skin on *(for skinless thighs, see the variation below)*

1½ teaspoons salt

1 medium clove garlic, finely crushed

1 teaspoon fresh thyme leaves, or ½ teaspoon dried thyme

freshly ground black pepper

¼ teaspoon hot red pepper flakes

1 teaspoon olive oil, plus more for sautéing

Wrap the bricks in 2 layers of aluminum foil, shiny side facing out. Make sure there is a clean, seamless side to each one.

Bone, but don't skin, the chicken legs. Warning: this procedure offers many opportunities for poking and cutting oneself—*be very careful; always point the knife toward the surface of the cutting board, not your fingers!* Put the leg on a clean cutting board, skin side down. First, visually and with your fingers, locate the bones, then make a cut along their length with a boning knife or small, sharp knife. Keep making shallow cuts along the bone and around the joint until the bone is separated from the meat, trying to avoid piercing the skin. It's fine if the meat is not too neat-looking—rips or shreds will be hidden in the cooking. Repeat with the remaining legs.

Season the chicken with the salt, garlic, thyme, black pepper to taste, red pepper flakes, and 1 teaspoon olive oil. Let marinate, covered, for an hour, turning the pieces a few times. Heat a large, heavy skillet over a medium flame for several minutes. Lightly brush the clean side of each brick with olive oil, and drizzle a little oil into the skillet. Pat the skin side of the chicken dry with paper towels. Lay 2 of the legs, skin side down, in the hot skillet (they should sizzle happily), and place the 2 bricks on top, weighting the chicken down. When the skin is golden brown and crisp, after about 2 minutes, they are ready to turn. Cook on the other side, without the brick, for about 2 more minutes. Cook the remaining 2 pieces of chicken in the same manner. Serve immediately, while the skin is still crisp.

BACON-WRAPPED CHICKEN COOKED UNDER A BRICK

In a hurry, and have only boneless, skinless chicken thighs available? Just replace the crispy fat of chicken skin with the crispy fat of bacon. Using 6 boneless, skinless thighs and a lighter hand with the salt, carefully wrap a thin strip of bacon (cheaper bacon is usually thinner) around each marinated, seasoned thigh, and cook as directed in the master recipe. The bacon will render its fat and become crisp during the cooking.

Herbed Braised Chicken, with Five Variations

serves 3 to 4

To *braise* meat means to cook it slowly in a small amount of flavorful liquid. Often, meat to be braised is first browned on the stovetop, but in this easier method, the chicken skin browns and crisps in the heat of the oven while the meat beneath slowly cooks to a melting tenderness. Most people who think they don't like dark meat find they love it prepared this way. This recipe (and all variations) may be prepared a day ahead and then popped back into the oven on serving day to heat through and re-crisp the skin.

If you wish to use boneless, skinless chicken thighs, the result will be more of a stew than a proper braise but will still be good. Use about 8 boneless, skinless thighs, and submerge the meat completely in the liquid before putting it into the oven.

4 whole chicken legs or 6 large bone-in, skin-on chicken thighs, about 2¼ pounds total

1½ teaspoons plus a pinch of salt

freshly ground black pepper

2 teaspoons chopped fresh thyme, or ½ teaspoon dried thyme

2 teaspoons chopped fresh sage, or ¼ teaspoon dried sage

1½ teaspoons chopped fresh rosemary, or ½ teaspoon dried rosemary

1 tablespoon olive oil

1 yellow onion, sliced

2 carrots, peeled, split lengthwise, and sliced on the diagonal

1 stalk celery, split lengthwise and sliced on the diagonal

2 to 3 cloves garlic, crushed

½ cup dry white wine

about 2 cups chicken stock

1 bay leaf

2 tablespoons chopped parsley

FOR SERVING (CHOOSE ONE)

Rice *(page 238)*

Handmade Egg Noodles *(231)*

Polenta *(242)*

Spaetzle *(237)*

Scallion-Buttermilk Potatoes *(142)*

Heat the oven to 350°F. Pat the chicken dry with paper towels. Trim off any excess fatty skin around the thigh, if you like. Season with 1½ teaspoons salt and black pepper to taste. Rub the thyme, sage, and rosemary all over the chicken; if using dried herbs, crumble them first in your hand. Let the chicken sit at room temperature while preparing the vegetables.

Heat the olive oil in a large saucepan over medium-high heat. Throw in the onion, carrot, celery, and garlic with a good pinch of salt. Cook the vegetables briefly, stirring frequently, until they begin to go limp, about 3 minutes. Transfer to a 9-by-13-inch baking dish or other dish in which the chicken pieces will fit without crowding. Arrange the seasoned, herbed chicken over the vegetables. In the same saucepan, bring the wine and stock to a boil with the bay leaf, and pour into the dish (don't pour it directly over the chicken, or you'll rinse off the herbs and seasoning) until the chicken is halfway covered with the liquid. Put the dish in the oven, uncovered. Let the chicken bake for about 30 minutes, then turn the oven temperature down to 300°F. It shouldn't boil hard or the end result could be dry (chicken, however, is more forgiving in this respect than beef). Let the chicken simmer until it is very tender, almost falling off the bone, 50 minutes to 1 hour more. Even after the chicken has cooked through, it still needs further simmering to become tender. Don't baste the chicken, or the skin won't be crisp. Serve soon after it emerges from the oven, while the skin is crisp.

Carefully pour off the pan juices into a deep bowl, let settle for a moment, then spoon most of the fat—the clear layer—off the top. Serve the chicken in wide bowls over rice, polenta, noodles, spaetzle, or potatoes, with plenty of the flavorful broth spooned around and parsley sprinkled on top. The vegetables will have given much of their flavor to the broth and chicken. Serve them, or not—they are still tasty, in a homely way.

BRAISED CHICKEN WITH FENNEL

Select a large fennel bulb with feathery fronds attached. Separate the bulb from the young fronds. Omit the herbs from the master recipe, adding instead a strip of lemon zest, a pinch of hot red pepper flakes, and ¾ teaspoon crushed fennel seeds. Quarter the fennel bulb and braise it alongside the chicken, serving a quarter to each person. Garnish the finished dish with the coarsely chopped fennel fronds.

CHICKEN PAPRIKASH

Follow the master Herb Braised Chicken recipe, omitting the herbs, carrots, and celery. Use lard in place of the olive oil. Use red or white wine. When seasoning the chicken, include a teaspoon of sweet Hungarian paprika. Include 2 to 3 tablespoons of paprika with the onions. Whisk together some of the defatted liquid with enough sour cream to make a slightly thick, rich sauce. Serve the chicken, onions, and sauce over noodles, Spaetzle (page 237) or potatoes, garnished with chopped parsley or dill.

BRAISED CHICKEN IN RED WINE WITH MUSHROOMS

This variation is in the spirit of the French classic, *coq au vin*. Omit the sage and rosemary from the master Herb Braised Chicken recipe. Instead of white wine and chicken stock, use a full bottle of good-tasting, fruity red wine. Marinate the chicken in the wine overnight, draining it well (reserve the wine) and patting it dry before seasoning with the salt, pepper, and thyme. Cut 4 ounces of thick bacon crosswise into ½-inch strips. Slowly brown the bacon in the skillet. Remove and reserve the cooked bacon, and cook the vegetables in the rendered fat. Transfer the vegetables to the baking dish, add the chicken and reserved wine, and braise as directed in the master recipe. While the chicken is braising, sauté 6 to 8 ounces sliced mushrooms in butter until golden brown (page 135). Add the bacon and mushrooms to the braise in the last 15 minutes of cooking. Serve with boiled buttered potatoes, and spoon plenty of the dark, flavorful sauce over it. If you have dried wild mushrooms, you may use them in this dish, in place of or in addition to the fresh mushrooms: reconstitute them in some of the wine and braise them with the chicken. Depending on their texture and flavor after cooking, you may or may not want to serve them with the chicken. Once my friend Elge and I made a startlingly good *coq au vin* using dried lobster mushrooms, pinot noir, pearl onions, and a strip of orange zest.

CHICKEN, CHORIZO, AND CHICKPEAS

Follow the master Herb Braised Chicken recipe, omitting the thyme, sage, and celery. Include 1 ½ cups of cooked chickpeas (see guidelines for cooking beans, page 106). Instead of chicken stock, use 2 cups of the chickpea cooking liquid. Include 2 Spanish chorizo sausages in the braising dish. Scatter ½ cup of whole green Mediterranean olives over the vegetables after transferring them to the baking dish. Serve in wide bowls, giving each person a good spoonful of chickpeas, 3 to 4 braised olives, and half of a chorizo along with the chicken.

CHICKEN CURRY

Follow the master Herb Braised Chicken recipe, omitting the celery, wine, and all herbs. Double the amount of garlic, and include with the garlic and onion 2 ounces (about the size of your big toe) of fresh ginger, minced, a teaspoon each of ground cumin and coriander, and 2 tablespoons curry powder (see page 102 for a recipe for homemade curry powder). Cook the vegetables in ghee (see page 37) or butter or vegetable oil. Serve over basmati rice—see page 101 for a recipe, and for other good accompaniments. If you like, lavishly sprinkle the finished dish with coarsely chopped cilantro.

Shoyu Chicken

serves 4 to 6

This savory dish is a staple of Hawaiian home cooking. In the islands, soy sauce is called by its Japanese name, *shoyu*.

3 pounds bone-in, skin-on chicken thighs *(about 8)*

3 cups chicken broth, boiling

1 cup Japanese soy sauce

¾ cup brown sugar

a 3- to 4-inch piece fresh ginger, peeled and thickly sliced

about 10 cloves of garlic, peeled and thickly sliced

1 whole star anise, broken into 3 or 4 pieces

1 teaspoon hot red pepper flakes

3 to 4 dried shiitake mushrooms

2 teaspoons salt

OPTIONAL, FOR THICKENING

3 tablespoons cornstarch

3 tablespoons water

FOR SERVING

plain Japanese steamed rice *(page 238)*

1 bunch scallions, trimmed, rinsed, and thickly sliced on the diagonal

toasted black and white sesame seeds *(page 176)*

Heat the oven to 350°F. Trim the chicken thighs of any excess fat. In a wide, shallow pot or baking dish, blend the hot broth, soy sauce, brown sugar, ginger, garlic, star anise, pepper flakes, shiitakes, and salt together, until the sugar and salt are dissolved. Place the thighs (unseasoned) in the liquid; the skin of the thighs should remain slightly above the level of the liquid. Bring to a simmer on the stovetop, then put the pot in the oven. Let cook, uncovered, for about 1½ hours, or until the meat is tender and the skin is browned.

If you like, strain and thicken the soy broth: first, transfer the chicken to a plate, then strain the solids out of the broth through a screen sieve, and return the strained broth to the pot. In a small bowl, whisk the cornstarch and 3 tablespoons water together until dissolved, and then whisk this slurry into the broth. Bring the broth to a boil, whisking frequently, until bubbling and slightly thickened. Return the chicken to the thickened broth. In wide bowls, serve the chicken and a ladleful of thickened broth over plain Japanese steamed rice. Scatter each serving generously with scallions, and sprinkle with toasted sesame seeds.

Chicken and Dumplings

serves 6 to 8

When I serve this at Deep Springs, many students ask, "So...what exactly is a dumpling?" Dumplings, bits of dough simmered in broth or water to enrich soups or stews, are the great-grandmother of pasta. They are an all-but-extinguished art in American cooking; the appeal of the simple, savory softness of a dumpling has been forgotten in our *al dente* age. If you have snooty guests who would wrinkle their noses at the mention of "dumplings," just say you're serving gnocchi. These Southern-style dumplings are cooked separately in water for a lighter, cleaner-tasting result than if they were cooked directly in the broth.

CHICKEN STEW

1 whole chicken, about 3½ pounds, with giblets

2 cups chicken stock *(page 217)*

5 cups water

2¾ teaspoons salt, or more as needed

1 bay leaf

¼ teaspoon dried thyme, or several sprigs fresh thyme

2 inner celery ribs with leaves

½ large yellow onion, thickly sliced

¼ teaspoon hot red pepper flakes

pinch of dried sage, or 1 to 2 fresh sage leaves

1 tablespoon butter

1 large carrot, peeled and cut into chunks on the diagonal

1½ large yellow onions, cut into medium dice

2 stalks celery, cut on the diagonal into thin slices

6 tablespoons all-purpose flour

1 cup cold water

freshly ground black pepper

DUMPLINGS

2 cups sifted all-purpose flour

1 teaspoon salt

⅛ teaspoon black pepper

1½ teaspoon baking powder

2 tablespoons butter

2 large eggs, beaten

½ cup broth from chicken

4 tablespoons (½ stick) butter

FOR SERVING

3 to 4 tablespoons chopped fresh parsley

To make the stew, remove some of the excess fat from the neck area and from the main cavity of the chicken. Using kitchen scissors, trim away the fatty parts of the skin around both openings. If there are giblets, remove the skin from the neck. Put the whole chicken, neck, giblets, chicken stock, water, and 2½ teaspoons of the salt in a large stockpot (the liquid will almost, but not quite, cover the chicken). Bring to a boil over high heat, then immediately reduce the heat to a simmer. As the chicken begins to boil, skim off any scum that collects on the surface. Once the chicken and broth have settled down to a simmer (with small bubbles appearing not too rapidly here and there on the surface of the liquid), skim any remaining scum and add the bay leaf, thyme, celery, onion, pepper flakes, and sage. Cook for 30 minutes from the time the chicken reaches a simmer, turning the chicken in the broth three or four times. Remove from the heat, cover the pot, and let sit for 5 minutes. With 2 large, sturdy spatulas or spoons, carefully remove the chicken to a deep platter to cool. Reserve ½ cup of broth for the dumplings.

Meanwhile, cook the vegetables. In a large saucepan big enough to hold the finished stew (a 4-quart pan is ideal), melt the tablespoon of butter over a medium-high flame. Throw in the carrot, onion, and celery with the remaining ¼ teaspoon salt. Cook the vegetables, stirring frequently but otherwise keeping the pan covered, until they are translucent, about 5 minutes. Pour the hot chicken broth through a wire-mesh strainer over the vegetables, and bring to a simmer. (Don't wash the stockpot yet; it will be used to cook the dumplings.) Vigorously shake the flour and water together for a full minute in a jar with a tight-fitting lid. Quickly whisk this slurry into the hot vegetables and broth, and simmer until the liquid is thickened and the vegetables are tender, 10 to 15 minutes. Add pepper and taste for seasoning, adding salt if necessary. Once the chicken is cool enough to handle, remove and discard the skin and tear the meat off the bones, discarding any remaining visible fat. Cut the meat into large bite-size chunks, and add to the broth and vegetables. Keep the stew warm.

To make the dumplings, sift the flour, salt, pepper, and baking powder together into a large bowl. Cut the butter into small pieces and rapidly work it into the flour mixture with your hands, pressing the butter into smaller and smaller pieces, until the flour is slightly moistened and there are few visible bits of butter. Slowly whisk the eggs into the warm chicken broth, then pour this mixture into the flour. Stir with a wooden spoon until you have a soft dough. Transfer to a floured board, and gently roll ½ inch thick. Using a sharp, flour dipped knife, cut dumplings about 1 inch wide and 3 inches long. Handle the dumplings gently, and keep them well-dusted with flour.

Fill the stockpot with ample fresh water and bring to a boil. Salt the water until it tastes lightly salty. Add the 4 tablespoons of butter to the water, let it melt, and drop in the dumplings all at once, stirring gently with a wooden spoon to separate them. Once the water has returned to a boil and the dumplings are floating, cook about 3 minutes more, gently stirring so the dumplings cook evenly. Using a slotted spoon, transfer the dumplings from the water to the chicken stew. Stir in the parsley, and serve in wide bowls.

CHICKEN POT PIE

In this farmhouse supper dish, a paprika-dusted biscuit covers a rich chicken stew. Prepare the chicken stew with vegetables in the master recipe above, removing about 2 cups of the broth prior to thickening, to achieve a gravy consistency in the finished stew. After adding the chicken meat, add the chopped parsley also, transfer the stew to a 9-by-13-inch baking dish, smooth the surface, and keep the stew warm. Heat the oven to 375°F, and prepare a recipe of rolled Biscuits (page 65), rolling out the dough into a rectangle that will just fit into the dish, about 8½ by 12½ inches. Draping the dough over the rolling pin, carefully position it atop the warm stew. Using a small, sharp knife dipped in flour, score the dough to demarcate 6 or 8 portions, not cutting all the way through the dough. Sprinkle the top surface of the dough with paprika. Bake until the stew is bubbling and the biscuit is cooked all the way through, about 25 minutes. Let the pot pie rest 10 minutes before serving.

Matzoh Ball Soup

serves 8 to 10; makes about 30 matzoh balls

Here you have the king of chicken soups, with fluffy dumplings reposing in a luxurious, golden, rich chicken broth.

RICH CHICKEN BROTH

- 1 large roasting chicken, about 4½ pounds, kosher if preferred
- 1 medium onion, sliced
- 1 medium carrot, peeled
- 1 stalk celery
- 4 sprigs parsley
- 8 black peppercorns
- 1 bay leaf
- a 3-inch piece of lemongrass *(optional)*
- 2 teaspoons salt

MATZOH BALLS

- ¼ cup rendered chicken fat, at room temperature
- 4 large eggs, separated, at room temperature
- 1 cup matzoh meal
- 2 teaspoons salt
- ¼ cup chicken stock, at room temperature

FOR SERVING

- 2 to 3 tablespoons chopped parsley

First, render the chicken fat. Rinse the chicken well and pat dry with paper towels. Remove and reserve the large fat pockets from the main cavity and the excess fat from around the neck flap. Using kitchen shears, snip the fat into small pieces. Put the fat in a small saucepan with about ¼ cup water and cook over medium heat until the water has boiled away (the bubbling sound will give way to a sizzling sound). Pour off the liquid fat through a wire-mesh strainer into a heatproof cup, to use in the matzoh balls—you should have at least ¼ cup.

Meanwhile, to make the broth, heat the oven to 450°F. Roast the chicken, whole and unseasoned, in a roasting pan until the skin is deep brown and crispy, about 45 minutes. Put the chicken and any juice that has accumulated in the pan in a large stockpot, cover by 3 inches with cold water, and bring to a boil over high heat, skimming off any scum that rises to the surface. As soon as the broth reaches a boil, reduce the heat to low and add the onion, carrot, celery, parsley sprigs, peppercorns, bay leaf, lemongrass, if desired (quite untraditional but subtly delicious), and salt to the pot. Adjust the heat as necessary to maintain a simmer—if the broth boils hard, the fat will emulsify into the liquid and the broth will be cloudy and not as clean-tasting. Gently simmer the broth for 1 hour, breaking up the chicken and stirring from time to time. Strain the broth through a mesh strainer, allow the fat to rise to the surface, and skim much, but not all, of it off with a spoon. Stir the broth and taste for salt—it may need several pinches more, especially if a non-kosher bird was used—the taste should be rich and deep and very good. The meat of the chicken is quite overcooked by this point; most of its flavor and value have been given over to the broth.

To make the matzoh balls, combine the chicken fat and egg yolks in a large bowl. Stir in the matzoh meal, salt, and stock. In a perfectly clean, separate bowl, beat the egg whites with clean beaters until soft peaks form. Fold a third of the whites into the matzoh meal mixture to lighten it, then gently fold in the remaining egg whites, just until the mixture is uniform. Chill, covered, for 1 hour. Wet your hands and lightly form 30 balls about 1 inch in diameter, placing them on an oiled plate. Bring a gallon of water to a boil in a wide 8-quart pot. Add 1½ tablespoons salt—the water should taste lightly salty. Slide the matzoh balls into the rapidly boiling water, all at once. Bring up to a simmer. Cover the pot and simmer gently for about 20 minutes. Remove the matzoh balls to warmed bowls with a slotted spoon. Bring the chicken stock to a boil. Place 3 hot matzoh balls in each bowl, cover with hot chicken broth, sprinkle with a bit of chopped parsley, and serve.

Gin Chicken Liver Pâté

serves 4 to 6 as an hors d'oeuvre

This pâté is adapted from a recipe by Elizabeth David, one of my favorite cookbook authors. (Strictly speaking, it is not pâté, but "chicken liver spread" just doesn't sound good, and "gin chicken livers," as Elizabeth David calls this recipe, brings to mind a dish of whole livers.) Whenever you ply your guests with wine, beer, or especially cocktails, it's wise to serve munchy food that is high in fat, helping the alcohol to metabolize more slowly in the body. Otherwise, if your drink is strong, your empty-stomached guests may pass out before you've had a chance to serve dinner. This simple liver spread, served with crackers or bread, will work splendidly. Pickled fruit (page 258) or a dish of olives complement it well.

4 ounces *(weighed after trimming)* **very fresh chicken livers, trimmed of veins and fat**

6 tablespoons unsalted butter, at room temperature

1 pinch salt, plus ¾ teaspoon

3 tablespoons gin

a few twists of black pepper

FOR SERVING

crackers *(pages 79 to 81)* **or toasts**

pickled fruit *(page 258)* **or olives**

In a medium-sized skillet over a medium-high flame, sauté the livers in 1 tablespoon of the butter with a good pinch of salt until brown on the outside and still a little pink on the inside, about 2 minutes. Remove from the heat and transfer the livers to the jar of a blender. Let the pan cool for just a moment. Pour the gin into the hot pan to deglaze, using a wooden spoon to scrape up the browned bits and letting them dissolve into the gin. Blend the livers, gin, remaining 5 tablespoons butter, ¾ teaspoon salt, and pepper until completely smooth. Pack into a small, deep glass or china bowl, cover, and chill.

Serve thickly spread on crackers or toasts and accompany with pickled fruit or olives.

Chicken Stock

makes about 12 cups

This basic chicken stock is a perfect base for soups, stews, or risotto. The chicken leg meat is sacrificed; when it emerges from the stockpot it has given its flavor to the stock and is not especially tasty.

1 whole chicken, including gizzard, heart, and neck *(liver gives a strong flavor; you may include it or not)*

12 cups cold water

1 medium onion, coarsely chopped

1 medium carrot, peeled and coarsely chopped

1 stalk celery, cut into a few pieces

1 sprig thyme

1 bay leaf

1 teaspoon peppercorns

½ teaspoon crushed fennel seed

1 teaspoon salt

Using a boning knife or other narrow, sharp knife, cut out the 2 breast halves from the chicken and reserve for another use (such as Sautéed Chicken Breasts, page 205). Make a few gashes in the meaty parts of the chicken legs, to better release the flavor. Remove any chunks of fat around the cavity and neck. Put the chicken and giblets in a stockpot with the water and bring just to a boil. Immediately reduce the heat to medium. With a wide spoon, skim off the scum (as well as some, but not all, of the fat) that rises to the surface.

Add the onion, carrot, celery, thyme, bay leaf, peppercorns, fennel seed, and salt. Raise the heat to quickly return the liquid to a boil, then immediately reduce to a lively simmer, with bubbles here and there in the pot. Don't let the stock boil hard. Covering the pot helps hold in the heat, but leave the lid slightly ajar. Let the stock simmer, skimming at times and stirring once or twice, for about an hour, then strain it through a fine-mesh sieve. Cool to room temperature, stirring occasionally, and refrigerate until needed.

STOCK FROM LEFTOVER ROAST CHICKEN

A cooked chicken carcass, with most of the leg meat as well as the breast meat gone, will yield less flavor than a fresh chicken with much of the meat left on. Follow the recipe above, using 6 cups of water instead of 12.

TURKEY STOCK

A 12-pound turkey is more or less the equivalent of four 3-pound chickens. Multiply either of the recipes above accordingly to make some good turkey stock.

Apple- and Rosemary-Scented Roast Turkey

serves 8 to 10 with leftovers

And here is how we prepare the Thanksgiving turkeys at Deep Springs, using apples from the orchard. Some of the apples are scattered in the main cavity, but most are stuffed into the neck cavity, providing moisture and aroma for the breast meat. The apples scent the bird while it roasts but are not necessarily meant to be eaten.

12-pound fresh turkey *(natural, not brined or flavor enhanced)*

¼ cup apple cider vinegar

¼ cup salt, plus more for seasoning apples

2 tablespoons freshly ground black pepper, plus more for seasoning apples

1½ pounds flavorful cooking apples

4 sprigs rosemary

PAN GRAVY

1 cup water

⅔ cup all-purpose flour

3 cups chicken stock or giblet broth, cooled

salt and black pepper

chopped cooked giblets *(optional)*

¼ cup applejack *(American apple brandy; optional)*

If possible, season the turkey 2 days in advance (on Tuesday of Thanksgiving week). First, remove any excess fat from just inside the main cavity of the turkey and from inside the neck flap. Soak a paper towel in the cider vinegar and rub the turkey all over with it. Mix the salt and pepper in a small bowl and rub it evenly all over the turkey, inside and out. Put a greater proportion of salt and pepper on the breast. Cover and refrigerate the seasoned turkey for 2 days, turning it over a couple of times.

If you will be using the turkey giblets to enrich the gravy, cook them shortly after bringing the turkey home; they will keep better cooked than raw. I usually throw away the liver unless I knew the turkey when it was alive, but it may. Simmer the giblets in water to cover in a small saucepan until tender. When tender, drain, reserving the stock, and remove as much meat as possible from the neck, then chop the neck meat and the rest of the giblets finely. Store the stock and chopped giblets separately in the refrigerator until you make the gravy. Set the turkey out at room temperature for about 3 hours before roasting. This will help it cook more evenly. (Once it's coming to room temperature, don't change your mind and decide to roast it another day!)

Heat the oven to 375°F. Choose a sturdy roasting pan of the proper size: it shouldn't be so small that the turkey has to be crammed in, nor so large that the juices cook away and burn in the heat of the oven. Tuck the wings behind the neck of the turkey and put the turkey in the pan, breast side up. Quarter, core, and slice the apples, and toss them with a little salt and pepper. Stuff most of the apples, along with 2 of the rosemary sprigs, into the neck flap. Scatter the remaining apples and rosemary into the main cavity. Roast the turkey, uncovered, for about 2 hours. When an instant-read thermometer inserted into the thickest part of the thigh registers 160°F, the turkey is done.

Alternately, you may peek into the interior of a thigh with a small knife—no pink should remain. Put the turkey in a warm place to rest for 10 minutes, then turn it breast side down, remove to a serving platter, and allow it to rest for another 10 minutes before turning it breast side up and carving.

To make the gravy, while the turkey is resting, pour all the juices from the roasting pan into a deep bowl. Carefully spoon off some, but not all, of the fat (the clear layer) from the top. In a jar with a tight-fitting lid, shake the water and flour together vigorously for a full minute, until no flour lumps remain. Pour this slurry into the roasting pan, along with the chicken stock and the defatted juices, set the pan on medium-high heat, and bring to a boil, stirring and scraping the browned bits off the bottom of the pan with a wooden spoon, until thick. There should be no floury taste. Season the gravy with salt and pepper, and add the cooked giblets, if you have them. If you like, splash in a little applejack.

CHAPTER 11
FISH & SHELLFISH

Welcome to one of the briefest chapters in the book. Fish, rarely served at landlocked Deep Springs, is among the only truly wild foods we still eat regularly. When I was a student, I always wanted seafood on visits home. Occasionally, a student will catch a trout in one of Deep Springs' reservoirs—these taste astonishingly sweet and fresh. On rarer occasions, a Deep Springs community member, returning from a trip to California's coast, will drive triumphantly into the Valley with much fanfare, bearing a fresh whole wild salmon or a chest full of just-caught shellfish, and everyone will gratefully feast.

If you obtain very fresh fish and don't overcook it, you are virtually guaranteed to make a delicious meal, even with the plainest cooking methods and seasonings. If you feel inexperienced, know that your nose is not; it's always a good idea to insist on smelling any fish you wish to buy. Fresh fish smells clean and briny, not fishy—you will know.

Clay's Broiled Trout

At home, "catching" trout in a market, I'm never tempted by the boneless trout; bones add flavor, character, and juiciness to the delicate flesh. Allow a one-pound whole trout for each person. Preheat your oven's broiler. Pat the fish dry with paper towels. Lightly prick the skin here and there with the tip of a knife. Generously salt and pepper the fish inside and out, put it in an oiled, shallow pan, and stick it under the broiler, a few inches from the flame. Broil for less than 5 minutes on each side, until the skin on each side is a nice bronze color. When the flesh of the fish is opaque throughout, it's done.

If you have just caught, gutted, and stream-cleaned your trout in the wild, say, somewhere in the Sierra Nevada, do as my brother Clay, an avid fisherman, does: wrap the salt-and-peppered trout in aluminum foil (shiny side facing in), seal well, and cook it, turning occasionally, for about 5 minutes on the roaring flames of your campfire. Excellent.

Whole Roasted Trout with Herb Salad

serves 2

A whole roasted fish, with the skin and head and everything, horrified me as a child, but now is my idea of a truly marvelous dinner. I love navigating through the various, and very different, parts: the skin, the crunchy tip of the tail, the cheeks. I love the gelatinous, succulent quality the bones give the delicate meat. After consuming the first side, I love lifting out the backbone and ribs all in one piece, like unzipping a zipper, laying bare the now boneless, juicy second side. It's a very intimate encounter with a fish. I'm fortunate to know a generous fisherman who regularly offers me trout so fresh they smell only of water and sunlight. He remembers to leave the heads on.

2 whole, very fresh trout, gutted, cleaned, and scaled, heads left on, about ½ pound each

¾ teaspoon salt

few twists of freshly ground black pepper

zest of ½ lemon

¼ teaspoon crushed fennel seed

1 to 2 tablespoons olive oil

lemon wedges for serving

HERB SALAD

about 1 cup loosely packed arugula, washed and spun dry

½ cup loosely packed Italian parsley leaves, coarsely chopped

1 small inner stalk celery, sliced very thin on the diagonal

¼ cup loosely packed pale green celery leaves, coarsely chopped

1 small shallot, very thinly sliced shortly before serving

big squeeze of fresh lemon

¼ teaspoon red wine vinegar

about 2 teaspoons extra-virgin olive oil

big pinch of salt

few twists black pepper

Heat the oven to 475°F. Blot the trout dry with paper towels inside and out. Mix the salt, pepper, lemon zest, and fennel together in a small bowl, and rub all over the trout, inside and out, including on the head, fins, and tail. Place the trout on a foil-lined rimmed baking sheet, and drizzle lightly with olive oil. Roast for about 10 minutes, or until the flesh of the fish is opaque throughout.

Meanwhile, make the herb salad: combine the arugula, parsley, celery, celery leaves, and onion in a medium bowl. Quickly toss the salad with lemon juice, vinegar, olive oil, salt, and pepper—taste a bite to be sure the flavors are lively and balanced, and adjust as necessary.

When the fish is done, transfer the whole fish to large, warmed plates. Tuck a lemon wedge alongside. Pile the salad atop and alongside the fish, and serve immediately. Provide damp towels on the table, and a big bowl for the bones and leavings.

Baked Salmon

serves 1

The only key to cooking fish (presupposing, of course, that the fish is impeccably fresh) is not over-cooking it. While pan-frying or grilling will produce an appealing brown, crusty exterior, sometimes you want to cook it in the simplest way possible. Baking is the most transparent method: the natural flavor of the fish is all that's there, with no supports or embellishments, no chef's ego. A good method for a beginner, baking makes it easy to observe the fish while it cooks. Served with an appropriate flavorful sauce or accompaniment (see the following list), baked fish shows how honest, clean, and delicious something very simple can be.

Wild Pacific salmon comes into season in late spring, continuing through the summer. *Halibut*, a variety of white-fleshed fish popular on the West Coast of the United States, is also very good simply baked, and enjoys a longer season.

5- or 6-ounce portion freshest wild salmon fillet, skinless (see Note)

olive oil

about ¼ teaspoon salt

Heat the oven to 400°F. Rub the salmon all over with olive oil and salt. Put on a foil- or parchment-lined baking sheet and stick the sheet in the oven. Depending on the thickness of the fish, it will cook in 9 to 10 minutes. You may peek into the interior of the fish with a small knife: it should flake easily but still be very moist and retain a faint translucency. Some people like their salmon a little rarer; others prefer it a bit more well-done.

Note: In late spring, when salmon season begins, the flesh is leaner and benefits from cooking with the skin on. Later in the season, in the heat of summer, the flesh is fattier and may be successfully baked without the skin. If you bake the salmon with its skin, remove the skin after cooking (it peels right off), flip the fish over, and serve skin side down on the plate. Salmon skin, seared over high heat, is delicious, but skin cooked at the low temperature called for here will be flabby and unappealing to most diners.

FOR SERVING (CHOOSE ONE)

- lemon wedges, a sprinkle of fresh dill, and Scalloped Potatoes (page 140)
- Marinated Beets (164) and Aioli (253) thinned with a little water and lemon juice
- Corn Salad (166)
- Meyer Lemon–Olive Relish (254) and Simple Roasted Potatoes (141)
- sweet ripe tomatoes tossed with salt and fresh dill, with boiled red potatoes and drizzles of sour cream
- warm bacon and curly endive salad with Shallot Vinaigrette (173)
- Green Bean Salad with Cherry Tomatoes and Basil (164)
- sautéed summer vegetables and Pesto (254)
- Pickled Summer Vegetables (256) and slices of avocado
- Snap Peas (139) and basil
- shell bean and corn succotash (122)

THREE MORE SIMPLE COOKING METHODS FOR SALMON

Salmon is delicious *poached in wine:* season skinless fillets well with salt several hours in advance. Bring a cup or two of dry, flavorful wine, red or white, to a gentle simmer, and poach the fish in the wine—just drop the seasoned fish into the hot wine and let it sit on the lowest flame, swirling the wine around the fish, until the fish is just barely cooked through, but still moist and translucent in the center. Include sprigs of basil or other herbs—whatever is appropriate—in the wine while poaching, if you wish. Dribble a little of the poaching wine over each serving.

Or, salmon can be *slow-baked:* rub a larger fillet of skin-on salmon with olive oil and salt, and bake it skin side up in a 200°F oven for 45 minutes to an hour, until the flesh is creamy and barely opaque throughout—watch it carefully. Remove the skin and serve the fish in rough chunks with lemon wedges, Shaved Fennel (page 167), Watercress Salad (page 162), and Roasted Potatoes (page 141).

Or, if you want to serve salmon with beautifully bronzed, *crispy skin,* use this method: season skin-on fillets with salt a couple of hours in advance. Heat a well-seasoned cast-iron pan (large enough to hold the portions of fish without crowding) in a 400°F oven for about 20 minutes. Blot any excess moisture from the salmon skin using paper towels, then rub the skin, as well as the flesh of the fish, with olive oil. Place the fish skin side down in the hot skillet—it will sizzle furiously. Put the pan back in the oven and bake without turning, until the fish's flesh is just barely cooked through. Timing will depend on the thickness of the fish—slim coho fillets might take less than 10 minutes, while thick king salmon could take up to 20 minutes. Err on the side of underdone, as fish cooked at this high temperature will continue to cook off the heat. The salmon should easily lift from the surface of the pan; use a thin spatula to loosen it if necessary. Invert the fish onto a warmed platter, so that the skin side is facing up.

Gravlax

serves 4

This splendid cured salmon hors d'oeuvre is at once simple and sophisticated.

4-ounce portion freshest wild salmon fillet, skin on

2 heaping teaspoons kosher salt

½ teaspoon brown sugar

3 or 4 cracked peppercorns

3 or 4 crushed juniper berries

2 or 3 sprigs fresh dill

FOR SERVING

sliced cucumbers

sour cream

chopped fresh dill

tomatoes

rye crispbread

Season the salmon generously all over with the kosher salt. Sprinkle with the brown sugar, peppercorns, and juniper berries. Bruise the fresh dill and press it into the flesh of the fish. Wrap with a layer of cheesecloth, then with several layers of paper towels (to absorb liquid), and finally with plastic wrap. Put the wrapped fish between two plates, and place a weight over the top plate. Refrigerate, weighted, for 4 days.

Unwrap and remove the dill and large chunks of pepper or juniper. Slice the salmon very thinly against the grain with a sharp knife. The skin helps the flesh keep its shape during slicing, but it is not good to eat in this form. Serve the sliced gravlax arranged on a platter, alongside sliced cucumber, a dish of sour cream, chopped fresh dill, tomatoes, and caraway-studded rye crispbread.

Pan-Fried Sole

serves 2

This delicate, simple dish is quite similar to the French classic *sole meunière*. An ode to butter, the recipe uses both clarified and brown butter.

8 to 10 ounces sole fillets

½ teaspoon salt

⅓ cup flour

about 4 tablespoons clarified butter (see page 37) **for sautéing**

2 tablespoons butter

¼ lemon

Pat the fish dry with paper towels, and season with salt. Sprinkle the flour onto a plate, and dredge the fish in the flour, shaking off the excess. Over a medium-high flame, heat a heavy skillet of ample size to accommodate the pieces of fish without crowding: it may be necessary to cook the fish in two batches. Add enough clarified butter to generously coat the bottom of the skillet. When the butter is very hot, almost smoking, carefully lay the fish in the pan, without crowding it (cook in batches if necessary). Cook until golden brown on one side, 1 to 2 minutes, then gently flip with a wide spatula (being careful not to spatter yourself with oil) and cook the other side for about a minute more. The timing will, of course, depend on the thickness of the fish—the inside of the thickest part of the fish should be opaque and should flake easily. Lift the fish onto a warmed plate, browner side up. Pour out the butter and use fresh clarified butter if you are cooking the fish in batches.

When all the fish is cooked, pour off the butter and return the skillet to a high flame. Melt the 2 tablespoons butter in the skillet. Watch the butter—when it turns a fragrant hazelnut brown, squeeze in a little fresh lemon juice. Drizzle the lemony browned butter over the fish. Serve immediately.

Sole Stuffed with Leeks

serves 3 to 4

This is a clean-tasting, elegant, old-fashioned dish. The delicate flavors are best appreciated with a simple accompaniment, such as buttered white rice, or alone in a meal of a few courses. For instance, start with Handmade Egg Noodles (page 231) tossed with butter, herbs, and Sautéed Mushrooms (page 135); then serve this stuffed sole all by itself; then serve a green salad with sliced oranges and Citrus Vinaigrette (page 173). For most occasions, I like this sole unadorned with any sauce besides the butter-enriched pan juices. But on occasions when a sumptuous sauce is appropriate, try Lemon Butter Sauce (page 252).

about 8 thin English sole fillets
(about 1½ pounds)

1 teaspoon salt

1 large or 2 medium leeks

about 3 tablespoons butter

1 lemon

Sprinkle the sole fillets with ¼ teaspoon of the salt, and keep cold.

Cut out any discolored, shriveled, or browned parts of the leeks. Cut away all the darker-green top parts, keeping them separate from the white and pale-green bottom portions. Rinse a handful of the longest dark-green leek tops (discard the rest or save for stock), and arrange them in a mat over the bottom of an 8-by-8-inch baking pan. These provide moisture and deepen the leek flavor. Trim the dirty root end from the white and pale-green bottom part of the leeks, then halve lengthwise. Under cool running water, rinse the leeks, making sure all the outer layers get thoroughly rinsed—they easily trap sand and dirt. Drain, then cut the leeks into small dice.

Heat the oven to 350°F. Melt a tablespoon of the butter in a small saucepan over medium heat. Add the diced leeks with the remaining ¾ teaspoon salt and stew, stirring frequently but otherwise keeping the pan covered, until tender, 7 to 10 minutes. If the leeks seem dry, add teaspoonfuls of water as necessary—the leeks shouldn't brown. Remove from the heat. You should have about 1 cup of tender, cooked leeks. Stir the finely grated zest of about half the lemon into the leeks. Cut the lemon into wedges, to be served with the fish.

Remove the sole fillets from the refrigerator. Spread the warm leek mixture evenly over the fillets, and roll the fillets up, starting with the thicker end. Place the rolls on the bed of leek tops in the baking pan, the smaller rolls toward the center. Put a thin slice of butter atop each roll. Bake for about 20 minutes, or until the fish is cooked through. Using a wide spatula, carefully transfer 2 or 3 rolls to each person's plate. Some juice will have accumulated in the baking pan; remove the mat of leek tops, letting the liquid remain in the pan. Whisk a final tablespoon of butter into the liquid, spoon this sauce over the fish, and serve with the lemon wedges.

Pan-Fried Cod or Snapper

If you have cod or snapper (or other thick-filleted, mild white fish) and would like to pan-fry it with a golden, crispy breadcrumb coating, use the Crispy Pan-Fried Chicken recipe on page 209. A pound of fish will serve about 3 people. Serve with lemon wedges and Slovenian Fennel and Potatoes (page 130).

Fried Catfish

serves 4 to 6

Catfish suffers from a somewhat lowbrow reputation, but these delicate, golden, cornmeal-dusted fillets will please the most discriminating palates. Other fish varieties are also delicious cornmeal-fried. For information about cornmeal, see page 40.

1 cup fine white or yellow cornmeal

2½ teaspoons salt

¼ teaspoon cayenne pepper

¼ teaspoon paprika

¼ teaspoon black pepper

about 6 cups safflower oil, peanut oil, or other vegetable oil appropriate for deep-frying

1¾ pounds thin catfish fillets

FOR SERVING

Tabasco sauce

lemon wedges

In a big, wide bowl, mix the cornmeal, salt, cayenne, paprika, and black pepper. Heat the oil in a deep, heavy pot to 350°F. Dredge the catfish fillets thoroughly in the seasoned cornmeal, then drop them, a few at a time, in the hot oil. As soon as they float in the oil, they're done. Lift out with a wire skimmer and drain on brown paper bags or paper towels. Serve immediately, with coleslaw (page 163), Skillet Cornbread (67), Tabasco sauce, and lemon wedges.

Seared Tuna

Obtain steaks (5 to 6 ounces for each person) of very fresh tuna, about 1 inch thick. Pat dry with paper towels, and season well with a big pinch of salt on each side of each steak. Heat a tablespoon of olive oil or vegetable oil in a heavy skillet over a medium-high flame until very hot. When the oil smokes, gently lay the tuna steaks in the skillet (be careful not to spatter yourself with oil). Let the steaks cook for about 1 minute on one side, then carefully flip with a wide spatula and cook on the other side for about 50 seconds more. Remove to a warmed plate, browner side up. The tuna steaks will be very, very rare, but warm, inside. For medium-rare tuna, leave the steaks in the pan but take the pan off the heat. Let them continue to cook for about 20 more seconds on each side. Want well-done fish? Choose another fish variety—fresh tuna becomes dry and stringy when seared to well-done. Grind a good shot of fresh pepper over the fish, sprinkle with a pinch more salt, drizzle with a little extra-virgin olive oil, and serve immediately, with simple salads and vegetables. Aioli (page 253), thinned to sauciness with a little water, is always a great accompaniment.

Mussels

Fresh mussels are a good and relatively inexpensive delicacy. Though available year-round, they are best in the cooler months of the year. Most of the mussels sold in the United States these days are sustainably farmed in the cold Atlantic waters off Prince Edward Island in Canada. When buying them, make sure they are quite fresh and alive; they should smell briny, not fishy, and if there are a lot of cracked or open mussels, it is perhaps best to wait until your fish market gets a fresh shipment.

Mussels lend themselves to almost any flavor combination you could imagine. Use the three recipes below as a guide and introduction, but do not feel bound by them. I have had exquisite mussels with Asian and Latin American flavors, with red wine instead of white, with beer, with sausage or bacon, with a plethora of herbs, or with almost no adornments at all. Mussels are traditionally served with bread to soak up the flavorful juices; you may toast the bread, if you like, and rub it with olive oil and a cut clove of garlic. All three recipes below are good served in wide bowls over linguine or other thin, long pasta. Serve with knife, fork, and spoon, and plenty of napkins. Accompany with a big, cheerful green salad, full of vegetables and croutons.

MOULES MARINIÈRE DE BRETAGNE

This is a traditional recipe from the windswept coast of Brittany, in northwestern France. Allow 25 to 30 fresh mussels per person. They should smell fresh, like the ocean. Wash well in cold water. Discard any that are cracked or broken, and any open mussels that do not close when agitated. Pull out any bits of rough "beard" that are sticking out of the shells. For each serving, have ready a good pat of butter, about ¼ cup finely chopped shallot or onion, ¼ cup dry white wine, ¼ cup heavy cream, a big tablespoon of chopped parsley, and a thick slice or two of fresh bread. Over a high flame, melt the butter in a big pot (with a tight-fitting lid) that will accommodate the entire pile of mussels. When the butter sizzles and foams, add the shallot and sauté for a moment. Add the mussels, and flip them around to coat with the butter and shallot, letting them cook for about a minute. Splash in the wine and cream, and immediately cover the pot. Steam the mussels, shaking the pot frequently, just until they open, 1 to 2 minutes. Divide the mussels into serving bowls, pour the precious liquid over each serving, sprinkle with parsley, and serve immediately, with bread to soak up the liquid. Serve with small forks, and put a big empty bowl on the table for the shells. Don't underestimate the deliciousness of the winy-creamy-briny liquid. A fishmonger once told me, "I have a great recipe for mussels: I steam them with olive oil, garlic, and white wine, then I throw out the mussels and just drink the liquid."

MUSSELS WITH LEEKS AND ORANGE ZEST

For a sprightly, fresh, natural marriage of flavors, use olive oil instead of butter, diced leeks instead of onion, and all white wine, no cream. When you splash in the wine, throw in about ¼ teaspoon of finely grated orange zest for each serving.

MUSSELS WITH SPICY TOMATO SAUCE

Cook the mussels as described, using olive oil instead of butter, minced garlic instead of onion, and a thin, flavorful tomato sauce (see Fresh Summer Tomato Sauce, page 249) instead of wine and cream. Throw in a good pinch of hot red pepper flakes a moment before you add the mussels. For extra richness, brown a little crumbled hot Italian sausage in the pot first. Accompany with plenty of olive-oil–toasted, garlic-rubbed bread.

Oysters on the Half-Shell

Oysters to be eaten raw should be *impeccably fresh, and taken from clean, cold waters*. Scrub oysters well under cold running water. Shucking oysters quickly and easily requires practice. Take an oyster knife and hold the oyster, its more rounded side down, folded in a thick kitchen towel. With determination, insert the knife into the "hinge" at the pointed part of the shell, and wiggle it from side to side. Once that tendon is severed, the top shell should loosen. Remove the top shell, cutting loose the place on it where the oyster attaches. Still using the knife, loosen the oyster from its bottom shell, but keep it in the shell, retaining as much of the liquid in the shell as possible. Place the opened oyster on a bed of crushed ice. When all the oysters are opened, serve them on the ice.

When you eat an oyster, smell it first: it should smell briny and fresh. This is not only a safeguard against ingesting a bad oyster, but a great part of the pleasure. Spoon a little sauce over, or not, and slurp the oyster and all liquid from the shell. Chew. Some people prefer their oysters completely unadorned, with perhaps just a wedge of lemon. Some prefer fresh lime, accompanied by amber Mexican beer. Others favor the following strong, traditional French accompaniment.

MIGNONETTE SAUCE

For every dozen oysters, macerate a tablespoon of minced shallot in a mixture of 2 tablespoons red wine and 2 tablespoons red wine vinegar. Add a pinch of salt and a healthy pinch of cracked black pepper. Let the flavors develop while you open the oysters. Some dip their oysters in the sauce, while others drizzle a few drops of sauce over each oyster.

Seared Scallops with Gremolata

Gremolata is a simple topping of finely chopped fresh parsley, garlic, and lemon zest. Traditional atop braised veal shanks in northern Italian cuisine, it can also be strewn over steak, chicken breast, or any other dish that needs a final fresh element. It's especially good on fish and shellfish. The marinade for these scallops echoes the elements of the gremolata.

First, choose fresh, pristine, "dry-packed" sea scallops that have not been treated with sodium tripolyphosphate. Keeping the scallops cold, remove the tough little "foot" attached to each one. Don't worry if some of the scallops are an orange color. Blot the scallops dry with paper towels, then marinate in a bowl with olive oil, a dribble of white wine, strips of lemon zest, thinly sliced fresh garlic, and parsley stems bruised to release their flavor. Toss the scallops in the marinade a few times, otherwise keeping them covered and refrigerated.

Make the gremolata immediately before cooking the scallops: using your big chef's knife, finely chop some fresh parsley, then stir in a generous amount of finely grated fresh lemon zest, and a little finely chopped fresh garlic, tossing well.

To cook the scallops, heat a skillet until very hot. Scatter half the gremolata over the bottom of a warmed serving dish that will accommodate the scallops. Remove the scallops from the marinade, pat dry with paper towels, and salt them judiciously. Oil the skillet very lightly using a wad of paper towels that have been moistened with vegetable oil. Place the scallops, flattest side down, in the skillet with tongs, about 2 inches apart. They must not be crowded in the skillet or they will release liquid and won't sear; cook in batches if necessary. Let the scallops sear without disturbing them until they are a deep golden brown underneath, about 1 minute, then turn them with tongs to sear the other side for about 30 seconds. When cooked, they should be still faintly translucent inside. Remove the scallops to the gremolata-strewn platter, brownest side up, then add a splash of wine to the skillet to release the fond left by the scallops. Dribble this over the cooked scallops. If you're cooking the scallops in batches, wipe the skillet with a paper towel, heat it up again with fresh olive oil, and cook the remaining scallops in the same manner. Once they are all cooked, scatter the scallops with the remaining gremolata, and serve.

Boiled Shrimp

serves 2 to 3

This is the most delightfully direct shrimp experience. Technically, these peel-and-eat shrimp are poached, not boiled; gentler heat keeps the shrimp tender. Cooking shrimp in their shells retains more of their integrity; the shell imparts a deeper flavor to the meat and keeps the meat moist. Even if I intend to serve the shrimp peeled, I still cook them in their shells and peel them when they are cool. Although the "veins" along the shrimps' backs are not harmful to eat, the experience is more aesthetic if they are removed. This method works for best medium shrimp—they have a good shell-to-meat ratio.

1½ pounds medium shell-on shrimp

1 gallon water

½ cup kosher salt

2 bay leaves

1 teaspoon hot red pepper flakes

1 teaspoon whole allspice

1 teaspoon black peppercorns

FOR SERVING

melted butter

lemon wedges

If you can find shell-on, deveined shrimp, use them. More likely, you'll have to devein the shrimp yourself. Lay a shrimp on your cutting board, stabilizing it with one hand, and cut a shallow incision through the shell with a small, sharp, serrated knife, along the whole length of its back. The vein should be easily removable with the tip of your knife. As you work, keep the shrimp cold.

In a large pot over a high flame, bring a gallon of water to a boil. Add the salt, bay leaf, red pepper flakes, allspice, and black peppercorns and let boil for 1 minute. With the water at a furious boil, throw in the shrimp, give the pot a stir, slap on the lid, and let the water return almost to a boil. When the shrimp begin to float and the water is beginning to bubble again, the shrimp are cooked. Quickly rinse a shrimp in cold water, then peel and eat, to make sure they are cooked to your liking—leave them in the water for another minute if necessary. Drain and serve immediately; peel-and-eat, with melted butter, lemon wedges, and plenty of napkins.

The heat contained in a gallon of boiling water is sufficient to cook 1½ pounds of shrimp. If you have more shrimp, adjust the water and seasonings accordingly.

If you want to serve your shrimp chilled, plunge them into a bath of salted water and ice after draining. Once they are well chilled, drain and peel. If they are to be picked up with the fingers, leave the tails on. Chilled shrimp are superb in a salad with avocado cubes and Lemon Vinaigrette (page 174). Aioli (page 253), thinned with a little water, is a good but rich sauce for chilled shrimp. Meyer Lemon–Olive Relish (page 254), all the components especially finely chopped, is also successful. But if American tradition is your bent, try the following flavorful, basic cocktail sauce.

COCKTAIL SAUCE

½ cup bottled "chili sauce" *(or ketchup)*

½ cup very finely diced fresh tomato

¼ teaspoon Tabasco sauce or other hot sauce

2½ teaspoons freshly squeezed lemon juice

⅛ teaspoon salt

good twist of black pepper

1 teaspoon vodka *(optional)*

1 tablespoon finely grated fresh horseradish

Mix everything in a small bowl and let sit for about 30 minutes at room temperature before serving.

Grilled Shrimp with Shrimp Essence

serves 2 to 3

In this method, the flavor from the shrimp shells is extracted into a scant, flavorful sauce, or "essence," that dresses the shrimp after they're grilled.

1 pound jumbo shrimp, shell-on

BRINE

1 tablespoon plus 2 teaspoons kosher salt

1 tablespoon sugar

2 cups cold tap water

FOR THE SHRIMP ESSENCE

the reserved shrimp shells

1 tablespoon sunflower oil or other light vegetable oil, plus more for grilling the shrimp

1 cup dry white wine, or water

2 to 3 cloves garlic, crushed

Peel each shrimp carefully, removing all bands of shell down to the tail. Once the entire body is peeled, the shell on the tail can often be gently pulled off, leaving the tail meat tips attached to the shrimp. Reserve all the shells. Using a small, sharp knife, devein each shrimp. As you work, keep the shrimp cold. Dissolve the salt and sugar in the cold water to make a brine, and immerse the shrimp in it. Let them soak in the brine for about 30 minutes.

Meanwhile, prepare the shrimp essence: heat a medium saucepan over a medium high flame, and add the tablespoon of oil. When it shimmers, add the shrimp shells and sauté, stirring constantly, until the shells turn pink and they release a deep shrimp aroma. Add the wine or water, stirring, then reduce the heat to a simmer. Let the shells cook for about 15 minutes, then let cool for about 10 minutes. Strain the shells out of the liquid, using your hands to carefully squeeze as much liquid as possible back into the pan—you want to get every drop. Add the garlic to the liquid, and bring the liquid back up to a boil. Cook until the liquid is reduced to about 3 tablespoons—this is your shrimp essence. Keep it warm while you're grilling the shrimp.

Drain the shrimp from the brine and thread them onto two parallel metal skewers, all facing the same direction, close together but not touching one another, creating a "raft" of shrimp that is easy to flip on the grill. Heat your grill thoroughly with a high flame. Pat the shrimp dry with paper towels, and brush them lightly with vegetable oil. Clean the grill grates, and oil them with a wad of paper towels that has been lightly saturated with vegetable oil. When the grill is hot, grill the shrimp on one side for about 2 minutes, then flip and cook the other side until barely cooked through—the shrimp will continue to cook off the grill. Remove the shrimp to a clean, warmed platter, and drizzle with the shrimp essence. Or pull out the skewers and toss the shrimp in the essence. Serve immediately.

Sautéed Spicy Squid

Squid populations are abundant in ocean waters, and squid is inexpensive, nutritious, and delicious when briefly sautéed. You may call it "calamari" if you like. This squid can be served by itself, or alongside a simple piece of baked mild fish, or atop risotto or pasta with olive oil, garlic, and herbs. Sautéed squid is excellent on a bed of white beans with generous drizzles of pesto, or with polenta and tomato sauce.

Start with small, fresh squid, the bodies measuring anywhere from 3 to 8 inches. Hold a squid by the body, letting the tentacles hang free. Lay the squid on your cutting board, and cut off the ring of tentacles just below the eyes—the tentacles should stay in one piece. Grasp around the eyes, and pull out everything remaining from the cone-shaped body. Using the back of your knife, squeeze out any remaining insides from the body, like crimping a tube of toothpaste. Using a finger, catch hold of the clear, plastic-like "quill" that runs the length of the inside of the body, and pull it out. Cut the body into bite-sized rings. Set tentacles and bodies together into a bowl, and discard everything else. Marinate the squid with a few pinches of hot red pepper flakes, a well-crushed clove or two of garlic, and a good drizzle of olive oil.

Get a big skillet very hot over a high flame. The skillet should be able to accommodate all the cleaned squid in a single layer without crowding. Add a bit of olive oil to the skillet, and swirl it around in the pan—the oil should begin to smoke. Add the squid all at once, spreading it out in the pan. Let the squid cook, undisturbed, for at least 30 seconds. After this initial sear, toss the squid around in the pan for 10 to 15 more seconds, just until all the pieces have turned opaque. Transfer the squid to a warmed bowl, and lightly salt to taste. Splash a little white wine into the skillet—it will dissolve the flavorful residue in the pan. Let it reduce to a tablespoon, drizzle this over the squid, and serve immediately.

CHAPTER 12

PASTA, DUMPLINGS, RICE, & STUFFING

This chapter tackles what might be called the "bones" of cooking. Carbohydrate-rich grains (wheat, rice, corn) and dough products form the backbone of every traditional cuisine. Meat and vegetables lend themselves to the simplest of treatments, but rice, pasta, dumplings, and other starch dishes often require technique and skill. While roast beef or baked salmon may be superb provided the cook has merely taken them out of the oven at the right moment, the excellence of a dish of homemade noodles sauced with cream depends on a whole succession of judgments and decisions by the cook.

Potato dishes are in the hot vegetables chapter (beginning on page 118), and other starchy dishes are found in the Great Lunches chapter (beginning on page 84). You'll find Chicken and Dumplings and Matzoh Ball Soup (pages 214 and 216) in the Chicken & Turkey chapter. Keep in mind, too, that beans (pages 106 to 116) are rich in starch and may deliciously accompany meat, fish, and vegetable dishes in place of rice, pasta, or potatoes.

Handmade Egg Noodles with Cream

serves 4 to 6

Fresh pasta takes practice to make well. This recipe aims to describe the process clearly, but ultimately, the only guarantor of success will be your own tactile experience. Mastering fresh pasta will teach you about the properties of gluten (the protein in wheat responsible for its elasticity), imparting an excellent "dough sense" that carries over to bread and pastry baking. I always use a stainless-steel, hand-crank pasta roller device from Italy to make fresh pasta. Many Italian purists think the metal devices are rubbish, and that rolling out your dough on a wooden countertop with a wooden rolling pin is the only way to proceed, but I am neither Italian nor a purist. If you want to roll these out with a rolling pin, by all means try—it is possible, but it takes work, patience, and space.

If you go to the trouble of making fresh pasta, you don't want a complex sauce to overwhelm it. These wide noodles are wonderful underneath braised chicken (page 212) or beef stew (page 184). But I think I like them best on their own, just with cream. Since this is an extremely simple (which is different from "easy") recipe, you'll get great results if the ingredients are of good quality. At Deep Springs we are lucky to have good farm-fresh eggs to make the noodles and our astonishingly thick, aromatic farmhouse cream to sauce the noodles. It's that simple: no cheese, no onion, no garlic, no parsley... just cream, a little butter, salt, and pepper.

EQUIPMENT

hand-crank pasta roller

pizza cutter

NOODLES

1¾ cups all-purpose flour, preferably unbleached

½ teaspoon olive oil

2 large eggs

1 egg yolk

1 to 2 teaspoons water *(only if necessary)*

semolina flour for dusting *(if unavailable, use all-purpose flour)*

SAUCE

1¼ cups heavy *(whipping)* **cream**

¼ teaspoon salt, plus more as needed

2 tablespoons butter

freshly ground black pepper

To make the noodles, before beginning to mix, bear in mind that pasta dough is much denser and more resilient than bread dough. In a sturdy mixer fitted with the paddle attachment, using its slowest speed, or by hand in a medium bowl using a wooden spoon, mix the flour and olive oil together for a moment, then add the eggs and yolk. The mixture will at first appear dry and crumbly. Keep mixing until it becomes more uniform. If it still seems too dry, add just enough water—a few drops at a time—for the dough to begin to cohere. You should need no more than a teaspoon or, if your flour is especially dry or your eggs small, two. The dough should not be so wet that it comes together in a ball by itself in the mixer, only moist enough that when you take a handful of the crumbles and squeeze they stick together readily. If there's too much water, the noodles will be sticky and flabby. Don't overwork the dough—it will make the pasta tough. Wrap the dough well in plastic wrap and let it rest at room temperature for 1 to 2 hours.

Divide the dough into 4 pieces, each slightly bigger than a golf ball. Keep the pieces you aren't using well wrapped. Take a piece of the dough and flatten it with your hand. If it seems sticky, dust it well with semolina flour. Using a hand-crank pasta machine, roll the dough first through the thickest setting. You will have an oval-shaped piece of dough. Fold this in thirds to make a square-shaped piece of dough, and run it through the rollers again at the thickest setting. Roll the dough through successively thinner settings until it is about as thick as 4 or 5 sheets of paper. Some cooks like to roll out each ball of dough partway and then let them rest, well covered, before rolling them through the thinnest setting. If your dough is soft and would rather stick than not, keep it well coated with flour at all times and hope for the best. If your dough is hard, has lots of white streaks, and tends to crumble and break, try misting it lightly with water before re-flouring and re-rolling. If your dough is elastic but firm, with a silky suppleness to it, and if it rolls out easily with only a slight crack here and there, you have made perfect pasta dough.

Before cutting all the noodles, make a test batch: take a sharp pizza cutter (or a knife) and cut a few inch-wide crosswise strips, slightly on the diagonal, from your sheet of pasta. Boil up a small pot of salted water and cook these noodles for 20 to 30 seconds. Drain the noodles well and turn them out onto a plate. If they fall completely flat, tear easily, and seem insubstantial, the dough has been rolled too thin—this can be remedied somewhat by reducing the boiling time. If they look thick and sturdy and taste tough and chewy, the dough is too thick—roll it thinner. If the noodles stand up nicely on the plate and taste good, with just the right balance of tenderness and firmness, they are just right. Proceed with rolling the other 3 pieces of dough, keeping any dough you're not handling at the moment covered with plastic wrap so it doesn't dry out. Cut all the noodles into 1-inch-wide strips with your pizza cutter, as described previously. Toss them with extra semolina flour and place them in loose clumps on a floured tray or baking sheet. Don't pile them heavily on top of each other. Keep the noodles on this tray, covered with a dish towel or with plastic wrap, refrigerated, until just before cooking/serving time.

To make the sauce and cook the noodles, pour the cream into a wide skillet, add the salt, and set over a low flame to warm. Bring a large pot of water (about 1½ gallons) to a furious boil. Add enough salt to the water so that it tastes lightly salty, and throw in the noodles all at once. Gently stir them around in the pot. Once the water returns to a boil, the noodles should take only about a minute to cook—to test, taste one. Drain well (don't rinse), and transfer the noodles to the skillet with the warmed cream, adding the butter, cut into small pieces, and salt and pepper to taste. Raise the flame to medium-high, and toss gently to coat. Taste for salt. Divide the pasta and sauce among wide, shallow bowls. Twist a little more black pepper over each, and serve immediately.

Ricotta Ravioli with Sage Brown Butter

makes about 50 ravioli; serves 4 to 6

Once you have made the noodles in the previous recipe a few times, try these classic, simple ravioli. When you have less time, use small wonton wrappers, sold refrigerated in many grocery stores.

EQUIPMENT

hand-crank pasta roller

pizza cutter

water mister

PASTA

1 recipe dough for Handmade Egg Noodles *(preceding page)*

FILLING

1½ cups whole-milk ricotta cheese

¼ teaspoon salt

few twists of black pepper

pinch of cayenne pepper

¼ teaspoon ground nutmeg

1 tablespoon extra-virgin olive oil

SAUCE

6 tablespoons unsalted butter

6 to 8 fresh sage leaves, coarsely chopped

freshly ground black pepper

Parmesan cheese for grating

While the pasta dough is resting, spread the ricotta in a rectangle about ¼ inch thick directly on a clean, white, dry dish towel. Wrap the towel gently around the cheese and let the towel absorb excess moisture from the cheese for about 30 minutes.

Roll out the pasta into sheets a little thinner than described in the egg noodles recipe, keeping it well covered at all times. Ideally, the sheets should be about 4 inches wide, resulting in 2-inch ravioli—no trimming necessary.

To make the filling, unwrap the ricotta and transfer it to a medium bowl. Season well with the salt, black pepper, a little cayenne, a few good scrapings of nutmeg, and a tablespoon of good olive oil. Taste—it should be rich and well-seasoned.

Have ready a clean water mister filled with water. Cut the pasta sheets into manageable lengths. Using one sheet at a time, place teaspoonfuls of ricotta filling 2 inches apart, off-center, along the sheet of pasta. Mist the pasta sheet lightly with water, then fold it over lengthwise, enclosing the filling. Carefully and systematically press out any air pockets, pressing firmly to fuse the pasta together. Using a pizza cutter, cut the ravioli apart. Trim if necessary. Transfer the ravioli to a sheet pan well dusted with semolina flour.

When all the ravioli are made, bring a large pot of water to a boil. Salt the water generously, and gently throw in half the ravioli. Let the ravioli cook for 40 to 45 seconds after the water returns to a boil, gently stirring the pot from time to time. Don't fret if a couple of them break. Rinse one in cold water and taste—it might need more cooking time to become tender. Scoop the ravioli out with a wire skimmer, drain briefly, then turn out into a buttered serving dish. Save some of the pasta-cooking water in case it's needed for the sauce.

To make the sauce, in a skillet, melt 3 tablespoons of the butter on high heat. When the butter turns golden brown and smells nutty, throw in half the sage—it will sizzle. Tip the ravioli into the skillet, toss gently, then slide them back into the dish. Repeat with the remaining ravioli, butter, and sage. If the ravioli seem in need of a little moisture, add a spoonful or two of the pasta-cooking water. Lightly grind black pepper and grate a little Parmesan over the ravioli, and serve immediately.

Whole-Wheat Pappardelle with Corn and Chiles

serves 4

This elegant summer garden pasta evokes the time I worked at Chez Panisse—David Tanis (DS'71) had earlier introduced it into the repertoire from a recipe by Diana Kennedy, and chef Catherine Brandel often put this sumptuous version on the café menu. Although tender, young cilantro is very good in this recipe, "bolted" cilantro is even better: summer heat causes the delicate plant to go to seed; in this transformation, the leaves become more fernlike and their characteristic citrusy flavor intensifies. If the plant has produced seed-heads, the immature green coriander berries are delicious—coarsely chop a teaspoon's worth and add to the sautéing vegetables.

NOODLES

1 pound fresh egg noodles *(see page 231)*, **made with a portion of whole-wheat flour, cut about ½ inch wide**

SAUCE

3 large ears white or yellow sweet corn, or a combination *(enough to yield 3 generous cups of kernels)*

4 tablespoons butter, divided

1 medium red onion, finely diced

about ½ teaspoon salt, in all

1 pound assorted small summer squash, finely diced *(enough to yield 3 generous cups)*

1 to 2 serrano or other small, hot green peppers, finely minced

juice of 1 lime

1½ cups loosely-packed cilantro leaves and slender stems, coarsely chopped

freshly-ground black pepper

5 tablespoons sour cream, thinned with 1 tablespoon milk or heavy cream

First make the noodles, following the recipe on page 231, using 1¼ cups white flour and ½ cup of whole-wheat flour in the dough. Have ready a large pot of boiling water.

Shuck the corn, wipe with a damp towel to remove the silk, and cut the kernels off the cobs with a sharp knife into a large bowl. With the back of your knife, thoroughly scrape out the remaining juice and corn germ from the cobs into the bowl. In a large skillet over a high flame, melt half the butter; when it sizzles, add the onion with a pinch of salt and sauté, stirring constantly, until the onion is almost tender. Add the squash with another big pinch of salt and cook, stirring, another minute. Add the serrano pepper and the corn, including all the corn's juice, and cook the mixture, stirring frequently, for about 2 minutes more, until the corn is heated through.

Meanwhile, salt the boiling water and cook the noodles briefly—once the water returns to a boil, they should only take an additional 30 seconds to a minute to cook. Drain, saving a cup of the cooking water, and add the pasta to the vegetables. Add the lime juice, remaining butter, 1 cup of the cilantro, and pepper to taste. Gently toss everything together, moistening as necessary with the reserved pasta cooking water. Taste for salt. Divide the pasta and sauce into warmed bowls, top each with a heaping tablespoon of the thinned sour cream and the remaining cilantro, and serve immediately.

Manicotti

makes about 16 crêpes; serves 4 to 6

In this recipe, sheets of "pasta" are cooked like crêpes, filled with seasoned ricotta, and baked with a simple bacon-tomato sauce.

CRÊPES

3 eggs

1 egg yolk

2 cups water

½ teaspoon salt

1½ tablespoons olive oil, plus more for cooking

1¼ cups all-purpose flour

FILLING

2 cups whole-milk ricotta cheese

1 egg white

1 tablespoon olive oil

⅛ teaspoon salt

several twists of black pepper

⅛ teaspoon ground nutmeg

SAUCE (OR USE FRESH SUMMER TOMATO SAUCE RECIPE, PAGE 249)

3 strips bacon

½ medium onion, finely diced

2 cloves garlic, crushed

one 28-ounce can whole plum tomatoes in tomato purée

3 to 4 tablespoons chopped flat-leaf parsley

salt and freshly ground black pepper

FOR SERVING

about ½ cup freshly grated Parmesan cheese

To make the crêpes, using a blender, blend the eggs, yolk, water, salt, and 1½ tablespoons olive oil together. Add the flour, and blend on high speed for 1 full minute. Let the batter rest for at least 1 hour before making the crêpes. Heat a small omelet pan (nonstick is ideal) over a medium-high flame. Brush a scant film of olive oil in the pan, then pour in 3 tablespoons of the batter. I find it easiest to use a ¼-cup measure, filling it three-fourths full. Scoop the batter from the bottom of the bowl, as the flour in the batter tends to settle. Swirl the pan so the batter evenly covers the bottom, and cook until the top of the crêpe has lost its glossiness. Flip and cook on the other side for a few seconds, until the crêpe puffs, then flip it onto a plate. This takes skill—the recipe makes enough to allow for a few mess-ups. Don't let the crêpes brown. Continue cooking the crêpes until the batter is used up, stacking the crêpes atop one another.

To make the filling, mix the ricotta, egg, olive oil, salt, pepper, and nutmeg together in a medium bowl.

Have the filling at room temperature when you assemble the manicotti.

For the sauce, freeze the bacon for about 30 minutes, then chop it into fine dice. Open the can of tomatoes, pour the contents into a bowl, and using your clean hands, lightly crush the whole tomatoes until no large chunks remain. Heat a medium-sized, heavy, nonreactive pot over a medium flame. Add the bacon, and let cook until some of the fat renders out, about 2 minutes. Add the onion and garlic and let cook, stirring frequently, until the onion is tender. Add the tomatoes and their liquid. Simmer the sauce for about 10 minutes, stirring frequently. Add the parsley, and taste for salt and pepper.

Heat the oven to 350°F. Spread some warm tomato sauce in the bottom of a wide, shallow casserole dish. Spread about 1½ tablespoons of ricotta filling across a crêpe. Roll the crêpe up cigar-style, and place in the casserole. Repeat, lining up the crêpes snugly in the pan, until the crêpes and filling are used up. Drizzle about half of the remaining sauce evenly over the manicotti, cover, and bake for about 30 minutes. Allow to rest for 5 minutes before serving. Serve with the remaining sauce, heated, and freshly grated Parmesan cheese.

Pasta Cookery

The preceding recipes address fresh pasta preparations; the following ones concern packaged, "dry" pasta, typically made with harder durum wheat: spaghetti, linguine, penne, and many other forms. Deep Springers consume great quantities of pasta; beginning Student Cooks and experienced chefs alike rely on "spaghetti and meat sauce" for its ease of preparation, just as our mothers did. Everyone knows how to boil dry pasta; it is one of the most basic cooking operations. But here are a few pointers: for every pound of pasta, bring 3 to 4 quarts of water to a boil. When the water reaches a full, rolling boil, add a tablespoon of salt for every 4 quarts of water—the water should taste lightly salted. Throw in the pasta all at once, and stir frequently as the water returns to a boil; this prevents the pieces of pasta from sticking to one another or to the bottom. For cooking times, use the times specified on the package as a guideline, from 3 to 4 minutes for angel hair pasta to 8 to 10 minutes for penne. Taste a piece of the pasta toward the end of the cooking time: it should be neither raw and hard in the center nor completely soft and yielding throughout. The center should be just firm but cooked through (if you want an old-fashioned American pasta dish, overcook the pasta).

Drain the pasta in a colander, retaining a bit of the cooking water in a cup; this water is frequently necessary to adjust the consistency of the sauce. Do not rinse cooked pasta in running water. For tomato sauce recipes, see pages 247 to 249. For best results, toss the pasta with sauce immediately and serve immediately. If it is necessary to serve the plain cooked pasta and the sauce separately, toss the pasta with a bit of olive oil first. Most pastas are enhanced with a sprinkling of freshly grated Parmesan cheese over each serving.

Toasted Pasta with Garlic
serves 6 to 8

This treatment transforms dry linguine or spaghetti into a new species of pasta, especially inviting in cool weather.

1 pound dry spaghetti or linguine

1 tablespoon olive oil

salt

4 to 6 cloves garlic, crushed

2 tablespoons butter

1 tablespoon extra-virgin olive oil

½ cup chopped parsley

½ cup freshly grated Parmesan cheese, plus more for serving

black pepper

Heat the oven to 300°F. Line up the uncooked pasta on a sheet pan. Drizzle the oil over it and work the pasta around until evenly coated. Spread the pasta out in an even layer. Bake until the pasta is toasted to a deep golden brown, 15 to 20 minutes. Once it begins to change color, it burns quickly, so keep checking it. While the pasta is toasting, put a gallon of water on to boil.

When the water comes to a boil, salt it until it tastes lightly salty, and boil the pasta just until cooked in the center. This will take several minutes longer than cooking untoasted pasta. Being sure to retain 2 or 3 ladlefuls of the cooking water, drain the pasta. Return it to the pot with a ladleful of pasta-cooking water and the garlic, butter, extra-virgin olive oil, parsley, and Parmesan, quickly and thoroughly tossing everything together. Taste for salt and moisture, adding a bit more hot cooking water, olive oil, or butter, if necessary. Sprinkle with a little more Parmesan and black pepper, and serve immediately.

You may add up to 3 cups of cooked cool-weather vegetables to this pasta, such as sautéed chopped Greens (page 132), stir-fried carrot slivers, or steam-sautéed broccoli and cauliflower (pages 123 and 126). Or toss in pitted, oil-cured black olives, thinly sliced fennel sautéed in olive oil, the chopped inner fennel fronds, and a squeeze of lemon.

Wide Noodles with Broccolini, Feta, Lemon, & Pine Nuts
serves 2 to 3

This pasta contains a simple, bright, healthy balance of flavors. Broccolini is a long-stemmed cross of kale and broccoli, sometimes marketed as "asparagus broccoli." In the Deep Springs broccoli patch, the gardeners harvest the little shoots that the plant continues to put out after the large heads are cut—this recipe is a perfect use for those.

You could make this with Handmade Egg Noodles (page 231), but it's also well-suited to dried egg noodles, often sold packaged in serving-sized nests. This good pasta product lacks the long shelf life of more common durum wheat pastas (such as spaghetti or macaroni), so make sure what you're using is fresh. If the pasta seems brittle, it might be old.

⅓ cup pine nuts

3 to 4 ounces feta cheese

1 bunch broccolini

salt

about 6 ounces dry wide egg noodles (2 servings)

½ teaspoon grated lemon zest

pinch of hot red pepper flakes

2 tablespoons olive oil

few twists of black pepper

Set a big pot of water on the stove to boil. Toast the pine nuts in a small skillet over a medium flame, tossing frequently, until they are pale gold, 6 to 7 minutes. Transfer to a small plate to cool. Crumble the feta onto a small plate. Trim the broccolini if necessary, and cut each one in half lengthwise. When the water boils, salt it until it tastes lightly salty, and boil the pasta. Near the end of cooking, throw the broccolini into the water with the pasta. When both the broccolini and pasta are just tender, drain, retaining just a sheen of the cooking water, then toss in a large bowl with the pine nuts, lemon zest, red pepper flakes, a tablespoon of the olive oil, and pepper to taste. Add half the feta cheese, toss again, and serve, topping the pasta with the remaining feta cheese and drizzling with the remaining tablespoon of olive oil.

Garlic Bread

American, not Italian, tradition dictates serving garlic bread with pasta. Of the many possible ways to make it, the approach known in Italy as *bruschetta* is my favorite: drizzle thick slices of well-textured bread with olive oil, sprinkle lightly with salt and pepper, and grill or toast until golden. While the toast is hot, rub the surfaces of the bread with a clove of freshly peeled raw garlic, rubbing the garlic into the pores of the bread. For a light garlic flavor, rub lightly. Drizzle with a little more olive oil and serve immediately.

Pecan Couscous

serves 4 to 5

Couscous is a traditional Moroccan wheat product, somewhat like tiny bits of pasta. Traditional recipes, using regular couscous, specify a lengthy steaming and fluffing process, but this very simple method works well using whole-wheat couscous, and tastes delightful with Marmalade Chicken (page 206).

1 tablespoon butter

1 clove garlic, finely crushed

¾ teaspoon paprika

1 cup water

½ teaspoon salt, plus a pinch

1 cup whole-wheat couscous

½ cup pecans, lightly toasted *(page 176)* **and finely chopped**

1 teaspoon olive oil

black pepper

Melt the butter in a small saucepan over a medium-high flame. When it sizzles, add the garlic and paprika. Stir and cook for just a moment, letting the garlic sauté, then add the water and ½ teaspoon salt. Bring to a boil, then pour in the couscous. Stir once, remove from the heat, and cover the pan. Let sit for 5 minutes or longer, keeping the pan in a warm place.

Toss the toasted, chopped pecans in a small bowl with the olive oil, a pinch of salt, and a twist of black pepper. Just before serving, fluff the couscous with a fork and toss in the pecans.

Spaetzle

serves 6 to 8

Spaetzle are little pasta-like boiled dumplings, traditionally served with slow-cooked meats, Sautéed Mushrooms (page 135), and other wintry food. Perhaps you have seen spaetzle makers: a small hopper, holding the batter, moves back and forth over graterlike holes, releasing the spaetzle into the boiling water. Lacking a spaetzle maker, you need a vessel with widely spaced perforations (holes about ¼ inch in diameter, ¾ inch apart) and a scraper to extrude the batter through the perforations and into the boiling water below. In the Deep Springs kitchen, I use a shallow, perforated "hotel" pan set over a deeper hotel pan containing the water, and a metal dough scraper. In home kitchens, some improvisation and experimentation may be necessary.

To make *herbed spaetzle,* add the finely-chopped herb of your choice to the batter, or a combination: 2 tablespoons of parsley, dill, or chives; and/or a tablespoon of thyme, sage, savory, or rosemary. To make *green spaetzle,* using a blender, purée a large handful of fresh spinach leaves with the recipe's milk or water.

2¼ cups all-purpose flour *(up to ⅓ cup can be replaced with whole-wheat flour)*

½ teaspoon salt

1¼ cups milk or water

1 egg

3 egg yolks

1 tablespoon butter, plus more as needed

Whisk together the flour and salt in a medium bowl. In small bowl, whisk the milk, egg, and yolks together. Whisk the milk mixture into the flour mixture just until uniform. Let the batter stand for 30 minutes before cooking the spaetzle. While the batter is resting, bring a large, wide pot of water to a boil. Have a wide, buttered dish ready to receive the hot spaetzle. Add the tablespoon of butter to the water and enough salt to make the water taste lightly salty. Reduce the heat to medium-high if the water is boiling violently. Take up about one-fourth of the batter, transfer it to the hopper of your spaetzle maker, and extrude the batter through the holes into the boiling water. After the water returns to a boil, let the spaetzle cook for about 30 seconds. Scoop them out with a wire skimmer or a slotted spoon, drain briefly, and toss into the buttered dish. Repeat with the remaining batter in three more batches. Toss with a bit more butter (use brown butter, see page 123, if you like) and serve.

If you won't be serving the spaetzle immediately, toss with a little butter and let them cool in the dish. Once cool, they may be put in a container and refrigerated. To reheat, brown them in butter in a skillet.

Cornmeal-Egg Soup Dumplings

serves 2 to 3

These quick, simple, noodlelike dumplings will enrich virtually any brothy soup or stew. You make crêpes from a simple cornmeal batter, then cut them into squares and toss them in the soup. Soup possibilities include any of the braised chicken recipes (page 151) made with extra broth, the chicken stew base for Chicken and Dumplings (214), Soupe au Pistou (151), or Brothy Vegetable Soup (133).

- **2 eggs**
- **¼ cup fine cornmeal** *(preferably stone-ground; see page 40)*
- **2 teaspoons olive oil, plus more for cooking the crêpes**
- **1 tablespoon white wine or orange juice**
- **¼ teaspoon salt**
- **freshly ground black pepper**

In a medium bowl, whisk together the eggs, cornmeal, 2 teaspoons of the olive oil, wine, salt, and pepper into a batter. Heat about ½ teaspoon olive oil in a small (preferably nonstick) skillet over a medium-high flame. Add ¼ of the well-stirred batter, swirling to coat the pan. Let cook about 20 seconds on one side, then flip and cook the other side just until solid—the crêpe shouldn't brown. Make three more crêpes, using up all the batter. As they are done, turn them onto a cutting board. Cut the crêpes into 1-inch squares and stir the dumplings into your pot of soup.

Rice

serves 4 to 5

When you want to serve plain rice, there are a few options for cooking it: on the stovetop in a good, heavy, heat-conducting pot; in a rice cooker; or in a tightly covered pan in the oven. At home I use a rice cooker, but I often find the oven method most convenient in the Deep Springs kitchen. For all these methods, the ratios are the same: 1 part white rice to 1½ parts water, or 1 part brown rice to 2¼ parts water. For brown rice, the cooking time is about 50 percent longer.

The most foolproof method of all dispenses with rice-to-water ratios entirely: just cook rice in ample boiling, salted water until tender, then drain well, exactly like pasta. This "pasta method" sacrifices some vitamins and flavor, however.

This plain, pilaf-style recipe is best when a highly flavored, sauced dish, such as one of the braised chicken recipes, is to be served over it. For rice to accompany Gumbo (page 99), use long-grain white rice and butter.

For simple *Asian-style steamed rice,* use short-grain white rice (I favor Japanese brands, or those labeled "sushi rice") and omit the oil and salt (and the sautéing)—simply cook the rice in water.

- **1 tablespoon butter or olive oil**
- **1 cup uncooked white or brown rice, long- or short-grain**
- **1½ cups water** *(for brown rice: 2¼ cups water)*
- **¼ teaspoon salt**

OVEN METHOD

Heat the oven to 400°F. On the stovetop, melt the butter in a medium (large), oven-safe saucepan. Add the dry rice and sauté, stirring constantly, until very hot, 2 to 3 minutes. Add the water and salt, stir once, and bring to a boil. Cover the pan tightly with aluminum foil (shiny side facing in) and put in the oven. Bake for 20 to 30 minutes (50 minutes to 1 hour for brown rice). Check for doneness, using a fork; the liquid should be completely absorbed and the rice should be evenly tender; re-cover with foil and return to the oven if necessary. Fluff the rice with a fork and serve.

STOVETOP METHOD

In a medium (large), heavy, heat-conducting pot with a well-fitting lid, melt the butter over medium-high heat. Add the rice and stir to coat the grains. Sauté for 2 to 3 minutes, stirring constantly. Add the water and salt, stir once, and bring to a boil. Turn the heat down to medium-low, maintaining a lively simmer. Cover the pot and let the rice cook, undisturbed, for about 20 minutes (40 minutes for brown rice), or until the water is absorbed. It's best not to peek at the rice until it's done; to tell if the water is absorbed, tilt the pan slightly. If you hear a hissing, boiling sound, there is still unabsorbed water in the pan, and the rice needs more time. If there is no sound, all the water is absorbed and the rice is ready. Fluff the rice with a fork and serve.

RICE COOKER METHOD

Sauté the rice in the butter in a skillet as described, then transfer it to the rice cooker, adding the water and salt. Turn on the cooker—it will shut off automatically when the rice is done. Fluff the rice with a fork and serve.

PASTA COOKING METHOD

If you have an unusual variety of rice and are uncertain of its rice-to-water cooking ratio, simply cook the rice in a pot of boiling salted water, like pasta. Watch the rice carefully as it boils, tasting it frequently. When it is as tender as you like, immediately drain it and spread the rice on a tray or plate to stop the cooking. Toss with a little butter or oil. Once it has cooled to warm, put it in a serving dish. Rice cooked this way reheats well.

If you want to enrich the rice or make it more of a dish in itself, sharing equal weight in your menu with other foods, there are many, many possibilities for deepening its flavor. Here are just a few:

- more butter or extra-virgin olive oil, and salt and pepper (gently tossed in at the end, using a fork)
- chicken stock or other stock instead of the water
- chopped onion (sautéed in the butter at the beginning, before adding the rice)
- saffron (crushed and whisked with a little lemon juice and added at the beginning with the water)
- chopped fresh herbs (gently folded in at the end, using a fork)
- citrus (juice and finely grated zest, gently folded in at the end using a fork; a little extra salt will be needed)
- finely chopped scallions (sautéed in more butter and folded into the cooked rice at the end)

Golden Basmati Rice Pilaf

Most varieties of white rice need not be rinsed in water prior to cooking. Indian basmati rice, however, benefits from a good rinse, then a 30-minute soak in cool water before draining and cooking. This procedure causes the rice grains to lengthen considerably in the cooking. After rinsing and soaking a cup of basmati rice, drain it very well. Sauté about a teaspoon each of whole mustard seed, coriander seed, cloves, and whole cardamom pods, plus a couple of bay leaves and a whole cinnamon stick, in ghee (see page 37). When the spices have released their scent, toss in the drained rice and continue to sauté for a moment more. Add a teaspoon of ground turmeric to the pot, then add 1½ cups water and ½ teaspoon salt. Cook the rice as directed in the recipe above, using the oven, stovetop, or rice-cooker methods. For plain basmati rice, see the curry recipe on page 100.

Brown, White, and Wild Rice Pilaf with Mirepoix

serves 6 to 8

Once you have experienced the simple rice-cooking procedures in the previous recipe, try this more complex one: three different rices, all requiring different cooking times, are initially cooked separately, then allowed to finish cooking together with the classic trio of aromatic vegetables known as *mirepoix*. The result is more than the sum of its parts. To ensure correct timing, be sure the vegetables are cut and ready before beginning.

½ cup uncooked wild rice

1½ teaspoons salt, or more as needed

4¾ cups water

6 tablespoons butter

1 cup uncooked brown rice

2 bay leaves

1 large yellow onion, cut into medium dice

2 carrots, peeled and cut into medium dice

1 large stalk celery, cut into medium dice

1 cup uncooked long-grain white rice

black pepper

In a small saucepan, bring the wild rice, ¼ teaspoon of the salt, and 1 cup of the water to a boil. Cover the pan, remove from the heat, and set aside; do not drain the rice.

In a large, heavy saucepan, heat 2 tablespoons of the butter over medium-high heat. When it sizzles, throw in the brown rice with another ¼ teaspoon salt. Sauté the brown rice in the butter, stirring constantly, until the rice begins to smell nutty. Add 2¼ cups water, the wild rice and the water it cooked in, and the bay leaves. Bring to a boil, reduce the heat to a simmer, and let the rice cook for about 15 minutes, covered, while you prepare the white rice and the vegetables.

As soon as the wild–brown rice mixture settles to a simmer, heat the remaining 4 tablespoons butter in a large saucepan over medium-high heat. Add the onion, carrot, and celery with the remaining teaspoon of salt and stew, stirring frequently, until the vegetables begin to soften, about 3 minutes. Add the white rice to the vegetables and sauté for 3 to 4 minutes more. Add the vegetable–white rice mixture and the remaining 1½ cups water to the saucepan containing the brown and wild rice. Stir briefly to combine, raise the heat to bring to a boil again, then reduce the heat to maintain a simmer. Cover the pan and let the rice simmer gently until all the liquid is absorbed, 15 to 20 minutes more. To check for doneness without removing the lid, tilt the pan slightly and listen for a sizzling sound; if there is no sound, the liquid has all been absorbed.

Sprinkle a bit of fresh pepper over the rice, taste for salt (if salt has been added at the various stages as specified, it probably won't need any more) and correct if necessary, fluffing the rice gently with a fork; if you stir it, it could become mushy. Remove the bay leaves and serve.

Green Rice with Peas and Pea Greens

A fresh springtime accompaniment to roast beef or steak. For every cup of rice, allow a big bunch of fresh pea greens and about 1 pound (in-shell weight) of English peas. Boil long-grain white rice in plenty of boiling salted water until the rice is tender. In the last minute of cooking, add the shelled peas. Drain the rice and peas in a fine-screen colander. Meanwhile, wash and chop the pea greens coarsely, and sauté them in butter with a little salt until tender and tasty. In a food processor, purée about a third of the greens, then scrape the purée into a square of cheesecloth. Transfer the hot, drained rice and peas to a large bowl. Take up the corners of the cheesecloth and squeeze as much pea-green liquid into the rice as possible. Gently fold the green liquid and the remaining sautéed pea greens into the rice, along with butter, salt, and pepper to taste, and transfer to a serving dish. Serve immediately.

Risotto

serves 6 to 8

Risotto [ree-SO-toe], quintessentially Italian, is a specific, easy technique for cooking a particular kind of rice. The result—tender grains cloaked in a flavorful, velvety sauce—is unlike any other rice dish in the world. Virtually all risotto recipes call for stock, most often chicken stock. In a pinch, some cooks just use water, building up the flavor with extra onion and garlic. But if you use good homemade chicken stock in this recipe or any of the variations, you will not be disappointed. A plain risotto made with good Italian Parmesan, butter, and homemade chicken stock is a culinary touchstone. Serve risotto immediately, or the rice becomes mushy and the surrounding sauce becomes too thick.

8 cups chicken stock

4 tablespoons cold butter

1 large yellow onion, finely diced *(ideally, the onion bits should be similar in size to the grains of rice)*

2 pinches of salt, plus more as needed

2 cups uncooked Arborio rice or other Italian risotto rice

1 cup dry white wine

about ⅓ cup freshly grated Parmesan cheese, plus more for topping

freshly ground black pepper

Fill a large stockpot with the chicken stock and bring to a boil. Keep it at a simmer while you are making the risotto. In a large, heavy saucepot, melt 2 tablespoons of the butter over medium heat. Add the onion with a large pinch of salt and sauté until it just loses its crunch, about 4 minutes. Throw in the rice with another good pinch of salt and cook for about 1 minute, stirring well, lightly sautéing the rice in the onions and butter. Add the wine and stir, enjoying the wonderful aroma, until it is absorbed. Add the stock, 1 to 2 ladlefuls at a time, to your pot of rice, keeping the rice very moist, a thin film of stock over the surface of the rice, and stirring from the bottom frequently. Keep stirring and adding stock as necessary. When finished, after about 20 minutes, the risotto should be almost pourable in consistency, each grain of rice cooked through and soft (taste to find out), but not split out from too much liquid. Depending on the size and shape of your pan—a wider pan will permit more evaporation—and the absorbency of your rice, you will probably use up all the broth.

At the moment the risotto is done, add the cheese and stir in the remaining 2 tablespoons cold butter. Carefully salt and pepper to taste. Serve immediately, with extra Parmesan grated over the top.

SAFFRON RISOTTO

Crush a generous pinch of saffron threads to a powder in a mortar and pestle. Add a tablespoon of lemon juice and mix well. Add this mixture to the risotto when you start adding the stock, rinsing out the last bit of saffron from the mortar with some of the stock.

WILD MUSHROOM RISOTTO

Soak about ½ ounce of dried porcini mushrooms for 30 minutes in 2 cups of the hot chicken stock. Drain the mushrooms and squeeze dry, reserving all the liquid. Chop the mushrooms finely and add to the pot before adding the wine. Use the strained soaking liquid in the risotto. Substitute ½ cup heavy cream for the Parmesan (cream's simple richness allows the complex mushroom flavor to shine through). Garnish with a little chopped parsley. If you are fortunate enough to find fresh porcini mushrooms or other fresh wild mushrooms (page 135), chop them coarsely, sauté them in butter with a little salt, pepper, and garlic, and add to the risotto at the end.

BUTTERNUT SQUASH RISOTTO

Halve 1 small butternut squash or other sweet winter squash, scoop out the seeds (you may infuse the simmering stock with the seeds, straining them out before adding the stock to the risotto), and bake in a 350°F oven until the flesh is soft, about 1 hour. Scoop out the flesh and add to the risotto in the last 10 minutes of cooking. The squash purée will dissolve into the risotto, turning it a beautiful orange. Add a little chopped fresh sage at the beginning, and garnish with whole sage leaves briefly sizzled in butter. This risotto is good with roast chicken, roast pork, or ham.

Polenta
serves 4 to 6

Polenta, a creamy, savory porridge made from coarse yellow cornmeal, may seem new to American cuisine, but it is a close cousin to the grits and cornmeal mush well known in the American South. I first encountered it in western Slovenia, a stone's throw from Italy. There, it is served with beef goulash or other rich accompaniments, and is made only with water and salt, nothing else. American cooks typically enrich polenta with Parmesan cheese, but I increasingly prefer it plain, especially when made with good, stone-ground cornmeal. Polenta takes a long time, but is quite easy to cook, with none of the timing particulars of rice or pasta.

BLACK TRUFFLE RISOTTO

Perhaps, in fall or winter, at your produce market or specialty food store, you spot fresh black truffles from the Périgord region of France, nestled in cups of Arborio rice. You decide to buy a small one—for such a small, unassuming object, it is quite expensive. Back home in your kitchen, prepare a basic recipe of risotto, using the rice in which the truffle was packed. With a small knife, peel the truffle thinly. Save the peelings and infuse the simmering chicken stock with them. Carefully cut the truffle into fine julienne. At the moment the risotto is finished, stir in the truffle. Keeping the truffle's pungent flavor clear and uncluttered, omit the Parmesan and enrich the finished risotto with a shot of heavy cream. Serve immediately, and take in the extraordinary aroma.

One winter, when the Deep Springs biology professor Jack Murphy (DS'78) offered a mycology class, I made black truffle risotto with a golf ball–sized $20 truffle I bought on a trip to San Francisco. Virtually no one in the community had ever tasted or smelled a truffle before. The chocolaty, pheromone-y scent of the truffle filled the Boardinghouse, and we feasted.

I love freshly made creamy polenta with beef stew, especially Goulash (page 186), or with garlicky cooked Greens (132). Sautéed Mushrooms (135) are especially succulent atop polenta. Other choices are Roasted Red Peppers (140), Roast Chicken (205), Herbed Braised Chicken (212), or any preparation of pork (pages 197 to 201).

In summer, add a cupful of freshly cut corn kernels to the pot of polenta in the last 10 minutes of cooking. For another variation, pour the hot polenta into a buttered shallow dish, let cool to room temperature, then cover and refrigerate for several hours. Cut the firm polenta into squares or triangles, and sizzle them in a nonstick skillet with olive oil and butter.

5 cups water

1 cup polenta or coarse cornmeal, preferably stone-ground *(see page 40)*

1 teaspoon salt, or more as needed

3 to 4 tablespoons butter

½ cup freshly grated Parmesan cheese *(optional)*

¼ teaspoon black pepper, or more as needed *(optional)*

pinch of cayenne pepper *(optional)*

Heat the oven to 325°F. Bring the water to a boil in a heavy 2-quart saucepot. Slowly whisk in the polenta, and keep whisking as the mixture comes back up to a boil. When it reaches a boil, allow it to cook for about a minute, whisking a few times, until it begins to thicken. Cover the pot and put it in the oven. Let it cook for 1 to 1½ hours, taking it out and stirring thoroughly with a wooden spoon every 30 minutes or so. This gentle long cooking brings out the flavor of the corn; polenta may be cooked start to finish on the stovetop but requires constant stirring and vigilance against burning on the bottom.

Stir in the salt and butter, and, if you opt for them, the Parmesan, black pepper, and cayenne. Taste carefully (it's very hot), and adjust the seasoning if necessary. The polenta may be held on the lowest heat, or in a double boiler over hot water, for another 30 minutes. Polenta continues to thicken as it sits.

Southern Spoon Bread

serves 4 to 6

Should you be able to find stone-ground, whole-grist cornmeal, this is an excellent use for it. Although the additions of cheese or green chile suggested in the variations are flavorful and delicious, spoon bread is traditionally kept plainly-flavored when sharing the plate with saucy meats and other highly-flavored dishes.

3 cups milk

1¼ cups cornmeal *(stone-ground and whole-grain, if available, see page 40)*

3 eggs

2 tablespoons butter, at room temperature

1 teaspoon salt

1 teaspoon baking powder

2 pinches of cayenne pepper

In a medium-size, heavy saucepan over medium-high heat, bring the milk to a boil. Watch carefully—milk readily boils over. Stir in the cornmeal, and continue stirring. When the cornmeal thickens, reduce the heat to low, continuing to stir until very thick. Remove from the flame and let cool, stirring occasionally, until you can comfortably hold your hand on the bottom of the pot. Heat the oven to 375°F while the mixture is cooling. Butter an 8-by-8-inch baking dish. Add the eggs, butter, salt, baking powder, and cayenne to the cooled cornmeal mixture. Beat for several minutes with a wooden spoon, then scrape into the baking dish. Bake for 30 minutes, or until lightly puffed and set. Serve from the dish, using a large spoon.

VARIATIONS

If you're serving spoon bread by itself and want to punch up the flavor, you may stir grated cheese into the batter (and sprinkle more cheese over the top halfway through baking), or some freshly cooked corn kernels, or a little Green Chile Relish (page 251)…or all of the above.

Quinoa

serves 3 to 4

This delicate grain has sustained the Incas of Peru and other Andean peoples for millennia. Besides having a unique, herbal flavor, it is very high in protein and minerals. This plain recipe is a good introduction; if you like, augment in the same ways as rice: with more butter, sautéed onions, sliced scallions, garlic, herbs, or finely chopped toasted nuts.

1 cup quinoa

2 cups water

½ teaspoon salt

2 teaspoons butter

Put the quinoa in a screen sieve and rinse well under cold running water—this removes the bitter saponin that coats and preserves the grain. Put the quinoa, water, salt, and butter in a heavy, heat-conducting pot with a well-fitting lid and bring to a boil. Reduce the heat to medium, maintaining a lively simmer. Cover the pot and let the quinoa cook undisturbed for about 20 minutes, or until all the water is absorbed. You may also cook quinoa in the oven or in a rice cooker—see the basic Rice recipe, page 238.

Farro Salad with Cherry Tomatoes and Pecorino

serves 4 to 6

This bright summer picnic dish contains *farro,* a delicious grain that has recently enjoyed a revival in Italy. It is a form of emmer, quite similar to wheat, with a bit of the outer husk removed, a process called "semipearling." It is simply boiled in salted water, like pasta, until tender but toothsome. If whole, non-semipearled farro is what you have, it will take about twice as long to cook.

- **1 cup semipearled farro**
- **1 tablespoon salt, plus more as needed**
- **3 tablespoons extra-virgin olive oil**
- **2 handfuls arugula, washed and spun dry**
- **1 basket assorted cherry tomatoes, cut in half lengthwise**
- **2 to 3 ounces pecorino cheese, cut in very small dice**
- **2 to 3 sprigs mint, stems removed and coarsely chopped**
- **¼ cup finely diced red onion**
- **3 tablespoons balsamic vinegar**
- **juice of ½ lemon**
- **freshly ground black pepper to taste**

In a large saucepan, bring 2 quarts of water to a rolling boil. Add the farro and 1 tablespoon of salt. Reduce the flame to maintain a boil, and cook the farro, stirring frequently, until tender, but still firm (taste a few grains to determine doneness), about 20 minutes. Drain well, and spread the farro out on a tray. Drizzle with about half the olive oil, toss thoroughly to distribute the oil, and let cool to room temperature. In a large bowl, toss the cooled farro with the remaining olive oil, arugula, cherry tomatoes, pecorino, mint, onion, balsamic, lemon, and pepper. Taste for salt—it may need a little more. Taste for bright acidity, adding a little more lemon juice or balsamic vinegar, if necessary. Mound in a shallow bowl and serve at room temperature.

Clio's Stuffing

serves 6 to 8

I love participating in live theater; once, I appeared in Tina Howe's *One Shoe Off,* an absurdist comedy about a zany dinner party, where the hostess cooks a Thanksgiving menu because it's all she knows how to cook—and even then, she forgets to put the turkey in the oven. The character Clio, a young actress, pigs out on stuffing in the second act. She moans, "I can't stop eating this stuffing!" I made this recipe for our production of the play—I also played Clio's husband.

Stuffing is best baked in a dish, not inside the turkey. Turkey cooks more evenly when the main cavity is empty—by the time the stuffing in a stuffed turkey reaches a safe internal temperature, the turkey itself will be irredeemably overcooked.

Any bread that's not too sour (such as sourdough) or too sweet (such as sliced supermarket sandwich bread) makes great stuffing; the bread recipes in this book are ideal. I prefer bread that contains a good proportion of whole-wheat flour. You may use a blend of cornbread and regular bread (my usual practice for Deep Springs Thanksgivings), or use all cornbread—in that case, since cornbread is rich, use less butter to cook the onions and celery. There is no need to toast cornbread along with the vegetables—just crumble it coarsely and gently combine with the other stuffing ingredients. An all-cornbread stuffing is so Southern that it's usually called "dressing." The herbs may be varied—although sage is traditional, rosemary and thyme are excellent, too. Sautéed Mushrooms (page 135) are great in stuffing. You may include the giblets from the turkey, simmered until tender and chopped finely, if you opt not to use them in the gravy.

- **½ cup butter** *(1 stick)*
- **4 or 5 stalks celery, cut into large dice, plus some leaves, coarsely chopped**
- **1 fat yellow onion, cut into large dice**
- **1 teaspoon salt, plus a pinch or more as needed**
- **1 tablespoon finely chopped fresh sage** *(or 2 teaspoons dry rubbed sage)*

1 large loaf wheat bread, cut into cubes
¾ teaspoon freshly ground black pepper
about ¾ cup milk, heated, or turkey broth

Heat the oven to 375°F. Melt the butter over medium-high heat in a large, heavy skillet. When it sizzles, throw in the celery, celery leaves, and onion with ½ teaspoon of the salt. Cook, stirring frequently, until the celery and onion are soft. Add the sage with a pinch of salt and cook for a minute more. Add the bread cubes, stirring gently to incorporate everything. Continue to cook, letting the bread lightly toast in the skillet. Season with ½ teaspoon more salt and the black pepper. Taste—if the bread is on the sweet side, it might need more salt. Moisten the stuffing with about ¾ cup hot milk or turkey broth—it should be neither sopping wet nor dry. Taste for salt and pepper again. Arrange the stuffing in a buttered baking dish and bake until lightly browned on top. "What *is* it about this stuffing?" Clio asks, helping herself to more.

STUFFED WINTER SQUASH

A whole winter squash stuffed with this stuffing is very good, and not just for vegetarians. Stuffable varieties include turban, acorn, dumpling, red kuri, kabocha pumpkin, and table pumpkin. Heat the oven to 350°F. Carefully cut out the top of your squash around the stem, as though you were going to make a jack-o'-lantern, scoop out the seeds, rub the inner cavity with a little olive oil and salt, then gently pack in the hot stuffing, just after you've added the milk or broth. Replace the top, put the squash on a foil-lined baking sheet, and bake for 1½ to 2 hours, depending on the size of the squash, or until the squash is soft to the touch. Use the foil to carefully transfer the squash to a serving platter. To serve, remove the top and scoop from the inside, getting some of the squash's flesh along with the stuffing.

CHAPTER 13

SAUCES, RELISHES, PICKLES, & JAM

Often, you don't need a sauce; the food itself is delicious enough, flavorful and juicy enough, to stand alone, simple and unadorned. Much good food sauces itself. The rich, flavorful skin on roast chicken "behaves" like a sauce, its fatty, salty qualities enhancing the flavor of the meat. However, a sauce clearly expresses the cook's thoughtfulness and attention. A sauce might bring all the elements of a meal together or, in fact, might be the whole point of the meal (see Aioli, page 253).

Sauce recipes appear throughout this book, not just in this chapter. Frequently, the sauce is an integral part of a recipe; meat is often drizzled with its own pan juices, perhaps enriched with a little wine or butter. When a separate sauce is specific to a particular recipe, it is found next to that recipe: a cocktail sauce recipe follows Boiled Shrimp (page 227), brown butter is part of the Brussels sprouts recipe (page 123), lemon butter is included with the Artichokes (page 119), and a few of the soup recipes include their own specific garnishing sauce or relish. Versatile vinaigrettes and creamy dressings are found in the Salads & Dressings chapter, beginning on page 173.

This chapter includes tomato sauces for pasta and pizza; three different horseradish sauces for beef, fish, and vegetables; fresh salsa and guacamole; and marvelous recipes for silky New Mexico green and red chile sauces. Homemade mayonnaise and aioli are cornerstones of skillful cooking, and Lemon Butter sauce (page 252) employs a technique used in restaurant kitchens everywhere. Heaps of fresh herbs go into Salsa Verde and Chimichurri sauces (254 and 255).

Pickles, found toward the end of the chapter, enhance other foods on the plate in the same way a sauce does. The fruit jams are good on buttered toast, of course, but marmalade makes a great glaze for chicken (page 206), and quince jam enhances poultry or pork.

Dad's Steak Sauce

serves 2

Based on recollections vague and various, I've reconstructed a sauce my father made decades ago. It's extremely simple and quick to put together, melting into and magnifying the honest flavor of simple salted-and-peppered steaks. The garlic remains subtle, true to an era when garlic was permitted in American cooking but treated with caution, as if too much could cause harm, whereas fully crushing the garlic and letting it remain in the sauce will deliver a more powerful, modern punch. Pork chops, chicken breasts, burgers, and other simple meats may also be enhanced by this sauce.

1 small clove garlic

2 teaspoons Worcestershire sauce

2 teaspoons honey

¼ teaspoon soy sauce

¼ teaspoon cider vinegar

2 or 3 drops Tabasco or other hot sauce

pinch of salt

1 tablespoon cold butter

Lightly smash the garlic clove so it stays all in one piece. Put the garlic in a small skillet with the Worcestershire sauce, honey, soy sauce, vinegar, Tabasco, and salt. Bring just to a bubbling boil over a high flame, then remove from the heat. Let sit for 1 minute, then remove and discard the garlic. Add the cold butter. Swirl the pan, slowly melting the butter into the warm sauce. Return the pan to the lowest flame if there is not enough residual heat to melt the butter. Once the butter is all melted, whisk the sauce, if necessary, to remove any lumps or flecks of butter, and pour into a small serving dish. Keep the sauce slightly warm, and serve over warm steaks.

Tomato Sauce

makes about 4 cups; serves 4 to 6

This simple tomato sauce for pasta is quick, charged with garlic, and not too sweet. It glows with Italian red-pepper-flake warmth. Neither too thick nor too watery, it is a staple of my cooking at Deep Springs, suited to many purposes. It will keep, covered, in the refrigerator for several days before the garlic starts to taste tired. It also freezes well.

Generally speaking, canned tomatoes are a pure, sound, and consistent product; not bred for shipping or shelf life, tomatoes grown for canning are usually full-flavored, fully ripened, and processed soon after harvesting. If you have a bumper crop of garden-fresh, ripe summer tomatoes, make a couple of pounds of them into Tomato Concassé (page 148), substituting the concassé for the large can of diced tomatoes in this recipe. Or use the simpler Fresh Summer Tomato Sauce recipe on page 249.

2 tablespoons olive oil

2 or more large cloves garlic, finely crushed

¼ teaspoon dried oregano, crumbled

¼ teaspoon hot red pepper flakes, or more to taste

⅓ cup dry red wine

one 28-ounce can diced tomatoes in juice

one 15-ounce can tomato sauce

black pepper

¼ cup coarsely chopped fresh basil or ½ teaspoon sweet-smelling dried basil or dried marjoram

salt, if needed

CHAPTER 13: SAUCES, RELISHES, PICKLES, & JAM

LARGE QUANTITY RECIPE: MAKES ABOUT 2½ GALLONS; SERVES 40 TO 50

½ cup olive oil

2 to 3 entire heads of garlic, cloves peeled and finely crushed

1 tablespoon dried oregano, crumbled

2 teaspoons hot red pepper flakes, or more to taste

1½ cups dry red wine

two #10 cans *(each 6 pounds 6 ounces)* diced tomatoes in juice

one #10 can *(6 pounds 6 ounces)* tomato sauce

black pepper

1½ cups coarsely chopped fresh basil or 2 tablespoons dried basil

salt, if needed

Have the ingredients prepared, measured, and ready—they all go into the pot in rapid succession. Heat the olive oil in a large, heavy saucepot over medium-high heat until it shimmers. Stir the garlic into the oil with a wooden spoon, and cook until the sizzling bits of garlic turn from a translucent yellow to an opaque ivory color. It will release an explosion of aroma. Do not let the garlic brown. Immediately add the oregano and red pepper flakes, then the wine. Let boil for a moment, then add the diced tomatoes with their juice. Do not add the can of tomato sauce yet. Stirring occasionally, bring to a boil, then reduce the heat to a lively simmer and cook until the sauce is reduced a little, about 10 minutes. Stir in the can of tomato sauce, black pepper to taste, and basil. Heat through and taste, adding salt if necessary (the canned tomatoes usually contain enough).

THICK TOMATO SAUCE

This formula works well on pizza: instead of a large can of diced tomatoes, use a smaller, 15-ounce can, and include a 15-ounce can of tomato purée, adding it with the tomato sauce. (For a large-quantity batch, use one #10 can of diced tomatoes, one #10 can of tomato purée, and one #10 can of tomato sauce.)

Tomato Sauce with Meat

makes about 6 cups; serves 6 to 8

Ground beef tomato sauces have their place, but you'll love this one with ground pork. Italian sausage is the flavor inspiration, but actual sausage is too fatty. For best results, use coarsely-ground pork.

1 pound coarsely-ground pork

½ teaspoon crushed fennel seeds

¼ teaspoon hot red pepper flakes

¼ teaspoon salt

¼ teaspoon black pepper

1 recipe Tomato Sauce *(preceding recipe; household-quantity version)*

Before you begin making the tomato sauce, cook the pork: heat a wide skillet over medium heat. Put the meat in the skillet, gently breaking it up as it cooks. The heat should not be so high that the meat browns. When about half the meat still has its pink color, evenly sprinkle the fennel seed, red pepper flakes, salt, and pepper over it. Continue cooking until the pork is cooked through and well flavored, breaking it up into small chunks. (If there is a lot of fat, drain some of it off.)

Prepare the tomato sauce, stirring the pork in—juice and all—when adding the diced tomatoes.

Fresh Summer Tomato Sauce

makes 3 to 4 cups; serves 5 to 6

This sauce, though thin, is full of flavor. Instead of basil, you may add sprigs of fresh marjoram. To paraphrase St. Ignatius, *Add marjoram, Dei gloriam.*

2 pounds fresh, ripe, sweet summer tomatoes, trimmed of any bad spots and cut into large chunks

1 small onion, thinly sliced

2 sprigs fresh basil or marjoram

2 tablespoons olive oil

1 teaspoon salt, or more as needed

freshly ground black pepper

Heat the oven to 350°F. In a 9-by-13-inch or other wide, shallow baking dish, toss together the tomatoes, onion, basil, olive oil, salt, and pepper to taste. Bake in the oven, uncovered, for about 1½ hours, or until everything is bubbly and there are little browned bits of tomato and onion on the surface. Strain through a screen sieve into a large bowl. Using the back of a ladle, force as much of the tomato pulp as possible through the sieve and into the bowl. Scrape the pulp clinging to the outside surface of the sieve into the bowl. A hand-crank food mill works very well for this task. Stir the sauce and taste for salt and pepper.

Fresh Salsa

makes about 4 cups

Once, in a mischievous mood, making this salsa in the usual way in the Deep Springs kitchen, I noticed the big pile of jalapeño pith and seeds to be discarded. Instead of throwing them into the compost, I ground up this searingly hot material in the food processor, added a little of my prepared salsa so it looked right, and labeled it: "Warning: Extremely HOT Salsa! Eat at Your Own Risk!" Inevitably, and much to my amusement, the students ended up having a salsa-eating contest, complete with painful repercussions vividly reported the following day.

To dice a tomato, use a serrated knife; I prefer the long blade of an offset bread knife. For a mild salsa, use only the outside of the jalapeño or serrano chile, not any of the inside, light-colored pith. For a hotter salsa, include some of the pith.

Beware, when working with hot chiles, of getting the chile's volatile capsaicin oils on your hands. Just washing your hands with soap doesn't get it all off—as you'll find if you rub your eyes or other sensitive areas. The trick is to first rub your hands well with a spoonful of vegetable oil. The oil will dissolve the capsaicin. Then wash the oil off with soap.

3 to 4 large, red, ripe tomatoes (about 1½ pounds), **finely diced** (about 4 cups)

½ small white or yellow onion, finely diced (about ⅓ cup)

1 jalapeño or serrano chile, seeded and very finely minced (use more for extra heat)

½ cup coarsely chopped cilantro

1 small clove garlic, well crushed

juice of ½ lime, or more if needed

1 teaspoon salt, or more if needed

Combine all ingredients in a medium bowl. Taste for acidity, heat, and salt, adjusting as necessary.

GUACAMOLE

Mash about 6 large, perfectly ripe avocados with 1 cup of the fresh salsa above, plus the juice of another lime, another ½ teaspoon salt, 3 to 4 dashes of hot sauce, and (here's the secret) a small pinch of crumbled dried oregano. Don't mash the avocados too thoroughly—a little chunkiness is good. Taste for balanced salt and acidity. Serve with corn tortilla chips.

MEDITERRANEAN AVOCADO DIP

For a surprisingly delicious change, add ½ cup of coarsely chopped fresh mint to guacamole, and serve with oven-crisped triangles of wheat flatbread.

HORSERADISH-TOMATO RELISH

This light and sparkling salsa turns roast beef into a summer dish. It is also good with pot roast, pork chops, leg of lamb, and baked salmon. Omit the jalapeño and cilantro from the master salsa recipe. Use lemon juice instead of lime. Finely grate a generous amount of fresh horseradish—about ½ cupful—into the salsa. Add a good twist of black pepper.

Fresh Horseradish Cream

serves 4 to 6

This fluffy, creamy, sharp sauce is traditional with an English Roast Beef dinner (page 183), enhancing medium-rare slices of beef, rich Yorkshire pudding, and watercress. But it has other uses—a dollop is delicious in the center of a plate of sliced Marinated Beets (164), floating in a bowl of Russian Beef Borscht (186), or atop a chunk of Baked Salmon (222) with fresh dill and cucumbers.

4 ounces fresh horseradish, peeled and finely grated

1 cup cold heavy (whipping) **cream**

¼ teaspoon sugar

½ teaspoon salt

Combine the ingredients in a mixing bowl and whip (using an electric mixer, or by hand with a whisk) until soft peaks form. Taste for balanced salt, sweetness, and sharpness. Serve in a chilled silver dish, if you want to be especially English.

SLOVENIAN HORSERADISH SAUCE

This horseradish sauce is both leaner and smoother than the creamy English version above, and may be put to the same uses. In Slovenia, it's served with tender braised beef; traditionally the egg is cooked by simply dropping it into the pot with the beef for about 8 minutes. Mash about 4 ounces of finely grated horseradish with a hard-cooked egg yolk until the mixture is uniform, then season with salt and a few drops of red wine vinegar.

New Mexico Red Chile Sauce

makes about 4½ cups

The people of New Mexico cultivate a vibrant, distinct cuisine. The two fundamental sauces, the starting points for many traditional dishes, are red and green chile sauce. Red chile is almost always dried, while green chile is almost always fresh (or frozen or canned). Chiles not harvested green are allowed to stay on the plant a little longer. Once they redden, they are picked and dried. Though they are the same fruit from the same plant, red and green chile are very different in character and flavor. Chicken usually goes with green chile, while red meats are most often served with red chile, but often you'll find the opposite. Sometimes the green is hotter, sometimes it's the red. Often, it depends on your mood: the official New Mexico State Question, asked many times a day in restaurants all over the state, is "Red or green?"

Here is a beautiful, authentic, deeply flavored red chile sauce from my Aunt Mary Nell's recipe file— she was a great New Mexico cook. For Thanksgiving, many New Mexico families serve this sauce in addition to gravy, naturally resulting in day-after-Thanksgiving turkey enchiladas.

Although I usually make this sauce (and the following green chile sauce) for enchiladas (pages 96 to 98), they have many other uses. Both are superb drizzled over eggs; stirred into beans to make a simple chili; as a medium for braising chicken or beef (pages 212 or 184); or served alongside Skillet Cornbread (67), Polenta (242), Southern Spoon Bread (243), or any other dish containing corn. Try a plate of whole-wheat pasta tossed with garlic, sweet corn, sautéed summer squash, and cilantro, topped with either red or green chile sauce.

¾ to 1 cup pure ground New Mexico red chile (see Note)

2 cups water

2 cups chicken stock

6 tablespoons lard or vegetable oil

¼ cup all-purpose flour

4 cloves garlic, crushed

1½ teaspoons salt, or more as needed

⅛ teaspoon black pepper

Blend the chile, water, and stock in a medium saucepan. Bring to a boil, remove from the heat, and let sit for 20 minutes. In a small skillet over medium heat, melt the lard, blend in the flour and garlic, and cook this roux just until it turns from a pasty white color to a pale beige. Let it cool for a few minutes, then whisk it into the chile mixture. Add the salt, bring to a simmer, and cook the sauce for about 10 minutes. Add the black pepper—it may seem redundant to put pepper in chile sauce, but it brings the flavors into focus. Taste, adding more salt if necessary.

Note: This recipe requires *pure ground chile*, not chili powder. Chili powder is a spice blend containing cumin and oregano and sometimes salt in addition to mild ground red chile (see page 108). Instead of ground chile, you may use 14 to 16 whole dried chile pods: rinse briefly in cold water if they are dusty; remove the stems, seeds, and pale veins; and tear the chiles into 1-inch pieces. Put in a saucepan with the water and stock and bring to a boil. Remove from the heat and let sit for 20 minutes, then transfer to the jar of a blender. Quickly pulse the mixture several times—do not purée. Strain through a screen sieve. Using the back of a ladle, press as much flavorful chile pulp through the sieve as possible, then discard the skins. This more laborious method results in a very smooth sauce that is easier on some people's stomachs. Finish the sauce with the roux made from the lard, flour, garlic, salt, and pepper, as described.

New Mexico Green Chile Sauce

makes about 4 cups

See the description of chile sauces at the beginning of the preceding recipe. Green chiles must be roasted and carefully peeled before using. Many New Mexicans buy and roast bushels of fresh green chiles in late summer during harvest, freezing them whole in zipper-lock bags, 6 to 8 chiles to a bag. See the next recipe, Green Chile Relish, for detailed instructions on roasting chiles.

This recipe, also from my Aunt Mary Nell, makes enough sauce for Green Chile Enchiladas (page 97). Canned diced green chiles are fine to use, but be sure to pick out any bits of chile skin—these become apparent as you're stirring the sauce. If you have real, fresh, fire-roasted New Mexico green chiles that you've peeled and cleaned yourself, the resulting sauce will be very, very good indeed.

6 tablespoons lard or vegetable oil

¼ cup all-purpose flour

4 cloves garlic, crushed

½ cup finely diced onion

1 cup water

1 cup chicken stock

1½ cups roasted, peeled, seeded, and chopped New Mexico green chile *(from about 8 chiles; see following recipe)*

1 teaspoon salt, or more as needed

⅛ teaspoon black pepper

In a medium-sized, heavy saucepan over medium heat, melt the lard, blend in the flour, and cook this roux just until it turns from a pasty white color to pale beige. Add the garlic and onions and cook for about a minute more, then remove from the heat and let cool for about 5 minutes. Slowly whisk in the water and stock. Add the chiles and salt, bring to a simmer, and cook gently for about 15 minutes. Add the black pepper, bringing the flavors into focus. Taste, seasoning with more salt if needed.

Green Chile Relish

makes about 1 cup; serves 4 to 6

This simple mixture of chile, garlic, and salt is the most direct green chile experience, though in New Mexico they don't call it "relish"—it's just "green chile." It is addictively good in many things: in Southwestern and Mexican dishes, to be sure, but also mixed into mayonnaise for sandwiches, swirled into corn soup (page 128) or Corn Chowder (89), or stirred into a small carton of sour cream for an extraordinary dip for tortilla chips. Add a spoonful to Blue Cheese Dressing (175) or cornbread batter (67).

If New Mexico chiles are unavailable, roast a blend of three more commonly available green chile varieties to echo the distinctive heat, flavor, and complexity of New Mexico chiles: a few mild Anaheims, a few zippier pasilla chiles (larger and darker green), and a couple of small, hot serrano chiles.

Roasting chiles is similar to roasting peppers (see page 140). Arming yourself with tongs, roast 6 to 8 large chiles directly over the gas flame of your stove, or put them on a sheet pan and roast them close to your oven broiler, or, most deliciously, char them over a hot charcoal fire. Whichever heat source you use, allow the chiles to blacken and char evenly on all sides, but always watch them carefully. Do not let them burn so much that the outer skin turns ashy gray. When they are evenly charred, put them in a heatproof glass bowl, and cover with a dampened paper towel. Seal the container and let the chiles sweat for 20 to 30 minutes. Being careful not to lose any of the juice that has accumulated, break open the chiles and allow any juice inside to run back into the bowl. Using your hands, remove the skin, stems, and most of the seeds. Do not rinse the chiles in running water—a few bits of charred skin are part of the charm, as well as a few seeds. Sometimes it helps to wipe your hands with paper towels a couple of times during the process. Put the peeled, seeded chiles on a cutting surface. (Strain and save the flavorful juice for another use, or for stirring into the finished relish if you would like a wetter consistency.) Chop the chiles finely with a good pinch of salt and a well-crushed clove or two of garlic. Put the relish into a bowl and serve. It will keep, refrigerated, for a few days.

Lime-Pickled Red Onions

These crisp, refreshing onions are good company to rich Mexican meat dishes (see Mexican Braised Beef, page 187), tacos, beans, avocados, and enchiladas, and their dazzling color enlivens any table. Slice red onions thinly and soak in enough fresh lime juice to just cover them. Cover and let macerate in the refrigerator for several hours. The onions will turn bright pink. Bring to room temperature to serve.

Yogurt-Shallot Sauce

Need a great-tasting, quick, not-too-rich, versatile sauce? This yogurt sauce is very good on fish, chicken, ground meat dishes, vegetables, or grains, or tossed with freshly boiled potatoes for an excellent, simple potato salad. Start with plain, whole-milk yogurt. Stir in salt and pepper to taste, and a small, minced shallot for every cup of yogurt. (Sometimes I grate the shallot—quick and effective, but fumy.)

Lemon Butter Sauce

serves 6

When a rich, warm butter sauce is wanted for lean, white fish, this is it. Though not traditional, it is also a superb sauce for Asparagus Pasta (page 121). The more sophisticated classic French *beurre blanc* is made with champagne vinegar in the reduction instead of lemon juice, and no zest. For a *beurre rouge,* use a fruity, bright-tasting red wine and red wine vinegar. For other variations, you can add a tablespoon or so of finely chopped herbs, or a tablespoon of crushed dry green peppercorns.

1 shallot, minced

¼ cup dry white wine

finely grated zest and juice of 1 lemon (about ¼ cup fresh lemon juice)

1 cup cold unsalted butter (2 sticks), **cut into 1-tablespoon pieces**

¼ teaspoon salt, or more if needed

Put the shallot, wine, 3 tablespoons lemon juice, and half of the lemon zest in a small, nonreactive saucepan. Bring to a boil over high heat, and boil until the liquid is reduced to about 2 tablespoons. Reduce the heat to low. Whisk the cold butter into the warm liquid, 1 or 2 tablespoons at a time. Let each addition of butter incorporate before adding the next. The butter will emulsify into a creamy, rich sauce. Add ¼ teaspoon salt and taste—the richness of the butter should be balanced by the tartness of the lemon. Add more salt if the sauce is bland or too tart, more lemon juice if sharpness is needed. For a more potent lemon flavor, add the rest of the lemon zest.

Mayonnaise

makes about 2 cups

This is a flavorful whole-egg mayonnaise. The eggs are lightly soft-boiled, then "pickled" with generous amounts of mustard, vinegar, and salt before the oil is added. It will keep, refrigerated, for about 2 weeks.

2 eggs

2 teaspoons mustard of choice: yellow, Dijon, coarse, or brown

1 tablespoon plus 2 teaspoons red wine vinegar

¾ teaspoon salt

2 or 3 dashes Tabasco or other hot sauce

1½ cups sunflower oil, peanut oil or other light vegetable oil

Lightly soft-boil the eggs: put the uncracked eggs in a small pan of cold water, bring to a boil, remove from the heat, and let stand, covered, for exactly 2 minutes. Pour off the hot water and rinse the eggs in cold water. Let them stand in cold water for 2 to 3 minutes. Using a small spoon, gently break the eggs and scoop the white and yolk into the jar of a blender. Add the mustard, vinegar, salt, and hot sauce. Cover the blender and blend the egg mixture on the lowest setting for about 10 seconds. For the mayonnaise to emulsify properly, begin adding the oil to the egg in a very thin stream. After a third of the oil has been added, increase the speed of the blender to medium and add the rest of the oil in a thin stream. If the mayonnaise gets so thick that the oil just pools at the top, transfer the mayonnaise to a bowl, and incorporate the rest of the oil gradually with a whisk until the mayonnaise is smooth. Spoon the mayonnaise into a clean jar and chill to thicken before using.

GARLIC MAYONNAISE

Traditional aioli (see recipe below) is always hand-made, with garlic pounded to a smooth purée and slowly "mounted" with olive oil, but this lighter homage to aioli will not disappoint garlic lovers. To the master mayonnaise recipe, add 1 or 2 well-crushed garlic cloves to the blender with the eggs, and use olive oil for ½ cup of the oil, adding it after the light oil. If you want a thinner consistency, stir in a few drops of water.

MUSTARD MAYONNAISE

Mix Dijon mustard and mayonnaise in any proportion. Mustard is virtually fat-free, while mayonnaise is almost all fat; mustard is spiky and sharp, mayonnaise is billowy and enveloping: strike the appropriate balance. This combination is good with vegetables, hot or cold fish, hot or cold meat, burgers....

Aioli

makes about 2½ cups

When I demonstrated the preparation of aioli to a cooking class at Deep Springs, it was such a hit that several of the students whipped up their own big batch and threw an aioli party in the Boardinghouse kitchen late that night!

Aioli is wonderful with any simple, savory food. For a traditional southern French meal, serve a generous bowl of aioli surrounded by an array of cooked and raw vegetables, boiled potatoes, and simply cooked fish or shellfish. You may use the Garlic Mayonnaise variation above with very good results, but here is a more authentic, unctuous aioli, made in a mixer. The tireless will enjoy making it by hand with a whisk.

2 large cloves garlic

¾ teaspoon salt, plus more as needed

3 egg yolks

2 teaspoons Dijon mustard

2 teaspoons red wine vinegar

2 cups extra-virgin olive oil

¼ cup water

juice of ½ lemon

Split the garlic cloves lengthwise, and inspect the inner sprout in each clove—if it is distinct and green in color, remove it—it tastes bitter and harsh. If it's too small or too tender to be easily removed, it's fine to leave it in. Crush the garlic finely in a mortar with a pinch of salt until it's completely smooth, or use the back edge of a knife. Put the garlic, yolks, mustard, vinegar, and ¾ teaspoon salt in the bowl of an electric mixer, and mix well with the whisk attachment. Drizzle 1 cup of the oil into the garlic mixture in a very thin stream while the mixer is running. The mixture will lighten in color and thicken. Mix in the water to loosen the mixture. Reduce the speed of the mixer, and drizzle in the remaining 1 cup olive oil in a thin stream. Mix in the lemon juice. Taste for seasoning. If you want to serve the aioli with something rich, like Baked Salmon (page 222), or fried food, thin it with a little more water and lemon juice.

CHAPTER 13: SAUCES, RELISHES, PICKLES, & JAM — 253

Toasted Nut Olive Oil

Olive oil infused with toasted nuts enhances summer green beans, summer squash, beets, winter squash, broccoli, cauliflower, and many other vegetables. It may be used to make a vinaigrette (page 173) or as the basis for Salsa Verde (see below). Walnuts, almonds, pecans, pine nuts, or hazelnuts may be used. Lightly toast about a cupful of your chosen nut (page 176). While the nuts are still warm, chop finely, and stir them into a cupful of olive oil. Add a pinch of salt and pepper, and let sit at room temperature for several hours. Stir well before using.

Pesto

makes about ⅔ cup; serves 2 to 3

I prefer making pesto in small batches as needed, using a large stone mortar and pestle (see illustration on page 247)—the weight of the pestle does most of the work. If you're serving pesto with pasta, retain a cupful of the pasta cooking water before draining the pasta, and don't rinse the pasta after cooking. Toss the hot pasta together with the pesto in a large bowl—allow 3 to 4 tablespoons of pesto per serving. Use a little of the reserved water to adjust the moisture and "sauciness."

2 cloves garlic

about ¼ teaspoon salt

2 tablespoons pine nuts or coarsely chopped walnuts

1 bunch fresh basil *(3 cups loosely packed leaves)*, **coarsely chopped**

about ⅓ cup extra-virgin olive oil

2 tablespoons freshly grated Parmesan cheese

black pepper

Split the garlic cloves lengthwise, and inspect the inner sprout in each clove—if it is distinct and green in color, remove it. If it's too small or too tender to be easily removed, it's OK to leave it in. Pound the garlic in a large mortar with the salt until it is smooth. Pound in the nuts until smooth, then the basil, with a pinch more salt. Adding olive oil as necessary, keep pounding until the basil is reduced to a chunky purée. Add the Parmesan and dilute with enough olive oil to make a runny consistency. Add pepper to taste.

You may also make the pesto in a food processor, but the flavors are subtly truer when the garlic and basil are pounded, rather than cut by whirling knives. Using the food processor, first thoroughly process the garlic, half the oil, the walnuts, and salt to a smooth purée. Next, add the basil (coarsely chopped) and pulse the machine until the basil is mostly incorporated. Add the Parmesan, remaining oil, and pepper to taste, and pulse to a chunky purée.

Meyer Lemon–Olive Relish

makes about 1 cup; serves 2 to 3

This fresh, herb-packed, lemony sauce is well suited to the Crispy Pan-Fried Chicken on page 209. It's also superb drizzled over a plate of baked mild white fish, new potatoes, and artichoke hearts. It's closely based on Italian *salsa verde,* traditionally used to accompany roast pork. For classic *salsa verde,* omit the lemon peel and olives from this recipe, and add 3 finely chopped anchovy fillets. For an excellent *dill salsa verde,* substitute fresh dill for half the parsley, and drizzle it over a plate of baked fish, boiled potatoes, and carrots.

Meyer lemons, ubiquitous in parts of China and prized by Californian cooks, have a complex floral fragrance and sweeter juice than regular lemons. The soft, aromatic peel can be eaten as well—it is sweet, not bitter like that of other citrus.

1 Meyer lemon or 1 regular lemon

1 large shallot, finely diced

1 tablespoon red wine vinegar

pinch of salt, plus more as needed

2 teaspoons capers, chopped

1 medium bunch parsley, very finely chopped *(about ¾ cup)*

½ cup extra-virgin olive oil, or more if needed

¼ cup pitted green olives, coarsely chopped

freshly ground black pepper

If using a Meyer lemon, remove about three-fourths of the peel with a sharp paring knife—the outer zest as well as the white pith. Cut the peel into fine dice and put it into a medium bowl. If using a regular lemon, finely grate the zest into a medium bowl. Put the shallot in the bowl, and squeeze the lemon juice over the peel and shallot. Add the vinegar and a generous pinch of salt. Let sit for about 10 minutes. Add the capers, parsley, oil, olives, and salt and pepper to taste. To retain the bright, fresh flavor of the parsley, this sauce must be served soon after it's mixed. If necessary, you may make the different components of the sauce in advance: the lemon, shallot, vinegar, and salt in one bowl, and the capers, parsley, oil, and olives in another. Combine just before serving, with pepper and more salt, if needed, to taste. Or just assemble the sauce as directed, but don't stir it until serving time.

Green Chimichurri Sauce

makes about 1 quart; serves 10 to 12

This sauce, the punchier South American cousin of the Italian *salsa verde* above, is marvelous with grilled meat of all types. It could be made in a food processor, but I prefer the more intricate, layered flavor that results from chopping the ingredients by hand.

- 8 cloves garlic, well crushed
- ½ cup red wine vinegar
- 2 small sweet onions, finely chopped
- ½ teaspoon salt
- 4 to 5 green serrano chiles, most, but not all, of the seeds and white pith removed, very finely minced
- 1 bunch flat-leaf parsley
- 1 bunch cilantro
- 3 to 4 sprigs fresh oregano, or 1 tablespoon dried oregano
- ½ teaspoon freshly ground black pepper
- generous 1 cup extra-virgin olive oil

Mix the garlic, vinegar, onions, salt, and minced serrano chiles in a bowl. Stir from time to time while preparing the herbs.

Wash the herbs well and discard the thickest stems. Using a big, sharp knife and methodical patience, chop the herbs very finely. Mix the chopped herbs with the pepper and oil. Keep the vinegar mixture and the herb mixture separate until you are ready to serve the sauce. You can even layer the herb and oil mixture atop the vinegar mixture in a quart jar, then stir the two together at serving time.

Dill Pickles

makes 2 quarts

These fresh, crunchy dill pickles are based on a recipe in *Saving the Season*, a splendid, intelligent book on home preserving, written by my friend and Deep Springs classmate Kevin West (DS'88). At your summer farmers market, choose slender, bumpy Kirby cucumbers; fresh, aromatic dill heads; and, if possible, new-crop garlic. During pickle-making time, wild fennel is typically in bloom on roadsides and pathways. I often can't resist using a few fennel blossom heads in place of the flowering dill; the wild-fennel flavor has dilly undertones.

- 3 pounds pickling cucumbers
- ¼ cup kosher salt, plus an additional ½ teaspoon
- 6 cups lukewarm water
- 2 teaspoons whole coriander seeds
- 1 teaspoon whole fennel seeds
- 3 large flowering dill heads
- 3 cloves garlic, split in half
- 1¾ cups apple cider vinegar *(5% acidity)*

Scrub the cucumbers under cold running water. Trim a little of the tough skin off the tip-ends of each cucumber, then slice in half lengthwise. In a large bowl, dissolve the ¼ cup of kosher salt in the water, and add the coriander, fennel, dill heads, and cucumbers. Cover the bowl and let sit for 24 hours, stirring a couple of times.

The next day, scald two quart mason jars and their lids with boiling water, and let air-dry. Measure and reserve 2¼ cups of the cucumber brine. Using a slotted spoon, remove the cucumbers from the remaining brine, and pack them neatly into the jars. Strain the seeds and dill from the brine, and divide between the jars. Add 3 garlic clove halves to each jar. In a saucepan, bring the reserved 2¼ cups brine and the vinegar to a boil. Stir in the additional ½ teaspoon of salt, and pour the brine over the cucumbers. Put the lids on the jars, let cool to room temperature, and refrigerate. The pickles will be ready after 1 week.

Pickled Summer Vegetables

makes about 8 cups

These sprightly, colorful vegetables are irresistible. Try Baked Salmon (page 222) topped with avocado slices, with a big spoonful of these vegetables—and a little of their juice—strewn over and around. Or chop them up and mix into tuna, egg, or potato salad.

BRINE

1½ cups red wine vinegar

3½ cups water

½ cup kosher salt

1¼ cups sugar

1 teaspoon whole black peppercorns

2 bay leaves

6 whole cloves

½ teaspoon mustard seed

½ teaspoon allspice berries *(about 10)*

¼ teaspoon hot red pepper flakes

VEGETABLES

1 medium carrot, peeled and cut on the diagonal into ⅛-inch slices

1 green zucchini, cut in half lengthwise, then cut on the diagonal into ¼-inch slices

1 yellow zucchini, cut in half lengthwise, then cut on the diagonal into ¼-inch slices

1 fennel bulb, trimmed and cut into ¼-inch slices

4 ounces green beans, tops and tails cut off, cut on the diagonal into thirds

4 ounces yellow wax beans, tops and tails cut off, cut on the diagonal into thirds

1 small red onion, cut into ¼-inch slices

1 bunch red radishes, trimmed and cut into quarters

1 small cucumber, halved and cut on the diagonal into ¼-inch slices

To make the brine, bring the vinegar, water, salt, sugar, and spices to a boil in an enameled or stainless-steel pot (the vinegar will adversely react with other metals). Boil for 1 minute. Drop the carrots into the boiling brine, cooking just until tender-crisp (20 to 30 seconds after the brine returns to a boil) and removing with a slotted spoon to a heatproof glass or plastic container (you may use 2 quart-size canning jars). Repeat with the remaining vegetables, one variety at a time, in the order given. Cut as specified, the vegetables should each take about 30 seconds to cook. The beans might require more time (taste to tell), and the cucumber should cook for only about 10 seconds. Between batches of vegetables, remove the pan from the heat if necessary to keep the brine from becoming overly concentrated. When the vegetables are all cooked, boil the brine for 30 seconds longer, then pour it over the vegetables. Let cool to room temperature, then refrigerate. They are ready to eat the following day and will stay fresh tasting for several days.

PICKLED WINTER VEGETABLES

Use the following combination of vegetables in the colder months:

2 medium carrots, peeled and cut on the diagonal into ⅛-inch slices

1 fennel bulb, trimmed and cut into ¼-inch slices

1 small red onion, cut into ¼-inch slices

1 small head cauliflower, cut into ¼-inch-thick florets

1 bunch red radishes, trimmed and cut into quarters

Blond Barbecue Sauce

makes 1⅓ cups sauce; serves 6 to 8

This sweet, spicy sauce is easy to throw together with kitchen staples and makes a wonderful glaze for pork or lamb ribs (or chicken). Just salt the meat, slather with sauce, and roast on a baking sheet at 325°F, basting occasionally with the sauce, until the meat is tender and the glaze is golden brown.

½ cup honey

¼ cup Dijon mustard

¾ cup apricot jam *(or tart plum jam; see page 259 for recipes)*

3 tablespoons red wine vinegar

1 tablespoon salt

½ teaspoon black pepper

¼ teaspoon cayenne pepper

Combine everything in a pan and heat, stirring, until bubbling and the preserves are dissolved.

Oven Applesauce

Some years, the Deep Springs orchard produces an extraordinary bumper crop of peaches, pears, and, most of all, apples. Other years, a late freak snowstorm will demolish all the blossoms, and there will be no fruit. Once, during a bumper year, longtime Deep Springs farmer and fellow alumnus Andy Jennings (DS'89) walked into the Boardinghouse kitchen bearing an armload of apples — an assortment of the orchard's finest. We cut into each one, tasting their various sweet, crunchy qualities—some were harder, some were denser, some were tarter, and one was spicy, with a hint, almost, of cayenne.

Any kitchen besieged with apples, as mine was that year, should have this easy recipe in its arsenal. This applesauce is perfect to accompany pork chops, or potato pancakes, or both at the same time, or to be eaten all by itself.

Core Golden Delicious, McIntosh, Gravenstein, or other sweet-tart apples, cut them into big chunks, and put them in a baking dish, crowding them slightly. Dot with a little butter and sprinkle with a small pinch of salt. Cover the dish tightly with aluminum foil (shiny side facing in) and bake at 400°F until the apples are completely soft, 30 to 40 minutes. Remove the foil and gently stir the applesauce to a medium chunky consistency. Scrape into a storage container, let cool, and chill. The applesauce's full flavor often does not develop until the following day.

You may peel the apples, but the peel contributes a deeper apple flavor—the large pieces of peel are easily picked out once the applesauce has cooled. Don't be alarmed if some apple varieties turn pink when cooked into applesauce. Quince, apple's old relative, has aromatic, astringent, yellow-white flesh that turns anywhere from pale pink to wine-dark crimson through long cooking (see page 260).

Cranberry Sauce

makes about 2½ cups; serves 10 to 12

For some people, the full glory of cranberry sauce is realized not at Thanksgiving dinner but the following day, in the requisite cold turkey sandwich, thickly overlaying—not mixed into—the mayonnaise.

one 12-ounce bag fresh cranberries

¾ cup sugar, or more as needed

⅛ teaspoon salt

½ teaspoon finely grated tangerine or orange zest

Rinse the cranberries in a colander, discarding any soft ones. Drain thoroughly and put in a medium-sized, heavy saucepan. Add the sugar, salt, and zest and heat on a medium-high flame, stirring frequently. When the cranberry sauce begins to boil, reduce the flame to medium, and cook for 8 minutes more, stirring frequently. Taste for sweetness—I like it quite tart; add more sugar to taste. Cover and remove from the flame. Let sit, covered, for 10 minutes. Stir again and transfer the sauce to a medium bowl. Cool, cover, and refrigerate. Bring to room temperature before serving.

CRANBERRY RELISH

This is the classic uncooked relish; many people like both kinds for Thanksgiving. Make it the Tuesday of Thanksgiving week, as it needs a full 2 days to mellow. Use the same ingredients as in the master recipe, but for the citrus element, use 2 whole tangerines or 1 small orange. Rinse the cranberries and discard any soft ones. Drain thoroughly. Rinse the tangerine and cut into chunks, removing any seeds. Pulse cranberries, sugar, salt, and tangerine—peel and all—to a coarse purée in a food processor, or put through a meat grinder. Cover and chill for 48 hours before using. After 24 hours, taste the relish—if you think it needs to be sweeter, stir in a tablespoon of additional sugar. Bring to room temperature before serving.

Pickled Plums

makes 4 quarts

There was always a cut-glass bowl of pickled peaches at Thanksgiving when I was growing up. They were from a can but were different from regular canned peaches—they were whole, with their pit, and the syrup had a whiff of vinegar and spice to cut the sweetness. My first year away from home, cooking Thanksgiving dinner in the Boardinghouse kitchen as a Student Cook at Deep Springs, I found a recipe for those peaches and made it using plums instead. Later, I found the same recipe, handwritten, in my grandmother Nell's big recipe box.

These are wonderful with turkey or ham. The treatment also lends itself to many other types of fruit (see the following list), and the syrup curiously enhances Baked Custard (page 304).

Sweet, firm-fleshed French or Italian-style "prune" plums, arriving in the market in late summer, are preferred in this recipe. Tarter, earlier, more delicate varieties of plum might fall apart in the pickling but are still delicious.

2 cups apple cider vinegar

4 cups sugar

2 cinnamon sticks

1½ teaspoons whole cloves

¾ cup water

4 quarts fresh small prune plums or other fruit (see list below), **washed**

Bring the vinegar, sugar, cinnamon sticks, cloves, and water to a boil in a large, heavy pot and boil for 5 minutes. Remove and set aside the cinnamon sticks and cloves. Poach the plums in the syrup in batches. When the syrup returns to a boil after the fruit has been added, let boil for about 30 seconds, longer for larger plums. Using a slotted spoon, gently remove the fruit to sterilized glass jars or any heatproof glass or plastic container.

When all the plums are poached, return the whole spices to the syrup, boil for a minute more, then pour the syrup and spices over the fruit. When cool, refrigerate. The fruit will be ready to eat the next day, but it is best after a week or two.

OTHER PICKLED FRUIT

The following fruit may be pickled in the same way:

- cherries, sour or sweet varieties (whole; use allspice berries and black peppercorns instead of cinnamon and cloves; this is particularly good accompanying Gin Chicken Liver Pâté, page 217)
- apricots (whole)
- peaches or nectarines (whole if small, halved or quartered if large)
- figs (halved; omit spices but add a few slices of lemon to the liquid)
- Bosc or Asian pears (thick slices; add a piece of peeled fresh ginger to the liquid along with the spices)

Pickled Black Grapes

makes 1 quart

These uncooked pickled grapes take only moments to make, and are a delicious accompaniment to grilled sausages or other flame-kissed meats.

about 1½ pounds black or red seedless grapes

1 bay leaf

½ teaspoon whole black peppercorns

1 cup boiling water

6 tablespoons sugar

2¼ teaspoons kosher salt

½ cup red wine vinegar

Wash the grapes well, drain thoroughly, and pluck them from their stems. With a small, sharp knife, cut each grape in half lengthwise. Pack the grapes into a quart jar (or two pint jars). Put the bay leaf and the peppercorns into a heatproof glass measuring cup and cover with the boiling water. Let steep for about two minutes, then add the sugar and salt, stirring to dissolve. Stir in the vinegar, then pour the warm brine, including the bay leaf and peppercorns, into the jar with the grapes. Put the lid on and let cool, then refrigerate. They're good the day they are made, but they will last for months in the refrigerator.

Kevin's Apricot Jam

makes 3 pints

We tend to think of jam-making as a big, all-day project, requiring crates of fruit to be simmered slowly in giant pots in a sweltering hot kitchen. But, in fact, to best "capture" the intense, fresh flavor and color of good fruit, jam is best cooked rapidly, in small, manageable batches. To further streamline the process, I don't put finished jars of jam through a boiling-water bath to make them shelf-stable; I simply store the jars in the refrigerator. Please see the information about sugar and its crucial role in jam-making, page 43.

Apricots have a fleeting, early-summer season—when you come across good ones, get a big bag and hurry home to make this silky, simple jam, from my Deep Springs classmate Kevin West (DS'88) and his book *Saving the Season*. It can be used in the Blond Barbecue Sauce recipe (page 257), or as an accompaniment to Pound Cake (288) or Cheesecake (274), whether combined with fresh apricots or on its own, or it may simply be spooned over cottage cheese.

For excellent *plum jam,* choose sweet-tart plums, such as the Santa Rosa variety. Plums do not give up their pit as neatly as apricots; to prepare plums for jam, I use a small, sharp knife to cut neat "lobes" of the flesh away from the pit. Then I take small handfuls of the pits and squeeze them very well over the bowl, using both hands, to get as much of the extra-tart pulp clinging to the pit as possible. Tart plum jam makes an excellent Jam Pie (page 273).

3½ pounds sweet summer apricots

2 tablespoons freshly-squeezed lemon juice

2¾ cups sugar

Using a small knife, halve the apricots and remove their pits. Cut each half in half again. In a large bowl, toss the apricots together with the lemon juice and sugar, and let sit for at least 30 minutes. Turn the mixture into a large, heavy, nonreactive pot (I use a large enamel Dutch oven), and quickly bring to a boil over a high flame, stirring often. After the jam reaches a boil, let it continue to cook and reduce, stirring frequently, for 8 to 10 minutes. Remove from the heat, and let the jam sit a few minutes longer, stirring once or twice. Pour the hot jam into 3 sterilized pint jars (or 6 half-pints), cap with sterilized lids, let cool to room temperature, then store in the refrigerator.

Marmalade

makes about 4 pints

Marmalade on hot buttered toast, with tea, is one of Britain's gifts to the world. But marmalade has other uses—it makes a superb glaze for chicken (page 206), and it lifts the peanut butter sandwich into a whole new realm. Make marmalade in January or February, when citrus fruits are at their peak. This method discards some, but not all, of the bitter white pith of the citrus fruit, allowing the fruit's friendlier flavors a clearer voice. The ginger and tea could be considered optional but highly recommended—they beautifully enhance the strong citrus flavors.

- **3 pounds mixed citrus fruit: about three-quarters sweet varieties** *(oranges, mandarins, kumquats)*, **and one-quarter sour/bitter varieties** *(lemons, Seville oranges, limes, grapefruit)*
- **1 ounce** *(a 2- to 3-inch piece)* **fresh ginger, peeled and finely grated**
- **3 cups water**
- **3 Earl Grey teabags**
- **about 5 cups sugar**

Wash the citrus in cool water and towel dry. Remove all colored outer zest of all the thick-rinded fruit with a vegetable peeler. Kumquats, Meyer lemons, and small mandarins or tangerines need only to have their seeds removed but may otherwise be used whole. Patiently cut this zest into small, confetti-like strips with a sharp knife. Using a serrated knife, cut off and discard most, but not all, of the bitter white pith from the fruit (if you're including a grapefruit in the mix, remove all of its white pith, as it can be especially bitter). Chop the flesh of the fruit coarsely, removing any seeds.

Save all of the juice. Mix the citrus zest, citrus flesh, citrus juice, ginger, and water together in a large, heavy, nonreactive (stainless-steel or enamel) pot, and bring to a boil. Reduce the heat slightly and let boil, stirring frequently and making sure nothing sticks to the bottom of the pot, for about 20 minutes, or until the bits of zest are tender (taste to find out). Add the teabags, remove from the heat, and let the tea steep for 5 minutes. Remove the teabags and immediately add the sugar to fix the fresh tea flavor, stirring to dissolve. The amount of sugar depends on your own taste and on the tartness of the fruit; fruit that is more sour and bitter will need more.

Briskly simmer the marmalade, stirring frequently, until it is thick enough to form a gel when a small spoonful is put on a chilled plate and cooled for a few minutes in the refrigerator. Pour the hot marmalade into sterilized jars, cap with sterilized lids, let cool to room temperature, then store in the refrigerator.

Quince Jam

makes about 2½ cups

The full promise of quince, a very old ancestor of apples and pears, is revealed only through long and careful cooking. This Greek-style jam is good on buttered toast or biscuits, or stirred into yogurt, or with cream cheese (or other, sharper cheese) on crackers, but it's particularly good with rich meats such as pork, duck, turkey, or lamb. Another way to use quince is to slice a peeled, seeded quince into paper-thin slices and combine it with apples for Apple-Walnut Crisp (page 277) or Apple Pie (page 265).

- **1 large, fragrant quince** *(enough to yield 3 cups diced)*
- **10 whole cloves**
- **2 strips lemon zest**
- **juice of ½ lemon**
- **⅓ cup sugar**
- **⅔ cup honey**
- **2 pinches of salt**

Rinse the quince and peel carefully with a vegetable peeler or sharp paring knife—quinces have strangely hard flesh; the knife can skip and jag. Save a few large strips of peel to deepen the flavor of the jam. Cut the quince lengthwise into quarters, then cut each quarter crosswise in half. Cut out the seeds and the tough, pale flesh around the seeds. Cut the quince into small dice. Put in a medium-sized, heavy, nonreactive saucepan with the reserved strips of quince peel and the cloves, lemon zest and juice, sugar, honey, and salt. Bring to a simmer over medium heat, stirring occasionally. Lower the heat and simmer very slowly for about ½ hour—the quince will turn a lovely red-pink color. Cool the jam slightly and pick out and discard the quince peels, lemon zest, and most of the cloves. Pack into a sterilized jar, cool, and refrigerate.

CHAPTER 14

PIES & FRUIT DESSERTS

Pie, like jazz or Shaker furniture, is a time-honored, uniquely American craft, a definitive statement of generosity and skill. No European-style tart contains as much fruit as an American pie. It is a fundamental part of our national traditional meal, Thanksgiving. In Bishop, California (Deep Springs' closest big town), the Labor Day Tri-County Fair always features a homemade pie contest judged by a plain-spoken, grandmotherly expert in front of a live audience. It's a rare and beautiful sight: more than a hundred freshly baked pies, each one unique, lined up on picnic tables. One year, Deep Springs garden manager Karen Mitchell won the grand prize, a 4-day ocean cruise for two, with her lemony white peach pie, using peaches from a pampered tree in the Deep Springs orchard.

At Deep Springs Thanksgivings, with many visitors, we sometimes make and consume forty or more pies. Some years, I collect the community's several school-age children and instruct them to quickly bring all the pies out onto the freshly cleared serving table in the dining room. At this much-anticipated moment, the drama heightened by playing Wagner's "Ride of the Valkyries" or the opening of Orff's *Carmina Burana* loudly on the Boardinghouse stereo, the room always erupts into applause.

The first part of this chapter aims to demystify the piemaker's craft, with recipes for Apple Pie and many other double-crust fruit pies. Recipes for single-crust pies follow, including chocolate and vanilla cream pies. The second part offers fruit desserts simpler than pie, including irresistible crisps, puddings, shortcake, and cobblers. The chapter ends with many suggestions for fruit served in its solitary glory or minimally adorned.

Butter Piecrust

makes one 10-inch double-crust pie shell or two 10-inch single-crust pie shells

Finishing up my college degree after Deep Springs, I spent much time learning how to make good pies with my friend Elge (raised on an apple and cherry farm in rural upstate New York, she knew her pie). We fantasized about opening a pie bakery in New York City.

Producing light, flaky piecrust is tricky—its reputation for being difficult is somewhat justified. However, once you get a feel for it and understand the reasons behind the various steps, there is no reason to fear it.

Piecrust owes its character to the fat it contains, and from how the fat is incorporated. Many prevailing recipes call for vegetable shortening, a highly processed substance quickly falling out of favor in American kitchens. It gives a good, flaky texture, thanks to its high melting point, but it is difficult to digest and has no flavor whatsoever. Many recipes calling for shortening also call for a little butter, to remedy the blandness. Pork lard, for which shortening was originally developed as a substitute, makes superlative piecrust, especially for apple, pear, and cherry pies. Like shortening, it has a high melting point. Its flavor is neutral, but it nonetheless gives pies a rich, rounded character. But many people today are afraid or unwilling to eat lard piecrust, and virtually all store-bought lard is full of preservatives.

Vegetable oil piecrust has a loyal following. The dough is quite easy to mix and roll—good for beginners, or for when you just don't have the fortitude to make a traditional flaky crust. For single-crust pies, an oil crust is perfectly fine. But its texture will be sandy, rather than flaky, as it is chunks of solid fat layered in the dough that create flakes.

I believe all-butter crusts are the best compromise. They are delicate, tender, flavorful, and every bit as flaky as shortening or lard crusts. A bite of butter piecrust tastes delicious all by itself. What is the best way to incorporate your chosen fat into the dry flour? Although many recipes specify using two knives or a pastry blender, I find that I have the most direct control over the process when I use my hands.

When flour comes into contact with water and is then worked, it develops springy, elastic, tough strands of wheat protein called *gluten*. With yeast bread, you want maximum gluten development—that's why you knead bread dough. With cookies or cake, you want very little gluten development, which is why you typically mix such doughs or batters "only until combined." With piecrust you want enough developed gluten in the structure to create flakes but not so much that the dough becomes tough. In this recipe, some of the butter becomes fine enough in the mixing process to moisten the flour, but there are also pea-sized chunks of butter in the finished dough. When the piecrust is rolled out, the chunks flatten into tiny disks. In the heat of the oven, these disks melt, creating a flaky structure.

Then there is the question of liquid: too much makes for a tough crust; too little, and the crust is difficult to roll out. The amount of liquid can never be exactly specified, as the moisture content of flour and fat varies. Most recipes call for ice water, but my grandmother, brilliantly, always used freshly squeezed orange juice, which provides a touch of acidity that inhibits excessive gluten formation. Elaine Teel, wife of the longtime Deep Springs mechanic, used 7-Up. I have used milk and lemonade. Once I considered using beer. It seems that when you use some kind of slightly acidic liquid, you can make a crust that is easy to roll but still tender and flaky. Orange juice also gives a bit of extra sweetness and contributes a rich, golden color. It will not impart a discernible orange flavor to your piecrust.

The last important point: a *glass pie plate* ensures a golden-brown bottom crust. Ten-inch glass plates seem to have become the standard, so that is the size specified for all these recipes. For single-crust pies, I use a regular 10-inch pie plate—one that holds 5 cups of water all the way up to the rim before it starts to overflow. For double-crust fruit pies, I use a slightly deeper 10-inch pie plate—one that holds 7 cups of water before it starts to overflow.

This recipe makes a generous amount of dough, enough for one double-crust pie or two single-crust pies. After trimming your finished crust, you will have a handful of dough left over. Squeeze this into a ball, roll it out into a rectangle, sprinkle it well with cinnamon sugar, roll it up like a jelly roll, and slice into ¼-inch-thick pinwheels. Bake them on a greased baking sheet while baking your pie, for 10 to 15 minutes. Cook's treat.

2¾ cups all-purpose flour

1 teaspoon salt

¼ teaspoon sugar

1 cup (*2 sticks*) **plus 1 tablespoon cold unsalted butter**

6 to 8 tablespoons cold orange juice, ideally freshly squeezed

Combine the flour, salt, and sugar in a large bowl. Slice the cold butter into the dry mixture, tossing to coat the slices. Using your hands, rapidly work in the butter, breaking up large chunks of butter and smearing clumps of the mixture between your palms until the visible chunks of butter are pea-sized. To keep the texture of the crust light and flaky, do this quickly—don't let the mixture warm up from the heat of your hands. As the flour is moistened by the butter, it will darken slightly in color, turning from cream white to pale ivory.

Sprinkle in the orange juice and, using a fork, lightly toss and combine just until the mixture coheres. *Do not overmix.* If the mixture seems dry, sprinkle in a bit more orange juice, but do not add so much that the dough becomes sticky. Divide the dough into 2 balls of equal size. Wrap each tightly in plastic wrap and press each wrapped ball into a disc. Let the dough rest in the refrigerator for at least 1 hour (this lets the gluten relax), then unwrap it and roll it out on a floured surface with a floured rolling pin, flipping it frequently so it doesn't stick, to a large circle. When rolling the dough, apply outward, not downward pressure. Rolling piecrust takes practice.

Fold the circle gently in quarters, lay it in a 10-inch glass pie plate, and unfold. Gently press the crust into the pie plate so there are no air pockets. Patch any holes or tears with bits of excess dough, lightly moistened with water. If your crust is for apple pie or another double-crust fruit pie, roll out the second (top) crust, and reserve it between 2 sheets of plastic wrap. Proceed as directed in the recipe.

If your crust is for a single-crust pie, trim off all but an inch of overhanging crust. Fold the crust in toward the rim, and crimp the edge of the crust in an attractive, even scallop pattern. This is not merely a decorative touch; the structure of this fluted edge helps keep the crust from sliding down off the rim. For single-crust pies, freeze the crust for at least an hour before proceeding—this discourages the crust from shrinking during baking. (This step may also benefit double-crust pies, though it is not as crucial.) Now you have a pie shell ready for filling and baking.

To *pre-bake* or *blind-bake* your single crust (as for lemon meringue or cream pies), remove the crust from the freezer and heat the oven to 325°F. Gently press a sheet of aluminum foil over the inner surface of the piecrust, shiny side down. Fill the foil with about 4 cups of dry beans to weight the crust as it bakes. Bake the crust, checking frequently, until it is an even, pale gold color from the fluted rim to the bottom, 30 to 35 minutes. Carefully remove the beans and foil and return the crust to the oven for 8 to 10 minutes more, to crisp the inner surface of the crust. Cool completely—the pie shell is now ready to be filled.

LARD PIECRUST

This is especially good with apple and pear pies in the colder months, and with cherry and other stone fruit pies in summer. Use the preceding method and ingredients, substituting ¾ cup (6 ounces) of cold lard for the butter. A little more liquid might be needed. To render your own lard, obtain some fresh pork kidney fat and use the instructions for rendering beef tallow in the Deep Springs Soap recipe on page 343. One Deep Springs Thanksgiving, in the piecrust for some of the pies, we used home-rendered lard from a student's rural Wisconsin family.

VEGETABLE OIL PIECRUST

This doesn't need the prolonged resting periods that a butter crust demands. For a single crust, mix ½ teaspoon salt and 6 tablespoons sunflower oil or other vegetable oil into 1⅔ cups all-purpose flour (part whole wheat is good here) until smooth. With a fork, mix in 2½ tablespoons orange juice or other sweet-tart liquid (see the introduction to the master recipe). Mix just until blended—6 or 7 strokes. The dough will at first seem gooey and far too wet, but soon the flour will absorb the liquid. Pack it into a ball, wrap with plastic wrap or wax paper, and refrigerate for about 30 minutes. Roll out between two sheets of wax paper.

VEGETABLE OIL–BUTTER PIECRUST

This hybrid recipe is not quite as flaky as an all-butter crust but is certainly easier and quicker, and still very good. Mix 1 teaspoon salt, 6 tablespoons sunflower oil, and 6 tablespoons softened butter into 2 ¾ cups all-purpose flour (part whole wheat is good here) until uniformly crumbly (there will be bits of butter in the mix). With a fork, mix in 5 tablespoons orange juice or other sweet-tart liquid (see the introduction to the master Piecrust recipe). Mix just until blended. Divide the dough into 2 balls of equal size, wrap well with plastic wrap, press the dough into discs, and refrigerate for about 30 minutes. Roll out each crust between two sheets of wax paper.

DOUBLE-CRUST PIES

Apple Pie

serves 6 to 8

The best apple pies are made during apple-harvesting season. Certain apple varieties are ready for harvest in late summer, while others continue through the fall. Granny Smith and Golden Delicious are both good, tart, commonly available cooking apples, and may be used alone or in combination. Other excellent regional varieties include Gravenstein, Sierra Beauty, McIntosh, Winesap, Arkansas Black, and Pippin. If you are going to the trouble of making a pie by hand, in-season fruit is essential. Once I made an apple pie in July, with heavily waxed Granny Smith apples from a supermarket. Those apples had likely been in cold storage for most of the year by that point. They cooked down to a very scant, lackluster brown sludge. What was I thinking? That time of year, I should have made berry or peach pie.

Apple pies should be generously filled. The apples cook down and the top crust buckles beautifully. I like a tart pie and use the lesser amount of sugar; you may add more if you like. I like the subtle flavor profile of the spices listed; you may change the amounts or the combination to suit your taste.

Despite the time-honored pie-with-ice-cream tradition, I've always thought the coldness and extreme sweetness of ice cream compete with the subtle goodness of a homemade pie. I suggest serving your pie simply, with lightly sweetened whipped cream flavored with vanilla (1 cup heavy cream, 1 tablespoon sugar, ¼ teaspoon vanilla extract).

1 recipe Butter Piecrust *(page 263)*, **rolled out for a double-crust pie**

FILLING

7 or 8 large, tart cooking apples, peeled, cored, and sliced ¼ inch thick *(for 7 or 8 cups sliced apples)*

grated zest and juice of ½ lemon

1 tablespoon all-purpose flour, or as needed

⅓ to ½ cup firmly packed brown sugar

¼ teaspoon ground cinnamon

¼ teaspoon ground nutmeg

¼ teaspoon ground allspice

1 to 2 teaspoons finely grated fresh ginger, or ¼ teaspoon ground ginger

pinch of salt

ASSEMBLY

1 egg, separated

1 tablespoon butter, cut into small pieces

1 tablespoon milk

1 tablespoon granulated *(white)* **sugar**

As you slice the apples, toss them with the lemon juice in a large bowl to sharpen the flavor and prevent them from browning. Judge the juiciness of the apples—very juicy apples will need about ½ tablespoon more flour than specified; drier, greenish apples will need about ½ tablespoon less flour.

The following assembly instructions apply not only to Apple Pie, but to all of the double-crust fruit pie recipes in this chapter:

Toss the fruit and all filling ingredients together until thoroughly combined. Taste the fruit, adding more sugar if it's tart.

Heat the oven to 425°F. Have the unbaked pie shell ready. Before filling the pie shell, lightly beat the egg white and brush the entire inside surface of the pie shell with it, making sure to apply a good coat around the rim. This will help keep the bottom crust from getting soggy and will also "glue" the top and bottom crusts together at the edge. Give the fruit mixture a final toss, then dump it into the prepared pie shell, arranging it in an even layer, slightly mounded in the center. Dot the fruit with the butter and gently drape the top crust over the fruit, pressing around the rim to fuse the top and bottom crusts. Using a knife or kitchen shears, cut away the excess crust around the rim, leaving about 1 inch of overhang. Working your way around the pie, fold the overhanging crust over the edge of the bottom crust and crimp, pinching the folded edge of the crust in an attractive, even scallop pattern. This is not merely a decorative touch; the structure of this fluted edge helps keep the crust in place.

Make an egg wash: thoroughly mix the egg yolk and milk together in a small bowl. Brush the top and rim of the pie with the egg wash, sprinkle the top with the sugar, and cut 3 vents in the center of the top crust. Bake in the center of the oven for 15 minutes, then turn down the oven temperature to 325°F. Bake for 40 minutes longer, rotating the pie once or twice, or until the fruit is thoroughly cooked, and the juices are thickened and bubbly. Test by inserting a small knife into a vent; the fruit should offer no resistance when pierced. Peering through a vent, you should be able to see bubbling juices. The bottom of the pie should be golden—this is why you use a glass pie plate. Let the pie cool on a rack for a couple of hours at least, until room temperature or barely warm—the juices will continue to thicken as the pie cools.

APPLE AND CANDIED ORANGE PIE

A friend says the oranges in this pie turn the apples into peaches. Navel oranges have firm flesh that holds together well in this treatment. Rinse an orange well, and take several strips of zest (using a vegetable peeler) from the top and bottom of the orange—from its "polar regions," if you will. Cut 6 thinnish (less than ¼ inch thick) crosswise slices from the orange's "equatorial region," carefully removing any seeds. Cover the slices with 1½ cups water in a small saucepan, add the strips of zest, and squeeze in all the juice from the ends. Bring to a boil, reduce the heat, and simmer, stirring very gently from time to time, for about 20 minutes, or until the orange rind can be easily pierced with the tip of a knife. Add 1 cup sugar to the saucepan, and simmer for 30 minutes more. Carefully drain the 6 orange slices and layer them among the apples in the master Apple Pie recipe. No need to include the grated lemon zest the recipe calls for. Reserve the orange-flavored syrup for another use. This pie is a great conclusion to a winter holiday lamb dinner; for a festive occasion, add a little splash of cognac to the whipped cream.

APPLE AND CANDIED LEMON PIE

Proceed as directed for Apple and Candied Orange Pie, using a large, fragrant lemon.

APPLE AND QUINCE PIE

Peel and core a quince, slice it paper-thin, and add it to the apples. This addition will deepen, hauntingly, the flavor of the apples.

BACON-APPLE PIE

This pie is the crowning glory of an old-fashioned ranch breakfast, when you want to pull out all the stops. Omit the butter, lemon zest, and salt from the filling ingredients in the master Apple Pie recipe. Cut 5 to 6 ounces of bacon (4 to 5 thick strips) into small dice. Fry slowly in a small skillet until much of the fat is rendered out and the bacon is beginning to crisp. Drain on a paper towel, then toss the bacon with the apples and proceed with the remainder of the recipe.

Other Double-Crust Fruit Pies

(All serve 6 to 8; use the master Apple Pie recipe for assembly instructions)

Pear Pie

This is one of my favorite pies. Ripen Bosc pears on your kitchen table for several days, until their brown skin takes on a golden hue and a matte finish, then make this pie. Follow the assembly and baking instructions in the master Apple Pie recipe.

1 recipe Butter Piecrust *(page 263)*, **made with a small portion of whole-wheat flour**

FILLING

7 ripe Bosc pears, peeled, cored, and sliced ½ inch thick

grated zest and juice of ½ lemon

pinch of cinnamon

1 teaspoon grated fresh ginger

1½ tablespoons flour

⅓ cup brown sugar

pinch of salt

ASSEMBLY

1 egg, separated

1 tablespoon butter, cut into small pieces

1 tablespoon milk

1 tablespoon sugar

Blackberry Pie

Pure summer celebration in a flaky crust! For pies using summer fruit, quick-cooking tapioca gives a cleaner-tasting result than flour; cornstarch is the next best option. Follow the assembly and baking instructions in the master Apple Pie recipe.

1 recipe Butter piecrust *(page 263)*

FILLING

6 cups blackberries *(include a few underripe ones to deepen the flavor)*

grated zest and juice of ½ lemon

1 tablespoon merlot wine *(optional)*

3 tablespoons quick-cooking tapioca

½ cup sugar

pinch of salt

ASSEMBLY

1 egg, separated

1 tablespoon butter, cut into small pieces

1 tablespoon milk

1 tablespoon sugar

Blueberry Pie

Lime juice and zest curiously enliven the blueberry flavor. Follow the assembly and baking instructions in the master Apple Pie recipe.

1 recipe Butter piecrust *(page 263)*

FILLING

6 cups blueberries *(include a few underripe ones to deepen the flavor)*

grated zest and juice of 1 small lime

3 tablespoons quick-cooking tapioca

⅓ cup sugar

pinch of salt

ASSEMBLY

1 egg, separated

1 tablespoon butter, cut into small pieces

1 tablespoon milk

1 tablespoon sugar

Peach, Nectarine, Apricot, or Plum Pie

Pies made with stone fruit are one of summer's finest culinary pleasures, but the amount of sugar can vary widely. Yellow peaches and nectarines are tarter than white varieties and will require less lemon juice and more sugar, while white peaches and nectarines need much more lemon juice, and a more restrained hand with the sugar. Rub peaches with a cloth under cold running water to remove the fuzz; they need not be peeled. Apricots may taste very sweet when fresh, but "tarten" as they cook. For an excellent plum pie, use sweet Italian-style prune plums. All pies made of stone fruit have their silkiest texture the day they're baked. Follow the assembly and baking instructions in the master Apple Pie recipe.

1 recipe Butter piecrust *(page 263)*

FILLING

5 to 6 cups pitted peaches, nectarines, apricots, or plums, cut into large chunks

grated zest and juice of ½ lemon

3 tablespoons quick-cooking tapioca

⅓ to ½ cup sugar

¾ teaspoon ground cinnamon

¼ teaspoon ground nutmeg

¼ teaspoon ground allspice

1 to 2 teaspoons finely grated fresh ginger, or ¼ teaspoon ground ginger

pinch of salt

ASSEMBLY

1 egg, separated

1 tablespoon butter, cut into small pieces

1 tablespoon milk

1 tablespoon sugar

Diana's Cherry Pie

Sour cherries, so beloved in pie that they're also known as pie cherries, possess an extraordinary flavor, quite distinct from the sweet varieties. They are small and fragile, their season is short, and their pale juice leaves stubborn stains, but if you can find them, they are worth the effort. My sister Diana makes this in the early summer in Oregon, using sour cherries from the tree in her yard, pitting them with a big paper clip. Follow the assembly and baking instructions in the master Apple Pie recipe; if you like, create a lattice-top crust, so the cherry filling shows through.

1 recipe Butter piecrust *(page 263)*

FILLING

6 cups pitted sour cherries

¾ cup sugar

½ teaspoon almond extract

3 tablespoons quick-cooking tapioca

pinch of salt

ASSEMBLY

1 egg, separated

1 tablespoon butter, cut into small pieces

1 tablespoon milk

1 tablespoon sugar

Rhubarb Pie

This pie is beautiful with a lattice-top crust, the better to show off the red rhubarb. Include strawberries if you must; rhubarb alone is more beguiling. Follow the assembly and baking instructions in the master Apple Pie recipe.

1 recipe Butter piecrust *(page 263)*

FILLING

5½ cups sliced, unpeeled red rhubarb

¾ to 1 cup sugar

½ teaspoon cinnamon

2½ tablespoons quick-cooking tapioca

pinch of salt

ASSEMBLY

1 egg, separated

1 tablespoon butter, cut into small pieces

1 tablespoon milk

1 tablespoon sugar

Single-Crust Pies

Lemon Meringue Pie

serves 6 to 8

Meringue topped virtually any sort of pie in our grandmothers' day. Today, lemon meringue is the sole survivor of this tradition—the lightness of meringue marries beautifully with a tart lemon filling. Many recipes for meringue call for a hefty dose of sugar, giving the whites good stability but making the pie quite sweet for my taste. Here, a layer of dry white breadcrumbs (undetectable in the finished pie) absorbs excess moisture from the tender, lightly sweet meringue.

The tart lemon curd is also good by itself, on French toast with berries, spread onto biscuits or scones, or between the layers of a cake. Replacing a couple of tablespoons of the lemon juice with fresh lime juice will curiously pique the lemon flavor without announcing its own presence.

For best results, whip the egg whites for the meringue at the same time the lemon filling goes on the heat. The filling should be piping hot to help the bottom of the meringue set.

½ recipe (single crust) Butter Piecrust (page 263), blind-baked

FILLING

6 egg yolks (save the whites for the meringue; see Note)

2 whole eggs

¾ cup sugar

1 tablespoon finely grated lemon zest (from about 3 lemons)

¾ cup plus 2 tablespoons fresh lemon juice (from 4 to 5 lemons)

⅛ teaspoon salt

2 tablespoons butter, cut into small pieces

MERINGUE

6 egg whites, at room temperature

¼ cup sugar

⅛ teaspoon fresh lemon juice

pinch of salt

¼ teaspoon vanilla extract

¼ cup panko crumbs or other dry, white breadcrumbs

Heat the oven to 350°F, and have the baked piecrust ready. When separating eggs, be careful with any whites intended for beating: even a tiny speck of egg yolk or grease will prevent them from beating properly. To make the filling, in a medium bowl, thoroughly whisk together the egg yolks, whole eggs, and sugar until completely uniform. In a medium-sized, heavy saucepan, combine the egg mixture with the lemon zest, lemon juice, and salt. Add the butter, and set the pot over low heat. (If possible, start whipping the egg whites for the meringue now; see the next paragraph.) Gently heat the mixture, whisking frequently, to 170°F, or until hot and thick. For stirring, alternate between a wooden spoon (to scrape the thickened mixture from the bottom of the pot) and a whisk (to dissolve lumps).

As the lemon mixture starts heating up, make the meringue: in a perfectly clean metal or glass bowl, using an electric mixer, beat the egg whites. When they begin to foam, add the sugar, lemon juice, salt, and vanilla. Beat until soft peaks form, then beat just a moment more, until the meringue is between the soft-peak and stiff-peak stages. Let the meringue sit while you finish cooking the filling.

As soon as the lemon filling is ready, spoon it into the crust and smooth the top. Scatter the panko crumbs evenly over the filling—this layer will absorb excess moisture from the meringue (a common problem with lemon meringue pie). Spoon the meringue in globs all over the lemon filling, gently spreading it all the way to the crust, sealing in the lemon filling completely. Swirl the meringue in big swirls, creating peaks and valleys. Don't fuss over it too much. Bake in the oven until the meringue is thoroughly golden on top, 15 to 20 minutes. Let the pie cool completely, about 2 hours, and serve at room temperature. Serve this pie just as it is—no accompaniment or final garnish is necessary.

Chocolate Cream Pie

serves 8

This delectable, old-fashioned pie has offered succor to many a homesick Deep Springs student.

½ **recipe** *(single crust)* **Butter Piecrust** *(page 263)*, **blind-baked**

FILLING

1¼ **cups firmly packed brown sugar**

3 **tablespoons cornstarch**

½ **teaspoon salt**

½ **cup plus 1 tablespoon unsweetened cocoa powder** *(preferably dark or Dutch-processed)*

3 **cups whole milk**

3 **egg yolks**

2 **tablespoons butter**

1½ **teaspoons vanilla extract**

TOPPING

1 **cup heavy** *(whipping)* **cream**

1½ **tablespoons granulated** *(white)* **sugar**

¼ **teaspoon vanilla extract**

dark chocolate for shaving over the top

Have the baked piecrust ready. To make the filling, in a medium-sized, heavy saucepan, mix the brown sugar, cornstarch, salt, and cocoa powder. Gradually stir in the milk. Over medium heat, bring the mixture to a boil, whisking frequently. Beat the egg yolks in a bowl, whisk in some of the warm chocolate mixture, then whisk the yolks into the remaining chocolate mixture in the pan. Slowly bring back to a gentle boil and cook for 1 minute, stirring frequently. For stirring, alternate between a wooden spoon (to scrape the thickened mixture from the bottom of the pot) and a whisk (to dissolve lumps). Remove from the heat and add the butter and vanilla. Let cool for about 10 minutes, then pour into the baked pie shell. Let cool completely, then chill.

To make the topping, whip the cream with the sugar and vanilla, using an electric mixer, until almost stiff but still supple. Spread the cream over the pie, not too fussily but completely covering the chocolate filling. Make swirls and peaks and valleys. Using a vegetable peeler, generously shave dark chocolate shavings all over the surface of the cream.

Custard Cream Pie

serves 8

This old-fashioned pie celebrates the simple goodness of eggs, cream, butter, and milk.

½ recipe *(single crust)* **Butter Piecrust** *(page 263),* **blind-baked**

FILLING

- **⅔ cup sugar**
- **¼ cup cornstarch**
- **⅛ teaspoon salt**
- **4 large egg yolks**
- **2½ cups whole milk**
- **3 tablespoons cold butter, cut into 3 or 4 pieces**
- **2 teaspoons vanilla extract**

TOPPING

- **1 cup heavy** *(whipping)* **cream**
- **1½ tablespoons granulated** *(white)* **sugar**
- **¼ teaspoon vanilla extract**

Have the baked piecrust ready. To make the filling, sift the sugar, cornstarch, and salt together. In a medium-sized, heavy saucepan, beat the egg yolks until smooth, then add the milk and beat together until uniform. Pour in the sugar mixture, and stir to dissolve. Put the pan over medium heat and slowly bring to a simmer, stirring very frequently. For stirring, alternate between a wooden spoon (to scrape the thickened mixture from the bottom of the pot) and a whisk (to dissolve lumps). As soon as the mixture begins to bubble gently, reduce the flame to low. Cook for a minute, stirring constantly, then remove from the heat. Stir in the butter slowly, one piece at a time, then add the vanilla. Pour the hot custard into the baked pie shell. Let cool to room temperature, then chill.

To make the topping, whip the cream with the sugar and vanilla, using an electric mixer, until almost stiff but still supple. Spread the cream over the pie, not too fussily but completely covering the filling. Make swirls and peaks and valleys.

BANANA CREAM PIE

Slice and layer 2 to 3 large, perfectly ripe bananas (they should have a few brown speckles and no green at the stem) with the hot custard filling. Shave bittersweet chocolate over the whipped cream topping.

BANANA PUDDING

For a good old-fashioned banana pudding, layer sliced bananas, Vanilla Wafers (page 327), and the master Custard Cream Pie recipe's hot custard filling in a tall glass bowl or trifle dish. Chill overnight, then top with whipped cream.

Pumpkin Pie

serves 6 to 8

Large jack-o'-lantern pumpkins are bred for size, not flavor. For pumpkin pie, use small pumpkins bred for sweet, flavorful meat. The Japanese kabocha pumpkin, squat and heavy, with a dark green outer rind, is excellent for pumpkin pie: its sweet, velvety, dense flesh does not need the final drying step, and it mashes beautifully into a stringless purée. Other types of hard winter squash make good pies—the difference between pumpkin and squash is quite subtle—and yes, you may still call it pumpkin pie. For a *breakfast pumpkin pie,* reduce the sugar to about ⅓ cup, and use some whole-wheat flour and a little wheat germ in the crust.

- **½ recipe Butter Piecrust** *(page 263)***, rolled out for a single-crust pie**
- **1 small sugar pumpkin or other sweet-fleshed winter squash, enough to yield 2 cups purée** *(or one 15-ounce can pumpkin)*
- **1 teaspoon ground cinnamon**
- **¼ teaspoon ground cloves**
- **¼ teaspoon ground allspice**
- **2 teaspoons finely grated fresh ginger** *(or ¼ teaspoon ground ginger)*
- **¾ cup firmly packed brown sugar**
- **3 eggs**
- **¼ teaspoon salt**
- **1½ cups evaporated milk** *(one 12-ounce can)*

FOR SERVING

barely sweetened whipped cream flavored with vanilla extract

Have the unbaked pie shell ready. Heat the oven to 375°F. Cut the pumpkin in half, remove the seeds and stringy material, and put cut side down on a foil-covered baking sheet. Bake until the flesh is completely soft, about 45 minutes, depending on the thickness of the flesh. If the flesh is juicy (this depends on the variety), it needs to be dried out slightly. Scoop the flesh from the shells back onto the baking sheet, mash into an even layer, and return to the oven. Bake until the pumpkin is drier and denser, about 20 to 30 minutes. Measure out 2 cups.

Heat the oven to 400°F. In a medium bowl, mix the spices and sugar with the warm pumpkin, beating well to break up any pumpkin lumps. Let cool slightly. Beat in the eggs, then the salt and milk, whisking until uniform. Pour into the unbaked shell. Bake for 10 minutes, lower the oven temperature to 300°F, and bake until the filling is set but still slightly jiggly in the center and the crust is golden on the bottom, about an hour more. Let cool to room temperature and serve with barely sweetened vanilla-flavored whipped cream.

Sweet Potato Pie

serves 6 to 8

This is an outstanding Thanksgiving pie—although it resembles pumpkin pie, the flavoring is quite different. Accompany with barely sweetened, vanilla-flavored whipped cream, laced with a spoonful of bourbon, if you wish.

½ recipe Butter Piecrust *(page 263)*, **rolled out for a single-crust pie**

about 3 orange-fleshed sweet potatoes or yams, enough to yield 2 cups

½ cup firmly packed brown sugar

1 tablespoon finely grated fresh ginger, or ½ teaspoon ground ginger

¼ teaspoon ground nutmeg

2 eggs, lightly beaten

¼ teaspoon salt

1¼ cups half-and-half

¼ cup bourbon

½ teaspoon vanilla extract

Have the unbaked pie shell ready. Heat the oven to 400°F and roast the sweet potatoes whole on a foil-covered sheet until they are completely soft. Let cool until you can handle them, remove the skin, mash well, and measure out 2 cups. In a medium bowl, combine the warm sweet potatoes with the brown sugar, ginger, and nutmeg, beating well to break up any lumps. Beat in the eggs, salt, half-and-half, bourbon, and vanilla. Pour into the pie shell, and bake for 10 minutes. Lower the oven temperature to 325°F and continue baking until the filling is set, 45 minutes to an hour. The filling will be slightly puffed around the edges and barely firm in the center. Serve slightly warm or at room temperature.

Pecan Pie

serves 8 to 10

Here is a wonderful, old-fashioned version of this classic, rich Southern pie. If you dare, make the crust with lard (page 264) or better yet, with the extra bit of beef tallow you happen to have left over from soapmaking (page 343). Cane syrup or golden syrup provides a deeper, truer sweetness than the more ubiquitous corn syrup. Cane syrup is found in the American South, and many variations of it (such as golden syrup) are common in Canada, England, and much of northern Europe.

Cutting the pecans in half lengthwise is a chore, but they look more attractive than if they were simply chopped, and the finished pie will slice more neatly. This sweet, rich pie really only needs a cup of strong coffee for accompaniment, but for festive occasions, you can't go wrong with a dollop of barely-sweetened, bourbon-laced whipped cream atop.

½ recipe Butter Piecrust *(page 263)*, **or Lard Piecrust** *(264)*, **rolled out for a single-crust pie**

4 eggs, at room temperature

1 cup cane syrup or golden syrup

¾ cup sugar

¼ cup butter, melted

2 teaspoons vanilla extract

¼ teaspoon salt

1½ cups pecan halves *(about 5 ounces)*, **each halved lengthwise**

Heat the oven to 425°F. Have the unbaked pie shell ready. Beat the eggs slightly in a medium bowl. Add the syrup, sugar, butter, vanilla, and salt. Stir in the pecans and pour into the pie shell. Bake for 15 minutes, then reduce the oven temperature to 350°F. Bake for another 30 to 35 minutes, until the filling is set—a silver knife, inserted near the center, should come out clean, with only a buttery film.

Rhubarb Custard Pie

serves 6 to 8

This excellent pie will convince even those who are dubious about rhubarb. Though traditionally baked with a lattice top crust, I prefer it in just a single crust—the red rhubarb forms a beautiful mosaic-like pattern. A Deep Springs student's aunt sent me this recipe after the family visited and cooked with us in the Boardinghouse kitchen. "Tom," she wrote on the back of the recipe card, "this pie is awesome."

½ recipe Butter Piecrust *(page 263)*, **rolled out for a single-crust pie**

1¼ cups sugar

¼ cup all-purpose flour

¾ teaspoon ground nutmeg

⅛ teaspoon salt

3 eggs, lightly beaten *(my friend Elge likes to add an extra yolk)*

¼ teaspoon vanilla extract

1½ pounds red rhubarb, unpeeled, cut diagonally into thin slices *(4 cups)*

1 tablespoon butter, melted

Have the unbaked pie shell ready. Heat the oven to 425°F. Blend the sugar, flour, nutmeg, and salt together in a medium bowl. Add the eggs, vanilla, rhubarb, and butter, and stir to combine. Pour into the pie shell. Bake for 15 minutes, then reduce the oven temperature to 325°F. Bake for 40 to 45 minutes longer, or until the filling is set, the rhubarb is tender, and the crust is browned on the top and bottom. If the pie's top is browning too much, lay a sheet of aluminum foil over the top, shiny side up. Let cool completely, or until just warm, and serve plain or with whipped cream.

Jam Pie

serves 6 to 8

My mother still talks about a delicious pie her frugal mother once made during the World War II years, using up odd bits of jam and jelly from several jars. Tart Plum Jam (page 259) is very good in this pie.

½ recipe Butter Piecrust *(page 263)*, **rolled out for a single-crust pie**

3 eggs, at room temperature

1⅓ cups sour cream

3 tablespoons butter, melted

2 cups great-tasting, tart jam: 1⅓ cups for the pie, about ⅔ cup for the topping

1 teaspoon vanilla extract, or a combination of vanilla and almond extracts

4 teaspoons sugar

¼ teaspoon salt

4 teaspoons cornstarch

Have the unbaked pie shell ready. Heat the oven to 350°F. In a medium bowl, lightly beat the eggs, then mix in the sour cream, butter, 1⅓ cups jam, and vanilla until the mixture is uniform. Whisk together the sugar, salt, and cornstarch in a small bowl until no lumps remain, and blend thoroughly into the jam mixture. Pour into the pie shell and bake for 30 minutes. Turn down the oven temperature to 325°F and bake for another 15 to 20 minutes, until the filling is puffed around the edges and just barely set in the center. Let cool completely. Just before serving, spread the remaining ⅔ cup jam over the top of the pie.

Maple Syrup Pie

serves 8 to 10

I prefer dark grade-B maple syrup, with subtle but deliciously bitter notes, to the lighter varieties. For several years at Deep Springs we mail-ordered giant tins of this syrup from Maine. This unusual, rich pie is excellent served with fresh fruit and whipped cream.

½ recipe Butter Piecrust (*page 263*)**, rolled out for a single-crust pie**

2 eggs

1 egg yolk

3 tablespoons all-purpose flour

1 teaspoon salt

2 cups dark maple syrup

1 cup heavy (*whipping*) **cream**

1½ teaspoons apple cider vinegar

Have the unbaked pie shell ready. Heat the oven to 425°F. Beat the eggs and yolk together briefly in a medium bowl. Add the flour and salt, beating well. Add the syrup, cream, and vinegar. Pour into the pie shell and bake for 10 minutes. Reduce the oven temperature to 325°F, then bake for 40 minutes more, or until the filling is slightly puffed and bubbly. Let the pie continue to set up and cool completely— 2 or 3 hours—before slicing.

Aunt Lela's Buttermilk Pie

serves 8 to 10

This rich pie is best served with only a cup of good, strong coffee. My Great Aunt Lela brewed her coffee strong by pouring it back through the grounds— only twice for herself, but three times for company.

I entered this pie in the Professional Baked Goods division at the Tri-County Fair in Bishop (Deep Springs' nearest town)—it won Best in Show.

½ recipe Butter Piecrust (*page 263*)**, rolled out for a single-crust pie**

¼ cup all-purpose flour

1¾ cups sugar

½ teaspoon salt

½ cup butter (*1 stick*)**, melted**

3 large eggs, at room temperature

½ cup buttermilk

1 teaspoon vanilla extract

1 teaspoon lemon extract

nutmeg for sprinkling on top

Have the unbaked pie shell ready. Heat the oven to 325°F. Mix the flour, sugar, and salt in a medium bowl. Add the melted butter and beat (the mixture will be stiff). Add the eggs, one at a time, then add the buttermilk and extracts. Pour into the pie shell, sprinkle the top evenly with nutmeg, and bake for about 40 minutes, or until set. Let the pie cool completely on a rack—at least 2 hours—before serving at room temperature.

Cheesecake

serves 12 to 16

Structurally speaking, cheesecake is a kind of pie; before springform pans were ubiquitous, people baked their cheesecakes in pie plates and often called them "cheese pie." Here is a classic recipe for this beloved American dessert. It's easy to put together, but keep in mind that it requires a good deal of time. The baking and cooling period takes 4 hours, and it must be baked at least one day before you serve it. It's even better 48 hours after baking, when the cheese flavor reaches its zenith.

While this cheesecake tastes glorious simply served plain, the glazed fruit is delicious and pretty. Don't be tempted to garnish rich and creamy cheesecake with rich and creamy whipped cream, as chain restaurants often do—one does not enhance the other.

CRUST

1 cup fine graham cracker crumbs

2 tablespoons sugar

3 tablespoons butter, melted

FILLING

2½ pounds cream cheese (five 8-ounce packages)**, at room temperature**

1⅔ cups sugar

2 tablespoons all-purpose flour

¼ teaspoon salt

6 eggs

½ cup heavy (whipping) **cream**

1 teaspoon vanilla extract

2 tablespoons fresh lemon juice

½ teaspoon finely grated lemon zest

GLAZED FRUIT TOPPING (OPTIONAL)

¾ cup fruit jelly, jam, or preserves, corresponding to the type of fresh fruit you are using

2 tablespoons water

2 to 3 cups fresh fruit: sweet or sour cherries (pitted)**, berries, plums** (cut into chunks)**, nectarines or peaches** (cut into chunks)

Heat the oven to 350°F. To make the crust, blend the graham cracker crumbs, sugar, and melted butter together. Lightly butter a 10-inch springform pan, and press the crust mixture evenly on the bottom of the pan. Bake the crust for about 10 minutes. Set aside to cool while you mix the filling. Leave the oven set at 350°F.

To make the filling, be sure the cream cheese is at room temperature—set the packages out on your kitchen counter for at least an hour before you mix the filling. In a large bowl, gently stir up the cream cheese with a few strokes of a wooden spoon. Sift together the sugar, flour, and salt and blend into the cream cheese thoroughly. Using a wire whisk or the low setting of an electric mixer, gently beat until the mixture is perfectly free of lumps. Do not violently beat the mixture, or the cheese could turn grainy. Add the eggs one at a time, incorporating each egg thoroughly into the batter before adding the next. Add the cream, vanilla, lemon juice, and lemon zest. Pour into the crust.

Put the cheesecake into the oven and bake for 10 minutes. Lower the oven temperature to 225°F and bake for 1½ to 2 hours, or until the cheesecake is no longer jiggly in the center and is pulling away from the sides of the pan. Leaving the cheesecake in the oven, turn off the oven (do not open the oven door) and let it rest in the oven for another hour. Cool on a rack for yet another hour, then wrap and refrigerate overnight (2 days is even better). For the best flavor and texture, let the cheesecake come to room temperature before serving.

To make the glazed fruit topping (if using), melt the jelly with the water in a medium saucepan, just until the jelly is melted. The fruit may be prepared ahead of time, but combine it with the glaze shortly before serving. Toss the fresh fruit with the glaze, immediately pile the fruit on the cheesecake, and serve.

GINGERSNAP CRUST

When the mother of one of my Deep Springs classmates visited the Valley to teach an informal pottery class, she made gingersnap-crusted cheesecake for us all. Instead of graham crackers, use a generous cup of finely crushed Gingersnaps (page 324), and since gingersnaps are decidedly sweeter than graham crackers, use only 2 teaspoons sugar rather than 2 tablespoons.

Other Fruit Desserts

David's Baked Apples

serves about 4

I was never particularly interested in baked apples until I discovered this simple, yet extraordinary recipe in Deep Springs alumnus David Tanis' (DS'71) wonderful cookbook *A Platter of Figs*. Choose tart, smaller-sized apples. Instead of the cognac David calls for, I once used fresh lemon juice, with a little grated fresh ginger stirred in—they were superb.

8 small, tart baking apples

sugar

about ⅓ cup brandy or cognac

Heat the oven to 375°F, and position one of the oven's racks at the top level. Using a small, sharp knife, neatly cut out each apple's stem area in one cone-shaped piece, as if you were going to make a jack-o'-lantern out of the apple. Set the tops aside—you'll put them back on the apples later. Using a small melon baller, hollow out the seeds and tough core membranes from each apple, taking care not to pierce the bottom of the apple. Fill each apple hollow with sugar, then trickle a teaspoon or two of brandy or cognac into each one. Replace the tops, arrange the apples in an attractive shallow baking dish, and sprinkle additional sugar generously over the apples. Bake on the top rack of the oven for about 30 to 45 minutes, until the apples have burst and released juice. Let the apples cool completely in the dish. Serve two apples, plus some of the flavorful juices, to each person. Serve the apples plain, or accompany with a little sour cream, or ice cream.

Orange Bread Pudding

serves 4 to 6

If you find the usual cinnamon- and vanilla-flavored bread pudding dull, try this more sprightly one, made with fresh citrus and almond extract.

1 tablespoon butter

4 cups white bread cubes

2¼ cups whole milk

finely grated zest of 2 medium oranges *(about 1 tablespoon)*

juice of 2 medium oranges *(½ cup)*

4 eggs

1 tablespoon fresh lemon juice

⅓ cup sugar

¼ teaspoon salt

1 teaspoon almond extract

⅓ cup dried fruit, such as golden raisins, cherries, prunes, or cranberries

Heat the oven to 325°F. In a large skillet over medium heat, melt the butter and add the bread cubes. Stir the bread around until it is lightly toasted, about 10 minutes. Add the milk (it will boil up) and the orange zest. Remove from the heat. In an 8-by-8-inch baking dish, gently beat together the orange juice, eggs, lemon juice, sugar, salt, and almond extract. Slowly stir in the milk-bread mixture and the dried fruit. Bake for about 40 minutes, or until a knife inserted near the center comes out clean. This is good served warm, at room temperature, or chilled.

Ginger Peach Crisp

serves 6 to 8

Rather than topping fruit crisp with ice cream or whipped cream, I love to serve it piping hot in a bowl with fresh, cold, unsweetened, unwhipped heavy cream poured over. I don't bother peeling the peaches; under cool running water, rub them with a cloth to remove the fuzz.

8 cups pitted sliced fresh peaches

3 to 4 tablespoons granulated *(white)* sugar

juice of ¼ lemon—more if using white peaches

1 tablespoon finely grated fresh ginger, or more to taste

pinch of salt

2 tablespoons quick-cooking tapioca or all-purpose flour

TOPPING

1½ cups all-purpose flour *(up to ½ cup may be whole wheat)*

½ cup rolled oats

½ cup firmly packed brown sugar

2 tablespoons granulated *(white)* sugar

⅛ teaspoon salt

12 tablespoons salted butter *(1½ sticks)*, at room temperature

FOR SERVING

plain, unwhipped heavy cream

Heat the oven to 350°F. Combine the peaches, sugar, lemon juice, ginger, salt, and tapioca in a large bowl. Taste—the topping is cookie-sweet, so the fruit mixture should be tart. For a bolder flavor, add more ginger. Dump the peaches into a 9-by-13-inch pan.

To make the topping, combine the flour, oats, brown and granulated sugars, and salt in a large bowl, then work in the softened butter until the mixture is crumbly and there is no dry flour left. Sprinkle the topping evenly over the peaches. Do not pat the topping down—the pebbly appearance is much of the charm. Bake for 40 to 50 minutes, or until the topping is golden brown and thick fruit juices are bubbling up from below. Serve warm with plain, unwhipped heavy cream.

Pear, Ginger, and Lemon Crisp

serves 6 to 8

I made this crisp for the Deep Springs community on my visit to interview for the chef's job, and included the recipe in the earliest version of this book. Post–Deep Springs, students reported back to me that they had become very popular potluck party guests on the strength of this recipe. For a more traditional *apple-walnut crisp*, simply substitute apples for the pears and walnuts for the almonds, and go easy on the ginger.

FILLING

2½ pounds just-ripe, flavorful pears

juice and finely grated zest of 1 lemon

2 to 3 tablespoons finely grated fresh ginger

3 tablespoons sugar

1 tablespoon all-purpose flour

pinch of salt

TOPPING

¾ cup sliced almonds, lightly toasted *(page 176)* and chopped medium fine

¾ cup plus 1 tablespoon all-purpose flour

¼ cup rolled oats

⅓ cup firmly packed brown sugar

2 tablespoons granulated *(white)* sugar

½ cup salted butter *(1 stick)*, at room temperature

FOR SERVING

whipped cream or plain, unwhipped heavy cream

Heat the oven to 350°F. To make the filling, peel, core, and cut the pears into ½-inch slices. Toss with the lemon juice and zest, ginger, sugar, flour, and salt in a 9-by-13-inch baking dish and arrange in an even layer.

To make the topping, combine the toasted, chopped almonds with the flour, oats, and brown and granulated sugars, then work in the softened butter until the mixture is crumbly and there is no dry flour left. Sprinkle the topping evenly over the pears. Do not pat the topping down—the pebbly appearance is much of the charm. Bake for 40 to 50 minutes, or until the topping is browned and the fruit syrup is bubbling up around the edges. The pears should be completely soft, offering no resistance to a small knife poked through in the center. Let the crisp cool slightly, and serve in shallow bowls with whipped cream, or simply with cold, unwhipped, unflavored heavy cream (my favorite).

OTHER FRUIT CRISPS

Take a cue from the array of fruit pie recipes (beginning with Apple Pie, page 265), and create the crisp of your choice: rhubarb crisp, cherry crisp with almonds in the topping, winy berry crisps—all may be known and loved.

Poached Pears with Chocolate Sauce

serves 6

Pears and chocolate? It's an almost magical combination. Serve this dessert as is, or with a few Almond-Butter Cookies (page 319). Add a scoop of vanilla ice cream, plus a couple of candied violets, and you have the French classic *poires belle Hélène*.

PEARS

1 lemon
1¼ cups sugar
1 cup dry white wine
2 cups water
½ vanilla bean, split lengthwise, or 2 teaspoons vanilla extract
6 ripe, fragrant Bartlett pears

CHOCOLATE SAUCE

2 cups water
⅓ cup light corn syrup
1½ cups unsweetened cocoa powder
1 cup granulated (*white*) **sugar**
pinch of salt
⅔ cup bittersweet chocolate chips

To poach the pears, first wash the lemon well. Using a vegetable peeler, remove the zest from the lemon in long strips and put it in a large, heavy saucepan. Add the juice of the lemon, sugar, wine, water, and vanilla bean. Bring to a simmer over medium-low heat, stirring occasionally to dissolve the sugar. Using a small, sharp knife, peel the pears, reserving the peels. Cut the pears in half and remove the core, keeping the pear halves intact. Put the peels and the pears in the warm poaching liquid. The peels will deepen the pear flavor. Raise the heat to medium, and bring to a simmer. Poach the pears, stirring gently, until the pears are soft and well heated all the way through, about 10 minutes. Let the pears cool to room temperature in the liquid, then refrigerate overnight in the liquid.

To make the chocolate sauce, heat the water and corn syrup together in a medium-sized, heavy saucepan. Combine the cocoa powder and sugar in a bowl, working out any lumps in the cocoa, and add to the pan, whisking well. Bring to a boil, whisking frequently. Remove from the heat and add the salt and chocolate chips, whisking to dissolve the chocolate. Keep warm, or rewarm in a double boiler before serving.

Carefully remove the chilled pear halves from the liquid, and put in attractive individual glass bowls. (Strain the flavorful pear liquid and reserve for another use.) Spoon about ⅓ cup of warm chocolate sauce around, rather than over, the pears—make sure some of the bare pear's cheek shows through the dark sauce. Serve immediately, while the pear is cool and the sauce is hot. The sauce reheats well; there will be a little left over.

My Mother's Strawberry Shortcake

serves 6 for dessert or 3 for dinner

Every spring when I was little, when strawberries were at their peak, my mother would purchase an entire 10-pound lug of strawberries, just for the two of us. She didn't make jam or anything with them—we would just eat our fill of fresh berries all week long. But on the evening she brought the berries home, we would have nothing but strawberry shortcake for dinner, served in big, shallow, blue-and-white china bowls that belonged to my grandmother. You may sweeten and lightly whip the cream if you prefer, but I love this farmhouse version with cold, unwhipped cream poured over the hot buttered biscuit and room-temperature berries. This temperature differential, and the butter on the biscuit, are the heart of this recipe. "You have to see the little globules of butter floating in the cream," my mother says.

2 baskets *(about 1¾ pounds total)* **fresh strawberries in season, hulled and thickly sliced**

4 to 5 tablespoons sugar

2 teaspoons fresh lemon juice

SHORTCAKES

2 cups all-purpose flour

2½ teaspoons baking powder

½ teaspoon baking soda

½ teaspoon salt

1 tablespoon sugar, plus about 4 teaspoons more for sprinkling over the tops

6 tablespoons cold unsalted butter

¾ cup cold buttermilk

FOR SERVING

butter, at room temperature, for spreading on the shortcakes

2 cups heavy *(whipping)* **cream, well chilled**

Toss the strawberries with the sugar in a medium-sized glass or stainless-steel bowl. Taste the berries, adding more sugar, if you like, or if a little more sharpness is needed, a few drops of lemon juice. Cover and let sit at room temperature while you make the shortcakes.

To make the shortcakes, first heat the oven to 425°F. Sift together the flour, baking powder, baking soda, sugar, and salt into a medium bowl. Cut the cold butter into slices and rapidly work the butter into the dry mixture with your hands. Work until the flour is somewhat moistened and there are no large, but many small, pieces of butter in the mixture. Pour in the buttermilk and gently combine with a wooden spoon just until mixed.

Turn the dough out on a floured board and knead (in other words, flatten, fold over, flatten, fold over) only four or five times, sprinkling flour on the board as necessary to prevent sticking. In flattening and folding, work the dough into a rectangle, about 8 by 6 inches. Gently roll the dough, using flour as necessary to keep it from sticking, to a ¾-inch thickness and cut 4 or 6 large shortcakes. Brush the top of each shortcake with a little water to moisten, then sprinkle each with about a teaspoon of sugar. Place 1 inch apart on an ungreased baking sheet, let rest for a few moments, and bake in the center of the oven until golden brown on the bottom and top, 8 to 10 minutes. Once the shortcakes are cut and placed on the baking sheet, they may be refrigerated until you are ready to bake them.

Have everything ready to assemble when the shortcakes emerge from the oven. Let the shortcakes rest on the baking sheet for a few moments, then transfer them to shallow china soup bowls. Carefully split the shortcakes apart, setting the tops gently to the side. Spread a little softened butter on each shortcake, spoon a generous amount of room-temperature strawberries over each shortcake, then pour the cold cream over and around the strawberries. Place the shortcake tops back over everything. Serve immediately, with knife, fork, and spoon.

Canned-Fruit Cobbler

serves 4 to 6

My grandmother made this cobbler with canned pears, but it's good with canned peaches or pineapple, too. It is also a great use for a pint jar of home-canned fruit in light syrup. Juicy fresh fruit may be used, also, such as berries, plums, or peaches, sweetened with sugar and allowed to sit to draw out the juices.

½ **cup butter** *(1 stick)*

⅔ **cup sugar**

¾ **cup all-purpose flour**

1 teaspoon baking powder

¼ **teaspoon salt**

⅛ **teaspoon ground mace or nutmeg**

¾ **cup milk**

one 14-ounce can fruit in light syrup, or about 2 cups juicy, sweetened fresh fruit

Heat the oven to 350°F. Melt the butter in the oven in a 9-by-13-inch baking dish. Sift the sugar, flour, baking powder, salt, and mace together in a medium bowl. Whisk the milk into the batter, just until uniform. Pour the fruit, syrup and all, into the melted butter, distributing the pieces of fruit evenly over the bottom of the pan. Pour the batter over the fruit. Don't stir.

Bake for 20 to 25 minutes, until the top is pale golden brown. Let the cobbler set up for about 5 minutes before serving.

Simplest Fruit Desserts

Apples and Oranges

Serve crisp, flavorful apples and juicy oranges together as a very simple winter dessert. Satsumas and other small, sweet, seedless, easy-to-peel mandarin oranges come into season in December—these are ideal. Bring the whole fruit to the table in a bowl, then slice the apples with a small knife, arranging the slices on a plate. Peel the oranges, twisting the peel over the apples—the citrus oil from the peel will agreeably flavor the apples. A few sweet, gooey Medjool dates are most welcome here, too.

Cherries with Almond Paste

Serve a big bowl of fresh sweet cherries (or apricots) alongside a slab of almond paste or marzipan—almond paste has more almonds and less sugar than marzipan, and is less refined. Let people cut slices or chunks of almond paste to eat with their cherries.

Citrus Compote

In the coldest months of the year, bright citrus comes into season. Choose large, sweet navel oranges, plus a few ruby-red grapefruits. The sweetest, juiciest fruits are heavy for their size, and have smaller pores. Rinse the fruit well, and finely grate the zest of about half of the fruit into a glass bowl. With a small, sharp knife, peel all the fruit, taking care to remove all the inner light-colored pith, then cut each fruit segment out of its membrane, into the bowl. Remove seeds as you go. Once the sections are cut out, squeeze all remaining juice from the "carcass" of membrane, into the bowl. Continue until you have a bowl of jewel-like segments swimming in zesty juice. Squeeze the juice of a lime into the bowl to sharpen the flavors. Take about a cupful of the juice and stir sugar into it to dissolve the sugar—you want just enough sugar to lightly sweeten the whole amount of juice. Add a small amount of vanilla extract, then add this sweetened, vanilla-scented juice back into the bowl. Stir gently, chill lightly, and serve in bowls with spoons.

Dulce De Leche with Fresh Fruit

Traditional Mexican recipes for the delectable caramel concoction known as *dulce de leche,* which could be translated as "sweet of the milk" or "milk candy," call for slowly simmering sweetened milk in a heavy, open pot, stirring constantly, until the liquid is greatly reduced, and the milk's sugars and the added sugar both begin to caramelize. In this shortcut recipe, you cook unopened cans of sweetened condensed milk in water in a slow cooker, and the resulting caramel is thick, dark, and superb. Choose sound cans of sweetened condensed milk, with no dents. Take off the labels and wash off the glue. Shake the cans very well to dissolve the sugary sediment that forms on the bottom, then arrange them in a slow cooker. Cover with hot tap water so the cans are completely submerged, turn the slow cooker on high, cover, and let cook for about 6 hours. *Never lift the lid or touch or disturb the cans during cooking, and never remove a hot can from the water.* Let the cans cool in the water for about 1 hour, then run cold water over them to cool completely before opening. Open the cans, and carefully stir in about ¼ teaspoon sea salt into each one. Eat the caramel with a spoon, accompanied by fresh fruit—crisp apples, sweet pears, ripe bananas, cut fresh pineapple....

Dried Fruit in Sweet Wine

Sun-drying is probably the oldest form of fruit preservation. If you're serving this simple dessert in a large quantity, cook each type of dried fruit separately—their various flavors will remain distinct. For household quantities, it's fine to cook the fruit all together. Put any combination of dried pears, apricots, cherries, prunes, and golden raisins in a pot and cover with sweet muscat wine, or other sweet wine. Heat over a medium flame, stirring occasionally, just until the wine is hot and steaming, then remove from the heat and let the pot sit until both syrup and fruit have cooled to room temperature. In Serve an assortment of fruit, plus a big spoonful of the winy syrup, to each person in a bowl. Top with a dollop of sour cream, and serve with a spoon.

Figs, Honey, and Feta

Ripe figs are thoroughly soft; if you have figs that are still a little firm, set them on a plate (not touching one another) and let them ripen at room temperature for a few days. Serve ripe figs, a block of room-temperature feta cheese, and a dish of honey. Put a slice of feta atop half a fig, dab with honey, and eat.

Melon with Rosewater

Procure an array of sweet, ripe summer melons, different varieties and colors, if possible: cantaloupe, green- and orange-fleshed honeydew, red and yellow watermelon.... Cut the melon into large, attractive chunks, rind removed or not. Cover and chill. Sprinkle the melon lightly with rosewater and serve.

Nuts from the Shell

In the fall, the new crop of tree nuts arrives in the market, typically almonds, walnuts, pecans, hazelnuts, and Brazil nuts. Whole nuts in their shell are a traditional Christmastime treat. When my mother and her sisters were young, every year for Christmas their dad gave them each a big tin of perfect, unbroken pecan halves he'd shelled himself. Cracking nuts is a developed skill, the object being to apply just enough pressure to crack the shell without damaging the nutmeat. You may wonder, with shelled nuts readily available, why go to the trouble of cracking them yourself? A nut's shell, as any squirrel will tell you, is nature's best way of preserving a nut, better than any refrigerator or plastic wrapping. Nuts right out of the shell have a full, complex sweetness. You rediscover their character and flavor. With a little cheese or fruit, they can be a delightful, participatory hors d'oeuvre or dessert. Bring a bowl of nuts to the table, along with a nutcracker and several nut picks, and an empty bowl for the shells. One person cracks, and the others pick.

Peaches and Cream

Slice sweet ripe peaches (peeled if you like, or simply rubbed with a cloth under running water to tame the fuzz), toss them with a little sugar, and let sit a few minutes. In the bottom of each person's bowl, put a generous dollop of lightly sweetened, vanilla-flavored whipped cream (1 cup cream, 1 tablespoon sugar, ¼ teaspoon vanilla extract). Arrange the sliced peaches over the whipped cream, and drizzle over any peach juice that has accumulated. Finally, pour a couple of tablespoons of cold, unwhipped heavy cream into each bowl. Eat with a spoon. I love the loft and lightness of whipped cream, and the sauciness of liquid cream; here, you have both. Nectarines, apricots, blackberries, blueberries, and raspberries may be enjoyed the same way.

Warm Pears with Chocolate Ice Cream

Peel, core, and cut a couple of ripe, sweet, good-smelling pears into ½-inch slices, and sauté them in a big skillet with butter, sugar, and a pinch of salt, just until the pears are heated through. Add a little lemon juice to balance the sweetness, and a few drops of vanilla extract. Spoon the warm pears and all their juice around and alongside scoops of chocolate ice cream, and serve immediately.

Persimmons

Persimmons, still considered an oddity by many Americans, come into season in the fall and early winter. They are sweet—very low in acid, with a lush, nutty, pumpkin-like flavor. There are two principal varieties: the teardrop-shaped Hachiya must be slowly ripened after picking until the flesh is completely soft (a process known as *bletting*), while the smaller, flatter Fuyu needs only minimal ripening. Usually, both varieties are seedless. Ripen a Fuyu persimmon at room temperature until just beyond crisp but still firm. Peel, and slice crosswise to reveal a star pattern in the fruit's core. Arrange on a plate. They are perfect on the Thanksgiving table accompanied by a few lightly toasted pecans. Ripen a Hachiya persimmon on a windowsill, stem side down, until it is deeply translucent and completely soft. It could take weeks. Serve chilled or at room temperature. On a small glass dessert plate, slice the persimmon lengthwise down to the stem, at right angles, to make 4 quarters. Open out the quarters on the plate to make a flower, and serve with a spoon. The texture is slippery, like pudding.

Pineapple

This method of cutting a fresh pineapple reveals the fruit's beautiful geometry, and keeps waste to a minimum. In the market, choose a pineapple that is heavy for its size, more golden than green, with healthy green leaves, and an appealing, light pineapple aroma at the base. Twist off the crown of leaves, wash the pineapple well in cool running water, and pat it dry. Using your chef's knife, cut about 1 inch off the top, and about ½ inch off the bottom. The skin and "eyes" are removed in two separate processes: first, using your knife, slice away the outer layer of skin, leaving only the pitted "eyes." Then, using a small knife, remove the "eyes" two at a time, following their natural lines, resulting in a spiral ridged pattern. Cut the cleaned pineapple lengthwise in quarters, then cut the tough core out from each quarter. Slice each quarter into 3 or 4 lengthwise slices, and serve slightly chilled.

Pomelo

This regal ancestor of the grapefruit is especially prized, and in season, around Chinese New Year, in January or February. The largest, most golden specimens are put on display, adorning the home or altar; the fruit is said to bring wealth and prosperity. Bring home a large, yellow pomelo, heavy for its size, and display it on a plate (I use a small polished-wood pedestal) for several days, appreciating its beauty and fragrance. When you're ready to consume it, tear off the thick, soft peel with your hands, revealing the inner ball of segments. Separate the segments, then carefully remove the tough membrane from each segment with the aid of a small knife, leaving only the bare cells of the fruit. Twist pieces of peel over the cells so they are flavored with the peel's oil. Eat the clusters of cells plain, or dip in a small dish of salt (as the Chinese do), or sugar, or a combination.

Rhubarb

Scandinavians find this familiar and comforting. Just wash your rhubarb; don't peel it. Slice it thick, and throw it in a saucepan with a pat of butter, a few drops of water, a pinch of salt, a bit of grated orange zest if you like, and as much sugar as it takes to make the juices taste good but still tart. Heat to a gentle bubble and cook for a few minutes, stirring gently from time to time, until the rhubarb is juicy and tender. Serve warm in a bowl with a little cold cream, sour cream, or a scoop of vanilla ice cream.

Watermelon

On the hottest summer day, chill a large, ripe watermelon, preferably a flavorful, old-fashioned variety with seeds. Wipe the outside clean with a damp towel. Using a knife, cut two intersecting channels across the blossom end of the melon, creating an "X" pattern, as if you were going to cut it into quarters, but only cutting through the toughest part of the rind, not into the flesh. Now place your fingers into one of the channels and *break* the entire melon in half lengthwise. Breaking the melon in this manner, rather than cutting it, retains more of the melon's juice, and also reveals the pockets of seeds along their natural lines. Using the knife to guide the breaks, break each half lengthwise to make quarters, then break each quarter into pieces appropriate for hand-held eating outdoors. For an especially appealing presentation, serve the chunks of melon on a bed of ice. Serve with a dish of sea salt—it's delicious on watermelon.

The Strawberry

A man walking across a field suddenly encounters a ferocious, hungry tiger. The man flees, and the tiger chases him. Coming to a cliff, the man grasps a wild vine and swings over the edge. The tiger sniffs at him from above. Terrified, the man looks down and sees another tiger, pacing and growling below. At that moment, two mice, one white and one black, begin to gnaw away at the vine, bit by bit. The man notices a big, ripe, luscious red strawberry growing on the cliffside nearby. Grasping the vine in one hand, he plucks the strawberry with the other. How sweet it tastes!

—Traditional Buddhist story

CHAPTER 15

CAKES

When my mother was a girl, she'd sometimes arrive home from school to find a large homemade birthday cake on the counter, complete with frosting and candles. Knowing that all the family birthdays were months away, she'd ask, "Whose birthday is it?" "Well, it's somebody's birthday somewhere in the world!" my grandmother would say, brightly. After supper, she would serve the cake with the lights dimmed, the candles lit, and the whole family singing "Happy Birthday, Dear Someone."

My criterion for a good cake is simple: it should taste good enough to be thoroughly enjoyed without frosting. You'll find a good recipe for cream cheese frosting accompanying the carrot cake, but there are no standard buttercream-type frosting recipes in this book. When a cake accompaniment is needed, I usually serve a dollop of lightly sweetened, vanilla-flavored whipped cream (1 cup cream, 1 tablespoon sugar, and ¼ teaspoon vanilla extract, whipped just to soft peaks)—it allows the flavors, richness, and light texture of the cake to shine through. For birthday cakes and other special occasions when a frosted cake is called for, I use whipped cream to frost the cake (see Whipped Cream Cake, page 290, and Big Pink Cake, page 297).

Please see the information on flour (page 40), on buttermilk (page 38), and on baking powder and baking soda (page 37).

Baking a cake from scratch has the reputation of being difficult, but there are only a few things to bear in mind:

Pay attention to the temperature of your ingredients, especially the eggs and butter. Cake batter should be room temperature when it goes into the oven; it bakes more evenly than a chilled batter. Eggs should always be at room temperature (warm cold eggs for a few minutes in hot tap water). Butter should be pliable but still firm enough to trap tiny air bubbles when whipped—a bit cooler than room temperature.

Don't overmix the batter. Mix just until the batter is uniform; overmixing activates the gluten in the flour, resulting in rubbery, tough cake.

Don't slam the oven door at any point during baking. Until the cake is cooked through, its structure is delicate. Any jostling could deflate the tiny bubbles of air that give the cake its light texture.

Don't overbake or underbake your cake. Remove it from the oven when a toothpick inserted in the center just comes out clean, with maybe a few crumbs clinging, but no raw batter. If overbaked, the cake will be dry. If the cake is underbaked, with a patch of wet batter in the center, it can't be put back in the oven to finish baking—it will dry out.

Cool cakes on a rack. Let your cake sit in the pan, on a rack, for about 10 minutes after taking it out of the oven, then remove it from the pan and let it cool completely on the rack. This allows heat and steam to readily escape, preventing sogginess and making for the best, lightest texture.

Goose Egg Pound Cake

makes 1 large cake; serves 8 to 10

One late-summer day, a particularly grumpy and ill-tempered gander appeared in Deep Springs Valley under still-unexplained circumstances. In the face of Christmas roast goose jokes, Deep Springs rancher/animal rescuer Iris Pope named him Louis, gave him the run of the apple orchard, and, from friends in town, fetched a lovely, sweet-tempered Edith of a goose for this Archie of a gander. He is still nasty, but more tractable. She radiates in his presence. Iris named her Babette, and we use her eggs in baking. They seem to produce a subtly richer result than hens' eggs in egg-heavy preparations such as this pound cake. But don't wait to get goose eggs to make this cake—you may use 5 hens' eggs instead.

While many modern pound cake recipes call for sour cream, buttermilk, or some such dairy product, and leavening such as baking powder, this one contains little besides the classic four ingredients: eggs, butter, sugar, and flour. It has no leavening other than the air whipped into the butter and eggs. The rosewater adds a subtle aroma and just a bit of moisture. A little honey is included for two reasons: to deepen the sweetness and to retain moisture. It is a beautifully dense, tender, creamy-tasting cake with a delectable brown outer crust.

The flavorings may be varied to suit your taste. The honey and rosewater are my additions, but I also love citrus zest, almond extract, and mace. The presence of lemon extract, a favorite Southern ingredient, and perhaps its unique cold-oven baking method, bespeak its Texas pedigree. My mother says, "This was my favorite cake to bake in Houston in the summer. I could pop it in the oven and then leave the house while it baked!"

1 cup unsalted butter *(2 sticks)*, **at cool room temperature**

1¾ cups sugar

1 teaspoon vanilla extract

1 teaspoon lemon extract

1 tablespoon rosewater, or just plain water

1 tablespoon honey

¼ teaspoon salt

2 or 3 goose eggs or about 5 regular large hens' eggs, at warm room temperature *(about 1¼ cups)*

1 cup sifted cake flour, sifted again after measuring

1 cup sifted all-purpose flour, sifted again after measuring

Don't preheat the oven. Butter and dust with flour 1 large tube pan or 2 loaf pans, tapping the pan to remove excess flour. Using an electric mixer, cream the butter and sugar together very well for 3 full minutes, until the mixture is very fluffy and lightened in color. "It should look like whipped cream," my mother says. Beat in the eggs one at a time, beating for a full minute after adding each one. Beat in the vanilla and lemon extracts, rosewater, honey, and salt. Add both kinds of flour, and gently blend the batter on low speed until the flour is mostly incorporated. Remove the bowl from the mixer, and finish mixing by hand, using a rubber spatula. Mix just until the batter is uniform—do not overmix. Scrape the batter into the prepared pan, spread evenly, and put into the cold oven. Turn on the oven to 300°F and bake for 1 hour, or until a toothpick inserted in the center comes out clean. Let cool in the pan for 15 minutes, then turn the cake out onto a rack. Enjoy warm or cooled.

GOOSE EGG POUND CAKE CINNAMON TOAST

Twenty of us enjoyed these little toasts with vanilla ice cream on New Year's Eve, 1999, after a dinner of saffron risotto, spicy roast chicken, beet and carrot salad, chickpea salad with lemon and parsley, and rich dinner bread, before an appropriately amazing fireworks display. The cake contained Babette the goose's eggs and butter from the Deep Springs Dairy.

Heat the oven to 400°F. Mix about 2 teaspoons ground cinnamon into ¼ cup sugar. Generously butter thin slices of day-old pound cake, sprinkle heavily with cinnamon sugar, and toast on a baking sheet in the oven until the sugar is melted and the cake is crisp and golden brown on the bottom. Serve like a cookie with vanilla ice cream.

Carrot Cake

makes one 9-inch cake; serves 6 to 8

This was the cake I always relied on early in my professional cooking days. It's *the* classic American cake, appropriate for any occasion, from rustic picnics to elegant weddings. I love the delicate, moist crumb that results when the carrots and nuts are very fine. Like all the cakes in this book, it is perfectly good eaten plain. But as much as I love unfrosted cakes, I'd be the last to deny that cream cheese frosting is perfect with carrot cake. If you want a double-layer carrot cake, double the cake and frosting recipes.

1 cup walnuts *(about 3¼ ounces)*, **lightly toasted** *(page 176)*

1 cup sifted all-purpose flour

1 teaspoon baking soda

1 teaspoon baking powder

½ teaspoon ground cinnamon

½ teaspoon salt

⅔ cup sunflower oil or other vegetable oil

¾ cup firmly packed brown sugar

2 eggs, at room temperature

1 teaspoon vanilla extract

1¾ cups grated carrots, grated on the small holes of the grater

CREAM CHEESE FROSTING (OPTIONAL)

8 ounces cold cream cheese

finely grated zest and juice of ½ lemon

1 teaspoon vanilla extract

1½ cups sifted powdered sugar

Heat the oven to 325°F. Butter a 9-inch round cake pan or springform pan. To ensure that the cake doesn't stick to the pan, cut a circle of parchment and place it in the bottom of the pan. Butter the parchment and dust the pan well with flour, tapping out the excess.

With your hands, lightly rub some of the excess papery brown skin off the toasted walnuts. Chop the walnuts very fine with a sharp knife, or quickly pulse them in a food processor to a fine meal. In a medium bowl, whisk together the flour, baking soda, baking powder, cinnamon, and salt, then whisk in the walnuts. In a large bowl, whisk the oil, brown sugar, eggs, vanilla, and carrots together, then fold the dry mixture into the wet mixture with the whisk, just until the mixture is uniform. Scrape into the prepared pan, smooth the top, and bake for about 30 minutes, or until a toothpick inserted in the center of the cake comes out clean. Let cool for 10 minutes in the pan, then turn out onto a plate. Peel off the parchment, and invert the cake onto a rack to cool completely. *If you opt to frost the cake, make sure it's completely cool before applying frosting.*

To make the frosting (if using), gently and patiently stir the cold cream cheese by hand together with the lemon juice, zest, and vanilla in a medium bowl. Don't overbeat the cream cheese, or the texture might become grainy. Add the sugar in three or four parts, blending each addition partway before adding the next. Blend until smooth, and then spread on your completely cooled carrot cake.

Parsnip Cake

makes one 10-inch cake; serves 6 to 8

Ginger, almonds, and vanilla contribute their character to the unique perfume of parsnip in this wintertime cake, a favorite of one of my successors in the Deep Springs Boardinghouse, Jon "Dewey" DeWeese (DS'07). Lacking almond meal, you may grind blanched (page 176) or whole almonds to a fine meal in the food processor. Pecans or walnuts may be used instead of almonds, if you like.

1 cup sifted all-purpose flour

1 teaspoon baking soda

1 teaspoon baking powder

½ teaspoon salt

1 cup almond meal *(or fine meal of pecans or walnuts)*

⅔ cup sunflower oil or other vegetable oil

¾ cup sugar

2 eggs, at room temperature

½ teaspoon vanilla extract

½ teaspoon almond extract *(omit if using other nuts than almond)*

1½ tablespoons finely grated fresh ginger

2 parsnips, peeled and finely grated *(to yield 1¾ firmly- packed cups)*

powdered sugar for dusting *(optional)*

Heat the oven to 325°F. Butter a 10-inch springform pan. To ensure that the cake doesn't stick to the pan, cut a circle of parchment and place it in the bottom of the pan. Butter the parchment and dust the pan well with flour, tapping out the excess. In a medium bowl, sift together the flour, baking soda, baking powder, and salt. Whisk in the almond meal. In a large bowl, whisk the oil, sugar, eggs, vanilla, almond extract, ginger, and parsnips together very well. Add the dry ingredients to the wet ingredients, and fold together with the whisk until the batter is uniform. Scrape the batter into the prepared pan, smooth the top, and bake in the center of the oven for about 30 minutes, or until a toothpick inserted in the center comes out clean.

Allow the cake to cool in the pan for 10 minutes, then remove the cake from the pan, and let cool completely. If you wish, dust the cake with powdered sugar before serving: put some powdered sugar into a screen sieve, and lightly tap the sieve over the cake.

Whipped Cream Cake

makes one 12-inch cake; serves 6 to 8

Rather than butter in the batter, this simple, old-fashioned cake starts with a bowl of whipped cream. It's delicious warm, topped with—what else?—more whipped cream.

1¼ cups well-chilled heavy *(whipping)* **cream**

1 cup sugar

2 eggs, warmed in hot tap water

1 teaspoon vanilla extract

1¾ cups sifted all-purpose flour or cake flour

2 teaspoons baking powder

½ teaspoon salt

TOPPING

1 cup well-chilled heavy *(whipping)* **cream**

1 tablespoon sugar

¼ teaspoon vanilla extract

Heat the oven to 350°F. Butter a 12-inch springform pan or two 9-inch round cake pans. To ensure that the cake doesn't stick to the pan, cut a circle of parchment paper and place it in the bottom of the pan. Butter the parchment and dust the pan with flour. Or, more simply, you may bake the cake as a sheet cake, in a buttered 9-by-13-inch pan.

Using an electric mixer, whip the cold cream in a large bowl with half the sugar until soft peaks form, then whip in the eggs and vanilla, then the remaining sugar. Sift together the flour, baking powder, and salt, and gently fold into the cream mixture, just until the batter is uniform. Scrape the batter into the prepared pan, smoothing the top. Bake for 25 to 30 minutes, or until a toothpick inserted in the center comes out clean. (The timing will be a few minutes less if using two cake pans.) Let cool for about 10 minutes in the pan, then turn it out onto a plate. Peel off the parchment, and invert the cake onto another plate (if serving warm) or onto a rack to cool completely. If you have baked the cake in a 9-by-13-inch pan, leave it in the pan.

To make the topping, whip the cream with the sugar and vanilla until soft peaks form. On each person's plate, top slices of warm cake with dollops of cold whipped cream. Or cool the cake completely and frost with the whipped cream, beaten until it holds its shape, then refrigerate until serving time. If you have baked the cake in two 9-inch pans, stack the layers with a good layer of whipped cream between them. Serve alone or with fresh fruit.

Chocolate Mayonnaise Cake

makes two 9-inch cakes; serves 10 to 12

When I first served this cake at Deep Springs, I announced that it contained a secret ingredient and joked that whoever guessed correctly would get a kiss from beloved professor Ross Peterson. Absolutely no one in the community could guess what it was, until the visiting girlfriend of a student suddenly remembered making a mayonnaise cake in a home economics class. "Mayonnaise!" she blurted out. Before Ross could even jump out of his chair, everyone in the dining room howled with laughter. I will never forget the slapstick image, post-kiss, of the grinning Ross, his wife Kay who had tried unsuccessfully to intervene, the student's girlfriend, and the student, all four of them red-faced, finally sitting down to enjoy the rest of their cake. I'd had my doubts when I mixed in the mayonnaise, but was amazed to discover what a good, tender cake it was. It's as easy as making a cake-mix cake, but if you use dark or Dutch-processed cocoa powder (see page 39), the result is superb. And you don't need to tell all your secrets; you may just call it chocolate cake.

3 cups all-purpose flour

1½ cups granulated *(white)* **sugar**

¾ cup unsweetened cocoa powder *(preferably dark or Dutch-processed)*

1 tablespoon baking powder

¾ teaspoon baking soda

1½ cups hot strong coffee

1½ cups mayonnaise

2 teaspoons vanilla extract

1 tablespoon finely grated orange zest *(optional)*

powdered sugar for dusting *(optional)*

whipped cream for serving *(optional)*

Heat the oven to 350°F. Butter two 9-inch round cake pans. To ensure that this delicate cake is easily removed from the pans, lining the pans with parchment is recommended. Cut circles of parchment to fit the bottoms of the pans. Butter the pans thoroughly, then put the parchment in the bottom and butter the parchment. Mix together a little cocoa powder with an equal amount of flour, and dust the lined pans with this mixture, tapping the pans to release the excess. Lacking parchment, just thoroughly grease the pans—especially the bottoms—and dust them well. You may also simply bake the cake in a buttered 9-by-13-inch pan as a sheet cake.

Sift the flour, sugar, cocoa powder, baking powder, and baking soda together in a medium bowl. In a large bowl, whisk together the coffee, mayonnaise, vanilla, and orange zest (if using). Add the dry ingredients and mix just until uniform. Scrape into the prepared pans and bake just until a toothpick inserted in the center comes out clean, about 25 minutes. Let cool for 10 minutes before turning the cakes out onto plates. Peel off the parchment, then invert the cakes onto a rack. If you have used a 9-by-13-inch pan, leave the cake in the pan. Cool completely and dust with powdered sugar in a sieve, if you like, tapping the sieve over the cake. Or, you may serve it with whipped cream—in that case, the powdered sugar isn't necessary.

Pinky's Jewish Apple Cake

makes 1 large cake; serves 10 to 12

This autumn gem comes from my friend Elge's mom—the family operates an apple farm in rural upstate New York. The brown sugar and orange juice concentrate give the cake a golden-yellow color that warms the soul on chilly days.

- 1 cup granulated (*white*) sugar
- 1 cup firmly packed brown sugar
- 1 cup sunflower oil or other vegetable oil
- ⅓ cup orange juice concentrate (*undiluted*)
- 4 eggs, at room temperature
- 2 teaspoons vanilla extract
- 3 cups sifted all-purpose flour
- 1 tablespoon baking powder
- ¾ teaspoon salt

APPLE FILLING

- 1 tablespoon ground cinnamon
- ⅓ cup granulated (*white*) sugar
- 5 or 6 tart, flavorful apples, peeled and sliced 1/8 inch thick (*about 6 cups sliced*)

Heat the oven to 350°F. Thoroughly grease a large tube pan and dust with flour, tapping out the excess. Using an electric mixer, beat the granulated and brown sugars, oil, and orange juice concentrate together. Add the eggs, one at a time, beating for a full minute after the addition of each one. Add the vanilla. Sift together the flour, baking powder, and salt, and gently fold the dry ingredients into the egg mixture, just until the batter is uniform.

To make the filling, combine the cinnamon and sugar in a small bowl. Gently pour just enough batter into the prepared tube pan to cover the bottom. Add half the apples. Just drop the apples in—don't rearrange or flatten them. Sprinkle evenly with half of the cinnamon-sugar mixture. Pour half the remaining batter over the apples, then repeat with the remaining apples and cinnamon sugar, ending with the remaining batter. Bake the cake for half an hour, then lower the oven temperature to 325°F and bake for 40 minutes more. When done, the top of the cake, lightly pressed with a finger, will spring back. The toothpick test is not reliable for this recipe, because of the apple filling. Let the cake cool for 10 minutes before removing it from the pan. It's extraordinary while still warm. Wrap the remainder well after it's completely cool. It will still be delicious and moist the next day.

Elge's Three-Ginger Gingerbread

makes 1 large cake; serves 10 to 12

Ginger is always welcome after a rich meal—it aids in digestion. This dense, intense cake contains three different forms of ginger: fresh, powdered, and candied. Though great the day it's made, there is a subtle blending and smoothing of flavors after it sits for a day.

- 3 cups sifted all-purpose flour
- 1 teaspoon baking soda
- 1 teaspoon baking powder
- 1 tablespoon ground cinnamon
- 1½ teaspoons ground cloves
- 2 teaspoons ground ginger
- ¾ teaspoon salt
- 1½ cups granulated (*white*) sugar
- 1 cup sunflower oil or other vegetable oil
- 1 cup molasses
- ½ cup water
- 2 large eggs, at room temperature, beaten
- 2 tablespoons finely grated fresh ginger
- ½ cup chopped candied ginger
- powdered sugar for dusting (*optional*)

LEMON CREAM (OPTIONAL)

- 1 large, juicy, fragrant lemon, or 1½ small lemons
- 3 tablespoons granulated (*white*) sugar
- 2 cups well-chilled heavy (*whipping*) cream

Heat the oven to 350°F. Butter a 12-inch springform pan. To ensure that the cake doesn't stick to the pan, cut a circle of parchment and place it in the pan's bottom. Butter and flour the parchment and dust the pan with flour, tapping out the excess. You may also bake the cake in a buttered 9-by-13-inch pan. Whisk the flour, baking soda, baking powder, cinnamon, cloves, ground ginger, and salt together in a medium bowl. In a large bowl, whisk together the sugar, oil, molasses, water, eggs, fresh ginger, and candied ginger. Add the dry ingredients to the wet, and gently fold together with a whisk just until thoroughly combined. Scrape into the prepared pan. Bake just until a toothpick inserted in the center comes out clean, about 45 minutes. Let the cake cool in the pan for about 10 minutes, then turn out onto a plate. Peel off the parchment, and invert the cake onto a rack to cool completely. If you've used a 9-by-13-inch pan, leave the cake in the pan. Wrap well and age for 1 day before serving.

Dust the top with powdered sugar through a sieve, or leave plain. Serve with hot tea as an afternoon restorative, or serve as a dessert with the lemon cream. To make lemon cream, into the bowl in which you intend to whip the cream, finely grate the zest of the lemon. With the back of a wooden spoon, mash the lemon zest with the sugar. Add the cream and whip it until soft peaks form. Fold in the juice from the lemon, and serve immediately.

Fresh Ginger Cake

makes 1 large cake; serves 10 to 12

Another excellent ginger cake, based on a famous recipe by my old Chez Panisse friend (and renowned cookbook author) David Lebovitz. It must be aged a day before serving—as with the preceding recipe, the ginger-molasses flavor doesn't reach its full bloom until the next day.

4 ounces fresh ginger, peeled and thinly sliced before weighing

1 cup sunflower oil or other vegetable oil

1 cup sugar

1 cup molasses

1 cup hot strong coffee

2 eggs, at room temperature, beaten

¼ teaspoon vanilla extract

2½ cups sifted all-purpose flour

½ teaspoon baking soda

1 teaspoon baking powder

¼ teaspoon salt

¼ teaspoon ground cinnamon

¼ teaspoon black pepper

Heat the oven to 350°F. Butter a 12-inch springform pan. To ensure that the cake doesn't stick to the pan, cut a circle of parchment and place it in the pan's bottom. Butter the parchment and dust the pan with flour, tapping out the excess. In a blender or food processor, blend the ginger and oil with the sugar until the ginger is completely pulverized into the mix—there should be no chunks.

Reduce the speed of the blender, and pour in the molasses, coffee, eggs, and vanilla. Pulse just until blended. Sift the dry ingredients into a large bowl and add the wet ingredients, carefully mixing just until the batter is uniform. Scrape the batter into the prepared pan. Bake just until a toothpick inserted in the center comes out clean, about 40 minutes. Let the cake cool in the pan for about 20 minutes, then turn it out onto a plate. Peel off the parchment, and invert the cake onto a rack to cool completely. Wrap well and let age for 1 day before serving. It will stay moist and delicious for 3 days. For a great topping for this cake, David suggests lemon curd lightened with whipped cream. Take a cup or two of the filling for Lemon Meringue Pie (page 269), let it chill, then fold it into an equal amount of barely sweetened whipped cream. Chill the mixture for a few hours to let the lemon flavor intensify.

Currant Cake

makes two 9-inch cakes; serves 10 to 12

Toasted, ground walnuts add richness and depth to this elegant cake.

1 cup walnuts *(about 3¼ ounces)***, lightly toasted** *(page 176)*

1 cup dried Zante currants

1 cup dry white wine

¾ cup unsalted butter *(1½ sticks)***, at room temperature**

1⅓ cups firmly packed brown sugar

3 large eggs, at room temperature

1 teaspoon vanilla extract

1⅓ cups sifted all-purpose flour

1½ teaspoons baking powder

½ teaspoon baking soda

¼ teaspoon salt

1 cup buttermilk

powdered sugar for dusting *(optional)*

Heat the oven to 350°F. Butter two 9-inch round cake pans, or a 9-by-13-inch rectangular pan. To ensure that the cake doesn't stick to the pans, cut circles of parchment to fit the bottoms of the pans.

Butter the parchment and dust the pan with flour. Take handfuls of the toasted walnuts and rub lightly to release excess papery brown skin. Chop the walnuts fine, or pulse to a fine meal in a food processor. Don't overgrind or you will have walnut butter. Combine the currants and the white wine in a small saucepan and heat until the wine steams. Remove from the heat and let the currants steep and plump in the wine for about 20 minutes, then drain them. Reserve the currant-sweetened wine for another use. (Use it for part of the water in Focaccia, page 77. Or baste roasting pork with it.)

Using an electric mixer, cream the butter well, then add the sugar and beat on high speed for about 3 minutes. Add the eggs, one at a time, beating each one in thoroughly before adding the next. Add the vanilla. Sift the flour, baking powder, baking soda, and salt together and blend in the ground walnuts. Gently fold this dry mixture into the butter mixture in three parts, alternating with the buttermilk. At the end, just before the batter is completely uniform, fold in the currants. Scrape the batter into the prepared pans and bake for about 20 minutes, or until a toothpick inserted in the center comes out clean. Let the cakes cool in the pans for about 10 minutes, then turn them out onto a plate. Peel off the parchment, and invert them onto a rack to cool completely. If you've used a 9-by-13-inch pan, leave the cake in the pan. If you like, dust the cake with powdered sugar through a sieve.

Cherry-Pork Cake

makes one large cake; serves 10 to 12

This unusual cake derives from old, Depression-era farmhouse cake recipes that used salt pork or pork sausage in place of butter. These recipes contained a multitude of spices, and whopping amounts of sugar, to mask the salty sausage flavor. Here, I started with good fresh pork and pork fat, and included a reasonable amount of salt, cake-friendly spices, and dried cherries. The result is a richly delicious, surprisingly light cake, studded with cherries.

1½ cups dried, lightly sweetened sour cherries

1 cup boiling water

½ pound lean fresh pork

½ pound fresh pork fat

1 teaspoon salt

1 teaspoon powdered ginger

¼ teaspoon ground white pepper

2½ cups sugar

2 large eggs

3 cups cake flour

1 teaspoon baking powder

1 teaspoon baking soda

1 cup coarsely chopped pecans

powdered sugar for dusting *(optional)*

Heat the oven to 350°F, and butter and flour a large bundt pan. Pour the boiling water over the cherries, letting them soak for about 15 minutes, then drain, saving the soaking water. Freeze the pork for about ½ hour, then cut it into small pieces and place in the bowl of a large, heavy-duty food processor with the salt, ginger, and white pepper. *(If you only have a standard-sized food processor, blend the pork mixture in two batches, then fold the two batches together before adding the dry ingredients.)* Process the pork until smooth, scraping down the bowl as necessary. Add the sugar and blend well, then the eggs, then the cooled cherry-soaking water. Process very well.

Sift the flour, baking powder, and baking soda into a large bowl. Fold the pork mixture into the flour mixture until almost uniform, then add the cherries and pecans and blend just until uniform. Scrape the batter into the prepared pan and bake for 1 hour. Let the cake rest in the pan for 10 minutes before turning it out onto a rack to cool. Let cool completely, then dust the cake with powdered sugar through a sieve, if you like. Well-wrapped, this cake stays moist and delicious for 2 days.

Prune Cake

makes 1 large cake; serves 8 to 10

Good old prunes—I always like to have them around. They are less sweet and more complexly flavored than raisins. You can add cut-up prunes to oatmeal or cereal or coffeecake batter (even salads!); you can simmer them in Constant Comment tea and serve as a compote with cream; you can cut a small hole and stuff them with sweetened, orange-flavored cream cheese and maybe a toasted almond to mimic the pit; or you can make this old-fashioned, moist cake, which you could call "plum cake" if you think "prune cake" would make your guests wrinkle their noses. For the holidays, serve with whipped cream, dressed up with a tablespoon or two of cognac.

1½ cups pitted prunes

1 cup prune juice *(orange juice may be substituted)*

3 large eggs, at room temperature

1 cup sunflower oil or other vegetable oil

1 teaspoon ground cinnamon

½ teaspoon ground nutmeg

2 tablespoons unsweetened cocoa powder

1 teaspoon vanilla extract

¾ teaspoon salt

1½ cups sugar

2 cups sifted all-purpose flour

½ teaspoon baking soda

½ teaspoon baking powder

1 cup walnuts *(about 3¼ ounces)*, **lightly toasted** *(page 176)* **and excess papery skin rubbed off** *(optional)*

FOR SERVING (OPTIONAL)

sweetened whipped cream, with or without a little cognac stirred in

Heat the oven to 350°F. Butter a 12-inch springform pan or a 9-by-13-inch pan. If you are using a springform pan, cut a circle of parchment and place it in the bottom of the pan, to ensure that the cake doesn't stick. Butter the parchment. Dust the pan with flour and tap out the excess. Using kitchen scissors, snip the prunes into quarters. Put them in the jar of your blender, and add the prune juice, eggs, oil, cinnamon, nutmeg, cocoa powder, vanilla, and salt. Blend on a lower speed for about 30 seconds, then raise the speed and slowly add the sugar while the motor is running. If this seems to be too much for your blender, transfer the mixture to a bowl and whisk in the sugar by hand. Sift together the flour, baking soda, and baking powder into a large bowl. Gently fold the prune mixture into the flour mixture with a whisk, being sure to sweep the bottom and all sides of the bowl. When the mixtures are mostly combined, sprinkle in the toasted walnuts, if using (I like to leave them whole), and continue to fold the batter with the whisk just until it is uniform. Scrape the batter into the prepared pan and bake just until a toothpick inserted in the center comes out clean, 35 to 40 minutes. Let the cake rest in the pan for 10 minutes before turning it out onto a plate. Peel off the parchment, then invert the cake onto a rack. If you've used a 9-by-13-inch pan, leave it in the pan. Let cool completely, then cut into small squares or wedges with a sharp knife. Serve unadorned or with cognac-laced whipped cream.

Milk and Honey Cake

makes two 9-inch cakes; serves 10 to 12

Deep Springs maintains beehives and produces honey redolent of desert wildflowers. The lush Mediterranean flavor of this cake is enhanced by a few toasted walnuts and a scattering of jewel-like fresh pomegranate seeds.

- 2½ cups all-purpose flour
- 1½ teaspoons baking powder
- ½ teaspoon salt
- ½ teaspoon white pepper
- 1¼ cups honey
- 1 cup extra-virgin olive oil
- ¾ cup milk, heated
- 2 eggs, at room temperature
- ½ teaspoon vanilla extract

GLAZE

- 2 tablespoons milk
- 2 tablespoons honey

FOR SERVING

- 1 cup toasted walnuts *(page 176)*
- ½ cup fresh pomegranate seeds

Heat the oven to 350°F. Butter two 9-inch round cake pans or a 9-by-13-inch pan. If you use round pans, cut circles of parchment and place them in the bottoms of the pans, to ensure that the cake doesn't stick. Butter the parchment. Dust the pans with flour and tap out the excess. Sift together the flour, baking powder, salt, and white pepper. Whisk the honey, olive oil, hot milk, eggs, and vanilla in a large bowl until uniform; the eggs will emulsify the mixture. Gently fold the dry mixture into the wet mixture just until blended. Scrape into the prepared pan and bake for about 25 minutes, or until a toothpick inserted in the center comes out clean. Let cool for 10 minutes in the pan, then remove the cake from the pan. Peel off the parchment, and invert the cake onto a rack. If you've used a 9-by-13-inch pan, leave the cake in the pan. To make the glaze, stir the milk and honey together in a small bowl until the honey is dissolved. Using a spoon, drizzle and spread the glaze all over the warm cakes, especially around the edge. Let the cakes absorb each application of glaze before applying the next, using the entire amount of glaze. Cool the cakes completely on a rack. Wrap well; this cake will be just as good the next day. Serve in wedges with a few toasted walnuts and a sprinkle of fresh pomegranate seeds.

Poppyseed Cake

makes one 12-inch cake; serves about 8

This is the cake I often choose for my February birthday during the peak of blood orange season: the singular poppyseed flavor invites a citrusy topping. Poppyseeds are very perishable—ascertain that those you are buying smell fresh and sweet, with no taint of rancidity, then store them in an airtight container in the freezer. For best results, have all cake ingredients at room temperature. It's best to have the butter at cool room temperature—softened, but still pliable. Be careful when separating the eggs—even a speck of egg yolk, or a trace of oil in the bowl, will inhibit the whites' proper beating.

- ¾ cup Dutch blue poppyseeds
- 1 cup whole milk
- 1 teaspoon vanilla extract
- 2 cups sifted cake flour
- 2½ teaspoons baking powder
- ¼ teaspoon salt
- ⅔ cup salted butter *(10 tablespoons plus 2 teaspoons)*, at cool room temperature
- 1¼ cups granulated sugar
- 4 egg whites

FRESH CITRUS TOPPING

- 2 juicy blood oranges
- 3 tablespoons citrus marmalade
- 1 tablespoon water
- 5 to 6 kumquats, thinly sliced, seeds removed

In a medium bowl, mix the poppyseeds, milk, and vanilla. Cover and let sit for 2 hours, or overnight in the refrigerator. If refrigerated, bring the mixture to room temperature before mixing the batter. Heat the oven to 375°F. Butter a 10- or 11-inch springform pan. Cut a circle of parchment to fit the bottom, and butter the parchment. Dust the pan with flour, tapping out the excess.

Sift the flour, baking powder, and salt together into a medium bowl. In a large bowl, cream the butter well, then slowly add the sugar, creaming again until very light and fluffy. Using a rubber spatula, alternately fold the flour mixture and the poppyseed–milk mixture into the butter in 3 to 4 additions, continuing to fold until the mixture is almost uniform. In another medium bowl, using clean beaters, whip the egg whites until soft peaks form (do not beat the whites until stiff), then fold the egg whites into the batter until the batter is uniform.

Scrape the batter into the prepared pan, smoothing the top. Bake 35 to 40 minutes, or until a toothpick inserted in the center comes out clean. Cool on a rack for 10 minutes, then remove the cake from the pan.

To make the topping, finely grate the zest of the blood oranges into a bowl. Peel the blood oranges with a sharp knife, removing all the white pith, saving all juice. Cut in half lengthwise, then cut each half crosswise into slices, removing any seeds. Put the slices in the bowl with the zest, along with any reserved juice. Blend the marmalade with the water and warm gently in a small saucepan or in a small bowl in the microwave to dissolve the marmalade, then let cool. Just before serving, gently combine the marmalade, kumquat slices, and blood orange. Serve a small spoonful of fruit with each slice of cake.

Big Pink Cake

makes 1 large cake; serves 10 to 12

For some occasions, nothing but a Big Pink Cake will do. A Deep Springs favorite for years, this raspberry whipped cream layer cake is as dramatically impressive as it is delicious. The buttermilk cake base is also terrific plain.

2⅓ cups sifted all-purpose flour or cake flour

1½ teaspoons baking powder

½ teaspoon baking soda

pinch of salt

¾ cup salted butter *(1½ sticks)***, at room temperature**

1⅓ cups sugar

3 large eggs, at room temperature

1 teaspoon vanilla extract

1 tablespoon finely grated lemon zest

1 cup buttermilk

RASPBERRY WHIPPED CREAM

8 ounces frozen raspberries *(or fresh, in season)*

¼ cup sugar

3 cups heavy *(whipping)* **cream**

3 drops lemon extract

¼ teaspoon vanilla extract

multicolored nonpareil sprinkles for decoration *(optional)*

Heat the oven to 350°F. Thoroughly butter two 9-inch round cake pans. To ensure that the cake doesn't stick, cut circles of parchment and place them in the bottoms of the pans. Butter the parchment, and dust the pans well with flour, tapping out the excess. Sift the flour, baking powder, baking soda, and salt together. Using an electric mixer, beat the butter until creamy, then gradually add the sugar and beat thoroughly until light, about 3 minutes. Add the eggs, one at a time, then the vanilla and lemon zest. To this liquid mixture alternately fold in half the dry ingredients, then half the buttermilk, repeating with the remaining dry ingredients and buttermilk. Mix just until blended. The batter tastes excellent. Scrape the batter into the prepared cake pans, spreading it evenly. Bake in the center of the oven, rotating if necessary, until the cake feels springy to the touch and a toothpick inserted in the center of the cake comes out clean, 20 to 25 minutes. Let the cakes cool in the pans for about 10 minutes. Run a small knife around the edges to loosen the cakes, then invert them onto plates. Peel off the parchment, flip the cakes onto a rack, and *let cool completely*. If you want many layers of cake and whipped cream, you may slice the cakes evenly across, using a long, sharp knife, so you have 4 thin rounds. I usually don't bother.

To make the raspberry whipped cream, in a small, nonreactive saucepan over low heat, gently thaw the berries for a few moments, then raise the heat, add the sugar, and bring the berries to a simmer. If using fresh berries, simply mash the berries and sugar together and heat. Set a screen sieve over a bowl, and dump the berries and juice into the sieve. Using the bottom of a ladle or the back of a large spoon, press as much pulp from the berries as possible. Discard the dry, seedy solids left in the sieve. Cool the berry purée in the refrigerator. In a large bowl, mix the cream with the berry purée and the lemon and vanilla extracts and whip until the cream holds its shape. Place a cake round, bottom side up, on a nice-looking plate. If the cake seems in danger of sliding around on the plate, anchor it with a small dab of whipped cream. Cover the top with a thick layer of whipped cream. Place the other round atop the first, and cover the top and sides with more whipped cream. Slather the excess whipped cream over the sides and top of the cake— it should look rather free and easy, not fussed over. The cake will keep in fine condition, refrigerated, for several hours. If you wish, shortly before serving, toss small handfuls of multicolored nonpareil sprinkles on the sides and top of the cake.

CHAPTER 16
GOOEY DESSERTS

In this chapter you will find some of the most gratifying, indulgent, comforting dessert recipes in the book. Pies and cakes reveal the skill of the cook, crisps and cobblers showcase good seasonal fruit, cookies deliver big flavor in portable little bites, but the elemental bowl-and-spoon desserts in this chapter—custard, ice cream, sherbet, pudding, even Jell-O—often elicit a long, closed-eyed sigh, down to the last spoonful.

Chocolate Pudding

serves 6 to 8

This makes a deep, dark chocolate pudding. The skin that forms on the top as it cools is some people's favorite part: choose a wide, shallow bowl for the pudding, to allow more surface area for skin to form. If you want to avoid a skin forming, choose a deep container and cover the pudding with plastic wrap when cool, pressing the wrap directly on the pudding's surface. Serve alone or with whipped cream.

¾ cup sugar

3 tablespoons cornstarch

¼ teaspoon salt

½ cup unsweetened cocoa powder

3 cups whole milk

3 egg yolks

1 ounce *(1 square)* **unsweetened chocolate**

¾ teaspoon vanilla extract

In a medium-sized, heavy saucepan, mix the sugar, cornstarch, salt, and cocoa powder until there are no lumps. Gradually stir in the milk. Over medium-low heat, slowly heat the mixture, whisking frequently, until it steams and thickens slightly. Beat the egg yolks in a small bowl, whisk in a few spoonfuls of the warm chocolate mixture, then whisk the yolk mixture into the remaining chocolate mixture in the pan. Bring to a gentle simmer and cook for 1 minute. Remove the pan from the heat and add the chocolate and vanilla. Stir to melt the chocolate. Let cool for about 10 minutes, then pour into a bowl. Let cool completely, then chill.

Butterscotch Pudding

serves 4 to 6

Artificially flavored butterscotch products have prevailed for so long that few of us know that "real" butterscotch is a close relative of caramel and toffee. *Caramel* is simply pure white sugar heated until it darkens (see page 43 for more on caramel). As it transforms, the sugar takes on the deep, dark, wonderfully complex flavors we associate with caramel. *Toffee* and *butterscotch* also involve the caramelization of sugar, but with butter added—as the sugar caramelizes, the butter browns, creating ever more complex flavors. While toffee (see page 328 for a recipe) is made with white sugar and butter, the essence of butterscotch is brown sugar and butter. The molasses in brown sugar adds complexity, and seems to jump-start the caramelization process. This recipe begins with making extra-dark brown sugar out of white sugar and molasses.

¾ cup plus 1 tablespoon granulated *(white)* **sugar**

2 tablespoons molasses

¼ cup cornstarch

¾ teaspoon salt

2½ cups whole milk

3 large egg yolks

4 tablespoons salted butter

1 cup heavy cream

¾ teaspoon vanilla

TOPPING

1 cup heavy cream

¼ teaspoon vanilla

Put the sugar—including the extra tablespoon—in a large, heavy saucepan, and add the molasses, stirring with a wooden spoon until the mixture is uniform. Reserve 1 packed tablespoon of this dark brown sugar to sweeten the cream for the topping.

In a large bowl, blend the cornstarch and salt. Add the milk, whisking to dissolve the cornstarch completely. Whisk the yolks in a small bowl, then add them to the milk mixture, whisking until uniform. Keep the whisk in the mixture—you'll need it later.

Add the butter to the brown sugar in the saucepan, and set the pan over low heat to melt the butter. Have the cup of cream ready nearby. When the butter is melted, raise the flame to medium, and let the mixture cook, stirring almost constantly with a wooden spoon, taking care to go over the bottom of the pot constantly with the spoon. Let the mixture rapidly bubble, continuing to stir. At the beginning, the mixture will give off steam, as the moisture in the butter cooks off. Then the bubbling will lessen somewhat, and the mixture will begin to emit little puffs of smoke. Immediately remove the pan from the flame. *Be very careful at this stage—the sugar-butter mixture is extremely hot.* Carefully pour in the cream, a little at a time, stirring as you pour. Some of the butterscotch will clump—that's OK. When all the cream has been added, return the pot to a medium flame, stirring to dissolve as much of the solid butterscotch as possible. Pour most of the butterscotch-cream mixture into the milk mixture in the large bowl, whisking as you pour. Now pour the tempered milk mixture into the pot with the remaining butterscotch, and whisk until uniform. Heat over a medium-high flame, whisking almost constantly, until the pudding boils. Let the pudding cook for 2 minutes, continuing to whisk. Whisk in ¾ teaspoon vanilla, then pour the pudding into an 8-by-8-inch glass baking dish, or into individual serving dishes. Let cool to room temperature, then cover with plastic wrap and chill.

For the whipped cream topping, whip 1 cup of cream together with ¼ teaspoon vanilla and the reserved tablespoon of dark brown sugar, until soft peaks form. Top large spoonfuls of pudding with spoonfuls of whipped cream.

Pearl Tapioca Pudding

serves about 4

Here is a good, old-fashioned, not-too-rich tapioca pudding recipe using real pearl tapioca, not the quick-cooking type.

⅓ cup small pearl tapioca

¾ cup water

2¼ cups whole milk

¼ teaspoon salt

½ cup sugar

1 egg, beaten

¾ teaspoon vanilla extract

½ teaspoon orange flower water *(optional)*

In heavy saucepan, soak the tapioca in ¾ cup water for 30 minutes. Add the milk and salt, and gradually bring to a boil over medium heat, stirring frequently. Turn the flame to low and simmer, stirring frequently, for 20 minutes: the mixture should be thickened and the pearls should be tender, but still intact. Stir in the sugar. In a small bowl, slowly whisk about ¼ cup of the hot milk mixture into the egg, then slowly whisk this mixture back into the saucepan. Add the vanilla and orange flower water, if using, and let the pudding simmer another minute. Pour into bowls, let cool, then chill. Serve plain or with fruit.

Peach Leaf Custard Sauce

makes about 2¼ cups; serves 4 to 5

Several peach trees thrive in the Deep Springs orchard. Their leaves lend a delicate almond flavor to this "pouring custard." It is excellent served warm over a wedge of plain cake, generously topped with sliced, lightly sugared peaches and plums.

20 fresh, unsprayed peach leaves, washed

2 cups milk

4 egg yolks

¼ cup sugar

⅛ teaspoon salt

Heat the milk with the peach leaves in a medium-sized, heavy saucepan over a low flame until the leaves release an almond scent into the milk. Strain the milk, squeezing the leaves gently. Put the milk in a double boiler over, not in, boiling water, and heat. In a small bowl, beat the yolks, sugar, and salt together. Whisk a few spoonfuls of the hot milk into the yolks to temper them, then whisk the yolks into the hot milk. Cook in the double boiler, whisking frequently, until thickened. Let stand, off the heat, whisking frequently, for about 5 minutes.

Vanilla Bean Crème Brûlée

serves 8

I've always thought of crème brûlée as a modern dessert, but I found this recipe on yellowed paper, written in my grandmother's inimitable backhand script, in her old box of recipes. It is the use of the blowtorch, I think, that makes this recipe so perennially appealing to Deep Springs students.

½ vanilla bean

3 cups heavy *(whipping)* **cream**

6 tablespoons sugar, plus about ½ cup

pinch of salt

6 egg yolks

Heat the oven to 350°F. With a small knife, split the vanilla bean lengthwise. Pour the heavy cream into a small, heavy saucepan. Scrape the fine seed paste from the vanilla bean into the cream, and put the bean pod into the cream also. Add the 6 tablespoons sugar and salt, and gently warm the cream over medium heat, stirring frequently, until the sugar is dissolved.

In a medium bowl, whisk the egg yolks. Slowly whisk a couple of spoonfuls of the hot cream into the yolks, then whisk the yolks into the rest of the cream in the saucepan. Strain the custard through a screen sieve into a pitcher. Pour the custard into 8 wide, individual custard dishes (4- or 5-ounce capacity; wide dishes mean there is more top surface area for the brûlée crust). Place the dishes in a deep baking pan, place the pan in the center of the preheated oven, and then carefully pour boiling water into the baking pan, being careful not to splash water into the custard. Pour in enough water to come halfway up the sides of the custard dishes. Gently close the oven and bake for 30 to 40 minutes, or until the custards are just set, still jiggly in the center. Carefully remove the custards from the pan and set on a wire rack to cool—you may bake and refrigerate the custards, covered, well ahead of serving time.

Before applying the remaining sugar and serving, bring the custards to room temperature. To serve, evenly sprinkle about 1 tablespoon of sugar over the surface of each custard. Using a propane blowtorch, burn the sugar until it is a deep mahogany brown, moving the flame of the torch over the sugar until it beads, bubbles, and finally caramelizes. For best results, let the sugar get fairly dark. Let the sugar cool and harden for a moment or two, then serve immediately.

Don't have a blowtorch? Here is my grandmother's alternative: Turn on your oven's broiler. Sieve 1½ tablespoons brown sugar onto a buttered baking sheet. Spread the sugar out with a spoon into a circle, about ⅛ inch thick. Do 4 of these at a time. Put in the oven, turn the oven to broil, and watch very carefully. When the sugar is melted and has run together, let cool for a minute, test with a spatula, lift quickly onto wax paper, and let cool until hardened. Repeat with the other 4. Place a disc of hardened sugar onto each custard and serve immediately.

Baked Custard

serves 3 to 4

Here is a glimpse into the past from my grandmother's recipe file: the simplest baked custard imaginable, crème brûlée's good country ancestor. Serve it unadorned at those times when you want something gloriously plain. It's also good with maple syrup, melted jam or jelly, or the syrup from pickled fruit (page 258).

2 cups whole milk

⅓ cup sugar

pinch of salt

3 eggs, lightly beaten

¾ teaspoon vanilla extract

Heat the oven to 325°F. Scald the milk by heating it in a medium-sized, heavy saucepan over a medium-high flame, stirring frequently, until steaming. Remove from the heat, add the sugar and salt, and stir until dissolved. Slowly whisk about ½ cup of the hot milk into the eggs in a small bowl, then slowly whisk the eggs into the pan of hot milk. Add the vanilla. Pour (straining through a sieve if you like, to remove tough bits of egg) into a 4-cup loaf pan or other medium-sized baking dish, and set the dish in a larger pan. Place the whole thing in the center of the preheated oven, then carefully pour boiling water into the larger pan, being careful not to splash water into the custard. Pour in enough water to come halfway up the side of the custard dish. Gently close the oven and bake for 20 to 30 minutes, just until a knife inserted in the center comes out clean. The custard will still be slightly jiggly in the center. Remove from the water bath and let cool for a few minutes before serving warm. The custard is also good cold; cool to room temperature before putting it in the refrigerator.

COLOSTRUM CUSTARD

To ensure healthy calves, cows (and other mammals) produce a special milk called colostrum, pale yellow in color and especially high in protein, when calves are born. Deep Springs' dairy cows, by their nature, produce more colostrum than their calves are able to drink. Most of the excess is collected and frozen, reserved for the struggling calves of Deep Springs' main cattle herd, typically born in winter. When those who work closely with the calves can be persuaded to part with a precious gallon of colostrum milk, the community is treated to this rare delicacy. The yellow milk tastes very rich and slightly thick, as if eggs were already whisked in. When you heat it, it firms up exactly like egg custard. Proceed as directed in the master recipe, using colostrum milk and omitting the eggs and the milk-scalding step: just whisk sugar into the milk until dissolved, stir in the vanilla, and bake in a water bath.

Gooseberry Fool

serves 4

"Fool" was a term of endearment hundreds of years ago. This traditional English way of preparing tart fruit is very simple and very good. This recipe reflects my preference for a tart fool; adjust the sugar to your taste. Serve in wineglasses or other tall goblets.

2 cups gooseberries

2 tablespoons water

pinch of salt

3 to 4 tablespoons sugar

1 cup heavy (whipping) **cream**

¼ teaspoon vanilla extract

Pinch off the tough little stem ends from the gooseberries. Put the berries in a small, heavy, nonreactive saucepan with the water, salt, and 2 tablespoons of the sugar. Heat over a high flame, stirring constantly, until the berries have broken down to a purée and the sugar is dissolved.

Let cool to room temperature, then chill thoroughly. Taste the gooseberries for sweetness and add another tablespoon of sugar, if you like. Using an electric mixer, whip the cream with the vanilla and remaining 1 tablespoon sugar until soft peaks form. Fold in the gooseberry purée somewhat imperfectly—it's fine if there are streaks of purée. Spoon into goblets, chill, and serve.

OTHER FRUIT FOOLS

Plums, huckleberries, rhubarb, raspberries, other berries—any fruit with a strong flavor and a pronounced tartness is an excellent candidate for making into a fool. For well-pigmented fruit, fold only three-fourths of the purée into the cream, then layer the cream with the remaining purée in the glass.

Vanilla Ice Cream

makes about 1 quart

This is just a bit leaner than most recipes for vanilla ice cream, and so feels more satisfyingly cold on the tongue. A bit of cornstarch keeps it creamy, while an imperceptible touch of honey haunts the sweetness. My mother loves vanilla ice cream with a little bourbon poured over.

½ cup sugar

1 tablespoon cornstarch

3¼ cups half-and-half

1 tablespoon honey

pinch of salt

4 egg yolks

1½ teaspoons vanilla extract

Mix the sugar and cornstarch together in a medium-sized, heavy pot until there are no visible lumps. Pour in the half-and-half, and add the honey and salt. Slowly bring to a simmer over medium-low heat, stirring frequently, until foamy on top and steaming. Whisk the egg yolks in a small bowl. Very slowly whisk in about 1 cup of the hot half-and-half mixture into the yolks, then slowly whisk this mixture back into the pot of hot half-and-half. Cook for 1 to 2 minutes more over medium-low heat, stirring frequently, until steaming hot and slightly thickened. Remove from the heat and let cool, continuing to stir frequently for about 5 minutes. Let cool to room temperature. Stir in the vanilla and chill thoroughly, preferably overnight. Freeze the mixture in your ice cream maker according to the manufacturer's instructions. Serve immediately, while still soft and creamy, or pack the ice cream into a container, put it in the freezer, and let it freeze hard. Hard-frozen ice cream tastes best when allowed to "temper" slightly; it should be served a few degrees above freezing. If you are serving ice cream for dessert, move the container of ice cream from the freezer to the refrigerator just as you are sitting down to begin dinner. By dessert time, the ice cream should be perfectly tempered.

COFFEE ICE CREAM

This requires 3 or 4 shots of fresh espresso. As soon as the espresso is made, stir in a heaping tablespoon of the recipe's sugar to fix the fresh-brewed flavor. Let cool to room temperature. Follow the master Vanilla Ice Cream recipe, using only 3 cups half-and-half and only 1 teaspoon vanilla, and add the cooled espresso when adding the vanilla. This ice cream is delightful with Chocolate Sauce (page 278) or with fine chunks of bittersweet chocolate folded in when the ice cream is finished churning.

STRAWBERRY ICE CREAM

Crush fresh, perfectly ripe, red-all-the-way-through strawberries (enough to yield 1¼ juicy cups) with 2 tablespoons of sugar until the sugar is completely dissolved (don't crush the fruit to a smooth purée; some chunks should remain). Add a few drops of lemon juice and chill well. Follow the master Vanilla Ice Cream recipe, using only 3 cups half-and-half, 2 egg yolks, and 1 teaspoon vanilla. As soon as the ice cream is solid in the ice cream maker, fold in the strawberries.

PEACH ICE CREAM

Crush enough perfectly ripe, peeled, sweet summer peaches with 2 tablespoons of sugar to yield 1¼ cups (don't crush the fruit to a smooth purée; some chunks should remain). Add a few drops of lemon juice. Chill the peaches well. Follow the master Vanilla Ice Cream recipe, using only 3 cups of half-and-half, 2 egg yolks, and 1 teaspoon vanilla. Once the ice cream is solid in the ice cream maker, fold in the crushed peaches. A little almond extract is particularly good with peaches or any other stone fruit.

BUTTERMILK ICE CREAM

This is an excellent and appropriate use for the "true" cultured buttermilk that results from butter making (page 79), but storebought cultured buttermilk is delicious, too. Follow the master Vanilla Ice Cream recipe, using 1 cup of heavy cream and ½ cup of whole milk for the base (instead of the 3¼ cups of half-and-half), and an additional 2 tablespoons of sugar. Immediately prior to churning the ice cream, slowly whisk in 1¾ cups buttermilk. So that the good buttermilk flavor stands out, use only ½ teaspoon of vanilla.

CINNAMON ICE CREAM

For an excellent ice cream to accompany plum desserts, follow the master Vanilla Ice Cream recipe, adding 2 fragrant cinnamon sticks to the pan when you add the half-and-half, and leaving them in as the mixture cooks, cools, and chills. Fish the cinnamon sticks out just before churning. Use only ½ teaspoon of vanilla.

WHISKEY ICE CREAM

For the sugar in the master Vanilla Ice Cream recipe, use a dark-brown muscovado sugar (or regular brown sugar). In place of the vanilla, use 5 tablespoons of Irish whiskey (or bourbon). Don't add more whiskey, or the ice cream will be too soft.

BUTTER PECAN ICE CREAM

For the half-cup of white sugar in the master Vanilla Ice Cream recipe, substitute ⅔ cup of brown sugar. In a 325°F oven, lightly toast 1 cup of coarsely chopped pecans with 1 tablespoon of butter and a good pinch of salt for about 10 minutes (page 176)—the butter will brown as the nuts toast. Flavor the ice cream with 1½ tablespoons of bourbon, reducing the vanilla extract to 1 teaspoon—bourbon and pecans go very well together. Fold about three-quarters of the pecans into the ice cream after it's churned, and top servings of ice cream with the remaining pecans.

Lemon Ice Cream

makes about 1 quart

This ice cream, so lemony it's almost sherbet, goes superbly with Gingersnaps, page 324, but is good enough to be served on its own. I can't imagine a dinner that wouldn't be well concluded with a small dish of lemon ice cream.

1 tablespoon finely grated lemon zest

½ cup plus 1 tablespoon fresh lemon juice *(from 4 to 5 lemons)*

1 cup sugar

3 large eggs

2 cups half-and-half

½ teaspoon vanilla extract

In a medium-sized, heavy, nonreactive saucepan, whisk together the lemon zest, lemon juice, sugar, eggs, 1 cup of the half-and-half, and vanilla. Cook over medium heat, stirring constantly and going over the entire bottom of the pan with your spoon, until the mixture just comes to a simmer. Remove from the heat, stir for a moment longer, cover, and let sit for about 5 minutes. Stir again and strain the custard through a fine sieve into a bowl, pressing hard on the zest to extract as much of its flavor as possible. Chill, covered with plastic wrap pressed on the surface, until completely cold. Whisk in the remaining cup of half-and-half and freeze the mixture in your ice cream maker according to the manufacturer's instructions. Serve immediately, while still soft and creamy, or pack the ice cream into a container, put it in the freezer, and let it freeze hard. If frozen hard, allow the ice cream to "temper" in the refrigerator for about an hour before serving.

Blackberry Ice Cream

makes about 1 quart

On a hot, midsummer's day, find a wild blackberry bush on a sunny hillside. The ripe, sweet berries are purple-black and slightly dull, not shiny; they are often hidden among the foliage, hanging like tiny clusters of grapes. A ripe berry will easily separate from the stem—if you have to pull it off with any force, it isn't ripe yet. However, for this intensely flavored ice cream, adapted from a recipe in Lindsey Shere's *Chez Panisse Desserts,* a few underripe ones will keep the flavor bright. Of course, raspberries or any other tart-sweet berry would be very good treated this way. If your berries taste a little tired, a teaspoon of rosewater will enhance their flavor considerably—blackberries, raspberries, and roses are all in the same botanical family.

3 cups ripe, juicy wild blackberries

⅔ cup sugar

2 cups heavy *(whipping)* **cream**

pinch of salt

¼ teaspoon vanilla extract

Blend the blackberries to a purée in a blender. Pass the purée through a sieve to remove the seeds, pressing it through the mesh of the sieve using the back of a ladle. Heat the sugar and 1 cup of the cream in a heavy saucepan until the sugar dissolves. Add the blackberry purée, the remaining cup of cream, salt, and vanilla. Chill thoroughly and freeze in your ice cream maker according to the manufacturer's instructions. Serve immediately, while still soft and creamy, or pack the ice cream into a container, put it in the freezer, and let it freeze hard. If frozen hard, allow the ice cream to "temper" in the refrigerator for about an hour before serving. Serve this ice cream alone, or alongside a scoop of Lemon Ice Cream (preceding recipe).

Pear Sherbet

makes about 1 quart

This refreshing sherbet is pure essence of pear. Make it when pears are at their best, in fall and early winter. I love Bartlett pears—they are fragrant and yellow when ripe, and widely available in their season (September through December), but Comice, French Butter, and slightly overripe, nutty Boscs are worth trying, too. Pear sherbet needs little accompaniment: perhaps an almond cookie, some biscotti, or, for very special occasions, a scant scattering of painstakingly collected fresh rosemary flowers.

3 pounds ripe Bartlett pears, in season

¼ cup water

¾ cup sugar

pinch of salt

2 teaspoons fresh lemon juice

Peel and core the pears, and cut into ½-inch chunks. Heat the pears, water, sugar, and salt in a medium-sized, heavy, nonreactive pot until the mixture is bubbling and the pears are heated through. Purée in a blender or food processor. Let the purée cool to room temperature, add the lemon juice, and chill thoroughly in the refrigerator. Freeze in your ice cream maker according to the manufacturer's instructions. Serve immediately, while still soft and creamy, or pack the sherbet into a container, put it in the freezer, and let it freeze hard. If frozen hard, allow the sherbet to "temper" in the refrigerator for about an hour before serving.

PEAR AND BLACK PEPPER SHERBET

Using a fine-mesh wire strainer and a regular-mesh strainer, sift freshly ground black pepper into three grinds: fine, medium, and coarse. Stir 1 teaspoon of the medium-grind pepper into the purée in the master recipe when you are ready to freeze it. In place of the lemon juice, use white balsamic vinegar, if you like. This sherbet is wonderfully refreshing in the middle of a long dinner of small courses, should you be so ambitious. Serve with a couple of toasted, salted pecans or almonds.

Snow Ice Cream

serves 2 to 3

Every other winter or so, enough snow falls in and around Deep Springs Valley to close the mountain passes, and the community is stranded for a few days. This recipe is a very good exercise in seizing such a moment. Snow varies like any natural product—some snow will immediately go slushy in the bowl; other snow will stay resolutely fluffy.

1 egg yolk

½ teaspoon vanilla extract

1 tablespoon brandy

¼ cup heavy (whipping) **cream**

¼ cup sugar

about 8 cups perfectly clean, freshly fallen snow

In a small saucepan, whisk together the egg yolk, vanilla, brandy, heavy cream, and sugar, in that order, to make a custardy syrup. Heat gently, stirring frequently, until the mixture is hot and the sugar dissolved. Let cool to room temperature, then chill until cold. Minutes before you want to serve the ice cream, take a large mixing bowl, a clean thing to scoop snow with, the custard-syrup, and a wire whisk outside with you. Collect the snow in the bowl, drizzle the cold custard-syrup over it, and gently mix with the whisk to combine—there should still be lumps of snow. Bring the snow ice cream in and consume immediately. People should be waiting by the door, spoons in hand.

MAPLE SNOW ICE CREAM
This is quicker and no less delicious.

¼ teaspoon vanilla extract

1 tablespoon bourbon

¼ cup dark maple syrup

¼ cup heavy (whipping) **cream**

Whisk the ingredients together and chill thoroughly. Mix with snow as directed in the master recipe. Of course, anything sweet and liquid poured over fresh snow could be a delightful dessert.

GELATIN DESSERTS

My grandmother believed in the healing powers of gelatin—when anyone was sick, she'd say, "Oh, I'll make you some nice Jell-O." In antique French and English cookbooks, there are dessert recipes that involve simmering fresh veal bones for hours to extract their natural gelatin, laboriously clarifying the resulting stock, flavoring it with fruit, and setting it in a bed of ice to gel. These are the ancestors of the now-ubiquitous packaged gelatin, known to most Americans as Jell-O.

This section aims to describe the full spectrum of gelatin-based desserts, starting with nostalgic concoctions using sweetened, packaged gelatin. Recipes and ideas for more sophisticated desserts based on unflavored gelatin follow, including *gelées*. The chapter ends with several elegant recipes for cream-based gelatin desserts, known as *panna cotta* in Italian cuisine.

Savory gelatin preparations, called aspic, were once common but are now quite rare. Decades ago, American housewives put all kinds of things in sweet gelatin: not only fruit and dairy products but vegetables, nuts, mayonnaise, and sometimes even ham and turkey, calling such concoctions "salad," to be served with the meal. Such traditions continue in some circles, but at the behest of nutritionists, purveyors of packaged gelatin are now careful to emphasize that their product is a dessert. Despite its toy-like colors and equally garish flavors, very few of us truly dislike Jell-O. We ate it as children, and we appreciate its cool, light qualities as adults.

Whatever the type of gelatin dessert, I prefer a soft texture. For packaged gelatin, I add about 2 extra tablespoons of water for every cup of water called for on the package. This more delicate, melting texture means the gelatin can't be successfully unmolded—it must be served out with a big spoon. As many learn in college, vodka, tequila, or other booze can replace some of the water. When using canned fruit with gelatin, always drain it first. Don't use the liquid from the fruit in place of the water for the gelatin—it will cloud the gelatin and make it too sweet. If you're using fresh pineapple, it needs to be simmered first to destroy an enzyme that would otherwise dissolve the gelatin's protein and prevent it from setting. The same is true for fresh figs, fresh ginger, guava, kiwi, and papaya.

Here are some great, simple combinations of packaged, sweetened gelatin with fruit. If you are in an experimental mood, let your imagination—or old cookbooks—be your guide:

- strawberry gelatin with sliced bananas
- cherry gelatin with peeled fresh peaches, apricots, plums, or nectarines
- cherry gelatin with canned fruit cocktail
- raspberry gelatin with canned pears
- lemon or lime gelatin with canned pineapple
- lemon or orange gelatin with canned crushed pineapple and grated carrots ("Golden Glow Salad"—very 1930s!)

And here are three representative dairy-based preparations made with packaged gelatin:

Tangy Lemon Sour Cream Gelatin

In a small saucepan, bring to a boil 1 cup water with the finely grated zest of 1 large lemon, and remove from the heat. Completely dissolve a 3-ounce package of lemon-flavored gelatin in the water. Add the juice of the lemon and ¼ cup cold water. Let cool for 5 minutes. Whisk ½ cup sour cream and ½ cup buttermilk together in a medium bowl until smooth. Whisk in about ¼ cup of the gelatin mixture, then whisk in the rest of the gelatin mixture. Chill until set.

Lime Yum

This is an updated version of something I loved when I was very little. In a medium bowl, using an electric mixer, whip 1 cup heavy cream with ¼ teaspoon vanilla extract until soft peaks form. Fold in 1 cup (one 8-ounce can) drained unsweetened crushed pineapple, one 3-ounce package lime-flavored gelatin (dry, not mixed with water), 1 cup (one 8-ounce carton) sour cream, and the finely grated zest and juice of 1 small lime. Chill thoroughly. The texture is creamier the first day, but the flavor is better the next.

Creamy Orange Gelatin

In a small saucepan, bring to a boil ¾ cup water with the finely grated zest of 1 large orange, and remove from the heat. Completely dissolve a 3-ounce package of orange-flavored gelatin in the water. Gradually add the warm gelatin to an 8-ounce package of softened cream cheese in a medium bowl, whisking out any lumps. Add the juice of the orange and 1 tablespoon of fresh lemon juice. Chill until set.

Gelatin desserts can be made from scratch, not from veal bones, but using unflavored powdered gelatin and clear fruit juice—I like to call these *gelée* (zhay-LAY). I usually use a ratio of 1 envelope (or 2¼ teaspoons) to 2¼ cups clear, sweetened fruit juice. First, prepare the fruit juice. Clear apple juice works very well—it combines well with other juices, or can be infused with other flavors. Wine, (hard) cider, or pomegranate juice can also be made into good gelées. Naturally tart juice will provide the liveliest flavor. Carefully sweeten the juice to taste with sugar; it should be only a little sweeter than if you were to drink a cup of it. Next, put about ¼ cup of the juice in a small dish. Sprinkle the gelatin evenly over the surface of the liquid—the gelatin will rapidly absorb much of the juice. Heat another portion of the juice (about 1 cup) in a small saucepan until hot and steaming, and stir in the gelatin mixture, dissolving the gelatin completely. Remove from the heat and stir in the remaining amount (about 1 more cup) of juice. A little liqueur or other spirit may be included in the volume of liquid.

To serve gelée elegantly, first make the gelée base and chill it to set. Cut the accompanying fresh fruit close to serving time. Layer spoonfuls of gelée with cut fruit in wineglasses or goblets. Top, or not, with whipped cream.

Here are some ideas for gelées:

- sparkling apple cider gelée with Poached Pears (page 278)
- summer berry–red wine gelée with whipped cream and fresh berries
- pomegranate and red wine gelée with fresh oranges
- lemon-mint gelée with fresh strawberries

Carol's Fresh Fruit Gelée

serves 4 to 6

This recipe, relatively low in sugar, is excellent get-well comfort food. When I brought a big bowl of it to my neighbor Carol when she was ill, she loved it so much that she asked for the recipe. She was surprised to learn that it was made with fruit juice and unflavored gelatin. "I never thought of making jello out of anything but Jell-O," she wrote in her thank-you note. "This opens up a whole new vista!" The fruit may be varied; any fruit that tends to brown (such as pears) must first be poached in the juice.

2 cups good apple juice

2 fresh, ripe pears, peeled and sliced

1 envelope *(2½ teaspoons)* **unflavored gelatin**

2 tablespoons of your favorite tart fruit jelly

finely grated zest and juice of 1 lemon

1 to 2 tablespoons sugar

1½ cups red seedless grapes, halved *(or use the small grapes called Zante or "champagne" grapes)*

1½ cups fresh seedless tangerine sections

Bring 1 cup of the apple juice to a boil in a small saucepan. Add half the pear slices, and bring to a boil again. Let boil for 20 seconds, stirring gently, to cook the pears through. Using a slotted spoon, remove the pears to a large glass bowl. Repeat with the remaining pears. Put a few tablespoons of the remaining apple juice in a small bowl. Sprinkle the gelatin over the juice—it will absorb the juice.

Add the jelly to the hot pear-infused juice in the saucepan. Put the pan back over a low flame, stirring to thoroughly melt the jelly. Add the lemon zest, lemon juice, and sugar. Stir the gelatin mixture into the hot, sweetened juice until the gelatin is thoroughly dissolved. Add the remaining apple juice. Put the grapes and tangerine sections into the bowl with the pears. Pour the juice mixture over the fruit. Chill for several hours or overnight, until set.

Blood Orange Gelée

serves 6 to 8

This could be considered the queen of gelées; it's perfect after a rich, spicy winter meal. Regular oranges may be used; the total volume of sliced oranges should be about 3½ cups.

8 to 10 blood oranges, enough to yield 3½ cups of fruit and juice

2¼ teaspoons plain unflavored gelatin *(1 envelope)*

1¼ cups plain apple juice or other clear fruit juice

1 stick cinnamon

3 cardamom pods

⅔ cup sugar, or more to taste

juice of ½ lemon

1 teaspoon orange flower water

Using a fine rasp-style grater, grate the brightly-colored zest off half the blood oranges into a medium nonreactive saucepan. Using a small, sharp knife, peel all the light-colored pith off all the oranges, then carefully slice the oranges into thin rounds, putting them (and all juice) in a large, attractive glass bowl or white china serving dish.

Sprinkle the gelatin over about ¼ cup of the apple juice, and let sit. Add the remaining cup of apple juice to the pan with the orange zest, and add the spices. Bring the juice and spices to a simmer, and gently simmer, covered, for 10 minutes. Stir in the sugar and lemon juice and simmer for 5 minutes more. Remove from the flame, and stir in the gelatin mixture, stirring well to dissolve the gelatin completely. Stir in the orange flower water. Pour the gelatin mixture over the oranges in the bowl, picking out the cardamom and cinnamon, if you like. Gently stir to distribute the gelatin evenly throughout the oranges. Let cool, then refrigerate for several hours. To serve, use a wide spoon to scoop servings into goblets or glass bowls.

Almond Cream

serves 4 to 6

This creamy dessert (also known as *Russian cream*) and the variations that follow are some of gelatin's finer manifestations, quite similar to Italian *panna cotta*. They are always accompanied by fresh fruit; this almond-scented version goes especially well in the fall with the nutty, pumpkin-y flavor of persimmons. Ripe pears are excellent, too.

1½ teaspoons unflavored gelatin *(not a full envelope)*

3 tablespoons water

1 cup heavy *(whipping)* **cream**

½ cup sugar

small pinch of salt

1 cup natural sour cream *(no thickeners or stabilizers)*

½ teaspoon vanilla extract

½ teaspoon almond extract

¼ teaspoon lemon extract

FOR SERVING

Fuyu persimmons *(page 282)* **or ripe pears, peeled and cut attractively**

Sprinkle the gelatin over the water in a small bowl. Mix the cream, sugar, and salt in a small saucepan. Set over a low flame and heat, stirring almost constantly, until the sugar is dissolved. Add the gelatin mixture, whisking until the gelatin is completely dissolved: when you tilt the pan, you should not see any granules of gelatin. Let cool for about 30 minutes, or until room temperature. Put the sour cream (or yogurt) in a large bowl and whisk it smooth. Whisk the gelatin mixture into the sour cream until smooth, then stir in the flavorings. Pour into a wide bowl or into individual serving dishes, and chill until set.

To serve attractively, using a wide spoon, spoon the cream carefully into glass dessert bowls, and spoon a few pieces or spoonfuls of fruit alongside. Or if you've used individual serving dishes, simply spoon the fruit over the cream.

ROSE-SCENTED CREAM WITH RASPBERRIES

Raspberries and blackberries are botanically related to roses, so their flavors pair especially well with rosewater-flavored cream in this elegant, refreshing summer dessert. Gently toss a pint of raspberries, blackberries (or a combination) with 1 tablespoon sugar, and let sit until the berries are juicy and the sugar is dissolved. Use the following ingredients for the cream, following the instructions in the master Almond Cream recipe. Serve the berries and cream side-by-side in a bowl.

1½ teaspoons unflavored gelatin *(not a full envelope)*

3 tablespoons water

1 cup heavy *(whipping)* **cream**

½ cup sugar

small pinch of salt

1 cup Greek-style plain yogurt

1 teaspoon rosewater

FRESH BAY LEAF CREAM WITH CITRUS

The green, fresh scent of bay leaf is surprisingly delicious in desserts. California bay leaves, especially the young ones that emerge in the winter, are considered overly strong for many cooking applications, but I love to use them, albeit sparingly. Here, the cream and citrus temper their assertiveness to make a memorable winter dessert. For the citrus fruit accompaniment, follow the Citrus Compote recipe on page 280, or make the citrus topping for Poppyseed Cake, page 296.

4 fresh English bay leaves, or 2 fresh, young California bay leaves

1 cup heavy *(whipping)* **cream**

1½ teaspoons unflavored gelatin *(not a full envelope)*

3 tablespoons water

½ cup sugar

small pinch of salt

1 cup sour cream or Greek-style plain yogurt

Citrus Compote *(page 280)*, **for serving**

Crumble the bay leaves in your hand to release their scent, then put them in a small saucepan with the cream. Heat over low heat, stirring occasionally,

CHAPTER 16: GOOEY DESSERTS

until the cream is steaming and infused with the flavor of the bay leaves. Strain out the bay leaves, and finish making the cream following the instructions in the master Almond Cream recipe above. Serve the cream in a bowl with the Citrus Compote spooned around it.

Goat Milk Panna Cotta with Cherries

serves 4 to 6

One spring, a friend in town ("town" meaning Bishop, an hour's drive from the college) gave Deep Springs a young milk goat, named Tinker-bell. Though her nasty temperament inspired us to re-christen her "Stinker-smell," she gives abundant milk, which we make into fresh, flavorful white cheese, and feature in desserts like this. This panna cotta was inspired by *fior di latte* (literally "flower of the milk") gelato, the simplest traditional Italian gelato flavor, composed only of sweetened milk, no vanilla, so you can really taste the flavor of the milk.

Cherries are always delicious, but any good fresh fruit and a corresponding or complimentary flavor of jam may be used.

2½ cups fresh goat milk, in all

¼ cup plus 3 tablespoons granulated sugar, in all

3 tablespoons water

2 teaspoons powdered gelatin *(not a full envelope)*

½ cup heavy cream

pinch of salt

CHERRY TOPPING

3 tablespoons sour cherry jam

1 tablespoon water

1 pint fresh sweet cherries, pitted

1 tablespoon cherry brandy, or kirsch, or cognac *(optional)*

In a small, very clean skillet or sauté pan, boil 1 cup of the fresh goat milk together with ¼ cup sugar over a medium flame, frequently going over the bottom of the pan with a wooden spoon to ensure the milk isn't sticking, until the mixture is reduced to one-half cup.

Meanwhile, measure the water into a small bowl, sprinkle the gelatin evenly over the water, and set aside to allow the gelatin to absorb the water. Measure the remaining 1½ cups fresh goat milk, heavy cream, 3 tablespoons granulated sugar, and salt into a saucepan. Add the reduced milk mixture. Heat gently to steaming, and add the gelatin mixture. Whisk to dissolve the gelatin completely. Pour into a large bowl or into individual serving dishes, let the panna cotta cool, then cover and chill several hours or overnight. If poured in individual serving dishes, it will set up in less time.

To make the cherry topping, dissolve the jam in the water to make a syrup, heating slightly if necessary. Toss the pitted cherries in the syrup, stir in the optional cherry brandy, spoon over the panna cotta, and serve.

CHAPTER 17

COOKIES & CANDY

Cookies are an emblem of American hospitality and nurturing. I prefer them between meals, as a snack with a cup of coffee or tea, rather than for dessert following a big meal. Deep Springs students disagree; chocolate chip cookies are made and served for dessert at Deep Springs more frequently than any other sweet—and several different recipes head up the chapter.

Many cookie recipes call for brown sugar. For *home-mixed brown sugar* that possesses more character than the store-bought variety, blend dark molasses into granulated (white) sugar. For light brown sugar, use 1 teaspoon molasses for each cup of sugar. (For darker brown sugar, use 1 tablespoon molasses.) Blend with your clean fingers until the mixture is uniform.

All these cookies are easy to make; most may simply be mixed, dropped by spoonfuls onto a greased sheet, and baked right away. Most recipes call for butter that is at room temperature. If you have only cold butter, just slice thinly and spread the slices out in a single layer in your mixing bowl. The butter will quickly soften.

The most important moment in cookie making is taking the cookies out of the oven at just the right time—*always watch cookies carefully while they're baking*. Lining your baking sheet with a lightly greased sheet of parchment paper ensures the cookies' easy removal.

An often-overlooked step in cookie baking is *removing the baked cookies from the hot sheet to a rack to cool*. This allows steam to escape more readily, so the cookies will have their best texture, whether crispy or chewy. Once completely cooled, the cookies can be stacked on a platter.

Chocolate–Chocolate Chip Cookies

makes about 3 dozen 2-inch cookies

I made these on my first night as the chef at Deep Springs.

2 cups well-sifted all-purpose flour

½ cup unsweetened cocoa powder

¾ teaspoon baking powder

¾ teaspoon salt

1 cup butter *(2 sticks)***, at room temperature**

1 cup plus 2 tablespoons firmly packed brown sugar

3 large eggs

2 teaspoons vanilla extract

1 teaspoon almond extract

2½ cups semisweet or bittersweet chocolate chips

Heat the oven to 350°F. Lightly grease 2 baking sheets. In a medium bowl, sift together the flour, cocoa powder, baking powder, and salt. Using an electric mixer, cream the butter and sugar well, then beat in the eggs and extracts. Mix in the dry ingredients and chocolate chips until the dough is uniform. Drop heaping tablespoons of dough 2 inches apart on the baking sheets. Bake just until the tops are no longer shiny, 10 to 12 minutes. Let the cookies rest on the baking sheets out of the oven for a moment, then transfer to a rack to cool. When cooled completely, store in an airtight container.

CHOCOLATE–WHITE CHOCOLATE CHIP COOKIES

Use white chocolate chips instead of semisweet in the master recipe. To get the full color effect, reserve a handful of the white chips and place them randomly over the tops of the cookies before baking.

CHOCOLATE-PEANUT COOKIES

Follow the master recipe, omitting the almond extract, reducing the salt to ½ teaspoon, and adding 1½ cups of salted peanuts (red-skin or Spanish are my favorite) along with the chips.

DARK CHOCOLATE WAFERS

When an elegant, simple chocolate cookie is called for, try this variation. Proceed with the master recipe, using bittersweet chocolate chips. In a double boiler (or in a 250°F oven), slowly melt the chocolate chips, stirring occasionally until completely smooth. Let the melted chocolate cool to warm room temperature, then mix it into the creamed butter and sugar. Continue to mix the dough and bake the cookies as driected in the master recipe, watching carefully while baking. This method makes good small cookies (teaspoon-sized drops of dough).

Ella's Chocolate Chip Cookies

makes about 2½ dozen large cookies

These cookies, originally from the kitchen of Ella and Pete Rock (the latter a novelist, professor, and Deep Springs alumnus, DS'86), have become a timeless classic in the Deep Springs kitchen. Ella advises, "This recipe also makes good *oatmeal cookies,* substituting raisins for the chips, and adding a tablespoon of cinnamon to the dry ingredients. The dough freezes well and, in fact, tastes great straight out of the freezer, with vanilla ice cream."

1 cup butter *(2 sticks)***, at room temperature**

¾ cup granulated *(white)* **sugar**

1 cup firmly packed brown sugar

2 large eggs

1½ teaspoons vanilla extract

1 to 1½ cups coarsely chopped walnuts *(3 to 5 ounces; optional)*

2 cups semisweet or bittersweet chocolate chips

2 cups sifted all-purpose flour

2½ cups rolled oats, ground to a fine meal in a food processor or blender

¼ teaspoon salt

2 teaspoons baking powder

LARGE QUANTITY RECIPE: MAKES ABOUT 5 DOZEN LARGE COOKIES

2 cups butter *(1 pound or 4 sticks)***, at room temperature**

1½ cups granulated *(white)* **sugar**

2 cups firmly packed brown sugar

4 large eggs

1 tablespoon vanilla extract

2 to 3 cups coarsely chopped walnuts *(6 to 10 ounces; optional)*

4 cups semisweet or bittersweet chocolate chips

4 cups sifted all-purpose flour

5 cups rolled oats, ground to a fine meal in a food processor or blender

½ teaspoon salt

4 teaspoons baking powder

Heat the oven to 375°F. Using an electric mixer, cream the butter, granulated sugar, and brown sugar. Add the eggs and vanilla and blend until uniform. Mix in the nuts, if you're using them, and chocolate chips. In a very large bowl, combine the flour, ground oats, salt, and baking powder. Add the wet mixture to the dry and fold together until you have a uniform dough. Roll into golf ball–sized balls and bake on ungreased baking sheets until light brown all over, about 15 minutes. Let the cookies rest on the baking sheets out of the oven for a moment, then transfer to a rack to cool. When cooled completely, store in an airtight container.

Pistachio Chocolate Chip Cookies

makes about 4 dozen 2-inch cookies

Every member of the nut family has its own special affinity for chocolate, and pistachios are no exception. Here, the lovely green nuts show up among the chocolate chips while the pistachio flavor somehow charms the cookie to a new and elegant realm. You'd love to eat these cookies on New Year's Eve, perhaps made with white chocolate chips.

The base recipe, a classic buttery-sugary American chocolate chip cookie, is delicious featuring other nuts (I especially like pecans, left whole), or with no nuts.

1 cup butter *(2 sticks)***, at room temperature**

¾ cup firmly packed brown sugar

6 tablespoons granulated *(white)* **sugar**

¾ teaspoon vanilla or almond extract

1 egg, at room temperature

2¼ cups sifted all-purpose flour

½ teaspoon salt

¾ teaspoon baking powder

1½ to 2 cups bittersweet, semisweet, or white chocolate chips

1 to 1½ cups shelled unsalted pistachios *(4 to 6 ounces)*

LARGE QUANTITY RECIPE: MAKES ABOUT 8 DOZEN 2-INCH COOKIES

2 cups butter *(1 pound or 4 sticks)***, at room temperature**

1½ cups firmly packed brown sugar

¾ cup granulated *(white)* **sugar**

1½ teaspoons vanilla or almond extract

2 eggs, at room temperature

4½ cups sifted all-purpose flour

1 teaspoon salt

1½ teaspoons baking powder

3 to 4 cups bittersweet, semisweet, or white chocolate chips

2 to 3 cups shelled unsalted pistachios *(8 to 12 ounces)*

Heat the oven to 350°F. Lightly grease at least 2 baking sheets. Using an electric mixer, cream the butter and both kinds of sugar until fluffy and light in color. Beat in the vanilla and eggs. Sift the flour, salt, and baking powder together. Add to the wet mixture and combine on low speed until there are only a few streaks of dry flour left. Add the chocolate chips and pistachios and combine until the mixture is uniform. Drop heaping tablespoons of dough onto the baking sheets, and bake for 10 to 12 minutes.

If you want soft cookies, bake them just until they are no longer shiny on top. For crisper cookies, bake until they are pale golden brown.

Let the cookies rest on the baking sheets out of the oven for a moment, then transfer to a rack to cool. When cooled completely, store in an airtight container.

FRUIT AND NUT COOKIES

Instead of chocolate chips, use a greater proportion of nuts, and include dried or candied fruit. Often, to let the nut and fruit flavors prevail in such cookies, I use all white sugar, no brown sugar. One of my favorite combinations is almonds and dried cherries, with almond extract added. Also very good are pistachios with chopped candied orange peel.

Chocolate Chip–Hazelnut Shortbread Bars

makes sixteen 2-inch bars

"Shortbread" denotes a cookie containing only flour, sugar, and plenty of butter, but no egg, leavening, or liquid ingredients. The name comes from the effect of butter on flour: when flour is mixed with water, as with bread dough, the flour's gluten, or protein, forms long, resilient strands that account for the strong, elastic structure of bread dough. But in cookie baking, a generous amount of butter or other fat "shortens" the strands of gluten, keeping the final product tender and crumbly.

- **1½ cups hazelnuts** *(about 5½ ounces)*, **lightly toasted** *(page 176)*
- **1 cup butter** *(2 sticks)*, **at room temperature**
- **1 cup firmly packed brown sugar**
- **1 teaspoon vanilla extract**
- **1¼ cups semisweet or bittersweet chocolate chips** *(one 8-ounce package)*
- **⅛ teaspoon salt**
- **2 cups sifted all-purpose flour**

Heat the oven to 350°F. Put the toasted hazelnuts on a wire rack and rub them to release the excess brown skin. Let cool, and chop the nuts coarsely. Cream the butter and brown sugar in a large bowl until light and fluffy. Mix in the vanilla and the chocolate chips. Sift the salt and flour together, add to the butter mixture, and blend just until uniform. Press the dough evenly into an 8-by-8-inch pan. Bake for about 25 minutes, or until pale golden brown. With a small, sharp knife, cut the cookies into bars while warm. Let cool completely, then remove from the pan.

Sheet Pan Brownies

makes about 4 dozen 2-inch brownies

This has proven to be *the* recipe for a quantity of brownies. The larger recipe makes enough to fill a restaurant-size 24-by-17-inch sheet pan. Made with cocoa powder and chocolate chips, they are less expensive than brownies made of solid chocolate, but they are amazingly rich, chewy, and satisfying. It may seem odd to use brown sugar, but it underscores the deep chocolate flavor. I think these brownies are at their best the day after they're baked.

USING A 12-BY-17-INCH PAN (WITH AT LEAST A ¾-INCH RIM)

- **7 ounces unsweetened cocoa powder** *(about 1¾ cups; almost a full can)*
- **¾ cup vegetable oil**
- **2 cups** *(1 pound or 4 sticks)* **plus 2 tablespoons butter**
- **8 large eggs**
- **4½ cups firmly packed brown sugar**
- **1 tablespoon vanilla extract**
- **⅛ teaspoon salt**
- **12 ounces all-purpose flour** *(3 cups sifted)*
- **1 pound whole pecans** *(about 5 cups)*, **lightly toasted** *(page 176)*
- **2 cups bittersweet or semisweet chocolate chips** *(12 ounces)*

LARGE QUANTITY RECIPE: MAKES ABOUT 8 DOZEN 2-INCH BROWNIES, USING A FULL SHEET PAN (24 BY 17 INCHES)

14 ounces unsweetened cocoa powder *(about 3½ cups)*

1½ cups vegetable oil

4 cups *(2 pounds or 8 sticks)* plus 4 tablespoons butter

16 large eggs

9 cups firmly packed brown sugar

2 tablespoons vanilla extract

¼ teaspoon salt

1½ pounds all-purpose flour *(6 cups sifted)*

2 pounds whole pecans *(about 10 cups)*, lightly toasted *(page 176)*

4 cups bittersweet or semisweet chocolate chips *(1½ pounds)*

Heat the oven to 325°F. Butter a 12-by-17-inch pan (or 24-by-17-inch sheet pan for large quantity), line the bottom with baking parchment, then lightly butter the parchment. Combine a handful of flour with a handful of cocoa powder. Shake this mixture around in the pan, coating the entire greased inner surface. Shake out the excess flour-cocoa mixture, tapping the pan.

Combine the cocoa powder, oil, and butter in a large saucepan and heat over a low flame until the butter is melted. Whip together and heat the eggs, brown sugar, vanilla, and salt in the top of a double boiler (I use a large stainless-steel mixing bowl set over, not in, a pot of gently boiling water), stirring frequently, until the mixture reaches 110°F, about the temperature of a warm bath. Combine the two mixtures in a very large bowl and whip with an electric mixer (or by hand with a whisk) for about 5 minutes. Begin to fold in the flour, then add the nuts and chips, continuing to fold just until the batter is uniform. Spoon the batter in globs into the prepared pan, then spread gently with a rubber spatula. The batter will fill the pan to the brim. Bake, rotating the pan every 10 minutes, until a toothpick comes out clean, 35 to 40 minutes. Let cool completely on a rack. Wrap well and let sit overnight.

To cut, first run a small knife all around the edge of the pan to loosen the edges. Invert the uncut brownies onto a large tray, or onto the back of another sheet pan. Peel off the parchment, then invert onto a cutting board. Cut into squares of the desired size with a long knife.

Mexican Chocolate Cookies with Almonds

makes about 4 dozen 2-inch cookies

I devised this recipe as an alternative way to enjoy the distinct character of Mexican "drinking chocolate." These cookies are dark and very flavorful, but also light and crispy, the distinctive cinnamon finish of the chocolate coming through. See page 39 for more information on Mexican chocolate.

one 1-pound, 3-ounce package Mexican chocolate

2 sticks *(8 ounces, or 1 cup)* salted butter, softened

1 cup granulated sugar

2 eggs

1 teaspoon vanilla extract

1 teaspoon almond extract

2 cups all-purpose flour

1 teaspoon baking powder

¼ teaspoon baking soda

¼ teaspoon salt

1⅓ cups lightly toasted, coarsely-chopped almonds *(page 176)*

Unwrap the chocolate and place it in a saucepan set over a larger pan of boiling water. Let the chocolate soften completely (this type of chocolate does not melt), stirring it around from time to time. Let the chocolate cool for about ½ hour, until still soft, but almost at room temperature.

Meanwhile, heat the oven to 325°F. In a large bowl, with an electric mixer, cream the butter and sugar together well, until lightened in color and very fluffy, 4 to 5 minutes. Beat in the chocolate, then the eggs, one at a time, and finally stir in the extracts. Sift the flour, baking powder, baking soda, and salt together, and fold into the chocolate mixture. When the batter is almost uniform, add about ¾ cup of the chopped almonds, and fold until the batter is uniform.

Using a small (1-ounce) ice-cream scoop, drop even, 1-ounce balls of dough onto lightly greased cookie sheets. Sprinkle the tops with the remaining chopped almonds, and bake about 15 minutes. While baking, the cookies will puff up a bit, then flatten when they cool. Let the cookies rest on the sheet for a moment to set up, then transfer to racks to cool.

Peanut Butter Cookies

makes about 4 dozen 1½-inch cookies

Traditional recipes for peanut butter cookies use vegetable shortening and processed peanut butter that contains more vegetable shortening and added sugar. This recipe calls for natural peanut butter and butter—less-processed ingredients. They are rich, crumbly, and deeply peanutty.

¾ cup butter *(1½ sticks)*, **at room temperature**

1 cup natural peanut butter, chunky or smooth, well stirred

1½ cups firmly packed brown sugar

1 large egg plus 1 egg yolk, beaten

½ teaspoon vanilla extract

¼ teaspoon salt

2 cups sifted all-purpose flour

Heat the oven to 350°F. Lightly grease 2 baking sheets. Cream the butter well in a large bowl. Add the peanut butter and cream well. Add the sugar and cream well. Add the egg, yolk, vanilla, and salt, and whip until smooth. Sift the flour, add it to the bowl, and mix just until the dough is smooth and uniform.

Form the dough into 1-inch balls, and place them 1 inch apart on the baking sheets. Press each ball down with a flour-dipped fork, once in each direction to make a grid pattern, to a thickness of about ½ inch. Bake just until slightly puffed, lightly brown on top, and golden brown underneath, 10 to 12 minutes. Let the cookies rest on the baking sheets out of the oven for a moment, then transfer to a rack to cool. When cooled completely, store in an airtight container.

ALMOND-BUTTER COOKIES

Use chunky almond butter in place of the peanut butter, and use 2 teaspoons of almond extract in place of the vanilla extract. To signal the cookies' identity as distinct from their peanut butter brethren, form them into almond-shaped ovals, and press with a fork in only the long direction, evoking the shape and appearance of almonds.

Oatmeal-Coconut Bars

makes sixteen 2-inch bars

These are very good with vanilla ice cream. My mother saved this recipe decades ago, annotating it with just one word: "Divine."

2½ cups rolled oats

¾ cup sweetened flaked coconut

¼ cup granulated sugar

¼ teaspoon salt

¾ teaspoon baking powder

¾ cup butter *(1½ sticks)*, **at room temperature**

¼ cup firmly packed brown sugar

Heat the oven to 375°F. Butter an 8-by-8-inch baking pan. Sprinkle 2 tablespoons of the oats evenly into the pan. Combine 2¼ cups of the oats with the coconut in a medium bowl. Combine the granulated sugar, salt, and baking powder in a small bowl. Sift if there are any lumps. Cream the butter with the brown sugar in a large bowl, then add the granulated sugar mixture and cream again. Add the oat mixture and combine with your hands until uniform. Press the dough evenly into the pan without disturbing the coating of butter and sprinkling of oats. Sprinkle the remaining 2 tablespoons oats over the surface of the dough.

Bake for 20 to 25 minutes, or until pale golden brown. For the neatest results, let cool completely and refrigerate for several hours before using a sharp knife to cut the cookies in a 4-by-4 grid into 16 square bars, or whatever shape and size you please. Let the cookies come to room temperature before serving.

Wedding Cookies

makes about 30 small cookies

Call these cookies *Mexican wedding cakes* if you make them with pecans, popular in Texas and the Southwest. If made with walnuts, call them *Russian tea biscuits*. Made with pistachios and served with hot, strong tea, call them whatever you like; they will be delicious.

1 cup unsalted butter *(2 sticks)*, **at room temperature**

¼ cup granulated *(white)* **sugar**

scant ¼ teaspoon salt

2 teaspoons vanilla extract

2 cups unsifted all-purpose flour

1 cup finely chopped pecans, walnuts, or pistachios *(about 3¼ ounces; if salted, reduce the salt to a pinch)*

about 2 cups sifted powdered sugar for coating cookies

Heat the oven to 325°F. Cream the butter, sugar, and salt in a large bowl until light in color and fluffy. Add the vanilla, then the flour and nuts. Form into balls the diameter of a bottle cap. Bake on an ungreased baking sheet for 10 to 12 minutes. Do not let the cookies brown. Let them sit for a moment, then carefully remove from the baking sheet and roll in sifted powdered sugar while warm. Let cool on a rack. Re-roll the cookies in powdered sugar before serving.

Sesame Cookies

makes about 200 small cookies

These little cookies are loved by everyone. Southern in origin, they still manage, like many Southerners themselves, to feel at home in a variety of settings. They not only admirably conclude a down-home, no-holds-barred meal of Southern barbecue, they taste great after an authentic Asian dinner, a Southwestern fiesta, or a mosaiclike feast of grains and garden vegetables. You may include black sesame seeds in the quantity of sesame seeds called for; don't use all black sesame seeds or you won't be able to tell when they are toasted.

1¼ cups sesame seeds *(a combination of white and black, if you like)*

¼ cup butter, melted

1¼ cups firmly packed brown sugar

1 teaspoon vanilla extract

1 large egg

1¼ cups sifted all-purpose flour

¼ teaspoon baking powder

¼ teaspoon salt

Heat the oven to 350°F. Toast the sesame seeds in a shallow baking pan in the oven, stirring and redistributing several times, until they are fragrant and a uniform pale gold, 15 to 20 minutes. Keep in mind that they burn easily. Remove the pan from the oven. The sesame seeds make a very subtle and exquisite crackly sound as they cool. Cool them thoroughly in the pan before you mix the dough. Raise the oven temperature to 375°F. Lightly grease 2 or more baking sheets. Beat the butter and sugar in a large bowl until light, then beat in the vanilla, egg, and toasted sesame seeds. Sift the flour, baking powder, and salt together, and stir into the butter mixture just until the dough is uniform. Drop half teaspoonfuls of dough 1 inch apart on the baking sheets. Bake just until the edges and bottoms are brown, about 5 minutes. Watch carefully; since these cookies are so rich in sugar, they burn easily. Let the cookies set up on the sheet for a moment, then transfer them to racks to cool. Cool the baking sheets between batches.

Cashew Cookies

makes about 3 dozen small cookies

These cookies are mostly cashew, with just enough cookie to hold them together. If you are feeling bold, add a pinch—or two—of cayenne pepper to the dough. If you're starting with "raw" cashews, toast them to a very pale golden brown according to the guidelines on page 176, then toss with a little melted butter and a teaspoon of fine salt per pound of cashews.

2 cups roasted, salted cashews

¾ cup sifted all-purpose flour

1 to 2 pinches cayenne *(optional)*

¾ cup unsalted butter *(1½ sticks)*, **at room temperature**

½ cup sugar

2 teaspoons finely grated lemon zest

1 large egg

Heat the oven to 350°F. Lightly grease 2 baking sheets. Using a food processor, pulse and grind the cashews to a medium-fine meal. Add the flour to the cashews and process for a second or two longer. Transfer this mixture to a large bowl. In the emptied food processor, cream the butter, sugar, and lemon zest together until light, scraping down the sides of the bowl frequently. Add the egg and process until uniform. Scrape the butter mixture into the cashew-flour mixture, and mix until you have a uniform dough. Cover with plastic wrap and chill for 1 hour.

Keeping your hands slightly damp with cold tap water, form the dough into 1-inch balls, then roll into oblongs about 2 inches long, bending them into an arc shape when placing them on the baking sheet—the finished cookies will look somewhat like cashews.

Bake until lightly browned around the edges and on the bottom and cooked through, about 12 minutes. Let the cookies rest on the baking sheets for a moment before removing them to racks to cool. Let them cool completely before arranging or storing. These cookies are quite delicate; they will not withstand much handling.

Walnut Biscotti

makes about 4 dozen cookies

For walnut lovers, here is a heap of lightly toasted walnuts bound in a biscotti matrix. In the late afternoon, my Aunt Jean loves to dip walnut biscotti in a glass of pinot noir. For the holidays, add a quarter-cup of finely chopped dried cranberries to the dough.

1 pound walnut halves and pieces *(about 5 cups)*, **lightly toasted** *(page 176)*

1 cup minus 2 tablespoons sugar

1 egg

2 egg whites

½ teaspoon vanilla extract

½ teaspoon orange or lemon extract

1½ teaspoons anise seed *(optional)*

2 cups sifted all-purpose flour

1 teaspoon baking powder

¼ teaspoon salt

Heat the oven to 350°F. Grease a large baking sheet (you can use the baking sheet you toasted the walnuts on). When the toasted walnuts are cool, rub handfuls lightly between both hands to release the excess papery brown skin. Do not chop the walnuts—they should be whole for this recipe.

Using an electric mixer, beat the sugar, egg, and egg whites for about 3 minutes, until fluffy and light in color. Add the extracts and anise seed, if desired. Sift the flour, baking powder, and salt together. Fold the dry ingredients into the egg mixture until just combined, then fold in the walnuts, coating them with dough. It will seem like too many walnuts and not enough dough, but all is well.

Divide the dough in half and shape each portion into a log on the baking sheet, making sure the logs are at least 3 inches apart. The dough will be lumpy from the walnuts. Slightly flatten the top and pat the outer surface of the logs as smooth as possible with your hands. Bake, rotating the pan once, until the loaves are golden, about 35 minutes.

Let the loaves cool for 10 minutes and lower the oven temperature to 325°F. Transfer the loaves to a cutting board. Cut each loaf diagonally into half-inch slices with a sharp knife. Lay the slices back on the baking sheet, cut side up (you might need to use a second baking sheet), and bake until crisp and lightly gold around the edges, 15 to 20 minutes longer. Cool the biscotti on a rack. When cool, store in an airtight container.

Lemon-Anise Biscotti

makes about 3 dozen cookies

These are hard, but not tooth-cracking, true Italian biscotti. The Deep Springs student irrigation team stuffs handfuls of these biscotti into the pockets of their overalls before going out to the alfalfa fields to move the big, unwieldy irrigation lines. Even when the biscotti get soaked, they're still good, and they don't make such a crumbly mess as other cookies.

2 cups sifted all-purpose flour

1 teaspoon baking powder

¼ teaspoon salt

2 large eggs

1 cup minus 2 tablespoons sugar

¼ teaspoon vanilla extract

⅛ teaspoon lemon extract

1 tablespoon finely grated lemon zest

1 tablespoon anise seed

Heat the oven to 350°F. Grease a baking sheet. Sift the flour, baking powder, and salt into a medium bowl. Using an electric mixer, beat the eggs with the sugar for about 3 minutes, until light and lemon-colored, then add the extracts, zest, and anise seed. Fold in the dry ingredients until just combined. Divide the dough in half and shape each portion into a log, about a foot long and 3 inches wide, on the baking sheet, making sure the logs are at least 3 inches apart. Bake, rotating the pan once, until the loaves are golden and slightly cracked on top, about 35 minutes.

Let the loaves cool for a few minutes and lower the oven temperature to 325°F. Cut each loaf diagonally into ¼-inch slices with a sharp knife. Lay the slices back on the baking sheet, cut side up, about ½ inch apart, and bake until crisp and golden around the edges, about 15 minutes longer. Cool the biscotti on a rack. When cool, store in an airtight container.

Lime Bars

makes sixteen 2-inch bars

These bars are brownielike in texture, with a deep lime flavor.

¾ cup granulated sugar

1 tablespoon finely grated lime zest *(from about 3 limes)*

⅓ cup butter, melted and hot

2 ounces cream cheese, at room temperature

1 egg

1 egg yolk

¼ cup fresh lime juice *(from about 2 or 3 limes)*

1 teaspoon vanilla extract

½ cup plus 2 tablespoons sifted all-purpose flour

¼ teaspoon salt

powdered sugar for dusting

Heat the oven to 350°F. Generously butter and flour an 8-by-8-inch pan. Put the sugar in a large bowl, and grate the lime zest into it. Work the zest and sugar together with your fingers. Using a hand-held mixer, blend in the hot butter and cream cheese until uniform. Add the egg and egg yolk, and beat for a full minute. Beat in the lime juice and vanilla. Sift the flour and salt together into the wet ingredients and fold to combine, just until uniform. Scrape into the prepared pan and bake for about 25 minutes. Let cool, and cut into bars. Put a few spoonfuls of powdered sugar into a screen sieve and tap the sieve over the lime bars, dusting them generously.

Lemon Slice Cookies

makes about 3 dozen 1½-inch cookies

An old recipe from my Aunt Jean, these pale half-moon cookies are wonderfully buttery and lemony. I almost never have the urge to decorate cookies, but I love to paint the curved outer rim of these with a simple egg yolk glaze so they resemble half-slices of lemon.

2 cups minus 2 tablespoons all-purpose flour

¼ teaspoon baking powder

¼ teaspoon salt

¾ cup butter *(1½ sticks)*, **at room temperature**

½ cup granulated sugar, plus more for sprinkling

½ cup powdered sugar

1 tablespoon finely grated lemon zest

3 tablespoons fresh lemon juice

½ teaspoon vanilla extract

EGG YOLK GLAZE (OPTIONAL)

2 teaspoons egg yolk

2 teaspoons sugar

¼ teaspoon fresh lemon juice

2 or 3 drops lemon extract

Sift together the flour, baking powder, and salt. In a large bowl, cream the butter, ½ cup granulated sugar, and powdered sugar. Beat in the lemon zest, lemon juice, and vanilla. Add the dry mixture to the wet mixture and combine until you have a uniform dough.

Roll the dough into 2 logs about 6 inches in length, using plastic wrap or waxed paper. If you want perfectly shaped cookies, the logs must be perfectly round. Freeze the logs for at least 1 hour, or chill overnight. Heat the oven to 350°F. Lightly grease 2 baking sheets. With a sharp knife, carefully slice the frozen logs into even halves lengthwise, then cut ¼-inch-thick slices from each half. Place the half-moons 1 inch apart on the baking sheets. Lightly sprinkle granulated sugar over the surface of each cookie. Bake for about 10 minutes—they will remain pale, as the lemon juice inhibits browning. Let the cookies set on the baking sheets out of the oven for a moment, then carefully remove them to racks to cool.

If you opt to glaze the cookies, heat the oven to 300°F. Combine the egg yolk, sugar, lemon juice, and extract in a small bowl and stir until the sugar is dissolved. Using a small pastry brush, apply a thick line of glaze to the curved rim of each cookie. There should be just enough glaze to paint all the cookies. To set the glaze, put the cookies back on the baking sheets and place in the warm oven for about 5 minutes. Let the cookies cool completely before arranging them on a plate.

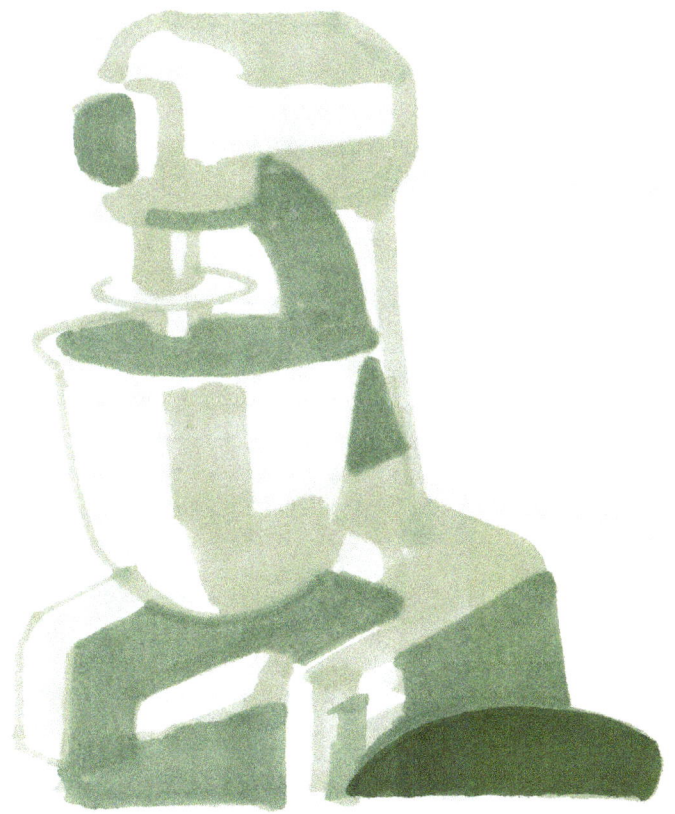

Italian Orange Cookies

makes about 3 dozen 2-inch cookies

These iced, cakelike cookies are perfect with espresso or tea after a big Italian dinner.

¾ cup butter *(1½ sticks)*, at room temperature

½ cup granulated sugar

¼ cup firmly packed brown sugar

3 eggs

1 teaspoon vanilla extract

1 tablespoon finely grated orange zest

¼ cup fresh orange juice

¼ cup orange juice concentrate *(undiluted)*

3 cups sifted all-purpose flour

2½ teaspoons baking powder

¼ teaspoon baking soda

¼ teaspoon salt

ICING

3 tablespoons orange juice concentrate *(undiluted)*

1 teaspoon finely grated orange zest

pinch of salt

½ teaspoon vanilla extract

4 tablespoons butter

2 cups powdered sugar, sifted

Have all ingredients at room temperature. Heat the oven to 350°F. Lightly grease 2 baking sheets. Using an electric mixer, cream the butter, granulated sugar, and brown sugar until fluffy. Add the eggs, one at a time, then add the vanilla, orange zest, orange juice, and orange juice concentrate.

Sift the flour, baking powder, baking soda, and salt together, and blend into the wet mixture just until the dough is uniform. Let the dough rest, covered, in the refrigerator for 20 minutes, then drop by neat tablespoonfuls 2 inches apart on the baking sheets. Bake until the cookies feel springy to the touch and are pale golden brown around the edges, about 8 minutes. Allow the cookies to set on the pan for a few minutes, then remove to racks to cool while making the icing.

To make the icing, combine the orange juice concentrate, orange zest, salt, vanilla, and butter, cut into small pieces, in a small, thick-walled pan. Warm over medium-low heat, stirring occasionally, until the butter is melted. Stir in the powdered sugar and heat the mixture gently, stirring occasionally, for 5 minutes. Remove from the heat and let cool for 5 minutes, stirring a few times as it cools. Ice the cookies, and let the icing dry and harden for an hour or so before arranging the cookies on a platter or stacking them in a tin.

Gingersnaps

makes about 8 dozen 2-inch cookies

These gingersnaps are quite snappy, with a hefty, but balanced, dose of spice. Containing only a little butter, they keep well.

¾ cup butter *(1½ sticks)*, at room temperature

2 cups sugar

2 eggs, beaten

½ cup molasses

2 teaspoons apple cider vinegar

3¾ cups sifted all-purpose flour

¾ teaspoon baking soda

¾ teaspoon baking powder

1 tablespoon ground ginger

½ teaspoon ground cinnamon

¼ teaspoon ground cloves

¼ teaspoon black pepper

Cream the butter and sugar in a large bowl. Beat in the eggs, molasses, and vinegar. Sift the flour, baking soda, baking powder, ginger, cinnamon, cloves, and pepper, and add to the butter mixture. Mix just until thoroughly blended. For easiest handling, chill the dough for an hour. Before baking, heat the oven to 325°F, and lightly grease at least 2 baking sheets. Form the dough into ¾-inch balls and place 1½ inches apart on the baking sheets. Bake for about 12 minutes, or until crinkled and no longer moist on top. Remove the cookies to racks to cool. As they cool, they will become crisp and snappy. Store in an airtight container.

GINGERSNAPS, VANILLA ICE CREAM, AND BOYSENBERRIES

When you have perfect sweet boysenberries or blackberries, make Gingersnaps and churn up a quart of Vanilla Ice Cream (page 305). We served this at Deep Springs' graduation one year, following a dinner of grilled pork chops and corn on the cob. If the berries are superlative, this is one of the best summer desserts of all. For every person, generously allow a cup of ice cream, a heaping half-cup of berries, and 5 or 6 cookies. Serve the ice cream in chilled bowls. Heap the berries in a glass bowl, with the cookies on a platter. Give people small plates and let them help themselves to berries and cookies to go with their ice cream. Eat the ice cream using a succession of gingersnaps as a spoon, relieving the sweetness with tart berries now and again.

Ginger Cookies

makes about 4 dozen 2-inch cookies

This is your best recipe for soft, chewy ginger cookies—they are more kid-friendly than the previous Gingersnaps. In Deep Springs' desert climate, they will harden if left uncovered.

- ¾ cup *(1½ sticks)* **plus 1 tablespoon butter, at room temperature**
- **1 cup firmly packed brown sugar**
- **¼ cup molasses**
- **1 large egg**
- **1 teaspoon cider vinegar**
- **2⅓ cups sifted all-purpose flour**
- **1 teaspoon baking soda**
- **1 teaspoon baking powder**
- **1½ teaspoons ground ginger**
- **1 teaspoon ground cinnamon**
- **½ teaspoon ground cloves**
- **pinch of salt**
- **granulated sugar for rolling**

In a large bowl, cream the butter and brown sugar until fluffy. Add the molasses, egg, and vinegar and beat well, about 1 minute. Sift the flour, baking soda, baking powder, ginger, cinnamon, cloves, and salt, and add to the butter mixture; mix just until thoroughly blended. Chill the dough for 1 hour. Before baking, heat the oven to 375°F, and lightly grease 2 baking sheets. Form the dough into 1-inch balls and roll in granulated sugar. Place 2 inches apart on the baking sheets. Bake for about 10 minutes—do not overbake. Once they form their crinkly top and are just barely browned, they are done. Remove the cookies to a rack to cool. Keep in an airtight container.

Butter Cookies

makes about 30 small cookies

Why are these plain cookies so good, the dough so irresistible? It's the yolk.

- **1 cup unsalted butter** *(2 sticks)*, **at room temperature**
- **¾ cup sugar**
- **1 egg yolk**
- **1½ teaspoons vanilla extract**
- **2 cups sifted all-purpose flour**
- **⅛ teaspoon salt**

Cream the butter and sugar together in a large bowl until fluffy and light in color. Beat in the yolk and vanilla. Sift in the flour and salt and mix until combined. Roll into logs about 1 inch in diameter, wrap well in plastic wrap, and chill for at least 1 hour.

Before baking, heat the oven to 350°F. Lightly grease 2 baking sheets. Slice the dough into ¼-inch-thick slices and arrange at least 1½ inches apart on the baking sheets. Bake the cookies until they are the palest brown around the edges, about 10 minutes. Transfer to a rack and let cool completely. Store in an airtight container.

CARDAMOM BUTTER COOKIES

Remove the inner dark seeds from cardamom pods until you have about 2 teaspoons of seeds. Crush with ¼ cup sugar in a mortar until the seeds are completely powdered. Mix in an additional ½ cup sugar and use this sugar in the recipe above. These make a superb, sophisticated after-dinner digestive.

Biscochitos

makes about 4 dozen small cookies

These rich cookies are a traditional Christmas specialty of New Mexico. Made with lots of pork lard, they have a full, creamy flavor. In the more frugal days of our great-grandmothers, many cakes and cookies were made with lard or other animal fats, a practice surviving only in traditional recipes like this. In a diplomatic gesture disclosing the controversial main ingredient, my mother always uses her pig-shaped cookie cutter for biscochitos, and places a single silver dragée for the pig's eye.

Superlative biscochitos are made with lard rendered from Deep Springs pork. To render your own lard, follow the instructions in the Deep Springs Soap recipe (page 343) for rendering beef tallow, using fresh pork kidney fat instead of beef kidney fat.

The anise seeds are controversial—those who dislike them dislike them intensely and might call them *piojos,* Spanish for "head lice," prompting many biscochito bakers to make two batches, *con piojos* and *sin piojos,* pleasing the whole family. If anise is not to your liking, omit it and add a couple of teaspoons of vanilla extract instead. My sister Diana won a blue ribbon at the county fair for these biscochitos.

2 teaspoons anise seed *(omit if hated, or replace with vanilla extract)*

¼ cup dry white wine

2 cups lard, at room temperature

2 cups sugar

3 eggs

6 cups sifted all-purpose flour

4 teaspoons baking powder

1 teaspoon salt

TOPPING

1 teaspoon ground cinnamon

¼ cup sugar

Crack the anise seed coarsely in a mortar, or place it in a fold of waxed paper and gently pound with a heavy object. In a small dish, mix the anise seed into the wine and let sit, covered, for several hours or overnight.

Using an electric mixer, beat the lard until creamy and fluffy, until it has become snow-white and opaque. Add the sugar and cream again. Beat in the eggs, one at a time, then beat in the wine-anise mixture. Sift the flour, baking powder, and salt together, and fold into the lard mixture, mixing until the dough is uniform. For easiest rolling, chill the dough for about 2 hours.

Before baking, heat the oven to 350°F, and lightly grease at least 2 baking sheets. On a floured surface, roll the dough into a rectangle about ½ inch thick. For light-textured cookies, avoid overhandling the dough. Using a sharp knife dipped in flour, cut into 1½-inch diamond shapes, or cut into desired shapes with cookie cutters. Place the cookies 1 inch apart on the baking sheets. For the topping, blend together the cinnamon and sugar, and sprinkle some on each cookie. Bake for 10 to 12 minutes, or until pale golden brown on the bottom. Gently transfer the biscochitos to a rack to cool. Store in an airtight container.

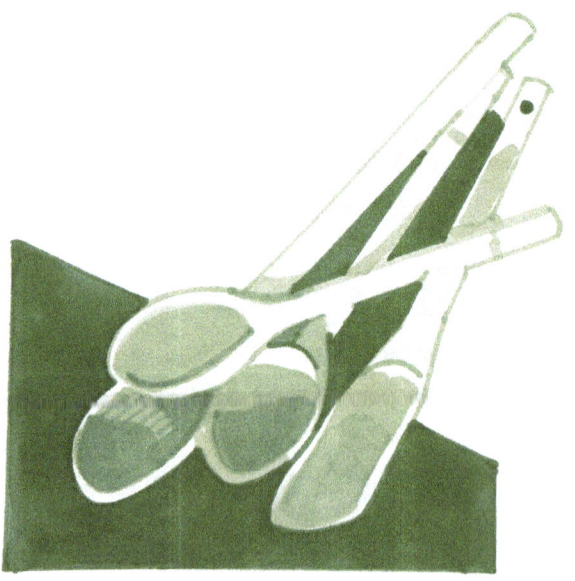

Vanilla Wafers

makes about 4 dozen 1½-inch cookies

Plain and simple, these cookies are taken from a cookbook published in 1917—the year Deep Springs was founded. They are good for homemade Banana Pudding (page 271), or for making Mama Nell's Kentucky Bourbon Balls (page 328).

5 tablespoons butter, at room temperature

1 cup sugar

1 egg

2 teaspoons vanilla extract

¼ cup milk

2 cups sifted all-purpose flour or cake flour

2 teaspoons baking powder

½ teaspoon salt

Heat the oven to 350°F. Grease 2 baking sheets. Cream the butter in a medium bowl; add the sugar and cream again. Beat in the egg, vanilla, and milk. Sift the flour, baking powder, and salt together. Add the dry mixture to the wet mixture and combine until uniform. Drop scant teaspoonfuls of dough about 1½ inches apart on the baking sheets. Or put the dough into a heavy-duty zipper-lock bag, cut a small hole at the corner, and squeeze out evenly shaped wafers. Bake for 12 to 15 minutes, or until brown around the edges and pale gold in the center. Remove to a rack to cool. Store in an airtight container.

Old-Fashioned Vinegar Taffy

makes 1 pound, about 70 pieces

For many years when I was a kid, my mother and I made taffy on the last day of school. Here are three good candy-making rules:

For best results, *use a leading brand of cane sugar*. It should say "100 percent pure cane sugar" on the label. They are formulated to ensure success.

Make this or any other candy using *very clean equipment, in a kitchen that is otherwise unoccupied*. Spattering grease or steam from boiling pots might jeopardize the delicate, controlled crystallization of sugar.

Choose a dry day for candy making (there is no other kind of day at Deep Springs); a humid environment can result in sticky candy.

½ cup water

2½ cups granulated pure cane sugar

¼ cup apple cider vinegar

¼ teaspoon salt

1 tablespoon butter

1 teaspoon vanilla extract

cornstarch for pulling

Butter a shallow glass baking dish. Combine the water, sugar, vinegar, salt, and butter in a very clean, medium-sized, heavy saucepan over medium-high heat, stirring constantly until the sugar dissolves. Wipe the sugar crystals from the side of the pan if necessary, using a moistened paper towel. Continue to cook over medium-low heat, without stirring, to 272°F, or the soft-crack stage. Do not let the mixture go above this temperature or the candy will be too hard. Remove from the heat and add the vanilla extract. Pour the candy into the buttered baking dish. Let cool for about 30 minutes, turning the edges toward the center several times with a spatula to prevent hardening.

When cool enough to handle, dust your hands well with cornstarch. Gather the taffy into a ball and pull and fold, pull and fold, over and over, until it holds its shape. Divide into two parts. Pull and twist each part into a 1-inch rope. Rub a little butter onto your kitchen shears and cut each rope into 1-inch pieces. Place on waxed paper and let harden in a dry place at room temperature for several hours. Wrap each piece in a 4-inch square of waxed paper. Store in an airtight container.

English Toffee with Sea Salt

makes about 2½ pounds

This is a deep, dark toffee, with dark chocolate and a light sprinkle of sea salt. Given how extraordinarily good this adult candy is, it is quick and easy to make.

Please see the notes about candy making in the previous recipe.

2 cups granulated pure cane sugar

1½ cups butter *(3 sticks)*

2 tablespoons water

2½ cups whole raw almonds *(about 10 ounces)*

2 cups semisweet or bittersweet chocolate chips *(12 ounces)*

¾ teaspoon sea salt

Lightly butter a big flat metal platter or rimmed baking sheet (big enough to allow the candy to spread and not end up too thick; a 12-by-18-inch sheet pan is ideal). If you have baking parchment, line the platter or sheet with lightly buttered parchment.

In a very clean, medium-sized, heavy saucepan, heat the sugar, butter, and water over a medium flame, stirring occasionally. When the butter is melted, stir in the almonds. Without stirring, continue to cook the candy over medium heat until the mixture registers a toasty 285° to 290°F on an instant-read thermometer or a candy thermometer (the syrup will be a deep golden color, and the nuts will be toasted). Immediately pour the toffee onto the buttered platter. Let the toffee spread out and set for a few seconds, tilting the pan if necessary, then evenly sprinkle the chocolate chips over the hot toffee. Let the chocolate soften for about 30 seconds, then spread it smooth. While the chocolate is still soft, sprinkle it evenly with sea salt.

Let the toffee harden at room temperature for at least 2 hours, then put the pan in the freezer for several minutes. Secure the pan in a bag and drop the whole thing on the floor. The toffee should separate easily into lovely, randomly shaped, bite-size pieces.

Sesame Candy

makes about 1½ pounds

Sesame seeds have been cultivated for millennia, are rich in vitamins and minerals, and are enjoyed throughout the world. Many versions of this brittle-like candy exist; this is one of my favorites.

2 cups white sesame seed *(or a combination of white and black, if you like)*

¼ teaspoon salt

½ cup brown sugar

½ cup honey

Heat the oven to 350°F. Lay two large sheets of non-stick baking parchment on a wooden board or a metal sheet pan, for cooling the candy. Spread the sesame seeds out on a baking sheet and carefully toast them in the oven, removing the sheet and stirring the sesame seeds around every 5 minutes, until they are a uniform, pale golden brown, about 15 minutes total. Let cool slightly, then transfer the seeds to a bowl, so that they can be quickly dumped into the hot syrup. Stir the salt into the sesame seeds to evenly distribute it.

In a large, heavy saucepan, combine the brown sugar and honey, and bring to a boil over a high flame. Reduce the flame slightly, and boil for exactly 2 minutes. Off the heat, dump in the toasted sesame seeds with the salt, and stir quickly with a wooden spoon to coat the seeds evenly with the syrup. Immediately transfer the candy onto the bottom sheet of parchment, and spread it out with a lightly-buttered spatula. Lay the other parchment sheet atop the candy, and roll the candy with a rolling pin to a uniform thickness. Peel off the top sheet of parchment, and let the candy cool completely. Remove the candy from the parchment, and break into large, irregular pieces. Store in an airtight container.

Mama Nell's Kentucky Bourbon Balls

makes 20 to 30 small cookies

I knew my maternal grandmother as Mama Nell. This is perhaps the most treasured old family recipe I have—I always make bourbon balls at Christmas, if only to retell an oft-told family anecdote: when she lived in Texas, Nell once hosted a Ladies' Aid Society luncheon—the most proper, teetotaling, hard-shell Baptist ladies in town would be in attendance. This was one of her favorite recipes, so she decided to serve them despite their unmistakable whiff of whiskey. The president of the society—the staunchest, most proper one of all—popped a bourbon ball in her mouth and exclaimed, "Nell, these cookies are simply delicious; what is that familiar flavor?" Without missing a beat, my grandmother replied, "Nutmeg!"

1½ cups pecans *(about 5 ounces)*, **very lightly toasted** *(page 176)*

1 cup vanilla wafers *(see page 326 for a recipe)*, **crushed to a powder**

1 cup powdered sugar, plus more for coating cookies

2 tablespoons unsweetened cocoa powder

¼ cup Kentucky bourbon

1½ tablespoons cane syrup, golden syrup, or light corn syrup *(see the Pecan Pie recipe, page 272)*

When the toasted pecans are cool, chop them very finely with a sharp knife—you should end up with 1 cup of chopped pecans. Combine the pecans with the crushed wafers, 1 cup powdered sugar, and cocoa powder in a medium bowl. Mix in the bourbon and cane syrup. Form into small balls about ½ inch in diameter, and roll them in powdered sugar. Cover tightly and chill for an hour or two. Let them come to room temperature before serving. Store the cookies tightly covered and refrigerated, or else the alcohol will evaporate.

CHAPTER 18

MENUS

This is important: a menu is where it all comes together. More than the list of foods served at a meal, a menu is the experience of the foods themselves taken as a whole. A good menu is more than the sum of its parts; the various offerings complement and enhance one another, with a sense of contrast on one hand and balance on the other. A menu may include several courses, or may be as simple and everyday as this:

- *Grilled Cheese Sandwich*
- *Tomato Soup*

Menu writing is its own kind of poetry—I could sit on my couch all afternoon sipping tea and writing menus. However, the trick is to get up from the couch and proceed to cook those lovely-sounding menus, turning out meals that fulfill or exceed every expectation.

This book deals almost exclusively with informal, "family-style" menus, where all the foods appear on the table at the same time and everyone helps themselves. In the Deep Springs Boardinghouse, meals are served buffet-style, with the day's menu written on a board. But ambitious cooks may choose to serve a meal in a more formal, restaurant style, sometimes known as French service, where courses are presented already plated, in succession: first an hors d'oeuvre, then maybe a soup, then the main course, then a salad, then dessert. While much more labor is involved in serving a menu of courses, it opens up greater possibilities for the food: risotto is served the moment it's finished; meat or fish is fresh from the pan, still sizzling; the salad has no chance to wilt or the soufflé to fall.

A basic American family-style dinner menu typically consists of a protein; a starch; a vegetable or two, including a salad; sometimes bread; and a dessert. This simple formula may be infinitely varied.

Here are some rules for menu making:

Keep it simple. Overambition is the downfall of many a well-intentioned dinner. Very often, less is more. A dinner consisting of only two excellent dishes is far better than a dinner of those same two excellent dishes plus three more not-so-good ones.

Balance the richness. If one course—usually the meat course—is especially rich, make sure the salad and other courses are on the light and refreshing side. Don't follow a goat cheese–laden salad with a steak topped with blue cheese. Both are delicious, but not in the same menu. If the main offerings are rich, a light dessert is welcome. If the main courses are kept light, it's a great opportunity for a rich dessert. Any composed, complex dish is usually best on its own. Lasagna, pot pie, enchiladas, assorted pizzas, beef stew with potatoes—such dishes are meals in themselves and need only the simplest accompaniments: tossed green salad, vegetables in vinaigrette, a bowl of radishes. . . .

Maintain ethnic continuity. In other words, don't follow barbecued chicken wings with Chinese noodle stir-fry, or sushi with enchiladas. With sufficient experience, however, you can successfully break this rule: many foods adapt beautifully to other ethnic contexts. Once I slipped a rather European salad of roasted beets, sliced oranges, and tarragon into a Middle Eastern falafel dinner, and it tasted right at home. I love menus that contain many ethnic flourishes but where freshness and simplicity define the meal rather than a discernible ethnic "stamp."

Pay attention to the season and the weather. Hot weather demands the simplest cooking: sliced ripe garden tomatoes with salt, peaches and plums sprinkled with flavored sugars, simple salads of homegrown greens and herbs, boiled fresh corn on the cob, hot chiles and cilantro to cool the body. Cool-weather cooking is more nuanced and complex: long-cooked dishes, braises, beets, hard squash, piquant greens, elaborate starches, spinach, onions, pork, cream, the astonishing brightness of citrus, the precious season of persimmons.

Cooking dinners in the highly unpredictable spring or fall months at Deep Springs can be tricky. Sometimes I commit myself to wintry rib-sticking fare, such as pot roast, before I realize it's going to be a sweltering scorcher of a day. So I heap on the chopped herbs and flavor the gravy with a good splash of vinegar to make a heavy dish taste lighter. Or sometimes I have planned a light, salad-y menu on a day that starts off sunny but ends up with snow falling at four in the afternoon. So I hustle to throw together a soup and bake the bread late so it's still warm. Cooking, I maintain, is fundamentally an interaction with nature; the good cook must pay attention and respond to the environment to produce soul-satisfying food. Finally, consider the sensibilities of your guests. I say "consider" and not "cater to"; I love to expand, very gently, my guests' comfort zones, to introduce them to new foods or to compel them, with a warm smile, to reconsider foods they thought they hated.

Many sample menus follow; for the dishes marked with an asterisk (*), you will find the recipes in this book. Some of them are from my "archive" of actual meals I cooked at Deep Springs. Other menus evoke that time, or otherwise suggest especially simple, everyday, home-cooked meals.

Breakfasts

Oatmeal* with Dried Fruit Compote* & Pecans
Yogurt with Orchard Peaches

Dutch Babies*
Santa Rosa Plums
Maple Yogurt

Soft-Boiled Eggs*
Cornmeal Biscuits*
Tomatoes with Salt*

Scrambled Eggs*
Warm Corn Tortillas
Fresh Salsa*
Pinto Beans* with Sour Cream

Freshly Baked Granola*
Yogurt with Fresh Berries
Doughnuts*

Baked Bacon*
Scrambled Eggs*
Jack's Buttermilk Pancakes* with Maple Syrup
Fresh Fruit

Fresh Breakfast Sausage*
Biscuits and Gravy*
Fried Eggs*
Eloise's Cornmeal-Buttermilk Pancakes*
    with Maple Syrup

Shirred Eggs*
Elaine's Baked Grits*
Ham Slices
Griddle Toast*
Grandma Z.'s Coffeecake*

Cornmeal-Cherry Scones*
Ham and Cheese Omelets*
Grapefruit*

Poached Eggs*
Cream Biscuits*
Griddle-Cooked Sirloin Steak with Green Onions
Crispy Breakfast Potatoes*

Breakfast Pumpkin Pie*
Mixed-Grain Porridge with Pumpkinseed Butter
Sliced Pears
Yogurt Smoothies

Lunches

Egg Salad* Sandwich on Wheaty Bread*
Watercress Soup*

Soupe au Pistou*
Rosemary Focaccia*
Roast Beef Salad*

Grilled Cheese Sandwiches*
Tomato Soup*
Green Salad* with Hard-Boiled Eggs*

Chef's Salad*
Catherine's Corn Soup*
Tomato Focaccia*

Marinated Steak*
Celery Root Salad*
Minted Iced Tea*

Reatha's Macaroni and Cheese*
Sliced Cold Glazed Ham*
Green Salad* with Green Apples

Pasta with Summer Tomato Sauce,*
    Queso Blanco,* and Basil
Iceberg Wedge Salad with Blue Cheese Dressing*
    and Bacon
Whey Lemonade*

Mama Nell's Chili con Carne*
condiments: sour cream, grated cheese,
    green onions
Skillet Cornbread*
Dill Pickles*
Limeade*

Green Chile Enchiladas*
Green Salad* with Radishes

Asparagus and Mushroom Frittata*
Leek and Gruyère Frittata*
Bacon and Onion Frittata*
Green Salad* with Avocado and Toasted Seeds*
Soft Wheat Rolls

Sorrel Omelet*
Baby Mixed Green Salad*
Garlic Toast*

Gumbo* with Rice*
Green Salad* with Shallot Vinaigrette*

Split Pea Soup* with Ham
Warm Wheaty Dinner Bread*
Pickled Winter Vegetables*

Tacos de Carne Asada*
Black Beans* with Sour Cream
Green Salad* with Radishes and Oranges
Hibiscus Iced Tea*

Tracy's Caesar Salad*
Cheesecake*

Tortilla Española*
Gazpacho*
Fennel, Orange, and Black Olive Salad*
Focaccia*

Pepperoni Pizza*
Zucchini and Red Onion Pizza*
Tomato, Basil, and Ricotta Pizza*
Green Salad* with Ranch Dressing*

Pork and White Bean Chili*
Black Bean Chili*
condiments: tomato, chopped white onion,
    sour cream, Jack cheese
Skillet Cornbread*
Chilled Radishes*
Jícama*

Tuna Salad* Melts
Curry Tofu Salad* Melts
Carrot-Raisin Salad*
Green Salad*

Sandwich Bar:
Freshly Baked Wheaty Dinner Bread*
Sliced Cold Roast Beef*
Sliced Cold Roast Pork
condiments: cheese, tomato, shaved onion, lettuce,
    mayonnaise, mustards
Dill Pickles
Butternut Squash Chips*
Green Salad*
Nettle Broth* Soup with Garden Leeks and Potatoes

Fresh Clam Chowder*
Corn Chowder*
Homemade Crackers*
Green Salad*

Baked Potatoes*
condiments: butter, sour cream, sharp cheddar cheese,
    sliced green onion, bacon, cooked broccoli
Egg Salad* with Herbs
Cold Roast Chicken*
Green Salad* with Tomatoes

Toasted Pasta with Garlic,* Broiled Cauliflower,*
    Tomato, and Toasted Breadcrumbs
Winter Lettuce Salad
Sliced Salami

Gâteau de Crêpes*
Green Salad*

Chicken Soup
Whole-Wheat Cheddar Biscuits*
Deviled Eggs*
Shaved Vegetable Salad

Italian Meatballs*
Mushroom "Meat" Balls
White and Brown Rice*
Tomato Sauce* and Parmesan
Tossed Green Salad* with Chopped Vegetables

Gunhild's Chicken Curry*
Garden Eggplant Curry
Golden Basmati Rice Pilaf*
Red Lentil Dal
Cantaloupe and Black Pepper Raita*
Papadums*

Dinners

Rico's Tacos* with Avocado and Sour Cream
Green Salad* with Red Onion and Sweet Balsamic
    Vinaigrette*

Cayenne-Rubbed Chicken with Potatoes and Garlic*
Broccoli* with Garlic and Sesame

Pork Chops Slow-Cooked in Olive Oil*
Polenta*
Greens*

Chicken Paprikash*
Herbed Spaetzle*
Spinach Salad* with Lemon Vinaigrette*

Boiled Shrimp* with Lemon and Melted Butter
Red Beans and Rice*
Cornmeal-Fried Okra*
Big Tossed Salad with Avocado, Tomatoes,
    and Croutons*

Roast Lamb*
Potato, Fennel, and Celery Root Gratin*
Escarole, Frisée, and Radicchio Salad
Apple and Candied Orange Pie* with
    Cognac Whipped Cream

Gravlax* with Rye Bread, Shaved Onion,
    and Tomatoes
Whole Wheat Pappardelle with Corn and Chiles*
Blackberry Ice Cream* and Peach Ice Cream*

Artichokes* with Lemon Mayonnaise
Pork Tenderloin*
Snap Peas*
Broiled Asparagus*
Rhubarb Fool
Lemon Slice Cookies*

Roasted Eggplant,* Roasted Red Peppers,* and
    White Beans with Pesto*

Mixed Green Salad with Shaved Parmesan, Fresh
    Artichoke Hearts,* and Toasted Pine Nut Vinaigrette
Tomato Focaccia*
Lemon Ice Cream* with Gingersnaps*

Goulash*
Polenta*
Chicory Salad with Apple Cider Vinaigrette*
Whipped Cream Cake* with Assorted Winter Fruit

Pan-Fried Cod*
Spicy Sautéed Squid*
Slovenian Fennel and Potatoes*
Red Radicchio Salad*

Baked Salmon* with Meyer Lemon–Olive Relish*
Sautéed Green Beans* with Toasted Walnut Olive Oil*
Green Pasta with Sautéed Corn* and Roasted Peppers
Milk and Honey Cake*
Cinnamon Ice Cream*

Wild Mushroom Risotto*
Seared Tuna* with Marinated Beets,* Cucumber,
    and Aioli*
Fennel, Blood Orange, and Toasted Almond Salad*
Pear Sherbet* with Sesame Cookies*

Carrot Soup with Ginger*
Flank Steak with Blue Cheese*
Brown, White, and Wild Rice Pilaf with Mirepoix*
Arugula Salad* with Toasted Walnuts*
Pinky's Jewish Apple Cake*

Roast Beef*
Horseradish-Tomato Relish*
Steamed Red Potatoes
Minty Peas*
Gooseberry Fool*

Butternut Squash Soup with Diced Pear*
Cynthia's Garlic-Studded Milk-Braised Pork Loin*
Olive Oil Mashed Potatoes*
Sautéed Rainbow Chard
Kohlrabi-Apple Slaw*
Almond Cream* with Persimmons

Pinto Beans* with Onions and Cilantro
Carne Asada* with Warm Corn Tortillas
New Mexico Posole with Pork and Green Chile*
Chayote* with Garlic
Fresh Salsa*
Jícama* and Radishes*
Lime Bars*
Fruit with Rosewater

Gin Chicken Liver Pâté* on Thyme Crackers*
Olives
Boeuf Bourguignonne* with Parsley Potatoes
Red Lettuce Salad with Asparagus* and
    Lemon Vinaigrette*
Currant Cake*

Chicken and Dumplings*
Southern-Style Braised Green Beans*
Garden Lettuce Salad with Ranch Dressing*
Lemon Meringue Pie*

Apple-Marinated Pork Chops*
Roasted Potatoes, Apples, and Onions*
Watercress Salad*
Fresh Ginger Cake*

Tarragon-Roasted Chicken with Tomatoes*
Wild Mushroom Risotto*
Stuffed Artichokes* with Sherry Vinegar Butter
Green Salad* with Blue Cheese Dressing*
Orange Bread Pudding*

Glazed Meatloaf*
Minty Peas*
Honey-Glazed Rainbow Carrots*
Mashed Cauliflower*
Dinner Bread*
Tossed Garden Salad with Creamy Dressing
    and Croutons*
Diana's Cherry Pie*

Braised Chicken in Red Wine with Mushrooms*
Parsley Farm Potatoes
Pear and Walnut Salad
Fresh Bay Leaf Cream with Citrus* and
    Cardamom Cookies*

Marmalade Chicken*
Pecan Couscous*
Sautéed Green Beans* with Red Onion
Mixed Green Salad* with Toasted Cumin–Mint–
    Yogurt Dressing*
Rich Dinner Bread*
Goat Milk Panna Cotta with Cherries*

Gazpacho* of Fire-Roasted Vegetables
Roast Beef*
Horseradish Cream*
Scallion-Buttermilk Potatoes*
Arugula, Mushroom, and Walnut Salad with
    Lemon-Walnut Vinaigrette
Sourdough Bread
Italian Orange Cookies*

Tender Cured Pork Chops* with Fresh Sage
Corn on the Cob*
Roasted New Potatoes with Garlic
Fuji Apple Coleslaw*
Tomatoes with Salt,* Feta, and Basil
Sweet Potato Bread
Gingersnaps, Vanilla Ice Cream, and Boysenberries*

Grilled Skirt Steak with Salsa Verde*
Tomato Cobbler*
Green Bean and Cherry Tomato Salad*
Butter Pecan Ice Cream*

Carbonnade Flamande*
Saffron Risotto*
Rosemary Salt Potatoes
Garden Tomatoes, Summer Squash, and
    Green Beans Tossed with Torn Basil
Sourdough Bread
Garden Salad* with Dijon-Yogurt Dressing
Ginger Peach Crisp* with Whipped Cream

Leek and Vegetable Purée Soup*
Asparagus-Mushroom Frittata*
Red-Leaf Lettuce and Radicchio Salad
Potato Focaccia*
Apples and Oranges*

Falafel*
Hummus*
accompaniments: tahin sauce,* pita bread,
    cucumbers, tomatoes, red onion, shredded lettuce,
    green salad* with rose petals
Marinated Beets* with Tarragon
Milk and Honey Cake* with Walnuts and
    Pomegranate Seeds

CHAPTER 18: MENUS — 335

Slow-Roasted Pork*
Roasted Potatoes* with Garden Herbs
Whole Roasted Cauliflower*
Mixed Green Salad* with Baby Garden Onions
Sourdough Bread
Ginger Cookies*

Skillet Hamburgers* with Hamburger Buns*
accompaniments: lettuce, thin-sliced onion,
　　sliced tomato, mustards, mayonnaise
Potato Chips*
Chopped Vegetable Salad
Tangy Lemon Sour Cream Gelatin*

Russian Borscht*
Sour Cream
Rye Bread
Dill Pickles*
Fresh Cucumbers
Poached Pears with Chocolate Sauce*

Goulash*
Polenta*
Dinner Bread*
Mixed Green Salad*
Walnut Biscotti*

Aioli* with Garden Vegetables: beets, carrots,
　　green onions, green beans, cherry tomatoes,
zucchini, broccoli
Mediterranean Meatballs*
Rice*
Plum Fool*

Deep Springs Thanksgiving, 1998

Apple-and Rosemary-Scented Roast Turkey*
　　with Gravy*
Mashed Potatoes*
Clio's Stuffing*
Stuffed Giant Turban Squash with Cornbread Stuffing
Brussels Sprouts with Brown Butter*
Roasted Yams with Pears and Bourbon*
Roasted Garden Carrots with White Mountain
　　Pine Nuts
Leek and Cabbage Sauté
Sweet Onions Cooked in Cream*
Watercress-Persimmon Salad
Pickled Cauliflower
Pickled Plums*
Cranberry Sauce* and Cranberry Relish*
Sweet Potato Bread
Deep Springs Sourdough Bread
Apple and Quince Pie* with Lard Piecrust*
Pumpkin Pie*
Pecan Pie*
Pear-Persimmon Crisp
Deep Springs Dairy Whipped Cream
Sparkling Water with Fresh Lime

A Dinner at My House, Passover, 1999

Matzoh Ball Soup*
Roast Leg of Lamb* with Garlic, Lemon, and
　　Rosemary
Boiled Artichokes* with Citron Mayonnaise
Italian Tzimmes*
Shaved Fennel* Salad
Coconut Macaroons
Strawberries in Sweet Wine

Christmas Eve, 1999

Jícama, Radish, Orange, and Pomegranate Salad
Mexican Braised Goat Stew* with Saffron
Goat Tamales with New Mexico Red Chile Sauce*
Lime-Pickled Red Onions*
Refried Beans*
condiments: pico de gallo, tomatillo salsa, cilantro, limes, sour cream
Tortillas
Winter Fruit and Custard Tart

New Year's Eve, 1999

Ginger and Paprika Roast Chicken
Saffron Risotto*
Beet and Carrot Salad
Chickpea Salad with Lemon and Parsley
Potato Bread*
Green Salad with Croutons*
Goose Egg Pound Cake Cinnamon Toast* with Vanilla Ice Cream*

Festival of Organ Meat Pleasure, Fall 2001

Beef Liver with Bacon, Onions, and Mushrooms*
Beef Heart Fritters
Goat Cheese, Spinach, and Green Chile Soufflé*
Mixed Green Salad* and Tomatoes
Sesame Bread*
Chocolate–Chocolate Chip Cookies*

Garden Dinner Offered in Memory of Deep Springs Student Michael Pihos, September 17, 2006

Cucumber-Basil-Yogurt Cooler
Handmade Egg Noodles* with Sautéed Mushrooms,* Garden Greens, and Feta
Chickpeas with Tomatoes, Lemon, and Mint*
Spinach Salad* with Parmesan, Croutons,* Hard-Boiled Egg,* and Lemon Vinaigrette*
Marinated Beets* with Fennel Flowers, Arugula, and Oranges
Warm Bread and Farm Butter*
Chocolate Cream Pie*

CHAPTER 19

AFTERMATH: LEFTOVERS, DISHES, SOAP, & STAINS

Dinner is finished. Your happy, well-fed guests have retired...now what? The hardworking cook's final task is to take care of the leftovers. For aesthetic and economic reasons alike, good management of leftovers—what the French call "les restes"—is vitally important to any kitchen. When you bring leftovers into the equation, you find that cooking for a household, even just for yourself, is an ongoing, ever-evolving process, not a matter of following a series of isolated recipes.

To begin with the bad news about leftovers, cooked food loses flavor and nutritional value when it sits and is then reheated. While many dishes such as chili or curry do taste particularly good the following day, no food is improved by a week in the refrigerator. Vitamins and minerals degrade, onions and garlic oxidize, potatoes and other starches develop unappealing textures, and bright, distinct layers of flavor become muted and one-note.

There are three principal modes of procuring, cooking, and eating food, each with a different approach to leftovers: I like to call them "No Refrigerator," "Small Refrigerator," and "Big Refrigerator." In the "No-Refrigerator" mode, the economical cook prepares only enough food for each meal, so there are almost never any leftovers. Portions are restrained; there is always exactly enough; every freshly-cooked bite is savored. Meat and produce are purchased (or otherwise obtained), cooked, and eaten fresh every day. This mode prevails in many cultures around the world, and derives from a time when home refrigeration was less prevalent, or non-existent.

By contrast, in "Big-Refrigerator" homes, food is usually cooked in quantities large enough for several meals. Servings are large, second helpings are available, and overeating is acceptable. There is always ample leftover food, and oftentimes, this food ages in the refrigerator to the point of spoilage before it can be used. In this mode, food is purchased less often, and in larger quantities. A "well-stocked refrigerator" is seen not merely as a necessity, but as a virtue. This mode is familiar to most North Americans—household refrigerators in the United States and Canada are much larger than anywhere else. With this approach, you're often eating leftovers, and almost always eating food that is less fresh than your No-Refrigerator neighbors.

I try to achieve the middle ground between those two extremes: the "Small-Refrigerator" mode. It means strategically planning meals, always "cooking ahead" to produce the building blocks for future meals. I might serve Green Chile Beef Stew (page 188) in bowls on the first night, then layer the chile with tortillas and cheese to make enchiladas the following night. Or, beans are served plain the day they're cooked, then become refried beans the next day. When soft-boiling eggs, if you throw in extra eggs and leave them in the water, you'll have hard-cooked eggs for another meal with almost no extra effort. Roast beef begets roast beef sandwiches with homemade aioli. Roast chicken begets a bright chicken salad, full of cilantro and lime juice. Author Tamar Adler drives this point home in her wonderful book An Everlasting Meal. Nowadays, cooking for our small household, I supplement a weekly large shopping trip with two or three additional trips to the market for fresh ingredients. Other than a small "bank" of leftovers at any given time, and the raw ingredients for one or two meals at most, my refrigerator mostly contains drinks and condiments…and yes, it could be much smaller than it is.

That's the good news about leftovers: strategically planned and well-utilized, they not only save money and energy, but they present wonderful opportunities for creative cooking. I once cooked a whole side of salmon on a big griddle; it came out moist and delicious, with bronzed, crispy skin. The next night, with the leftover salmon, I made old-fashioned croquettes, bound with a thick béchamel sauce, rolled in breadcrumbs, and shallow-fried. The fresh salmon was exquisite and simple, but the croquettes, with their deep seasoning and crispy crumbs, were truly outstanding. Cooking the salmon expressly to make croquettes would have been too much work, but it took no extra effort to cook the double portion of salmon on the first night. Often, when grilling meat for a meal, I make extra, then use the leftover meat for especially delicious tacos or enchiladas, or sandwiches or salads. Leftovers can provide an opportunity to focus on other parts of the meal: to make a batch of fresh noodles or dumplings, finesse a salad, or chop up a fresh relish.

Some tips for the good management of leftovers:

Take care to store leftover food promptly and properly. Put away leftover food as soon as you can, ideally, as soon as the food has cooled to room temperature. Use sealable storage containers—my favorite are glass containers with well-fitting plastic lids. Sturdy zipper-lock bags are also very effective, if the air is pressed out before sealing. Don't store foods in the metal pots they were cooked in, including enamelware; moisture from the food can penetrate fine cracks in the enamel and rust the metal beneath. Transfer food in half-empty containers to smaller containers, and it will keep better. Wrap large pieces of food well in plastic wrap, ensuring it isn't exposed to the direct air of the refrigerator.

Often, I will press a sheet of plastic wrap directly on the surface of the food in a storage container before putting on the lid, giving it double protection from the air. Plastic wrap is a food-saver's friend; I save money by buying large rolls from restaurant-supply stores.

Under refrigeration, food loses seasoning and moisture. This is why more liquid dishes, especially long-cooked brothy meats, such as stews and braises, keep and reheat especially well. When reheating leftover food, add additional salt, and a little water, stock, milk, cream, or other liquid.

The gentle, radiant heat of the oven (or toaster oven) is almost always preferable to a microwave oven for reheating food. If you must reheat food in a microwave, take the food out and stir it, or turn it, every 30 seconds or so, just until it's heated through. Often, a lower microwave power setting is preferable to the highest setting.

To revive leftover quick breads such as biscuits, scones, or cornbread, brush their tops with milk or cream, then heat through in a hot oven.

Sprinkle unsliced day-old loaves of bread with water, then heat for several minutes in a hot oven.

To reheat leftover rice, first gently break up the clumps of cold rice with your hands, then toss it with a few spoonfuls of water, just enough to moisten. Put it in a shallow, ovenproof dish in a layer about 1 inch thick, cover with foil, and put in a hot oven for about 15 minutes, until heated through.

Many a reheated dish is enlivened with a sprinkle of fresh parsley or other herbs, and a squeeze of fresh lemon juice. Sautéed Greens (page 132) always brighten a leftover stew or soup.

If you're making a large pot of stew, soup, or chili to last for a couple of meals, add the chopped parsley or other fresh ingredients only to the portion you'll consume right away. Promptly refrigerate the leftover portion. When reheating it, check its seasoning carefully, and add the parsley or other fresh element at that time.

As an attentive, creative cook, you know the power and potential of leftovers. You decide to put those last three tablespoons of chicken braising liquid into the warm hummus, and it's the most delicious hummus you and your family have ever tasted. Or the time you heated that last tiny serving of tomato soup, added butter and fresh herbs, and turned it into a sauce that tasted lovely with the roast chicken and potatoes. Or when you chopped up the leftover leg of lamb and made shepherd's pie. No single recipe can lead you to these brilliant moments—you have to find them for yourself. You'll discover a golden secret: those unplanned, spontaneous moments when you use odds and ends of leftovers can yield some of your very best meals, all the better for being impossible to duplicate.

How to Wash Dishes

Wherever good, homemade food abides, there is always a pile of dirty dishes. That's just the way it is. Settle into your dishwashing, appreciating the task's meditative simplicity. Every Deep Springs student must perform at least one 2-month tour of duty scrubbing pots and plates in the Boardinghouse kitchen.

Here is an excellent, thorough method for washing dishes at home:

1. *De-particle-ize:* rinse off all visible particles of food and excess grease, using hot water and a nylon scrubber if necessary. Be careful of the type of scrubber you use. Some will abrade metals, glass, and glazes. Even softer types can easily abrade plasticware—inexpensive, open-mesh nylon scrubbers are best for most purposes. The mesh bags in which onions and garlic are sometimes packaged make good scrubbers.

2. *Scrub:* put a tablespoon or two of dish detergent in a small basin and fill with about 2 quarts of hot water. Saturate a dishcloth in your soapy water, and scrub all grease, oil, and any remaining food particles from the dishes. Rinse the cloth frequently in clean water, re-saturating it with the soapy water. Sponges contain an enormous surface area within their pores and so are traps for bacteria. They are very difficult to clean thoroughly. If you do use sponges, it's a good idea to sterilize them frequently in the microwave (about 1½ minutes) or in boiling water, and replace them at regular intervals. I think small, sturdy cotton dishcloths are better, as they can be thrown in the washing machine.

3. *Rinse:* using hot running water, thoroughly rinse the detergent off the dishes, arranging them in a dish rack. Let dishes air-dry, or thoroughly towel-dry with a clean kitchen towel.

Always wash sharp knives or anything with a blade separately; never put sharp objects in a basin of soapy water.

A *baking soda solution* will sometimes help remove the black residue of burned food from the bottom of a pot, depending on the type of food and how badly it was burned. Fill the pot with a few inches of hot water, stir in a couple of heaping spoonfuls of baking soda, and let soak overnight. Bring the water to a boil (watch carefully—don't let it boil over) and cool again to room temperature—the residue should easily scrape off.

In the Deep Springs Boardinghouse and other large-scale kitchens, it's more efficient to use the industrial three-basin method: first, rinse particles off the dishes thoroughly, then immerse them and scrub the grease off in (1) a basin of soapy water, then (2) in a basin of hot water to rinse, then (3) in a basin of lukewarm water with a glug of bleach added to sterilize. Arrange the dishes on a rack and let air-dry completely.

Laundry Stains

Cooks need to know about stains. Our clothes get stained with food, with grease from various appliances, with soot from the ovens, and with our own blood. Never rinse any protein-based stain (blood, egg, milk) in warm or hot water—always cold. Use bleach only occasionally if you want your clothes to last. For a large load of white or light-colored clothes, add about ½ cup bleach—a large glug—to the water, making sure it disperses before adding clothes (you should do this with detergent, for that matter, too). If you are away from home and get a stain on an article of clothing you care about, treat the spot as soon as possible with cold water and a little hand soap.

STAIN GUIDE

For most stains: saturate the area of the stain with cold water, then rub well with a bar of Fels-Naptha soap (an antique brand still available in most supermarkets). Rub the soap-saturated fabric vigorously against itself all around the area of the stain. Launder in cold water. Repeat until the stain is gone.

Fresh blood: rinse with cold water, rubbing the fabric against itself around the area of the stain. On white fabrics, treat any residue with hydrogen peroxide. On colored fabrics, treat any residue with Fels-Naptha soap.

Dried blood: rinse with cold water, rubbing well. For white fabrics, saturate the stain with hydrogen peroxide, rub thoroughly, then rinse well with cold water. Repeat until the stain is gone, then launder. On colored fabrics, rinse and rub well under cold running water, then treat with Fels-Naptha soap.

Egg: use cold water to dissolve the egg (even if dried), rubbing under running water until all visible residue is gone, then launder in cold water. Treat any residue with Fels-Naptha soap.

Dirty kitchen towels and chef's jackets: use a powdered oxygen-action stain remover, soaking the soiled items overnight. (This same product is good for removing stains from enameled cookware, coffee cups, or your porcelain kitchen sink.)

Handkerchiefs: soak your dirty white hankies for 20 minutes in enough lukewarm water to cover with 2 or 3 glugs of hydrogen peroxide mixed in, then launder in hot water.

Stinky items—socks, washable footwear, nasty bedsheets: wash in hot or warm water, with about ¼ cup baking soda in addition to the detergent.

Ball-point pen ink: rub fabric against itself around the area of the stain with rubbing alcohol, then rinse out the alcohol with cold water. Repeat until the stain is gone.

Non-Edible Recipes

Toothbrushing Powder

This simple powder contains thyme oil, prized for centuries as an antimicrobial agent. Blend four tablespoons fine sea salt (preferably unrefined, see page 42) with about 8 drops of essential oil of thyme, and about 4 drops essential oil of peppermint or cinnamon, blending well until the oils are evenly dispersed throughout the salt. Blend in 2 tablespoons of baking soda. Store in a small bottle with a cork, or other airtight container, away from light or moisture. To use, sprinkle about ½ teaspoon onto your moistened toothbrush, and brush your teeth with a little warm water. A couple of teaspoons of this powder dissolved in a small cup of equal parts hydrogen peroxide and warm water makes a good gargling rinse.

Cut Flower Solution

Most varieties of cut flowers, in most circumstances, will stay fresh longer in a weak solution of bleach and sugar, rather than in plain water. For every quart of water, stir in ¼ teaspoon of laundry bleach, and 2 teaspoons of sugar, until the sugar is dissolved. When the water begins to look cloudy, replace it with fresh solution.

Hummingbird "Nectar"

Stir ½ cup granulated (white) sugar into 2 cups boiling water until dissolved, then let cool completely. Wash the feeder well each time you fill it. Don't be tempted to use honey instead of sugar—a honey solution readily ferments, which can harm the little birds' systems. Flower nectar (and the "nectar" in feeders) is like an energy drink: the sweet liquid gives them the bursts of energy they need for hunting insects.

Deep Springs Soap

makes about 10 pounds of soap, or 50 big bars

As any Deep Springs student butcher will tell you, a whole cow contains an astonishing amount of fat. The fat surrounding an animal's kidneys is the purest, highest quality fat. Skillfully rendered, it's a splendid medium for deep-frying, and may even be used in baking, as our ancestors did. But what about all the other fat, not just the prime kidney type? What do enterprising Deep Springers do with all this fat, besides throw it away? Make soap! This recipe—one used at Deep Springs for years—yields mild hand and body soap of a quality and purity money just can't buy. All soap is made of fat and lye: the quality and purity of the fat determine the quality of the soap. Often, in commercial soap, the fat, chemically purified, is of questionable origin. While most soaps contain perfume to hide the smell of the fat, the olive oil in this soap imparts an appealing, clean, naturally soapy scent. We developed this recipe from formulas in an excellent little book published in the 1970s called simply *Soap: Making It, Enjoying It,* by Ann Bramson.

If you require instant gratification in your endeavors, soapmaking is not for you. The ingredients are difficult to find, rendering the tallow takes hours and makes a mess, the temperatures and weights must be exact, the mixing itself requires long, patient stirring, and the soap must cure for at least a month before it's ready to use. Nonetheless, the whole process—including, at last, the satisfying use of the finished soap—offers a fresh appreciation and understanding of an ordinary, everyday product.

We use soap constantly, but rarely pay it much attention.

For success, follow each step precisely; soapmaking is not an improvisatory craft.

Dogs have been known to eat this homemade soap, with very unfortunate, messy after-effects, so keep it out of their reach.

EQUIPMENT/SUPPLIES

meat grinder (or have the butcher grind the fat for you)

large stainless-steel or enamel cooking pot

slow cooker (optional)

screen sieve

cheesecloth or old dish towel

scale accurate to the half-ounce

2-quart glass jar with metal lid (juice jars are ideal; they will withstand the high reaction temperature of the lye)

large wooden spoon (okay to use for cooking afterward—just wash it well)

insulated cooler, about 2-gallon capacity

large plastic garbage bag

2 steel-tipped thermometers with an accurate 60° to 120°F range (1 will suffice, but 2 are more convenient)

large kitchen knife

Ingredients for Soap

6½ pounds fresh, raw beef kidney fat (to make exactly 5.63 pounds, or 5 pounds 10 ounces, or 90 ounces of rendered tallow; a custom butcher will have this; kidney fat is easier to work with than other types of fat)

16½ ounces pure lye crystals (properly known as sodium hydroxide; available by mail order)

48 ounces (by weight) **water** (3 pounds exactly)

39 ounces (by weight) **olive oil** (2 pounds 7 ounces; extra-virgin oil is great but not necessary)

½ ounce vitamin E oil (available in body-care stores)

2½ ounces extra-virgin olive oil (added at the end to scent and "superfat" the soap, making it extra mild)

To render the tallow: in a meat grinder, grind the fat, or have the butcher do this for you. Or chop it into small pieces with a large knife. Put it in a large, heavy pot (a slow cooker works well). Set over a very low flame, and allow the fat to render, stirring from time to time. As it renders, the pure fat melts into a clear liquid, and the chunks of solid fat become translucent. After 3 to 4 hours, pour the contents of the pot through a screen sieve set over another pot. Press on the solids left in the sieve to squeeze out more of the liquid fat, then discard the solids.

Now line the sieve with 2 to 3 thicknesses of cheesecloth (or an old dish towel) and place it over a large bowl. Pour the liquid fat through the cheesecloth to filter out any remaining debris. Allow the tallow to cool to room temperature, then refrigerate overnight. Pry the hardened tallow from the bowl. Weigh it—you will need exactly 90 ounces. (Ann Bramson, the soap book author, suggests mixing any leftover tallow with an equal amount of butter and using this blend of fats to make a superlative crust for pecan pie. You may also fry steak in beef tallow; see page 180.)

To mix the lye solution: weigh the lye and water precisely. Put the lye crystals in a 2-quart glass jar with a tight-fitting metal lid. Slowly pour in the water—the reaction will produce a lot of heat. With the handle of a wooden spoon, stir to completely dissolve the crystals in the water. Wash the spoon well afterward.

To prepare the insulated mold: with scissors, cut open one side seam and the bottom seam of the garbage bag, to make one large sheet of plastic. Use this to line the insulated cooler. Drape the flaps of the sheet over the edge of the cooler.

To make the soap: both the lye and the tallow mixture should be within a degree or two of body temperature (98°F). Put the tallow, the 39 ounces of olive oil, and the vitamin E oil together in a large stainless-steel or enamel pot, and heat over the lowest heat of the stove for just a few minutes, just to begin melting the tallow; the residual heat will melt the rest. Or place the pot in a basin of hot water.

If you have just made the lye solution, let it cool for at least 30 minutes, then cool it further, if necessary, by placing the jar in a basin of cold water. Poke 2 holes in the metal lid of the jar for the lye solution (one for the solution to exit, the other for air to enter) so the solution can be dispersed in a thin, even stream.

When both lye and fat are at about 97°F, begin stirring the fat with your large wooden spoon while dispersing the lye into the fat. Keep stirring until all the lye is in the fat and the mixture thickens, keeping the mixture at 97°. If the mixture cools down, place it in a basin of hot water to warm it back up. When you can dribble a stream or droplets of the mixture across its surface and the shape remains for a moment (called tracing), it is ready. Add the 2½ ounces of extra-virgin olive oil to the mixture and stir for about 5 minutes more. Pour the mixture into the prepared mold. Press the flaps of plastic evenly and gently over the surface of the mixture and close the cooler. Do not open the cooler for 48 hours.

To finish and cure the soap: After 48 hours, remove the block of solid soap from the cooler, and peel away the plastic. Scrape away any white, powdery residue on the surface. If the soap is still quite soft, let it air-cure on a sheet of plastic on a tray until it firms up—a day or longer. If it seems firm enough to cut, go ahead and cut it into bars with a large kitchen knife. Arrange the bars on a sheet of plastic on a tray to allow for maximum air circulation, and let the soap air-cure in a clean, dry place for about a week. If the bars are still soft to the touch at this point, let them cure for another week, until they are hardened. Wrap each bar individually in butcher paper or waxed paper, and let cure for 3 to 4 more weeks before using.

CHAPTER 20

BIBLIOGRAPHY

When I was a teenager, I discovered *The Chez Panisse Menu Cookbook* on my friend Cathleen's kitchen shelf, sat down, and read the whole thing from cover to cover, like a novel. Duck fat, truffles, fennel, chervil, salt-packed anchovies—I had never encountered such ingredients before. I was fascinated by the French techniques and repertoire, the menu-crafting principles, and the deep respect for vegetables. That evening, I successfully made a carrot-and-shallot soup from the book, garnished with chervil cream. My imagination was ignited, and the seeds of a culinary career were planted in that moment.

Even as a young kid, I spent hours reading the many informational passages in my own copy of *The Joy of Cooking*, absorbing as much as I could. I read dessert cookbooks. I read the recipes in my mother's women's magazines. At Deep Springs I discovered M.F.K. Fischer's compilation of her early writings, *The Art of Eating*, and read every word, immersing myself in her world where food serves as a lens for seeing, well, everything. I pored over Deborah Madison's and Paul Bertolli's first cookbooks during those years, too.

Later, in my professional cooking era, no task was more satisfying on a free afternoon than getting an armload of cookbooks off the shelf and perusing them for menu ideas. I especially loved cookbooks with a distinctive, personal voice: when I returned to Deep Springs to be the chef there, a friend I'd known from Chez Panisse, David Lebovitz, published his first cookbook, *Room for Dessert*, and reading it felt like spending time with David himself. Nowadays, although I no longer cook for a living, cookbooks still inspire my passion for the craft. If I'm not careful, stacks of cookbooks start to take over the tabletops in my house.

Following is a list of my idiosyncratic favorite cookbooks, that have well withstood the vicissitudes of time and trends, and that continue to inspire my culinary imagination today. Additionally, I'm proud to mention excellent, recent books written by fellow Deep Springs alumni: Chef David Tanis' cookbooks, Kevin West's book on seasonal preserving, and L. Jackson Newell's long-awaited history of Deep Springs.

Cookbooks

These fourteen cookbooks, my idiosyncratic favorites, have all well withstood the vicissitudes of time and trends, have influenced my cooking, and continue to inspire my culinary imagination.

THE BETTY CROCKER PICTURE COOKBOOK
published by McGraw-Hill, 1956
This is the first cookbook I used when I was growing up—it was my mother's principal cookbook. A little more approachable than *The Joy of Cooking*, it is a lushly illustrated, encyclopedic treasury of good, mid-century American cooking. It contains many charming "tips" for the "busy housewife," including the admonition to "harbor pleasant thoughts" while scrubbing the kitchen floor.

CHARLESTON RECEIPTS
published by The Junior League of Charleston, 1950
This book is the final word on the cookery of the coastal American South. Most of the recipes (or "receipts") are simple, elegant, and still thoroughly appealing. Though published in 1950, the book vividly evokes earlier ages (for example, a recipe for "Regent's Punch," containing rock sugar candy, green tea [!], champagne, sherry, brandy, and a sliced lemon, notes "As mixed at Lewisfield Plantation, 1783"). Very few convenience foods are called for—virtually everything is from scratch. The "Seafoods" chapter is particularly excellent, as is "Pickles & Relishes."

CHEZ PANISSE COOKING
Paul Bertolli, Random House, 1988
This is among the most beautifully written cookbooks. Of persimmons, he writes, "There are few things as striking as a persimmon tree in autumn—fruit clinging like Christmas ornaments to the dark arms of the bare tree in the quickening air. Melancholy, fruition, and the close of the circle of seasons are summed up in this image of withering branches and ripening fruit." Many of the ingredients (rabbit, pigeon, black truffles, walnut oil, Meyer lemons) are hard to find in supermarkets, and many of the recipes have multiple, exacting steps. Nonetheless, each recipe, if followed closely, is a valuable, multifaceted culinary lesson.

CHEZ PANISSE DESSERTS
Lindsey Shere, Random House, 1985
This collection of elemental, classic, European-inflected preparations has long been my favorite dessert cookbook. These desserts are always thought of in the context of the whole meal—there are virtually no complex showstoppers, just simple preparations—tarts, mousses, compotes, crisps—showcasing the main ingredient's best qualities. Most of the chapters deal with seasonal fruit: "Citrus Fruit," "Apples, Pears, and Quinces," "Berries," "Summer Fruits," "Figs, Melons, and Other Fall Fruits." The ice creams and sherbets are especially wonderful and timeless.

THE CHEZ PANISSE MENU COOKBOOK
Alice Waters, Random House, 1982
When I was a teenager, I discovered this book on my friend Cathleen's kitchen shelf shortly after it was published, sat down, and read the whole thing from cover to cover, like a novel. Duck fat, shallots, fennel, chervil, salt-packed anchovies—I had never encountered such ingredients before. That evening, I successfully made a carrot soup from it. My imagination was ignited, and the seeds of a culinary career were planted in that moment. The book thoroughly explores the idea of a good, balanced menu (the recipes are arranged in menus, not organized into the usual categories of salads, meats, desserts, and so on) and offers a superb introduction to the idea of cooking seasonally.

ENGLISH FOOD
Jane Grigson, Penguin Books, 1974
When the food of the British Isles was still the butt of many jokes, this book quietly and intelligently proved the subtlety, complexity, and overall deliciousness of this cuisine. Celery in cream; Welsh supper herrings; crumpets; steak, kidney, and oyster pie; chicken with mussels; poor knight's pudding; and gooseberry fool are only a few of the book's many unexpected delights.

THE GREENS COOKBOOK
Deborah Madison, Bantam Books, 1987
This cookbook broke new ground—it proved that elegant, satisfying, painstakingly crafted food need not contain meat. Madison's clear, poetic enthusiasm for her subject shines from every page. These well-written recipes are more exacting than those in

her more recent cookbooks, but each recipe, followed closely, supplies a wealth of culinary information.

HONEY FROM A WEED: FASTING AND FEASTING IN TUSCANY, CATALONIA, THE CYCLADES AND APULIA
Patience Gray, North Point Press, 1986
A fascinating, erudite compendium of Mediterranean peasant food. The author's life-partner, a sculptor, sought out sources of marble and stone for his work in remote areas around the Mediterranean. While he sculpted in these rural areas of northern and southern Italy, Greece, and Spain, she closely and brilliantly studied the local foodways. Many of the recipes use foraged, fished, or hunted wild ingredients from these places, but a few translate to modern kitchens and tastes, such as ewe's cheese with pears, fried chicken in walnut sauce, "widowed" potatoes, Tuscan loin of pork, and wild peach jam.

THE JOY OF COOKING
Irma S. Rombauer and Marion Rombauer Becker, 13th edition, Bobbs-Merrill, 1975
By almost anyone's estimation, this is *the* essential American kitchen reference, written not by a committee, a club, or a corporation, but by a mother and her daughter, over a period of several decades. The recipes themselves are not necessarily unique, but the book contains a staggering amount of information on food and cooking. Cookbook historian Anne Mendelson wrote an absorbing, harrowing biography of Irma, Marion, and their book.

THE MOOSEWOOD COOKBOOK
Mollie Katzen, Ten Speed Press, 1977
I heavily relied on this book when I cooked at Deep Springs as an inexperienced Student Cook, and came to trust it as a friend. The hand-lettering, the funky illustrations, and the personal conversational nature of the recipes all make for an excellent beginner's cookbook, with many recipes that are still fresh and exciting.

NOTHING FANCY
Diana Kennedy, North Point Press, 1984
This is my favorite example of a good, working cookbook that is also highly personal and idiosyncratic. It contains an entire chapter called "Crispy Things." While many of the recipes spring from the author's beloved, adopted Mexico, the teatime and holiday favorites from her native England—hot cross buns, cucumber sandwiches, gingerbread, bitter orange marmalade, lemon curd, rock cakes, barley water, ginger beer—form the spirit and backbone of the book.

RECIPES FROM THE REGIONAL COOKS OF MEXICO
Diana Kennedy, Harper & Row, 1978
Her great, earlier cookbook, *The Cuisines of Mexico,* was one of the first to prove unequivocally the depth and breadth of one of the world's most exciting and intriguing cuisines. This book, focused more on individual cooks and regional specialties, is more personal. It contains a long, wonderful account of an elaborate Oaxacan goat *barbacoa*, full of rich culinary detail.

SUMMER COOKING
Elizabeth David, Museum Press/Knopf, 1955
Of the many intelligent, evocative cookbooks on the food of France and the Mediterranean penned by David (*Mediterranean Cooking* [1950], *French Country Cooking* [1951], *Italian Food* [1954], *French Provincial Cooking* [1960]), designed to bring Britons out of their postwar culinary depression, *Summer Cooking* extols, in concise, poetic paragraphs, the culinary virtues of eating appropriately to the season. Ease, lightness, and simplicity prevail. Her work continues to inspire generations of English and American chefs and cooks.

WHITE TRASH COOKING
Ernest Matthew Mickler, Ten Speed Press, 1986
At first glance, this book seems like a joke, but on closer examination, a sensitive, warmhearted cultural document of Southern food emerges. Some of the recipes are great fun to read but not necessarily feasible to cook and eat ("Butt's 'Gator Tail" comes to mind), but many others are genuinely appealing. In the recipes, people's voices are allowed to be just as they are. Haunting, evocative photographs supplement the recipes.

Deep Springs Authors

DAVID TANIS (DS'71):

A PLATTER OF FIGS AND OTHER RECIPES
Artisan, 2008

HEART OF THE ARTICHOKE AND OTHER KITCHEN JOURNEYS
Artisan, 2010

ONE GOOD DISH: THE PLEASURES OF A SIMPLE MEAL
Artisan, 2013

David's books are treasures—I can't look at any of them for long without wanting to jump up and go into the kitchen. The first two are arranged in sumptuous, seasonal menus, while *One Good Dish*, as the title suggests, offers simpler recipes that stand alone. Throughout, David shares his inner creative thought processes, opinions, inspirations, and anecdotes. Green lasagna with greens, with puréed greens in the lasagna noodles plus more sautéed greens and béchamel in the filling (probably my favorite version of lasagna), and simple baked apples (my version is on page 276 of this book) are only two among many favorites in *Figs*. *Artichoke* is full of inspiring recipes, from a series of small essays on such simple fare as beans on toast, to showstoppers such as roast suckling pig. And I could never do without the radishes a la crème from *One Good Dish*.

KEVIN WEST (DS'88):

SAVING THE SEASON: A COOK'S GUIDE TO HOME CANNING, PICKLING, AND PRESERVING
Knopf, 2013

In this meditation on aesthetics via the craft of seasonal preserving, Kevin weaves elements of literature, classical art, and philosophy together with excellent preserving recipes and methods. His rural Southern background provides an authoritative foundation for the culinary lore, but his keenly developed senses of refinement, balance and restraint are manifest not only in the recipes, but also in his poetic photographs.

L. JACKSON NEWELL (DS'56):

THE ELECTRIC EDGE OF ACADEME: THE SAGA OF LUCIEN L. NUNN AND DEEP SPRINGS COLLEGE
University of Utah Press, 2015

This essential history of Deep Springs and its fascinating founder was painstakingly researched and compiled over a period of many years by Jack and his wife, Linda (also an historian and author). In his roles as a member of the Deep Springs class of 1956, as Dean of Liberal Education at the University of Utah, and as a professor, trustee, and President at Deep Springs over decades, Jack was uniquely poised to write this book.

Sources

FOR SOUTHERN STONE-GROUND GRITS AND CORNMEAL:
Logan Turnpike Mill
706-745-5735 or 800-84-GRITS
loganturnpikemill.com

FOR NEW MEXICO GROUND RED CHILE, WHOLE DRIED RED CHILE PODS, AND FRESH GREEN CHILE:
The New Mexican Connection
800-933-2736
newmexicanconnection.com

FOR TRULY UNREFINED SEA SALT:
Salt Works, Inc.
800-353-SALT (7258)
seasalt.com

FOR SUPERB FLOUR AND AN ALL-AROUND BAKING RESOURCE:
King Arthur Flour
800-827-6836
kingarthurflour.com

FOR GRAINS OF MANY TYPES:
Bob's Red Mill
800-349-2173
bobsredmill.com

FOR EXCELLENT-QUALITY MEAT, SEEK OUT:
a family-run butcher shop
a local, family-owned small farm
   with a livestock program

FOR GOOD, FRESH FRUITS, VEGETABLES, AND HERBS, OR FOR FARM-FRESH EGGS, INVESTIGATE:
farmers markets
roadside farm stands
"U-pick" places
raising chickens in your backyard
growing a garden

Acknowledgements

I would like to express my gratitude to the many people who, knowingly or unknowingly, directly or indirectly, have helped *The Deep Springs Cookbook* through its many incarnations, from "seed" to "tree."

To longtime Deep Springs President David Neidorf for envisioning this edition long ago, and to Development Director David Welle for producing it. To Justin Kim for the beautiful artwork, and to Jena Scholten for realizing the book's design. To Bill LeBlond, Sarah Billingsley, and the team at Chronicle Books for publishing the earlier edition of the book, *The Commonsense Kitchen*.

To L. J. "Elge" Bridwell, for delicious friendship, unstinting critical honesty, and intimate involvement with the book over so many years. To Charis and Mark Takaro, for countless excellent home-cooked meals and steadfast support. To Mona Talbott for constant inspiration on the culinary path.

To Deep Springs College community members past and present, including Geoff and Iris Pope, Andy and Heather Jennings, David and Jane Steidel, Jack and Linda Newell, Ross and Kay Peterson, Chuck and Elaine Teel, the Badkar family, the Copelin family, the Mitchell family, Jack Aldworth, Donna Blagdan, Jonathan "Dewey" DeWeese, Brad Edmondson, Priscilla Freeman, Abram Kaplan, Cecilia Lopez, Don Read, Bill Scott, David Tanis, Ella Vining, and Kevin West. To Deep Springs students past and present, especially the classes of 1986 to 1989, 1996 to 2001, and 2005 to 2009.

To friends and family behind many of the recipes, including Carol Adair, Paul Airoldi, Ann Hanchey Applegarth, Diana Applegarth, Joel Baecker, Mary Nell Brown, Ann Tracy Drummond, Clay Drummond, Jean Glover, Nellie Maybelle Hanchey, Iris Ann Hudgens, Michael Thomas Hudgens, Eloise Humphrey, Reatha Jones, David Lebovitz, Eric "Rico" Luna *(el corazón de mi alma)*, Emily Marshall, Scott Miller, Dana Nesbitt, Laura Laylin Nichols, Michael Polek, Linda Rael, Joan Rinaldi, Cynthia Shea, Lela Hanchey Thompson, Amy Toder, Adra Valentine, Katherine White, Elizabeth "Lee" Zavadil, and Tom Zavadil.

Finally, to all my teachers—transmitters of information, experience, spirit, drive, wisdom, and love—including writing coaches Ruth Lewis, June Wolfe, Pam Perryman, Tim Hunt, and Lydia Fakundiny; science guides Edie Anderson, Carla Scheidlinger, and Gordon Wardlaw; meditation masters Donald Rothberg (a deep bow), Sylvia Boorstein, and Christopher Titmuss; and culinary exemplars Elizabeth Alderson, Catherine Brandel, Kazue Carlson, Eve Felder, Mirka Grbec, Gilbert Pilgram, Cynthia Shea, Peggy Smith, Carole "Cookie" Tam Sing, Alice Waters, and, of course, my mom.

INDEX

A

Acorn squash, stuffed, 245
Aioli, 253
Allspice-Scented Pot Roast, 188
Almond(s)
  Blanched, 176
  – Butter Cookies, 319
  Cream, 311
  Mexican Chocolate Cookies with Almonds, 318
  Mixed Salted Nuts, 176
  Parsnip Soup with Toasted Almond Olive Oil, 138
  Paste, with Cherries, 280
  Toasted, 176
  Toasted, with Fennel and Blood Orange Salad, 167
Andouille sausage, 98, 111
Appetizers see Hors d'oeuvres
Apple(s)
  Cake, Pinky's Jewish, 292
  cider, about, 197
  Cider Vinaigrette, 174
  David's Baked Apples, 276
  Dutch Babies, 68
  Fuji Apple Coleslaw, 163
  – Kohlrabi Slaw, 169
  – Marinated Pork Chops, 197
  Oranges and Apples, 280
  Oven Applesauce, 257
  – Pear Salad, 163
  Pie, with variations, 265 – 266
  Roasted Potatoes, Apples, and Onions, 141
  Turkey, Roast, Apple – and Rosemary-Scented, 218
  – Walnut Crisp, 277
Applegarth, Ann, 154
Apricot Jam, Kevin's, 259
Apricots, Pickled, 258
Artichokes, 119
Artichoke Hearts, Fresh, 120
Arugula Salads, 161
Asparagus
  Broiled, 121
  Grilled, 121
  – Mushroom Frittata, 93
  Pan-Roasted, 120
  Pasta, 121
  Salad, 164
  Spring Pasta with Snap Peas and Asparagus, 139
Aunt Lela's Buttermilk Pie, 274
Avocado(es)
  Dip, Mediterranean, 249
  Guacamole, 249
  Toast, 104
  Tortilla, 104

B

Bacon, 54
Bacon and Onion Frittata, 93
Bacon-Apple Pie, 266
Bacon Fat, Green Beans Cooked in, 122
Bacon-Wrapped Chicken Cooked Under a Brick, 211
Baked Apples, David's, 276
Baked Bacon, 54
Baked Custard, 304
Baked Potatoes, 85
Baked Salmon, 222
baking powder, about, 37; home-mixed, 62
baking soda, about, 37
Balsamic Vinaigrettes, 174
Banana
  Bread, 72
  Cream Pie, 271
  Pudding, 271
Barbecue Sauce, Blond, 257
Basil
  Green Bean Salad with Cherry Tomatoes and Basil, 164
  Pesto, 254
  Watermelon Salad with Feta and Basil, 173
Basmati Rice, 101
Basmati Rice Pilaf, Golden, 239

Bay Leaf, Fresh Bay Leaf Cream with Citrus, 311
BEANS, 106 – 116; See also individual varieties
    Black, 108
    Fresh Shell Beans, 122
    Guidelines for cooking, 106
    Pinto, 108
    Refried, 108
    Sauerkraut, Sausage and Bean Soup (Jota), 143
    White Bean Gratin with Fennel, 115
    White Bean Soup with Escarole, 114
    White Bean Soup with Fried Sage, 114
Beans, Green, 121, 122
Béchamel sauce, 95
BEEF, LAMB, & PORK, 178 – 202
Beef
    Allspice-Scented Pot Roast, 188
    Carne Asada, 182
    Carpaccio, 194
    Chicken-Fried Steak, 55
    Flank Steak with Blue Cheese, 181
    Grilled Skirt Steak with Salsa Verde, 181
    Liver with Bacon, Onions, and Mushrooms, 196
    Marinated Steak, 180
    Porcini-Dusted Steak, 182
    Posole, 98
    raw beef, 193, 194
    Roast Beef Salad, 184
    Roast Beef, 183
    Steak Fried in Beef Tallow, 180
    Steak Tartare, 193
    Stew, 184 – 188
        Boeuf Bourguignonne, 186
        Carbonnade Flamande, 186
        Goulash, 186
        Green Chile Stew, 188
        Italian Stew, 186
        Mexican Braised, 187
        Russian Borscht, 186
Beef, ground
    Burger Steak Salad, 192
    Glazed Meatloaf, 189
    Italian Meatballs, 190
    Mediterranean Meatballs, 191
    Rico's Tacos, 192
    Skillet Hamburgers, 192
Beet, Kale, and Leek Salad with Orange Oil, 169
Beets, Marinated, 164
Bertolli, Paul, 205, 347
Betty Crocker Picture Cookbook, The, 347
Beurre blanc, 252
Beurre rouge, 252
BIBLIOGRAPHY, 346 – 349
Big Pink Cake, 297
Biscochitos, 326
Biscotti, Lemon-Anise, 322
Biscotti, Walnut, 321
Biscuits, with variations, 65 – 66
Biscuits and Gravy, 66
Black Beans, 108
Black Bean Chili, 110
Black Kale, Golden Beets, and Leeks with Orange Oil, 169
black pepper, about, 41
    Cheese Crackers, 79
    in Pear Sherbet, 307
Blackberry Ice Cream, 307
Blackberry Pie, 267
Blanched Almonds, 176
Blond Barbecue Sauce, 257
Blood Orange, Fennel, and Toasted Almond Salad, 167
Blood Orange Gélée, 310
blowtorch, for Crème Brûlée, 303
Blue Cheese Dressing, 175
Blue Cheese, Flank Steak with, 181
Blueberry
    Coffeecake, 71
    Pancakes, 63
    Pie, 267
Boardinghouse, Deep Springs, 24
Boeuf Bourguignonne, 186
Boiled Peanuts, 138
Boiled Shrimp, 227
Boiling water, about, 30
Borscht, Russian, 186
Bourbon, Roasted Yams with Pears and, 149
Bowl-Dressed Salad, 159
braise (definition), 30

Braised Beef, Mexican, 187
Braised Chicken
    Chorizo, Chicken, and Chickpeas, 213
    Curry, 213
    Fennel-, 213
    Paprikash, 213
    in Red Wine with Mushrooms, 213
Brandel, Catherine, 128, 233
Brassicaceae (cabbage family), 132
BREAD, BUTTER, CRACKERS, & CHEESE, 74 – 82
Bread, quick, 62 – 63
    Banana Bread, 72
    Biscuits, with variations, 65 – 66
    Coffeecakes, 71
    Cornbread, Skillet, 67
    Irish Soda Bread, Joan's, 70
    Pancakes, 63 – 64
    Pumpkin Bread, 70
    Scones, 68 – 69
    Southern Spoon Bread, 243
Bread, using in recipes
    Bread Pudding, Orange, 276
    breading, three-step process, 209, 225
    Croutons, 175
    French Toast,
    Garlic Bread, 237
    Garlic Soup, 131
    Griddle Toast, with variations, 53
    Stuffing, Clio's, 244
Bread (yeast), 76 – 78
    Dinner Bread, with variations, 76 – 77
    Focaccia, with variations, 77 – 78
    Hamburger Buns, 77
    Lunch Bread, 77
    Pizza dough, 86
Bready Egg (soft-boiled egg and toast), 53
BREAKFAST: OATS, GRITS, BACON, & EGGS, 50 – 60
Breakfast
    Eggs, 56 – 60
    Grapefruit, 56
    Potatoes, Simple, 54
    Sausage, Fresh, 55
Brick, Chicken Cooked Under a, 210

brine (definition), 30
brines for chicken or pork, quick, 198, 206
Brizendine, Wendell and Ginny, 184
Broccoli, 123
Broccolini, Wide Noodles with Feta, Lemon, Pine Nuts, and, 236
Broiled Asparagus, 121
Broiled Cauliflower, 126
Broiled Trout, Clay's, 221
Broth see Stock
brown butter, 38, 123, 232
Brown, White, and Wild Rice Pilaf with Mirepoix, 240
Brownies, Sheet Pan, 317
Bruschetta, 237
Brussels Sprouts with Brown Butter, 123
Buckwheat Pancakes, 63
Buddhist story: "The Strawberry", 284
Buns, Hamburger, 77
Burger Steak Salad, 192
Butter
    about, 37
    Brown Butter, 38, 123, 232
    clarified, 38
    Cookies, 325
    homemade (Farm Butter), 79
    Jalapeño-Lime Butter, 127
    Lemon Butter (for Artichokes), 119
    – Pecan Ice Cream, 306
    Piecrust, 263
    Radishes with Butter, 171
    Sauce, Lemon Butter, 252
Buttermilk
    about, 38; homemade, 79
    Ice Cream, 305
    Pancakes, Jack's, 63
    Pie, Aunt Lela's, 274
    – Scallion Potatoes, 142
Butternut Squash
    Chips, 145
    Risotto, 241
    Soup with Diced Pear, 144
Butterscotch Pudding, 301
Butter–Vegetable Oil Piecrust, 265

Cabbage with Juniper, 124
Cabrito (goat meat), 187
Caesar Dressing, Creamy, 162
Caesar Salad, Tracy's, 161
CAKES, 286 – 298
   Banana Bread, 72
   Big Pink Cake, 297
   Blueberry Coffeecake, 71
   Carrot Cake, 289
   Cherry-Pork Cake, 294
   Chocolate Mayonnaise Cake, 291
   Currant Cake, 294
   Funnel Cakes, 73
   Grandma Z.'s Coffeecake, 71
   Milk and Honey Cake, 296
   Parsnip Cake, 290
   Pinky's Jewish Apple Cake, 292
   Poppyseed, 296
   Prune Cake, 295
   Pumpkin Bread, 70
   Whipped Cream Cake, 290
Calamari see Squid
Candy
   English Toffee with Sea Salt, 327
   Old-Fashioned Vinegar Taffy, 327
   Sesame Candy, 328
Canned-Fruit Cobbler, 280
capsaicin oil (chile), 249
Caramel, 44, 281, 301
Carbonnade Flamande, 186
Cardamom Butter Cookies, 325
Carne Asada, 182
Carnitas, 201
Carol's Fresh Fruit Gélée, 310
Carpaccio, Beef, 194
Carpaccio, Summer Squash, 171
Carrot(s)
   Cake, 289
   Honey-Glazed Rainbow Carrots, 125
   Italian Tzimmes, 125
   – Raisin Salad, 165
   Soup with Ginger, 125

Cashew Cookies, 321
Catfish, Fried, 225
cattle, raising at Deep Springs, 304
Cauliflower, 126
Cayenne-Rubbed Chicken with Potatoes and Garlic, 208
Celery Root, Fennel, and Potato Gratin, 130
Celery Root Salad, 166
chard, 132
Chard and Mushroom Frittata, 93
Chayote, 127
Cheese
   about, 81
   Blue Cheese Dressing, 175
   Crackers, 79
   Flank Steak with Blue Cheese, 181
   Sandwich, Grilled Cheese, 89
   Queso Blanco, 82
   Reatha's Macaroni and Cheese, 85
Cheesecake, 274
Chef's Salad, 160
Cherries with Almond Paste, 280
Cherries, Pickled, 258
Cherry-Cornmeal Scones, 69
Cherry Pie, Diana's, 268
Cherry-Pork Cake, 294
Chez Panisse, 24, 128, 149, 166, 233, 293, 347
Chez Panisse Cooking, 205, 347
Chez Panisse Desserts, 307, 347
CHICKEN & TURKEY, 204 – 218
Chicken
   Braised in Red Wine with Mushrooms, 213
   Braised with Fennel, 213
   Breast, Sautéed, 206
   brines for chicken, 205 – 206
   Cayenne-Rubbed Chicken with Potatoes and Garlic, 208
   Chorizo, Chicken, and Chickpeas, 213
   Cooked Under a Brick, 210
   Crispy Pan-Fried Chicken, 209
   Curry, 100, 213
   Curry, Gunhild's, 100
   Double-Herbed Grilled Chicken, 207
   and Dumplings, 214
   fat, rendering, 216

Gin Chicken Liver Pâté, 217
Herbed Braised Chicken, with variations, 212
Holiday Roast Chicken, 205
Marmalade Chicken, 206
Paprikash, 213
Pot Pie, 216
Roast Chicken, 205
Shoyu Chicken, 214
Stew, 214
Stock, 217
Tarragon-Roasted Chicken with Tomatoes, 210
Chicken-Fried Steak, 55
Chickpea(s)
Chicken, Chorizo, and Chickpeas, 213
Falafel, 103
Hummus, 104
Salad with Tomatoes, Lemon, and Mint, 116
Chile
Beef Stew, Green Chile, 188
"chile" vs. "chili", 30
hot chiles, working with, 249
New Mexico chile, 108, 250, 251
Relish, Green, 251
Sauce, New Mexico Green, 251
Sauce, New Mexico Red, 250
Whole-Wheat Pappardelle with Corn and Chiles, 233
Chili
Black Bean Chili, 110
con Carne, Mama Nell's, 108
Frito Pie, 109
Pork and White Bean Chili, 111
Chimichurri Sauce, Green, 255
Chips, Butternut Squash, 145
Chips, Potato, 145
Chivo (goat meat), 187
Chocolate
about, 39
Cookies with Almonds, Mexican, 318
Cream Pie, 270
Mayonnaise Cake, 291
Pudding, 301
Sauce, 278
Wafers, 315

Chocolate Chip Cookies
Ella's, 315
Pistachio, with variations, 316
Hazelnut Shortbread Bars, 317
Chocolate–, with variations, 315
Chorizo, Chicken, and Chickpeas, 213
Chowder, Corn, 89
Chowder, Fresh Clam, 88
cider, apple, about, 197
cilantro, "bolted," 233
Cinnamon Ice Cream, 306
Citrus
about, 38
Compote, 280
Marmalade, 260
Topping (for Poppyseed Cake), 296
Clam Chowder, Fresh, 88
clarified butter, 38
Clay's Broiled Trout, 221
Cobbler, Canned-Fruit, 280
Cobbler, Tomato, 147
Cocktail Sauce (for shrimp), 228
cocoa powder, about, 39
Coconut Bars, Oatmeal–, 319
coffee, about, 39
Coffee Ice Cream, 305
Coffeecake, Blueberry, 71
Coffeecake, Grandma Z.'s, 71
Coleslaw, Fuji Apple, 163
Coleslaw, Kohlrabi-Apple, 169
collard greens, 132
Colostrum Custard, 304
Compote, Citrus, 280
Compote, Dried Fruit, 52
Concassé, Tomato, 148
Cook's Illustrated magazine, 189
COOKIES & CANDY, 314 – 329
Cookies
Almond-Butter, 319
Biscochitos, 326
Butter, 325
Cardamom Butter, 325
Cashew, 321

Chocolate Chip–Hazelnut Shortbread Bars, 317
Chocolate–Chocolate Chip, with variations, 315
Chocolate-Peanut, 315
Ella's Chocolate Chip, 315
Ginger, 325
Gingersnaps, 324
Lemon Slice, 323
Lemon-Anise Biscotti, 322
Lime Bars, 322
Mexican Chocolate with Almonds, 318
Oatmeal, 315
Oatmeal-Coconut Bars, 319
Orange Italian, 324
Peanut Butter, 319
Pistachio Chocolate Chip, with variations, 316
Sesame, 320
Vanilla Wafers, 326
Walnut Biscotti, 321
Wedding, 320
cooking greens, 132
Corn
    Chowder, 89
    on the Cob, 127
    Salad, 166
    Sautéed Kale and Corn, 133
    Sautéed Corn, 128
    Soup, Catherine's, 128
    Whole-Wheat Pappardelle with Corn and Chiles, 233
Cornbread, Skillet, 67
Cornmeal
    about, 40, 67
    Biscuits, 65
    - Buttermilk Pancakes, Eloise's, 63
    - Cherry Scones, 69
    - Egg Soup Dumplings, 238
    - Fried Okra, 136
    - Fried Summer Squash, 145
    Polenta, 242
    seasoned cornmeal (for Fried Catfish), 225
    Southern Spoon Bread, 243
Couscous, Pecan, 237
Cowboy Pancakes, 63

Crackers, 79 – 80
    Black Pepper Cheese, 79
    Cheese, 79
    Thyme, 80
    Puffy Salties, 80
    Whole-Wheat, 80
Cranberry Relish, 258
Cranberry Sauce, 257
Cream Biscuits, 65
Cream Cheese Frosting, 289
cream, churning butter from, 79
Cream Pie
    Banana, 271
    Chocolate, 270
    Custard, 271
Cream Scones, 69
Cream, Fresh Horseradish, 250
Cream, Handmade Egg Noodles with, 231
Cream, Lemon (for gingerbread), 292
Cream, Sweet Onions Cooked in, 136
Cream, Whipped, 265, 286
Creamy Caesar Dressing, 162
Creamy Gelatin Desserts
    Almond Cream, 311
    Creamy Orange Gelatin, 309
    Fresh Bay Leaf Cream with Citrus, 311
    Rose-Scented Cream with Raspberries, 311
Crème Brûlée, Vanilla Bean, 303
Crêpe Cake with Spinach, Gruyère, and Béchamel, 94
Crêpes (Manicotti), 234
Crisp
    Apple-Walnut, 277
    Ginger Peach, 276
    Pear, Ginger, and Lemon, 277
crisps, potato see Potato Chips
Crispy Pan-Fried Chicken, 209
Crispy Pork, 201
crookneck squash see summer squash
Croutons, 175
Cucumber Salad, Summer, 166
Culinary Terms, 30
Cumin–Mint–Yogurt Dressing, 175
Currant Cake, 294

Curry Powder (home-blended), 102
Curry Tofu Salad, 91
Curry, Chicken, 213
Curry, Gunhild's Chicken, 100
Custard Cream Pie, 271
Custard Sauce, Peach Leaf, 303
Custard, Baked, 304
Custard, Colostrum, 304
Cut Flower Solution, 342
cutting boards, 34
Cynthia's Garlic-Studded Milk-Braised Pork Loin, 199

D

Dad's Steak Sauce, 247
Dark Chocolate Wafers, 315
Date and Orange Salad, 170
David, Elizabeth, 348
David's Baked Apples, 276
Deep Springs College
    about, 20
    Boardinghouse, 24
    contact information, 25
    Dairy, 22
    raising meat at, 178, 184, 187, 204
Deep Springs Soap, 343
Desserts, Fruit (other than pie), 276 – 283
Deviled Eggs, 92
DeWeese, Jonathan "Dewey", 290
Diana's Cherry Pie, 268
Dill Pickles, 255
Dill Salsa Verde, 254
Dinner Bread, 76
Double-Crust Pies, 265 – 269
Doughnuts, 72
Dressings, Salad, 173 – 174
Dried Fruit Compote, 52
Dried Fruit in Sweet Wine, 281
Drop Biscuits, 66
Dulce De Leche with Fresh Fruit, 281
Dumplings, Chicken and, 214
Dumplings, Cornmeal-Egg Soup, 238
Dumplings, Spaetzle, 237
Dutch Babies, 68

E

Eggs
    Breakfast Eggs
        about, 56
        Bready Egg, 53
        Fried, 57
        Fried Egg Sandwich, 58
        Gashouse Egg, 53
        Knothole Egg, 53
        Omelets, with variations, 58
        One-Eyed Egyptian, 53
        Poached, 60
        Scrambled, 57
        Shirred, 60
        Soft-Boiled, 60
        Sorrel Omelet, 59
    Other egg dishes
        Deviled Eggs, 92
        Egg Pizza, 88
        Egg Salad, 92
        Frittata, with variations, 93
        Handmade Egg Noodles with Cream, 231
        Hard-Boiled Eggs, 91
        Tortilla Española, 94
Eggplant, Roasted, 129
Elaine's Baked Grits, 52
Elge's Three-Ginger Gingerbread, 292
Elizabeth's Beef Stew, 186
Ella's Chocolate Chip Cookies, 315
Eloise's Cornmeal-Buttermilk Pancakes, 63
Enchiladas, 96 – 98
    Green Chile, 97
    My Mother's, 96
    Red Chile, 98
English Toffee with Sea Salt, 327
equipment, kitchen, 32, 36
equivalents of common ingredients, 46
Escarole and White Bean Soup, 114

F

Falafel, 102
Farm Butter and Buttermilk, 79
Farro Salad with Cherry Tomatoes and Pecorino, 244

fat, beef, 343; Steak Fried in, 180
fat, chicken, rendering, 216
fat, pork
   Cherry-Pork Cake, 294
   Biscochitos, 326
fats, cooking, about, 41
Felder, Eve, 149
Fennel
   Fennel, Blood Orange, and Toasted Almond Salad, 167
   Fennel, Celery Root, and Potato Gratin, 130
   Fennel, Orange, and Black Olive Salad, 168
   Roasted Potatoes and Fennel, 141
   Shaved Fennel, 167
   Slovenian Fennel and Potatoes, 130
   White Bean Gratin with Fennel, 115
   wild fennel, 255
Feta cheese
   Fig and Feta Salad, 106
   Figs, Feta, and Honey, 281
   Watermelon Salad with Basil and Feta, 173
   Wide Noodles with Broccolini, Lemon, Pine Nuts, and Feta, 236
Fig and Feta Salad, 106
Figs, Feta, and Honey, 281
Figs, Pickled, 258
Filberts, Toasted, 176; see also Hazelnuts
FISH & SHELLFISH, 220 – 229
Fish
   Baked Salmon, 222
   Clay's Broiled Trout, 221
   Fried Catfish, 225
   Gravlax, 223
   Pan-Fried Cod, 225
   Pan-Fried Snapper, 225
   Pan-Fried Sole, 223
   Seared Tuna, 225
   Simple Cooking Methods for Salmon, 222
   Sole Stuffed with Leeks, 224
   Whole Roasted Trout with Herb Salad, 221
Flank Steak with Blue Cheese, 181
flour, about, 40
Flower Solution (for cut flowers), 342
Focaccia, with variations, 77 – 78

fond, about, 207
Food likes and dislikes, 26, 196
Fool, Gooseberry, 304
Freeman, Priscilla, 146
French Toast, 53
French-style Potato Salad, 171
Fresh Artichoke Hearts, 120
Fresh Bay Leaf Cream with Citrus, 311
Fresh Clam Chowder, 88
Fresh Ginger Cake, 293
Fresh Horseradish Cream, 250
Fresh Salsa, 249
Fresh Shell Beans, 122
Fresh Summer Tomato Sauce, 249
Fried Catfish, 225
Fried Egg Sandwich, 58
Fried Eggs, 57
Fried Green Tomatoes, Priscilla's, 146
Fried Okra, 136
Frijoles borrachos (drunken beans), 108
Frito Pie, 109
Frittata
   Asparagus and Mushroom, 93
   Chard and Mushroom, 93
   Leek and Gruyère, 93
   Onion and Bacon, 93
Frosting, Cream Cheese, 289
Fruit Compote, Dried, 52
Fruit Desserts (other than pie), 276 – 283
Fruit Desserts, Simplest, 280 – 283
Fruit, Dried, in Sweet Wine, 281
Fruit Fools, 305
Fruit Gélée, Carol's Fresh, 310
Fuji Apple Coleslaw, 163
Funnel Cakes, 73

G

Galette, Red Onion, 136
Garlic
   about, 40
   Aioli, 253
   Bread (bruschetta), 237
   Cayenne-Rubbed Chicken with Garlic, 208

Mayonnaise, 253; see also Aioli
Pasta, Toasted, with Garlic, 236
Pork Loin, Garlic-Studded Milk-Braised, Cynthia's, 199
Roasted Garlic, 131
Soup, 131
Gashouse Egg, 53
Gâteau de Crêpes (Stacked Crêpe Cake with Spinach, Gruyère, and Béchamel), 94
Gazpacho, 168
Gelatin Desserts, 308 – 312
    Almond Cream, 311
    Blood Orange Gélée, 310
    Creamy Orange Gelatin, 309
    Fresh Bay Leaf Cream with Citrus, 311
    Gélée, Carol's Fresh Fruit, 310
    Goat Milk Panna Cotta with Cherries, 312
    Lime Yum, 309
    Rose-Scented Cream with Raspberries, 311
    Tangy Lemon Sour Cream Gelatin, 309
German Potato Salad, 171
ghee, 38
Gin Chicken Liver Pâté, 217
Ginger Cake, Fresh, 293
Ginger, Carrot Soup with, 125
Ginger Cookies, 324
Ginger Peach Crisp, 276
Gingerbread, Elge's Three-Ginger, 292
Gingersnap Crust (Cheesecake), 275
Gingersnaps, 324
Glazed Ham, 201
Glazed Meatloaf, 189
Glossary of Culinary Terms, 30
Goat Milk Panna Cotta with Cherries, 312
Goat, Mexican Braised, 187
Golden Basmati Rice Pilaf, 239
GOOEY DESSERTS, 300 – 312
Goose Egg Pound Cake, 288
Goose Egg Pound Cake Cinnamon Toast, 288
Gooseberry Fool, 304
Grandma Z.'s Coffeecake, 71
Granola, 52
Grapefruit for Breakfast, 56
Grapes, Black, Pickled, 258

Gratin, Leek, 133
Gratin, Potato, with Celery Root and Fennel, 130
Gratin, White Bean with Fennel, 115
Gravlax, 223
Gravy, Biscuits and, 66
Gravy, Turkey, 218
GREAT LUNCHES, 84 – 105
Greek Salad, 159
Green Bean(s)
    Cooked in Bacon Fat, 122
    Salad with Cherry Tomatoes and Basil, 164
    Sautéed, 121
    Southern-Style Braised Green Beans, 122
Green Chile
    Beef Stew, 188
    Enchiladas, 97
    Posole with Pork, 98
    Relish, 251
    Sauce, New Mexico, 251
Green Chimichurri Sauce, 255
Green Rice with Peas and Pea Greens, 240
Green Salads, 157 – 162
Greens (cooked), 132
Greens Cookbook, The, 110, 169, 347
Gremolata, Seared Scallops with, 227
Griddle Biscuits, 66
Griddle Toast, 53
grill, outdoor, 35
Grilled Asparagus, 121
Grilled Cheese Sandwich, 28, 89
Grilled Chicken, Double-Herbed, 207
Grilled Okra, 136
Grilled Shrimp with Shrimp Essence, 228
Grilled Skirt Steak with Salsa Verde, 181
Grilled Summer Squash, 146
Grits, 52
Grits, Baked, Elaine's, 52
Gruyère and Leek Frittata, 93
Guacamole, 240
Gumbo, with variations, 98
Gunhild's Chicken Curry, 100

Halibut, Baked, 222
Ham, Glazed, 201
Ham, Lima Bean Soup with Kale and, 112
Hamburger Buns, 77
Hamburgers, Skillet, 192
Handmade Egg Noodles with Cream, 231
Hard-Boiled Eggs, 91
Hazelnut Shortbread Bars, Chocolate Chip–, 317
Hazelnuts, Toasted, 176
Herbs
   about, 43
   Double-Herbed Grilled Chicken, 207
   Herbed Braised Chicken, with Five Variations, 212
Hibiscus Iced Tea, 105
Holiday Roast Chicken, 205
homemade butter and buttermilk, 79
homemade cheese (Queso Blanco), 82
homemade Curry Powder, 102
homemade Soap, Deep Springs, 343
hominy (New Mexico Posole), 98
Honey, Feta, and Figs, 281
Honey, Milk and Honey Cake, 296
Honey-Glazed Rainbow Carrots, 125
Hors d'oeuvres
   Aioli, 253
   Blue Cheese Dip, 175
   Butternut Squash Chips, 145
   Cheese, 81
   Deviled Eggs, 92
   Gin Chicken Liver Pâté, 217
   Gravlax, 223
   Guacamole, 249
   Hummus, 104
   Mediterranean Avocado Dip, 249
   Nuts from the Shell, 281
   Oysters on the Half-Shell, 226
   Radishes, 171
   Ranch Dip, 174
   Red Onion Galette, 136
   Roasted Eggplant, 129
   Roasted Garlic, 131
   Shrimp with Cocktail Sauce, 227
   Steak Tartare, 193
Horseradish
   Cream, Fresh, 250
   Sauce, Slovenian, 250
   – Tomato Relish, 249
hot chiles, working with, 249
HOT VEGETABLES & VEGETABLE SOUPS, 118 – 151
How to Wash Dishes, 341
Howe, Tina, 244
Huckleberry Pancakes, 63
Hummingbird Nectar, 343
Hummus, 104

Ice Cream
   Blackberry, 307
   Butter Pecan, 306
   Buttermilk, 305
   Cinnamon, 306
   Coffee, 305
   Lemon, 306
   Peach, 305
   Snow, 308
   Strawberry, 305
   Vanilla, 305
   Whiskey, 306
Iced Tea, Hibiscus, 105
Iced Tea, Minted, 104
ingredients, about, 37
Irish Leek and Oat Soup, 134
Irish Soda Bread, Joan's, 70
Italian Beef Stew, 186
Italian Meatballs, 190
Italian Orange Cookies, 324
Italian Tzimmes, 125

Jack's Buttermilk Pancakes, 63
Jalapeño-Lime Butter, 127
Jam
   Apricot, Kevin's, 259
   Marmalade, 260
   Pie, 273

Quince, 260
Jello see Gelatin Desserts
Jennings, Andy, 257
Jícama, 168
Joan's Irish Soda Bread, 70
Jota (Sauerkraut, Sausage, and Bean Soup), 143
Joy of Cooking, The, 348
julienne (definition), 31
Juniper berries, Cabbage with, 124

K

Kabocha pumpkin, 271
Kale, 132
    Lima Bean and Ham Soup with Kale, 112
    Salad of Beets, Leeks, Orange Oil and Kale, 169
    Sautéed Corn and Kale, 133
Kennedy, Diana, 80, 348
Kevin's Apricot Jam, 259
kielbasa, 202
Kimchi Deviled Eggs, 92
KITCHEN BASICS, 26 – 49
knives, about, 33
Knothole Egg, 53
Kohlrabi-Apple Slaw, 169

L

Lamb
    Stew, 187
    Roast, 184
    Shepherd's Pie, 187
Lard
    Biscochitos, 326
    Piecrust, 264
Large Quantity Recipes
    Ella's Chocolate Chip Cookies, 316
    Tomato Sauce, 247
    Sheet Pan Brownies, 318
Laundry Stains, 341
Lebovitz, David, 293
Leek(s)
    Gratin, 133
    – Gruyère Frittata, 93
    Mussels with Orange Zest and Leeks, 226
    Salad of Black Kale, Beets, Orange Oil and Leeks, 169
    Sole Stuffed with Leeks, 224
    Vegetable and Leek Purée Soup, 133
Leftovers, 345
Lemon
    – Anise Biscotti, 322
    Butter (Artichokes), 119
    Butter Sauce (beurre blanc), 252
    Cream (for gingerbread), 292
    Ice Cream, 306
    Meringue Pie, 269
    Relish, Meyer Lemon–Olive, 254
    Slice Cookies, 323
    Vinaigrette, 174
Lemonade, 105
Lemonade, Whey, 82
lettuce, types, 157
Liberty Café, 133
Lima Bean and Ham Soup with Kale, 112
Lime Bars, 322
Lime Yum, 309
Limeade, 105
Lime-Pickled Red Onions, 252
Liver, Beef, with Bacon, Onions, and Mushrooms, 196
Liver, Gin Chicken Pâté, 217
Lopez, Cecilia, 76

M

Macaroni and Cheese, Reatha's, 85
Macaroni and Cheese, Spicy, 85
Madison, Deborah, 110, 347
Manicotti, 234
Maple Snow Ice Cream, 308
Maple Syrup Pie, 274
Marinated Beets, 164
Marinated Steak, 180
Marmalade Chicken, 206
Marmalade, 260
Mashed Cauliflower, 120
Matzoh Ball Soup, 216
Mayonnaise, 252
    Aioli, 253
    Cake, Chocolate Mayonnaise, 291

Garlic, 253
Mustard, 253
measuring, about, 45
measuring equivalents of common ingredients, 46
Meat, raising at Deep Springs, 178, 184, 187, 204
Meatballs, Italian, 190
Meatballs, Mediterranean, 191
Meatloaf, Glazed, 189
Mediterranean Avocado Dip, 249
Mediterranean Meatballs, 191
Mediterranean Tuna Salad, 90
Melon with Rosewater, 281
MENUS, 330 – 337
Meringue Pie, Lemon, 269
Metric equivalents of U.S. measurements, 47 – 49
Mexican Braised Beef (or Goat), 187
Mexican Chocolate Cookies with Almonds, 318
Mexican Wedding Cakes, 320
Meyer Lemon–Olive Relish, 254
Mignonette Sauce (for oysters), 226
Milk and Honey Cake, 296
Milk-Braised Pork Loin, Cynthia's, 199
Milk Toast, 53
Milk, sweetened condensed, 281
Mint, Chickpea Salad with Tomatoes and, 116
Minted Iced Tea, 104
Minty Peas, 139
mirepoix (definition), 31
Mirepoix, Brown, White, and Wild Rice Pilaf with, 240
mirliton (Chayote), 127
Mixed Salted Nuts, 176
"Modern Man" by Ann Applegarth (poem), 154
Mongold, Rex and Susan, 125
mortar and pestle, 35, 247 (illustration)
Moules Marinière de Bretagne, 226
Murphy, Jack, 242
Mushroom(s)
  Chicken Braised in Red Wine with Mushrooms, 213
  Frittata, with variations, 93
  Risotto, Wild Mushroom, 241
  Sautéed, 135
  Steak Sauce, 135
Mussels
  with Leeks and Orange Zest, 226
  Moules Marinière de Bretagne, 226
  with Spicy Tomato Sauce, 226
Mustard Mayonnaise, 253
Mustard Vinaigrette, 174
mutton, 187
My Mother's Enchiladas, 96
My Mother's Polish Sausage Stew, 202
My Mother's Strawberry Shortcake, 279

Nectar, Hummingbird, 343
Nectarine Pie, 268
Nettle Broth, 135
New Mexico
  Biscochitos, 326
  Enchiladas, 96 – 98
  Green Chile Relish, 251
  Green Chile Sauce, 251
  Red Chile Sauce, 250
New Orleans (Red Beans and Rice), 111
Newell, L. Jackson, 349
nonreactive (cookware), 31
Noodles
  Handmade Egg Noodles with Cream, 231
  Whole-Wheat Pappardelle with Corn and Chiles, 233
  Wide, with Broccolini, Feta, Lemon, and Pine Nuts, 236
Nothing Fancy, 80, 348
Nunn, Lucien L., 21
Nuts
  from the Shell, 281
  Mixed Salted, 176
  Toasted Nut Olive Oil, 254
  Toasted, 176

Oats
  Irish Leek and Oat Soup, 134
  Oatmeal Cookies, 315
  Oatmeal Scones, 68
  Oatmeal (breakfast), 51
  Oatmeal-Coconut Bars, 319

Steel-Cut Oatmeal, 51
oils, cooking, about, 41
Okra
   Cornmeal-Fried, 136
   Grilled, 136
   Gumbo, 98
Old-Fashioned Vinegar Taffy, 327
Olive Oil
   Pork Chops Slow-Cooked in, 198
   Toasted Almond, 138
   Toasted Nut, 254
Olives, Black, with Fennel and Orange Salad, 168
Omelets, 58
   Sorrel, 59
   Spanish Potato (Tortilla Española), 94
One Shoe Off (play), 244
One-Eyed Egyptian Egg, 53
Onion(s)
   about, 40
   – Bacon Frittata, 93
   Lime-Pickled Red Onions, 252
   Red Onion Galette, 136
   Roasted Potatoes, Apples, and Onions, 141
   Sweet Onions Cooked in Cream, 136
Orange(s)
   Apples and Oranges, 280
   Apple and Candied Orange Pie, 266
   Blood Orange Gélée, 310
   Blood Orange, Fennel, and Toasted Almond Salad, 167
   Bread Pudding, 276
   Cookies, Italian Orange, 324
   – Date Salad, 170
   Mussels with Leeks and Orange Zest, 226
   Salad of Black Kale, Beets, Leeks, and Orange Oil, 169
   Salad of Fennel, Black Olives, and Oranges, 168
Oysters on the Half-Shell, 226

P

PANCAKES, BISCUITS, & CORNBREAD, 62 – 73
Pancakes
   Blueberry, 63
   Buckwheat, 63
   Cowboy, 63
   Dutch Babies, 68
   Eloise's Cornmeal-Buttermilk, 63
   Huckleberry, 63
   Jack's Buttermilk, 63
   Ricotta, 64
   Whole Wheat, 63
Pan-Fried Chicken, Crispy, 209
Pan-Fried Cod or Snapper, 225
Pan-Fried Sole, 223
Panna Cotta
   Almond Cream, 311
   Fresh Bay Leaf Cream with Citrus, 311
   Goat Milk with Cherries, 312
   Rose-Scented Cream with Raspberries, 311
Pan-Roasted Asparagus, 120
Pan-Toasted Seeds, 176
Papadums or Papads, 102
parchment paper (baking), 35
Parmesan, with Shaved Fennel and Pears, 167
Parsnip Cake, 290
Parsnip Soup with Toasted Almond Olive Oil, 138
PASTA, DUMPLINGS, RICE, & STUFFING, 230 – 245
Pasta
   dry pasta, about, 235
   fresh pasta
      Handmade Egg Noodles with Cream, 231
      Manicotti, 234
      Ricotta Ravioli with Sage Brown Butter, 232
      Whole-Wheat Pappardelle with Corn and Chiles, 233
   Asparagus Pasta, 121
   Spring Pasta with Snap Peas and Asparagus, 139
   Toasted Pasta with Garlic, 236
   Tomato Sauces, 247, 248
   Wide Noodles with Broccolini, Feta, Lemon, and Pine Nuts, 236
Pâté, Gin Chicken Liver, 217
pattypan squash see summer squash
Pea Soup, 110
Peach(es)
   – Ginger Crisp, 276
   Ice Cream, 305
   Peach Leaf Custard Sauce, 303

Peaches and Cream, 282
Pickled, 258
Pie, 268
Peanuts, Boiled, 138
Peanut Butter Cookies, 319
Peanut Soup, 139
Pear(s)
   and Apple Salad, 163
   and Black Pepper Sherbet, 307
   Butternut Squash Soup with Diced Pear, 144
   Crisp, Pear, Ginger, and Lemon, 277
   Pickled, 258
   Pie, 267
   Poached Pears with Chocolate Sauce, 278
   Roasted Yams with Pears and Bourbon, 149
   Shaved Fennel with Pears and Parmesan, 167
   Sherbet, 307
Pearl Tapioca Pudding, 302
Peas and Pea Greens, Green Rice with, 240
Peas, Minty, 139
Peas, Snap, 139
Pecan(s)
   Butter Pecan Ice Cream, 306
   Couscous, 237
   Pie, 272
   Toasted, 176
Pecorino, Farro Salad with Cherry Tomatoes and, 244
pepper, black, about, 41
Peppers, Red, Roasted, 140
Persimmons, 282
Pesto, 254
Pesto, Potatoes and Tomatoes, 141
Peterson, Ross and Kay, 291
Pickles
   Dill Pickles, 255
   Lime-Pickled Red Onions, 252
   Pickled Black Grapes, 258
   Pickled Fruit, 258
   Pickled Plums, 258
   Pickled Summer Vegetables, 256
   Pickled Winter Vegetables, 256
PIES & FRUIT DESSERTS, 262 – 283

Pie
   Apple and Candied Lemon, 266
   Apple and Candied Orange, 266
   Apple and Quince, 266
   Apple, 265
   Aunt Lela's Buttermilk, 274
   Bacon-Apple, 266
   Banana Cream, 271
   Blackberry, 267
   Blueberry, 267
   Chicken Pot, 216
   Chocolate Cream, 270
   Custard Cream, 271
   Diana's Cherry, 268
   Jam, 273
   Lemon Meringue, 269
   Maple Syrup, 274
   Nectarine, 268
   Peach, 268
   Pear, 267
   Pecan, 272
   Plum, 268
   Pumpkin, 271
   Red Onion Galette, 136
   Rhubarb Custard, 273
   Rhubarb, 268
   Shepherd's, 187
   Sweet Potato, 272
Piecrust
   Butter, 263
   Lard, 264
   Vegetable Oil, 264
   Vegetable Oil–Butter, 265
Pies, Double-Crust, 265 – 269
Pies, Single-Crust, 269 – 274
Pine Nuts, Wide Noodles with Broccolini, Feta, Lemon, and, 236
Pineapple, 282
Pinky's Jewish Apple Cake, 292
Pinto Beans, 108
Pistachio Chocolate Chip Cookies, 316
Pizza, with variations, 86
A Platter of Figs and Other Recipes, 276, 349

Plum Pie, 268
Plums, Pickled, 258
Poached Eggs, 60
Poached Pears with Chocolate Sauce, 278
poem: "Modern Man" by Ann Applegarth, 154
Poires belle Hélène, 278
Polenta, 242
Polish Sausage Stew, My Mother's, 202
Pomelo, 282
Pope, Geoff, 33, 180, 186
Pope, Iris, 85, 186, 288
Poppyseed Cake, 296
Porcini-Dusted Steak, 182
Pork
   and White Bean Chili, 111
   brines for pork, 198
   Cherry-Pork Cake, 294
   Chops, Apple-Marinated, 197
   Chops, Slow-Cooked in Olive Oil, 198
   Chops, Tender Cured, 197
   Crispy, 201
   Glazed Ham, 201
   Loin, Cynthia's Garlic-Studded Milk-Braised, 199
   Posole with Green Chile, 98
   Red Chile Posole, 98
   Slow-Roasted, 200
   Tenderloin, 199
Pot Pie, Chicken, 216
Pot Roast, Allspice-Scented, 188
Potato(es)
   Baked, 85
   Bread, 77
   Breakfast Potatoes, Simple, 54
   Cayenne-Rubbed Chicken with Garlic and Potatoes, 208
   Chips, 145
   Focaccia, 78
   Gratin, with Fennel and Celery Root, 130
   Roasted, Simple, with variations, 141
   Salad, 170
   Salad, French-style, 171
   Salad, German, 171
   Scallion-Buttermilk Potatoes, 142
   Scalloped, 140
   Slovenian Fennel and Potatoes, 130
   Tomatoes, Potatoes, and Pesto, 141
   Tortilla Española (Spanish Potato Omelet), 94
Potatoes, Sweet, 149
pots and pans, 34
poultry, 204
Pound Cake, Goose Egg, 288
Powder, Toothbrushing, 342
Priscilla's Fried Green Tomatoes, 146
Prune Cake, 295
Pudding
   Banana, 271
   Butterscotch, 301
   Chocolate, 301
   Orange Bread, 276
   Pearl Tapioca, 302
   Summer Tomato, 148
Puffy Salties, 80
Pumpkin
   Bread, 70
   kabocha, 245
   Pie, 271
   Seeds, Pan-Toasted, 176
   table, 245

Q

Queso Blanco, 82
quick breads, 62 – 63
   Banana Bread, 72
   Biscuits, with variations, 65 – 66
   Coffeecakes, 71
   Cornbread, Skillet, 67
   Irish Soda Bread, Joan's, 70
   Pancakes, 63 – 64
   Pumpkin Bread, 70
   Scones, 68 – 69
   Southern Spoon Bread, 243
Quince and Apple Pie, 268
Quince Jam, 260
Quinoa, 243

R

Radicchio, Roasted, 142
Radishes, 171
Raisin-Carrot Salad, 165
Raitas, 102
Ranch Dressing, 174
Raspberry whipped cream (Big Pink Cake), 297
rasp-style grater, 34
Ratatouille, 150
Ravioli, Ricotta, with Sage Brown Butter, 232
raw beef, 193, 194
Reatha's Macaroni and Cheese, 85
Red Beans and Rice, 111
Red Chile Enchiladas, 98
Red Chile Posole, 98
Red Chile Sauce, New Mexico, 250
Red Onion Galette, 136
Red Peppers, Roasted, 140
Refried Beans, 108
Refritos (Beans), 108
Relishes see Sauces
Rhubarb, 283
Rhubarb Custard Pie, 273
Rhubarb Pie, 268
Rice (see also Risotto)
    basic cooking methods, 238
    Basmati, 101, 239
    Brown, White, and Wild Rice Pilaf with Mirepoix, 240
    Green Rice with Peas and Pea Greens, 240
    Red Beans and Rice, 111
Rice Pilaf, Golden Basmati, 239
Rico's Tacos, 192
Ricotta Pancakes, 64
Ricotta Ravioli with Sage Brown Butter, 232
Risotto, 241
    Black Truffle, 242
    Butternut Squash, 241
    Saffron, 241
    Wild Mushroom, 241
Roast Beef, 183
Roast Beef Salad, 184
Roast Chicken, 205
Roast Lamb, 184
Roast Pork, 200
Roast Turkey, Apple – and Rosemary-Scented, 218
Roasted Eggplant, 129
Roasted Garlic, 131
Roasted Potatoes, with variations, 141
Roasted Radicchio, 142
Roasted Red Peppers, 140
Roasted Yams or Sweet Potatoes, 149
Rock, Pete, 315
Romano Beans, Sautéed, 122
Rosemary Oil (for White Bean Soup), 114
Rose-Scented Cream with Raspberries, 311
Rosewater with Melon, 281
roux (definition), 31
Russian Borscht, 186
Russian Cream, 311
Russian Tea Biscuits, 320

S

Sage, Fried, with White Bean Soup, 114
Salad, Egg, 92
Salad, Roast Beef, 184
Salad, Tuna, 90
SALADS & DRESSINGS, 156 – 176
Salad Dressings
    creamy, 175
    vinaigrettes, 173 – 174
Salads, Leafy Green, 157 – 162
    Arugula, 161
    Bowl-Dressed Salad, 159
    Chef's Salad, 160
    Greek Salad, 159
    Lettuce, How to Wash, 158
    Lettuce, types, 157
    Toppings for Green Salads, 158
    Tracy's Caesar, 161
    Spinach, 161
    Watercress, 162
Salads, Vegetable and Fruit, 163 – 173
    Apple and Pear, 163
    Asparagus, 164
    Carrot-Raisin, 165
    Celery Root, 166

Chickpea with Tomatoes, Lemon, and Mint, 116
Corn, 166
Cucumber, 166
Curry Tofu, 91
Farro with Cherry Tomatoes and Pecorino, 244
Fennel, Blood Orange, and Toasted Almond, 167
Fennel, Orange, and Black Olive, 168
Fig and Feta, 160
Green Bean with Cherry Tomatoes and Basil, 164
Black Kale, Beets, and Leeks with Orange Oil, 169
Orange and Date, 170
Potato, 170, 171
Watermelon, Feta, and Basil, 173
Salmon
  Baked, 222
  Gravlax, 223
  Simple Cooking Methods for, 222
Salsa Verde, 254
Salsa Verde, Grilled Skirt Steak with, 181
Salsa, Fresh, 249
salt, about, 42
Salt, Thyme, 173
Salted Nuts, Mixed, 176
Sandwich(es)
  about, 89
  Fried Egg, 58
  Grilled Cheese, 28, 89
  Summer Tomato, 173
SAUCES, RELISHES, PICKLES, & JAM, 246 – 260
Sauce
  Blond Barbecue, 257
  Chocolate, 278
  Cocktail (for shrimp), 228
  Cranberry, 257, 258
  Dad's Steak, 247
  Fresh Horseradish Cream, 250
  Fresh Summer Tomato, 249
  Green Chile Relish, 251
  Green Chimichurri, 255
  Horseradish-Tomato Relish, 249
  Lemon Butter, 252
  Meyer Lemon–Olive Relish, 254
  Mignonette (for oysters), 226
  Mushroom Steak, 135
  New Mexico Green Chile, 251
  New Mexico Red Chile, 250
  Oven Applesauce, 257
  Peach Leaf Custard, 303
  Salsa Verde, 254
  Slovenian Horseradish, 250
  Thick Tomato (for pizza), 248
  Tomato, 247
  Tomato-Horseradish Relish, 249
  Tomato with Meat, 248
  Yogurt-Shallot, 252
Sauerkraut, Sausage, and Bean Soup (Jota), 143
Sausage Stew, Polish, 202
Sausage, Fresh Breakfast, 55
sauté (definition), 32
Sautéed Cauliflower, 126
Sautéed Chicken Breast, 206
Sautéed Corn, 128
Sautéed Green Beans, 121
Sautéed Kale and Corn, 133
Sautéed Mushrooms, 135
Sautéed Romano Beans, 122
Sautéed Spicy Squid, 229
Sautéed Spinach, 144
Saving the Season, 255, 259, 349
Scallion-Buttermilk Potatoes, 142
Scalloped Potatoes, 140
Scallops, Seared, with Gremolata, 227
Scones
  Cornmeal-Cherry, 69
  Cream, 69
  Oatmeal, 68
Scrambled Eggs, 57
Sea Salt, English Toffee with, 327
Seared Scallops with Gremolata, 227
Seared Tuna, 225
seasoned cornmeal (for Fried Catfish), 225
seasoning food, 32
Sesame
  Bread, 77
  Candy, 328
  Cookies, 320

Seeds, Pan-Toasted, 176
shallots, about, 40
Shallot Sauce, Yogurt-, 252
Shallot Vinaigrette, 173
sharpening knives, 33
Shaved Fennel, 167
Shea, Cynthia, 133, 199
Sheet Pan Brownies, 317
Shell Beans, Fresh, 122
Shellfish
    Boiled Shrimp, 227
    Grilled Shrimp with Shrimp Essence, 228
    Mussels, with variations, 225
    Oysters on the Half-Shell, 226
    Sautéed Spicy Squid, 229
    Seared Scallops with Gremolata, 227
Shepherd's Pie, 187
Sherbet, Pear, 307
Shere, Lindsey, 307, 347
Sherry Vinaigrette, 174
Shirred Eggs, 60
Shortbread Bars, Chocolate Chip–Hazelnut, 317
Shortcake, Strawberry, My Mother's, 279
Shoyu Chicken, 214
Shrimp
    Boiled, 227
    Grilled with Shrimp Essence, 228
    Gumbo, 98
Simple Roasted Potatoes, 141
Single-Crust Pies, 269 – 274
Skillet Cornbread, 67
Skillet Hamburgers, 192
Skirt Steak, Grilled, with Salsa Verde, 181
slaw see Coleslaw
Slovenia, 186, 193
Slovenian Fennel and Potatoes, 130
Slovenian Horseradish Sauce, 250
slow cooker, 35
Slow-Baked Salmon, 222
Slow-Roasted Pork, 200
Snap Peas, 139
Snow Ice Cream, 308
Soap, Deep Springs (homemade), 343

Soda Bread, Joan's Irish, 70
Soft-Boiled Eggs, 60
Sole Stuffed with Leeks, 224
Sole, Pan-Fried, 223
Sorrel Omelet, 59
Soup
    Black Bean Chili, 110
    Butternut Squash with Diced Pear, 144
    Carrot with Ginger, 125
    Catherine's Corn, 128
    Chili con Carne, 108
    Clam Chowder, 88
    Corn Chowder, 89
    Garlic, 131
    Gazpacho, with variations, 168
    Gumbo, with variations, 98
    Irish Leek and Oat, 134
    Leek and Vegetable Purée, 133
    Lima Bean and Ham with Kale, 112
    Matzoh Ball, 216
    Nettle Broth, 135
    Parsnip with Toasted Almond Olive Oil, 138
    Peanut, 139
    Polish Sausage, My Mother's, 202
    Pork and White Bean Chili, 111
    Posole, 98
    Red Beans and Rice, 111
    Sauerkraut, Sausage, and Bean (Jota), 143
    Soupe au Pistou, 151
    Split Pea, 116
    Tomato, 147
    Watercress, 149
    White Bean and Escarole, 114
    White Bean with Fried Sage, 114
Soup Dumplings, Cornmeal-Egg, 238
Sour Cream Biscuits, 65
Sources (for special ingredients), 350
Southern Spoon Bread, 243
Southern-Style Braised Green Beans, 122
soy sauce, Shoyu Chicken, 214
Spaetzle, with variations, 237
spices, about, 43
Spicy Macaroni and Cheese, 85

spinach, 132
Spinach Salads, 161
Spinach, Sautéed, 144
Split Pea Soup, 116
sponge (breadmaking), 32
sponges (dishwashing), sterilizing, 341
Spoon Bread, Southern, 243
Spring Pasta with Snap Peas and Asparagus, 139
Squash, Butternut
   Chips, 145
   Risotto, 241
   Soup with Diced Pear, 144
Squash, Summer
   Carpaccio, 171
   Cornmeal-Fried, 145
   Grilled, 146
Squash, Winter
   acorn, 245
   dumpling, 245
   kabocha, 245
   red kuri, 245
   Stuffed, 245
Squid, Sautéed Spicy, 229
Stains, Laundry, 341
steak see also beef
Steak Sauce, Dad's, 247
Steak Tartare, 193
Steak, Chicken-Fried, 55
Steel-Cut Oats, 51
Stew, Beef, with variations, 184 – 188
Stew, Chicken, 214
Stew, Lamb, 187
Stock
   Chicken, 217
   Nettle Broth, 135
   Turkey, 218
   Vegetable, 151
Strawberry Ice Cream, 305
Strawberry Shortcake, My Mother's, 270
"Strawberry, The" (Buddhist story), 284
Stuffed Artichokes, 119
Stuffed Winter Squash, 245
Stuffing, Clio's, with variations, 244

Succotash, 123
sugar, about, 43
Sugar Snap Peas, 139
Summer Cucumber Salad, 166
Summer Squash
   Carpaccio, 171
   Cornmeal-Fried, 145
   Grilled, 146
Summer Tomato Pudding, 148
Summer Tomato Sandwich, 173
Summer Vegetables, Pickled, 256
Sunflower Seeds, Pan-Toasted, 176
Sweet Onions Cooked in Cream, 136
Sweet Potato Pie, 272
Sweet Potatoes, Roasted, 149
sweetcorn see corn
syrup, cane or golden,
Syrup, Maple
   Snow Ice Cream, 308
   Pie, 274

T

Tacos
   de Carne Asada, 182
   Crispy Pork, 201
   Rico's, 192
Taffy, Old-Fashioned Vinegar, 327
Tahin Sauce for Falafel, 103
Talbott, Mona, 166
Tangy Lemon Sour Cream Gelatin, 309
Tanis, David, 24, 233, 276, 349
Tapioca Pudding, Pearl, 302
Tarragon-Roasted Chicken with Tomatoes, 210
Tartare, Steak, 193
Tartare, Lamb, 193
tasso, pork (Red Beans and Rice), 111
tatsoi (cooking green), 132; (in Green Salads), 157
Tea, Hibiscus Iced, 105
Tea, Minted Iced, 104
Tender Cured Pork Chops, 197
Tenderloin, Pork, 199
Texas Beans, 108
Texas Toast see Griddle Toast

Thanksgiving
   Apple – and Rosemary-Scented Roast Turkey, 218
   at Deep Springs, 262, 336
   Cranberry Relish, 258
   Cranberry Sauce, 257
   Pumpkin Pie, 271
   Stuffing, Clio's, 244
   Sweet Potato Pie, 272
Three-Ginger Gingerbread, Elge's, 292
Thyme Crackers, 80
Thyme Salt, 173
Toast, French, 53
Toast, Griddle, 53
Toast, Milk, 53
Toasted Cumin–Mint–Yogurt Dressing, 175
Toasted Nuts, 176
Toasted Nut Olive Oil, 254
Toasted Pasta with Garlic, 236
Toasted Seeds, 176
toasted sugar, 44
Toffee, English, with Sea Salt, 327
Tofu Salad, Curry, 91
Tomato(es)
   about, 172
   Cherry Tomatoes, Farro Salad with Pecorino and, 244
   Cherry Tomatoes, Green Bean Salad with Basil 164
   Chickpea Salad with Tomatoes, Lemon, and Mint, 116
   Cobbler, 147
   Concassé, 148
   Fresh Salsa, 249
   fresh tomatoes, peeling and dicing (Concassé), 148
   Gazpacho, 168
   – Horseradish Relish, 249
   Mussels with Spicy Tomato Sauce, 226
   Potatoes, Tomatoes, and Pesto, 141
   Priscilla's Fried Green Tomatoes, 146
   Pudding, Summer Tomato, 148
   Sandwich, 173
   Sauce, 247
   Sauce with Meat, 248
   Sauce, Fresh Summer, 249
   Sauce, Thick (for pizza), 248
   Soup, 147

Tarragon-Roasted Chicken with Tomatoes, 210
   with Salt, 172
Toothbrushing Powder, 342
Tortilla Española, 94
Tortillas, corn,
Tracy's Caesar Salad, 161
trichina parasite (trichinosis) in pork, 178
Trout, Clay's Broiled, 221
Trout, Whole Roasted, with Herb Salad, 221
Truffle, Black, Risotto, 242
Tuna Salad, with variations, 90
Tuna, Seared, 225
Turkey, Apple – and Rosemary-Scented Roast, 218
Turkey Stock, 217
Turnips, in Leek and Vegetable Purée Soup,
Tzimmes, Italian, 125

U

Umbelliferae (carrot family), 130

V

Vanilla Bean Crème Brûlée, 303
Vanilla Ice Cream, 305
Vanilla Wafers, 326
Vegetables see also individual varieties
   about, 118
      hot vegetable dishes and soups, 118 – 151
      cold vegetable dishes and salads, 156 – 176
   Pickled Summer, 256
   Pickled Winter, 256
   summer, 150, 151
Vegetable and Leek Purée Soup, 133
Vegetable Oil Piecrust, 264
Vegetable Oil–Butter Piecrust, 265
Vegetable Stock or Broth, 151
Vinaigrette
   Balsamic, 174
   Cider, 174
   Lemon, 174
   Mustard, 174
   Shallot, 173
   Sherry, 174
Vinaigrette Potato Salads, 171

vinegar, about, 45
Vinegar Taffy, Old-Fashioned, 327

W

Wafers, Dark Chocolate, 315
Wafers, Vanilla, 326
Walnut Biscotti, 321
Walnuts, Toasted, 176
Warm Pears with Chocolate Ice Cream, 282
water, how to boil, 30
Watercress Salad, 162
Watercress Soup, 148
Watermelon, 283
Watermelon, Feta, and Basil Salad, 173
Waters, Alice, 347
Wedding Cookies, 320
West, Kevin, 255, 259, 349
Whey Lemonade, 82
Whipped Cream, 265, 286
   Big Pink Cake, 297
   Gooseberry Fool, 304
   Cake, 290
Whiskey Ice Cream, 306
White Bean
   Chili, Pork, 111
   Gratin with Fennel, 115
   Soups, 114
Whole Roasted Cauliflower, 126
Whole Roasted Trout with Herb Salad, 221
Whole-Wheat Pancakes, 63
Whole-Wheat Pappardelle with Corn and Chiles, 233
Whole-Wheat Crackers, 80
Wide Noodles with Broccolini, Feta, Lemon, and Pine Nuts, 236
Wine, red
   Boeuf Bourguignonne, 186
   in Butter Sauce (beurre rouge), 252
   Chicken Braised in Red Wine (coq au vin), 213
   Salmon poached in, 222
Wine, white
   in Butter Sauce (beurre blanc), 252
   in dough for Focaccia, 77
Winter Squash, Stuffed, 245
Winter Vegetables, Pickled, 256
Worcestershire sauce, about, 45

Y

Yams, Roasted, 149
Yams, Roasted, with Pears and Bourbon, 149
yeast breads, about, 74
Yogurt
   Mediterranean Meatballs, 191
   Raitas, 102
   – Shallot Sauce, 252
   Toasted Cumin–Mint–Yogurt Dressing, 175

Z

zest (citrus), 32
zucchini see summer squash

He said: "It is all useless, if the last landing place can only be the infernal city, and it is there that, in ever-narrowing circles, the current is drawing us."

And Polo said: "The inferno of the living is not something that will be; if there is one, it is what is already here, the inferno where we live every day, that we form by being together. There are two ways to escape suffering it. The first is easy for many: accept the inferno and become such a part of it that you can no longer see it. The second is risky and demands constant vigilance and apprehension: seek and learn to recognize who and what, in the midst of the inferno, are not inferno, then make them endure, give them space."

—Italo Calvino, Invisible Cities

www.ingramcontent.com/pod-product-compliance
Lightning Source LLC
Chambersburg PA
CBHW080407300426
44113CB00015B/2424